Solutions Architect Interview Guide

Mastering solutions architecture and interview preparation with real-world examples and expert insights

Ramakrishnan Vedanarayanan

Arun Ramakrishnan

bpb

www.bpbonline.com

First Edition 2026

Copyright © BPB Publications, India

ISBN: 978-93-65894-608

To View Complete
BPB Publications Catalogue
Scan the QR Code:

Dedicated to

To my father, M.R. Vedanarayanan, my mother, Usha, and my family, Vani Krishnan and Shradha Ramakrishnan, for their constant support, sacrifices, and encouragement. This book would not have been possible without your love and belief in my dreams.

-Ramakrishnan Vedanarayanan

To my beloved parents who taught me that values in life are more important than valuables, to my affectionate wife SriPriya, who makes me believe in myself, and to my precious daughter Sanju, who lightens up every moment of my life.

-Arun Ramakrishnan

About the Authors

- **Ramakrishnan Vedanarayanan** is an accomplished solutions architect with over 20 years of industry experience, specializing in cloud computing, DevOps, automation, and artificial intelligence, including cutting-edge generative AI technologies. In his role at **Tata Consultancy Services (TCS)**, he has architected and delivered mission-critical, scalable solutions for global banking and enterprise customers. His expertise spans cloud-native development, infrastructure automation, and enterprise modernization, helping organizations achieve operational excellence, security, and agility.

  Ramakrishnan is a passionate mentor who has guided numerous professionals across cloud, DevOps, and AI domains. He actively fosters a culture of continuous learning and innovation. His leadership and contributions have been recognized through prestigious accolades, including the 'Golden Guru' award at TCS for technical excellence and mentorship. A firm believer in lifelong learning, he combines practical experience with forward-thinking strategies to help enterprises confidently navigate the evolving technology landscape.

- **Arun Ramakrishnan** is a chief architect at **Tata Consultancy Services (TCS)**, having close to 30 years of experience in global enterprises' technology transformation. He is a trusted advisor to multinational organizations, driving innovation through cloud adoption, digital modernization, distributed architectures, and AI/ML-based solutions. He has led the modernization of complex legacy systems, orchestrated large-scale cloud migrations, and helped organizations implement Agile, resilient, and cost-optimized technology ecosystems.

  Arun's distinguished career is marked by a blend of deep technical expertise and strategic leadership. His work has been recognized with multiple technology leadership awards and engineering excellence honors. He is passionate about simplifying complex systems, designing future-ready solutions, and empowering organizations to thrive in an ever-evolving digital world. As a hands-on architect, thought leader, and mentor, he brings a unique perspective on the convergence of technology and business success.

Together,

Ramakrishnan Vedanarayanan and Arun Ramakrishnan bring a combined wealth of over 50 years of practical experience. Their shared vision for this book is to equip aspiring and practicing solutions architects with the strategies, technical expertise, and real-world insights needed to build resilient, scalable, and impactful solutions in today's dynamic technology landscape.

About the Reviewers

❖ **Pravin Pandey** is a globally recognized solution architect leader, mentor, and thought leader with extensive professional experience and advanced certifications. He is passionate about technology innovation, transformational leadership, and guiding the next generation of talent. Currently working in the high-end luxury retail sector, Pravin specializes in managing architecture design globally, ensuring operational excellence and the seamless integration of cutting-edge technologies tailored to the unique demands of the industry.

An active member of IEEE and ACM, Pravin is also a mentor who shares his expertise to inspire and develop future leaders in datacenter transformation, modernization, and data analytics. His mentorship reflects his commitment to fostering innovation and helping individuals excel in their professional journeys.

Pravin's work in multi-cloud environments spans industries such as finance, retail, healthcare, technology, and manufacturing, where he has delivered tailored solutions resulting in significant cost savings, enhanced scalability, and optimized performance. He specializes in modernizing legacy systems, integrating AI-driven insights, and enabling data-driven decision-making, empowering organizations to achieve sustained growth and operational agility.

Known for his ability to merge technical expertise with business strategy, Pravin is a trusted advisor in managing complex systems and delivering future-ready architecture designs. His role as a mentor, coupled with his global impact, solidifies his reputation as a leader who not only drives transformational IT solutions but also inspires others to innovate, grow, and succeed in their careers.

❖ **Satish Prahalad Gururajan** is a passionate and highly skilled solutions architect with nearly two decades of professional experience in the tech industry. He has a strong foundation in application development, with a focus on Java technologies, and has played pivotal roles in software design, development, and delivery. Over the course of his career, Satish has excelled in diverse positions, ranging from developer to architect, product owner, and designer, which has allowed him to build a comprehensive understanding of both technical and business needs. Satish's expertise goes beyond development; he has consistently demonstrated a strong ability to bridge the gap between technical teams and business stakeholders, ensuring that solutions align with both strategic goals and user requirements. His experience spans a variety of industries, and he has a proven track record of successfully leading teams through the development lifecycle, from ideation and design to implementation and deployment. As a certified professional, Satish holds multiple industry-recognized certifications, including SAFe® Product Owner/Product Manager, CSPO® (Certified Scrum Product Owner), and CSM® (Certified Scrum Master), which have honed his skills in Agile methodologies and product management. These certifications have not only enriched his technical acumen but also enhanced his leadership and project management capabilities, enabling him to guide teams in delivering high-quality software in a collaborative and efficient manner. Satish is especially passionate about problem-solving and has a natural talent for distilling complex technical concepts into easily understandable terms. His ability to simplify intricate topics allows him to communicate effectively with both technical and non-technical audiences.

❖ **Chris Hinch** is a seasoned solutions architect and practice director, with over 25 years of experience, with a strong foundation in engineering. With a natural talent for solving complex challenges through technology, Chris transitioned from engineering to solutioning for clients. He pioneered a unique approach by prioritizing understanding the client's challenges and removing the technology bias to identify the most effective and cost-efficient solutions. Chris's dedication to listening and tailoring solutions has consistently delivered exceptional results for his clients.

API architecture patterns, offering practical insights for selecting an architecture pattern to build scalable and resilient applications.

Chapter 5: Aligning Technology with Business Goals - This chapter highlights the critical role solutions architects play in ensuring that technology directly supports business strategy and value creation. You will learn how to translate business requirements into technical solutions, manage costs and budgets, apply project management principles, and design integration strategies for mergers and acquisitions. Through real-world examples, this chapter builds your ability to bridge the gap between technical execution and business success.

Chapter 6: Agile Processes and Essentials - This chapter explores how Agile methodologies reshape the role of solutions architects. You will learn how to design flexible, modular architectures that support iterative delivery while maintaining long-term strategic alignment. Covering key frameworks like Scrum, Kanban, XP, and SAFe, along with essential tools such as Jira and Confluence, this chapter equips solutions architects to thrive in fast-paced, collaborative environments and effectively balance agility with architectural integrity.

Chapter 7: Legacy Modernization and Migration Strategies - This chapter highlights the critical need for enterprises to modernize legacy systems to stay competitive, meet evolving customer expectations, and support business growth. It covers the challenges of modernization, key drivers behind it, and strategies for modernizing outdated platforms, including mainframe migration and cloud adoption. You will also explore how artificial intelligence accelerates modernization efforts, along with practical roadmaps, checklists, and insights to guide successful legacy transformation initiatives.

Chapter 8: DevOps Essentials - This chapter equips solutions architects with the critical DevOps knowledge needed to design scalable, automated, and resilient systems. It covers the core practices of CI/CD pipelines, **infrastructure as code (IaC)**, monitoring, security integration (DevSecOps), AIOps, and FinOps. You will learn how to align DevOps practices with architecture design to support continuous delivery, enhance system reliability, optimize costs, and build secure, cloud-native solutions ready for real-world demands.

Chapter 9: Performance and Scalability - This chapter emphasizes the critical role of application performance and scalability in delivering exceptional user experiences. You will learn strategies to design systems that meet high performance standards, scale seamlessly under growth, and maintain reliability. The chapter covers key concepts such as observability, performance tuning, scalability techniques, cloud-based scaling, and the emerging role of AI in performance optimization, preparing you to architect systems that perform and scale efficiently in real-world environments.

Chapter 10: Data Management and Analytics - This chapter explores the critical role of data management and analytics in modern enterprise architecture. You will learn how to design scalable, secure, and efficient data architectures, implement integration strategies, and leverage big data solutions across hybrid and cloud environments. The chapter also highlights how to use analytics to drive business insights, equipping you to build data-driven systems that support informed decision-making and digital transformation initiatives.

Chapter 11: User Experience Considerations - This chapter emphasizes the importance of integrating **user experience (UX)** principles into solutions architecture. You will learn how to design systems that are intuitive, accessible, and user-centric while maintaining technical and business alignment. Covering human-centered design, accessibility standards, usability best practices, and ethical considerations, this chapter equips you to create architectures that enhance user satisfaction, foster engagement, and support seamless cross-platform experiences.

Chapter 12: Disaster Recovery and Business Continuity - This chapter focuses on designing resilient systems that maintain business operations during disruptions. You will learn how to develop **disaster recovery (DR)** and **business continuity (BC)** plans, implement effective backup and failover strategies, and apply key concepts like **recovery time objective (RTO)** and **recovery point objective (RPO)**. Covering techniques such as **infrastructure as code (IaC)**, **policy as code (PaC)**, and chaos engineering, this chapter equips solutions architects to build architectures that ensure operational stability, minimize downtime, and meet critical business objectives.

Chapter 13: Governance and Compliance - This chapter focuses on integrating governance frameworks and compliance requirements into solution designs. You will learn how to build secure, auditable systems that meet standards like GDPR, HIPAA, PCI DSS, and SOX, while supporting innovation and operational agility. Covering risk management strategies, **policy as code (PaC)**, and governance automation, this chapter equips solutions architects to design accountable, resilient, and regulatorily compliant architectures across modern enterprise environments.

Chapter 14: Communication and Collaboration - This chapter highlights the critical role of communication and collaboration in a solutions architect's success. You will learn how to effectively engage stakeholders, create clear documentation, present ideas confidently, and lead cross-functional teams. With practical strategies and real-world examples, this chapter equips you to navigate complex team dynamics, build trust, and transform technical solutions into impactful, organization-wide outcomes.

Chapter 15: Problem-solving and Innovation - This chapter develops the critical skills of analytical thinking, creative problem-solving, and innovation essential for solutions architects. You will learn structured approaches to tackle complex technical and business challenges, apply risk management strategies, and foster innovation through emerging technologies and collaborative team dynamics. By mastering these skills, solutions architects can drive impactful solutions that not only address immediate needs but also position enterprises for long-term success.

Chapter 16: Vendor and Stakeholder Management - This chapter focuses on the critical skills solutions architects need to manage vendors and stakeholders effectively. You will learn strategies for building strong vendor relationships, negotiating favorable contracts, integrating third-party solutions, and aligning diverse stakeholder expectations. By mastering vendor and stakeholder management, solutions architects can drive project success, reduce risks, and foster lasting partnerships that support scalable, reliable solutions.

Chapter 17: Continuous Learning and Improvement - This chapter emphasizes the importance of continuous learning as a strategic advantage for solutions architects. You will explore actionable strategies to stay relevant, including pursuing certifications, tracking industry trends, and building strong professional networks. By fostering a mindset of growth and innovation, solutions architects can enhance their expertise, stay competitive in a dynamic field, and position themselves as trusted leaders in technology and business transformation.

Chapter 18: Preparation for Solutions Architect Interview - This chapter prepares you to confidently navigate the solutions architect interview process. You will learn strategies to handle different types of interviews, including behavioral, technical, and design challenges, while showcasing your problem-solving abilities, business alignment skills, and technical expertise. From structuring responses effectively to presenting a strong portfolio, this chapter equips you with practical techniques to stand out and perform at your best during interviews.

Chapter 19: The 30-day Interview Preparation Plan - This chapter presents a structured 30-day roadmap to help you systematically prepare for solutions architect interviews. Covering technical mastery, real-world problem-solving, cloud-native patterns, and critical soft skills, the plan balances depth and breadth to ensure you are fully interview-ready. Through checklists, practical exercises, and mock scenarios, you will build the confidence and capability needed to succeed in both technical and stakeholder-driven aspects of the interview process.

Chapter 20: Expert Insights and Common Pitfalls - This chapter provides valuable insights from industry experts on what distinguishes successful solutions architect candidates. You will learn the key qualities top architects look for, how to avoid common interview mistakes, and strategies to demonstrate technical expertise, leadership, and strategic thinking. Drawing from real-world experiences, this chapter prepares you to navigate interviews with confidence, stand out from the competition, and position yourself as a top-tier solutions architect.

Chapter 21: Operational Excellence Considerations - This chapter explores the principles and practices of Operational Excellence critical to designing scalable, resilient, maintainable, and efficient systems. You will learn how to align technical design with evolving business needs, implement automation and continuous improvement strategies, and apply **site reliability engineering** (SRE) practices. By mastering operational excellence, solutions architects can deliver robust, high-performing systems that drive long-term business success.

Chapter 22: Cloud-native Architecture and Design - This chapter explores the principles and practices of designing cloud-native applications that fully leverage the scalability, flexibility, and resilience of modern cloud platforms. You will learn about containerization, orchestration, cloud-native design patterns, reference architectures, and best practices for migrating legacy workloads. The chapter also covers critical security considerations, equipping solutions architects to build robust, scalable, and secure cloud-native solutions ready for global scale.

Chapter 23: Production Support - This chapter focuses on the critical role of production support in maintaining application reliability and customer satisfaction after deployment. You will learn the responsibilities of solutions architects in production environments, types of support and maintenance, the production support lifecycle, and the growing role of AI and automation in modern support processes. The chapter also highlights **key performance indicators** (KPIs) and best practices to ensure efficient, scalable, and proactive production support operations.

Chapter 24: Strategic Future for Architects - This chapter reflects on the journey of becoming a solutions architect, highlighting the blend of technical mastery, strategic thinking, and leadership needed for lasting success. It reinforces the mindset of continuous growth, innovation, and business impact, preparing you not only for interview success but for a dynamic, evolving career. The chapter encourages embracing challenges, creating value beyond systems, and inspiring the next generation of technology leaders.

Chapter 25: Appendix - This chapter serves as a practical toolkit, providing essential resources, templates, and references to support solutions architects in real-world projects and interview preparation. From troubleshooting cheat sheets and cloud service comparisons to high-level design templates and recommended readings, the Appendix equips you with actionable materials to enhance problem-solving, design planning, and continuous career growth.

Coloured Images

Please follow the link to download the
Coloured Images of the book:

https://rebrand.ly/9496ef

We have code bundles from our rich catalogue of books and videos available at https://github.com/ bpbpublications. Check them out!

Errata

We take immense pride in our work at BPB Publications and follow best practices to ensure the accuracy of our content to provide with an indulging reading experience to our subscribers. Our readers are our mirrors, and we use their inputs to reflect and improve upon human errors, if any, that may have occurred during the publishing processes involved. To let us maintain the quality and help us reach out to any readers who might be having difficulties due to any unforeseen errors, please write to us at :

errata@bpbonline.com

Your support, suggestions and feedbacks are highly appreciated by the BPB Publications' Family.

Piracy

If you come across any illegal copies of our works in any form on the internet, we would be grateful if you would provide us with the location address or website name. Please contact us at business@bpbonline.com with a link to the material.

If you are interested in becoming an author

If there is a topic that you have expertise in, and you are interested in either writing or contributing to a book, please visit www.bpbonline.com. We have worked with thousands of developers and tech professionals, just like you, to help them share their insights with the global tech community. You can make a general application, apply for a specific hot topic that we are recruiting an author for, or submit your own idea.

Reviews

Please leave a review. Once you have read and used this book, why not leave a review on the site that you purchased it from? Potential readers can then see and use your unbiased opinion to make purchase decisions. We at BPB can understand what you think about our products, and our authors can see your feedback on their book. Thank you!

For more information about BPB, please visit www.bpbonline.com.

Join our Discord space

Join our Discord workspace for latest updates, offers, tech happenings around the world, new releases, and sessions with the authors:

https://discord.bpbonline.com

Table of Contents

CHAPTER 1
Setting the Stage

Introduction

This chapter introduces the role of a solutions architect, exploring the key drivers behind solution architecture and its alignment with organizational business goals. We will outline the core responsibilities expected of a solutions architect and highlight the essential skills needed to excel in this role. Additionally, we will discuss how a solutions architect can contribute beyond traditional boundaries, adding value to both project teams and the broader enterprise. Finally, we will provide guidance on staying current with evolving architectural and technical trends.

Structure

This chapter covers the following topics:

- Architects in an enterprise
- Solution architecture
- Need for a solution architecture
- Influences of a solution architecture
- Solution architecture build worthiness
- Effective solutions architect
- Responsibilities of a solutions architect
- Attributes of a good solution architecture
- Architectural assumptions and exclusions
- Required technical skills
- Learning architecture in a systematic way

Objectives

By the end of this chapter, we will understand the different architect roles prevalent in an enterprise. The chapter will cover the scope of solution architecture and the role of a solutions architect. We will learn business goals, business architecture, and how the solution architecture acts as a glue between the two. Readers will learn the responsibility of a solutions architect as expected by large enterprises and guidance for becoming a solutions architect in a systematic way.

Architects in an enterprise

Before we move on to look at specific aspects of a solution architecture and the responsibilities of a solutions architect, we will list down the common architect roles found in an organization. This will help us understand the type of activities that are carried out by each of the roles. We will later dive deeper into the responsibilities of a solutions architect.

Enterprise architect

The enterprise architect defines the overall IT strategy of the organization. The enterprise architect decides the boundary of the technical landscape within which all software applications will reside. They will recommend and oversee the technology stack to be used within the organization for different areas such as front-end, back-end, databases, middleware, data warehouses, etc. The enterprise architect provides a framework for IT governance within the organization.

Solutions architect

The solutions architect focuses on implementing the solution for a business problem. The solutions architect will choose the components required within the solution and define the mode of communication between those components within the solution. We will look at the responsibilities of a solutions architect in greater detail in the section *Responsibilities of a solutions architect* within this chapter.

Technical architect

The technical architect is concerned with the technical implementation of a specific component within the solution. They recommend the technologies to be used across layers and the components within a solution. The technical architect will provide the required technology leadership to the development team for software creation.

Data architect

The data architect manages the flow of data, security, privacy, and the persistence of data within the organization. They also work with the solution and technical architects for individual projects to recommend the tools and techniques to create database systems, data warehouses, and data lakes for individual projects.

Cloud architect

The cloud architect creates solutions for applications born in the cloud (called cloud-native applications) and applications that are migrated from an on-premises data center to the cloud. The cloud architect is conversant with different services offered by the cloud providers and chooses appropriate ones to create the required capabilities for the application on the cloud. They are also familiar with proven cloud architectures and select the right architecture based on the nature of the application to be deployed on the cloud.

In most customer organizations, the solution and technical architect roles overlap. The solutions architect also works with the development team to define the technology stack and underpinnings to build applications. The solutions architect is also expected to perform certain tasks of the data architect, such as choosing the right database for persistence to keeping the data private and secure within the application. For any complex tasks, such as the creation of a data warehouse or a data lake, the data architect is invited to take up the responsibility of guiding the solutions architect and the developers.

Apart from the common architect roles, some large enterprises also have the following specialized architect roles. This depends on the technical maturity of the organization and the scale of the specialized technical functions required:

- **Performance architect**: The performance architect devises the types and techniques of performance measurement within the project. Applications for which performance is a key indicator of success, the architect works full time with the solutions architect and the development team to define the key performance indicators to be measured and the thresholds for those indicators. They also recommend the tools required for the measurement of performance for the different layers and components within the system.

- **Security architect**: This is a specialized role to define the security strategy for applications. For some applications, data privacy is extremely important as a breach could potentially result in a penalty of millions of dollars for the organization. This role is extremely crucial for applications that deal with sensitive data, such as bank accounts, credit card information, health care data, and personally identifiable information, such as social security numbers and passport numbers.

- **Infrastructure architect**: This is a specialized role that exists within organizations where hundreds of applications exist, and an optimal infrastructure layout is required. The infrastructure architect decides the capacity of resources based on the quality of services required for the application, such as performance, availability, and disaster recovery.

Solution architecture

All enterprises, big or small, have become digital. They have their services rolled out to their customers through different channels such as the web, mobile, or their customer service centers. These services could be an independent application in themselves or be part of a larger application that comprises other services as well. Before these applications were created, they would have posed themselves as business problems which the enterprise would have wanted to solve. It could have been a new service or a product that the company wanted to introduce, or it could have been an effort to shorten the time taken for an existing service to be rolled out to their customers. Once we have these problems at hand, they are broken down into manageable chunks or requirements. These requirements are analyzed to be converted into software applications. Before this happens, many decisions are made in between. All these decisions taken to create a digitized version of the required service or product constitute solution architecture. The decisions include, but are not limited to, the number of components required to create the digitized version of the service and the communication enablement between the components. The communication enablement between these components, in turn, depends on the technical nature of those components and the format of data exchange. These decisions taken for solving individual problems are aligned with the rules defined by a technical governance framework called the enterprise architecture. These rules apply to the creation of any digitized version of products and services required for the successful functioning of the enterprise. A solutions architect not only needs to be aware of the general architectural and design patterns, but also the enterprise architecture framework of the organization within which they should create their architecture and design of the software system.

Defining a solutions architect

Solutions architects always need to expand the boundary of their knowledge spectrum to cope up with the pace of technology change. Apart from this, solutions architects also need to exceed the expectations of the customer for whom they will be working, depending on the technology stack their customer organization uses. There are areas of focus, preferences, and strengths for a solutions architect. However, the decisions a solutions architect is expected to take go far beyond the confines of creating a blueprint for a software system. The solutions architect is expected to work closely with different stakeholders from the business and technology areas. The architects are required to work with the business analyst in creating the requirements or user stories (as in an Agile environment). They are also expected to work with the development team to ensure that the system does not deviate from the original proposed solution. In addition, they coordinate with the test managers and the infrastructure team to define the test strategy and do capacity planning, respectively. There are projects in which developers are given additional responsibility to make technical decisions. However, there is a gap between what an associate does as a developer daily versus making decisions about how the different components interact with each other within a software system and their implication on the quality of services such as performance, security, and scalability. The developer churns out code in a language they are proficient in and tests the developed code before the software is rolled out for widespread use. There are situations in which a developer takes technical decisions involuntarily without knowing the long-term side effects on the quality of services of the software system.

The solutions architect takes informed decisions using their knowledge of architectural styles, design patterns, and design principles. The solutions architect also knows the impact of each one of these architectural styles on the software quality of services. The solutions architect is also knowledgeable about different methodologies of software development to devise ways to measure the quality of services like security, scalability, and performance. The architect is also conversant with tools for observability once the system goes into production.

Key principles

Given a problem statement, the solutions architect is expected to come up with a solution architecture for solving the problem. The following are the key principles that need to be applied while arriving at the solution architecture:

- **Simplicity**: The first important principle is to keep the solution simple. Do not over engineer the solution by introducing components and technologies that will make the solution complex. This is going to increase the total cost of ownership of the solution both in terms of development and postproduction support.

- **Loose coupling**: Build the solution as loosely coupled components. This enables us to independently replace the components in the future, if required. This also enables us to use the right technology for the individual layers or components without having to worry about the technology being used by a layer above or below.

- **Reusability**: Identify the capabilities or components that can be reused across the application. Develop the logic as common components and use a plug and play model to include the common components wherever required.

- **Modularity**: Make the solution as modular as possible so that the software components can be tested independently with reduced dependencies.

- **Extensibility**: The software is easily extensible without having to modify a lot of components.

- **Industry standards**: The solution makes use of industry standard best practices and design patterns. Using proven practices for known problems helps to reduce errors and save effort while implementing the solution for existing patterns.

- **Externalization of shared capabilities**: The shared capabilities are identified and externalized. Shared capabilities such as reporting, storage, and caching are pervasive throughout the system.

- **Clear role demarcation**: The system should have a clear demarcation of the operations and data based on the user roles defined for the system.

These principles serve as a foundation for building robust, scalable, and maintainable solutions.

Need for a solution architecture

Software systems are perceivably built to last; at the same time, they should also be flexible enough for changes to be plugged into easily as the business requirements change or evolve over a period after the initial version of the software is deployed into production. The changes that come into the system need not necessarily be with regard to the functionality that is embedded in the form of logic within the code. The change could be in terms of the type of users that would interact with the system. For example, the application could additionally be rolled out to mobile users along with the web users. There could be additional systems that could be integrated, or there could be new interfaces added to support new functionality, such as payments using payment gateways or payment processors. The way an architect visualizes and designs a system should be open enough to accommodate the changes coming into the system in the future. If the system is not able to absorb new changes with the passage of time or takes a considerable amount of time and effort to inject new changes into the system, it is not a well architected system. The structure of the whole system should be approached very cautiously, keeping in mind the future needs of the business. Along with it, the architect should also consider the different nonfunctional requirements that need to be satisfied by the system. If these are not addressed during the architectural stage, it will result in a very rigid system that will need a large maintenance budget, which increases the total cost of ownership.

In the given modern age of e-commerce and digitalization, products and services are offered at the doorsteps of the customer. Customers want a quicker and effortless service from enterprises. The solution architecture needs to support a quicker time to market. The architecture also needs to strike a balance between online and offline processes in the way customers are serviced. Though a straight through processing is always desirable, an architecture that strikes a balance between automated and manual touch point is more effective in increasing the time to market.

With the advent of cloud providers, the solution landscape seems to have undergone a major shift. A lot of capabilities are being provided out-of-the-box in the form of infrastructure, platform, and software, and the solutions architect's job seems to have been made simpler. Architect is required to weave the capabilities together to create the required blueprint in conjunction with the provided requirements. The responsibility only increases to gain an in-depth understanding of how these capabilities function beneath the visible surface. Apart from the business functionality, non-functional requirements play a very important role in the day-to-day operations of the system. Unless the solutions architect has this understanding of the services, the final product moved to production is bound to have implications in terms of maintenance, change management, and, more importantly, cost.

The onus is on the solutions architect to be even more prudent to use the right services for the required capability for the system to be operationally efficient and cost effective. To achieve this, the solutions architect should be able to understand the intent of the requirements before delivering a blueprint of the system for further design and development. If the complexity of the system is misunderstood, there is a chance that we add services that are far more humongous than what is required to build the system. This is where contextual knowledge becomes very important. Most of the time, the technical team and the business team work in isolation, and a set of requirements in the form of English statements is given to the architecture team. This isolation during the initial phase of the system blueprint starts to percolate through all the phases of the project and finally shows its ugly effect when the system is deployed into production. The architect can get help from domain experts to understand the functionality in greater detail before making decisions about what components are required to make up the whole system. Solution architecture is not just about a group of architects working independently, but working hand in hand with the stakeholders involved till the architecture blueprinting and design detailing are done for the software system.

Influences of a solution architecture

Before we discuss the basics of how to effectively architect the system, we should understand the drivers behind the demand for a technology-based intervention. These drivers help both the business and technology stakeholders to be convinced of the need for a new system to be built or a change to an existing system within the enterprise. The solutions architect needs to have a good grasp of the business goals of the organization and the existing business processes within the enterprise. Once the architect has a good understanding of the existing business process landscape and the enterprise business goals, the clarity about the technology system requirements comes automatically. This will further pave the way for the road map to build such systems for the enterprise's internal or end customer use.

Figure 1.1 gives an overview of how the business processes, business goals, and the solution architecture relate to each other. The solution architecture tries to address the gap between the existing processes and the business goals with technology intervention, as follows:

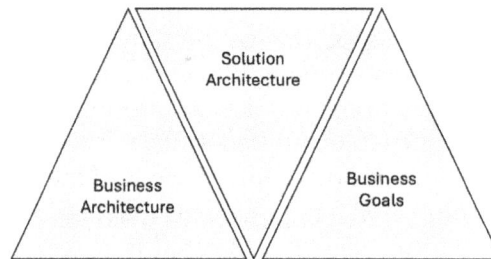

Figure 1.1: *Interconnection between business architecture, business goals, and solution architecture*

Business goals

All businesses exist to make profits. It is very important for them to have a clear vision of what they want to do on a continual basis. Unless an enterprise has short term and long-term goals, its very existence in the future will become bleak. Each enterprise has its goals set every year, which depend on the nature of the business they are in. Your bank might want to increase its deposits by 30% from the previous year. A retail organization might want to improve its sales by 25% on a yearly basis. The competition also sets the speed of the race in which the enterprises want to participate and always want to win. Understanding the business goals becomes paramount to creating a successful system architecture. The architect should have the ability to extract business problems that need to be solved for the enterprise to reach its goals. These problems must be clearly identified and should have enough details to address their relevance to one or more of the business goals of the enterprise. The problem could point to the lack of a product in the existing portfolio of the enterprise, the gap in the service provided, or a usability problem in the system that hampers customer retention or results in business reputation damage. The problems identified may sometimes be addressed as a technology change or a process change within the organization.

The solutions architect needs the ability to understand the difference between the two and has to address it accordingly. In certain cases, it would not help if a certain technical change is introduced into the enterprise without optimizing the business process. The solutions architect, hence, is not only an expert in understanding software systems but should also develop the ability to quickly understand the necessity of the requested functionality and should be able to respond either with a direct technology change or suggest an optimization of the existing process. Once we have the list of problems identified that correlate to the business goals to be realized, the problem statements must be clearly documented. The format prescribed to document the problem statements should clearly elucidate the business goal to be achieved. The description of the problem statement with relevant data points should prove that it is indeed a problem requiring a solution to move towards the end business goal.

The process flow diagram could be used to indicate the flow of data and work required to realize the process. Steps within the process should be marked clearly to indicate the bottlenecks that are hurdles in achieving the desired business objectives. Once the problem statements are documented, the stakeholders need to be identified for a walk through to get their consensus. The stakeholders might come from different departments of the enterprise, such as sales, servicing, and marketing. It is the job of the solutions architect, along with the domain expert, to clearly articulate the problem statement from a process perspective and convince them of the intervention required to resolve the problem. The consensus needs to be reached before we move forward to decide on a technological solution that could possibly alleviate the problem and help the enterprise to achieve the required goals. Workshops can be conducted with the required stakeholders to discuss the problem statements and possible solutions, and the feedback received from the stakeholders needs to be incorporated. The problem statement can then be broken down into a list of requirements or user stories with the help of the domain expert or a business analyst.

These discussions will help the solutions architect to firm up the understanding of the system requirements and translate them into technical interventions. The value derived from the implemented system is in direct proportion to the creation of the right set of problems and devising the right solutions to solve those problems. This inherently helps enterprises to achieve their business goals.

Business architecture

The business architecture of an enterprise is made up of multiple parts. It comprises the existing processes within the enterprise. The structure of the organization, how the processes and data flows within the enterprise, what kind of roles exist, and the type of empowerment these roles have. There is always a gap between the existing business architecture and the business goals that the enterprise wants to pursue. This constant pursuit to move from the current state to the desired state is the process excellence that each business wants to achieve. In many organizations, business hierarchy plays a very important role in the way the processes are laid out. That could be a possible hurdle in moving towards the required business goals. The solutions architect needs to be aware of the business architecture as well, though they may not have a lot of say in the way things could possibly be structured within the enterprise. However, it should be considered as an influencer while designing software systems and needs to be documented as criteria or parameters that are considered while coming up with the system blueprint.

Solution architecture as the glue

Once we understand the business goals and the current state of the business, the solution architecture comes into play to create the required bridge between where we are currently and where we want to be in the future. As discussed earlier, this could be the creation of a new product or service or a modification to existing products or services. The solution architecture aims to create new capabilities for the enterprise, modify existing ones, and sunset unwanted systems that unnecessarily cost money for the enterprise. It also optimizes existing services and products for the overall good of the enterprises and the customers served by the enterprise.

We will discuss in the following section how to measure the effectiveness of a solution architecture under the qualities required of a solution architecture.

Solution architecture build worthiness

The build worthiness of the architecture is another important aspect to ponder. It must be ensured that architecture can deliver the goods. We cannot wait until such a time that the rubber meets the road, when the system is deployed into production.

Proof of architecture is a very important activity that needs to be carried out before the architecture is finalized for use in building the system. Before this activity begins, the preparation phase becomes important to understand the scope of the exercise. The experiments need to be properly scoped and should clearly communicate the objectives of the exercise. The objectives could vary between finding the fitment of the architecture with regard to the requirements or understanding the granularity of the components participating in the solution. There are certain cases in which the proof of architecture is carried out to understand the behavior of the nonfunctional requirements. There are scenarios in which the solution may have to consume data or disseminate data to external systems. In such cases, the proof of architecture exercise focuses on collecting metrics around the quality of service, such as reliability, resilience, performance, and security.

The proof of architecture gives an exact picture of how the process and data flows within the system and how different components of the solution landscape gel with each other. It also gives a good idea of how the capabilities of the solution need to be opened for interaction with the outside world. Components that are in process have far fewer restrictions as they are going to be confined within a single large application process than components that are both used internally by other components of the application and by parties within and outside the enterprise. Another important aspect is the format of data exchange across different components within the system. Proof of architecture will help answer the questions about the data formats that need to be exchanged between layers or components that make up the overall system. The proof of architecture will address any data transformations required before the data flows from one component to another. It will also bring out any performance bottlenecks that need to be taken care of. It becomes more important when there are multiple integration touchpoints expected within the system. There could be applications external to our system that need to be communicated with, for the realization of a business capability. Sometimes, proof of architecture also throws light on the gaps within the existing processes. As an architect, you get questions in mind as to why certain steps are required within the whole process or if the mode of the step can be exchanged from manual to automated or vice versa, thereby paving the way to optimize existing workflows within the system. Once the proof of architecture is complete, the results need to be documented along with the data points that show the build worthiness of the system.

Effective solutions architect

There is a very thin line between a solution architecture and the details that make up the solution in its entirety. If you zoom into a certain portion of the architecture, then you get to see the details of a particular portion of the system. For instance, you may get the overall floor plan of a multi storied building as given by a civil architect. At the same time, the architect should also be able to clearly chalk out detailed plans of the individual floors of the building and the houses on each floor. Each house might be of a different size and may have a different layout for the rooms. Similarly, this software solutions architect should not only come up with an overall blueprint of the application but also detail out the individual components that make up the system in its entirety. There are architects who confine themselves to drawing solution diagrams on a slide and give them to stakeholders for further consumption. They graze the requirements of the system based on which they arrive at a solution architecture.

There is very little focus on the actual capabilities required within this system, let alone the nonfunctional requirements. These paper architects mostly thrive on their overall experience and are not conversant with contemporary design methodologies and technologies. For instance, there are cloud solutions architects coming up with cloud native architectures in a way that they familiarize themselves with a few required services of the cloud provider without understanding the essence of cloud native architectures or getting into the details of how the service is supposed to work, whether it is the right service to be used for the capability being built, the limitations of the service as against satisfying the requirements of the system. At the outset, the architecture will seem to satisfy the requirements of the overall system. When we start building the system, end-to-end flows wither out because of the limitations posed by the individual components or services used to realize the requirements. Therefore, it is very important for a solutions architect to map the detailed requirements of the system to the individual components or services that make up the overall system. This helps in two different ways, as follows:

- A solutions architect ensures that the solution is complete in all respects with regard to the requirement coverage of this system.
- It helps to ensure that we have chosen the right services to realize the requirements of the system.

A good solutions architect should also be familiar with a few contemporary programming languages, which will come in handy if they develop a quick proof of concept for some of the requirements. A good solutions architect is always hands-on and will be ready to participate in creating a quick proof of concept to prove a solution to convince both the business and technology stakeholders. This internally gives a sense of confidence about the architecture that is to be rolled out further for the buildup of the system. The solutions architect also decides the choice of the technical stack for each of the layers or components in the system. The architect should also be conversant with popular technology frameworks that exist in the market at the point in time of the architecture and design exercises.

The other quality required of a solutions architect is not to confine themself only to the solution required to build the system. They must adhere to the broader technology rules and contracts that are allowed at the enterprise level and incorporate them into the system being architected. This is to ensure non-violation of any principle that might put the organization overall at risk. Examples include designing an application that helps in conversations between a customer and a service agent that cannot be stored for more than three months, following payment card industry standards across all applications developed in a bank for any transaction that involves a credit card.

The solutions architect must not confine themselves to learning the architectural patterns and the design principles. Understanding of the domain becomes very important to create an architecture that is flexible to accommodate changes in the future and to reuse common components across capabilities within the domain. For example, an insurance policy premium calculation component may be used during the process of policy initiation and policy renewal, but with minor differences. A deep understanding of the domain will help to identify such places of reuse and will aid the architect to come up with a solution that is lighter, modular, and maintainable.

Responsibilities of a solutions architect

It is a customer facing role wherein you get to work directly with the business stakeholders to understand their business problems and provide solutions. At the same time, the solutions architect works with project managers, test managers, and operations staff and assists them in choosing the most optimal strategies to make the project successful.

The following are the responsibilities of a solutions architect from the point of view of business stakeholders and project teams:

- Understand the business goals and help business stakeholders to bridge the gap between the current and future states.

- Provide thought leadership to businesses for optimizing the existing business architecture with simplification of the steps in the existing processes.

- Understand existing processes within the enterprise, identify gaps in them, and suggest newer products or services that could bridge the gap.

- Work with business stakeholders to socialize the problem statement and firm up the clarity of the problem statement, refine and document the same.

- Work with their domain experts and business analysts to refine business problems and help them break them down into manageable chunks of requirements.

- Work out different solution options for the problem statement identified and choose the most appropriate one that best fits the requirements.

- Understand the IT governance framework at the organization level and ensure that decisions at the application level adhere to the rules prescribed by the enterprise architecture.

- Have knowledge of technologies and frameworks to provide technology consultancy to enterprises to choose the right technologies to solve problems.

- Conduct proof of architecture and proof of concept experiments to ensure that the end-to-end flow of the functionality works as per the defined architectural specifications.

- Gather nonfunctional requirements working with the business and make sure the solution designed meets the expectations set by the stakeholders.

- Suggest optimal development methodologies for the development teams to adopt during the build of the software system.

- Provide continuous support during the build of the solution to ensure that the product is built as per the defined architectural specifications and will help the enterprise to realize its business goals.

- Identify potential points of automation within the existing build and test processes and help the teams to build the same.

- Work with test managers to suggest the right tools for testing the solution components.

- Work with operations and assist them in creating the required hooks for the continuous build, test, and deploy pipelines.

- Work with infrastructure teams to suggest the requirements related to software services and infrastructure required for the deployment of the final product into production.

Being part of discussions during the takeover of the application for long term support and helping them write system operation manuals and decide on appropriate monitoring tools.

Attributes of a good solution architecture

The solution architecture should measure and refine itself against the given attributes for being a very effective blueprint to build a system, as follows:

- **Functionality**: The developed solution blueprint should be fit for purpose and address all the requirements of the system. The solution should not be made complicated than is required.

- **Extensibility**: This refers to the ease with which the solution lends itself to changes in the future. A rigid software architecture will resist changes and increase the total cost of ownership.

- **Scalability**: A good solution architecture lets the software scale well, whether it is vertical with the addition of resources, or horizontal with the addition of more nodes.

- **Performance**: A solution architecture should consider the performance **service level indicators** (**SLA**) specified for different transactions within the application. The architecture designed should not introduce performance bottlenecks as the load increases within the application.

- **Availability**: A solution architecture should promise a certain uptime of the system in each period. The system should be available at the time the software is being upgraded.

- **Security**: The architectural blueprint should ensure the privacy of the users as well as data during the flow of work and data within the system. The solution should recommend appropriate techniques for keeping data safe during transit and at rest.

- **Disaster recovery**: A solution architecture should have a minimum **recovery time objective** (**RTO**) and offer an effective **recovery point objective** (**RPO**). RTO is the time required to bring the system back to operation. RPO is the point from which the system can be recovered after failure.

- **Portability**: This attribute denotes how easy it is to port the solution to a different operating system, hardware configuration or a future version of the software runtime. This attribute is very important in a fast-changing technological world where operating systems and software runtimes evolve rapidly.

- **Maintainability**: This attribute denotes the ease with which the software can be maintained after it is deployed into production. The architecture should lend itself to generating metrics at different touch points within the software, which in turn can be used to monitor the system effectively.

- **Accessibility**: A solution architecture developed should provide well defined points of access to different capabilities of the software system. This will enable access to different functionality to stakeholders both within and outside the enterprise.

Architectural assumptions and exclusions

A solutions architect puts all this effort into making the solution as complete as possible and robust; practically, there are always a few areas for which complete information may not be available. This might include information about third party systems, integration touchpoints with systems owned by other divisions within the enterprise, and vendor supported third party applications, etc. In such cases, it is important to call out such dependencies or uncertainties and make way safely for other components to adjust themselves when things become clear down the line. For instance, the type of protocol may not be known for an external service that is accessible at multiple places within the application. This could be handled by applying a facade pattern, which acts as a point of access to the third-party system. This isolation will help to change the logic only at a single place instead of changing the application at multiple places where access to third party service is required.

Required technical skills

In this section, we will briefly list the skills required for a solutions architect.

A good solutions architect not only needs to possess sound technical skills but also have good soft skills. The right blend of the two makes the role of a solutions architect very effective while delivering value to the organization by solving problems and convincing multiple stakeholders of the decision-making process on the way to building software solutions.

The technical skills required for a solutions architect are as follows. We will go through each one of them in detail in *Chapter 3, Technical Proficiency Essential Knowledge*:

- Architectural styles
- Architectural patterns
- Design patterns
- Knowledge of technology frameworks
- Knowledge of cloud architectures
- Hands-on with contemporary programming languages
- Technologies of the past
- Being current with contemporary technologies
- Domain knowledge
- Development methodologies

Learning architecture in a systematic way

The best way to learn solution architecture is by doing. It is a very good way to be a part of solution discussions with other solutions architects and get to know what is being discussed and how the solution architecture evolves over time. The developer who has experience can also attempt to do solution architecture by learning common architectural and design patterns. They can apply their knowledge to problems in their own project and get it reviewed by the architects in their project team.

The other way to learn solution architecture in a systematic way is to take up an industry standard certification. There are good architecture certifications offered by organizations such as *The Open Group, Amazon, Microsoft,* and *Google.*

Learning from technology forums and blogs written by industry leaders will help a solutions architect to keep abreast of the latest developments in the architecture world. Industry leaders such as Microsoft and Google have created training material for associates with different levels of proficiency to master content related to solution architecture.

Signing up for courses on many of the online educational websites and apps is a good starting point to learn technology. There are overviews to give you a summary of the topic in about an hour, and courses running for tens of hours to give you an in-depth treatment of the topic of technology.

A picture is worth a million words. Likewise, in software, being hands-on is one of the most important skills for a solutions architect. Be proficient in one or more programming languages, design patterns, and architectural styles. Take a sample application or a scenario and code it end-to-end by applying the applicable architectural style and design patterns to internalize their usage.

Staying updated with emerging technologies and applying them to the solutions you develop is another way to keep evolving in this field.

Conclusion

In this chapter, we looked at the different architect roles in an organization and how the responsibilities of some of these roles overlap. We discussed what a solution architecture is and the drivers behind it. We then listed down the responsibilities of a solutions architect in an organization and the skills required for a solutions architect at the outset. We also looked at ways to systematically acquire and improve our solution architectural skills.

In the next chapter, we will use a checklist that an architect can use to ensure effective stakeholder engagement and communication, comprehensive requirements gathering, and architecting and designing a software system. We will also provide a checklist to ensure the quality of services, such as availability, security, performance, and scalability.

Join our Discord space

Join our Discord workspace for latest updates, offers, tech happenings around the world, new releases, and sessions with the authors:

https://discord.bpbonline.com

CHAPTER 2
Solutions Architect Checklist

Introduction

Designing a software system requires a multitude of skills. It requires good technology skills mixed with communication and interpersonal skills. If those skills are complemented with a systematic way of doing things, the software system created will be one that adds value to the enterprise in realizing its business goals. Many times, the architects will be technically good and possess good communication skills, but due to the lack of application of systematic thinking, the solution they create may have a lot of gaps in satisfying both functional and nonfunctional requirements. Even more important, the software system built should have the buy-in of all the stakeholders involved, without which it will not find any light at the end of the tunnel. Thus, it is critical to have the buy-in of all the stakeholders involved in the organization. A checklist will be very useful in inculcating a systematic thinking model into the minds of the solutions architect. This chapter introduces the reader to various checklists that can be used as a validation guide during the different phases of the software development lifecycle.

Structure

This chapter covers the following topics:

- Initiation to checklists
- Stakeholder communication and collaboration checklists
- Architecture, design, and development checklists
- Solution quality of service checklists
- Problem solving, innovation, and continuous improvement checklist

Objectives

The readers of the chapter will learn what a software architecture checklist is and the need for a checklist to be used by a solutions architect. The readers will get to know how to use a checklist. The chapter also covers checkpoints under different categories such as business stakeholder management, communication, requirements, architecture, design, and other quality of services, which are critical for developing a solution architecture. The chapter also contains solved questions at the end, which will help the reader to get an idea of the type of questions that will be asked in a solutions architect interview.

Initiation to checklists

A solution architecture checklist encompasses a list of checkpoints that are required to be verified by the solutions architect and the development team to ensure that the solution adheres to the needs of the business to realize the business goals of the organization. The checklist is created from industry standard best practices, proven architectural styles, design patterns, and commonly accepted software processes and procedures. They ensure that the system is well architected, flexibly designed, and at the same time, address the functional and non-functional requirements of the system.

A brief description of how each type of checklist will be useful is depicted in *Figure 2.1*:

Stakeholder management	Identify & Engage with business and Technology stakeholders in a meaningful way
Communications	Articulate Business value to key stakeholders in an effective way to get their buy-in
Architecture & Design	Architect & Design systems that conform to Industry as well as Enterprise standards
Software Development	Adding value throughout the software development lifecycle to multiple teams
Devops	Pipelines that help to standardize the build and quality of the software components
Availability	Ensure Availability of components to get maximum out of the designed system
Security	Provide Data Security during Transit and at Rest using Industry standard Practices
Performance	Ensure Optimum performance of System components for a great user experience
Scalability	Enable scalability using modern software design build and packaging processes
Usability	Build a modern but a usable system to provide a compelling user experience
Application Reliability	Application to be robust and provide fault tolerance and provide fault isolation
Problem Solving	Apply innovative approach to solve problems and identify opportunities for automation

Figure 2.1: Types of checklists

Need for a checklist

Consider the following scenarios:

- A solutions architect created an architecture that did not have enough controls to store the customer data securely. It was an application built for a healthcare provider. The customer data was compromised, which resulted in reputational damage to the company, and it ended up paying millions of dollars as a penalty.

- The software system created was tested for functionality, and it satisfied all the functional requirements. When it was deployed to production, it continued to work as expected, but when there was a special event and the load on the system spiked, the performance of the system degraded, resulting in a bad user experience and loss of business.

- A software system built for a retailer was not designed for redundancy of its critical services and was down for a substantial amount of time during a critical patching window, which resulted in a loss of business for the enterprise.

- A system was built for an insurance company, the navigation of which was very confusing for the users, resulting in an increase in call volume to its call center. The company had to spend a huge amount of money to maintain its call center resources.

All these scenarios resulted from a gap in one or more of the quality-of-service attributes of the software solution. This could have easily been prevented had the solutions architect followed a systematic approach to take care of the required qualities of service to be built into the system. A checklist will be useful to guide the architect and the development team to check if all the tasks pertaining to meeting the functional and nonfunctional requirements have been completed, for the system to be useful for the end users, thereby adding value to the enterprise.

Using the checklist

The checklist can be used by architects or by any stakeholder in the development team to verify the solution against each of the checkpoints in each category. This can be useful to identify gaps in the solution architecture to meet both its functional and non-functional requirements.

The following are the key points to keep in mind while using the checklist:

- Modify the checklist to suit your enterprise and project needs of functional and non-functional requirements.

- Apply principles of your enterprise architecture governance framework into each of the checklist categories, more so, while addressing the solution architecture and the quality of service attributes.

- The checklists have been created based on existing architectural and design principles, so refine the checklist because the principles evolve, and new ones arrive.

- Make a note of any exclusion from any of the steps given in the checklists, with a reason for the same, so that the decisions taken are well informed and data driven.

- Update or modify the checklists based on learnings from previous projects and suggestions from the stakeholders who are actively engaged in the design and building of the system.

- Review the checklist periodically and make sure it aligns with the goals of the software system being built.

Stakeholder communication and collaboration checklists

In this section, we will create checkpoints that a solutions architect can use to identify the problem statement, solidify it, and socialize it with the business and technology stakeholders of the enterprise. We will discuss how we can make the communication process more effective along the way so that there is consensus among the parties involved before a solutions architect can embark on the journey of architecting and developing the software system. We will also discuss a checklist for managing the requirements effectively.

Business stakeholder management checklist

Getting business stakeholders' buy-in is the key to any software project. The solutions architect must work with both the business and other technology stakeholders of the organization from the beginning to understand and redefine, if required, the business problem statement. Consensus among all the stakeholders in the organization is vital for the project's success.

The following is a checklist that the solutions architect can use as a reference to ensure proper stakeholder management at the start of the project:

- The architect has understood the business domain of the customer organization, which is the core of their existence.

- The architect has understood the business goals of your customer, for which they are ready to make business process and technology interventions.

- The architect has understood the existing business processes within the organization.

- The architect has understood the business and technology hierarchy within the organization.

- The architect has gained knowledge of the business architecture of their organization, where the business processes interact and collaborate with each other to offer value to their customers.

- The architect has understood the specific business problem of the customer, which needs technology or a process intervention.

- The architect has knowledge of the cost budget and timeline within which the business problem needs to be solved.

- Document the business problem that needs to be solved with sections such as the current and the desired states, impacted business units, goals that will be achieved, etc.

- The architect has identified the business and technology stakeholders that they need to work with.

- The stakeholders are apprised of the project's vision and how it helps to realize the enterprise business goals.

- The stakeholders are aware of the need to solve the business problem and have a consensus on the problem statement.

Having discussed the checkpoints to identify stakeholders and their business problems, we will move on to create a checklist to effectively plan and manage the communication channels with them.

Communication checklist

Once the stakeholders are identified, it is important to have meetings and workshops with different groups in the organization to elaborate and detail the problem statement. This will raise the problem space understanding of the solutions architect. The solutions architect also comes up with a mental model of the solution and socializes with different groups to get their consensus. It is very important for the solutions architect to use appropriate communication and collaboration platforms (Confluence, for example) to document the discussions during those meetings and workshops. The idea of this is to come up with a consensus on the problem definition and the overall process or technology intervention required. The checklist is as follows:

- The architect has grouped the stakeholders to whom the problem statement and the technology or process intervention need to be communicated.

- There is a clear plan of engagement with each of the stakeholder groups.

- The architect has identified the priority and order of meetings or workshops that need to be set up for communication with stakeholders.

- The problem is clearly articulated to the business and technology stakeholder groups with the relevant documents and presentations, including the data points and facts.

- The technology or process intervention that will be applied to solve the business problem has been clearly articulated.

- The stakeholders are convinced of the overall technology and process intervention suggested to solve the business problem.

- The possible technology choices that will be used for the solution have been discussed with the stakeholders.

- The suggested process interventions agreed by the stakeholders are in line with the business goals to be met.

- The business architecture impacts are communicated to all the stakeholder groups for an agreement.

- There is a consensus about the solution among the audience during those workshops or meetings.

- All the stakeholders are apprised of the timelines of the project and their engagement with respect to each of the project phases.
- The risks associated with the project and its impact on budget and timelines have been clearly communicated to all stakeholders.
- Risk mitigation plan is in place and has been articulated and shared with all the stakeholders.
- The key stakeholders that will have an influence on decisions throughout the project have been identified and engaged with.
- The key stakeholders have been communicated and have agreed on their involvement throughout the project based on fixed hours every week.
- Feedback has been received from the relevant customer stakeholders during those workshops or meetings.
- Documented the discussion during those meetings or workshops to get everybody on the same page. The minutes of meetings or notes are shared using a documentation platform like Confluence.
- Incorporated the changes based on the feedback received from the technology and business stakeholders.
- The revised technology and process intervention have been communicated to the stakeholders, including the executive management and project sponsor.
- Sign off is provided to proceed with the solution details to solve the problem.

Having seen the checkpoints to effectively engage with the business and technology stakeholders involved, we will move on to look at checkpoints that can help to efficiently manage requirements, which is the backbone of any software system.

Requirements management checklist

Once the problem statement is defined, the solutions architect works with the business analyst identified for the program and other business and technology stakeholders of the organization for requirement analysis. This requirement checklist will help the solutions architect to break down the problem statement into manageable chunks called requirements or user stories, in the case of Agile.

The following is a checklist that the solutions architect can use as a reference to effectively engage in the management of requirements at the start of the project:

- Helps project teams understand requirements as simple English statements.
- Helps businesses to prioritize requirements easily.
- Helps both the project and business teams to look at working software every two or three weeks and make amends as required to the application.
- The business analyst has started to refine the problem statement to break it down.
- Started to work with the technology stakeholders to understand the non-functional requirements like usability, security, performance, and scalability.
- The business analyst has written the user stories for both functional and non-functional requirements in the case of Agile development.
- In case of Waterfall, the business analyst has explicitly written the requirements as sections in a document that covers both functional and nonfunctional requirements.
- The business analyst has classified the user stories based on the area to which they belong, such as security, payments, accounts, operations, etc.

- Each of the requirements or the user story has been mapped to one or more of the business goals of the enterprise.

- The acceptance criteria have been identified for each of the user stories in consultation with the relevant stakeholders.

- The user stories are prioritized based on the criticality of achieving the business goals.

- A prototype has been created for the application to depict the functional and data flow within the application.

- A prototype has been socialized with all business stakeholders, and feedback received from them.

- Feedback received from the stakeholders has been incorporated into the prototype.

- The user stories are circulated to the business and technology stakeholders for sign off.

- Suggested changes by the customer, to re-prioritize the user stories, have been taken care of.

- The functional and non-functional requirements of user stories have been signed off by the business and technology stakeholders.

- A robust change management process has been created to incorporate the changes to the requirements or user stories during project execution.

Having discussed the stakeholder communication, collaboration, and requirement checklists, we will now discuss the technical checkpoints that a solutions architect can use to blueprint, design, and develop a software system.

Architecture, design, and development checklists

In this section, we will discuss checkpoints that a solutions architect can use to architect, design, and develop a system effectively. The solution architecture and design checklist will cover aspects to ensure that there are no gaps left when the solutions architect creates the architecture and design blueprint of the application. In the development checklist, we will talk about points the solutions architect needs to keep in mind to assist the development team in efficiently converting the design into a software system. We also have a DevOps checklist, which can be used to establish a mature DevOps culture within the project team to enable timeliness and quality of the software product.

We will first look at the architecture and design checklist that can be used by a solutions architect to blueprint the system.

Architecture and design checklist

Architecture and design checklist is the most important artefact that needs to be used by an architect to ensure that their solution is flexible, built to proven architectural styles, and meets the required quality of services. This checklist also addresses the required checkpoints to ensure that the software solution is designed in a parametrized way if it needs to support multiple lines of business or regions in which the organization operates. This checklist helps to ensure that various aspects of the software solution are thoroughly considered and addressed during the architecture and design of the application.

The following is a checklist that the solutions architect can use as guidelines for the architecture and design of a software application:

- The user stories for the functional and non-functional requirements are signed off.

- The functional and non-functional requirements are understood by the solutions architect.

- The architect has decided on the type of architectural style to be applied to the solution.

The following are examples of architectural styles:

- o **Model View Controller (MVC)**
- o REST-based
- o Microservices
- o Event-driven architecture

- The solutions architect has made sure that the layers are loosely coupled so that they can be replaced independently.

The following are examples of application layers:

- o Front end layer
- o Business layer
- o Database layer
- o Integration layer

- The architect has decided the type of functional and nonfunctional components required within the business layer.

The following are the examples:

- o Functional components include premium calculation, generation of a payment invoice, etc.
- o Nonfunctional components include logging from the application, storage to be used, etc.

- The architect has decided the type of communication required between the components.

The following are examples of communication types:

- o Synchronous **application programming interface (API)** and **remote procedure call (RPC)**
- o Asynchronous communication (queue based)

- The architect has decided on the format of the messages to be exchanged between the components.

The following are examples of message formats:

- o **JavaScript Object Notation (JSON)**
- o **Extensible Markup Language (XML)**
- o **Plain Old Java Objects (POJO)**

- The architecture created is flexible to absorb changes in the future without having to meddle with a lot of components in the system.
- The design is modular enough to ensure that they can be built, integrated, and tested independently once the development starts to build the application.
- The architecture caters to multiple lines of business, if required.
- The architecture and design externalize parameters that define the flow of the application based on the lines of business or regions.
- The architecture addresses the need to support multiple programming languages, if required.
- The architect has identified internal and external integration touch points that the application will communicate with.

The following are examples of internal and external integration touch points:

- o Internal authentication end point to authenticate users.

-     o   External API end point for valuation of a car given its model, make, year of manufacture, miles run, etc.

- The architect has understood the protocols with which the integration of the internal and external systems will happen.

- The architect has understood and documented the storage requirements of the system.

- The architect has understood and documented the security requirements of the system.

- The architect has understood and documented the availability requirements of the system.

- The scalability requirements of the system have been understood and documented.

- The architect has understood and documented the performance requirements of the system.

- The architect has understood and documented the usability and **user experience** (**UX**) requirements for the application.

- The architect has identified the shared capabilities required for the solution.

  The following are examples of shared capabilities in a software system:
    - o   Reporting tools for the application
    - o   Identity and access management system
    - o   Workflow software

- The architect has identified and documented the operational systems to be communicated with, to get enterprise level data for the application.

- The architect has identified foreseeable dependencies and risks for the application.

- The architect has documented and shared the foreseeable risks with the business and technology stakeholders and the project management team.

- The architect has made a choice of technologies to be included in the building of different types of components in the system.

  The following are examples of technology choices:
    - o   Angular or React JS, for the front-end components.
    - o   Spring Boot or .NET for the business components.

- The architect has considered the options of using a contemporary application framework versus build from scratch approach for the solution.

- The architect has conducted **Proof of Architecture** (**PoA**) experiments for critical components and integration touch points within the application to ensure protocol type, performance, and security guardrails are applied to data.

- The results of the proof of architecture have been documented and shared with all the stakeholders of the project.

- The architecture is socialized with the relevant business and technology stakeholders, and its salient features and limitations are articulated to them.

- The dependencies and risks are clearly articulated to all stakeholders.

- The feedback is received, incorporated, and a consensus is reached for the architecture to be used to build the solution.

- There is a sign-off received from the technology stakeholders of the organization to go ahead with the system build to resolve the business problem.

- The architecture is socialized with the project team, including project managers, developers, and testers who will build and test the system.

Having seen the checklist for architecture and design, we will now move on to discuss the software development lifecycle checklist that can be used by the solutions architect to mentor, monitor, and assist the development team.

Software development lifecycle checklist

In modern day enterprises, the role of the architect does not end with creating a blueprint of the system by applying their knowledge of architectural styles and design patterns. They are also expected to be part of the bigger project team during the whole development process, helping all development stakeholders like project managers to plan the sprints, to development leads for helping them with productivity improvements, to test managers to devise test strategy and to developers to help them with modern and safe coding practices. The solutions architect also works with the DevOps engineer to recommend to them the best practices for creating the DevOps pipelines for continuous integration, delivery, and deployment, as needed. They also work with different specialized teams like the performance team, security team, and the deployment team to arrive at optimum strategies for meeting the nonfunctional requirements of the solution. Apart from this, they also work with the infrastructure team to arrive at the layout of the services required for the application.

The following are the checkpoints that the software architect can use to add value during the different phases of the **software development lifecycle** (**SDLC**):

- The architect assists the project manager, Scrum Master, and the development team in planning the sprint.
- The architect assists the Scrum teams regularly to clarify details on the design of the specific feature functionality being built.
- The architect has come up with coding practices to be adopted by the development team.
- The architect conducts code reviews to assess the quality of the code being written.
- The architect helps the development team recommend unit testing frameworks to test the application code, depending on the type of component, like frontend, backend, and database components.
- The architect works with the development team to suggest ways to improve the velocity of the team.
- The architect assists the project manager in reassessing time and effort for components if a major change is foreseen for a functional or nonfunctional requirement.
- The architect conducts regular reviews of the development team's work for any deviations from the approved solution.
- The architect assists the test manager and testers to devise ways for testing different types of components, including frontend and backend components.
- The architect keeps a close watch on the quality of services being met by the solution built by the development team.

Having discussed the development checklist, we will move on to discuss the DevOps checklist. The DevOps culture has become inevitable for building quality solutions and is being adopted by large as well as small enterprises across the globe.

DevOps checklist

DevOps has become an integral part of the SDLC in most projects. In short, DevOps is an integration of tasks of the development and operations teams into a single bucket to improve the quality of the software developed and reduce the time to market the software. A DevOps pipeline encompasses different stages or hooks that the software component goes through and gets itself certified for meeting the functional and nonfunctional requirements. The DevOps team is mostly a shared services team that helps different projects in building the required pipelines.

The architect works closely with the DevOps team to create the required pipelines for their project. They ensure that the DevOps pipeline requirements are met for their project. They decide the different stages of the pipeline based on the nature of the components in the project. They work with the DevOps team to define the success or failure criteria for each of the stages of the pipeline. The essential knowledge required about DevOps for an architect is discussed in *Chapter 8, DevOps Essentials.*

The following is a checklist that the architect can use as a reference to ensure proper implementation of the DevOps culture in the project:

- The team delivers code to the version-controlled codebase repository at regular intervals.

  In small enterprises, the solutions architect decides the technology for building the pipeline. However, as stated before, in large enterprises, the DevOps team is a centralized team which builds the DevOps pipeline for multiple projects. In such a case, the solutions architect works with the DevOps team to define the stages of the pipeline for their project.

- The technology for the **continuous integration and continuous delivery** (**CI/CD**) pipeline is finalized for the project by the architect in consultation with the DevOps team.

  The following are examples of technology for CI/CD pipelines:
  - Jenkins
  - Gitlab
  - GitHub actions
  - Azure DevOps

- The DevOps pipeline is configured as code by using YAML, etc.

- The stages of the pipeline are finalized based on the nonfunctional requirements of the project engagement.

  The following are examples of the stages in the pipeline:
  - Unit testing
  - Functional test
  - Security test
  - Performance test
  - Parallel testing

- Each stage of the pipeline has its own measurements for success or failure, acting as a quality gate.

- Each quality gate has its own key success or failure criteria defined for it.

  The following is an example of success or failure for the performance test stage:
  - Transactions per second or throughput
  - Response time
  - Number of errors
  - Threads created

- Developers have a clear view of how their code flows within the pipeline and the success or failure of each stage.

- **Infrastructure as code** (**IaC**) is implemented for the project.

- Each component has its own code base and is independently versioned and baselined.
- Static code analysis is being carried out as part of the pipeline.

    The following are examples of static code analyzers:
    - SonarQube
    - Klocwork

- There are distinct environments for development and test (functional, security, performance).
- There is logging and auditing process in place for each of the build that happens through the pipeline.

A complex and sophisticated architecture may not add value unless it offers the required quality of services to its users. Having discussed the architecture, design, and DevOps checklists that can be used within the software development lifecycle. We will now discuss checklists for ensuring the quality of services of the software application.

Solution quality of service checklists

We will start by looking at the checkpoints that a solutions architect can use to ensure the availability of the software system as required by the enterprise.

Availability checklist

Availability is one of the key qualities of a software system. Each enterprise wants its services and products to be available to its customers on a 24/7 basis, and any downtime would mean a loss of business for the enterprise. Solutions architects are very particular about this attribute and make sure that their solution lends itself to the maximum availability (expressed as a percentage, such as 99.5% availability) of the system after it has been deployed in production. The solutions architect works with the infrastructure team to understand and recommend appropriate infrastructure layouts. They also work with the production support team to make sure that proper monitoring tools are in place to alert the production support staff and the developers concerned of any issues in production that might affect the system up time.

The following is a checklist that the solutions architect can use as a reference to ensure the continuous availability of the deployed application:

- SLA for availability has been discussed and agreed upon with the business and technology stakeholders of the organization.
- Disaster recovery plan is in place for the application in case of an outage to the application.
- RTO has been defined for the application.
- RPO has been defined for the application.
- The application has been redundantly deployed across two or more data centers to handle unforeseen outages.
- Application components are redundantly deployed within the same data center based on the peak load of the system.
- Load balancing techniques are in place to route requests to multiple servers to spread the load on the system.
- Monitoring mechanisms are in place to detect any failure of the application components and alert the development and production support teams.
- Appropriate procedures have been defined to heal the system, in case of alerts being triggered with respect to the health of the system.

- Failover tests are conducted to ensure that the switch happens to healthy instances of the components or servers in case of an outage.

- Appropriate patch management procedures are in place to not disrupt the system during the patching process.

- The software uses practices like blue green and canary deployment for moving new components into production to avoid application down time and increase reliability.

Having discussed the availability checklist, we will move on to see the checkpoints a solutions architect can use to ensure security of the software application being built.

Security checklist

Security is one of the key considerations for any software application. The application could be dealing with sensitive and confidential data like health information and bank information. It needs to have proper controls built into it to handle such information types. Apart from that, the application will use technical information for its internal use, like database passwords and encryption keys. It should consider using appropriate means of securing data when it is on the wire and during storage. Suitable transport layer security protocols can be used to encrypt data, be it customer information or internally used information like passwords. Information like passwords and encryption keys can be stored in vaults. In parallel, the customer data needs to be encrypted before it is stored. Refer to the following checklist:

- The security principles of the application adhere to the enterprise architecture governance framework of the organization.

- The users are authenticated before they are allowed to access the features of the application.

- The users have access to application features and data only based on the role defined for them within the application.

- **Personally identifiable information** (**PII**) is being stored securely by the application.

- Transport level security is enabled for communication between the components within the application, if the components are deployed independently and communication happens through the network.

  The following are the examples of Transport Layer Security protocols:

  o Transport Layer Security 1.x (TLS 1.2, TLS 1.3)

  o Secure Sockets Layer, (SSL 2.0, SSL 3.0)

  o Datagram transport layer security

- Secrets within the application are stored securely by the application; for example, **Amazon Web Services** (**AWS**) key store and Azure key vault can be used to store the secrets such as database passwords.

- Proper encryption algorithms are being used by the application to store confidential data within the application.

- All the inputs from the user are sanitized before they enter the application business components. The user input sanitization of data will help in preventing attacks such as cross site request scripting, SQL injection, and command injection attacks.

- The application passes inputs to the database query as parameters to avoid SQL injection.

- The application uses only enterprise authorized frameworks and libraries.

- The libraries and dependencies of the application are patched regularly to prevent any security attacks on the application.

- Exceptions are handled properly within applications and are not exposed to the users of the application.

- All entry points to the application are TLS enabled.

- All HTTP calls to the application are redirected to HTTPS within the application.

- The application follows the principle of least privileges, which warrants that the user should only have the minimum permissions to perform their tasks within the application.

- The application is tested for security vulnerabilities for every build that goes through the DevOps pipeline.

- The architect has created a security profile for the application.

- The code is being checked for vulnerabilities as listed in the **Open Web Application Security Project** (**OWASP**).

Having discussed the security checklist, we will now discuss the checkpoints a solutions architect can use to ensure the performance of the application, which is one of the top priorities before the application moves to production.

Performance checklist

Performance of an application becomes a key aspect for certain types of applications, like stock broking, flight booking, where even milliseconds could make a difference. In practice, the application is load tested for performance and is monitored for key performance indicators like throughput and response time. Profiling of the application is also done to assess the memory footprint of the components at run time. The code is changed to become more efficient if the time taken to execute a function is larger than expected.

The following is a checklist that the solutions architect can use as a reference to ensure that the application meets performance requirements:

- All external libraries and frameworks are tested for their performance before being used in the project.

- The application mainly uses asynchronous communication between the components via queues.

- A cache is used by the application to persist and read data that is required for quick references.

    The following are the examples of cache:

    o REDIS

    o Memcached

- The application uses NoSQL Databases to store unstructured data rather than a **relational database management system** (**RDBMS**).

- All critical components in production have **application performance monitoring** (**APM**) enabled for them to monitor and alert production and development teams to avoid failures becoming outages.

- Break point tests are conducted for each component to assess the maximum load that the component can take with a standard configuration of computing resources (CPU, memory, etc.).

- Load testing has been conducted for each component and all integration touch points to ensure that the system can take up the anticipated load.

- Profiling of components is being done for components where the response time exceeds the accepted service levels.

- **Content delivery network** (**CDN**) is leveraged, if the application serves users across multiple geographies.

- The network and deployment topology of the application is designed to have a minimum latency.

- Data partitioning is in place to split the data across multiple nodes to reduce the load on a single node.

- Long running tasks are identified and the system is designed to execute such tasks in an offline mode.

- For APIs, policies are in place to limit the number of requests per minute to prevent overloading of requests on the infrastructure.

Having discussed the performance checklist, we will move on to discuss a checklist to ensure scalability of the application.

Scalability checklist

Scalability of an application indicates its ability to replicate its components when a single instance of a component is unable to take the load coming into the system. The scalability of the system gives the required power to the application to function with optimum performance.

The following is a checklist that the architect can use as reference to ensure that the application developed and deployed is scalable based on load:

- All the services in the application are developed in a stateless manner.

- All the services in the application behave in an idempotent manner.

- The components of the application are deployed as containers.

- Auto scaling is enabled for the application which increases the number of nodes or instances during peak load and brings them down during reduced loads.

- The architecture supports addition of more resources to individual nodes or servers (vertical scaling).

- The architecture supports addition of more nodes or servers to the cluster as needed (horizontal scaling).

- There are monitoring mechanisms available in the production environment to alert the maintenance team of any issues related to performance or load on the system.

- The application does not use the local file system for writing and reading files from the application.

- The data storage system is designed to expand based on the increase in its volume.

- The database has one or more read instances or replicas to reduce the load on the write instance.

- The application uses expandable storage for artefacts like documents, images, and videos.

    The following are examples of expandable storage:

    o   AWS **Simple Storage Service (S3)**

    o   Azure Blob Storage

Having discussed the scalability checklist, we will now discuss a checklist to make the system usable for different types of users.

Usability checklist

User experience is one of the important criteria for an application to succeed. The user interface of an application must be intuitive and should guide the user to perform different transactions with ease in the system.

The following is a checklist that the architect can use to ensure that the application developed is user friendly and meets usability requirements:

- The application is designed as a single page application, and all the user interface elements loads within the page load time service level agreement.

- The software solution is built to be cross browser compliant as required by the business.

- The system supports all the form factors like web, mobile, and tablets as warranted by the system business requirements.

- The software system is responsive in nature, supporting different sizes and configurations of form factors.

- There are specific user personas for which specific navigational flows are built into the system.

- The application is designed to easily discover the most used features of the system.

- The software is designed to hint to the user during various stages of transaction progress and completion within the application.

- The system handles erroneous inputs gracefully and gives back simple and useful messages to the user for correcting them.

- Appropriate design patterns, like backend for frontend pattern, have been leveraged to expose the capabilities of the system to different form factors.

- The software architecture is designed for customization of features for the users of the system.

- The architecture offers switches to turn on and off features of the software system as per the needs of the business.

- The capabilities of the system can be easily rolled out to both internal business divisions and external enterprises, if required.

- The design of the system allows users to navigate without the need for any external assistance.

- The user flows are gamified within the application to make it appealing to users based on the target audience.

Application reliability is more about the robustness of the system. In the next section, we will discuss a checklist to ensure application reliability.

Application reliability checklist

Reliability ensures the correct and optimum performance of the system continuously over a period. The architect adopts several measures like rigorous testing practices, building fault tolerance, and isolation of failures to ensure reliability. Monitoring and alert mechanisms are enabled in the software system to continuously measure the performance of critical services in the application and alert appropriate teams if the application is starved of resources like CPU and memory. The solutions architect can also adopt distributed architectures like microservices to reduce the complexity of the individual components of the software system, which increases reliability.

The following is a checklist that the architect can use as a reference to ensure the reliability of the software designed:

- Services are classified based on their criticality (platinum, gold, and silver), and redundancy is built for them based on their criticality.

- The architect has broken down complex software components into multiple smaller and simpler ones to reduce the complexity within a single component and reduce the probability of application failure.

- Monitoring and alert mechanisms are in place for components that are critical to the functioning of the business.

- In the case of microservices, graceful degradation during failure of the individual microservice is ensured using the circuit breaker pattern.

- Chaos testing is in place for the application to check if the application behavior is predictable in case of a network or external application outage.

- Distributed tracing is enabled for distributed applications to understand the paths taken by each request to quickly debug problems.

The following are examples of traceability tools:

- o X-Ray in AWS
- o Azure Monitor
- o Google Cloud Trace
- o Zipkin (open-source)

- Centralized logging is in place for the application to correlate information, in case of a component failure, and a need to debug.

- Log index tools are in place to search the log dumps and identify issues pertaining to failed requests.

- Exception clustering from log files and causal analysis of those exceptions are being done on a regular basis.

- Mechanisms are made available to handle exceptions and errors so as not to interrupt the user flow within the application.

  The following is an example:

  - o In some of the travel booking portals, if a particular payment option is unavailable the users are requested to try other payment methods and are appropriately taken to that screen flow.

- The application is built to be fault tolerant and individual components can be isolated and fixed in case of failures.

We have looked at different checklists till now to ensure that the system offers the required quality of service to its end users. These checklists help the solutions architects to ensure that the software system built by them is available, reliable, performant, and usable. In the next section, we will discuss checkpoints solutions architects can use to be innovative in their problem-solving approach and continuously improve the quality of the solution.

Problem solving, innovation, and continuous improvement checklist

The solutions architect continuously works with the project team to help them realize their development goals. This, in turn, helps the overall enterprise to realize its business goals with optimum resources, effort, and cost. The architect helps the team improve their productivity. They are also smart enough to develop their own tools to perform certain tasks without depending on expensive licensed tools. For example, the architect might write their own utility to measure the network latency rather than depending on a licensed tool or an open-source framework, that may not be permissible by the enterprise architecture governance framework, as follows:

- The architect has applied a human centered approach to their solution for the problem being solved.

- The solutions architect has chosen the right tools to solve different problems during the process of architecture and design.

- The architect helps the project team identify the right development tools, for example, IDEs, to complete their development tasks in time and with quality.

- The architect foresees external dependencies during the initiation phase of the project and helps the project manager to plan accordingly.

- The architect makes workarounds for the dependencies during the design and development phase of the project, for example, creation of stubs for virtualizing unavailable external services.

- The architect prioritizes the order of technical activities to be done to solve a problem to optimize effort, time and cost. For example, the architect may apply the API first design principle to ensure that the contracts are defined, and all developers can code to those contracts before coding the front end or the backend services.

- The architect creates their own tools for automating tasks rather than depend on expensive tools.

- The architect helps the team to identify opportunities for automation to improve the productivity of the team.

- The architect helps the development team to build automation solutions/utilities to automate repeatable tasks in the project.

- The architect foresees potential risks to development of feature functionality and adopts techniques to mitigate them.

- The architect keeps an eye of the team's velocity and trains them to bridge skill gaps to improve the velocity.

Having seen the checkpoints to make the solution innovative and identify opportunities for continuous improvement, we will move on to discuss question and answers that a solutions architect might be asked in an interview about effectively engaging with stakeholders, manage requirements and provide the required software quality of services in the solution being built.

Conclusion

In this chapter, we looked at the composition of a software checklist and the need for using a checklist. We created checklists for different stages of the software development lifecycle, like stakeholder engagement, communication, architecture, and design. We also looked at the checkpoints for performance, scalability, security, availability, usability, and reliability for ensuring the quality of the services of the software components.

In the next chapter, we will look at the essential knowledge for building a software system. This will include the different design patterns and principles. We will list the critical services for the popular cloud platform providers. We will also learn about networking. We will also cover the usage of machine learning and AI in modern software systems.

Key takeaways

The takeaways are as follows:

- **Checklists and the need for a checklist**: Understand what a checklist is and why it is important for a solutions architect to have a checklist.

- **How to use a checklist**: How a solutions architect can make use of the checklists provided and contribute to a smooth flow of the SDLC.

- **Stakeholder management, communication and requirements management**: Understand checkpoints to be used to identify and communicate with the stakeholders to get their buy-in. Learn to manage changing requirements efficiently.

- **Technical knowledge checklist**: Understand checkpoints to be used to manage architecture and design. Learn the checkpoints that can be used during the development phase of the SDLC.

- **Quality-of-services**: Learn about check points to monitor and ensure quality-of-services like performance, scalability, availability and security.

- **Model interview questions and answers**: Model questions and answers for the reader preparing for the solutions architect interview.

Model interview questions and answers

1. **Can you provide an example of how you engaged with stakeholders to gain their buy-in for a design change in software?**

   Model answer:

   - You will identify the key business and technology stakeholders of the system to whom you need to communicate the change.

   - You will set up a discussion session with them to explain the design change that you are planning to make.

   - You will explain to them the criticality of the change to either the functionality of the application or the nonfunctional requirements.

   - You will explain the impact of the change on the existing architecture and design and its impact of the change on the timeline and budget.

   - You will ask for their consensus to go ahead with the change before it is made on the artefacts of the project.

   - You will make the changes to the system once you receive a confirmation note/email from them, which you will consider as a sign off.

2. **How will you contribute to the development phase of the project as a solutions architect?**

   Model answer:

   - Understand the software methodology being used in the project.

   - Assuming it is Agile based, you will work with the DevOps team to define the quality gates for the application.

   - You will also define the criteria for success and failure for the quality gates of the DevOps pipeline used by the components.

   - You will define best practices for coding to be used by the developers in line with industry-accepted best practices and the enterprise architecture framework.

   - You will work with the test manager to come up with the test strategy for testing the application end to end by suggesting test tools that will easily lend itself based on the architecture of the application.

   - You will conduct regular reviews of the design being used to build the application to ensure that it is based on the agreed architecture and call out any deviations to be corrected by the development team.

   - You will contribute to the change management process to assist the project management office to assess risks, ways to mitigate them and a build a framework to calculate the effort and costs associated with the change, based on their size.

3. **How will you ensure scalability of your end user application for an upcoming major sale festival when the load is expected to go up two-fold?**

   Model answer:

   - You will ensure that auto scaling for the components is enabled to scale up and scale down based on load.

   - You will ensure redundancy of the critical services in production and set up a load balancer to distribute the load between the redundant instances of the service.

- You will ensure that monitoring mechanisms are in place in production to alert the production support and the development team in case of any spikes in the resources used by the application, like memory, CPU, etc.

- You will closely monitor the log files using tools like Splunk to look for any unusual errors or exceptions and conduct a quick root cause analysis of those exceptions and errors.

- You will also enable auto healing mechanism on the servers, such as dynamic memory upgrade, based on the percentage of usage of the resources by the application.

- You will enable dynamic tracing using tools like AWS X-Ray or Zipkin to monitor the passage of requests across application components to find out the point of stall, in case few of the requests fail to go through.

- You will create read replicas of the database to reduce load on the write instance of the database.

4. **As an architect, how will you ensure the security of data within the application you are designing for a healthcare provider?**

   Model answer:

   - You will ensure two types of security within the application:

     o **Security of data during transit**: You will enable it using protocols like TLS and UDLS.

     o **Security of data at rest**: You will enable it by encrypting data before it is stored.

   - You will redirect all HTTP requests to use HTTPS for the end users.

   - You will store all the credentials used by the application like database passwords and secrets in a key vault to safeguard them.

   - The data can be encrypted before its stored in a database on a default encryption mechanism can be enabled before persisting any data on the database.

   - Access to supporting documents like medical records and prescriptions that will be stored in an object storage service like AWS S3 or Azure Blob Storage will be based on user roles with limited permissions like read only.

5. **How will you ensure that an application you are designing for school students is easy to use?**

   Model answer:

   - You will design the application to be supported for multiple channels like web, mobile and tablets.

   - You will ensure that the front end works on a variety of browsers and their versions.

   - The application is designed to easily discover the most used features of the system.

   - You will design the software to give explicit and user-friendly messages to the student when they are facing any usage related issue within the application.

   - The system is fault tolerant to handle erroneous inputs (auto corrects in possible cases) and gives back simple and useful messages to the user for correcting them.

   - You will gamify the user flows as much as possible to make usage of the application easy and fun for the students.

6. **How will you design an application for stock brokers, where performance and reliability are extremely important?**

   Model answer:

   - You will work with the business and technology stakeholders to understand the **key performance indicators** (**KPIs**) like throughput and response time.

   - You will architect the system as loosely coupled components so that they can be independently scaled.

   - You will enable asynchronous messages as the mode of communication between the components.

   - You will keep the payload to be lighter, that is passed between components during transactions.

   - You will work with the networking team to ensure that the latency of the network is kept to a minimum.

   - You will load test the system with the specified number of users, that corresponds to the maximum load expected on the system.

   - You will use monitoring tools like AppDynamics or Dynatrace to measure critical health parameters like memory and CPU consumption, errors and exceptions, when the system is subjected to maximum load.

   - You will perform a breakpoint test on a single instance of the component/server to measure the thresholds it can withstand.

   - Based on the breakpoint test results and the required KPIs, you will suggest the infrastructure capacity to be planned for the application.

   - You will setup alert mechanisms in production servers to monitor the performance of the application and alert the infrastructure and development teams in case of any deterioration to performance.

Join our Discord space

Join our Discord workspace for latest updates, offers, tech happenings around the world, new releases, and sessions with the authors:

https://discord.bpbonline.com

CHAPTER 3
Technical Proficiency Essential Knowledge

Introduction

In this chapter, we will begin by explaining the terminology used during the architecture and design phases of software applications. We will cover the essential knowledge required for an architect to design enterprise applications. We will discuss industry standard design patterns and principles. We will also provide essential knowledge on cloud, databases, security, and networking. We will also touch up on the emerging technologies that an architect needs to be aware of, to have meaningful discussions and apply them to the design of applications based on business requirements.

Structure

This chapter covers the following topics:

- Architecture and design vocabulary
- Application design patterns essential knowledge
- Design approaches essential knowledge
- Design principles essential knowledge
- Cloud computing essential knowledge
- Database management essential knowledge
- Application security essential knowledge
- Networking essential knowledge
- Emerging technologies essential knowledge

Objectives

In this chapter, readers will gain an understanding of the terminology used in architecture and design. The solutions architect will especially learn to apply industry standard design approaches and design patterns at the right places during the design of enterprise applications. The readers will gain essential knowledge on cloud computing, database management, security, and networking. Readers will get to know the emerging trends like generative AI and quantum computing that will help the solutions architect to have meaningful technical conversations and design modern day software applications. The chapter also covers questions and answers that a solutions architect might be asked in a technical interview.

Architecture and design vocabulary

In this section, we will look at the terminologies used in the architecture and the design space that a solutions architect is supposed to be conversant about. We will explain each one of these terms with examples. It is important that the architect understands the difference between these terms, as these are being used interchangeably in the realm of software architecture and design. Once the architect gets a clear grasp of the associated terminology, it becomes easier to have conversation with fellow architects and makes their thoughts clearer during documentation and articulation (socialization) of the solution architecture and design. The architect should know that the architectural styles, architectural patterns and design patterns can be applied together in a collective manner during the end-to-end design and implementation of a software system.

Architectural styles

An architectural style expresses at a high level as to how a software system is structured (blueprint), developed and deployed. They do not solve a specific architectural problem at hand. An architectural style expresses the ways in which the components or the code can be organized in an application, at a high level. Some of the architectural styles are as follows:

- Monolith architectural style
- Layered architectural style
- Distributed architectural style
- Messaging architectural styles

Let us understand architectural style with the following real-world examples:

- Building a manufacturing unit for producing cars
- Building a housing complex with hundreds or thousands of apartments in it

In these examples, the architect will use a totally different style to build them.

Architectural styles are abstract answers to the question or challenge of how different components in a software application can be arranged or stacked together. For example, an artist will draw the outline of a picture, which gives an idea of what the picture is going to look like when it is completed. The architectural style is not a readymade solution to an application architecture problem, and it helps the architect to decide the broader blueprint of the solution.

Architectural styles operate at a higher level of abstraction to provide a highly granular view of the layers or the components' arrangement and their mode of communication within the application. Choosing an architectural style gives clarity to the architect about the arrangement of modules in the application and the mode of communication between them. It is to be noted that the architect can mix two or more architectural styles to create their solution for the software.

Architectural patterns

Architectural patterns help us to implement architectural styles in a particular way. They provide industry proven solutions to solve specific architecture problems within an application. It expresses a zoomed in view of the modules that will be present in the application and defines the contract of responsibility and interaction of each one of those modules. The architectural pattern will draw its initial idea of the solutions architecture from its abstract architectural style parent and expand it for additional details. An application can be built with a chosen architectural style, and each architectural style can be realized with the application of one or more architectural patterns.

Some popular architecture patterns are as follows:

- Client server architecture
- MVC pattern
- Event-driven architecture

To conclude, architectural styles and patterns are interchangeably used in the architecture world, but there is a subtle difference between the two, which the architect needs to be aware of.

Design approach

Application design deals with the details of creating applications for the enterprise. Business problem statements are analyzed and elaborated by a business analyst. A solutions architect chooses a design approach that best suits the problem to be solved. It is chosen in such a way that it helps the enterprise to optimize design and development in terms of effort, efficiency, and cost. The design approach chosen is also dependent on the way the organization is structured. Key stakeholders are identified from business and technology groups, and they participate in the design and development exercise of the software application. The design approach chosen should also lend itself to meeting both functional and nonfunctional requirements of the application. The design approach should give the enterprise flexibility to change or extend the functionality without expending a lot of effort and cost. At the same time, it should also lend itself to meet the software quality of service attributes like scalability, performance, availability, security, and reliability.

For example, if scalability is important, a design approach that divides the software into multiple chunks will be a better option, as that will enable each chunk to scale independently. If the application developed has a need to work with several vendors accepting requests to offer its service, then a design approach that gives importance to the request-response contract will be a better choice.

We will look at the following design approaches in the section *Application design patterns essential knowledge*:

- **Domain-Driven Design (DDD)**
- API first design
- **Artificial intelligence (AI)** first design

Design patterns

Design patterns are solutions to commonly occurring problems during the design and development of object-oriented software applications. As a software architect, it is important to know the industry standard way of solving certain design problems that we encounter time and again in building applications. It is beneficial that the architect does not spend time trying to solve these problems that have already been solved in the best possible way. It is important that the architect identifies these problems or situations in design and development and applies appropriate patterns to overcome those problems. It not only helps the architect save time but trying to solve these common problems in software design, in their very own way might sometimes be incomplete and error prone. To use these patterns, it is important that the architect internalizes the pattern's usage to identify the right places and opportunities during software design and development.

We will look at the following design patterns in the section *Application design patterns essential knowledge*:

- Gang of Four design patterns
- Enterprise application design patterns

Application design principles

Design principles are industry proven and accepted guidelines for creating a flexible, reusable, and extensible software system. These principles aid loose coupling of the software components and enhance the quality of the software developed in terms of scalability, modularity, and maintainability. Unlike design patterns, they do not solve a problem on their own. However, they are the leading light that developers and architects should follow for the developed system to be flexible in the long term, after the software is deployed in production. The software systems following the proven design principles lend themselves to change very easily.

We will look at the following design principles in the section *Application design patterns essential knowledge*:

- SOLID design principles
- **Keep it simple, stupid (KISS)**
- **Don't repeat yourself (DRY)**

Note: **In this chapter, we will study in detail the foundational design patterns, enterprise application design patterns, and common approaches used for designing applications. We will also discuss design principles to be applied for cleaner and maintainable code. In the next chapter, we will discuss architectural patterns in detail and their applicability to the architecture of enterprise applications.**

Application design patterns essential knowledge

We discussed what design patterns are and how they are useful in the design of software components and applications in the previous section. Design patterns can be applied at multiple levels of abstraction. They are applied at a granular level within the scope of individual application components (foundational patterns) or across components to address design concerns (enterprise application patterns). In complex enterprise applications, we can use enterprise design patterns to address concerns regarding database access, inter component communication, log management, etc. we will discuss the following types of design patterns in this section:

- Gang of Four design patterns also called the foundational patterns
- Enterprise application design patterns used in the design of enterprise applications

Gang of Four design patterns

Gang of Four (GoF) are also called the fundamental design patterns and are applicable to the **object-oriented programming (OOP)** style. These can be applied to applications of any size that require creation of objects, structuring those objects to form complex ones and manage interaction between those objects. The fundamental design patterns promotes cleaner code with a set of principles that promulgate the idea of separation of concerns of different tasks (object creation and their behavior) within a software component. It is important to note that design patterns are not specific to any programming language, and they can be applied to any programming language to solve a specific object-oriented design challenge.

There are three different types of fundamental design patterns, as follows:

- Creational patterns
- Structural patterns
- Behavioral patterns

Creational patterns

Let us see creational design patterns that deal with the construction of objects in an application to address different types of design challenges.

We can use the creational patterns in the following scenarios:

- **Factory pattern**: Decouple object creation logic from business logic of the application; Create different object types based on input passed.

- **Prototype pattern**: Create a duplicate copy (clone) of an existing object in an application.

- **Builder pattern**: Create complex objects with a different set of properties (representation) every time.

- **Singleton pattern**: Want to manage only a single instance of an object in the application, thereby avoiding proliferation of objects in the system.

The following are examples of how creational patterns can be applied:

- Application needs to continue to work with a newer and older version of a feature functionality component (factory pattern).

- Create a complex credit card object (Visa or Master Card) with different properties and return to main application (builder pattern).

- Application needs to create a duplicate of an existing Bank Account Object and pass to a third-party interface (prototype pattern).

- A single object in the application that allows access to a particular resource like a printer (singleton pattern).

Structural patterns

Structural design patterns provide standard ways to organize objects in different ways using composition and create different object hierarchies as required by the application. They also provide ways to manipulate the structure and edit or delete objects from the existing structure.

We can use the structural patterns in the following scenarios:

- **Adapter pattern**: Allows an application component to work with another incompatible application component by using an adapter between them.

- **Bridge pattern**: Separate an interface from its implementation so that they can evolve independently.

- **Composite pattern**: Allow objects to be represented as hierarchies and build relationships between them using composition.

- **Façade pattern**: Allow a simplified interface to access more complex functionality underneath.

- **Decorator pattern**: Allow an objects behavior or functionality to be extended using a wrapper object that adds additional behavior.

- **Proxy pattern**: Need a placeholder interface or object to an underlying object and control access.

- **Flyweight pattern**: The flyweight pattern emphasizes the sharing of data between multiple instances of the same type of object.

The following are practical examples of how structural patterns are used:

- When an upgraded e-commerce application needs to continue to work with an older version of an inventory component, you create an adapter that translates the request to match the interface acceptable by the inventory application.

- In making a database connection in Java, we use the bridge pattern, JDBC drivers implement the driver interface and provide database-specific behavior (MySQL or Oracle). The `DriverManager` class acts as a bridge to identify the appropriate driver implementation based on the connection URL and delegates connection requests to the driver.

- If you are building an application for an automobile dealership aggregator that deals with different manufacturers and vehicle types, you can create an `AutomobileComposite` class that can hold objects like manufacturer details, automobile details to aggregate information pertaining to a particular manufacturer and the vehicle type (Car, truck, etc.).

- In an e-commerce application, when you want to place an order to an external partner that uses a proprietary interface, you create a façade to hide the complexity of interacting with the interface from the client.

- When you want to access a **Simple Object Access Protocol** (**SOAP**) web service, you use a proxy pattern and generate the required stubs to call the web service. The stubs makes the call to the web service on behalf of the client.

- In an e-commerce aggregator application, if you have multiple categories of products like books, electronics and grocery items, being sold by the same vendor, sharing common attributes like vendor ID, vendor address, tax ID, etc. Instead of creating a vendor object for each product category, we can use a flyweight pattern to create a single vendor object instance that are shared by different product categories.

- In a health care application, if you want to log the date and time of dispatch before sending different results reports to the patients, you can use a decorator pattern. Create a `dispatchResultDecorator` class, that can log the date and time of dispatch and then call a dispatch function on a `dispatchReport` instance. This prevents each type of dispatch report instance from having the implementation of logging the date and time of dispatch.

Behavioral patterns

Behavioral design patterns provide industry standard best practices for the objects in a software system to communicate with each other. They also assign responsibilities to the objects that communicate with each other and help to structure the model of interaction between them.

The following are the scenarios in which behavioral patterns are used:

- **Observer pattern**: A class and a method that gets notified of a change in another class it is observing.

- **Iterator pattern**: Iterate through a collection and process the objects one by one.

- **Command pattern**: Encapsulate a command as an object that can be processed consistently.

- **Chain of responsibility pattern**: Allow the request to be processed by a series of functions before it is finally serviced and a response is returned.

- **Visitor pattern**: You want to separate the operations on an object from its structure.

- **Template method pattern**: You want to define the steps of an algorithm as abstract methods and allow sub classes to define their implementation without changing its structure.

- **Interpreter pattern**: Interpreter pattern defines a way to evaluate grammar of a language or expression.

- **Memento**: You can use the memento pattern to capture and store an object's state so that it can be restored later without exposing its internal details.

- **Mediator**: The mediator object centralizes the communication between different objects in an application.

- **State**: A pattern in which the behavior of the object changes, when the internal state of the object changes.

- **Strategy**: The strategy pattern is a behavioral design pattern that defines a family of algorithms, encapsulates each one in a separate class, and makes them interchangeable with the implementation of a uniform interface.

The following are the practical examples of how behavioral patterns are used:

- In an e-commerce application, we can use an observer pattern to notify different components based on events. A shipping component can register itself with an order queue and get notified when a new order enters the order queue.

- In a retail application, we can create an **Iterator** class that takes a list of products and iterates to return each product to the caller till the list is empty. This abstracts the iteration logic to be implemented independently of each product class.

- In a healthcare provider application, a command interface with an execute method can be created. This interface can be implemented by multiple concrete commands like **prescribeTestCommand**, **CancelAppointmentCommand**, etc. These specific command objects can be used to execute specific tasks like prescribing a test to a patient or cancelling an appointment for a patient keeping the interface uniform.

- In a retail application, before an order is shown on the product landing page, different steps can be performed like customer's interest in specific product categories, recently bought items, their average order value, etc. Each step represents a responsibility and together constitutes a chain.

- In a retail application, before the value of the order is calculated and shown to the user, it is checked against different types of discounts applicable before the customer is asked to pay. Each discount type is created as a visitor which is accepted by the payment object of the application to calculate the discount.

- In an e-commerce application, a template method pattern can be used to process different types of orders like a physical order or an email coupon order. Certain steps of processing these orders are the same as order creation, inventory control. However, the method to dispatch these orders could be different. A template method pattern defines a class (**ProcessOrder**) that has both concrete steps like order creation and inventory checks. It also has abstract steps (methods) that can be implemented in a specific way by the concrete classes like a **ProcessPhysicalOrder** and **ProcessEmailOrder**.

- In an e-commerce application, use an interpreter pattern to create a system to break down and interpret the format and structure of the order request object before it is passed on to an external interface for processing.

- In an e-commerce application, a shopping cart can be created using a memento pattern, you let users add or remove items which is stored as the internal state. The object also provides access to the state only to the originator (user) that created it.

- In a retail application, a message queue acts as a mediator between different components like an order processor, Inventory controller and shipping.

- In an e-commerce application, an order can go through multiple statuses such as created, packaged, shipped, and delivered. We can model each of these statuses as a state object. Each state has specific behavior (the actions can be performed on the order).

- In a retail website application, different payment modes like credit card payment or UPI payment can be defined as an algorithm with each strategy implementing the same interface. The application during payment can use any one of the appropriate types of payment strategy to complete the payment.

Enterprise application design patterns

Enterprise application design patterns are industry standard design patterns that solve problems which arise during the development of complex enterprise applications. While the Gang of Four foundational design patterns deal with the creation and interaction of objects in an application, the enterprise application patterns act at a higher level of abstraction in solving problems that arise during the design of enterprise applications.

They provide industry accepted principles for efficient way of organizing business logic, data and transaction management, concurrency handling and log handling. These enterprise application patterns help to organize different application components in large scale enterprise applications.

Some of the commonly used enterprise application design patterns are as follows:

- **Domain model**: A domain represented as an object model with data and its behavior.

- **Foreign key mapping**: This pattern helps to map the database relationships as linkages between objects. This pattern is more often used in **Object Relational Mapping (ORM)** frameworks.

- **Active record pattern**: An object that hides database logic and represents the specific instance of an entity (record) from a database table and its methods to manipulate the data.

- **Front controller**: A component that acts as a doorway to the entire application through which all the requests are routed to the application logic.

- **Service locator pattern**: A pattern in which access to services within the application is encapsulated using a common entry point. This is to hide complex access logic to common services, **Java Database Connectivity (JDBC)** connections, **Java Naming and Directory Interface (JNDI)** look up used by business services within the application.

- **Query object**: An object that encapsulates a query within the application.

- **Remote façade**: It provides a unified interface to a set of other interfaces which allow access to internal and external resources of the application. An application might access the file storage device to retrieve a document and then call a third-party API. These two operations can be clubbed inside a single interface.

- **Data transfer object**: As the name suggests, data transfer objects are used to transfer data between two layers of an application. In a spring boot application, a data transfer object can carry data between the controller layer and the service layer. They are mutable by design.

- **Value object**: An object that acts as a data carrier within the application without an identity on its own. Value objects are immutable by design, i.e., their values cannot be changed once they are created.

- **Lazy loading**: A pattern in which the data required by the application is retrieved or loaded on a need basis or during the time of usage. It improves the performance of the application.

- **Service layer**: A pattern in which a service component acts as a layer of abstraction between business logic and the data access layer. It provides a separation of concern, making the code maintainable.

- **Unit of work pattern**: It keeps a list of all the components affected during a business transaction and orchestrates the updates as a single unit of work to keep the system in a consistent state.

- **Repository**: It is an abstraction provided for data access logic and an interface for entities of a domain. It hides the complexity of direct access to the underlying data storage, like a relational database.

- **Business delegate pattern**: This provides access to business logic within the application via simplified interfaces.

Design approaches essential knowledge

In this section, we will look at the following design approaches that are commonly used to design enterprise applications:

- Domain-Driven Design
- API first design approach
- AI first design approach

Domain-Driven Design

Domain-Driven Design is one of the most popular approaches to designing software. It brings a domain or business centric view to the way software is designed. In the earlier era of software design, the focus was more on the technical aspects of the software. The business requirements were coded in a sequential manner and the interconnections or relationships between requirements was largely ignored. This resulted in a software design and a product, which was a ball of mud. The software product though satisfied business needs at the outset. There was no thinking about a methodology in which the software components were rationally organized within the solution. The modularity adopted was more in terms of dividing the software solutions as technical layers that performed a specific task. For instance, the UI layer of the application was concerned with the rendering logic of the screens to the end user. The business logic layer would all be written as a single component without any demarcation between operations or behaviour of two different entities. Even if there was some amount of modularity built into it, it was more on technical lines rather than putting in some thinking to separate the business components based on business capabilities.

This kind of a design results in the following challenges:

- Changing one business requirement affects others, as a result the whole software has to be tested even if small changes were introduced into the system.

- A failure of a single module results in the whole application starting to fail because of the strong cohesion between software programs in the application.

- It is hard for the operations team to scale software independently. A spike in the use of a particular feature meant that the whole application needs to be made redundant and deployed to meet the spike in the load.

- If a particular component is not ready, the whole application has to wait to be deployed in production because of which the time to market largely increases.

- This leads to unmaintainable software products increasing the overall cost of ownership of the software system over years.

- The design affects the reusability of software as there is no compartmentalization of business logic.

DDD tries to prevent the abovementioned challenges by focusing on breaking the ball of mud into independent and manageable pieces of software components.

The methodology initially identifies the boundaries and sub boundaries within the business and organizes them as domains and sub domains.

Domains and sub domains

A domain is a core area of focus of a business. The business exists to offer products and services in that core area to its customers. Examples of domains include an order processing system, a flight reservation system or a hospital management system. The domain encompasses the different business divisions of the enterprise, the processes within each business division and the specific business language used within the business area. A software design that centers around the business domain is expected to add more value than a design that is more technology centric in which the business requirements are fitted into. This kind of design lends itself for a better understanding of the software system being developed, by the key business stakeholders of the enterprise and encourage them to take active participation in the development of the software system.

A domain is divided into sub domains in Domain-Driven Design. The sub domain represents a specific business capability in the larger business domain. This sub domain could be core sub domain or a supporting sub domain. A core sub domain supports the central business activities of the business, and a supporting sub domain supports the core sub domains. Each sub domain is self-contained and can exist on its own without any dependency on other sub domains. However, it can have a relationship with other sub domains.

Figure 3.1 shows the e-commerce domain with its sub domains (dark blue circles inside):

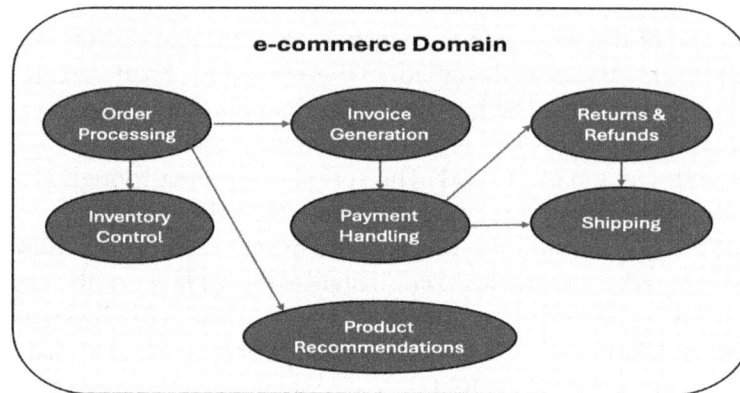

Figure 3.1: *Domains and sub domains of an e-commerce system*

Bounded context

Once the domain has been identified and divided into sub domains based on the core and supporting capabilities of the business, each sub domain is demarcated into a bounded context to mark its boundary and to define the technical artefacts like entities and aggregates (logical domain model) within the bounded context. The bounded context will be translated into one or more independent components or microservices at a later point in time. The idea of arriving at the bounded context is to break the complexity of the software into multiple chunks. Each bounded context will address a specific capability of the business like inventory, order processing, invoicing and payments, shipping, etc. The bounded contexts identified can have relationships among them. These relationships are called context maps.

The following are the relationship types:

- **Partnerships**: Bounded contexts and their teams share code of models between them, but the ubiquitous language used by different bounded contexts will be unique.

- **Customer-supplier**: In this model, one bounded context or team provides the required service to another bounded context, that consumes it.

- **Open host service**: A bounded context provides a service which is extended by other bounded contexts.

- **Anticorruption layer**: A layer of translation between two communicating bounded contexts, so that the model of one does not penetrate or impact the other bounded context.

- **Conformist**: The downstream system conforms to the models of the upstream systems.

Entities and aggregates

Within a bounded context which represents a sub domain, entities and aggregates need to be identified. Entities and aggregates represent the data, behavior and relationships required to realize the capabilities within a sub domain. This is referred as the logical domain model.

Entities are objects in DDD that hold data and behavior of real-world things. They are identified by a unique ID though the other attributes (data) of the entity instance (object) may be the same. For instance, customer is an entity in the above e-commerce example, and it may have attributes like customer ID, customer name, customer address, etc. Though the other attributes like name could be the same, the customer ID differentiates the instance of the specific entity.

The following are the high-level steps to applying DDD to design an application:

1. Identify the core domain you are working with. Identify the distinct business boundaries or sub domains within the core domain.

2. Establish relationships between those sub domains.

3. Establish the bounded contexts for each of the sub domains identified.

4. Establish relationships between bounded contexts using context map types such as partnerships, conformist, etc.

5. Identify entities, aggregates and value objects within each bounded context. The entities will model the data and behavior within each bounded context or sub domain. They will work together to make up a capability within a subdomain.

6. Map each of the bounded context to one or more components (microservices) providing the required capabilities for the application. Deploy these components independently.

API first design approach

API is an end point exposed by an enterprise for consumption of their services. APIs have become the backbone of modern-day software applications. They are effectively used by enterprises to offer their services to their customers and partners. Most of the applications are distributed and each application needs to expose their capabilities effectively and make known the contract for access of these capabilities. This is done with the help of APIs and a contract is made available for consumers to download and understand ways to access those APIs.

There are three types of APIs that are prevalent in the software application world as follows:

- **Private APIs**: These are APIs built for internal consumption within the enterprise by other business divisions or project teams.

- **Public APIs**: These are APIs exposed by the enterprise to the public. It is done to expose their services and data to be consumers such as developers to include the enterprise's capability or service as part of a larger application. This helps to foster innovation.

- **Partner APIs**: These are mostly commercial APIs that are exposed to the business partners of the enterprise. This helps the enterprise to offer their services through third party portals thereby allowing the enterprise to monetize their products and services.

  The API first design approach looks at the capabilities of the application as a set of APIs that are required to be exposed as private, public or partner APIs. The actual capability or functionality required is then implemented beneath these APIs. The API first approach helps to develop components and applications in a stateless manner as each of the APIs are self-contained and idempotent. This lets the APIs to scale very quickly without any external dependencies.

There are different architectural styles for exposing an application's capability as APIs. Some of them common ones are as follows:

- SOAP
- **Representational State Transfer (REST)**
- GraphQL developed by Facebook
- **Google RPC (gRPC)**
- Webhooks

We will look at each one of these in detail and their use cases in *Chapter 4, Technical Solutions Architecture and Design*.

Artificial intelligence first design

AI first design approach puts AI as the central point of architecture and design, around which all features of the applications are developed. With the advancement and affordability of high-performance computing hardware combined with availability of data, enterprises are slowly moving away from the conventional approach of coding technical components to machine learning models, that learns from the data on a continuous basis and provide the required functionality. Machine learning or AI is no longer seen as an exciting ingredient added to the list of nonfunctional requirements, but considered as an essential aspect to building modern software applications. The solutions architect should be conversant with machine learning algorithms and neural networks available to perform intelligent tasks within an enterprise. Enterprises are using AI for tasks as varied as recommending products for customers to converting legacy code to more modern software languages like Python and C-Sharp(C#). The architect working with large enterprises should identify opportunities where AI can make a sea of difference instead of conventional programming methods.

The following are the steps an architect could follow at the outset, for designing and implementing AI and machine learning based software solutions:

1. Identify opportunities in the enterprise where AI can be used.
2. Collect, consolidate and curate data for building the required AI solution.
3. Choose the right algorithms, neural networks, tools, frameworks for building the AI models.
4. Ensure the privacy, security and compliance of data being used and exposed to the solution.
5. Build the models with the curated data and the chosen algorithm or framework.
6. Tune the solution iteratively for accuracy, scalability and performance.
7. Validate the models using data for which the results are already known.
8. Tune the model's hyperparameters to make it more accurate.
9. Train the model continuously with data to make it usable on a continuous basis.
10. Collect feedback and finetune the model for adding business value to users.

With the world moving towards generative AI, it is very important that the architect has sufficient knowledge of how **large language models** (**LLM**) work and their application to solving problems for the enterprise. We will touch up on the topic of generative AI in the section, *Emerging technologies essential knowledge.*

Design principles essential knowledge

The following are the design principles that all architects must be conversant with, to guide the development teams towards building software systems that are maintainable:

- SOLID principles
- 12 factor app
- KISS
- **You aren't gonna need it (YAGNI)**

SOLID principles

SOLID principles help developers in building flexible and maintainable software. SOLID stands for the following:

- **Single responsibility principle**: It states that a class should have only a single reason for changes in it. It means that the class should focus on a single function or task. This allows for a clear delineation of functionality within the application. This promotes the principle of loose coupling between components.

- **Open close principle**: This principle emphasizes the guideline that a class should be open for extension and should be closed for modification. This enables development of an application wherein any changes to existing classes of functions does not break already existing and working functionality.

- **Liskov substitution principle**: This principle states that the objects of derived classes can replace the objects of a base class. This promotes polymorphism and makes sure all derived classes and objects of derived classes inherit a uniform contract for common functionality among them.

- **Interface segregation principle**: This principle states that we should not design a single interface with all the methods going into it. It makes the classes implementing such interfaces cluttered with unwanted functions or tasks. Instead, we should split the interface into smaller ones grouping related methods into each one of them. The classes can choose to implement one or more of those interfaces as appropriate.

- **Dependency injection**: This principle states that the higher-level modules should not be designed to depend on specific low-level modules. Instead, the higher-level modules should use abstractions (interfaces) for the lower-level modules to be injected into them. This results in cleaner code of feature functionality being developed and the lower-level modules can be easily replaced any time within the higher-level modules (containing feature functionality), depending on requirements.

12 factor app design

12 factor app design principles can be used to build scalable, maintainable and portable distributed applications. Though they are mostly used in the development of cloud ready applications and microservices, they can be applied to any modern-day software application embracing varied architectural patterns.

The following are the 12 design principles prescribed by the 12 factor app design methodology:

- **Single codebase per application tracked in version control with many deploys**: It means that each application or an independently deployable component should be managed with its own codebase using a version control system. This single codebase enables easy collaboration between development, testing and application support teams.

- **Explicitly declare and isolate dependencies**: This states that the dependencies such as libraries should be explicitly specified and managed by the application. For example, a spring boot application manages the libraries required using Maven.

- **Store config in the environment**: This principle recommends the configuration information used by the application to be stored outside the application. This enables the application to focus only on business logic and not on technical details of how it needs to run in different environments like development and testing.

- **Treat backing services as attached resources**: This principle emphasizes the fact to consider any support systems such as databases and storage required for the application as loosely coupled services. The loose coupling provides the different application components, the ability to scale independently.

- **Strictly separate build, release and run stages**: This principle requires the build, release and run stage to be independent. Build stage is where the application codebase is compiled and dependencies are resolved and a compilation unit (war or jar) gets created. The release stage enriches the application with configuration information so that it can run in different environments like development, testing and production. The run stage of this principle requires the application to be deployed and run in an automated manner with the built application code on which configuration has been applied.

- **Execute the application as one or more stateless processes**: Run each application or the service as a stateless process. This requires the application not to maintain a state that is used across requests between the service and the client. This enables easy scalability of the application without having to worry about loss of any state information.

- **Export services via port binding**: This principle emphasizes that any application or service developed should run by itself independently without the need for any external server. This can be achieved by the application binding to a port on its own and is able to receive requests from client. For example, a spring boot web app can independently receive and process requests without the need for it to be explicitly deployed in a web container.

- **Scale out via the process model**: This states that the application should be made up of multiple small processes instead of a single process. These small processes should able to be started and stopped independently. This principle aids in the easy scalability of those independent processes.

- **Maximize robustness with fast startup and graceful shutdown**: This principle emphasizes each service or application should start or shut down very quickly. The system should also be able to bring up or tear down other resources which will enable the application to be in a consistent state. This principle enables the application consumers not having to wait for a longer period to get their requests serviced.

- **Keep development, staging, and production as similar as possible**: It is important to keep environments such as development, testing and production as similar as possible. It aids the application to work consistently across environments. This also helps the developer team to identify issues quickly in the development stage itself and does not have to wait until testing or production which increases the cost of quality.

- **Treat logs as event streams**: This principle states that the applications should not be concerned with the storage and management of the logs produced by it. Logging and tracing requests are very important especially on the cloud, where the infrastructure is ephemeral.

- **Run admin or management tasks as one-off processes**: This principle requires that any administrative tasks required by the application such as setting up of the application configuration, etc., should be run as a separate process outside the application. This helps to segregate the application's business logic from other tasks required for the application to start and function normally.

Keep it short and simple

This principle is also referred to as KISS. It is one of the important principles, applied not just to software engineering, but also other engineering disciplines. It states that any solution should be made as simple as possible and should avoid unnecessary complexity built into it. It is more often applied to coding wherein programs should be short and readable. For example, a method should be readable in its entirety within the laptop screen and lengthy ones are to be refactored. This makes for an application that is modular, readable and maintainable.

You aren't gonna need it

This principle emphasizes the fact an application should only be made up of features that are required for the efficient functioning of the system. It calls for the prioritization of requirements as must haves, good to have, or excited to have. An application should address all the must have requirements and prioritize the other two categories. This again helps to keep the application simple, that lends itself well for future changes and ongoing maintainability.

Cloud computing essential knowledge

In this section, we will look at the types of services provided by the popular cloud providers like AWS, Azure, and **Google Cloud Platform (GCP)**.

We will also look at some of the services provided by them to ensure quality of services such as availability, scalability, security, and performance for the application deployed on them.

We will discuss cloud native patterns and their specific implementations on the cloud in *Chapter 22, Cloud-native Architecture and Design.*

Types of services

Each cloud provider, at the bare minimum, offers the following four types of services: Infrastructure, platform, software, and serverless. Let us take a closer look at these.

Infrastructure as a service

Each cloud provider offers infrastructure for deploying application workloads on the cloud. These are servers on the cloud that can either be rented as a whole by the customer or can be shared with other customers. The servers come in different configurations based on the memory and CPU requirements of the customer. These are all resources that are billed by the minute, depending on the service provider. These servers are virtual machines that are configured on the cloud and have their own name depending on the cloud service provider. Examples of infrastructure as a service include computing instances such as **Elastic Compute Cloud** (**EC2**) in AWS and **virtual machines** (**VM**) in Azure.

Apart from servers for application deployment, they also provide object storage for storing artefacts like files, images, and videos on the cloud. Some of such services include S3 from AWS, Blob Storage from Azure, and Google Storage from GCP.

These cloud providers also provide attachable block storage devices, much like a hard disk, to extend the storage capacity of the virtual machines. Each virtual machine can be attached to any number of block storage devices. Examples of storage services include **Elastic Block Store** (**EBS**) from AWS and GCP, and disk storage in Azure.

The advantage of using the cloud infrastructure is the infinite scaling they can provide virtually. It helps enterprises to expand or contract their infrastructure even on an hourly basis depending on their application needs. This ephemeral nature of the cloud infrastructure helps enterprises to save cost by not having to procure infrastructure permanently for their different environments like development, testing and production. The onus of managing and maintaining these infrastructures solely rests on the cloud provider. This is again a cost advantage for the enterprise. The cloud providers also present minimal cost options such as spot instances wherein the customers can bid for the unused infrastructure of the cloud providers at a very low cost. The other advantage of the cloud infrastructure is the back up and disaster recovery options they provide to protect the customers data, whenever there is a failure or outage at the infrastructure level.

The disadvantages of the **infrastructure as a service** (**IaaS**) model is that the customer may not have fine grained control over the cloud infrastructure procured. Though the cloud provider might offer a good amount of flexibility to configure the servers, it will not be the same as what could be achieved with servers procured and deployed in an on-premises environment. The other concern would be from a security stand point of the data stored in the cloud infrastructure. Though there are multiple security controls in place for the cloud infrastructure, the customers cannot control any compromise of data due to external security breaches happening on the cloud infrastructure.

Platform as a service

Platform as a service (**PaaS**) is another important service delivery model that solutions architects needs to be familiar with. It is a model in which the cloud provider not only provides the hardware infrastructure but also the required software for applications to be built and readily deployed on the cloud. PaaS on the cloud is available for all types of workloads on the cloud. It offers different types of environments to test and deploy web applications, analyze data using business intelligence tools, creating data warehouses and data lakes, running and managing containerized apps and monitoring them using sophisticated tools. For a developer, PaaS helps them pick the right tools (such as IDEs) for development, choose the operating system, install required application runtime libraries and build software. PaaS services are offered to enterprises over the internet. The extent of the services provided will depend on the type of subscription that the enterprise holds with the cloud provider. There are different types of PaaS such as Public PaaS where the platform is shared with multiple customers and private PaaS where the platform instance on the cloud is dedicated for one cloud customer.

Some examples of PaaS includes Elastic beanstalk in AWS, **Azure Kubernetes Service** (**AKS**) on Azure and Google Kubernetes Engine on GCP.

The following are the benefits of PaaS:

- The maintenance of the platform including constant patches to be applied lies with the cloud provider.

- Any licensing costs associated with the software platform are borne by the provider.

- PaaS offers a quick set up and a ready to deploy environment for applications, when the time to market for the customer is very short.

- Like IaaS, PaaS offers infinite scalability, and customers can increase or reduce their capacity based on the load on the application.

- PaaS is cost effective, and the customer needs to pay only for what is being used during the billing cycle.

The disadvantage of PaaS is the limited extent of customization that the cloud provider might allow for the architects and developers to do on the cloud platform. For instance, the relational database service is offered in a PaaS model by most of the popular cloud providers. However, they may not allow their customers to modify all the parameters of the database engine to the liking of the database administrators in the enterprise. In the scenario wherein the enterprise wants more control of such platforms on the cloud, the option is to go for the IaaS model and deploy the required software platform on the cloud to have fine grained control. The other disadvantage is the availability of the platform, the onus of which totally lies with the cloud provider. The architect needs to take an informed decision while deploying machine critical applications with PaaS. In a hybrid environment, the architect needs to be aware of challenges with regards to integration of the PaaS environment with that of the resources on premise.

Software as a service

Software as a service (**SaaS**) is a model in which the infrastructure, software platform and the application is provided by the cloud provider and the customer needs to only maintain the data required for the application and make use of the software services offered. This environment is more suitable for smaller enterprises which may not only have challenges with infrastructure and software platforms but may not have the skills to build applications using the right technologies. From a subscription perspective, SaaS providers offer a pay per use model, and they have different levels of service ranging from standard to premium based on the subscription. Like PaaS, SaaS providers offer services over the internet, and they offer APIs for applications either on the cloud or on-premises to be integrated with them. SaaS providers in general offer a multi tenancy model in which their services or applications are shared by many of their customers. Some of the SaaS applications include Google Gmail, Netflix entertainment platform and salesforce **customer relationship management** (**CRM**) platform.

The following are the advantages of using the SaaS models:

- The required capabilities are offered right out of the box, by the SaaS provider, which can readily be consumed with no effort.

- SaaS models have extreme capability to scale depending on the load they are subjected to.

- They provide very flexible subscriptions that caters to enterprise of different sizes, from small, medium to large.

- They offer a pay per use model which is very cost effective for consumers.

- They are a very good platform to quickly on-board or share ideas for smaller enterprise and startups, thereby fostering a culture of innovation.

The disadvantage of using the SaaS model is the risk that comes with sharing data with these third-party service providers. The onus of security of such services based on a SaaS model lies purely with the provider and any breach of the data could result in the consumer paying a huge amount of money as penalty to their end users. The solutions architect needs to be aware of these implications while trying to use SaaS models in the solution. With multi tenancy, the same instance of the application will be shared with multiple customers. The architect needs to consider the type of storage used by the SaaS provider and ensure that there is enough physical separation of data. This is especially important while using SaaS models for sensitive data like health information of individuals and bank information of customers.

Serverless computing

Serverless computing is a model in which the infrastructure and the required software is managed by the cloud provider, and it offers an environment for the developers to run and test the code without having to worry about the required hardware or software.

Serverless computing differs from the SaaS model, in which the user makes use of the readily built application and requires only their own data to make use of the application. Developers are offered different types of programming runtimes including Python, Node.js and Java. They write code within the serverless compute environment and the onus of managing the computing resources like CPU and memory lies with the cloud provider. The developer only needs to choose their platform of choice write code.

Though the developers do not have control over the hardware or the software runtime, they can request for additional CPU cycles or increased memory to improve the efficiency of the program. All the popular cloud providers offer a serverless computing model. The developers using a serverless computing model take the responsibility to code, test and deploy the application. However, the underlying infrastructure and the software runtime is totally managed by the cloud provider. The developers also needs to ensure that their code meets the quality of services required to be met like performance and security.

Serverless computing is used in scenarios where a piece of code needs to be executed as a precursor before a task is performed. For instance, a program can be written in the serverless model and can be wired as a request preprocessor to check and enrich the request for certain headers before it is sent to the web application. Another key feature of the serverless computing model is that the developers are charged only for the time their code runs in the cloud platform and the cloud resources consumed during that time. These serverless compute model programs can also respond to certain events in an application and hence make them a good candidate for event driven applications and microservices.

The following are the advantages of the serverless computing model:

- Developers concentrate only on writing code and the computing resources are provided by the cloud platform.
- The serverless compute platform automatically scales up or down depending on the number of instances of the function executed.
- Developers pay only for the time during which the resources are consumed.
- The software runtimes are provided for most of the popular programming languages and there are no licensing costs associated with their usage.
- It is an easier choice for developers to do quick proof of concepts before they try their programs on their managed infrastructure.

Some of the serverless computing models include AWS Lambda, Azure Functions and GCP Functions.

The main disadvantage with the serverless model is the limit they have on the execution time. If the code takes more time than the threshold execution time limit allowed by the serverless computing platform, the program will get terminated. The other challenge of the serverless model is the way they get warmed up to execute the code for the first time. The resources required are configured only when the code is run for the first time, which makes it slower for first time users of the functionality offered by the program deployed in a serverless model. Another disadvantage with this model is the kind of control that developers have over the infrastructure and software platform on which the code runs. The developers do not have any control over the type of servers or the efficiency of the platform on which the code is run although in some cases they can request for a higher memory, which proportionately increases the CPU cycle time, and the program gets executed faster.

Database management essential knowledge

Making a choice of databases for the application is one of the key responsibilities of a solutions architect. Though the solutions architect mostly works with the architecture and design of solutions, in many enterprises the solutions architect plays a very key role in choosing the right storage for the data that flows through the application. They should also be aware of the sensitivity of the data and should recommend appropriate controls to secure the data as required.

The following are the common type of databases that an architect can choose from, based on the type of data used by the application:

- **Relational databases**: This is the most common type of database used by many of the applications that are transactional in nature. They provide a strict schema and data is stored in tables as rows and columns with each row pertaining to an instance of an entity. The data stored in a relational database can be retrieved using relational operators. Examples of relational databases include Oracle, SQL server and Postgres which are offered as standalone version that can be installed on premise and all the cloud providers offer them on their cloud. The relational databases provide the required transactional capability to maintain consistency and integrity of data. Data can be created. Queried, updated and deleted from an application using database management frameworks. These frameworks provide a higher layer abstraction to the regular JDBC APIs. Popular database management frameworks include **Java Persistence API (JPA)** and hibernate. A few use cases for relational databases include banking transactions and storing health care data of patients.

- **NoSQL databases**: NoSQL or Not only SQL databases unlike relational databases do not have any fixed schema for storing data in them. This characteristic of the database makes them an ideal choice for storing semi structured data and unstructured data. So, they are not a best choice for running complex queries or joins. NoSQL databases also scale very well which makes them an ideal choice for applications, where the load is unpredictable and can grow very quickly. NoSQL databases are highly available as they are normally deployed across nodes. This makes NoSQL databases offer an eventual consistency model wherein the data becomes consistent a bit later (milliseconds) than it was stored. They are also very fast in returning the data queried as they do not need any complex queries to fetch the semi or unstructured data from them. The flip side to NoSQL databases is that they do not offer any transactional characteristics like consistency and integrity. NoSQL databases also do not have a standardized query language to retrieve from them unlike relational database which has the SQL to query or manipulate the data in them. Some of the popular NoSQL databases include Mongo DB, Cassandra, Couchbase, HBase, Dynamo DB from AWS and Big Table from Google Cloud Platform**.**

- **Graph databases**: A graph database is a special type of database which stores the data as nodes, edges and properties. It also establishes relationship between the nodes. The graph database uses mathematical graph structures for storing data in it. The graph databases use traversal algorithms like depth first or breadth first to query the data stored in them. Graph databases scale extremely well by storing data across different partitions or servers. Graph databases are useful for use cases where relationships between data is central to the storage. Social media applications, and recommendation engines are some of the places where a graph database would be a right choice. Some of the examples of graph database includes RedisGraph, ArangoDB, OrientDB, AWS Neptune, Azure Cosmos database and Neo4J.

- **Key value databases**: Key value databases store data as keys and their associated values. The key is unique and is used to retrieve the value from the database. Key value databases are ideal candidates for storing user sessions in an application. They can also be used as a caching mechanism to store data as key value pairs.

Any type of data can be stored and retrieved without complexity. These databases can scale very easily. On the flip side, they do not support a standardized query language to retrieve data and data cannot be retrieved without the keys. Examples of popular key value databases include Redis, Memcached and BerkeleyDB.

- **Event databases**: Some applications store events instead of the conventional data. An event database stores all the events over a period, which has resulted in the current state of the application. Each event along with it stores the date and time the event occurred, along with the information of what caused that event. Event databases also provide a notification feature. Popular event databases include Apache Kafka, EventStoreDB and Microsoft Azure Event Hubs.

Application security essential knowledge

Application security is one of the key quality metrics when architecting and designing applications. It is imperative for a solutions architect to understand the nature of data that is being dealt with by the application and the flow of it throughout the application. Any data breach through the application can result in a business loss or a penalty for the enterprise. The architect needs to be aware of the following data security aspects while the data is being transmitted across the wire and when it is stored:

- **Symmetric and asymmetric encryption**: Encryption is the process of transforming or scrambling data to a format that is incomprehensible to the human reader. Encryption is achieved using a key and an algorithm. A key (information or text that needs to kept as a secret) is chosen and using an algorithm the data is transformed with the help of the key and the output of this process can either be stored or transmitted to other applications. In the reverse, the same algorithm and keys are used to convert the incomprehensible text to the original text, which is called decryption. If the same key is used for both encryption and decryption, it is called a symmetric encryption. If two different keys are used, one for encryption and another for decryption, it's called asymmetric encryption. This is the basis for public key cryptography.

- **Hashing**: Hashing is the process of creating a hash value for the given text using a key and an algorithm. Hashing works in the same way as encryption but the generated hash cannot be converted into the original text. This makes hashing a feasible approach for storing and comparing secure data, like passwords.

- **Public key cryptography**: Public key cryptography uses asymmetric encryption as stated before. It uses two types of keys. A private key that is maintained as a secret by the server and is used to encrypt information served by the application. The other key is the public key which is given to all the clients or consumers of the application data. The data encrypted using the private key can only be decrypted using the public key. Again, the data encrypted by the public key can only be decrypted by the private key on the application side. This makes the data transmission over the wire secure. **Transport Layer Security (TLS)** protocols like TLS 1.2 and TLS 1.3 make use of public key cryptography.

- **Digital certificates**: Digital certificates are certificates issued in the form of a file to an enterprise to be used by its software applications. It identifies to the outside world, that the enterprise is legitimate and the applications hosted by it can be trusted by software clients. The digital certificate is issued by certification authorities for a specific period after which it becomes invalid. Digital certificates contain the public key of the enterprise application for which it was created. The digital certificate is sent to the consumer's browser or the application which uses the public key in it to encrypt the data to be sent to the server application. The server application decrypts the data using its private key.

- **Ensuring data security during transmission**: Data over the wire can be protected using protocols like TLS, formerly called **Secure Sockets Layer (SSL)**. TLS ensures security and privacy of data that is transmitted over a network. Apart from data, TLS can also be used to encrypt emails and **Voice over IP (VoIP)** data. TLS works with digital certificates issued by certification authorities like Verisign or Thawte, which are trusted by standard browser implementations like Microsoft Edge, Google Chrome and Apple Safari. Digital certificates are issued for an enterprise application that can be accessed by users using a desktop browser on a mobile phone. **Hypertext transfer protocol Secure (HTTPS)** that we commonly see in browser URLs is a TLS encryption implementation on top of the **Hyper Text Transfer Protocol (HTTP)** protocol.

- **Ensuring data security at rest**: Data at rest (stored on a disk) is always under constant threat from both internal and external parties. Data security at rest ensures the storage of customer data in a secure manner and there are controls in place to avoid breach of data security. One of the ways to keep data secure is to have a role-based access to ensure that each user only has access to the data they are entitled to view or modify. The second way to protect data that is stored is to use appropriate encryption algorithms with a suitable key size that can be used to encrypt data before it is stored in the database. Most of the popular databases offer default encryption techniques that can be used to encrypt the data before it is stored, without any explicit effort from the users. Using a Layered protection approach is another way of keeping the data secure. This is an approach in which the data layer is protected by multiple passwords which needs to be given one after the other to get access to the data. The architect also needs to classify the data based its sensitivity and apply proper controls for its view and modification.

Networking essential knowledge

It is important for a solutions architect to know how machines communicate over the network and the basic theory behind it.

The architect should be familiar with different application protocols that are commonly used in communication between application components or between applications. Though the solutions architect may not be expected to create or manage complex networks required by an enterprise, they should have the basic understanding of the network terminology and understand overall networking topologies in order for them to comfortably work with the network architects and infrastructure management teams.

The architect should be familiar with the **Open Systems Interconnection (OSI)** model and the simpler TCP/IP model, based on which most of the modern computer networks are designed.

Open Systems Interconnection model

The OSI model uses seven layers that computers use to communicate over the network. The OSI model is a vendor neutral logical framework that encompasses all the capabilities required to make the network function. The required capabilities are provided by components such as browsers, software runtimes, operating systems, routers, switches and network cables. The OSI model is useful in isolating different functions in a network and helps to address security issues associated with each function.

The following are the seven layers, top down, of the model:

- **Application layer**: The is the layer that the application makes use of to provide an interface with the end user of the application. This is the layer that is being used by the client applications such as web browsers or messaging clients to send and receive information. Some of the application layer protocols include HTTP, **File Transfer Protocol (FTP)**, **Simple Mail Transfer Protocol (SMTP)**.

- **Presentation layer**: This layer prepares the data required for the application layer. The presentation layer encrypts or decrypts the data based on the direction of the data flow.

- **Session layer**: This session layer is responsible for maintaining the connection between the nodes that are communicating. It helps to establish an uninterrupted session between the sender and the receiver. The session layer also provides check points for an optimized transfer of data from the sender to the receiver. If there are interruptions in the transfer of data, which is later resumed. This layer ensures that the data is transmitted from the last check point and only the untransmitted data is sent over the network.

- **Transport layer**: This layer popularly known as layer four in the OSI model, splits the data packets into segments for optimal functionating of the network. It handles communication between two nodes in a network by adding a **Transmission Control Protocol** (**TCP**) header. It also receives acknowledgement from the receiver if the data packets are received in order using sequence numbers and without errors. The data packets are transmitted again if there are any errors in the transmission. This is the layer hosting TCP and **Universal Datagram Protocol** (**UDP**) protocols.

- **Network layer**: This layer is responsible for routing data across different networks, The network layer finds the best path of data transmission between two hosts. It assigns a unique IP address within the data packets for the device.

- **Datalink layer**: This layer uses the **Media Access Control** (**MAC**) address to identify the node to which the packets should be routed next in the network. Devices in the datalink layer include switch and bridge. While sending, it creates the frames from the message to be sent and also adds the MAC address of the destination in the MAC header of the message.

- **Physical layer**: This physical layer is responsible for transmitting and receiving the data over the wire. The data is converted into electric signals (bits) and is sent across the network to other networks or machines. The physical layer also controls the rate at which the data is transmitted (bit rate control). The physical layer also determines the mode of transmission (simplex, duplex, and half duplex) of data across the network.

TCP/IP model

As mentioned earlier TCP offers a reliable way of transferring data across the network and the internet protocol handles the addressing and the routing of packets. The TCP/ IP model divides the framework into four different layers. It is different from the OSI model and was developed prior to it. TCP/IP defines how data is transmitted over the internet and how the data is broken down as packets, routed, transmitted, and decoded at the destination. Common TCP/IP protocols include HTTP and FTP. The TCP/IP collection of protocols is generally stateless, which means that each request from the client is treated independently. The following are the layers of the TCP/IP model. TCP/IP is independent of the operating system used and supports multiple routing protocols:

- **Application layer**: This is the layer of the network that is used by applications. This defines the format of data exchange that applications must adhere to while using specific protocols like HTTP and FTP.

- **Transport layer**: This layer exchanges acknowledgements of the data packets sent or received. This layer retransmits the missing packets of data to the destination. TCP and user datagram protocol are the protocols in this layer.

- **Internet layer**: The internet layer is responsible for routing data packets from one machine to another machine across a network. This is achieved by assigning each machine a unique IP address.

- **Network link layer**: This is also called the network access layer or the network interface layer. This layer assigns the MAC address for communication to the next destination for the data packets.

Emerging technologies essential knowledge

Apart from the knowledge to architect and design applications using industry standard architectural patterns, design approaches and principles, the solutions architect is expected to have an awareness of the technologies that are disrupting the industries overall.

The following are some of the topics, the architect needs to be educated with, though they may not be using these in their day-to-day work. This is required for them to understand their applicability, explore and include them in their solution, as appropriate.

Generative AI

Generative artificial intelligence (**GenAI**) is the technology that has taken the world by storm. It makes use of the data available on the internet, using which a model has been trained. The LLMs, as they are called, can generate text, images, and videos. As a result, they have found widespread usage in almost all areas, be it business, science, or the arts. The generative AI field is fast expanding with a wide variety of base models being made available by different technology companies and startups for use by businesses and developers. It is important that the architects have a grasp of the basic concepts related to GenAI to stay contemporary and have meaningful conversations with fellow architects and the businesses for which they build applications.

At a basic level, the architect needs to be aware of the following terminology and is expected to expand their knowledge further in this most exciting and happening area:

- **Conversational AI**: Conversational AI allows users to use common natural language to converse with AI models. It uses **natural language processing** (**NLP**) techniques to understand questions and provide answers.

- **Deep learning**: Deep learning uses neural networks (computer nodes arranged like neurons in the brain) to identify patterns in data to recognize images and predict outcomes based on the data with which it is trained.

- **Transformer**: Transformer are neural network architectures that work based on a mechanism called self-attention. It captures the context in the data provided and is able to generate output for questions asked based on the context.

- **Large language models**: LLMs are a broad category of models that are trained with a huge corpus of data and uses NLP to answer questions. There are LLMs which are pre-trained with data in a specific domain. For instance, a LLM pre-trained with medical and health care data can answer questions related to health disorders, their symptoms and treatment.

- **Generative pre-trained transformer (GPT)**: GPTs are a subset of the large language models that use the transformer architecture and are pre trained on a large corpus of data to provide answers to the questions asked. GPTs were developed by the OpenAI long term partnership.

- **Prompt engineering**: It is a way of asking a question to get the most relevant answer from a large language model. It is about framing a question about a particular topic that can get the best possible answer from the model. Zero shot prompting is a way in which we prompt the LLM with a question without any examples and we let the model answer based on its broad-based training. Few shots prompting is another method in which the prompt contains a few examples to get the response from the model.

Blockchain

Blockchain is a technology that allows information sharing in a distributed manner among participating entities. A relational database storing data as a central repository for an application or for a group of applications. However, a block chain database in not centralized and the database is maintained by all the parties involved in a transaction. A blockchain stores transactions in a block and these blocks are chained together sequentially. Blockchain creates a distributed ledger that is maintained by each of the interested parties or entities and any transaction in the block chain database must be approved by all parties before it is committed to the block chain database. Blockchain has a mechanism which does not allow unauthorized entries into the database.

The advantage of a blockchain is its ability to prevent data tampering as the transactions and its corresponding data are not centralized. This finds a lot of utility in businesses where trust plays a very important role. In trade finance, a block chain can be used to synchronize transactions between an exporter (seller), importer (buyer) and the bank. The transactions from shipping of goods, to guarantee provided by the bank and the payment by the buyer can all be synchronized using a blockchain. Similarly, a block chain will be very useful in the sale of properties in which the seller and buyer of the property needs to agree and perform transactions in a synchronized manner for the transfer of the property documents from the seller to the buyer and transfer of money from the buyer to the seller.

Quantum computing

Quantum mechanics is the study of behavior of the sub atomic particles in physics. Quantum computing is a field of computer science that makes uses of the principles of quantum mechanics to achieve computing power that are much beyond what is possible with the most powerful computers available now. Using the principles of quantum mechanics, a quantum computer will be able to solve a problem in seconds what it now takes hours for a super computer in the present-day world.

Like bits and bytes in today's computing world, data in quantum computing is stored as qubits. A qubit is a basic unit of information in quantum computing. Current day computing bits are binary and can hold only a value of zero or one, but a qubit can hold a superposition of multiple states. This makes information representation much more optimum. By adding multiple qubits and using a concept called entanglement (where multiple qubits influence each other, coordinate and synchronize), quantum computers can calculate exponentially more information and solve very complex problems that will take decades for the hardware available currently.

Conclusion

In this chapter, we looked at the essential knowledge required for a solutions architect to effectively architect and design solutions. We covered the topics of design patterns and approaches to architect and design software applications. We also looked at the different design principles that are commonly being used by software architects. We discussed the topics of cloud computing services, database management, application security and networking. We also briefly covered the emerging trends that a software architect should be knowledgeable about.

In the next chapter, we will cover different architectural patterns and their applicability to different scenarios and application types.

Key takeaways

The takeaways are as follows:

- **Foundational and enterprise design patterns**: Apply industry standard patterns practically for solving recurring problems during the design and coding of enterprise applications.

- **Design approaches and design principles**: Use standard design approaches to break complexity of enterprise application. Apply industry accepted design principles to applications during their architecture and design.

- **Learn essential knowledge**: Knowledge required in the areas of cloud computing, database management, security and networking for the architect to have a broader understanding of the landscape, apart from design patterns, approaches and principles.

- **Emerging technologies**: Understanding of the technologies like generative AI, Blockchain and quantum computing that are disrupting the industry at the present.

Model interview questions and answers

1. **How will you design a software component in which there should exist only one instance of a class?**

   Model answer:

   - You will use the Singleton design pattern which restricts the number of objects in the application to be only one in the application.

   - You will ensure that the singleton class does not have any instance variable to avoid threading issues in the class.

2. **What design approach would you use to break the complexity of software and design the application as distributed components?**

   Model answer:

   - You will use the DDD approach to break down the whole functionality (domain) into sub domains.

   - You will identify the capabilities required as part of the sub domains.

   - Each sub domain will have its own Ubiquitous (business) language.

   - You will create a bounded context for each of the sub domains identified.

   - Each bounded context will be associated with a set of entities and aggregates.

   - You will identify and establish relationships between the bounded contexts.

   - You will map each bounded context into one or more microservices.

3. **What is the design approach you will follow to an application that needs to open its services to lot of business divisions inside the enterprise and multiple business partners outside of the enterprise?**

   Model answer:

   - You will use the API first design approach.

   - You will study the external systems and the amount of granularity of data required by those systems.

   - You will design contracts APIs of the application, based on the need of the consumer entities that wants to consume data.

   - You will understand the subscription needs to the consuming entities and accordingly meter the APIs for avoiding excessive load on the system.

   - You will expose the contract to the consumers to access and understand the semantics for calling the exposed APIs.

4. **What are the design principles that you will adopt to architect and design an application that is distributed in nature?**

   Model answer:

   - You will decide the architectural pattern such as Event driven, multilayered or Microservices to use for the application based on requirements. you will also see if a combination of these patterns need to be used.

   - For the individual distributed components, you will try to keep their design as simple as possible avoiding unnecessary complexity in terms of additional frameworks or libraries.

   - You will use a design principle like 12 factor app design to follow industry standard best practices to improve modularity, flexibility and scalability of each distributed component.

5. **How will you ensure the security of data within the application during transmission and at rest?**

   Model answer:

   - You will ensure the security of data during transmission by using protocols like TLS between communicating components.

   - For the security of data at rest, you will use appropriate encryption algorithms to encrypt data before they are stored in persistent storage devices or databases.

6. **What are the different types of services offered by major cloud providers?**

   Model answer:

   - Infrastructure as a Service wherein the cloud provider is responsible for provisioning and protecting the hardware, such as virtual machines and elastic block stores. The customer or the consumer is responsible for installing the required software and build applications on the infrastructure provided. Azure virtual machines and AWS elastic compute cloud are examples of this type of service.

   - Platform as a Service in which the cloud provider provisions the hardware and the software platforms, and the customers can build applications on them and use it. AWS **Relational Database Service** (**RDS**) and **Azure Kubernetes Service** (**AKS**) are examples of this type of service.

   - Software as a service in which the hardware, software platform, and the applications are hosted by the provider, and the consumer just needs to consume the application with their own data.

   - Serverless computing is a model that is best suited for developers to write, test, and deploy code with popular programming languages. The hardware and the software runtime are provided by the cloud provider. AWS Lambda is an example of serverless computing.

Join our Discord space

Join our Discord workspace for latest updates, offers, tech happenings around the world, new releases, and sessions with the authors:

https://discord.bpbonline.com

CHAPTER 4

Technical Solutions Architecture and Design

Introduction

Application architecture is a key decision that plays a vital role in the success of a software project. There are multiple architectural patterns available which a solutions architect can choose from to blueprint a software system. The architecture of a system not only has its own technology implications but also highly influences the other phases of the software project, like development, testing, deployment, and monitoring. It is important to choose an architecture that not only has a technical advantage but also keeps the business goals of the organization in mind. Software solutions, most of the time, are built by enterprises to bridge the gaps between their existing business architecture and their aspirational business goals.

Structure

This chapter covers the following topics:

- Drivers of a solution architecture
- Influence of a solution architecture
- Application architectures
- Application programming interface architectures
- Architectural patterns summary
- Technology choices considerations

Objectives

In this chapter, readers will understand the factors that influence a solution architecture of a system. We will also discuss how a solution architecture can, in turn, influence the different phases of the software development lifecycle. We will cover different types of architectures that solutions architects need to be aware to prepare for a solutions architect interview and use the knowledge presented to effectively build solutions. The chapter will also cover the architectures for **application programming interfaces (API)**, which power many of the modern enterprises today.

Now that we have set the stage by understanding the significance of an application architecture in the success of a software project, let us explore the key factors that influence the design and selection of an appropriate choice of solution architecture. These drivers, both operational and technical, play a crucial role in determining the architecture best suited for a given project.

Drivers of a solution architecture

In this section, we will cover the factors that a solutions architect should consider while architecting a solution for an enterprise. A solution architecture, before being chosen and detailed, needs to consider various aspects that are both operational and technical in nature. Some of the operational drivers include organizational structure, stakeholder management, organizational culture, software budget, time to market, and, very importantly, their business goals. The technical influencers include functional and nonfunctional requirements, enterprise architecture governance, quality of services required, skillset of the available workforce, integration with other applications, and interface with third party systems.

The following are the operational factors to be considered by an architect:

- **Business goals**: Business goals are very important to keep in mind while architecting solutions. This emphasizes the fact that software architecture should not only address technical complexities but also consider optimizing the whole business process space to which the problem being solved belongs. A complex software solution is of little help if it does not optimize a business process that is taking a lot of time to complete. Business goals are thereby at the top of the list in choosing the right target architecture.

- **Organizational structure**: There are organizations with multiple divisions, including both business and technology. An application that has an impact on multiple business divisions needs to be more distributed in nature, and the respective components can be managed by the respective business divisions, governed by a contract for communication between them. From a technology standpoint, there could be multiple teams specializing in a particular area of technology. For instance, there could be a shared middleware services team that develops the middleware services for multiple business units in the enterprise using a specific suite of middleware tools. The architect needs to keep in mind the way the enterprise works and accordingly take architectural decisions.

- **Stakeholder management**: Functional requirements of the system play a key role in the chosen solution architecture used to build the system. At the same time, it is also important to understand the business stakeholders for whom the system is being built. If the requirements are simple, an architecture that can befit those requirements should be chosen. For example, an enterprise might want to build an application to manage leave applications and leave encashment. This application might not warrant a distributed architecture like microservices. The application can be built as a monolith with modularity built into it for segregation of major functions required. A solutions architect should clearly reason out and get the buy-in of both the business and technology stakeholders with regard to how the solution would solve their business problem, and the architecture chosen is the ideal fit for the solution to the problem being solved. The solutions architect should assess the complexity of the requirements given and should recommend an architecture that best fits the application requirements, rather than choosing an architecture that is very sophisticated or popular.

- **Organizational culture**: There are organizations that have a lot of resistance to change in adopting newer technologies. There could be multiple reasons for it. The enterprise could be dealing with very sensitive data and would want to stick with its proven technology stack for compliance reasons rather than trying out cutting edge technologies. For instance, enterprises dealing with financial information and patient health data might be very cautious about adopting newer technologies such as generative AI or blockchain for their core businesses. They may not adopt it until these are proven to be secure and are broadly accepted by the industry overall. However, they may be using them in their internal applications to optimize business tasks that may not involve sensitive customer data.

- **Cost and budget**: Enterprises more often do not want to spend a budget on a software project more than the money they can make out of it. The architecture chosen should enable the enterprise to build, test, and deploy the application within the stipulated cost and budget. The architecture should not prescribe components that are very expensive to procure and maintain in terms of their license cost. The architect should keep in mind the budget available for the enterprise to build the application.

- **Time to market**: Time to market is one of the key factors that a business considers while embarking on software project development. Many a time, the enterprise wants to introduce a service or a product before any of its competitors. The architect should keep in mind the timelines the business is considering for completing a software project. The solutions architect should use an architecture that strikes a balance between its applicability to the problem, the quality-of-service requirements, and the time to market the solution. A sophisticated software application or feature may not appeal to users if there are others like it in the market already.

The following are the technology factors to be considered by an architect:

- **Software system requirements**: The nature of the system requirements plays a very key role in the choice of application architecture. Application requirements can be complex, which requires a careful assessment and segregation of the functional capabilities required. An application that requires a compelling user experience will require a different architecture than an application that is compute intensive and needs to be extremely performant in the transactions carried out in the system. Another scenario could be an application that requires that an entire domain functionality be built that cuts across different business divisions in an enterprise. It is important for a solutions architect to choose an architecture that best fits the functional and nonfunctional requirements.

- **Enterprise architecture**: The overall technology governance in an enterprise plays a key role in the choice of architecture. There is a lot of emphasis on specific approaches to the way applications are built in an enterprise. The enterprise architecture will also have a big influence on the choice of the technology stack being used to build applications. This largely depends on the nature of the enterprise's business. The solutions architect should be aware of the enterprise architecture framework within which they should operate to build a blueprint of the system.

- **Quality-of-services**: Quality-of-services is bound by different service level agreements as dictated by the business stakeholders of the enterprise. The quality of service is also governed by the laws of the land in which the business operates. There could be a mandate to encrypt the data before it is stored or the continuous availability of the system, if the application offers an essential service being used by the public. An example could be an application hosted by the government to find the nearest hospital with the required facilities in case of an emergency.

- **Skillset of the available workforce**: The technology stack should be chosen based on the available skill set within an enterprise. Certain architectures lend themselves to a generic technology skill set, whereas others might need a specific skill set to realize the solution. For example, an event-driven architecture would require the team to have a good experience in message-oriented software like Kafka and messaging patterns to be put into use. The architect should accordingly strike a balance between the nature of the requirements, the available skillset, and the chosen architecture.

- **Integration with other applications**: Certain applications may need to work closely with other applications within the enterprise. Integration using an enterprise service bus or other middleware software would be the right approach to architect and design such applications. The architect should be able to decide the architectural pattern that would be the best fit for blueprinting such applications.

- **Interface with third party systems**: There are applications which require a heavy wiring with systems external to the enterprise. The protocol required to interface with each of those systems could be different, and the format for data exchange could vary. For example, a flight reservation system might interface with many other external data providers for the flight schedule and the fares that keep changing every hour. The solutions architect should be conscious of the contracts exposed by third party systems while designing those interfaces.

Having understood the factors that drive the choice of the solution architecture, it is equally important to recognize how the chosen architecture, in turn, influences the various phases of a software project. The architecture you select will impact not just the development approach but also the team structure, testing strategy, and deployment strategy.

Influence of a solution architecture

Like the way an organization's structure and its business goals drive the software architecture, the software solution architecture also has a profound impact on many aspects of software design and development.

The following are the phases of the software development that a solution architecture influences:

- **Development methodology**: The type of architecture decided by the architect has a direct impact on the development methodology used to build the software. For instance, if the application uses event-driven architecture wherein the software components are loosely coupled, the software can be built in an Agile fashion with multiple components being built in parallel and each component built incrementally. If the application architecture is a monolith, the software can be built using a traditional methodology like Waterfall.

- **Team structure**: The solution architecture also determines the way the teams are organized in a project. If the application architecture is distributed as in the case of microservices, each of the components can be built by individual functional delivery teams. Each team will be responsible for developing the capabilities pertaining to a domain. If the software architecture uses a three-tier pattern comprising user interface, controller, and business logic, there can be three specialized teams focusing on each of these layers. A microservices architecture will also mandate a specialized team, like a DevOps team, that will build the required pipelines to build, test, and deploy the software.

- **Test strategy**: The test strategy also gets influenced by the type of architecture chosen. A microservices architecture will lend itself easily to testing the components independently of each other. More so, the testing will depend on the type of microservice being developed, such as a business logic component or a database component. In a monolith, the focus is to heavily test the functionality of the application as there is very little segregation of the individual components within the application.

- **Deployment strategy**: Deployment strategy is another aspect that depends on the architecture of the application. Microservices architecture lends itself to the independent deployment of the developed services, and they can also be scaled independently. The hardware provisioning and scaling mechanism for this will be entirely different than a monolithic application, which is deployed and scaled as a single unit. The hardware provisioning for a monolith must accordingly be planned.

With an understanding of how solution architecture influences different aspects of a software project, let us now dive deeper into specific application architectures. Each architectural pattern brings its own advantages and challenges, and knowing when to apply them is critical for success in both project implementation and interview scenarios.

Application architectures

In this section, we will look at the different types of application architectures that a solution architect needs to be familiar with. We will look at the salient features of the architectural pattern discussed, their merits and demerits, so that the architect can take an informed decision on whether they will be a right fit for the given application. We will also look at the applicability of each one of those architectures so that the architect can easily identify the scenario in which one or more of those architectural patterns will be the right choice to be applied. Apart from the technology considerations, the architect also needs to keep in mind the operational and technology factors discussed in the section drivers of a solution architecture to choose an appropriate architecture.

Let us begin by discussing the pipes and filters architecture, which is a well-known pattern for organizing complex processes into modular, reusable components. This architecture can be particularly effective when processes need to be divided into independent tasks. Let us explore the details of this architecture.

Pipes and filters

The pipes and filters architecture is one in which the entire process is divided into multiple tasks, and each task is called a filter. Each task is carried out independently of the others. The tasks are connected using pipes that take the output of the previous filter to the next filter. Each filter is self-contained and works based on the input it receives and gives a specific output after processing. The filter could include any type of processing, like business validation, data transformation, or include a step of a batch process. Filters do not have any routing intelligence and send the output from them to the next filter in the line through the pipe. The filters consume data from a source, and after the data is processed through a series of filters, it is passed on to a target, which could be a business logic component in an application.

Figure 4.1 depicts the pipes and filters architecture:

Figure 4.1: *Pipes and filters*

The advantages of the pipes and filters architecture are as follows:

- Pipes and filters architecture promotes modularity of the software application.
- Each filter executes independently of the others, and they can easily be removed or replaced.
- Each filter can be reused any number of times in multiple flows.
- Filters can run in parallel, making them performant.
- Each filter can be made to run on different hardware and software, making them a flexible architectural choice.
- Each filter can be scaled independently.

The disadvantages of the pipe and filter architecture are as follows:

- Complete processing of a request end-to-end might depend on the slowest filter.
- A change of logic of a single filter warrants testing of the end-to-end flow.
- The pipes and filters solution might become difficult to maintain if they are run on completely different sets of hardware across multiple hyperscalers.
- Failure of a single filter while processing a request might cause application state related issues. It is important that all filters are designed to be stateless, and they are idempotent so that the failure to process a request by a filter can be taken up by another instance of the same filter.

The pipes and filter architecture can be used in the following scenarios:

- In a process of compute intensive application, the work can be divided against a series of tasks.
- Each task can best be run in its own choice of hardware and software. This lets computationally intensive tasks run on powerful hardware against others that are not computationally intensive.
- Filters can be run in parallel, making them an ideal choice to process huge amounts of data, as in an **extract, transform, and load** (ETL) application.
- Scenarios in which the tasks may have to be quickly removed or interchanged with others.

While pipes and filters focus on modularity through sequential task processing, a hexagonal architecture offers a different approach by isolating business logic from the technical concerns of an application. This separation ensures flexibility in how business logic is accessed and consumed by various interfaces.

Hexagonal architecture

The hexagonal architecture pattern, also known as the ports and adapters pattern, aims to isolate the business logic of the application from other technical components like data sources and protocols used to consume the business logic. The focus of this architecture pattern is to separate the business logic from other components of the application like database components or the user interface components. This helps to approach the application design more from a business requirements perspective rather than all other concerns that consume the business logic. Once the business components are built, they are integrated with other components or consumed by other applications through ports and adapters.

Adapters are specialized interfaces that can be used by other components or applications to consume the business logic through ports defined as part of the business components. The architecture enables multiple adapters to be integrated with the same port without impacting each other. For example, a business component exposed using a REST API can easily be consumed by a REST client and a GraphQL API.

The applications use adapters based on their convenience to consume the data from the port and use them in their very own way. Though hexagonal architecture appears more in line with microservices architecture, it deals with segregation of business logic as components within a single application, whereas microservices deal with applications having a wider business scope involving multiple business divisions within the enterprise.

Hexagonal architecture is depicted in the following figure:

Figure 4.2: *Hexagonal architecture*

The advantages of using the hexagonal architecture are as follows:

- Business logic is segregated from other technical concerns of the application, enabling developers to focus on core business requirements.

- Loose coupling of the components enables flexibility to add or remove components easily.

- The business components can scale independently based on the load on the system.

- Business logic can be independently tested in full without any dependencies.

- The architecture gives an advantage to choose the technology of choice for each of the components as they are loosely coupled.

- The ports and adapter pattern enables the business logic to be consumed by multiple clients at the same time.

The disadvantages of using the hexagonal architecture are as follows:

- Added complexity to write ports and adapters.

- The ports and adapters add another layer of abstraction, which may be a hurdle to the performance of the application.

- Tracing an application request might be a challenge because of the multiple layers involved.

- This architecture may be a complicated option for applications of simple and medium complexity.

- There could be a maintenance overhead because of the number of individual components and layers involved.

The hexagonal architecture can be used in the following scenarios:

- Hexagonal architecture fits in where a single business component must be consumed by multiple heterogeneous client applications.

- Applications that undergo frequent changes and need to be tested often.

- Hexagonal architecture can be used for systems which has high scalability requirements.

- This architecture pattern can be used for legacy modernization engagements where a newer component might have to work with a legacy component and vice versa.

- This architecture fits applications which need loose coupling, and components can evolve independently of each other but have well defined interfaces.

In contrast to the loosely coupled, flexible nature of hexagonal architecture, a monolithic architecture, discussed in the following section, bundles all components into a single deployment unit. While it may seem limiting, monolithic architecture has its place in certain scenarios, particularly for simpler applications or quick MVP builds.

Let us see when a monolithic approach makes sense and its trade-offs.

Monolith architecture

A monolithic architecture is a pattern in which all the components needed to realize the requirements of an application are bundled and deployed together. This architecture pattern does not segregate between different concerns like user interface, business, and database logic. There is a very tight coupling between different components of the system. Due to the lack of segregation of concerns in the application, all the components are developed using a common technology stack or programming language. The monolith applications are more suited for applications with simple requirements, and the testability of the application does not warrant a considerable amount of effort.

The monolith architecture is depicted in the following figure:

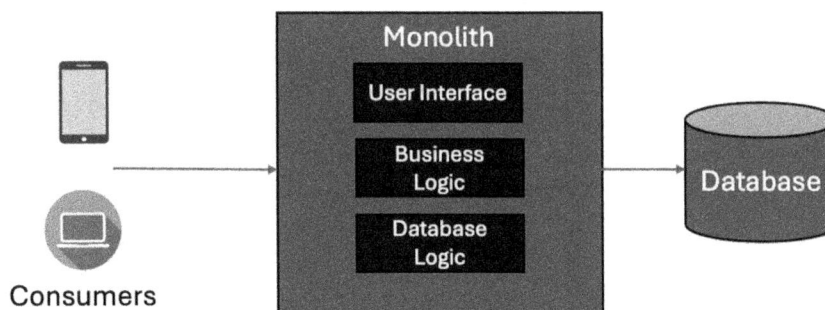

Figure 4.3: Monolith architecture

The advantages of the monolith architecture are as follows:

- An easy architectural pattern to blueprint and build applications.

- It is easy to deploy as the entire application is built as a single compilation unit.

- Offers a good performance as all the components run in a single process.

- Easier to deploy and manage as all components are bundled into a unified package.

The disadvantages of the monolith architecture are as follows:

- This architecture poses scalability issues as the whole package needs to be scaled, even for scaling a single component.

- The choice of technology poses limitations to developing specific component types like user interfaces and business logic components.

- Regression testing is a challenge, as even for small changes, a considerable portion of the application needs to be tested.

- As the codebase grows, it becomes difficult to deploy the application, and application start times could increase.

- Maintainability of the codebase is hard for large applications.

The monolith architecture can be used in the following scenarios:

- Simple applications where the number of features and components is limited.

- This architecture is suitable for applications where the user base is limited and does not change.

- It is a good candidate to quickly develop an application as a **minimum viable product** (**MVP**) that can be rolled out to users within shorter timelines.

Monolithic applications may provide simplicity, but when projects require clear separation between concerns like user interface, business logic, and data access, a layered architecture can provide the necessary structure. Let us explore the layered architecture below, one of the most widely adopted patterns, and its benefits.

Layered architecture

The layered architecture helps a solutions architect to conceptualize and blueprint the application as a set of distinct layers. This is one of the most popular architectural patterns that has been in the industry for a long time. The application using this architecture has multiple layers, each one responsible for a specific technology concern. There is a layer containing the user interfaces, there is a second layer containing the business logic of the application, and a third layer for database access logic. This makes the application more modular, and each layer is separated from the other two. This gives flexibility to the architect to choose a technology stack of choice for each of the layers. Client server and model view controller are specific cases of this architectural pattern. However, the communication between the layers depends on how the layers are segregated within the application. For example, if the business logic components are packaged together, they can communicate with each other directly by calling a method within the corresponding class. In this case, the user interface and business logic are segregated, and the two components could talk to each other using standard protocols like **Hyper Text Transfer Protocol (HTTP)**.

A layered architecture is depicted in the following figure:

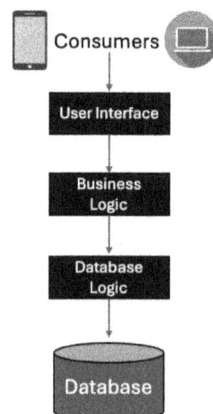

Figure 4.4: Layered architecture

The advantages of using a layered architecture are as follows:

- This architecture provides a clear segregation of concerns, such as user interfaces, business logic, and database logic, making the application more modular and maintainable.

- It lends itself to technology choices for each of the application layers concerned.

- It gives flexibility for different teams to work independently on each of the layers.

- Individual layers can be tested independently by mocking the other adjacent layer on which it is dependent.

- Individual layers can be scaled independently.

- Components in each layer can be reused depending on the context of feature functionality, for instance, a component developed to check the account status can be reused at multiple places like bill payments and fund transfers.

The disadvantages of the layered architecture are as follows:

- Though the individual layers can be scaled independently, it does not offer any segregation between components in each layer.

- The performance of the application depends on the performance of the individual layers.

- Introduction of a new feature requires development or a change across all the layers of the application.

Situations in which a layered architecture can be used are as follows:

- A good fit for applications that often require a technology change for each of the individual layers.

- The layered architecture can be used effectively for large applications, which makes it easier to maintain as the application is modular.

- This architecture can be used for applications where there are teams with skills for specific layers.

While layered architecture organizes an application by technology concerns, **service oriented architecture** (**SOA**) organizes services around business functionality. In an enterprise, SOA enables reuse and flexibility across multiple applications and business divisions. Let us look at the advantages and challenges of implementing SOA.

Service oriented architecture

The service oriented architecture allows services across multiple applications in an enterprise to communicate with each other. These applications could belong to different business divisions in an enterprise. The services exposed through SOA themselves are owned and maintained by the business division to which the process represented by the services belongs. The service oriented architecture brings in a lot of re-use in the way applications are conceptualized, designed, and developed. For example, the marketing division in an enterprise is responsible for the offers rolled out to its customers for a period. There are multiple applications that can consume these offers and present them to the customers. A customer using a mobile application can directly make use of the offers if interested. On the other hand, a front desk billing clerk using an internal desktop application can let the customers know of these offers at the time of billing the products.

The important feature of SOA is that each service is completely independent of each other and can be used by multiple client applications. These services can be exposed as **Simple Object Access Protocols** (**SOAP**) web services, **Representational State Transfer** (**REST**) services, and using a message queue. These services are bound by a contract that are made aware to the consuming applications for easy consumption of those services. These services are most popularly hosted on middleware products or an enterprise service bus through which the request response exchange happens.

A service oriented architecture is depicted in *Figure 4.5*:

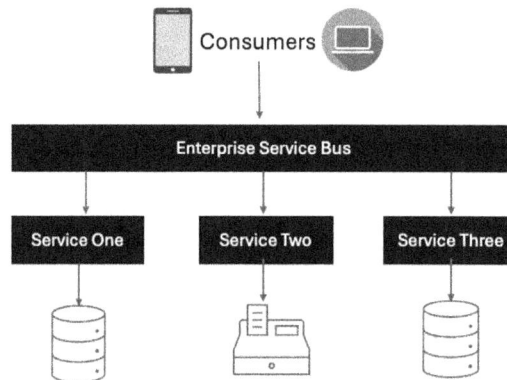

Figure 4.5: *Service oriented architecture*

The advantages of using SOA are as follows:

- Services are conceptualized and owned by business divisions which emphasize a joint ownership and business significance in realizing the business goals.

- The services can be developed and deployed independently improving their scalability.

- The services developed can be consumed by any number of channel applications that get added in the future.

- The services offer a definitive contract thereby enabling them to be consumed by any type of application that honors the contract.

- The services are loosely coupled because of which they can be enhanced independently without affecting other services.

- The architect can choose the technology that works best for the individual services.

The disadvantages of using SOA are as follows:

- The services in most cases are integrated using an **Enterprise Service Bus** (**ESB**) which adds additional hops and could be a hurdle for application performance.

- Increased license cost for the enterprise to procure and maintain the ESB and the individual services required.

- Complexity of development of the service and its contract to make them interoperable for consumption by multiple consumers.

- A strong SOA governance should be in place as the services could be owned by different entities within the organization.

- Versioning could become a challenge if multiple consumers want different versions of a service implementation.

Situations in which SOA can be used are as follows:

- Works extremely well for a large enterprise wherein a service needs to be consumed by multiple channel applications.

- SOA lends itself well where each business process is owned by separate business divisions within the enterprise.

While a SOA facilitates communication across services, at times, the application might need asynchronous, real-time responses to events. **Event-driven architecture** (**EDA**) addresses this by allowing components to react to events without being tightly coupled. Let us explore in the following section the benefits of EDA and when to use it.

Event-driven architecture

EDA is an architectural pattern in which the components of a system react based on events that happen within the application. An event is an action that is triggered by an end user or could be triggered by another component within the application. For example, an inventory component could check for sufficient goods in the warehouse on the receipt of an order within the system, which acts as an event to trigger the inventory validation process. The event-driven architecture encourages a loosely coupled model for applications in which communication between the components happens in an asynchronous fashion. Messages are exchanged between components using a message broker that helps to bind all the components together. There are two different approaches to implementing EDA.

A point-to-point model in which a producer sends a message to an event queue, and the message is consumed by a component designed to process that event. In the second approach, a producer publishes a message to a topic, and multiple consumers consume the message from the topic. This is called the publish subscribe model, in which a message can be broadcast to multiple subscribers that are interested in the event. Event-driven architecture also supports event streaming in which a continuous stream of messages gets written to the message broker or event bus, and they are continuously processed by event receivers in real or near real time. Some of the popular message brokers include Kafka, **Amazon Web Services** (**AWS**) **Simple Message Queue** (**SQS**), and RabbitMQ. *Figure 4.6* depicts an event-driven architecture:

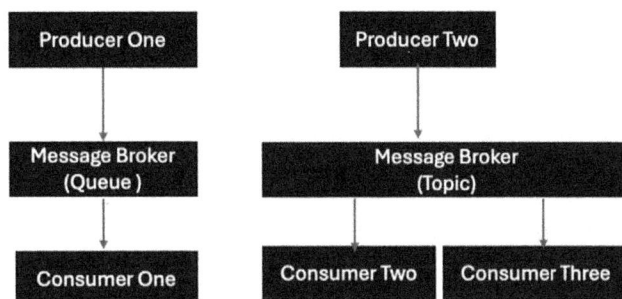

Figure 4.6: Event-driven architecture

The advantages of using event-driven architecture are as follows:

- Event-driven architecture encourages decoupling of components, making the application modular.
- Individual components can be replaced or changed without impacting others if the message structure for consumption does not change.
- Individual components have their choice to choose their own technology stack based on the problem they are trying to solve.
- Offers resilience and message (event) durability as the messages can be stored and processed later if the consumer is not available.
- Can be used for patterns like event sourcing that help to store state changes as events that can be later replayed if required. We will discuss the event sourcing pattern in *Chapter 22, Cloud-native Architecture and Design.*
- Helps in parallel development as individual teams can work on their components after the contract (message format) has been agreed upon.
- This architecture lends itself well to testing the individual components independently.
- This architecture is scalable as the individual components can be scaled based on their load.

The disadvantages of using event-driven architecture are as follows:

- This architecture may not be suitable for small or medium complexity applications due to the design intensity imposed by it.

- Traceability of the requests could be a challenge because of the asynchronous nature of message exchanges involving multiple components within the system.

- All transactions involve the message broker, which introduces an extra hop that could be the cause of concern for performance.

- This architecture will offer eventual consistency, and the data read could be slightly outdated before all the components process a message in a transaction.

Situations in which an event-driven architecture is applicable are as follows:

- This architecture is widely used by **Internet of Things (IoT)** applications where multiple devices emit data to be collated and processed.

- Event-driven architecture is commonly used by microservices architecture for communication between different components within the system. We will discuss microservices architecture in the next sub-section *Microservices architecture* of this chapter.

- This architecture is used in situations that require integration with other applications that use asynchronous communication.

- This is used by applications that require processing of data streams in real or near real time and decisions to be relayed back to the downstream systems.

While an event-driven architecture decouples components using events, in many modern enterprise applications, a more granular division of services is required. Microservices architecture builds on this idea by breaking down the application into independent, business-focused services. This architecture is foundational in cloud-native development. Let us explore how to effectively design microservices.

Microservices architecture

Microservices architecture is one of the most widely used architectural patterns in the industry today. It is very important for a solutions architect to understand this architecture and associated design approaches, design patterns, and design principles to successfully implement it the right way. In any solutions architect interview, there are always questions pertaining to the successful implementation of this architecture.

The microservices architecture starts with the division of a business domain into sub domains. In microservices architecture, the focus is more on the business domain than on the technology used to implement it. DDD that we covered in *Chapter 3, Technical Proficiency Essential Knowledge* is one of the most used design methodologies to split the overall business domain into sub domains. The sub domains represent the problem space, which at a high level represents the boundary of the different business functions required in an enterprise. The sub domains use ubiquitous language to create definitive meanings for the real-world entities that are used within the sub domain. The sub domain also gets associated with a domain model that represents the key participants, their relationships, and their behavior within the sub domain. The sub domains are later converted into a bounded context within which the required entities will live and operate (data and behavior) to realize the required business functions. The bounded contexts are then converted into microservices that represent the individual components providing one of the business capabilities. It is important to note that each microservice will have its own database. This is to ensure that all microservices are self-contained and their existence does not depend on a common data store of the application, thereby avoiding a single point of failure. Even though the data stores may be unique for each microservice, it is acceptable to have an overlap of data to a certain extent, as required for the business capabilities to operate in harmony with each other. For example, a shipping microservice might have some amount of order information to make sure that the order is shipped to the right customer with all the products ordered.

The whole process of coming up with the sub domains and the required microservices is called a decomposition strategy. This is one of the most important steps in microservices architecture. It is vital to get the right number of microservices for the system, at the same time ensuring that each microservice is of the right size. This determines the flexibility of the whole application to address changing market needs and a quick time to market. This also helps the individual microservices to scale independently and very quickly, as the size of the microservice is rightly managed. Microservices architecture is one of the most used architectures in cloud native applications. Microservices architecture lends itself very well to containerization. Clients access microservices using API gateway. It is important for the solutions architect to understand the concepts of containerization to effectively implement microservices architecture on the cloud. We will cover the containerization concepts and the microservices design patterns in detail in *Chapter 22, Cloud-native Architecture and Design*.

The following figure depicts a microservices architecture:

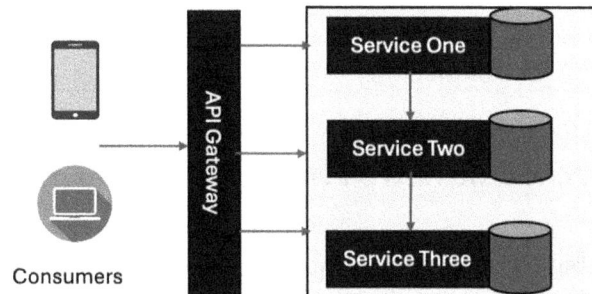

Figure 4.7: Microservices architecture

The advantages of microservices architecture are as follows:

- The architecture is driven by business focused design methodology.

  Note: **DDD approach that we covered in** *Chapter 3, Technical Proficiency Essential Knowledge* **is one of the popular methodologies to divide the entire business domain into sub domains.**

- Microservices are independently developed and deployed, thereby reducing the dependency on other parts or services of the application. The independent deployability is one of the key advantages that make microservices architecture the most adopted one by enterprises. This increases the time to market of any new features that the enterprise wants to roll out to its customers.

- Each microservice can be independently scaled very quickly because of its lighter weight.

- The startup of microservices is very quick as they are packaged with only limited functionality in them.

- Microservices enable the culture of DevOps that encourages the development team and the operations team to work together.

- Microservices are polyglots in nature, which means that each microservice can choose its own technology for development based on the type of problem they are trying to solve.

- Microservices architecture enables an organized team structure in terms of their role and responsibilities.

The following are the disadvantages of the microservices architecture:

- The microservices architecture is complex in nature to implement correctly, thereby making it difficult to adopt for smaller applications.

- The architecture might prove to be counterproductive if the team does not adopt a proper decomposition strategy.

  Note: **Decomposition strategy is a method used to come up with the Microservice components in a sub domain (divisions of a business domain). Each sub domain comprises of business capabilities; You can try to make each business capability a microservice. Be cautious neither to over split the services, which will make them very granular, nor assign them too many responsibilities, which will again make them a monolith on their own.**

- Microservices communicate with each other through network calls, which can be a hurdle to performance if the network latency is large.

- The enterprise needs to address additional technology complexity like DevOps pipelines, container orchestration tools (Kubernetes, for example), in addition to the development, deployment, and monitoring of each microservice.

- The microservice architecture could pose technical challenges like transaction management and service aggregation that need to be addressed by the solutions architect.

- Microservice might not be the right option for building applications that have a limited budget and have a very tight timeline for completion.

The following are the scenarios in which microservices architecture can be a right fit:

- The business is complex, and we need an architecture to address the business complexity in the technology solution.

- A large application that has high scalability requirements will benefit from a microservices architecture, which allows the business logic to be broken down into multiple independently deployable components.

- An enterprise that has a need to introduce newer services to its customers. After the initial build with microservices, it becomes easier to introduce new microservices to the application that constitute new feature functionality and products.

- Each microservice can be independently tested and deployed with a virtualization strategy for its dependencies.

Microservices are also being deployed using a serverless computing model in cloud native applications. Let us explore why serverless architecture has become one of the mainstays in a cloud native application architecture, along with its merits and demerits.

Serverless architecture

A serverless architecture is one in which the configuration of the hardware, and the software runtime are totally taken care of by the cloud provider. The developer can use the serverless computing model to deploy their code and test it. The developer can increase the efficiency of the program by requesting additional memory or computing power, depending on the service level agreements. All the popular cloud providers offer different software runtimes, such as Python, Java, and Node.js, in which code can be written. AWS Lambda and Azure Functions are some examples of serverless architecture.

The advantages of serverless architecture are as follows:

- The developer can directly deploy their code without having to worry about setting up their hardware and software environments.

- The developer can request additional memory and computing power to improve the efficiency of their code as required.

- There are no additional license costs to worry about.

- The developer is charged only for the time during which the code runs, optimizing the cost.

- Helps the developer to spin up a quick proof of concept.

- Fosters innovation for small enterprises and start-ups.

The disadvantages of the serverless architecture are as follows:

- The developer does not have a lot of control over the hardware and software runtime to configure them in a granular way as required.

- The security model of the serverless infrastructure is totally managed by the cloud provider.

- The cloud provider might provide only the popular and recent software runtime and may not support old technologies.

The serverless architecture is applicable in the following scenarios:

- Applications that need to be built in the shortest possible time without any infrastructure or software setup.

- Scenarios in which procuring a permanent license may be expensive for the enterprise.

While choosing the right application architecture is key to solving internal system challenges, APIs play a pivotal role in integrating services both within and outside of the enterprise. Let us now shift focus to API architecture and design to discuss the various approaches to exposing and consuming services in modern software applications.

Application programming interface architectures

API has become one of the important ways to expose the services of an organization to both internal business divisions and to the external world. APIs provide agility to businesses in staying competitive and increasing their reach to diverse partners across the world. APIs have evolved over the years, and their quality of services in terms of their security, scalability, and resilience has also seen a drastic improvement over the years.

APIs foster innovation at the same time, helping enterprises to monetize their digital assets. In *Chapter 3, Technical Proficiency Essential Knowledge*, we discussed the API first design approach in which applications are architected and designed with APIs as first-class citizens. Developers constantly use APIs to develop software that makes use of the services offered by large enterprises. The examples of web application that widely uses APIs are airfare comparison and booking portals, hotel bookings around the world, etc. We will discuss three major API architectures that are predominantly used that a solutions architect should be aware of.

Representational state transfer

REST is an architectural style for creating resource based, stateless API end points. The REST endpoints shield all the complexity of the underlying server implementation from the client and provide a unique **Uniform Resource Locator (URL)** to be used by the consumers. REST endpoints are typically resource based and they support operations that are required to query and manipulate the resources of the application. For instance, there would be specific APIs for customer and order resources of an application, and the API would support operations based on well-known HTTP verbs like post, get, put, and delete, mapping to create, read, update, and delete operations used commonly by server-side applications. The REST APIs are stateless in the sense that they do not hold any stateful data between any two requests in the same session. They are also idempotent and have the same effect on requests that carry identical payloads.

In essence, REST APIs are characterized by the following features:

- REST endpoints primarily operate on the resources, for example, customer, order, account, etc., of the application.

- Each REST API is identified using a unique URL or a URI.

- They are stateless by design.

- REST endpoints support HTTP verbs such as post, get, put, and delete.

- Responses from the REST end points are cacheable.

- They enable the approach of **Hypermedia as the Engine of Application State (HATEOAS)** wherein the transition to the next possible states of the application is dictated by the REST API in the form of hyperlinks in the response.

The following are the advantages of using REST APIs:

- They hide the complexity of the inner implementation, making them highly consumable.

- REST end points are interoperable with clients using disparate technologies for their front ends.

- They expose end points that are HTTP based and are easy to use by any type of client, like a web or mobile application.

- They follow the HTTP taxonomy for manipulating resources and are suitable for CRUD type of applications.

- Since they are stateless and idempotent, they lend themselves to caching of the generated responses.

- They are easily scalable given their stateless nature.

The following are the disadvantages of using REST APIs:

- Data aggregation could be a challenge given the fine grained (resource based) nature of the REST APIs.

- Though they expose their contracts through swagger files (API 2.0/API 3.0), there is no standardization of schema validation for REST endpoints.

- Applications requiring maintenance of state will not benefit from REST end points, given their stateless nature.

Simple Object Access Protocol

SOAP was one of the widely adopted protocols before REST came into being. Interoperability between clients and servers was the main challenge in the application integration space. Servers and clients were written in different programming languages, and integrating them became a challenge, and they could communicate only using a middleware. Web services became a popular choice to integrate applications, and SOAP served as a worthy candidate to integrate disparate systems. A set of associated standards (specifications) came along with SOAP for defining security, reliability, messaging, and interoperability.

SOAP defined the standard for defining the payloads that contained both data and operations, and the contract of the payload was defined using an interface definition file called the **web services description language** (**WSDL**). Any client that wanted to access the SOAP service could download the WSDL and create the stubs that hid the nuances of accessing the SOAP service. These stubs were able to be generated in multiple languages, depending on the technology stack used by the client. Another method that was available was the **dynamic invocation interface** (**DII**), in which the client did not have to generate stubs and was dynamically able to create SOAP requests and invoke services at runtime. SOAP services are still common in applications developed before the advent of REST, though their usage has almost stopped in contemporary software applications. The solutions architect might still have to deal with systems that use the SOAP protocol for inter system communication and should have an understanding of these types of services.

The following were the advantages of SOAP:

- Offers interoperability between applications using different technologies.

- Provided specifications for quality of services such as reliability, security, and interoperability.

- Removes the necessity of a middleware between the client and the server.

- The WSDL provided the clients with a schema that was used to validate request formats and content at compile time, making them efficient to be tested easily and debug errors.

The following were the disadvantages of SOAP:

- The SOAP and other related specifications are fairly complex to implement by applications.

- SOAP may not be the ideal choice for low latency applications, given their nature of invocation (DII especially).
- Since the SOAP services are tied to a WSDL, any changes to the payload will require a recompilation of the client stubs.

SOAP is applicable to the following types of applications:

- SOAP is an ideal candidate to integrate applications using different technologies in a large enterprise.
- Exposing third party partner systems becomes easier with the circulation of the related WSDL files to different consumers.
- Plays a significant role in exposing legacy systems to modern day application clients without a major change to the core of those legacy systems.

Google remote procedure call

gRPC is an open-source framework developed by Google for optimized and high-performance communication between client and server applications. gRPC is widely used by enterprises across the globe to build their APIs. gRPC uses a binary format as a payload(serialization) between the client and server. This binary format helps in the compression of the payload, thereby making communication faster. This is different between a REST and a SOAP service, where the payloads are sent in **JavaScript Object Notation** (**JSON**) and **Extensible Markup Language** (**XML**) formats, respectively. This makes gRPC useful for applications that need faster round trips between the client and the server.

gRPC uses a specific language called **protocol buffers** (**ProtoBuf**) to define the APIs. Later, the protocol buffer file is compiled to the programming language for both the server and the client applications based on their technology, like Java or Python. The protocol buffer file defines the contract between the client and server, just like WSDL for SOAP services and a Swagger file for REST endpoints.

The following are the advantages of using gRPC:

- gRPC makes applications interoperable with modern day software applications using a variety of technologies for their implementation.
- Suitable for low latency applications where the components interact over a network, like a microservices architecture.
- The binary format serialization compresses the payload, making the communication lighter between the client and server, improving performance.

The following are the disadvantages of gRPC:

- It is not suitable for simple applications due to the complexity of its implementation.
- Like SOAP services, the contract between the client and server is strictly dictated by the protocol buffer file. Any change in the contract will result in the recompilation of the server and client code that support gRPC.
- It may not be suitable for business-to-business integration (partner systems) because of its rigid nature to generate both server and client-side artefacts.

The following are the application types that will benefit from gRPC:

- Applications used by stock broking and currency exchange houses that require a very low latency, and gRPC could be a good fit for these kinds of applications.
- It is a good fit for cloud native applications that predominantly use microservices for their applications. Inter service communication will benefit from gRPC.

GraphQL

GraphQL was introduced by Facebook and is a query language used for APIs. GraphQL has a server engine and uses a declarative approach to define APIs. In the same way, there are client side libraries that are used to connect to the GraphQL APIs and get the required data. Apollo Server, Graphene, and GraphQL-JS are some of the popular server-side implementations of GraphQL. Apollo client is a popular client-side implementation that can be used by Angular or React front end applications to connect to the GraphQL APIs.

GraphQL was developed to be an efficient alternative to REST endpoints. APIs in GraphQL are defined using a schema that lets front end applications fetch the right amount of data they require for their different form factors (web, mobile, etc). GraphQL offers the capability to fetch required data in a single call from multiple resources across the enterprise. This avoids multiple round trips to the server, unlike in the case of RESTful APIs. GraphQL APIs can be designed to offer a single end point for the same scenario that requires multiple RESTful calls to get the same amount of data. GraphQL is strongly typed, which enables developers to validate the type of parameters passed in queries at the time of API invocation.

The following are the advantages of GraphQL:

- GraphQL can retrieve all of the data required in a single call from the client.
- GraphQL can help to fetch just enough data as required by the client application. Mobile applications can especially benefit, given their limited processing power, when compared to a desktop.
- GraphQL offers resolvers that can help to authorize users before they can fetch certain values as part of the API response.
- It has an efficient error handling mechanism that can return meaningful messages to the user.
- Offers notification of the client in real time when data is available in the API.

The following are the disadvantages of the GraphQL APIs:

- GraphQL may not be the right choice for systems requiring simple CRUD operations.
- GraphQL may pose performance related issues if the API schemas are deeply nested in terms of their structure to get data from multiple server resources.
- If the application requires fine grained security, REST will be a better choice to handle complexity than GraphQL resolvers.

The following are the scenarios in which GraphQL could be effectively used:

- APIs that fetch data from different resources, and the data needs to be returned to the client all at once.
- Applications that need to validate the query parameters at the API level and return meaningful responses to consumers.
- GraphQL is useful for applications supporting multiple form factors where the client needs to specify the data that it wants to consume.

Architectural patterns summary

Having discussed the patterns for application architectures and APIs, *Table 4.1* shows the salient features for a quick reference. This will help the readers as a refresher for preparing for the solutions architect interview:

Architecture pattern	Salient features
Pipes and filters	• This pattern divides a process as multiple steps. • Each step(filter) is connected to a pipe that takes the output of the filter to the next step(filter). • Filters can run in parallel. • Each filter can run in its own hardware and software, depending on requirements. • Each filter can be made redundant to reduce failures. • The data could come from multiple sources and go to a target after being processed by multiple filters. • Ideal for processes that need to be executed as a sequence of steps.
Hexagonal architecture	• The business logic is exposed to multiple clients in the form of a port. • Each port can be consumed by a diverse set of clients using custom adapters. • The adapters are written based on the protocol support required by the consuming applications. • Ideal for scenarios in which a business logic component needs to be consumed by disparate clients. • It is like a USB port in a laptop into which multiple devices can be plugged into like an optical mouse or a mobile charger.
Monolith	• All the components are packaged into a single compilation unit, such as a WAR or EAR file. • No clear segregation of layers within the application. • This poses a challenge on the technology choice for individual components like user interfaces, business, and data logic. • Ideal for simple applications with strict timelines.
Layered	• The application architecture is clearly demarcated by different layers. • Each layer addresses a specific technology concern like user Interface, business logic, and data access logic. • Each layer can be built with its own technology choice. • It is easy to replace the individual layers separately, making it very modular. • Ideal for applications wherein each layer undergoes lots of changes and also needs to be replaced often.
Service oriented architecture	• This architecture integrates different services of the enterprise. • The integration of services is enabled by an ESB. • Each service integrated can belong to different business divisions of the enterprise. • Ideal for scenarios where a business process is to be built as a sequence of services, with each service belonging to different divisions in a large business enterprise.
Event-driven architecture	• Applications generate events(messages) in response to a user action(quote, order, etc.). • The messages are posted to a message broker. • This will trigger an action on a business logic component. • This architecture enables both point-to-point and publish subscribe type of communication. • Ideal for decoupled systems and microservices.

Architecture pattern	Salient features
Microservices	• This architecture encourages a business driven approach using methodologies like DDD. • Application developed and deployed as individual components. • This architecture is highly scalable and hence suitable for cloud-native application architecture. • The communication between components can be synchronous or asynchronous. • Suitable for large applications with complex business requirements like e-commerce applications.
Serverless	• This model enables developers to deploy their code in their preferred software runtime on the cloud. • Developers can request additional hardware, such as memory and computing power. • Hardware and software platform is completely managed by the cloud providers. • Serverless computing model has come to be widely used with the microservices architecture. • This model is suitable for spinning up a quick proof of concept or a minimum viable product.

Table 4.1: *Application architecture patterns*

The following table covers the API architecture patterns:

API pattern	Salient features
REST	• Most widely used API pattern to integrate applications and expose application capabilities to internal and external partners. • Backed by HTTP, which makes it very consumable by disparate clients. • Supports create, read, update, and delete operations using the HTTP verbs of post, get, put, and delete. • REST APIs operate on resources of the application(order, customer, etc.). • The REST end points are identified by well-defined URLs. • REST APIs are stateless and idempotent. • The responses from REST end points are highly cacheable.
SOAP	• Makes use of an interface definition file called the WSDL to define the APIs. • APIs can be called dynamically or by generating stubs from the WSDL file. • The payload is a SOAP payload predominantly carried by http. • It has additional specifications for reliability messaging, security, and interoperability. • Used to create highly interoperable web services to integrate disparate applications and played a key role in enterprises using SOA.
gRPC	• Google RPC uses a binary format to carry payloads from the client to the server. • APIs are defined using an interface definition file called the ProtoBuf. • Stubs are generated for both clients and servers using the protocol buffer API definition file. • Very performant and is used for inter microservice communication. • May not be suitable for integrating external partners because of the rigid nature to generate stubs for both client and servers.

API pattern	Salient features
GraphQL	• GraphQL introduced by Facebook defines APIs in the form of a schema. • The user can define the depth of the query in the schema file depending on the data(response) requirements. • Helps to fetch all the data required from multiple sources in a single call. • It has resolvers that help with the authentication of APIs. • Could cause performance issues if the queries are deeply nested.

Table 4.2: *API architecture patterns*

We have, till now, discussed the different patterns for solution architectures and APIs. We will now examine the factors to be considered while choosing the technology stack for different layers of an application. This will help a solutions architect to quickly understand and use these while making a choice of a technology, and will help them to get prepared for the solutions architect interview.

Technology choices considerations

The solutions architect not only needs to be aware of the architectural patterns but also should be conversant with the considerations for choosing the technology across different layers of an architecture.

The following table lists the considerations along with the choice of software that is being used in the industry:

Category	Considerations	Technology choices
User interface	• Responsive web (web and mobile) • Cross browser compatibility • Performance (rendering time, data binding) • Plugins availability • Support and maintainability (community support, updates to the library) • Complexity and learning curve	Angular, React, Vue JS, Streamlit for python
APIs	• Protocol support (HTTP, Web Sockets) • Complexity (Stubs creation) • Security support (transport layer security, integration with identity providers) • Type of communication (synchronous, asynchronous) • Scalability (horizontal and vertical) • Licensing cost (open-source versus licensed)	Flask, Django, and Fast API for Python, .NET Web APIs, Spring Boot for Java
Middleware	• Type of integration (mainframes, databases, message-based systems). • Licensing cost (open-source versus licensed) • Flexibility (policy configuration and versioning) • Protocol support (HTTP, SOAP, MQ) • Support for compliance (PCI DSS, HIPPA)	Tibco Businessworks, MuleSoft anypoint, Azure Logic Apps, Red Hat Fuse

Category	Considerations	Technology choices
Message brokers	<ul><li>Messaging patterns supported (point to point, publish-subscribe)</li><li>Protocol support (AMQP, HTTP, MQTT</li><li>Delivery guarantee (at least once, exactly once)</li><li>Security (authentication, encryption)</li><li>Cost (commercial versus open source)</li><li>Durability (storage for a certain period)</li></ul>	Kafka, RabbitMQ, AWS Simple Queue Service, Azure Service Bus
Backend components	<ul><li>Requirements complexity (simple versus complex applications)</li><li>Performance</li><li>Cloud compatibility (ability to operate on the cloud)</li><li>Built-in security (authentication, authorization)</li><li>Database support (popular databases, object relation mapping)</li><li>Architecture support (microservices, layered architecture, etc.)</li><li>Ability to scale (horizontal and vertical scaling)</li><li>Library support (transaction management, error handling, resilience)</li></ul>	Spring Boot, Django for Python, .NET, Node.js
Databases	<ul><li>Nature of functional requirements (online transactions, data warehouse, caching)</li><li>Type of data stored (structured, semi structured, unstructured)</li><li>Security (authentication, authorization, encryption)</li><li>Ease and extent of administration (configuration, backup procedures)</li><li>Cost (license, maintenance cost)</li><li>Support for the cloud (on-prem and cloud)</li><li>Scalability (horizontal, vertical)</li></ul>	Oracle, Microsoft SQL server, Mongo DB, AWS DynamoDB, Redis

Table 4.3: *Technology choices considerations*

Now that we have covered key architectural patterns, API design strategies, and technology choices for different types of components in an application, it is time to prepare for common interview questions. The model interview questions and answers section will provide model answers to some of the most frequently asked architecture and design questions in solutions architect interviews.

Conclusion

In this chapter, we covered the operational and technology drivers for a solution architecture. We discussed how the business goals and the organizational hierarchy influence architectural decisions. We also discussed how the users' expectations for different quality of services, like performance and security, along with enterprise architecture governance, play a role in the architectural decisions being taken. We looked at the ways in which a solution architecture can influence different phases of a software project, like development, testing, and deployment of the application.

We looked at different architectural patterns that a solutions architect is required to know for effectively blueprinting software solutions. We discussed some of the most used patterns in the industry, like layered, microservices, event-driven architecture. We discussed the advantages and disadvantages of using each one of them, along with the scenarios in which they are applicable. We also discussed the architectural and design principles of creating APIs for applications. Finally, we looked at the considerations for making technology choices for different components like user interfaces, backend, and databases.

In the next chapter, we will look at how we can align technology covered with the business goals of the enterprise.

Key takeaways

The takeaways are as follows:

- **Drivers of a solution architecture**: Factors that influence a solution architecture that a solutions architect should be familiar with to strike a balance between the solution and the organization's structure and governance.

- **Architectural patterns**: Choose the best architecture based on the nature of the application. Different architectural patterns such as event-driven architecture, layered, pipes and filters, hexagonal, and microservices, along with their advantages, disadvantages, and the appropriate scenarios in which they can be applied.

- **Microservices**: Knowledge of what a microservice is and how to arrive at the required microservices for a business domain. Salient features of the microservices architecture that an architect is supposed to know to implement this widely used architectural pattern.

- **API architecture and design**: Knowledge required in the areas of API architecture and design. Different architectures available for implementing APIs like SOAP, REST, GraphQL, and gRPC, along with their merits and demerits.

- **Technology choice**: Be aware of the factors to be considered while choosing a technology stack for the different layers of the architecture, like presentation, APIs, middleware, and backend components.

Model interview questions and answers

1. **What is the architecture that you will prescribe for an application that generates lot of events?**

   Model answer:

   - You will prescribe an event-driven architecture for such an application.

   - You will choose a message broker through which the messages will be routed to the required microservices.

   - Each microservice could subscribe to the queue or topic that it is interested in to receive the events and process them.

   - Event-driven architecture enables a loose coupling of components and aids scalability of the individual components.

2. **What is the architecture you will choose if you want to segregate different technical responsibilities within an application?**

   Model answer:

   - A layered architecture will be more appropriate for this kind of a scenario.

   - You will suggest a separate layer for presentation, business logic, and data access within the application.

   - This architectural pattern will enable you to choose a technology that is fit for purpose for each of the layers.

   - In the future, it is easy to replace a single layer with an alternative technology stack without a lot of effort.

3. **What is the optimal architecture for an application that needs to execute a process as a sequence of steps, and each step requires a different software run time and a different hardware configuration?**

    Model answer:

    *   You will use the pipes and filters architecture for this application.

    *   The pipes and filters architecture pattern allows you to run the application as a series of filters (steps) connected through pipes.

    *   Each filter can be run in its own software run time and a hardware configuration that is suitable for the compute intensity required for it.

    *   Filters can also be run in parallel to make the architecture faster and efficient.

4. **What is the architecture you will recommend for an application to be developed for a large e-commerce giant that has multiple business divisions supporting the core business?**

    Model answer:

    *   An e-commerce application that has complex business requirements needs to be carefully designed.

    *   A methodology like DDD combined with a microservices architecture is the right choice for this application.

    *   DDD could be used to identify the sub-domains in the application. The sub-domains represent the business subdivisions of the business domain. The sub-domains within the e-commerce application include order management, payment processing, inventory control, and shipping, to name a few.

    *   Once you identify the sub-domains, you will identify the business capabilities required in each of the sub-domains. You will also create a boundary for the subdomain called the bounded context. For example, the order management subdomain and bounded context may require business capabilities like receiving an order, fulfilling an order, and canceling an order.

    *   You will identify microservices within each subdomain/bounded context for addressing the business capabilities required.

5. **What is the suggested architecture for an application in which the individual components need to be consumed by multiple disparate client applications supporting different protocols?**

    Model answer:

    *   You would use the hexagonal architecture to blueprint the application.

    *   You will understand the requirements of the different clients that need to communicate with the server application.

    *   You will develop the ports for the server-side component that provide the required function in the application. For instance, a port can interact with the business logic to fetch orders that were returned or cancelled in the last 6 months.

    *   Based on the nature of the clients, you would develop the required adapters that each of the clients can use to fit into the port and consume the business logic.

6. **What are the ways in which application components can communicate with each other in an event-driven architecture?**

    Model answer:

    *   In an event-driven architecture, the communication is asynchronous which means that the client and server are decoupled, and the client does not block to get the response from the server.

- The asynchronous communication can either be point-to-point or publish subscribe. In a point-to-point communication model, a producer posts a message(event) into a message broker queue and is consumed by another component.

- In a publish subscribe model, a producer posts a message (event) to the message broker topic, and all the interested components can subscribe to the topic and consume the message.

- Both point-to-point and publish subscribe model are used in the microservices architecture for inter service communication.

7. **What is the most common API architecture used by applications?**

Model answer:

- REST which is based on HTTP is the most widely used architectural style for designing and developing APIs.

- REST based on HTTP supports all the basic CRUD operations like create, read, update, and delete, used by most of the transactional business applications.

- REST APIs are easy to develop using modern day software application frameworks like Spring Boot.

- REST APIs are stateless, and they lend themselves to caching their responses.

8. **What is the API architectural pattern that will be used to fetch data from multiple sources in a single call?**

Model answer:

- GraphQL, the open-source API query engine, can be used to retrieve all the required data at once.

- You can define the schema for the API with the attributes required to be fetched from multiple sources in a single call.

- You would use an engine like an Apollo server or Graphene to implement the server-side APIs.

- You will ensure not to complicate the schema structure to ensure only the required data is fetched to avoid potential performance bottlenecks.

9. **What is the API model that you can use for integrating low latency applications?**

Model answer:

- As an architect, you would recommend gRPC as the protocol to implement the server and client-side code, as gRPC uses a binary format for serialization of data across the network.

- You will declare the required APIs or methods using Protocol buffers, which is the **interface definition language (IDL)** for gRPC.

- You will generate the server side and client-side code from the protocol buffer file, depending on the technology stack.

- The generated client stubs can be used to communicate with the server-side implementation.

- Be aware that gRPC can be used only for internal applications because of its design approach to generate both server and client-side code.

10. **How will you integrate your application with a SOAP web service?**

   Model answer:

   - You would request for the WSDL file for the server-side implementation. The WSDL file could be provided as a file or as a URL from a server.

   - You would generate the required client stubs from the WSDL file depending on the programming language used by the client application.

   - You will also go through the WSDL to understand the operations supported and the payload required for each operation.

   - You will use the generated client stubs from my application to communicate with the SOAP server.

Join our Discord space

Join our Discord workspace for latest updates, offers, tech happenings around the world, new releases, and sessions with the authors:

https://discord.bpbonline.com

CHAPTER 5

Aligning Technology with Business Goals

Introduction

Solution architecture goes beyond simply designing technical systems. It focuses on ensuring that technology directly aligns with business goals, creating tangible value. Solutions architects play a crucial role in bridging the gap between business strategy and technical execution. They ensure the architecture supports not only the organization's current growth and operational efficiency, but also its future strategic objectives.

This chapter explores the business aspects of solution architectures, including how to translate business requirements into technical implementation, manage costs, lead project management efforts, and integrate technology solutions during **mergers and acquisitions (M&A)**. Throughout the chapter, real-world examples and key interview questions will be provided to help readers prepare for discussions with hiring managers and technical leaders.

Structure

This chapter covers the following topics:

- Understanding business requirements
- Cost management and budgeting
- Project management essentials
- Integration solutions for mergers and acquisitions

Objectives

By the end of this chapter, readers will have the ability to translate complex business requirements into actionable technical solutions that are in alignment with overarching business goals. They will be equipped with the skills to effectively manage technology costs and budgets, ensuring that all expenditures are strategically aligned with business priorities. Additionally, readers will gain a solid understanding of applying project management principles to achieve the successful delivery of technical projects while minimizing associated risks. This chapter will also provide insights into developing integration strategies for mergers and acquisitions, ensuring that technical systems are seamlessly aligned with business objectives, while minimizing operational disruptions. Finally, solutions architects will learn how to build stronger communication and collaboration frameworks, enhancing their ability to bridge the gap between technical teams and business stakeholders. These skills are essential for aligning technology with business goals and achieving long-term organizational success.

Understanding business requirements

Effectively translating business needs into technical solutions is a core responsibility of a solutions architect. This process involves a deep understanding of the organization's business goals, operational challenges, and long-term vision. Solutions architects act as a bridge between business stakeholders, who focus on objectives such as increasing revenue, improving customer satisfaction, or expanding market reach, and technical teams, who transform these objectives into concrete solutions through technology, code, infrastructure, and systems design.

Translating business needs into technical solutions

One of the most critical responsibilities of a solutions architect is to ensure that business requirements are accurately translated into technical solutions. Solutions architects act as the bridge between business stakeholders, who focus on business objectives and operational needs, and the technical teams, who implement those objectives through code, infrastructure, and systems design.

Role of a solutions architect

Solutions architects play a vital role in understanding the business vision and then aligning technology to meet those goals. This involves breaking down complex business requirements into smaller, actionable technical tasks that the development team can execute. These tasks should contribute to building a system that is not only functional, but also capable of scaling as the business evolves. This process ensures that technical implementations are scalable, efficient, and aligned with the overall business strategy.

Let us consider an example. As a global e-commerce company prepares for rapid growth and regional expansion, the solutions architect is tasked with ensuring the platform can handle the anticipated surge in traffic. To address this challenge, the solutions architect must conduct a detailed analysis of the current infrastructure to identify areas requiring scalability improvements.

They would implement a cloud-native architecture that leverages auto-scaling to dynamically adjust resources during peak traffic periods. Additionally, the solutions architect should design a microservices-based architecture to isolate regional features, ensuring that performance in one region does not affect others.

To enhance the user experience, the checkout process would need to be optimized by introducing a distributed caching layer to reduce latency and improve transaction speeds. By executing these actions, the solutions architect ensures the platform is ready for future growth, aligns with the company's expansion strategy, and delivers a seamless experience for customers across all regions.

Gathering business requirements

To effectively translate business needs into technical solutions, solutions architects engage with stakeholders, such as business analysts, product owners, and department heads. Through collaboration, they develop a comprehensive understanding of the business's goals and how those goals translate into technical needs. This includes understanding what the business needs today and anticipating future requirements.

Let us consider an example. As a fintech company prepares to launch an instant credit scoring feature, the solutions architect's role is to gather business requirements from key stakeholders like product owners and compliance officers. This includes understanding regulatory compliance, security protocols, and expected system performance.

By facilitating workshops and conducting interviews, the architect collaborates closely with stakeholders to capture business goals and technical constraints. These insights are then translated into clear technical specifications, ensuring the system is secure, scalable, and compliant with industry standards.

Key techniques for requirements gathering

To gather accurate and comprehensive business requirements, solutions architects employ several techniques that help them understand the scope, goals, and challenges of the business as follows:

- **Workshops**: Workshops are collaborative sessions where stakeholders, business analysts, and technical teams come together to define requirements. During these workshops, solutions architects facilitate discussions that allow stakeholders to express their goals, pain points, and expectations. Workshops help ensure that everyone has a shared understanding of the project's objectives.

  For example, in a banking environment, a solutions architect might run a workshop with stakeholders from the credit department, legal teams, and customer service to define requirements for an automated loan approval system.

- **Interviews**: Interviews are one-on-one or small group discussions with key stakeholders. These conversations help gather in-depth insights into specific business processes or challenges. Interviews are particularly useful for capturing detailed requirements from stakeholders such as department heads or external partners who may have unique perspectives.

  For example, a solutions architect might interview the **Chief Financial Officer** (**CFO**) to understand the financial reporting requirements for a new **enterprise resource planning** (**ERP**) system, ensuring that the architecture supports both current and future reporting needs.

- **Business process modelling**: Business process modeling involves creating visual representations of how business processes work today and how they will function after implementing new solutions. Solutions architects use diagrams, such as flowcharts or use case diagrams, to break down processes into steps, highlighting where technical systems need to interact with business operations.

  For example, for an insurance company, the solutions architect might create a business process model that maps out the claim's approval workflow, identifying the key steps and data flows needed to automate the process efficiently.

Collaboration with business stakeholders

Frequent communication with business stakeholders is essential to ensure that the technical solutions remain aligned with evolving business needs. As business environments change, whether due to market dynamics, customer demands, or regulatory changes, so do the requirements for technical systems. This ongoing collaboration allows the solutions architect to adjust the architecture and technical approach as needed, as follows:

- **Maintaining open channels of communication**: Solutions architects establish regular touchpoints with business stakeholders to discuss progress, validate technical decisions, and adjust requirements as necessary. These conversations ensure that the architecture is aligned with the business's evolving strategy and that stakeholders are aware of any trade-offs being made.

  For example, in an Agile environment, solutions architects may participate in regular sprint reviews or demos where they present how technical solutions are aligned with user stories and business goals. This also gives business stakeholders an opportunity to provide feedback and request changes before the next sprint.

- **Validation of technical solutions**: Solutions architects must continuously validate that the technical implementation aligns with the agreed business requirements. Validation occurs throughout the project lifecycle, ensuring that the technical decisions remain consistent with the evolving priorities of the business.

For example, when building an inventory management system for a retail chain, the solutions architect would validate that the system tracks stock levels in real-time and integrates with the existing **point-of-sale (POS)** system, reflecting the original business requirement of real time visibility.

- **Addressing evolving business needs**: Solutions architects must be Agile in responding to changes in business priorities. For instance, a change in regulations may require modifications to data handling processes, or new market demands may call for accelerated delivery of certain features. Through frequent collaboration, the architect ensures that the technical solutions remain flexible enough to accommodate these changes without introducing significant technical debt.

  For example, if a regulatory change introduces new privacy requirements, the solutions architect may work with the legal team to adjust the system's data storage policies and ensure compliance with the new rules.

After accurately gathering and translating business requirements into technical solutions, the next key responsibility of a solutions architect is ensuring these solutions are not only effective but also financially viable. Managing costs and aligning technology investments with business goals is essential to the long-term success of any technical implementation.

In the following section, we explore how solutions architects can design cost-effective solutions and manage budgets effectively.

Cost management and budgeting

In the role of a solutions architect, designing cost-effective solutions is not just a matter of selecting the right technology; it is about ensuring that every technical decision is aligned with the organization's financial objectives. Solutions architects must carefully assess the cost implications of every component in the architecture, including hardware, software, cloud services, and maintenance costs, to ensure that the overall solution is financially sustainable in the long run. This requires a deep understanding of the cost structures associated with various technology choices and the ability to make strategic decisions that balance performance, scalability, and cost efficiency.

Designing cost-effective solutions

Managing costs effectively is a core responsibility of solutions architects. Every technical decision must meet the business's functional requirements while also being financially sustainable. Solutions architects carefully evaluate the cost implications of technical solutions, optimize infrastructure spending, and work closely with finance teams to ensure that technology investments align with the organization's broader financial goals.

Cost versus benefit analysis

Solutions architects play a key role in ensuring that technical solutions are not only effective but also financially justifiable. To achieve this, a structured approach to evaluating technology decisions is required, which involves weighing potential costs against anticipated business value. This framework helps to ensure that every investment in technology aligns with the organization's strategic objectives and delivers measurable business benefits.

The following list outlines the critical aspects of this evaluation process, including how to analyze costs, quantify benefits, and justify technology investments:

- **Evaluating technical decisions**: When proposing a new solution, whether it is a software platform, infrastructure upgrade, or cloud deployment, solutions architects must weigh the associated costs against the business value it delivers. The cost could include hardware, software licenses, cloud resources, and maintenance. The business value may come from increased efficiency, better performance, reduced time-to-market, or improved customer satisfaction.

For example, in a retail company, investing in a cloud-based recommendation engine might lead to an immediate increase in online sales due to better personalization. The solutions architect would compare the cost of implementing the recommendation engine, for example, development, cloud infrastructure, and ongoing maintenance, with the projected increase in sales revenue and customer retention.

- **Quantifying the benefits**: Benefits are often harder to quantify than costs. Solutions architects need to work closely with business stakeholders to understand the projected **return on investment** (**ROI**), whether through increased revenue, reduced operational costs, or better customer experiences. It is important to tie technical decisions to measurable business outcomes.

  For example, for a SaaS company, moving from a monolithic application to a microservices architecture might initially seem costly in terms of refactoring and redeployment. However, if the benefit is reducing downtime and enabling faster updates, which in turn, improves customer satisfaction and retention, the long-term gains outweigh the initial costs.

Cloud cost optimization

Solutions architects must consider multiple strategies to optimize cloud infrastructure and reduce overall costs without compromising on performance and availability. A comprehensive cost management approach involves leveraging cloud-native features like auto-scaling, selecting appropriate pricing models, and implementing storage optimization techniques. These strategies help organizations maintain efficient operations and align technology expenditures with business requirements.

The following list gets into specific tactics, such as auto-scaling, reserved instances, spot instances, and storage cost optimization, that solutions architects can employ to achieve cost efficiency while meeting performance demands:

- **Auto-scaling for efficiency**: Auto-scaling is a powerful cloud feature that allows systems to automatically adjust resources based on real-time demand. By configuring auto-scaling rules, solutions architects can ensure that the system dynamically adds or removes resources based on traffic or load, minimizing costs during periods of low demand while maintaining performance during high-demand spikes.

  For example, an e-commerce platform may experience traffic surges during the holiday season. The solutions architect can configure auto-scaling, like scale set in **virtual machine** (**VM**), App Services for PaaS, EKS, AKS, or GKE auto-scaling on AWS, Azure, or Google Cloud, to automatically provision additional servers during peak hours and scale down during off-peak times, ensuring cost efficiency without sacrificing performance.

- **Using reserved instances and spot instances**: Reserved instances allow companies to commit to using cloud resources (e.g., compute power, storage) over a one or three-year term, often resulting in significant cost savings compared to pay-as-you-go pricing. Solution architects can leverage these for workloads with predictable usage patterns. For non-critical workloads, spot instances can be used, allowing companies to take advantage of unused cloud capacity at reduced prices.

  For example, a financial services firm may use reserved instances for their core banking systems, which have consistent demand, while using spot instances for non-critical batch processing tasks that can run whenever spare capacity is available.

- **Optimizing storage costs**: Cloud providers offer various storage classes that cater to different needs, standard storage for frequently accessed data, and infrequent access storage for archival data. Solution architects must evaluate how data is used within the organization and move less frequently accessed data to lower-cost storage tiers.

  For example, a media company storing large amounts of video content may keep recently accessed videos in high-performance storage, while older, infrequently accessed videos are moved to a lower-cost storage tier, such as AWS S3 Glacier.

Tracking and managing technology budgets

In addition to optimizing costs, solutions architects need to actively manage technology budgets and work closely with finance teams to ensure that technology investments align with broader business goals, as follows:

- **Collaborating with finance teams**: Working with finance teams is essential to track and forecast technology expenses. Solution architects help finance teams understand the financial implications of technical decisions, especially when deploying new infrastructure, purchasing software licenses, or scaling cloud resources. Solutions architects must communicate the potential ROI of these technologies and ensure that expenses are budgeted correctly.

  For example, when proposing a new cloud-based data analytics platform, the solution architect will work with the finance team to forecast the costs of compute, storage, data transfer, and ongoing maintenance, ensuring the solution fits within the company's overall financial strategy.

- **Using cloud cost management tools**: Most cloud providers offer built-in cost management tools to help track expenses. Solutions architects use these tools, such as AWS Cost Explorer or Azure Cost Management , to monitor cloud spending in real-time. These tools allow architects to set budgets, create alerts, and provide detailed reports on where money is being spent, enabling proactive budget management.

  For example, a solutions architect managing multiple development environments can set a budget for each environment in AWS, Azure, or Google Cloud Cost Explorer. If the development environment exceeds its allocated budget, the system can send an alert to notify the team and trigger actions to optimize costs, such as scaling down unused resources.

- **FinOps**: In the context of cloud cost management, FinOps plays a crucial role by enabling organizations to optimize cloud spending through financial accountability and collaboration between finance, operations, and engineering teams. By implementing FinOps practices, solutions architects can gain better visibility into cloud usage and costs, helping them to allocate resources more efficiently while avoiding unnecessary expenses. This framework allows teams to continuously monitor and forecast cloud spending, ensuring that technical decisions are aligned with financial goals. FinOps promotes cost awareness and empowers teams to make data-driven decisions, ultimately maximizing the value of cloud investments. For a solutions architect, adopting FinOps practices helps maintain scalability and performance while keeping cloud budgets under control.

Forecasting future costs

Technology costs are not static, and as systems evolve, they often require increased resources. Solutions architects should work to forecast future technology costs based on expected business growth, product roadmaps, and any planned technology upgrades.

Let us consider an example. A social media platform expecting rapid user growth in the next year might forecast an increase in cloud usage and storage needs. The solutions architect would work with the finance team to predict future cloud expenses and negotiate with the cloud provider for better pricing or discounts.

While controlling costs is vital, it is equally important to ensure that technical solutions are delivered efficiently, on time, and within scope. This brings us to the role of effective project management, which allows solutions architects to keep projects aligned with business goals, minimize risks, and manage dependencies effectively.

In the next section, we get into project management essentials and how solutions architects can navigate different methodologies, such as Agile and Waterfall, to drive successful project outcomes.

Project management essentials

Solutions architects play a pivotal role in the successful delivery of technical projects by ensuring that project management practices align with the overall architecture and strategic objectives. Effective project management is essential not only for delivering on time and within budget, but also for ensuring that the solution meets business requirements and provides long-term value. Understanding different project management methodologies, their applicability, and how they impact architectural decisions, is key to driving successful outcomes.

Agile versus Waterfall

Solution architects play a critical role in aligning project management methodologies with technical implementation. Both Agile and Waterfall are widely used methodologies, and solution architects must understand when to apply each approach based on the project's needs and business context.

In *Chapter 6, Agile Processes and Essentials*, we discuss in detail Agile frameworks such as Scrum, Kanban, **Extreme Programming** (**XP**), and SAFe. These frameworks emphasize flexibility, iterative development, and collaboration across teams. In this section, we will briefly explore the key characteristics of Agile and Waterfall, providing examples of when each methodology is appropriate.

In *Chapter 6, Agile Processes and Essentials,* we will discuss the principles of Agile, such as iterative development, frequent feedback loops, and simplicity, along with how solutions architects can leverage these principles to design flexible, scalable architectures that evolve alongside the product.

The following are the key characteristics of Agile:

- **Iterative development**: Solutions architects design modular and scalable architectures that can evolve over time, often through continuous refactoring or architectural spikes. These incremental changes allow the architecture to remain flexible as new features are added.

- **Frequent collaboration**: In Agile environments, solution architects collaborate regularly with product owners and development teams, providing ongoing guidance and ensuring that the architecture aligns with changing business priorities.

  For example, in a product development team using Scrum, a solutions architect may work in short sprints, providing architectural input based on each sprint's user stories and goals. During sprint reviews, the architect presents how the design is evolving to meet both current and future needs.

The following are the key characteristics of Waterfall:

- **Comprehensive upfront design**: Solutions architects must deliver a fully designed architecture early in the project, which minimizes changes during later phases. This requires careful planning to ensure that the architecture accommodates long-term goals.

- **Clear phases**: Each project phase requires the solutions architect to ensure that architectural milestones are met before moving to the next phase. This method provides a more controlled and predictable approach, but may be less adaptable to changing requirements.

  For example, for a large government project where requirements are well-defined and stable, a solutions architect may be responsible for creating a complete architectural blueprint upfront, including detailed technical specifications for the entire system. This helps prevent major changes during the later phases of implementation.

Agile

Agile is characterized by its iterative and flexible approach, where requirements and solutions evolve through collaboration between cross-functional teams. This methodology is best suited for projects where requirements are dynamic or when rapid delivery of working software is critical. Solutions architects must be comfortable adapting their designs over time as Agile teams work through incremental sprints.

Figure 5.1 illustrates the Agile methodology, highlighting its iterative cycle that continuously loops through planning, design, development, testing, deployment, and monitoring for rapid feedback and incremental improvement:

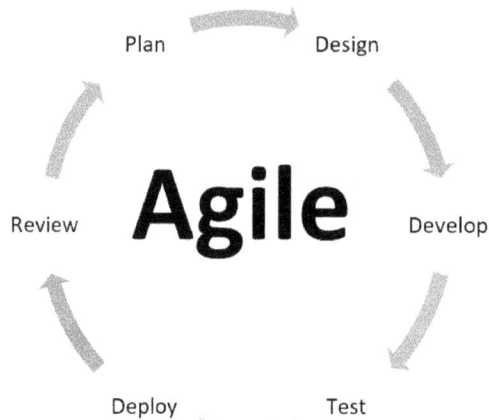

Figure 5.1: *Agile methodology*

Agile is typically preferred in dynamic environments such as product development, startups, or fast-changing industries. This methodology works best where requirements are likely to evolve over time, requiring frequent iterations, collaboration, and adaptability.

The advantages, disadvantages, and uses of Agile are as follows:

- **Advantages**: Agile can be more cost-effective in the long run due to its adaptability and flexibility. As changes are incorporated incrementally, the risk of expensive rework at the end of the project is reduced. The iterative nature of Agile also allows for early delivery of working software, which can provide immediate business value, allowing companies to start generating revenue or feedback before the final product is complete.

- **Disadvantages**: Agile can sometimes lead to scope creep if not managed properly, which may increase costs if requirements are continually added or changed. Additionally, because Agile teams often work in a continuous, iterative fashion, the total project duration may extend if new features or changes are constantly requested.

- **Usage**:
  - Requirements are likely to evolve, or you are dealing with uncertain or changing conditions.
  - Early value delivery is needed, and immediate feedback is critical.
  - Collaboration and flexibility are high priorities.

  For example, in a product development startup, Agile is often the best choice because it allows teams to adapt quickly to market feedback, build MVPs, and iteratively improve based on customer feedback, avoiding large upfront investments in features that may not align with market needs.

Waterfall

Waterfall is a linear, sequential methodology, where each phase of the project, for instance, requirements, design, implementation, and testing, must be completed before moving on to the next. This approach is best suited for projects with well-defined, stable requirements and a fixed timeline. Solutions architects must focus on designing comprehensive architectures upfront that account for all future requirements.

Figure 5.2 represents a detailed breakdown of the Waterfall methodology, showcasing its distinct phases and the sequential progression from one stage to another, emphasizing thorough planning and execution at each step before moving forward:

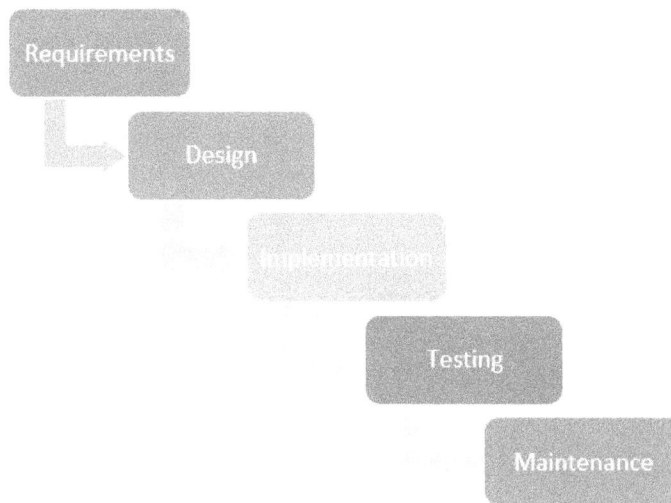

Figure 5.2: *Waterfall methodology*

Waterfall is more suitable for projects with stable requirements and fixed timelines, such as large-scale infrastructure deployments or compliance-driven projects, where all phases must be completed in a specific order.

The advantages, disadvantages, and uses of Waterfall are as follows:

- **Advantages**: Waterfall can be cost-effective when requirements are well-defined upfront, and there is little chance of significant changes during the project. With a clear timeline and scope, Waterfall allows teams to estimate project costs and timelines accurately. This is particularly valuable for compliance-driven projects, where strict guidelines must be adhered to, and there is little room for flexibility. Additionally, since all phases are completed before the next begins, there is lesser need for ongoing rework or adjustments, which can help control costs.

- **Disadvantages**: Waterfall's rigidity can lead to high costs if changes arise after the project has entered later phases. Since feedback is usually gathered only after the product is complete, any necessary changes at this point can require significant rework, leading to additional costs. Waterfall projects can also take longer to deliver value because stakeholders may not see working software until the final stages of the project.

- **Usage**:
  - The project has fixed, well-defined requirements and is unlikely to change.
  - The timeline and scope are strict, and the project must be completed in sequential phases (e.g., large infrastructure projects or compliance-driven initiatives).
  - Stakeholders are comfortable with receiving the final product at the end of the project lifecycle.

    For example, in a large-scale infrastructure deployment, where requirements are predefined (e.g., building a data center or upgrading an enterprise-wide ERP system), Waterfall may be the better choice due to its structured, phase-based approach. Since the scope is unlikely to change and each phase (design, build, deploy) needs to be completed before moving to the next, Waterfall ensures that costs and timelines are managed effectively.

Cost comparison

Agile tends to offer better long-term cost benefits when flexibility is essential, as it helps reduce the risks of large-scale rework by iterating in smaller cycles. However, Agile projects can see rising costs if the scope expands without proper management.

Waterfall can provide a clearer initial cost estimate and timeline, but its lack of flexibility can result in significant rework costs if changes occur late in the project lifecycle, making it less cost-effective in dynamic environments.

Ultimately, the decision on which methodology is more cost-effective depends on the nature of the project. Agile is often preferred when adaptability and early value delivery are needed, while Waterfall is more suited to projects where requirements are stable, and strict sequential phases are required.

Role in project delivery

Solutions architects are vital to the successful delivery of technical projects, regardless of the methodology used. They act as the bridge between the technical teams responsible for implementing the solution and the business stakeholders who define the project's goals.

The architect's role is to ensure that technical solutions align with both business objectives and the project's delivery model, as follows:

- **Connecting business and technology**: Solutions architects translate business requirements into technical specifications and guide development teams to ensure that the architecture meets both business and technical needs. This requires ongoing collaboration with product owners, project managers, and technical leads.

  Solution architects help manage expectations by clearly communicating the technical implications of business decisions, providing stakeholders with insights into how long certain features or architectural decisions will take to implement, and addressing potential trade-offs.

  For example, when tasked with upgrading an e-commerce platform, the solution architect's focus is on ensuring that the checkout system is scalable to accommodate future growth. This involves working closely with development teams to optimize database queries and backend performance, enabling the platform to handle high traffic spikes during peak seasons without compromising user experience.

- **Providing technical leadership**: Solution architects oversee the technical vision of the project, ensuring that the architecture remains scalable, secure, and aligned with the long-term business strategy. They also serve as a point of escalation when technical challenges arise, offering advice on architectural patterns, technologies, and solutions to unblock teams.

  For example, if a development team encounters performance bottlenecks, the solution architect may step in to recommend a caching strategy or database optimization to resolve the issue.

- **Ensuring stakeholder alignment**: Throughout the project lifecycle, the solution architect ensures alignment between the project's technical progress and the stakeholders' business expectations. This involves regular updates, sprint reviews, and demonstrations of technical solutions to business leaders.

  For example, in a healthcare system implementation, the solutions architect may present the progress of a new patient data module to executives, explaining how the system adheres to regulatory requirements while ensuring the patients' data is secure.

Managing risks and technical dependencies

A key aspect of project management for solutions architects is proactively identifying and managing risks that could jeopardize the success of the project. This includes both technical risks and dependencies that could impact timelines, quality, or alignment with business objectives.

Managing risks effectively is crucial to the success of any project. Solutions architects must adopt a proactive approach to identify, assess, and address risks throughout the project lifecycle to ensure that the solution aligns with business goals and is delivered on time and within budget, as follows:

- **Identifying risks early**: Solutions architects constantly assess potential risks in the architecture, such as scalability limitations, security vulnerabilities, or integration challenges with legacy systems.

  For example, during the early phases of a system migration project, a solutions architect might identify that the legacy database schema does not support the new system's data model. The architect then advises on a data migration strategy that minimizes disruption.

- **Mitigating technical risks through proactive design**: Solutions architects mitigate technical risks by designing systems that are scalable, modular, and fault-tolerant. They may implement strategies such as load balancing, automated testing, and failover mechanisms to reduce the risk of system downtime or performance degradation.

  For example, for a banking application that requires high availability, the solutions architect may design the architecture with redundancy and automatic failover, ensuring the system remains operational even in the event of server failure.

- **Managing technical dependencies**: In complex systems, there are often multiple technical dependencies that must be managed. Solutions architects must ensure that different components of the system can integrate seamlessly and that changes in one part do not negatively affect others.

  For example, during a cloud migration, the solutions architect is responsible for ensuring that the frontend seamlessly integrates with the newly designed microservices-based backend. This requires careful management of dependencies like API versioning and data synchronization to ensure smooth communication between systems without disrupting user experience.

The following are the risk mitigation strategies:

- **Prototyping and proof of concept (POC)**: Before fully committing to a particular technology or architectural pattern, solutions architects often recommend building a prototype or conducting a proof of concept to validate the solution and reduce risk.

- **Architectural reviews and code audits**: Regular reviews of the system's architecture and codebase can identify risks before they become critical, ensuring that technical debt is minimized.

- **Automation**: Automating testing, deployment, and infrastructure provisioning helps reduce human error and ensures that the system is reliable.

By integrating Agile frameworks discussed in *Chapter 6, Agile Processes and Essentials*, solutions architects can adapt their role to fit dynamic, fast-paced environments, while also leveraging Waterfall for projects requiring well-defined, sequential phases. Understanding when to apply each methodology is key to successful project delivery.

As solutions architects manage projects with varying complexities, some of the most challenging endeavors arise during mergers and acquisitions. Integrating disparate systems while maintaining business continuity is critical to the success of these transactions. In the following section, we will explore the strategies and best practices that solutions architects can apply to ensure smooth technology integration during mergers and acquisitions.

Integration solutions for mergers and acquisitions

M&A bring about complex technical challenges that can disrupt an organization if not properly managed. The role of the solutions architect in M&A is crucial for ensuring that the technology systems from both organizations are integrated seamlessly, aligned with business goals, and contribute to operational continuity. This section provides a detailed exploration of the challenges involved, strategies for integration, and best practices for ensuring successful system consolidation during mergers and acquisitions.

Challenges of technology integration during M&A

M&A present significant technical challenges, particularly when it comes to integrating disparate systems, applications, and infrastructures. Solution architects play a key role in assessing the technical landscape and ensuring that systems are integrated seamlessly and efficiently, aligning with business goals and minimizing operational disruption.

Let us consider an example. In a merger between two banks, the solutions architect prioritized integrating customer transaction systems first to ensure that banking operations continued uninterrupted. This was followed by the consolidation of internal systems such as HR and accounting platforms.

Assessing the technical landscape

The first step in any M&A technology integration is a thorough assessment of the technical landscape of both organizations. Solution architects must understand the existing systems, their purpose, and how they interact within the broader organizational infrastructure. This assessment includes identifying key systems such as ERP, **customer relationship management** (**CRM**), financial systems, and data warehouses, and determining how these systems overlap or differ between the merging entities.

Let us consider an example. In a merger of two e-commerce companies, company A operates a cloud-based CRM, while company B uses an on-premise solution. The solution architect's role is to assess both systems and determine the optimal approach, i.e., migrate company B's CRM fully to the cloud, retain the on-premise system for specific functions, or implement a hybrid architecture that integrates elements of both systems to meet evolving business needs.

Identifying redundancies and gaps

Once the systems have been assessed, solutions architects must identify redundancies and gaps. Redundancies occur when both organizations have similar systems serving the same function, such as two separate ERP systems. Gaps, on the other hand, occur when one organization lacks a critical system or functionality that the other has.

Let us consider an example. During the assessment of two merging banks, it was found that both organizations had separate but similar CRM systems. The solutions architect determined that consolidating these systems into a single platform would streamline customer management and reduce maintenance costs.

Case study: A global telecommunications company acquired a smaller regional player. The regional company had a legacy billing system that did not integrate well with the parent company's cloud-based billing infrastructure. The solution architect recommended migrating the legacy system to a cloud-based solution to align with the parent company's technology strategy while ensuring that the billing system could handle the increased customer base.

Prioritizing integration efforts

Given the complexity of M&A integrations, it is essential to prioritize the systems that need to be integrated first. Typically, business-critical systems such as customer management, financial reporting, and operational workflows are prioritized to minimize disruptions to daily operations. Non-essential systems, such as marketing automation or internal communication platforms, may be integrated later or retired altogether.

Let us consider an example. In a merger between two manufacturing companies, the solutions architect prioritized integrating the ERP systems to ensure continuity in supply chain and production operations. Other systems, such as internal HR platforms, were scheduled for integration in later phases to avoid disruption to mission-critical activities.

Navigating differing technology stacks

One of the most challenging aspects of M&A integration is managing differing technology stacks, programming languages, and infrastructure setups. In many cases, the two organizations may use entirely different technologies to perform similar functions, requiring careful planning to avoid creating inefficiencies.

Let us consider an example. If one company operates primarily on AWS and the other on Azure, the solutions architect must decide whether to standardize on a single cloud provider or adopt a hybrid cloud solution. This decision is based on factors such as cost, system compatibility, and long-term scalability.

Real-world scenario: A multinational healthcare company acquired a smaller competitor. The acquiring company had standardized on a microservices architecture deployed on Kubernetes, while the smaller company was using a business-intensive commerce application hosted on a private cloud. Given the high demand for scalability and flexibility in handling transactions, customer data, and real-time interactions, the solutions architect recommended breaking down the monolithic application into microservices. Migrating it to Kubernetes allowed the application to align with the acquiring company's existing infrastructure, ensuring better scalability, maintainability, and the ability to respond quickly to business demands.

Data and system integration strategies

One of the most critical components of M&A integration is ensuring that data and systems are integrated seamlessly and meet regulatory and compliance requirements. Solutions architects must consider factors such as data migration, system consolidation, regulatory compliance, and the potential need for re-engineering systems to fit into the new organization's architecture.

Effective data and system integration is essential for achieving a seamless merger, ensuring that critical business functions continue to operate smoothly and that the new organization can fully leverage combined data assets. Some strategies are outlined as follows:

- **Data consolidation and migration**: Data consolidation is often one of the most challenging aspects of M&A. Solutions architects must ensure that data from both entities is consolidated into a unified format, enabling the new organization to operate efficiently without losing critical information. This process often involves migrating data between systems, ensuring data integrity, and addressing potential duplication or inconsistencies.

  For example, when two healthcare organizations merged, the solutions architect oversaw the consolidation of patient records from both entities into a single data repository. Ensuring compliance with regulations such as **Health Insurance Portability and Accountability Act (HIPAA)** was a critical part of the process, and special attention was given to patient data security and privacy during the migration.

  Case study: In a financial merger, the solutions architect was tasked with consolidating two disparate loan processing systems. Both systems housed sensitive financial data that needed to be migrated to a single platform. Using an ETL process, the architect ensured data integrity, verified that no critical information was lost, and implemented real-time monitoring to track the progress of the migration.

- **Ensuring regulatory compliance**: Depending on the industry, M&A activities often trigger compliance issues related to data privacy, security, and storage regulations. Solutions architects must ensure that the integrated systems comply with all relevant regulations, such as **General Data Protection Regulation (GDPR)**, HIPAA, **Sarbanes-Oxley Act (SOX)**, and **Payment Card Industry Data Security Standard (PCI-DSS)**. Non-compliance can result in significant legal and financial penalties, making this a critical focus area during integration.

  For example, during the merger of two financial institutions, the solutions architect was responsible for ensuring that payment card information met PCI-DSS standards. This involved encrypting credit card data, implementing access controls, and creating audit trails to track data handling practices. For broader customer data, the solutions architect ensured compliance with other applicable regulations, such as GDPR or **Gramm-Leach-Bliley Act** (**GLBA**), by implementing strong data privacy measures, access controls, and encryption standards.

- **Middleware and APIs for system integration**: In many M&A scenarios, it may not be feasible to immediately replace or migrate legacy systems. In such cases, middleware or APIs can be used to bridge the gap between disparate systems, allowing them to communicate effectively while minimizing disruption to daily operations. Middleware serves as an intermediary layer that enables systems with different architectures or data formats to exchange information.

  For example, a global manufacturing company acquired a smaller firm with a legacy supply chain management system. Instead of immediately replacing the system, the solutions architect implemented a middleware to allow the legacy system to communicate with the parent company's modern ERP platform. This approach minimized downtime and allowed the parent company to continue monitoring and controlling supply chain operations without waiting for a complete migration.

Best practices for M&A integration

Given the complexity of integrating systems during M&A, solutions architects must follow a set of best practices to ensure a smooth transition. These best practices include developing phased integration plans, strategic prioritization, and careful coordination between teams.

Phased integration plans

A phased integration plan allows the organization to focus on integrating business-critical systems first while addressing long-term technological needs in subsequent phases. This approach reduces the risk of disruption to daily operations and allows for careful monitoring of the integration process.

The following are the phased integration plans:

- **Phase 1, integration of mission-critical systems**: In the first phase, the focus is on integrating systems that are essential to the organization's core operations, such as ERP, CRM, and financial reporting systems. These systems ensure that the business can continue operating smoothly during the merger.

  For example, in a merger between two telecommunications companies, the solutions architect prioritized integrating the CRM systems to maintain continuity in customer management and billing.

- **Phase 2, data migration and system consolidation**: After the mission-critical systems are integrated, the next step is to focus on data migration and system consolidation efforts. During this phase, non-essential systems are either retired or consolidated to reduce redundancy and ensure a unified infrastructure.

  For example, after completing the initial integration of an ERP system, a retail company began consolidating inventory management systems to ensure that product data from both companies could be managed in a single platform, improving operational efficiency and inventory accuracy.

- **Phase 3, long-term system integration and optimization**: The final phase focuses on addressing long-term system optimization, standardizing platforms, and developing new applications that leverage the expanded resources of the merged organization. This phase often involves consolidating and optimizing systems that support the broader business strategy, such as marketing platforms, customer management systems, or analytics tools.

  For example, after the initial integration of key systems, a solution architect worked to integrate the marketing campaign management and offer systems of two merging retail companies. This consolidation enabled the unified company to run coordinated, cross-platform marketing campaigns and provide consistent, personalized offers to customers. By integrating these systems, the business achieved improved customer engagement, streamlined operations, and reduced costs associated with managing redundant systems.

While *Phases 1* to *3* focus on the step-by-step integration of systems and data, it is crucial to maintain an overarching strategy that minimizes operational disruptions during these phases. Solutions architects must ensure that the integration process does not impede the day-to-day functioning of critical business activities. Therefore, minimizing disruption and managing long-term technological needs should be viewed as guiding principles that are applied consistently throughout all integration efforts, rather than as separate phases.

Key goals for minimizing disruption during integration

One of the key goals of M&A integration is minimizing disruption to daily operations. Solutions architects must ensure that system transitions occur smoothly by using strategies such as redundancy, backups, and staged rollouts to minimize downtime.

Let us consider an example. When integrating two retail companies' inventory systems, the solutions architect scheduled system updates during off-peak hours to avoid disruptions to online transactions and inventory management.

Ways of managing long-term technological needs

After the initial integration, solutions architects must consider the organization's long-term technological needs. This may include updating legacy systems, adopting new technologies, and ensuring that the integrated systems can scale to meet future business demands.

Let us consider an example. After merging with a smaller technology firm, a large software company's solutions architect led efforts to re-architect the unified platform to take advantage of emerging technologies such as machine learning and AI-driven analytics, ensuring that the system was prepared to handle future growth.

Conclusion

This chapter has covered the essential role that solutions architects play in aligning technical solutions with overarching business goals. From accurately gathering business requirements to managing costs and navigating complex mergers, solutions architects ensure that technology delivers real value to organizations. By balancing business needs with technical execution, they pave the way for long-term success and sustainable growth across all technical projects.

In the next chapter, we will get into Agile processes and essentials, exploring how solutions architects can effectively contribute to Agile teams, drive continuous improvement, and align architecture with Agile practices. Understanding the role of Agile methodologies in solutions architecture will enable you to design systems that are adaptable, responsive, and built for iterative development, helping you excel in fast-paced delivery environments.

Key takeaways

The key takeaways are as follows:

- **Translating business requirements**: Practical techniques for turning business needs into technical implementations.

- **Managing costs**: Best practices for optimizing budgets and minimizing technology expenses.

- **Project management**: How to manage technical projects, mitigate risks, and ensure stakeholder communication.

- **Mergers and acquisitions**: Strategies for integrating technology during organizational changes while ensuring continuity and alignment with business objectives.

Model interview questions and answers

1. **How do you translate business requirements into technical solutions?**

   Model answer:

   - You begin by engaging with key business stakeholders to fully understand their needs and objectives. Using techniques such as workshops, interviews, and business process modeling, you gather detailed requirements.

   - Once you have a clear understanding, you translate those requirements into technical specifications. This involves breaking down high-level business goals into modular, scalable, and efficient technical components, such as selecting appropriate infrastructure, designing APIs, and ensuring security and compliance.

   - Regular validation sessions with stakeholders ensure alignment throughout the project.

2. **How do you balance cost management while delivering scalable solutions?**

   Model answer:

   - To balance cost management with scalability, you conduct a thorough cost versus benefit analysis before selecting any technical solution.

   - You focus on cloud cost optimization techniques, such as using auto-scaling, reserved instances, and serverless architectures to minimize expenses during periods of low demand.

   - By continuously monitoring cloud usage and leveraging tools like AWS Cost Explorer or Azure Cost Management , you ensure that the project remains within budget while meeting scalability requirements.

3. **How do you ensure alignment between technical solutions and business goals?**

   Model answer:

   - You work closely with both business and technical stakeholders to understand the core business goals and translate them into technical objectives.

   - Throughout the project lifecycle, you ensure that the technical solutions are continuously validated against these goals through regular meetings, sprint reviews, and demos.

   - You also collaborate with product owners to prioritize features that bring the most business value while ensuring that the system remains flexible and scalable.

4. **What strategies do you use for managing technical debt in a fast-paced business environment?**

   Model answer:

   - Managing technical debt is critical to maintaining system health over time. You ensure that technical debt is treated as part of the regular backlog and is visible to both business and technical stakeholders.

   - During backlog refinement sessions, you work with the team to prioritize high-impact technical debt items alongside new feature development. This ensures that you address it incrementally without compromising project timelines.

   - You also advocate for continuous refactoring to keep the system maintainable and scalable.

5. **Can you provide an example of how you have handled cost overruns in a project?**

   Model answer:

   - In a previous project, you faced unexpected cost overruns due to increased cloud usage. You immediately assessed your cloud resource allocation and identified that some workloads were over-provisioned.

   - To mitigate the issue, you implemented auto-scaling and optimized your resource utilization.

   - Additionally, you worked with the finance team to revise the budget and forecast future usage more accurately. This helped you regain control over costs without affecting system performance.

6. **How do you manage the technical integration of systems during a merger or acquisition?**

   Model answer:

   - During M&A, the first step is to assess the technical landscape of both entities, identifying overlapping systems, technology stacks, and critical business processes.

   - You prioritize integrating business-critical systems like ERP and CRM first, ensuring minimal disruption to operations.

   - You use middleware or APIs to bridge disparate systems where necessary and develop a phased integration plan that focuses on consolidating systems over time.

   - Regulatory compliance and data migration are key concerns that are addressed early in the process to ensure a smooth transition.

7. **How do you handle differing technology stacks during mergers or acquisitions?**

   Model answer:

   - When merging organizations that have different technology stacks, you start by identifying the most critical systems and determining if it is more beneficial to migrate one system onto the other's platform or to adopt a hybrid solution.

   - You may implement middleware to connect systems for the short term while developing a long-term migration strategy.

   - The decision depends on factors like system compatibility, business needs, cost, and potential downtime.

   - A phased approach often works best, allowing critical systems to be integrated first while others are transitioned later.

8. **How do you ensure technology projects stay on budget while meeting business needs?**

   Model answer:

   - You ensure that all technology projects begin with a well-defined budget that accounts for both initial costs and ongoing expenses.

   - You work closely with finance teams to align the project's budget with the business's financial strategy.

   - Using tools like AWS Cost Explorer or Azure Cost Management , you continuously monitor expenditures, ensuring they stay within the allocated budget.

   - If you encounter budgetary issues, you reassess priorities with the product owner and stakeholders to adjust features or scope, balancing immediate business needs with long-term financial viability.

9. **How do you mitigate risks during project delivery?**

    Model answer:

    - Risk mitigation starts with identifying potential risks early in the project. You conduct risk assessments and identify areas such as system scalability, performance bottlenecks, and potential integration challenges.

    - Proactively designing fault-tolerant systems (e.g., using load balancers or redundancy) helps mitigate technical risks.

    - You also implement risk mitigation strategies like prototyping for high-risk features, setting up automated testing, and ensuring frequent communication with stakeholders to adjust project plans as new risks emerge.

10. **How do you manage project dependencies to ensure smooth delivery?**

    Model answer:

    - Managing project dependencies involves identifying and documenting all dependencies early in the project.

    - You work closely with cross-functional teams to ensure that these dependencies are clearly communicated and aligned across teams. You also track and manage them using project management tools like Jira.

    - For critical dependencies, you build in contingency plans (e.g., alternative solutions or workarounds) in case one dependency is delayed.

    - Frequent communication and stakeholder alignment are key to ensuring that dependencies do not derail project timelines.

11. **How do you ensure system compliance during mergers and acquisitions, especially with data privacy regulations?**

    Model answer:

    - During M&A, ensuring compliance with data privacy regulations like GDPR or HIPAA is critical.

    - You begin by assessing the data handling practices of both entities and ensuring that any combined system adheres to the strictest applicable regulation.

    - You collaborate with legal and compliance teams to map out requirements and implement data encryption, access control, and audit logging to protect sensitive information.

    - Where necessary, you recommend anonymization or pseudonymization techniques to ensure that data privacy regulations are met while enabling smooth data integration.

12. **How do you track and manage multiple project timelines across different business units?**

    Model answer:

    - To manage multiple project timelines across business units, you use project management tools like Jira or Microsoft Project to track dependencies, deadlines, and deliverables.

    - You also ensure that each business unit has clear visibility into their priorities and deliverables by maintaining transparent dashboards.

    - Regular status meetings with technical teams and business stakeholders help in tracking progress and adjusting timelines when necessary.

    - You also make sure that cross-team dependencies are well-managed by setting up proper coordination between teams.

13. **How do you communicate technical trade-offs to non-technical stakeholders?**

    Model answer:

    - When communicating technical trade-offs to non-technical stakeholders, you focus on using clear, business-focused language.

    - You explain the potential benefits and risks of each option in terms that resonate with the business, such as costs, time to market, or impact on customer experience.

    - For example, if a stakeholder requests a new feature that may compromise scalability, you will outline the trade-offs between delivering the feature quickly and ensuring long-term system performance, allowing the business to make informed decisions.

14. **How do you gather requirements in a collaborative environment?**

    Model answer:

    - In a collaborative environment, you facilitate workshops that bring together key stakeholders such as business analysts, developers, and product owners.

    - You ensure that everyone has an opportunity to voice their input while maintaining alignment on the project's goals.

    - Your approach focuses on fostering open communication to address potential challenges early and ensure that technical and business teams are aligned.

    - For instance, during a requirements-gathering session for a healthcare app, you might engage with both clinical staff and developers to gather diverse perspectives on user needs and system functionality.

15. **How do you handle changing business requirements during a project?**

    Model answer:

    - When business requirements change, you ensure that technical solutions remain flexible and adaptable to accommodate these changes.

    - You collaborate with stakeholders to reprioritize tasks, making necessary adjustments without compromising the system's overall integrity.

    - Additionally, you manage technical debt carefully to minimize disruptions, ensuring that short-term changes do not hinder long-term system performance.

    - For example, if a regulatory update requires changes to a system's data handling process, you will work with both legal teams and developers to implement the updates efficiently while preserving performance and scalability.

16. **How do you manage technology costs and budgets?**

    Model answer:

    - To manage technology costs and budgets effectively, you work closely with finance teams to track expenses and ensure technology investments align with the business's financial strategy.

    - You use tools like AWS Cost Explorer and Azure Cost Management to monitor cloud usage and optimize resource allocation.

    - Additionally, you incorporate FinOps practices to ensure that financial accountability is integrated with engineering decisions, allowing teams to balance costs while maintaining system performance.

    - For instance, during cloud migrations, you have implemented auto-scaling and reserved instances to minimize expenses while ensuring the infrastructure scales to meet demand.

Join our Discord space

Join our Discord workspace for latest updates, offers, tech happenings around the world, new releases, and sessions with the authors:

https://discord.bpbonline.com

CHAPTER 6

Agile Processes and Essentials

Introduction

Agile methodologies have transformed the landscape of software development and project management, shifting the focus from rigid, linear processes to flexible, adaptive, and collaborative approaches. These methodologies prioritize rapid delivery, continuous feedback, and the ability to quickly respond to change. For solutions architects, this requires a fundamental shift in how they design and architect systems. Instead of creating a static, one-off architecture, they must now focus on building flexible, scalable, resilient systems that can evolve iteratively to meet the changing needs of the business.

In Agile environments, solutions architects play a critical role in ensuring that technical architectures remain aligned with long-term business goals while still allowing teams to deliver value incrementally. This chapter gets into key Agile frameworks like Scrum, Kanban, XP, and SAFe and highlights the unique contribution of solutions architects within these methodologies. Additionally, it explores essential tools such as Jira and Confluence, which are crucial for enabling collaboration, managing architectural tasks, and maintaining project transparency in Agile environments.

Structure

This chapter covers the following topics:

- Agile
- Solutions architect role in Agile teams
- Decentralized decision-making
- Aligning architecture with Agile development
- Automation in Agile
- Agile tools

Objectives

By the end of this chapter, readers will gain a comprehensive understanding of Agile methodologies and how they impact the role of a solutions architect. The chapter will provide an in-depth look into Agile principles, values, and core frameworks such as Scrum, Kanban, XP, and SAFe, allowing readers to grasp when and how to apply each framework based on specific project requirements. Solutions architects will learn how their role adapts in Agile environments, balancing short-term delivery goals with long-term architectural vision. They will master key strategies for implementing modular designs, managing technical debt, and ensuring architectural integrity in iterative development cycles. Additionally, the chapter will cover the use of Agile tools like Jira and Confluence to efficiently manage backlogs, document decisions, and support team collaboration. Furthermore, solutions architects will explore the importance of defining Agile guardrails that guide teams without restricting their autonomy. By the end of the chapter, readers will also be equipped to tackle Agile-related interview questions with real-world examples and insights, ensuring they are well-prepared for discussions around Agile processes and strategies.

Agile

Agile is a dynamic software development approach that emphasizes flexibility, collaboration, and iterative progress. Unlike traditional methods that follow rigid and linear processes, Agile methodologies adapt to changing requirements, focusing on delivering value to customers through continuous feedback and incremental improvements. Agile framework breaks down complex projects into manageable pieces, allowing teams to respond quickly to change while delivering high quality and working software regularly.

Let us consider a real-world example. Imagine you are a solutions architect working on a multi-team project for an e-commerce platform. The business priorities shift based on market feedback, requiring quick adaptation. Agile allows you to continuously adjust the architecture and technical design while delivering high-priority features without disrupting ongoing development.

Agile methodologies

Agile methodologies are principles and practices that guide teams to deliver software, in short, iterative cycles called sprints. They encourage collaboration between cross-functional teams, the involvement of customers or end-users, and constant reassessment of the project. The primary goal of Agile is to deliver working software that evolves with changing stakeholder needs while reducing risks associated with long-term project planning.

Architect's role in Agile

As a solutions architect, you will prioritize incremental delivery, ensuring that each iteration moves the system toward long-term goals while allowing flexibility for changes. This requires designing an architecture that supports rapid delivery cycles without compromising on quality, scalability, and resilience.

Importance of Agile in modern software development

In today's fast-paced technological environment, businesses need to react swiftly to market changes, evolving customer needs, and emerging technologies. Traditional software development methods like Waterfall can be too rigid, making Agile a preferred choice for organizations seeking to enhance software delivery capabilities.

Agile focuses on collaboration and continuous delivery, enabling teams to deliver value faster while ensuring the product remains aligned with business goals. Agile methodologies help prioritize tasks based on immediate needs, respond quickly to feedback, and reduce risks such as scope creep or delays in responding to changing requirements.

Architect's consideration

While Agile fosters flexibility, for a solutions architect, it is crucial to ensure that rapid iterations do not compromise the system's overall architecture. You will need to maintain architectural integrity by balancing immediate needs with long-term scalability and performance.

With an understanding of the broader impact of Agile methodologies, it is essential to dive deeper into the specific principles and core values that define Agile. This foundational knowledge sets the stage for exploring different Agile frameworks and how solutions architects can apply them effectively.

Overview of Agile Manifesto and core principles

To fully grasp Agile methodologies, it is essential to understand the values and principles laid out in the Agile Manifesto, which serves as the foundation for all Agile practices.

The Agile Manifesto was introduced in 2001. It serves as the foundation for Agile methodologies. It provides a set of values and principles that guide how teams approach software development. The four key values of the Agile Manifesto are as follows:

- **Individuals and interactions over processes and tools**: Focus on communication and collaboration.

- **Working software over comprehensive documentation**: Deliver value through functional software.

- **Customer collaboration over contract negotiation**: Foster ongoing collaboration with customers.

- **Responding to change over following a plan**: Be flexible to changing requirements.

The following are the core principles of the Agile Manifesto:

- The highest priority is to satisfy the customer through the early and continuous delivery of valuable software.

- Working software is the primary measure of progress.

- Welcome changing requirements, even late in development. Agile processes harness change for the customer's competitive advantage.

- Agile processes promote sustainable development. The sponsors, developers, and users should be able to maintain a constant pace indefinitely.

- Deliver working software frequently, from a couple of weeks to a couple of months, with a preference for the shorter timescale.

- Continuous attention to technical excellence and good design enhances agility.

- Business people and developers must work together daily throughout the project.

- Simplicity, the art of maximizing the amount of work not done, is essential.

- Build projects around motivated individuals. Give them the environment and support they need, and trust them to get the job done.

- The best architectures, requirements, and designs emerge from self-organizing teams.

- The most efficient and effective method of conveying information to and within a development team is face-to-face conversation.

- At regular intervals, the team reflects on how to become more effective, then tunes and adjusts its behavior accordingly.

Now that we have established a clear understanding of Agile's core values and principles, let us examine some of the most widely used Agile frameworks, such as Scrum, Kanban, XP, and SAFe, and how these frameworks shape the role and responsibilities of solutions architects.

Key frameworks

Scrum is one of the most widely adopted Agile frameworks. It is designed to help small, cross-functional teams deliver work in sprints that typically last two to four weeks. Scrum provides a structured yet flexible approach, enabling teams to respond to changes while delivering valuable increments of the product at the end of each sprint.

Figure 6.1 illustrates the Scrum process, showcasing the flow of activities from product backlog refinement to sprint execution and delivery, ensuring continuous iteration and incremental delivery of high-value features:

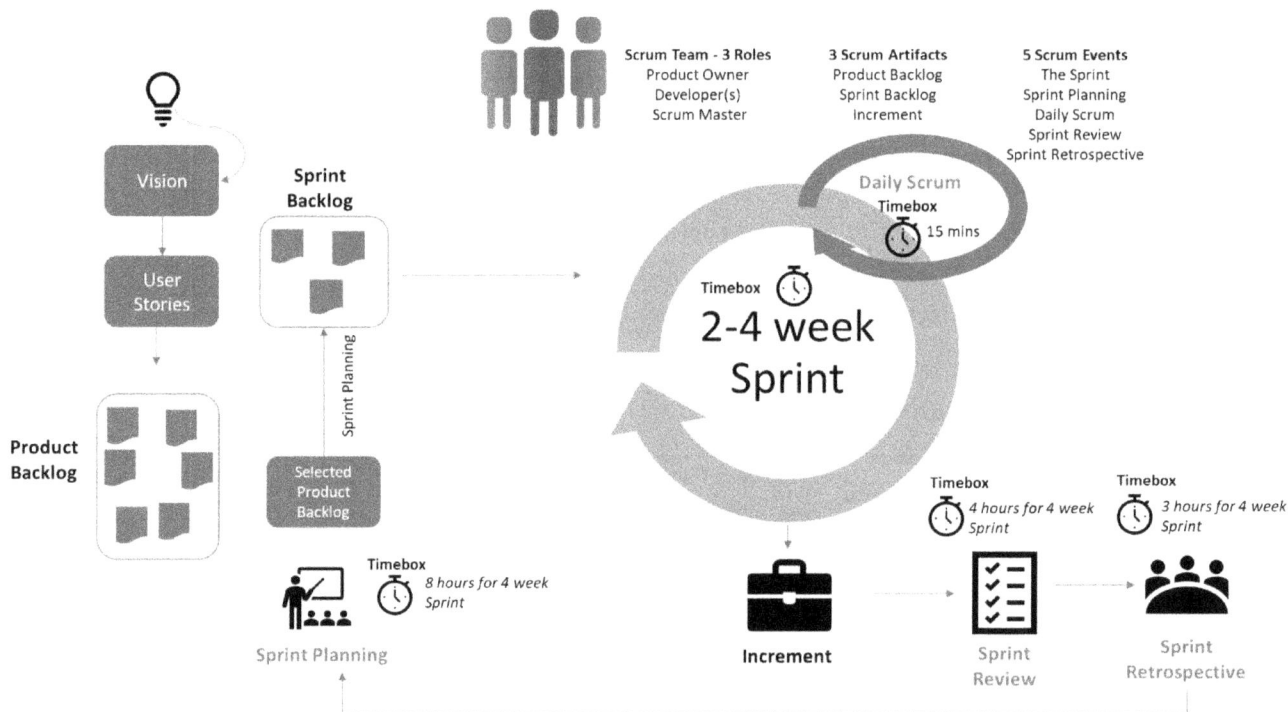

Figure 6.1: Scrum process

The following are the roles in Scrum:

- **Scrum Master**: Facilitates the process, removes impediments, and ensures the team follows Scrum principles.

- **Product owner**: Defines and prioritizes the product backlog (a prioritized list of project tasks), ensuring the team focuses on features that deliver maximum value.

- **Development team**: A self-organizing team responsible for delivering working software during each sprint.

Figure 6.2 depicts Scrum events, highlighting the key ceremonies such as sprint planning, daily standups, sprint reviews, and retrospectives, which facilitate effective communication, progress tracking, and continuous improvement throughout the sprint cycle:

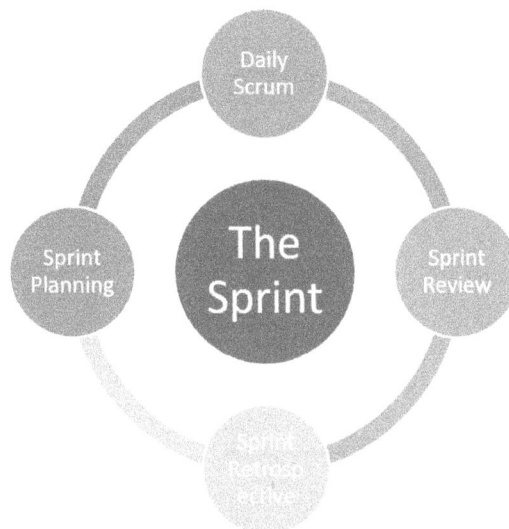

Figure 6.2: *Scrum events*

The following are the key concepts of Scrum:

- **Sprints**: Sprints are the heartbeat of Scrum, where ideas are turned into value. Time-boxed iterations (two to four weeks) during which teams work on a specific set of tasks.

- **Sprint planning**: Teams determine which backlog items will be completed in the upcoming sprint.

- **Daily standups**: Short, daily meetings (15 minutes or less) where team members provide updates and discuss blockers.

- **Sprint reviews**: Held at the end of the sprint to demonstrate the completed work and gather feedback from stakeholders.

- **Retrospectives**: After the sprint review, the team reflects on what worked and what did not, identifying areas for improvement.

The following are the ways in which Scrum helps in iterative delivery and adapting to change:

Scrum structure ensures that teams work in short, focused bursts, allowing them to deliver incremental changes. This approach makes it easier to adapt quickly to changes in requirements or feedback from stakeholders. Solutions architects play a vital role by ensuring the architecture aligns with iterative deliveries while keeping the qualities of service like flexibility, availability, security, performance, resilience, and scalability intact.

The following is a real-world architect's role:

As a solutions architect, you might conduct architectural spikes during sprints to explore and mitigate potential technical challenges, ensuring that the architecture supports both short-term delivery and long-term goals.

While Scrum follows structured sprints, Kanban offers a more continuous and visual approach to managing workflow.

Kanban

Kanban is a visual workflow management method designed to optimize the flow of tasks through a system. Unlike Scrum, Kanban does not use fixed-length sprints. Instead, it focuses on continuously pulling tasks into a Kanban board that visualizes stages of work (e.g., To Do, In Progress, Done).

Figure 6.3 illustrates a Kanban board, a visual management tool used to optimize workflow and track the progress of tasks through various stages, providing teams with a clear overview of ongoing, completed, and pending work items:

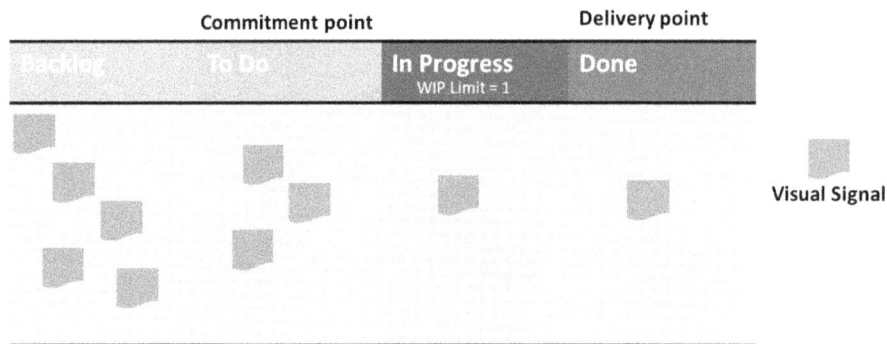

Figure 6.3: *Kanban board*

The following are the key elements of a Kanban board:

- **WIP limit**: Kanban emphasizes limiting **Work in Progress** (**WIP**). By setting a cap on the number of tasks in progress, teams avoid bottlenecks and focus on completing tasks before starting new ones.

- **Visual signal**: A Kanban board visually represents the flow of work. Each task is represented by a card that moves through different stages of the workflow, such as **To Do**, **In Progress**, and **Done**. This helps teams quickly identify task statuses at a glance.

- **Commitment point**: The point where tasks are committed to being worked on, signifying when a task moves from the backlog to active development.

- **Delivery point**: The point where tasks are considered complete and delivered, often marked as the **Done** column on the board. The goal of Kanban is to minimize the time taken to move tasks from the commitment point to the delivery point.

The following are the ways to use a Kanban board:

- The board is divided into columns representing different stages of the workflow as follows:

  o   To Do

  o   In Progress

  o   Done

- Tasks (cards) move across the board as they progress through the workflow, giving the team a clear, visual representation of how work is moving through the system.

The following are the benefits of Kanban:

- **Optimizes workflow**: By visualizing tasks and limiting WIP, teams can focus on completing tasks efficiently rather than starting new ones prematurely.

- **Continuous delivery**: Kanban promotes continuous delivery by avoiding rigid sprint cycles, allowing teams to push completed work at any time.

- **Flexible**: Teams can add, modify, or reprioritize tasks at any time without disrupting the workflow.

The following are the ways in which Kanban differs from Scrum:

Kanban offers more flexibility than Scrum, making it ideal for environments with unpredictable task flows, such as support or maintenance teams. While Scrum is more structured with time-boxed sprints, Kanban prioritizes flow efficiency and continuous delivery.

The following is the architect's role in Kanban:

As a solutions architect in a Kanban environment, your role would involve designing systems that can handle continuous updates without causing disruptions. You will focus on maintaining workflow visibility and optimizing throughput.

Extreme Programming

XP is a software development methodology aimed at improving software quality and responsiveness to changing customer requirements. XP focuses on collaboration and achieving a high standard of technical excellence through the following key practices:

- **Pair programming**: Two developers work together at one workstation, with one writing code while the other reviews it. This collaborative approach not only improves code quality by catching issues early but also facilitates continuous knowledge sharing between team members.

- **Test-Driven Development (TDD)**: TDD is a practice where developers write automated tests before writing actual code. This ensures that the system behaves as expected and helps catch issues early in the development process. It also leads to cleaner, more maintainable code by promoting the development of only the required functionality.

- **Refactoring**: Refactoring involves restructuring the codebase to improve its internal structure without changing its external behavior. This practice improves code maintainability, reduces technical debt, and ensures that the system can evolve over time without becoming brittle or difficult to modify.

- **Continuous integration (CI)**: XP emphasizes the importance of integrating code changes into the main branch multiple times a day. Continuous integration ensures that the system remains stable and functional as changes are made, reducing the risk of integration issues and maintaining a steady development cadence.

The following are the ways to focus on quality and engineering excellence:

XP's focus on these engineering practices ensures that teams produce high-quality software while remaining flexible in response to changing requirements. Practices like TDD and pair programming help reduce bugs, promote cleaner code, and improve overall software quality, while continuous integration ensures that small, frequent changes are integrated without breaking the system.

The following is the architect's role in XP:

The architect's role in XP involves ensuring that technical decisions align with business goals while maintaining the simplicity of design. They facilitate collaboration by guiding developers during pair programming and ensuring adherence to XP practices like TDD and continuous integration. The architect also monitors refactoring efforts to keep code maintainable and support iterative improvements. They act as a technical mentor, helping teams navigate complex challenges without compromising quality. Finally, they focus on building a scalable and adaptive architecture that can evolve seamlessly with changing requirements.

Scaled Agile framework

The **Scaled Agile framework (SAFe)** is designed to scale Agile practices across large enterprises, particularly in organizations where multiple teams work on the same product or portfolio. SAFe provides a structured approach for aligning Agile principles across different organizational levels, ensuring coherence and consistency in Agile adoption.

The following are the levels of SAFe:

- **Team level**: At this level, individual Agile teams operate using Scrum or Kanban, working in short sprints or cycles with daily standups to ensure rapid progress and alignment within the team.

- **Program level**: This level involves multiple Agile teams working together toward a shared objective, forming what's called an **Agile release train (ART)**. A release train engineer (similar to a Scrum Master for the program) coordinates the activities of all teams, ensuring they remain aligned with program-level objectives.

- **Portfolio level**: The portfolio level aligns Agile development efforts with the organization's overall strategy. It focuses on managing value streams, funding initiatives, and ensuring that development efforts support the organization's long-term goals. Governance and prioritization of initiatives occur at this level.

The following is the role of architects in SAFe environments:

Solutions architects play a crucial role in SAFe environments by ensuring that the architecture aligns with the long-term business goals. They coordinate across multiple Agile teams to ensure that systems are designed for scalability, reliability, and performance. Architects also help manage technical dependencies across teams, guiding them in following architectural best practices while ensuring that each team's solutions integrate seamlessly into the overall system.

Each Agile framework offers a unique approach to managing projects and delivering software incrementally, but the role of a solutions architect must adapt across all of them.

Solutions architect role in Agile teams

In traditional software development methodologies, solutions architects typically define the entire system architecture upfront. This approach, while suitable for linear models like Waterfall, can be too rigid for Agile environments, where requirements and priorities often change during development. In Agile, the role of a solutions architect shifts from delivering a comprehensive, static architecture to supporting an iterative, adaptive design process. Rather than creating a detailed architecture at the start, architects must ensure the system is flexible enough to evolve over time as new insights emerge.

The following are the key aspects of the shift:

- **Incremental architecture**: Instead of planning all details upfront, Agile solutions architects design modular systems that can evolve incrementally as each sprint delivers new features. This allows teams to make architectural adjustments based on real-time feedback and changing business requirements.

    For example, in a microservices architecture, rather than designing all services upfront, the architect might first create a few core services, then iteratively add more services as new business needs arise.

- **Early architecture planning with flexibility**: While some foundational architecture is still necessary early in the project, Agile solutions architects must recognize that initial designs may need to be revisited and adapted. The architecture must be flexible to accommodate evolving technical requirements and business priorities without creating unnecessary rework or technical debt.

    For example, in an e-commerce platform, the initial design might focus on scalability for user logins and payments, with flexibility to later incorporate more complex modules like product recommendations or inventory tracking.

- **Supporting Agile principles**: Agile architecture aligns with principles like simplicity, feedback-driven improvement, and continuous delivery. Solutions architects focus on maintaining a balance between immediate technical decisions and long-term architectural goals.

    For example, the solutions architect might simplify the data flow in the initial sprints by using a single data source for reporting, knowing that future iterations will introduce more complex data integration layers based on user feedback.

Continuous collaboration

Effective communication is crucial for the success of Agile teams, and solutions architects play a central role in ensuring that the architecture aligns with both business needs and technical capabilities. In Agile, collaboration between architects and cross-functional teams is ongoing and iterative.

The following are the ways for engaging with product owners and Scrum Masters during sprint planning:

- In Agile environments, sprint planning is a vital moment for ensuring that architectural considerations are addressed early in each iteration. Solutions architects work closely with product owners to understand business priorities and identify the technical implications of the user stories selected for the sprint.

- Architects also collaborate with Scrum Masters to remove any impediments related to architecture that could block the team's progress. By being part of sprint planning sessions, architects ensure that the architecture evolves in sync with the product roadmap and stakeholder expectations.

  For example, in a healthcare project, the product owner may prioritize building a user-friendly patient dashboard. The solutions architect helps identify the necessary backend systems that will support the data flow for the dashboard, while the Scrum Master ensures that technical blockers are cleared during the sprint.

The following are the ways for facilitating architectural discussions during sprints:

- Throughout the sprint, solutions architects engage in ongoing architectural discussions to ensure that the team is making the right technical decisions. These discussions focus on balancing immediate delivery goals with maintaining the system's long-term integrity.

- Architects also play a key role in refining the architecture as the sprint progresses, offering guidance on how to approach technical challenges without deviating from the broader architectural vision.

  For example, during the sprint, if the team faces performance issues with data processing, the solutions architect may suggest optimizing the database schema or implementing caching mechanisms to improve performance while staying aligned with the overall architecture.

The following are the ways for working with cross-functional teams:

- Agile teams are typically cross-functional, comprising developers, testers, designers, and business analysts, all of whom collaborate to deliver a product increment. Solutions architects bridge the gap between different team members by ensuring that architecture is aligned with business objectives, while still being technically sound and efficient.

- Architects often lead the development of technical solutions that fit within the Agile framework, ensuring that everyone, from front-end developers to backend engineers, understands the architectural strategy.

  For example, in a fintech project, a solutions architect might coordinate between the **user experience (UX)** or **user interface (UI)** designers and the backend development team to ensure that data security controls are built into the user interfaces for financial transactions.

With these responsibilities in mind, solutions architects must also maintain the balance between flexibility and long-term architectural goals.

Architectural spikes

In Agile, a spike is a type of exploratory task aimed at investigating a particular technical challenge. Architectural spikes, in particular, are used when the team needs to explore or evaluate different architectural options to mitigate uncertainty. Spikes allow teams to gain a deeper understanding of a technical issue or assess potential solutions without committing to full implementation.

The following are the ways to use architectural spikes:

- **High technical uncertainty**: When there is ambiguity or a lack of clarity about how to approach a complex technical problem, an architectural spike is a helpful tool. For instance, if there are multiple ways to implement a new feature and each presents different technical challenges, the team can run a spike to explore the pros and cons of each approach.

For example, in an AI-driven application, the team may run a spike to evaluate different machine learning models and their impact on system performance and scalability.

- **Evaluating new technologies**: If the team is considering adopting a new technology or framework, an architectural spike can be used to assess its feasibility, integration with the existing system, and potential risks.

    For example, a team evaluating whether to migrate from a monolithic architecture to a microservices-based system might run a spike to explore containerization technologies like Docker and Kubernetes.

The following are the steps to run a spike to evaluate technical solutions:

1. **Define the problem or uncertainty**: Identify the specific architectural challenge that needs investigation. This could involve a new integration, scaling challenges, or evaluating performance under different conditions.

2. **Set clear objectives**: Establish measurable goals for the spike, such as determining which architectural pattern to use, assessing the impact of a technology change, or identifying performance bottlenecks.

3. **Time box the spike**: Allocate a fixed period for the spike, typically one sprint or less. This ensures the spike remains focused and does not consume too many resources.

4. **Explore and experiment**: The team conducts experiments, runs tests, and gathers data to answer the spike's objectives. Solutions architects work with the team to explore different architectural options, often developing proof-of-concept implementations.

5. **Document and review the findings**: At the end of the spike, document the findings and make a recommendation for the way forward. These findings can then be used to inform future sprints or architectural decisions.

    For example, after running a spike on different database solutions for a highly transactional system, the team recommends switching to a NoSQL database like MongoDB due to its performance advantages.

While spikes help in managing uncertainty, empowering teams to make decisions independently is equally important for fostering agility.

Decentralized decision-making

One of the key principles in Agile is to empower teams to make decisions autonomously. However, to maintain architectural consistency and system integrity, solutions architects must provide teams with the right balance of freedom and guidance.

To support decentralized decision-making while maintaining architectural coherence, solutions architects need to set clear boundaries and guidelines for teams, as follows:

- **Defining architectural guardrails**: Rather than micromanaging every architectural decision, solutions architects provide guardrails, a set of architectural principles, guidelines, and patterns that ensure consistency across the system. These guardrails allow teams to make independent decisions within certain parameters, ensuring that the overall architecture remains cohesive.

    For example, for a large-scale e-commerce platform, the solutions architect may establish a guardrail that all APIs must conform to REST standards, ensuring consistent communication between services.

- **Empowering teams to own the design process**: With the right guardrails in place, Agile teams can make on-the-spot decisions about how to implement features, refactor code, or optimize performance. This speeds up development and reduces bottlenecks, as teams do not need to wait for approval from an architect for every decision.

For example, if a backend team needs to optimize performance for a specific service, they can adjust the database queries or caching strategy without waiting for detailed input from the architect, as long as they follow the established guardrails.

- **Providing architectural guardrails to maintain system integrity**: Guardrails are critical for ensuring that teams maintain architectural integrity while working independently.

  To set up effective architectural guardrails, solutions architects establish clear guidelines and best practices that allow teams to work autonomously while ensuring alignment with the overall system design and organizational standards, as follows:

  o **Established design patterns**: Teams follow predefined design patterns for solving common problems (e.g., microservices, event-driven architecture) to maintain consistency across the system.

  o **Technology stack choices**: Solutions architects define the tools, libraries, and technologies teams should use, ensuring compatibility and avoiding fragmentation within the system.

  o **Security and compliance requirements**: Architects establish security protocols and compliance requirements, for example, encryption standards, data privacy regulations that teams must follow.

However, even with guardrails, aligning the overall architecture with Agile development requires continuous monitoring and adjustment.

The following are the benefits of decentralized decision-making with guardrails:

- **Faster decision-making**: Empowering teams to make architecture-related decisions reduces delays and bottlenecks, as teams can move forward without waiting for top-down approval.

- **Innovation**: Allowing teams to explore different architectural solutions fosters creativity and encourages innovation.

- **Consistency**: While teams are empowered to make decisions, guardrails ensure that the system remains consistent, secure, and scalable.

The dynamic nature of Agile projects demands an architecture that evolves iteratively. As we move forward, we will look into strategies for aligning architecture with Agile development to ensure long-term scalability without compromising short-term goals.

Aligning architecture with Agile development

In Agile development, aligning architecture with iterative, fast-paced delivery cycles is a key challenge for solutions architects. The goal is to ensure that the architecture supports the short-term goals of Agile sprints while still evolving to meet long-term business needs. To achieve this, Agile architecture must be modular, continuously refactored, and supported by automation to balance speed with scalability and maintainability. This section explores how modular design, technical debt management, and automation are critical for aligning architecture with Agile development.

Modular and incremental design

Designing for Agility: Modular components, microservices, and loosely coupled systems. In Agile environments, designing architecture that is modular and loosely coupled is crucial for achieving flexibility and speed. Modular systems allow teams to build, test, and deploy features independently, aligning with the iterative nature of Agile development. Microservices, as a form of modular architecture, offer a scalable and resilient approach to system design, empowering teams to develop and deploy features independently while minimizing the risk of impacting the overall system.

Microservices offer a scalable and resilient approach to system design, empowering teams to develop and deploy features independently, as follows:

- **Microservices architecture**: Microservices are independently deployable components that perform specific functions. Unlike monolithic architectures, microservices allow teams to iterate quickly by updating individual services without affecting the entire system. This reduces deployment risks and speeds up time-to-market.

  For example, in an e-commerce platform, the product catalogue, shopping cart, and payment gateway can each be separate microservices. This enables the respective teams to deploy updates to their service without waiting for others.

- **Loosely coupled systems**: A loosely coupled system ensures that changes in one module have minimal impact on others. By decoupling components, architects enable independent development and deployment of various features or services, which supports Agile frequent release cycles.

  For example, in a banking application, the user authentication service can be decoupled from the payment processing service, allowing updates to authentication without affecting the payment service.

The following are the benefits of decoupling components:

- **Faster development cycles**: Teams can focus on specific components without being blocked by dependencies on other teams.

- **Independent deployment**: Each service can be deployed independently, enabling continuous delivery of features.

- **Enhanced scalability**: Loosely coupled systems scale more efficiently, as individual services can be scaled based on demand without affecting the entire system.

Continuous refactoring and technical debt management

In Agile, architecture must evolve with the product. As new features are added, the system's design may need to be adjusted to accommodate new requirements. **Continuous refactoring** is the process of improving the codebase without altering its external behavior, ensuring that the system remains maintainable, scalable, and performant over time.

For example, a team may discover that a module responsible for customer reporting has become too complex due to rapid feature additions. During a sprint, they may allocate time to refactor this module, simplifying its structure while maintaining its functionality. This reduces the risk of introducing bugs and making future updates easier.

The following are the strategies for managing technical debt in an Agile environment:

- **Incorporate debt management into sprints**: Allocate time in each sprint for addressing technical debt. This prevents it from accumulating and causing larger problems later.

- **Track technical debt**: Use tools like Jira or Trello to log and track technical debt, ensuring it remains visible to the team and is prioritized alongside new feature development.

- **Prioritize high-impact debt**: Not all technical debt needs to be addressed immediately. Solutions architects must work with teams to identify high-impact areas of debt, those that affect performance, scalability, or security, and prioritize fixing them.

  For example, a legacy authentication service may be identified as a high-impact technical debt, leading to a team prioritizing its refactoring over other lower-impact issues.

Prioritizing architectural improvements alongside product features are as follows:

Balancing the delivery of new features with the need for architectural improvements is critical. Solutions architects must work closely with product owners to ensure that architectural tasks (such as refactoring or addressing technical debt) are part of the backlog and prioritized appropriately.

For example, a team might allocate 70% of their time to delivering new features while dedicating 30% to architectural improvements during each sprint. This ensures continuous delivery while maintaining system scalability and maintainability.

Balancing immediate delivery with long-term scalability

To balance the need for immediate delivery with long-term scalability, solutions architects should take a pragmatic approach that ensures the architecture can evolve incrementally without incurring significant technical debt.

The following are the key strategies:

- **Design for change**: Ensure that the architecture can accommodate future changes without requiring major rework. This may involve using interfaces, APIs, or microservices that can be extended over time.

- **Regular architectural reviews**: Schedule periodic reviews of the architecture to identify areas that need improvement or refactoring. These reviews ensure that the system remains aligned with both current business needs and future scalability.

  For example, during monthly architectural reviews, a team might decide to refactor the data storage layer to support faster query performance as user traffic increases.

The following are the ways for creating a technical roadmap that aligns with sprint-by-sprint delivery cycles:

A technical roadmap is a long-term plan for how the system's architecture will evolve over time. Solutions architects should work with development teams to create a roadmap that outlines key architectural improvements and aligns with the product backlog.

Let us consider an example of a roadmap. In an e-commerce platform, the roadmap may outline the gradual migration from a monolithic architecture to a microservices architecture over the next six months. Each sprint includes incremental steps toward this goal, such as refactoring one component into a microservice during each iteration.

Let us now consider an example of balancing scalability, maintainability, and speed in Agile. A team may be tasked with delivering a new feature requiring heavy data processing. The immediate priority is to launch the feature, but the system must also be scalable to handle growing data volumes in the future. By using a modular design with cloud-native services like AWS Lambda or Azure functions, the team can deliver the feature quickly while ensuring that the architecture can scale as data volumes increase.

Automation in Agile

Automation is a cornerstone of Agile development. By automating repetitive tasks like testing, deployment, and infrastructure management, teams can focus on delivering value rather than manual tasks, as follows:

- **Automated testing**: Continuous testing is essential to Agile. Solutions architects must ensure that automated tests (e.g., unit tests, integration tests) are in place and integrated into the development pipeline. This ensures that the code is continuously tested and any issues are caught early.

- **Automated deployment**: Using tools like Jenkins or Azure DevOps, teams can automate the deployment process, reducing the risk of errors during manual deployment and enabling faster feature delivery.

- **Infrastructure automation**: **Infrastructure as code** (**IaC**) tools like Terraform, Azure ARM Templates, and AWS CloudFormation enable teams to manage and provision infrastructure automatically. This ensures consistency across environments and reduces deployment times.

The following is the role of **continuous integration** (**CI**) and **continuous deployment** (**CD**) pipelines in supporting Agile development:

CI is the practice of merging code into a shared repository multiple times a day, where automated builds and tests are run. This ensures that any issues are caught early and the system remains in a working state. CD extends CI by automatically deploying code changes to production once they pass all tests.

The following are the benefits of CI/CD in Agile:

- **Faster delivery**: Automating the build, test, and deployment processes enables faster and more reliable delivery of features.

- **Reduced risk**: Automated tests ensure that bugs are caught early in the development cycle, reducing the risk of introducing issues into production.

- **Frequent feedback**: CI/CD provides continuous feedback to the team, allowing them to quickly iterate their work.

Automating these processes ensures a stable foundation for maintaining architectural integrity in Agile environments.

There are numerous tools available for automating various aspects of the development lifecycle. The following are some of the widely used tools that are essential for implementing CI/CD practices, ensuring efficient builds, testing, and deployments:

- **Jenkins**: A widely-used open-source automation server for building CI/CD pipelines. Jenkins integrates with many tools and services to automate the entire development lifecycle.

- **DevOps on cloud**: Cloud-based DevOps platforms like AWS CodePipeline, Azure DevOps, and Google Cloud Build offer comprehensive support for managing development workflows, including automated builds, tests, and deployments. These platforms seamlessly integrate with cloud infrastructure, making them suitable for teams leveraging cloud-native services.

- **Docker**: A platform for containerizing applications, making them easier to deploy and run across different environments. Docker allows teams to package applications and their dependencies into containers, ensuring consistency across development, staging, and production.

- **Kubernetes**: An open-source container orchestration platform that automates the deployment, scaling, and management of containerized applications. Kubernetes allows teams to manage large-scale, distributed systems with ease, ensuring that containerized applications can scale and remain highly available across different environments.

While designing an adaptive architecture is crucial, managing and documenting this evolving architecture requires effective tools. This brings us to a discussion on some of the key Agile tools, such as Jira and Confluence, which help solutions architects maintain transparency, track architectural decisions, and foster team collaboration.

Agile tools

Agile methodologies prioritize collaboration, transparency, and continuous delivery. To achieve this, teams rely heavily on project management and documentation tools that support iterative development cycles. Tools like Jira and Confluence have become indispensable in Agile environments because they enable teams to organize work, track progress, document decisions, and maintain visibility across the organization. These tools not only help in managing day-to-day tasks but also play a crucial role in supporting long-term architectural goals.

The following is the importance of project management and documentation tools in Agile teams:

In Agile teams, the ability to track progress, adapt quickly, and communicate effectively is paramount. **Project management tools** such as Jira allow teams to plan sprints, manage backlogs, and visualize workflows. **Documentation tools** like Confluence provide a platform for teams to share knowledge, document technical specifications, and ensure alignment on architectural goals.

The following tools ensure that Agile teams maintain transparency and cohesion, even as requirements evolve rapidly:

- **Project management tools**: Enable tracking of tasks, sprints, and product backlogs.
- **Documentation tools**: Facilitate communication, documentation of decisions, and sharing of key insights across teams.

Jira for Agile project management

Use Jira to manage the product backlog, sprint planning, and tracking progress. Jira is a powerful project management tool specifically designed for Agile teams. It allows teams to manage their work through Kanban boards, Scrum boards, and backlogs. For solutions architects, Jira helps track architecture related tasks, manage technical debt, and ensure architectural goals align with product features.

Effective backlog management, sprint planning, and progress tracking are key activities where Jira plays a crucial role in ensuring that development efforts are aligned with both business priorities and architectural goals, as follows:

- **Product backlog management**: Jira helps manage the product backlog, which is a prioritized list of features, bug fixes, and improvements. Product owners, in collaboration with solutions architects, use Jira to define user stories and epics and prioritize them based on business needs and architectural considerations.

- **Sprint planning**: During sprint planning, Jira is used to allocate tasks to the development team based on their capacity. Solutions architects can create architecture-related tasks, such as implementing new design patterns or addressing technical debt, and ensure they are included in the sprint backlog.

- **Progress tracking**: Jira provides real-time visibility into the team's progress during a sprint. The burn-down chart helps track the completion of tasks, while the Kanban board visualizes the flow of work from To Do to Done. This helps the team identify bottlenecks and make adjustments as needed.

Jira is an excellent tool for managing architectural tasks alongside product features. To effectively track architectural work, solutions architects should do the following:

- **Create specific epics (large user story or feature) for architecture**: Group related architectural tasks under specific epics, for example, microservices refactoring or security enhancements, to maintain focus on long-term architectural improvements.

- **Track technical debt**: Use Jira to log and track technical debt by creating dedicated tickets or labels. This ensures that technical debt is visible to both the development team and product owners, and it can be prioritized alongside feature development.

- **Break down architecture tasks into user stories**: Even architecture-related tasks should be broken down into user stories or smaller tasks to fit within a sprint. This ensures that architecture improvements are delivered incrementally.

The following are the ways for integrating Jira with CI/CD tools to automate tracking of build and deployment status:

Jira integrates seamlessly with CI/CD tools like Jenkins and Azure DevOps. This integration allows teams to track the status of builds and deployments directly within Jira. Every time code is committed, Jira can automatically update the status of related tasks based on the build or deployment outcome, providing real-time feedback to the team.

It is essential to understand how automation within Agile tools like Jira can streamline workflow management and enhance traceability throughout the development lifecycle, as follows:

- **Automated status updates**: CI/CD integrations enable Jira to automatically move tasks between different statuses, for example, **In Progress**, **Ready for Review**, and **Done**, based on the results of the build and test pipelines.

- **Tracking build failures and deployments**: Teams can link Jira tickets to specific branches, commits, or builds, making it easier to identify which changes caused a build failure or deployment issue.

Confluence for documentation

Confluence is a collaborative documentation platform that complements Jira by providing a space for teams to document architecture decisions, technical specifications, and long-term roadmaps. For solutions architects, Confluence is vital for maintaining visibility into why certain architectural decisions were made and ensuring that all stakeholders have access to technical documentation. Let us take a look at how it can be used:

- **Architecture decision records (ADRs)**: Use Confluence to document key architectural decisions. This provides a historical record of the reasoning behind decisions, which can help future teams understand why certain technologies or designs were chosen.

- **Technical specifications**: Document technical requirements and specifications in Confluence, ensuring that both business and technical stakeholders have a clear understanding of the system's architecture. This includes APIs, data models, and security requirements.

- **Project roadmaps**: Confluence is also useful for creating long-term roadmaps that align architectural improvements with product releases. This roadmap ensures that the team balances feature delivery with maintaining system scalability and performance.

Confluence offers several features that help solutions architects share and document architecture styles, designs, and decisions, as follows:

- **Architectural diagrams**: Confluence integrates with tools like Lucidchart or Draw.io, allowing solutions architects to create and embed architecture diagrams directly into Confluence pages. These diagrams provide a visual representation of the system's architecture and help teams understand complex relationships between components.

- **Architectural styles**: Document common architectural styles (e.g., microservices, event-driven architecture) in Confluence, ensuring that teams have a consistent reference when designing new systems. This helps maintain alignment with the organization's overarching architectural principles.

- **Collaboration and feedback**: Solutions architects can use Confluence to create collaborative pages where team members can leave comments, ask questions, and suggest improvements. This fosters a culture of continuous feedback and improvement.

Best practices

The following are the best practices for Agile tool usage:

- **Keeping the backlog aligned with architectural priorities**: Solutions architects must work closely with product owners to ensure that the backlog reflects both business needs and architectural goals as follows:

  - **Regular backlog refinement**: Schedule regular backlog refinement sessions where architectural improvements and technical debt are reviewed alongside new feature requests. This ensures that architecture is continuously evolving while new features are delivered.

- Prioritize high-impact architecture work: Not all architectural tasks need to be addressed immediately. Solutions architects should help the team prioritize tasks that will have the most significant impact on system scalability, security, or performance.

- **Regular refinement of the backlog to include architectural improvements and technical debt**: It is important to treat architectural improvements and technical debt as part of the regular Agile workflow. This can be achieved as follows:

    - Incorporating architecture into user stories: Break down large architectural changes into user stories and prioritize them based on business needs and technical impact.

    - Maintaining a visible list of technical debt: Use Jira to track technical debt items and review them regularly to ensure they are addressed in upcoming sprints.

- **Using Jira and Confluence together to create transparency and ensure architectural concerns are visible to all stakeholders**: By using Jira and Confluence together, teams can ensure that architecture-related work is visible to both technical and non-technical stakeholders.

- **Link Jira tickets to Confluence pages**: Solutions architects can link Jira tickets to relevant Confluence pages, providing additional context for technical tasks and ensuring that stakeholders understand the architectural implications of certain features.

- **Use Confluence for documentation and Jira for execution**: Confluence serves as the central repository for architectural documentation, while Jira tracks the execution of related tasks. This separation of concerns ensures that the architecture is well-documented and that progress is tracked effectively.

Together, these tools offer a comprehensive approach to managing Agile projects and supporting architecture at every stage of development.

Agile best practices for solutions architects

The following are the Agile best practices for solutions architects:

- **Maintaining the architectural vision in an Agile environment**: Agile environments often focus on rapid delivery, which can sometimes lead to short-term decision-making that sacrifices architectural integrity. Solutions architects must balance agility with maintaining a strategic architectural vision as follows:

    - Continuous architectural reviews: Schedule regular reviews to ensure that the architecture remains aligned with long-term goals, even as the team focuses on delivering immediate features.

    - Guiding architectural evolution: Instead of enforcing a rigid upfront architecture, solutions architects should guide its evolution to adapt as the system grows.

- **Balancing Agility with a strategic architectural vision**: While Agile prioritizes adaptability and speed, it is crucial not to lose sight of long-term architectural goals. Solutions architects can balance these two as follows:

    - Using guardrails: Establish architectural guardrails (e.g., design patterns, best practices) that allow teams to move quickly while ensuring that their decisions align with the long-term architectural strategy.

    - Leveraging modular design: Design modular, decoupled systems that can evolve incrementally. This ensures that the architecture remains flexible enough to support rapid iterations.

With these practices in mind, it is essential to ensure the architecture's alignment across various Agile teams and frameworks. By adopting these best practices, solutions architects can successfully guide their teams and projects toward achieving both immediate and strategic goals.

In conclusion, maintaining the right balance between flexibility and architectural integrity is crucial for ensuring long-term success in Agile.

Conclusion

Agile methodologies have transformed how teams deliver software, and solutions architects play a vital role in ensuring that architectural decisions remain aligned with both business needs and technical realities. Architects in Agile environments must be adaptable, continuously refining the architecture as projects evolve, and collaborate closely with cross-functional teams. By leveraging iterative design, collaboration, and Agile tools like Jira and Confluence, solutions architects can ensure that systems are scalable, flexible, and resilient in fast-paced environments.

To summarize, the key takeaways from this chapter highlight how solutions architects can effectively contribute to Agile processes by focusing on modular design, managing technical debt, and leveraging the right tools and frameworks.

Key takeaways

The takeaways are as follows:

- **Understanding Agile methodologies**: Agile frameworks like Scrum, Kanban, XP, and SAFe provide a structured yet flexible approach for managing software development, allowing teams to adapt to changing requirements while delivering value incrementally.

- **Solutions architect's role in Agile**: Solutions architects play a vital role in guiding the architecture, ensuring it evolves with Agile principles, and aligning technical solutions with business goals. They serve as a bridge between stakeholders and development teams to maintain architectural integrity and enable fast-paced delivery.

- **Incremental and evolutionary architecture**: Embracing incremental and modular design allows solutions architects to support iterative delivery, accommodate changing requirements, and ensure long-term scalability and performance in an Agile environment.

- **Managing technical debt**: Solutions architects should proactively manage technical debt by making it visible, prioritizing it, and integrating refactoring tasks into sprints. This prevents technical debt from accumulating and hindering system scalability and maintainability.

- **Integrating NFRs**: Non-functional requirements such as performance, security, and scalability must be considered alongside functional requirements in Agile. Solutions architects should integrate **non-functional requirements** (**NFR**) into sprint planning and track them as part of the definition of done.

- **Collaborating across teams**: Effective communication and collaboration are critical. Solutions architects must regularly engage with cross-functional teams, participate in sprint planning, and use tools like Confluence to document architectural decisions, ensuring transparency and alignment.

- **Leveraging automation**: Automation is key in Agile. Implementing CI/CD pipelines, automated testing, and IaC practices can significantly improve the speed and reliability of deployments, enabling rapid iterations while maintaining quality.

- **Scaling Agile practices**: Scaling Agile with frameworks like SAFe requires aligning architecture and business strategy across multiple levels of the organization. Solutions architects should focus on creating a cohesive architectural vision that supports scalability and cross-team collaboration.

- **Security and compliance in Agile**: Security should be an integral part of Agile development, with security testing, compliance checks, and architectural reviews integrated into the CI/CD pipeline and the definition of done.

- **Living documentation**: Documentation should be treated as a living artifact, updated regularly to reflect the current state of the architecture. This ensures it remains useful without becoming a bottleneck, supporting continuous learning and improvement.

Model interview questions and answers

1. **How do you align Agile practices with long-term architectural goals?**

   Model answer:

   - You align Agile practices with long-term goals by creating an evolutionary architecture that supports continuous delivery and change.

   - This involves designing modular and loosely coupled systems that allow for flexibility in implementation while maintaining the integrity of the overarching architecture.

   - During sprint planning, ensure that architectural considerations are included and align with both current requirements and future scalability needs.

2. **What role does a solutions architect play in an Agile team?**

   Model answer:

   - In an Agile team, solutions architect ensures that the architecture supports iterative delivery and aligns with business goals.

   - You collaborate closely with product owners and Scrum Masters during sprint planning to prioritize architectural tasks.

   - Additionally, you provide technical guidance during development, help identify technical debt, and ensure that the evolving architecture maintains performance, security, and scalability.

3. **Can you describe how you have used Agile frameworks like Scrum or Kanban in your previous projects?**

   Model answer:

   - In a previous project, you used Scrum to manage a multi-team development effort for a financial application.

   - As the solutions architect, you created architectural spikes for complex user stories and collaborated with the Scrum Master to ensure technical blockers were addressed.

   - For maintenance and support tasks, you employed Kanban to visualize work items and manage workflow efficiently, maintaining visibility into ongoing technical debt and architectural improvements.

4. **How do you handle conflicting priorities between immediate sprint goals and long-term architectural integrity?**

   Model answer:

   - You address conflicting priorities by balancing short-term needs with long-term stability.

   - You advocate for architectural guardrails and incremental architectural improvements to ensure you do not accrue excessive technical debt.

   - During sprint planning, you work with the product owner to negotiate priority adjustments and ensure that essential architectural tasks are included, even if it is just small refactoring efforts that align with sprint goals.

5. **What is your approach to managing technical debt in an Agile environment?**

   Model answer:

   - You manage technical debt by ensuring it is visible, tracked, and prioritized.

   - During backlog refinement, you classify technical debt items based on their impact on performance, maintainability, and security.

   - You incorporate debt reduction tasks into sprints and ensure that high-impact debt is addressed first.

   - Continuous refactoring is key to keeping technical debt under control while delivering features incrementally.

6. **Can you explain how to scale Agile practices using frameworks like SAFe?**

   Model answer:

   - Scaling Agile using SAFe involves aligning architecture and business strategies across different levels, such as team, program, and portfolio.

   - As a solutions architect, you ensure that the architectural vision aligns with the program and portfolio levels, creating a shared understanding of non-functional requirements and architectural standards.

   - You also participate in **program increment** (**PI**) planning to ensure that architectural enablers are part of the roadmap.

7. **How do you ensure architecture consistency across multiple Agile teams?**

   Model answer:

   - You maintain architecture consistency through defined architectural guardrails, regular architectural sync meetings, and documentation in Confluence.

   - You establish architectural principles, reusable patterns, and shared components that teams can use to ensure consistency.

   - You also conduct architectural reviews and facilitate technical discussions to align teams with key decisions.

8. **Describe how you have used CI/CD in Agile.**

   Model answer:

   - You have implemented CI/CD pipelines using Jenkins and Azure DevOps to automate builds, testing, and deployments.

   - This ensures that code changes are integrated frequently and deployed in small batches.

   - For example, you set up automated testing in CI to catch issues early and use automated deployments in CD to roll out changes to production safely and quickly.

   - This process supports Agile's iterative delivery model.

9. **How do you approach architectural changes when requirements change frequently in Agile?**

   Model answer:

   - You approach frequent changes by designing for flexibility from the outset using modular, loosely coupled components.

   - You maintain an intentional architecture that provides direction while supporting emergent design patterns.

- When requirements change, you assess the impact on the existing architecture and update components incrementally to avoid disrupting ongoing development.

- Regular communication with stakeholders is crucial to managing expectations.

10. **What is your strategy for handling NFRs in Agile?**

Model answer:

- In Agile, you integrate NFRs like performance, security, and availability into the definition of done for each user story.

- You also create architecture enablers and technical stories specifically focused on NFRs.

- During sprint planning, you ensure that NFRs are considered alongside functional requirements to avoid compromising quality.

- For critical NFRs, you use architectural spikes to evaluate different options before committing to a design.

11. **How do you manage architectural documentation in an Agile environment?**

Model answer:

- You document architecture incrementally, focusing on lightweight, living documentation in tools like Confluence.

- You update architecture diagrams and design decisions as the system evolves, ensuring that documentation is current without being overly detailed.

- This living documentation approach allows the team to understand the architecture's evolution and supports continuous improvement without becoming a bottleneck.

12. **Can you provide an example of when you had to refactor a system in an Agile project?**

Model answer:

- In one project, you and your team noticed that a shared module was becoming a performance bottleneck.

- During the sprint, you led an architectural spike to analyze the issue and proposed a refactoring strategy that separated the module into independent microservices.

- This refactoring improved response times significantly without disrupting ongoing development, as it was planned and executed iteratively over several sprints.

13. **How do you ensure security and compliance in an Agile project?**

Model answer:

- You integrate security and compliance into Agile workflows by defining security requirements upfront and including them in the definition of done for each sprint.

- You use security testing tools (like OWASP ZAP for vulnerability scanning) as part of the CI/CD pipeline and conduct regular architectural reviews focused on security and compliance.

- This ensures that security is not an afterthought but a continuous focus throughout the project.

14. **What is your approach to ensuring system performance in Agile development?**

Model answer:

- You ensure system performance by defining performance criteria early and using automated performance tests in the CI/CD pipeline. During development, you monitor key metrics (e.g., latency, throughput) and use performance spikes to assess potential bottlenecks.

- You also design for scalability from the beginning, using microservices and cloud-native patterns to support dynamic scaling.

15. **How do you facilitate collaboration between architects and development teams in Agile?**

    Model answer:

    - You facilitate collaboration through regular technical syncs, joint backlog refinement sessions, and architecture discussions that involve developers early in the design process.

    - You also use Confluence to document architectural decisions and encourage team members to contribute ideas and feedback.

    - This collaborative approach ensures that the architecture reflects real-world constraints and supports team ownership.

Join our Discord space

Join our Discord workspace for latest updates, offers, tech happenings around the world, new releases, and sessions with the authors:

https://discord.bpbonline.com

CHAPTER 7

Legacy Modernization and Migration Strategies

Introduction

Software systems are built and maintained by enterprises to give their customers a compelling user experience. It is not only about a fancy application user interface but also more about introducing new product and service offerings to their customers. It is also to be noted that the user expectations from business houses in terms of new feature offerings only keep growing forever. Having said this, software systems built must be nimble for enterprises to roll out new service offerings to their customers on a regular basis. However, applications that are developed to serve hundreds of thousands of users slowly lose their sheen not only from a functionality perspective but also from a usability perspective. Users acquire new digital habits for the consumption of products and features offered by enterprises through their online channels. Moreover, the applications built by enterprises with the intent of realizing their business goals currently may no longer be their trusted envoy as the business horizon expands and the customer base increases.

Enterprises put their customers first and ensure that their content and delivery are more aligned with users' needs and their channels of delivery are at par with the current standards of the industry. It becomes inevitable for enterprises to keep their software systems up to date to ensure that their products and service delivery continue to delight their customers, and that they are not left behind their competitors in their area of operation. Apart from the customers' changing needs and the company's ever-changing appetite for expansion and growth, the hardware and software platforms hosting the application also evolves and we reach a point wherein the hardware and software are not able to put up with the changed demands of the customer and the enterprise and hence needs to be replaced. Legacy modernization is one area that is being discussed and pursued with a lot of rigor by modern day enterprises. Enterprises set aside millions of dollars in their budget for this very important exercise of future proofing their software systems and their business operations.

Structure

This chapter covers the following topics:

- Software application dynamics
- Role of a solutions architect in legacy modernization
- Challenges to legacy modernization

- Drivers for legacy modernization

- Legacy modernization to cloud

- Mainframe modernization

- Artificial intelligence in legacy modernization

- Roadmap to legacy modernization

- Checklist for legacy modernization

Software application dynamics

Software applications are built to last for a long period of time. Gaps between the enterprise business goals and the existing business processes trigger the setting aside of budgets for the development of new software applications. Requirements are gathered, analyzed, and refined iteratively before developing software applications. However, the business ecosystem continues to change with regard to the business goals being revisited and enhanced every quarter. The quality-of-service expectations from software systems, such as performance, usability, and security, also continue to change due to changing user needs and regulatory compliance. For instance, feature functionality that used to be a major driver a decade ago is only one of the main aspects of a software application now. Software application feature functionality among competitors has become table stakes now, with all leading business houses providing the same features and capabilities to users in their domain of expertise. For instance, if you want to get a quote for an insurance policy online, almost all the leading insurance companies provide features to generate a quote online. However, the current generation of software users is looking for something beyond application functionality. Users look for qualities of service like usability, performance, security, and reliability of the application before they choose a service provider. The continuous and combined effects of the functional changes along with upgrades for the nonfunctional aspects over time have a side effect of taking the application to a state where the application loses its nimbleness and the important quality of being fit for purpose. Fit for purpose lets a software application serve its users or customers without any friction in terms of functionality and other qualities of service.

Gartner defines a legacy application as an information system that may be based on outdated technologies but is critical for day-to-day operations. Enterprises spend millions of dollars to maintain these critical applications. However, maintaining these applications to keep them usable and fit for purpose for their customers becomes difficult both in terms of effort and cost, and a tipping point is reached wherein enterprises decide to rewrite or redevelop the application into a more modern avatar. Most enterprises go for a green field (from scratch) development to make use of the advancements in terms of hardware and software infrastructure. This also provides them with an opportunity to architect and design the application to ensure that it imbibes the required qualities of service, along with the option of optimizing their existing business processes and introducing new feature functionality as part of the redeveloped application.

Having seen what the legacy is and the need to modernize such platforms, let us see what the challenges are that come in the way of modernization efforts.

Role of a solutions architect in legacy modernization

With legacy modernization programs becoming more prevalent in both large and small enterprises, it is imperative for solutions architects to be aware of the proven strategies that are adopted industry wide for modernizing legacy workloads. Solutions architects are expected to recommend an appropriate modernization strategy, knowing well the structure of the organization they work for and the application landscape that the enterprise is planning to modernize. The solutions architects should also play a key role in anticipating risks involved in executing such programs and should set up necessary guardrails to mitigate the risks, just in case they happen.

The solutions architect also plays a key role in building a business case and socializing it with all stakeholders, including senior management, to procure the required budget for such programs.

Apart from recommending the appropriate modernization strategy and mitigating risks, the solutions architect should take the lead in the discovery phase of such engagements, wherein the requirements from the existing legacy application are culled out and refined. The architect should be aware of the different tools available to extract logic from applications that may be bereft of any functional specification documentation. The solutions architects also play a key role in the design of the new system based on the modernization strategy adopted and the new requirements frozen for the modernized version of the application.

The solutions architect plays an important role in the finalization of the architecture for the application to be modernized and the design required to realize the application. The architect suggests various accelerators, including AI-powered tools, to speed up the build and test phases of the application.

Finally, the architect is also responsible for coming up with the important KPIs, in consultation with the business and technology stakeholders, to measure the success of this modernization engagement and ensure a positive ROI to the enterprise carrying out such engagements.

Challenges to legacy modernization

Though modernization of applications comes with its own benefits, it also has its own challenges that need to be addressed while embarking on this journey or during the journey. If these challenges are not overcome, there is a good chance that the effort may get derailed midway after having spent a considerable amount of money. It is in the best interest of the enterprise to identify all challenges upfront and address them to complete the migration of an application from legacy platforms to the current-day modern platforms.

The following are the challenges that a solutions architect needs to be aware of and address when attempting to migrate legacy applications to modern day technical platforms:

- **Functional complexity**: Most of the applications that fall into the modernization bucket were developed at least a decade ago or even more. In many of these applications, there is no detailed documentation of the functionality, and due to the dynamic nature of the software industry, it is very likely that only a few people, or even fewer, know the overall functionality of the application. Some of the application components could be overly complex with integrations into systems outside of the enterprise.

- **Application criticality**: Applications could be mission critical for the overall running of the business. Hence, it becomes a very difficult decision to start the modernization exercise of these kinds of applications. The feasible way is to form a team of engineers and business analysts who go through the code and document the functionality of the application to the fullest, and get it vetted by the functional experts of the application. Any modernization exercise can only begin after this exercise is completed in a foolproof manner.

- **Interdependencies**: The application to be migrated might have dependencies on other systems within the enterprise. So, an upgrade to the current application might be difficult if the other systems still use older technologies. Though the current application can be overhauled or technically refreshed, all the integration points with the application will continue to use the older versions of the libraries to communicate with the dependent system. Analysis of these dependencies and making an inventory of applications that need to be upgraded, and the sequence also becomes equally important.

- **Software size**: Some of the applications could be massive in terms of the number of components they comprise. All these components could be tightly coupled with each other, which makes it difficult to adopt a phased approach to modernization. This kind of an application requires a lot of analysis and design before such applications are modernized to newer technology platforms.

- **Cost and budget**: Many of the enterprises may not have the required budget to modernize their applications. In medium and smaller enterprises, especially, they may be spending money to change the enterprise initiatives to grow the business. Depending on the nature of the application, with **software as a service (SaaS)** models becoming prevalent, it becomes a lot easier for enterprises to move to such models instead of spending a lot of money to rebuild such applications. However, the recommendations for a modernization strategy have to be arrived at after performing a careful cost-benefit analysis.

Having discussed the challenges on the way to application modernization and how to overcome them, we will now look at the drivers for legacy modernization, which help IT and business stakeholders to build business cases and procure funding from their senior leadership.

Drivers for legacy modernization

Software system continues to depreciate over a period. All applications, even those that are well maintained, will continue to depreciate because of continuous changes being made to both the codebase and the infrastructure platforms. The other major reason is the change in business priorities and goals. Specific business goals that were the drivers for a software system could change in a couple of years, and hence warrant a change to the application that could take a mammoth effort.

The drivers for legacy modernization are summarized in *Figure 7.1* for quick reference:

Figure 7.1: Drivers for modernization

The following are the major reasons that lead enterprises to modernize their legacy applications:

- **Shifted business goals**: All enterprises operate to make profits and want to continuously grow year by year. Each enterprise has its business architecture, representing the set of underlying business processes driving its products and services rolled out to its customers. These products and services are offered to their customers in the form of software applications. These underlying business processes need to undergo a change when the business goals change, and new business targets are set. As a result of this, the underlying software applications supporting these processes are also required to undergo changes. When business processes, which are the underpinning for any business, are getting overhauled, the applications that encompass the business logic (process) become outdated and warrant redevelopment.

- **Skill unavailability**: In the software space, hardware and software platforms undergo very rapid change. Programming languages and software frameworks used to build software systems also continue to change, with more feature rich, easy to understand, and modern languages quickly being adopted by developers. When enterprises start adopting a few of these languages or frameworks, there is a shift in the learning pattern among developers. Most of the development community starts to focus on a few of these newer languages and frameworks due to the demand for them, and the availability of skills for the older ones goes dwindling. For instance, when Spring Boot was introduced, it became a very popular replacement for **Enterprise JavaBeans (EJB)** based applications. Though new applications continue to be developed using Spring Boot in a RESTful way, there are requirements to maintain applications using EJB. However, the supply of skills for such technologies has become far and few.

- **Technology evolution**: Software platforms on which the application is hosted also continue to evolve, and there comes a point where the application either becomes too effort-intensive to maintain on the hosted platform or the application does not lend itself to newer versions of the hardware and software platforms. There are also newer technical paradigms or programming models whose development benefits far outweigh the existing application platform. For instance, Docker changed the way applications are developed and deployed as containers. If the application is a monolith with tightly coupled components, modernization becomes imperative to redevelop the application as microservices and deploy them as containers. The other reason is the vendor of the software platform deciding against making any further updates to the software platform or announcing the end of vendor support for the platform. These situations trigger the modernization effort of such an application within the enterprise.

- **Flexibility of change**: Applications are built to give the flexibility to add more functionality over a period after they move into production. Most of the applications do lend themselves to such an effort, but what happens is that, due to the constant changes made, the applications lose their nimbleness to support the addition of newer components to the overall unit. Solutions architects and developers technically bend these applications to introduce newer components to support the required functionality. However, after a period, the application starts to become frAgile and introduces brittleness in the components, which results in instability of the system in production.

- **Accrued technical debt**: All applications over a period continue to accrue technical debt. Technical debt gets introduced because of the code or design changes made to applications, either as quick fixes or to deliver a feature quickly within a timeline. Though these kinds of changes help to meet the deadlines for the team, many a time, they may be against the accepted patterns and principles of design and coding. These kinds of issues continue to accumulate in the code, and they increase the cost of testing and maintenance in the long term. Technical debts could also arise from incomplete or a lack of understanding of functional requirements when the team started developing the application.

- **Cost of maintenance**: As the application continues to accrue technical debt and becomes inflexible for change, it becomes difficult and expensive to maintain such applications. Due to the code complexities introduced over a period, the application might become unstable and might start to show up as unpredictable functional errors or issues in the agreed service levels for other attributes like performance and security. The enterprise continues to stack up its support team and needs to spend money to perform an excessive amount of testing, even for small changes introduced in the application. In the longer run, it becomes untenable to add changes to the application.

- **Quality of services**: Expectations over the application qualities of service continue to increase over a period after the application goes into production. There could be new security threats which might require a major upgrade to the application or the hosted platform. New laws could be enacted, forcing the application to become legally compliant with a host of changes made throughout the application. This continuous swarm of changes made to the application might introduce side effects affecting important qualities of service like performance and reliability. For instance, new business rules introduced to make the application legally compliant might introduce a performance lag, which becomes difficult to address with the current architecture and design of the application. Apart from this, the user interface world also changes at a rapid pace, which needs to be adopted by applications, failing to do so may leave them behind their competitors in terms of providing a compelling user experience.

Having discussed the drivers of legacy modernization, we will now discuss different strategies that are available for enterprises to modernize their legacy workloads. These strategies adopted depend on factors like the amount of money the enterprise is willing to spend, the skill availability of the enterprise for such programs, and, more importantly, the timeline they are looking for to complete the modernization of business-critical applications.

Modernizing legacy applications consumes time and effort. Not all the applications warrant the same type of transformation, and the approach adopted should be in alignment with the business goals of the enterprise. Few applications would just require movement to a modern-day hardware platform, whereas others might require a total rewrite of the application being modernized.

Legacy modernization strategies

In this section, we will look at the different strategies that enterprises adopt to modernize their legacy workloads. These strategies largely depend on the business goals of the enterprise, budget, and timelines. More importantly, customer experience takes center stage, and the enterprises embark on modernization journeys to make their application fit for purpose and provide their users with a compelling user experience. *Figure 7.2* depicts a summary of the different modernization strategies adopted by modern day enterprises:

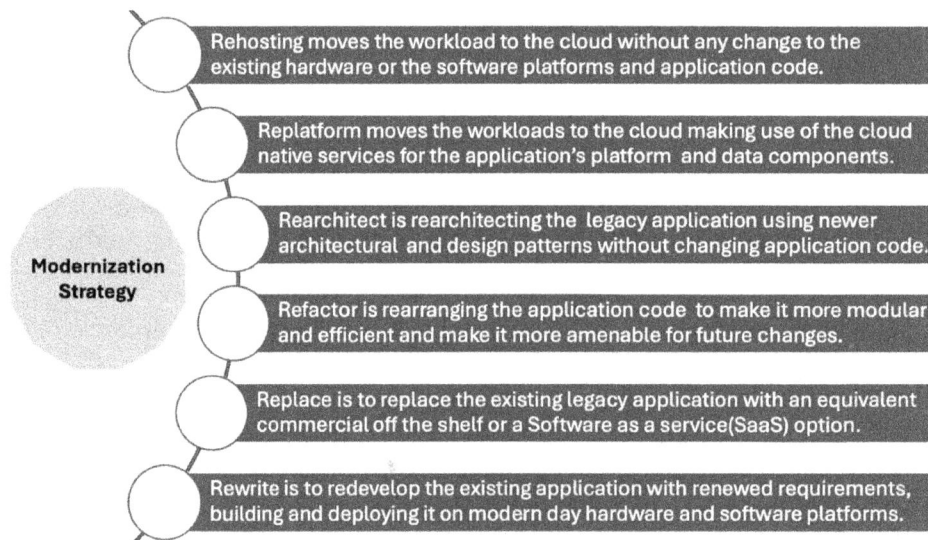

Rehosting moves the workload to the cloud without any change to the existing hardware or the software platforms and application code.

Replatform moves the workloads to the cloud making use of the cloud native services for the application's platform and data components.

Rearchitect is rearchitecting the legacy application using newer architectural and design patterns without changing application code.

Refactor is rearranging the application code to make it more modular and efficient and make it more amenable for future changes.

Replace is to replace the existing legacy application with an equivalent commercial off the shelf or a Software as a service(SaaS) option.

Rewrite is to redevelop the existing application with renewed requirements, building and deploying it on modern day hardware and software platforms.

Figure 7.2: Legacy modernization options

Rehost

Rehosting is also known as lift and shift. In this option, the application is redeployed to newer infrastructure, either on premises or on the cloud, without any changes. This is the simplest of the modernization options available to an enterprise. This can be done to launch services on a larger scale with a scaled-out infrastructure. This option also helps enable an enterprise to introduce improved services to customers within a short timeline. A very quick and easy migration to the newer infrastructure is the advantage of rehosting.

This option works best for enterprises that want to move their workloads to the cloud to benefit from the cost model of pay-as-you-go. The time, effort, and cost in this option are minimal to the enterprise, and there is also no business impact to the enterprise while rehosting applications to a newer environment. Enterprises embarking on a cloud journey choose this option to try out the cloud infrastructure and the associated cost. However, lift and shift is the easier option for the applications that do not have a lot of dependencies. If the application has a lot of moving parts, it takes a lot of effort for validation to ensure that all the parts rehosted work in harmony. Rehosting may not be the right option and will not yield any results if the application already has a lot of technical debt. In such cases, it makes a lot of sense to refactor or rearchitect the application to get any visible benefits of the modernization exercise.

The following are the major benefits of the lift and shift option:

- The lift and shift option helps to scale the infrastructure for the application being modernized.

- This option can also be used to enhance the security posture of the application being migrated to a newer environment.

- This is a good starting point for the enterprises that are embarking on a cloud journey.

- This also helps to save cost in terms of hardware licenses for enterprises while lifting and shifting their workloads to the cloud.

- Rehosting to a cloud provider could provide better capability for backup of the application and application data.

Replatform

Replatform is another key strategy to move applications to enable them to make use of newer versions of the operating systems, software runtimes, and powerful compute engines. This is a slightly expensive and more effort-consuming strategy than its rehosting counterpart. Replatforming can be done for both applications and databases. For applications, this option may require changes to the underlying application code for it to be replatformed. When an application is moving to a newer platform, the dependencies of the applications in terms of the different libraries they use might pose version-related challenges, and they may have to be refreshed to their latest versions before the application is deployed successfully on the newer platform run time. For example, a Java application using JDK 11 could be upgraded to Java 17, but there could be multiple libraries in the application, like parsers and utilities, that may not be compatible with Java 17. The versions of those libraries may have to change to a compatible version, and the application code might have to undergo changes.

For databases, it is about moving the schema and the data to a newer database platform. This is typically done to optimize cost, make use of certain out of the box features like parallelism in query execution, and benefit from better backup options. However, data migration in the replatform option could pose significant challenges in terms of the schema changes. The data types between the legacy source and the target platform should be mapped, and discrepancies in terms of their compatibility must be addressed. This can be done by using modern day schema migration tools that help to overcome such challenges. Another area that needs attention in replatforming databases is the difference in query syntaxes that may have to be resolved. For instance, DB2 and Oracle databases use different query syntaxes. Many legacy applications still do not use **Object Relational Mapping** (**ORM**) frameworks like Hibernate and have their SQL queries embedded in the application code. SQL queries embedded in the application code must also be changed to be compatible with the newer target platform.

When applications are replatformed to the cloud, other than the application code and database changes, there could be other components like batch jobs and integration layers that might also have to be replatformed, and these could have been written using proprietary software. There are chances that these may not be readily supported in the newer platform. The enterprise may decide to rearchitect or rewrite these incompatible components alone. In such situations, it needs to be taken care that they are rewritten in a platform-agnostic way so as not to be tied to a particular cloud provider.

The following are the advantages of the replatform strategy in the modernization of legacy applications:

- The application gets upgraded to the newer operating systems and runtime platforms, making it efficient to use modern day hardware platforms.

- The application also gets migrated to more powerful hardware platforms, which results in better efficiency of the application.

- It provides cost benefits in terms of maintenance of hardware and software platforms, as these are taken care of by the cloud provider in case applications are replatformed to the cloud.

- Replatforming will improve the security posture of the application, making it compliant with newer regulations.

- It improves the quality of services like performance and scalability of the application.

- Databases can make use of parallelism that improves query execution time, making the overall application performant, thereby improving the overall user experience.

- Improves the stability of the application because of improved hardware and software platforms, thereby reducing unplanned downtimes of the application.

- It provides improved backup and restore options than when the application was deployed on a proprietary legacy platform.

Rearchitect

Rearchitecture is a modernization strategy in which the architecture of the application is modified to take complete advantage of modern-day software architectural patterns and design principles. This option is considered by enterprises if their current business critical application is not fit for purpose to meet the increased expectations of both the enterprise management and its customers. Another major reason for rearchitecting an application is its high maintenance cost in production and the challenges related to the continued enhancement of the application with evolving business requirements. With the increasing demand for the quality of services to be on par with its competitors in terms of performance and reliability, this option becomes the right fit to address the required quality of services. Regulatory compliance and security are the next major reasons for enterprises to adopt this option. To improve the security posture and to comply with the laws of the land, it might be infeasible and expensive to redevelop the whole application, and may increase the total cost of ownership.

The rearchitect option provides an opportunity to make use of state-of-the-art hardware and software platforms and make the application distributed for ease of development and management postproduction. The strategy helps enterprises to align their IT systems with their contemporary business goals and accelerates the expansion of their business across multiple regions where they want to establish themselves. Many of the enterprises adopt this approach to reduce the time to market their products and services and make them available to their customers and their internal staff in a timely and usable way.

When the application is rearchitect for the cloud, the enterprise can make use of the out of the box services of the cloud and readily benefit from the scalability and the automation available to expand and shrink the infrastructure as required. Computing power, software run times, databases, and integration services like queues can be configured very easily with hardware infrastructure, and the configuration predominantly rests with the cloud provider. The enterprise can focus its energy on building the required business services. For the architecture, the applications can be rearchitected to make use of the cloud-native architectural patterns like microservices, which provide independent deployability of services and can easily be managed and monitored with contemporary container orchestration tools like Kubernetes. Cloud-native architecture is discussed in detail in *Chapter 22, Cloud-native Architectural and Design.*

The following are the advantages of an enterprise adopting the rearchitect strategy:

- Applications can make use of modern-day architectures like microservices (containerization), event-driven architecture, and design principles like SOLID and 12-factor design.

- Alignment of the IT systems with the changing business goals of the enterprise.

- Leverage automation for repetitive tasks like the provision of hardware, the configuration of software platforms, etc.

- Scale the system in or out based on the changing demands of the business thereby optimizing hardware and reducing the overall cost of ownership.

- Leverage modern day technologies like AI and ML to proactively monitor applications for failure and take appropriate actions.

- Leverage modern day management systems for container orchestration for efficient management of software platforms and available resources.

- Postproduction management in terms of fault isolation and management becomes easier with modularity being adopted for application architectures.

Having seen the option to rearchitect a legacy application, we will now move on to look at the strategy and the benefits of refactoring an existing legacy software system.

Refactor

Refactoring an application involves modification of application code to make it more modular. This option retains the existing functionality of the application and the hardware and software platform on which the current application resides. This option is chosen by enterprises to make the codebase more flexible for changes to future enhancements. This also includes cleanup of the codebase to remove dead or unreachable code, which reduces technical debt and the size of the application to make it accommodating for maintenance. Refactoring of the application also helps to simplify complex pathways in the code and makes it flexible for changes to the application in the future. During the refactoring exercise, developers also identify similar logic across the application and componentize those pieces of code logic so that it can be reused at multiple places within the application, as required.

The following are the advantages of the refactor option when applied to an application that is fit for purpose:

- Makes the application modular, thereby making it easier for maintenance and reducing cost.

- Improves the overall quality of the application by making it more performant and scalable.

- Improves the reusability of the code logic that is used at multiple places within the application.

- The complexity of the application gets addressed, thereby making it more amenable to accommodate future changes to the application.

- Technical debt is greatly reduced, thereby increasing maintainability of the application.

Rebuild

Rebuilding a legacy application involves rewriting the application completely from scratch with renewed requirements as per the current needs of the enterprise. In this approach, the project team can draw a plan to incrementally rebuild parts of the application with both the older and the newer application coexisting before the entire suite of the older components is rebuilt using the newer architecture and technology. This helps to have more control over the schedule and execute a plan in which the components can be prioritized and rebuilt based on the business criticality. This option gives the enterprise an opportunity to adopt modern day architectural and design patterns along with the choice of technology for each of the different layers of the application. Alongside this, this option gives the opportunity to introduce industry standard engineering principles like DevOps, containerization, and observability. In addition to an architectural and technology refresh, the organization can also optimize its business processes and can greatly improve customer delight with their product and services offered.

The following are the advantages of the rebuild option when applied to an application that is not fit for purpose:

- Opportunity to re-engineer business processes within the enterprise for an optimized product and service experience to its customers.

- Adopt state of the art technology to rebuild the modernized applications.

- Helps to future proof applications to become scalable and performant.

- Leverage technologies like AI and ML as part of application feature functionality.

- Adopt modern day user experience design principles to improve the usability of the application thereby improving customer's delight.

- Improved time to market by adopting modern day engineering practices for build, test, and deployment.

Replace

In the replace option of legacy modernization, the software application is replaced with a commercial off the shelf solution or a solution offered on the cloud in SaaS model. This is different from the rebuild option, in which the software application is redeveloped mostly in-house with renewed requirements that are aligned with the business and customer expectations.

In a replace strategy, different choices of platforms offering the required capabilities are evaluated, and the product to use is finally decided. The evaluation also takes into account the types of integration required with other systems in the enterprise. In many cases, the chosen product would require customization to fit the requirements of the enterprise. This customization is undertaken by the product vendors themselves, or the enterprise can employ a service integrator to customize the product to fit the requirements. This option helps the enterprise to quickly move to a more modern platform and retire the legacy application at the earliest. However, the enterprise should be very prudent in analyzing the features of the product and the amount of customization to be done before choosing the product for implementation. There are scenarios in which the product may have to be customized a lot to satisfy very specific requirements. Cost is another factor that plays a major role. Some of the product vendors have a plug and play model wherein the enterprise can choose only the components that are required for them and pay the license cost only for those components. Other product vendors might charge the enterprise the full license cost of the product, irrespective of the features used by the enterprise.

The following are the advantages of the replace strategy for modernizing legacy applications:

- It is easier to replace the application with a commercial off the shelf application than to rebuild the entire application.

- In a component licensing model, the enterprise pays only for the features that it uses rather than paying for the entire product.

- Industry popular products are mostly compliant with the laws of the land that enterprises like financial institutions must comply.

- Replace is an ideal option for medium size enterprises which may not have the necessary skills to rebuild the system.

- This option is an ideal choice for capabilities that are very much required but may not be the core competency of the enterprise to build them. For instance, an e-commerce company might buy a product for processing the payroll of its employees.

Best practices of legacy modernization

The following are the practices that many of the enterprises adopt during their journey of legacy modernization. These industry accepted guidelines help smooth the journey of modernization and also increase the success rate of such engagements. The following is a list of a few such best practices:

- **Conduct a discovery phase**: A discovery phase becomes very important in the path to modernize legacy applications. This phase helps to come up with the right number and size of the business capabilities required in the target modernized application. This also helps to zero in on the right modernization strategy to be adopted.

- **Build a roadmap**: Come up with a roadmap for the entire journey of the legacy modernization exercise. Plan and document each of the steps that are required in the pathway to successfully migrate legacy application to modern day architectures and technologies. At the same time, beware of the challenges and risks on the way and document the appropriate risk mitigation plan to be adopted.

- **Leverage automation**: Legacy modernization exercises deal with understanding existing application documentation, design, code, and database schemas. Make use of automation tools to extract business rules and logic from existing legacy applications. Refer to the section *Artificial intelligence in legacy modernization* for more on how AI can be used.

- **Retire unused applications**: Many enterprises continue to maintain applications that are no longer used by their staff. There is always a disconnect between the maintenance team and the business teams, which results in unused applications continuing to occupy the infrastructure landscape. Enterprises need to take an inventory of applications that are being maintained in production and also take stock of the applications being used by their users. The unused applications can be retired, thereby reducing the total cost of ownership.

- **Embrace Agile**: Break down the entire journey into manageable and measurable tasks and execute each one of them as independently as possible. This approach helps us to measure the effectiveness of the activity completed in the whole journey. Being Agile gives us an opportunity to course correct the direction of the whole journey, just in case certain aspects of the modernization exercise, like choosing a modernization strategy, identification of skills required, etc., need to be fine-tuned.

- **Track with KPIs**: Measuring a process is one of the important prerequisites to continuously improving it. Define key performance indicators to measure the effectiveness of the process being adopted for the legacy modernization exercise. KPIs can be defined and measured for different areas like project management, business process effectiveness, finance, and organizational change.

In this section, we discussed the best practices to get the most out of the legacy modernization engagements. We discussed the importance of building a roadmap for adopting automation and also making use of Agile practices to enable the success of such engagements. In the next section, we will see the role of cloud in the modernization of legacy workloads.

Legacy modernization to cloud

Many organizations follow a cloud first approach for their newer and transformation workloads. It becomes important for the solutions architects to understand how different workloads like applications, data, and processes can be migrated to the cloud. Cloud has an inherent quality of providing virtually infinitely scalable infrastructure, modern software runtimes, and a variety of services out of the box to transform workloads in the most effective way. The cloud also provides enterprises with the right opportunity to migrate their ageing workloads to hardware platforms with superior computing power and storage. Apart from the infrastructure, the cloud also provides the required tools that make the movement of applications to the cloud easier for organizations. Right from the phase of making an inventory of applications for cloud migration and up to the phase of development and deployment on the cloud, each cloud provider has their own set of tools to make modernization engagements a very seamless one.

The cloud also provides different models of computing, like SaaS and serverless computing, that break barriers of having to procure or provision the required infrastructure for applications. Cloud also accommodates with ease different styles of modernization approaches like rehosting, replatforming, or rearchitecting. This gives greater flexibility to enterprises, and they can choose the option that best works for them. The details of the cloud computing model and cloud architecture patterns are covered in detail in *Chapter 22, Cloud-native Architectural and Design*.

The following are the ways in which the cloud enables easier modernization of legacy applications, irrespective of the modernization strategy being chosen by the enterprise:

- **Serverless computing models**: Multiple cloud providers offer serverless computing models in which the infrastructure and software runtime are the responsibility of the cloud provider. Developers just need to deploy their code and run their application on the cloud. This offers an immense benefit to enterprises, especially the medium and smaller ones, to modernize their legacy workloads in the quickest and most efficient manner. AWS Lambda and Azure functions are some examples of serverless computing models. The serverless computing model was discussed in detail in *Chapter 3, Technical Proficiency Essential Knowledge*.

- **SaaS**: Software as a service enables direct consumption of the software application without having to worry about provisioning infrastructure or building applications. In this model, the infrastructure, application platform, and the application service are provided by the service provider. It enables a pay-as-you-use model for the enterprise. This model gives a great advantage for enterprises that quickly want to modernize their legacy workloads without having to worry about infrastructure, software installation, or application builds, and provides an opportunity to roll out their service to their customers. The data is owned by the enterprise, and this model is very useful for startups as well to roll out their minimum viable products in the quickest possible time.

- **Infrastructure migration**: Many of the enterprises move their legacy workloads to a suitable infrastructure on the cloud. This gives them an advantage of cost efficiency and maintenance ease, and provides the first essential step to modernize their workloads in terms of software at a later point in time. Many of the cloud providers like AWS, Azure, and Google Cloud Platform offer a variety of hardware infrastructure that enterprises can choose from and get cost benefits from the differentiated pricing models offered by these cloud providers. For instance, a batch job running in a dedicated hardware on premise can be moved to spot instances on the cloud, thereby decreasing the total cost of ownership of the application to the enterprise. Enterprises also get an advantage to switch hardware depending on the usage of the application at different points in time.

- **Cloud-native architectures**: Cloud-native architecture recommends that applications be divided into manageable chunks of software components called services (microservices), wherein the design is aligned more towards the business operations of the enterprise. These services are then containerized and deployed on container runtimes managed by a container orchestration engine like Kubernetes. These services are independently deployable and can be easily scaled in or out depending on the performance and scalability requirements of the system. Many of the enterprises are currently engaged in moving their legacy workloads to the cloud, adopting cloud-native architecture and design patterns.

- **Replatforming**: The cloud provides immense opportunities to move many of the legacy application components and services to equivalents on the cloud. All the major cloud providers offer hundreds of services in a pay-as-you-go model that can be utilized out of the box with a minimum amount of configuration. This offers a ready-to-use platform to enterprises to easily move their applications to the cloud. Apart from the application related services, the cloud also provides integration services for the application to easily connect with their partner systems outside of the enterprise.

In this section, we looked at why the cloud is a preferred platform for modernizing legacy workloads. However, many enterprises still have most of their core applications running on mainframe systems.

In the next section, we will discuss the approaches for modernizing mainframe applications.

Mainframe modernization

Mainframes continue to be at the core of major enterprises across the globe. Though there had not been any major operational and technical concerns with most of the workloads deployed and run on the mainframe ecosystem, mainframe modernization continues to be one of the most discussed topics in any technology forum. Many of them have been discussing this journey for years.

The following are the major reasons that enterprises are considering moving away from the mainframes:

- With modern-day enterprise applications being built on newer software platforms, agility in terms of integrating them with mainframe applications becomes a challenge, hampering innovation and future growth.

- Refactor code to achieve better control and quality over the application to induce the required functional changes within the application easily.

- Reduce the cost of maintenance of the mainframe hardware that is housed in enterprise data centres.

- Address the unavailability of skills to maintain the hardware and software platforms pertaining to mainframe applications.

- Leverage new hardware, software platforms, and engineering practices to improve the time to market aspect of mainframe applications.

- Improve the availability of applications by leveraging multiple regions and availability zones when such applications are deployed on the cloud.

- Better options for disaster recovery and business continuity for workloads when deployed on the cloud.

Mainframe modernization requires more than technology skills to ensure the success of such modernization engagements. It is not just a change of the mainframe platform to another equivalent on the cloud, but it requires a change in the IT culture of the enterprise. Enterprises have to understand and address challenges and risks to mainframe modernization and address these challenges in the flyway before these programs can be started.

The following are some of the important challenges that enterprises face when modernizing their mainframe applications:

- It is an effort intensive and an expensive exercise to modernize mainframe applications, from organizing a discovery to rewriting the code.

- Some cloud providers offer equivalent mainframe platforms for a lift and shift of those applications from the data centre. However, enterprises need to carefully weigh the options to modernize such applications.

- It requires a consensus among multiple business and technology stakeholders to start the modernization engagement of mainframe applications.

- It requires an expert team to lay down a roadmap of the phases and tasks and take them forward on the path to modernization.

In mainframe modernization, there are three different types of components to be modernized, as follows:

- Application logic written in **Common Business Oriented Language** (**COBOL**) and **Customer Information Control System** (**CICS**) to an equivalent modern programming language.

- User interface developed with technologies like **basic mapping support** (**BMS**) in mainframes should be rewritten to a contemporary UI technology supplemented with client-side frameworks and libraries.

- Moving data residing in DB2 and VSAM files to a relational database system like relational database service on the cloud.

As far as mainframe modernization is concerned, there are two different approaches that are being adopted by enterprises, namely, replatform and rearchitect.

Replatform

Many of the enterprises are looking at options for quickly moving their mainframe workloads to a platform on the cloud. This is a quicker option for the enterprise to retain their applications in their original form, but moving to a more distributed platform on the cloud, where they will get better agility at a reduced maintenance cost. **Million instructions per second** (**MIPS**) is a measure of the performance of the mainframe hardware systems. With an application using hundreds of MIPS to process customer transactions, the licensing cost of the mainframe operating systems and the software platforms goes up substantially. Enterprises want to move such workloads to other platforms on the cloud where they can reduce the cost of hardware and software hosting the applications. Small and medium applications can easily make use of this option, and the risk of rewriting complex code gets greatly reduced. This option of modernization helps enterprises to continue to maintain these applications with their existing workforce.

In the replatform option, the user interface and the business logic remain the same in the target platform. However, data residing on the mainframe database, such as DB2 or VSAM files, gets replatformed to a modern RDBMS platform like Oracle or PostgreSQL. This could warrant a minimum amount of changes to the code base. This option gives a quick return on investment and reduces the overall cost of ownership at the same time. Apart from replatforming the operating system and the database platform, the schedulers and tools of the legacy system will need a replacement in the target cloud platform. For instance, tools required for scheduling and monitoring jobs would need a replacement in the target platform. The platform for running batch jobs would also need to be replaced with an equivalent in the target.

The following table gives an idea of how the current and replatformed target will look for the major components being modernized:

Component type	Legacy platform	Modernized platform
User interface	(Basic mapping support/Green screens)	Basic mapping support/Green screens)
Business logic	COBOL, CICS, JCL	COBOL, CICS, JCL
Database	DB2, VSAM, IMS-DB	RDBMS
Operating system	Z/OS, AS/400	Cloud platform

Table 7.1: Replatforming a mainframe application

Rewrite

In this approach, there is an overhaul of the mainframe application, optionally combined with its movement to the cloud or a new data centre on premises. The application is rewritten using modern day software runtimes, including renewed user interfaces, business logic, data sources, and other systems of integration.

In the case of migration to the cloud, the mainframe application is rearchitected as a cloud-native application to fit into the cloud ecosystem, leveraging the capabilities of the cloud. The feature functionality of the mainframe applications written using COBOL and CICS is rewritten using the latest programming languages like Java or Python. The data sources used by the mainframe applications, like DB2 or VSAM, are migrated to cloud-native databases like Oracle or PostgreSQL. User interfaces developed using BMS are technically rewritten using Angular or React JS JavaScript frameworks.

The legacy applications migrated to the cloud follow a cloud-native architecture in which the business logic is converted into microservices, with each service offering a specific business capability. These microservices are then deployed as containers on the cloud with the application containers overseen by container orchestration engines like Kubernetes.

The following table gives an overview of how the application landscape looks when the legacy application has been rewritten:

Component type	Legacy platform	Modernized platform
User interface	(Basic mapping support/Green screens)	Angular/React JS
Business logic	COBOL, CICS, JCL	Java, Python, C#, NodeJS
Database	DB2, VSAM, IMS-DB	RDBMS
Operating system	Z/OS, AS/400	Linux, Windows, Docker

Table 7.2: Rewriting mainframe applications

The applications that have been modernized on the cloud can continue to integrate with applications in the enterprise data centre and with other third-party systems as before. This rewrite approach brings with it a high availability of the services and products to its customers, with an improved performance of customer transactions. The applications on the cloud communicate with the applications in the enterprise data centre through dedicated communication channels established between the cloud provider's availability zone and the enterprise data centre. For example, for AWS, a Direct Connect link could be used for a secure, fast, and reliable connection between the enterprise data centre and the cloud platform. AI plays a very crucial role in rearchitecting solutions in terms of extracting business logic from the existing application code to generate the target state technology and design artefacts that accelerate the legacy modernization engagements.

In the next section, we will discuss more about how AI is playing the role of an accelerator with regard to the different activities being done as part of the modernization exercise.

Artificial intelligence in legacy modernization

AI and ML are playing a key role in most of the phases of the green field software development lifecycle, and the area of legacy modernization is no exception. In modern day legacy modernization engagements, AI is used across multiple phases of the transformation program from identifying dependencies, business rules extraction from existing applications, analyzing and recommending modernization approaches, data migration, building and testing the modernized version, and reconciling the modernized version of functionality to that of the existing version. In case of applications with huge technical debt, they also help to analyze applications, identify technical debts, and recommend ways to clean them up and refactor them in a more modular way. These applications can be taken up for hosting in a newer environment that has the required hardware and software platform upgrades.

Figure 7.3 depicts the tasks that can intelligently be automated with the use of AI:

01 Modernization Recommendations

Analyze hardware infrastructure and application components to recommend modernization strategy

02 Technical Debt Reduction

Analyze existing code, understand patterns and identify areas contributing to technical debt

03 Dependency Analysis

Analyze dependencies between components in complex applications with no documentation

04 Business Rules Extraction

Parse application code and extract business rules for applications with no documentation

05 Code Generation

Convert legacy application code into modern day programming languages

06 Data Migration

Cleanse the data by identifying inconsistencies and dependencies of huge databases

Figure 7.3: Artificial intelligence in legacy modernization

The following are the tasks in the modernization journey that can hugely benefit from the usage of AI:

- **Modernization recommendations**: AI models can analyze hardware infrastructure and application platforms and recommend the appropriate strategy for modernization, like rehosting or rearchitecting. They help to deep dive into each one of the approaches and provide a cost-benefit analysis of each one of the options. They can also provide valuable information and support decisions on the architecture and design approach to be adopted to make the application modernized.

- **Technical debt identification and resolution**: AI language models can analyze existing code, understand patterns, and identify areas of the application that are overly complex, never visited, and deeply nested. It can also make recommendations to refactor code, enabling the re-use of logic that is being used at multiple points within the application.

- **Analyze dependencies**: AI models can be used to analyze dependencies between components in complex applications. This is especially useful in scenarios where there is no proper documentation of the existing application. Apart from identifying relationships between components, AI-powered code analyzers can pinpoint integrations with external systems and the places in the code where it is used. They can also identify internal dependencies to database systems and message queues, and unearth the integration touch points like APIs and service calls. AI models can also be used for What-If analysis to understand the impact on the application while changing a particular portion of the application.

- **Business rules extraction**: In case of applications written in languages whose skills are in demand, the language models can parse the code and extract business rules within the application. This can be a good starting point for the team to understand the business logic and create the requirements specification that can be used to build the modernized system.

- **Code conversion**: Models, when fed with the existing application code, can help to convert legacy into modern day programming languages. For instance, COBOL programs written decades ago with no subject matter expertise available within the enterprise can be fed to models, and the model can convert them into the required modern-day targets like Python or Java.

- **Data migration**: AI assistants can help cleanse the data by identifying inconsistencies and dependencies of huge databases before migration. It can help in the deduplication of data within databases and help sanitize huge datasets. They also help in creating schema design if they are fed with datasets along with metadata information. AI models can assist in mapping source to target data models and help simplification of the target schema. In microservices, AI models can assist in coming up with a schema for individual microservices if they are given domain specific and business capability related information about the application.

Having discussed the role of artificial intelligence in the transformation of legacy to modern architectures and design, we will now discuss a roadmap that enterprises can adopt and use as a reference for the execution of legacy modernization programs.

Roadmap to legacy modernization

The path to modernizing legacy applications needs to be carefully planned and executed. The discussion includes multiple stakeholders in the business and technology organization of the enterprise. It is one of the decisions that requires a strong business case and stakeholder consensus because the application has been in operation in a different older avatar till then and is getting replaced. Legacy modernization requires a careful analysis of the application landscape, and an informed choice needs to be made between what is necessary versus what can be deferred. Benefits and return on investments need to be discussed, documented, socialized, and approved before embarking on the journey of legacy modernization.

The following figure depicts the steps in the roadmap to modernization in an enterprise:

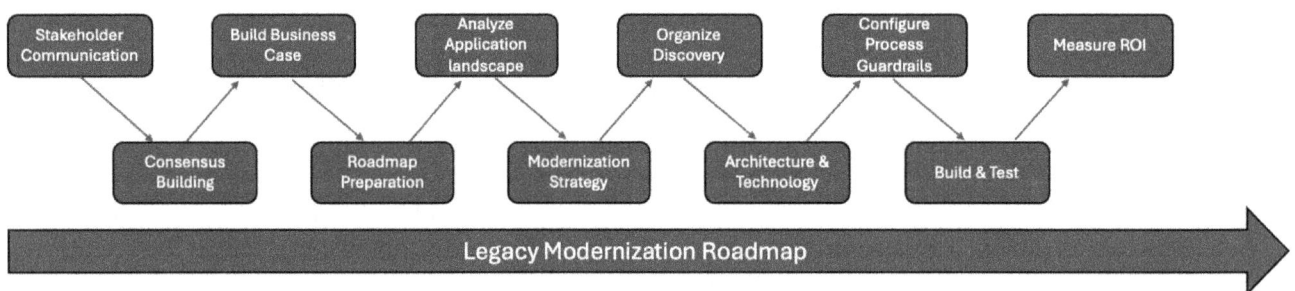

Figure 7.4: *Legacy modernization roadmap*

The following are the key steps that need to be addressed in the journey of legacy modernization:

- **Stakeholder communication**: All the stakeholders need to be identified and informed of the pain points in the existing application. This needs to be documented and socialized with leaders in the business and the technology hierarchy of the enterprise.

- **Build a consensus**: There needs to be consensus among the stakeholders involved in this journey of modernization. It is important to hold workshops with all the groups and associates that will be part of the journey and apprise them of the need to embark on this journey to overhaul the existing application. This helps to get everyone to understand the need for the engagement and garner support from the required parties within the enterprise.

- **Build the business case**: The reasons for the modernization of the application need to be clearly understood and documented. The reasons could be an ageing technology, higher cost of maintenance, or the inflexibility of the application to introduce new changes. This business case will form the basis for getting the required funding and for getting this software engagement moving forward.

- **Prepare a roadmap**: Create a roadmap that will guide the process of modernization. Based on the inventory prepared, prioritize different application components based on their complexity and business criticality. The roadmap should contain the sequence of high-level activities to be performed to embark on and successfully complete the modernization exercise.

- **Analyze existing application landscape**: Create an inventory of application components and it is dependencies. Make a list of hardware infrastructure (server types), software platforms, and application components. Get information related to each one of these from existing documentation, application code, and database schema. These are the candidates to start a discovery phase before the actual process of modernization.

- **Finalize the type of modernization**: Based on the nature of the application, its complexity, and criticality, decide on the type of modernization strategy. If the hosted application platform is nearing the end of support, a replatform strategy could be a suitable option to migrate the application to the latest version of the software platform. For example, a .NET application hosted on .NET framework version nearing end of support could be ported to .NET core latest version.

- **Organize a discovery phase**: This is one of the most important phases in the modernization journey. Based on the information available, like functional documentation, database schema, and application code, prepare the required functional specification for the new system and the technical design. Adopt a well-structured methodology to perform business decomposition of the existing application. For instance, if the enterprises decide to move from a monolith to microservices, DDD could be a good approach to be adopted. You can also use this phase to reengineer some of the business processes and optimize them. This is an optional step, but it presents a good opportunity to optimize existing business processes.

- **Finalize architecture and technology**: Blueprint the target architecture with all the dependencies and integrations explicitly called out. Finalize the versions of the software and the libraries intended for use by the target platform. Discuss with business and technology stakeholders and finalize the nonfunctional requirements that the modernized application needs to address. List the required design patterns to be used in the target and make the technology choices that will be used for the different capabilities required for the modernized application. For example, an existing web application can be modernized as containers and deployed on a Docker runtime.

- **Governance framework**: Create a governance framework for the modernization of engagements. The framework created should contain industry standard best practices, guidelines for modernization, and should align itself with the enterprise architecture governance framework. Based on the framework, configure checkpoints to measure the outcome of each stage of the roadmap by validating the deliverables. For example, ensure there is an API governance process in place to validate the APIs created as part of the modernization journey. Choose the required tools that will help both ease migration to the target and validate the individual components of the migrated application.

- **Build and test**: Construct the application with the choice of technology finalized for each of the layers. Adopt modern engineering principles like DevOps that could help in the early detection of issues before moving the application to the user acceptance test. Create a test strategy not only for testing application feature functionality but for other qualities of service like performance, security, and usability. Create a test strategy to compare the results of the modernized application with those of the old application to ensure that there are no gaps in the design and logic of the modernized version. Create a deployment strategy to perform a **friendly user test** (**FUT**) before the new application is opened up to a larger user base for consumption.

- **Measure return on investment**: Measure the return on investment of the modernization effort by creating reports with data that reflects the level of customer satisfaction. Also, measure the amount of money being spent on the modernized application and the number of tickets being raised by customers every week. At the enterprise level, measure ROI by analyzing customer retention percentage as well as newer customer registrations for the modernized application compared to those of the past periods. Measure the ease of deployment of the modernized application to newer geographies. Conduct a customer satisfaction survey to understand the customer satisfaction levels with regard to the overall quality of service of the newer application version.

Having discussed the roadmap for a legacy modernization program, let us now discuss a checklist that can be used by solutions architects to have checkpoints to ensure a smooth sailing in the journey of legacy modernization.

Checklist for legacy modernization

The following is the easy-to-use checklist for solutions architects and developers embarking on the journey of modernizing their existing IT applications:

- The business drivers have been identified and documented for the legacy modernization engagement.
- All the business and technology stakeholders have been identified and notified of the decision to modernize the legacy platform.
- The business case has been prepared and socialized with identified stakeholders.
- The business case for the legacy modernization program has been approved, and the budget has been allocated.
- Different options of legacy modernization have been evaluated, and an appropriate one chosen.
- A legacy modernization governance framework is in place (aligned to the enterprise architecture governance framework).
- A roadmap to modernize the legacy applications had been drawn and reviewed with the required stakeholders.
- A consensus has arrived with different teams, and buy-in has been received for the modernization journey.
- All applications have been prioritized based on complexity and business criticality.
- Applications of medium complexity, minimum business impact, and a good modernization cost benefit have been chosen for the modernization program (For enterprises embarking on a modernization journey).
- The legacy modernization option (rehost, rearchitect, or rewrite) has been chosen after a due diligence of the existing application platform and its dependencies.
- The target architecture has been blueprinted and approved by technology stakeholders.
- Appropriate technology choices have been finalized for different components of the application, like user interface, business logic, and databases.
- Equivalent tools for monitoring and scheduling are finalized in the target based on the requirements of the application being modernized.
- A plan has been drawn, socialized, and approved for the modernization project of the legacy application.
- The business processes are optimized for efficiency in case the legacy system is being rewritten.
- The application is built and tested based on the plan and SLAs agreed upon.
- Features and capabilities between the source and the target platforms are compared, and necessary changes are made to the system to become compatible with the target platform.

- The modernized system is tested for functionality and results compared with the legacy system for functional accuracy.

- The modernized system is tested for qualities of service like performance, security, and reliability.

- Modernized system is moved to production with suitable observability tools configured for continuous monitoring and improvement of the system.

- The ROI of the modernization program is measured using KPIs like customer retention percentage, new customer registrations, reduction in application downtimes, improved performance, and security postures.

Conclusion

In this chapter, we looked at different aspects of legacy application modernization. Legacy modernization is one of the areas that a lot of enterprises are paying attention to and are spending millions of dollars. It is important for solutions architects and developers to understand the legacy modernization strategies that are commonly used. They also need to be conversant with how AI can play a key role in the modernization of applications in the current day world. They also need to be aware of the benefits of moving enterprise workloads to the cloud using cloud-native architectures. The knowledge of these areas helps the solutions architect to add value to the enterprise along the way of their growth journey.

In the next chapter, we will discuss the topic of DevOps, one of the important ingredients to developing modern-day software applications for enterprises.

Key takeaways

The takeaways are as follows:

- **Legacy**: Learn what a legacy application is and why enterprises are spending millions of dollars in transforming legacy applications to modern day technology platforms, both on premise and the cloud.

- **Challenges to legacy modernization**: Learn about the different challenges that dampen the modernization of legacy applications to modern day architectures and technologies. Learn how business complexity, software size, cost, and budget pose different challenges to the modernization exercise.

- **Drivers to legacy modernization**: Learn the different drivers that speed up legacy modernization programs in an enterprise. Learn how shifting business goals, skills unavailability, and the evolution of technology play an important role in promoting the acceleration of modernization engagements.

- **Legacy modernization strategies**: Learn different strategies like rehost, replatform, rearchitect, refactor, replace, and rebuild for modernizing legacy applications. Learn the applicability of each of these strategies and the challenges with each of these options. Learn the advantages of each one of these options, as well.

- **Legacy modernization to the cloud**: Understand the different strategies like cloud-native architectures, SaaS model, serverless computing, and cloud platform services that enable modernization of legacy applications on the cloud.

- **Mainframe modernization**: Understand the challenges in the modernization of mainframe systems. Learn about the replatform and the rewrite options available for modernizing mainframe applications. Learn the different types of components that need to be migrated to a modern platform.

- **Road map to legacy modernization**: Learn how to systematically approach and execute a legacy modernization engagement. Learn the importance of organizing a discovery phase when choosing the modernization strategy, depending on the workloads to be modernized.

- **AI in legacy modernization**: Understand how AI is disrupting the legacy modernization space from extracting business rules from existing applications to generating design artefacts and code. They also aid in creating the required artefacts for testing and deployment.

- **Checklist for modernization**: Use a checklist to make sure that there are no gaps in ensuring a smooth legacy modernization journey. Solutions architects can use checkpoints to conduct reviews of legacy modernization programs.

Model interview questions and answers

1. **As a solutions architect, what is a legacy system in your opinion?**

    Model answer:

    - A software application that is not fit for the purpose of meeting the demands of its users or does not help the enterprise to meet its business goals.

    - The application that cannot support modern-day software platforms or hardware advancements.

    - A software application in which it is hard and expensive to make any architectural and design changes, and difficult to test and maintain.

    - An application that no longer meets the quality of services expected by the customers, like performance, reliability, and security.

    - A software that is not modular, and any code changes made manifest themselves as unpredictable errors during usage.

2. **What are the major challenges to migrating legacy systems?**

    Model answer:

    - **Functional complexity**: Most of the applications that fall in the modernization bucket are functionally complex and were developed at least a decade ago.

    - **Application criticality**: Applications could be mission critical for the overall running of the business. Hence, it becomes a very difficult decision to start the modernization exercise of these kinds of applications.

    - **Interdependencies**: The application to be migrated might have dependencies on other systems within the enterprise. So, an upgrade to the current application might be difficult.

    - **Software size**: Some of the applications could be massive in terms of the number of components they comprise. All these components could be tightly coupled with each other, making it difficult to adopt a phased approach to modernization.

    - **Cost and budget**: Many of the enterprises may not have the required budget to modernize their applications.

3. **What are the major strategies available to migrate legacy systems?**

    Model answer:

    - **Rehost**: A strategy in which the application is moved to a different environment with the same software and hardware platforms without any changes to the application. This applies more to migrating applications to the cloud with the same software and hardware environment.

    - **Replatform**: In this option, the operating system, software, or hardware platform is upgraded. For instance, a MySQL database in an on-premises application can be replatformed to use the Oracle relational database service on the cloud.

    - **Rearchitect**: In this option, the application is overhauled in terms of the architecture and the design. This is an option to entirely rearchitect the system to make it more distributed and efficient, making use of modern-day distributed architectures.

- **Refactor**: In this strategy, the application is refactored and made more modular without changing the application code. This makes the application performant and easy to maintain. This also reduces the cost of future changes, testing and maintenance.

- **Replace**: This option is to replace an application that is not fit for purpose with an option that offers features out of the box, like a commercial off the shelf or a SaaS solution.

- **Rebuild**: This option is to entirely rewrite the application using newer architectural patterns, design principles, and technology frameworks.

4. **What is the difference between rehosting and replatforming of a legacy application?**

Model answer:

- Rehosting is moving the application to the cloud without changing the software platform, architecture, or the application code.

- Rehosting is leveraged more in terms of moving workloads to the cloud as an initial step, after which the application can be refactored or rearchitected to improve the quality of the application's services.

- Rehosting helps enterprises to make use of the cloud in case the on-premises hardware license is very expensive or the usage is coming to an end.

- In the replatform option, the application is moved to the cloud, and it makes use of the out of the box platforms and services on the cloud. For instance, an application using an Oracle database on premise can be moved to the Amazon cloud to leverage the relational database service.

- Replatform helps the enterprise to adopt a pay-as-you-go model for the required services and not worry about the software or hardware licenses of those services on the cloud.

5. **How can artificial intelligence help in legacy migration?**

Model answer:

- AI has disrupted the area of legacy modernization, just like green field software development and testing of software.

- AI helps to extract business logic and rules from legacy applications for which no documentation is available.

- **Large language models (LLMs)** help to convert legacy code directly to modern-day programming languages. For example, LLMs can convert COBOL code directly to Java or Python.

- AI can analyze legacy applications and identify technical debt, along with recommendations to remove or reduce the technical debt.

- AI can also recommend the right strategy for modernization, like rearchitect, refactor, or rebuild, thereby helping organizations to review their decisions.

6. **As a solutions architect, how will you measure the effectiveness of a legacy migration project?**

Model answer:

- You will devise customer KPIs like customer retention ratio, new customers added, and new product registrations that will help to measure customer satisfaction levels.

- For the enterprise, we can measure the total cost of ownership and time to market before and after the migration of the legacy workloads.

- We can monitor the quality of services like performance improvement, improvement of security posture, and the usability of the application before and after migration to tangibly measure the efficiency added.

7. **What is the role of cloud with respect to legacy modernization?**

   Model answer:

   - Cloud-native architecture recommends splitting legacy applications as services (microservices) that are independently deployable.

   - Legacy applications can be migrated to better hardware infrastructure on the cloud as a starting point for rearchitecting legacy software platforms to the cloud.

   - Replatforming applications to cloud is done to make use of native cloud services by enterprises. This relieves enterprises of their responsibility to maintain those services and leverage the cost benefits associated with a pay-as-you-go model.

   - SaaS model offered by the cloud benefits enterprises to make use of applications offered readily on the cloud providers. In this model, only the data is owned by the enterprise, with the application and the hardware owned by the cloud provider.

   - In the serverless compute model, the enterprise can move their code to the cloud and execute it without provisioning any hardware or software platforms. Services like AWS Lambda and Azure functions are examples of serverless models offered by cloud providers.

8. **As a solutions architect, what is the roadmap you will propose for legacy modernization engagements?**

   Model answer:

   - Stakeholder communication and building a consensus are important steps in modernization exercises, as these are not just technology programs but an organizational change management that requires a buy-in from everyone involved.

   - Build the business case to get the required budget from the executive management and prepare a roadmap detailing all the steps to be performed to ensure completion and success of the modernization exercise embarked upon.

   - Analyze the existing application landscape and finalize the type of modernization that is suitable for the workload being moved. For instance, if an organization must quickly modernize a business-critical application within a short period of time, replacing it with a commercial off the shelf product will be the best option than a rebuild or a rearchitect option.

   - Organizing a discovery phase is very crucial to plan for the business logic and rules consolidation and finalization of modernization strategy, application architecture, and design.

   - Build and test the application as per the modernization strategy and architecture finalized.

   - Measure the return on investment by devising appropriate key performance indicators related to both operational and non-operational aspects of the system.

9. **As a solutions architect, what are the options available to modernize mainframe applications?**

   Model answer:

   - Replatform option in which enterprises want to move mainframe workloads to other platforms on the cloud, using which they can reduce the cost of hardware and software platforms hosting the applications.

   - Rewrite is another option available to modernize mainframe applications in which the application is rearchitected using cloud-native architecture patterns. Applications are split into components using methodologies like Domain-Driven Design, developed as containers, and deployed on cloud platforms managed by container orchestration platforms like Kubernetes.

CHAPTER 8
DevOps Essentials

Introduction

In today's technology landscape, DevOps has become an essential approach for building, deploying, and maintaining complex systems at scale. For solutions architects, understanding DevOps goes beyond just knowing tools and pipelines; it involves the ability to design resilient, automated, and scalable solutions that integrate seamlessly with development and operations workflows. As organizations increasingly adopt cloud-native architectures, DevOps has evolved into a core competency for delivering software that meets high standards of reliability, security, and agility.

This chapter focuses on providing solutions architects with the DevOps knowledge and skills necessary to succeed in real-world projects and to excel in technical interviews. Understanding CI/CD pipelines, **infrastructure as code** (**IaC**), monitoring and logging, security integration (DevSecOps), and automated testing are critical areas that are frequently assessed during interviews for this role.

Throughout this chapter, we will break down the essential components of a DevOps strategy from a solutions architect's perspective. This includes strategies for building secure pipelines, automating deployments, and ensuring that systems are designed for continuous integration and delivery. You will learn how to align DevOps practices with architecture design, how to respond to common interview scenarios, and how to address critical topics such as scalability, reliability, and security.

Structure

This chapter covers the following topics:

- DevOps culture and practices
- Platform engineering
- Implementing IaC with DevOps
- Continuous integration and continuous deployment
- Monitoring and logging
- AIOps

- FinOps in DevOps
- Security in DevOps
- QA and testing

Objectives

By the end of this chapter, readers will have a comprehensive understanding of the core principles and culture of DevOps, emphasizing its importance in modern, cloud-native software development. They will gain the practical knowledge to design and implement **continuous integration and continuous deployment (CI/CD)** pipelines, along with the ability to define and manage infrastructure using IaC tools like Terraform.

Readers will also learn how to enhance system reliability through effective monitoring, logging, and observability practices, utilizing tools. The chapter will get into advanced topics, including the integration of DevSecOps for embedding security at every stage of the pipeline and FinOps for managing cloud costs efficiently.

Moreover, the chapter will introduce cutting-edge concepts like **artificial intelligence for IT operations (AIOps)** for automating operational tasks and predicting system anomalies. It will also highlight the critical role of QA and testing within DevOps, providing strategies for continuous testing and quality assurance. By the end, readers will be well-prepared to design robust, secure, and cost-efficient DevOps solutions that deliver high-quality software at scale.

DevOps culture and practices

As a solutions architect, it is crucial to not only understand the technical aspects of DevOps but also to internalize its cultural principles. The role of a solutions architect often involves aligning technical solutions with business objectives, and DevOps bridges the gap between development and operations by emphasizing collaboration, automation, and continuous improvement. This section will cover what DevOps means in practice, how to adopt a DevOps mindset, and why mastering DevOps is a critical competency for solutions architects.

During interviews, solutions architects are often assessed on their ability to design end-to-end solutions that encompass the full software delivery lifecycle. It is not just about knowing tools and technology stacks but also demonstrating how these tools can be orchestrated to create a cohesive strategy that drives business value. When discussing DevOps in an interview, it is essential to present it as more than just a methodology; it is a cultural shift that fosters collaboration, innovation, and continuous delivery.

DevOps

DevOps is a set of practices and cultural philosophies aimed at integrating software **development (Dev)** and IT **operations (Ops)** teams. It focuses on automating processes, improving collaboration, and enabling continuous delivery and deployment. The goal is to shorten the development lifecycle and provide high-quality software in a consistent and repeatable manner.

DevOps principles

Understanding and implementing DevOps principles is a crucial part of a solutions architect's role. These principles guide the architect in designing systems that are efficient, reliable, and aligned with business goals.

Figure 8.1 provides a summary view of DevOps principles:

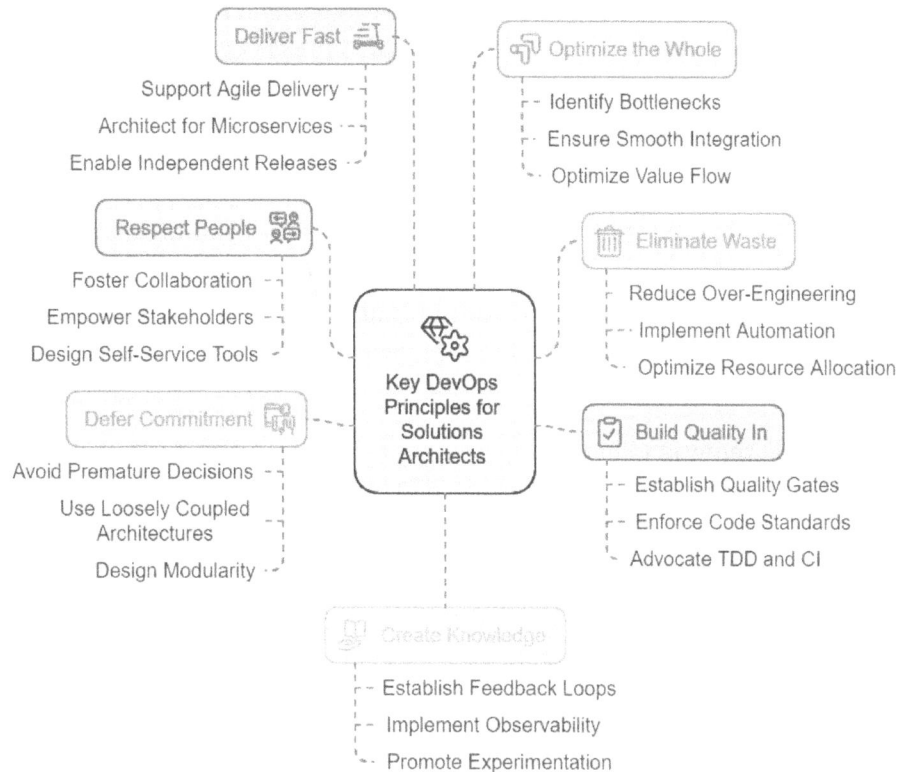

Figure 8.1: DevOps principles

The following is a concise overview of each key DevOps principle and its relevance for solutions architects:

- **Respect people**:
  - Respecting people and collaboration are at the core of DevOps. Solutions architects must foster a culture that values cross-functional teamwork and empowers all stakeholders.
  - Design self-service and automation tools to reduce friction between development, operations, and QA, enabling teams to work independently and improve productivity.

- **Eliminate waste**:
  - Reducing unnecessary work, such as over-engineering and redundant processes, ensures that solutions are lean and focused on business outcomes.
  - Implement automation for repetitive tasks, optimize resource allocation, and remove features or steps that do not directly add value.

- **Build quality in**:
  - Quality is everyone's responsibility. Solutions architects need to embed quality checks throughout the architecture to ensure robust and secure systems.
  - Establish quality gates in CI/CD pipelines, enforce code quality standards, and advocate **Test-Driven Development (TDD)** and continuous integration practices.

- **Defer commitment**:
  - Avoid premature architectural decisions. This principle encourages designing with flexibility to incorporate changes as requirements evolve.
  - Use loosely coupled architectures and modular designs, allowing components to be easily updated or replaced without impacting the entire system.

- **Deliver fast**:
  - Rapid delivery of new features and capabilities is essential for maintaining a competitive edge. Solutions architects need to design systems that support Agile delivery models.
  - Architect for microservices and modular deployments, enabling independent feature releases and minimizing the impact on other components.

- **Optimize the whole**:
  - Focusing on the efficiency of individual components can lead to suboptimal outcomes for the overall system. Solutions architects must adopt a holistic approach to optimization.
  - Use systems thinking to identify and address bottlenecks in the entire software delivery pipeline, ensuring smooth integration and value flow across all stages.

- **Create knowledge**:
  - Continuous learning is vital for improvement. Solutions architects should establish feedback loops and knowledge-sharing mechanisms to improve processes.
  - Implement observability and monitoring, document learnings, and promote a culture of experimentation and retrospectives to drive ongoing improvements.

By adhering to these key DevOps principles, solutions architects can design systems that not only meet technical requirements but also align with organizational goals, improve team collaboration, and support continuous innovation.

Need for DevOps

Solutions architects are responsible for ensuring that the solutions they design are not only aligned with business goals but also maintainable, scalable, and secure. DevOps provides the framework to implement and manage these attributes effectively. It also ensures that solutions architects can design systems that support agility, flexibility, and reliability, which are essential for modern software applications.

DevOps lays the foundation for efficient collaboration between development and operations teams by emphasizing automation, continuous integration, and delivery. However, as organizations scale, the complexity of managing infrastructure and environments increases. This is where **platform engineering** comes into play, building on DevOps principles to provide standardized, self-service platforms that abstract away the intricacies of underlying systems.

In the next section, we will explore how platform engineering enhances DevOps practices by enabling developers to focus on delivering value while operations teams manage a consistent and secure platform. This shift ensures streamlined workflows and accelerates the deployment process, further driving agility and efficiency in software development.

Platform engineering

While DevOps focuses on breaking down silos between development and operations, platform engineering takes this a step further by providing a standardized, self-service platform for developers. This ensures a consistent and streamlined experience, allowing teams to focus on delivering value rather than managing infrastructure complexities.

Platform engineering focuses on building internal developer platforms to streamline DevOps practices. These platforms abstract the complexity of underlying infrastructure, providing developers with self-service capabilities for deploying applications, managing environments, and accessing CI/CD pipelines.

Benefits of platform engineering

The following are a few benefits of platform engineering:

- **Enhanced developer productivity**: Developers can focus on building applications rather than managing infrastructure.

- **Standardization**: Ensures consistent practices across teams.

- **Accelerated delivery**: Reduces time to market by offering pre-configured environments.

While platform engineering streamlines the development process by providing standardized environments and self-service capabilities, IaC takes it a step further by codifying the infrastructure setup. This ensures that the environments provisioned through platform engineering are consistent, scalable, and easily replicable across multiple stages of the software lifecycle. Let us explore in the upcoming section how IaC enables this through automation and code-driven infrastructure management.

Implementing IaC with DevOps

IaC is a key practice for solutions architects, enabling them to define, provision, and manage infrastructure using machine-readable files. This approach provides a systematic way to build and maintain cloud infrastructure, ensuring consistency, scalability, and automation. In this section, we will get into how solutions architects can leverage IaC using tools like Terraform and other industry leading IaC tools to automate infrastructure management.

This section will focus on the strategic application of IaC, outlining the strengths of each tool, best practices, and how to incorporate IaC into CI/CD pipelines for automated deployments.

IaC and its relevance

IaC involves managing and provisioning infrastructure using code-based configurations. This approach helps solutions architects enforce repeatability, modularity, and automation in deploying infrastructure.

The following are the key benefits of IaC:

- **Consistency across environments**: Avoid configuration drift by ensuring that every environment is defined by the same code.

- **Scalability and automation**: Automatically scale resources and manage configurations for complex deployments.

- **Reduced human error**: Automate complex configurations to prevent manual errors.

- **Version control**: Track changes, rollback to previous states, and audit infrastructure configurations.

Comparison of tools

As a solutions architect, choosing the right IaC tool is crucial for creating scalable, repeatable, and consistent cloud environments. Each tool has its strengths and is suited for specific use cases depending on the cloud strategy, technology stack, and team familiarity. In this comparison, we will look at popular IaC tools such as Terraform, Pulumi, and the native solutions provided by hyperscalers, AWS CloudFormation, **Azure Resource Manager** (**ARM**) templates, and Google Cloud Deployment Manager.

The following table provides a comparative analysis of popular IaC tools, helping architects select the best fit for their specific project requirements:

Criteria	Terraform	Pulumi	CloudFormation	ARM templates	Google Cloud Deployment Manager
Language	**HashiCorp Configuration Language (HCL)**	Modern programming languages (Python, TypeScript, Go, C#)	JSON, YAML	JSON	YAML, Jinja
Multi-cloud support	Yes	Yes	No	No	No
Ease of adoption	Easy to learn with HCL language	Steeper learning curve for non-developers	Moderate learning curve for AWS beginners	Easy for Azure developers	Moderate learning curve for GCP users
State management	External state file stored locally or in remote backend (S3, Azure Blob)	Automatic state management, integrated with native cloud backends	Managed by AWS	No separate state file, state managed natively	No separate state file
Modularity and reusability	High (modules, reusable components)	High Leverages programming constructs like loops and functions)	Medium (nested stacks, StackSets)	Limited to linked templates	Limited (YAML templating support)
Language flexibility	Limited to HCL	High (Multiple languages supported)	Limited to JSON or YAML	Limited to JSON	Limited to YAML
CI/CD integration	Strong integration with Jenkins, GitHub Actions, Azure Pipelines	Strong integration with most CI/CD tools	Supported with AWS CodePipeline and Jenkins	Supported with Azure DevOps	Supported with GCP Cloud Build
Security and compliance	Sentinel policy as code, Checkov, Terrascan	Policy as code **Open Policy Agent (OPA)**, Checkov	AWS config rules, AWS CloudFormation Guard	Azure policy	Google Cloud Config
Community and ecosystem	Large community, well-documented modules	Growing community, extensive documentation	Strong AWS community support	Strong Azure support community	Limited community support
Configuration style	Declarative	Imperative and declarative	Declarative	Declarative	Declarative
Support for policy as code	Yes (sentinel, Open Policy Agent)	Yes (Open Policy Agent, Pulumi CrossGuard)	Yes (AWS Config, AWS CloudFormation Guard)	Yes (Azure Policy)	Yes (Google Cloud Policy Intelligence)
Best for	Multi-cloud, hybrid deployments	Multi-cloud with programming language flexibility	AWS-specific large-scale deployments	Azure-specific environments	GCP-specific environments

Table 8.1: Comparative analysis of IaC tools

Each IaC tool has its own strengths, limitations, and ideal usage scenarios depending on the project needs, cloud strategy, and team expertise. Based on the comparative analysis provided in *Table 8.1*, the following recommendations can help solutions architects determine which tool is most appropriate for specific use cases:

- Terraform is ideal for multi-cloud and hybrid deployments. It provides strong state management, modularity, and a large provider ecosystem. Use it when flexibility across cloud providers is a priority.

- Pulumi is best suited for teams familiar with modern programming languages like Python or TypeScript. It is particularly useful if you want to apply familiar language constructs (loops, conditionals) to infrastructure management.

- AWS Cloud Formation is the go-to choice for large-scale AWS-specific deployments. It integrates deeply with AWS services and offers strong governance through StackSets.

- ARM Templates are preferred for Azure-only environments. It is easy to adopt for Azure developers and integrates well with Azure Policy for compliance management.

- Google Cloud Deployment manager is suitable for GCP-centric projects. It supports YAML and Jinja templating but has a steeper learning curve compared to other tools.

Best practices for solutions architects

When designing IaC, solutions architects should follow best practices to ensure maintainability, scalability, and security as follows:

- **Use modules for reusability**: Create reusable components for networking, security groups, and other common resources.

- **Implement version control**: Use Git or Azure Repos for versioning, branching, and peer review.

- **Secure sensitive information**: Store secrets in tools like HashiCorp Vault or Hyperscaler based solutions like Azure Key Vault or AWS Secrets Manager.

- **Parameterize templates**: Use parameters to configure templates for different environments (dev, test, prod).

- **Apply policy as code**: Use tools like Terraform Sentinel or Azure Policy to enforce security and compliance.

Integrating IaC into CI/CD pipelines

Automating infrastructure deployments is a critical responsibility of solutions architects. Integrating IaC into CI/CD pipelines ensures that infrastructure is deployed consistently and verified before going live.

The following is the step-by-step implementation:

- **Author IaC code**: Write infrastructure code using Terraform or other IaC tools like ARM templates.

- **Version control**: Store the code in a repository like GitHub or Azure Repos.

- **CI/CD pipeline setup**: Define build and release pipelines in Azure pipelines or Jenkins.

- **Pre-deployment checks**: Implement linting, security scans, and unit tests.

- **Automate environment provisioning**: Deploy resources to test, staging, and production environments using pipeline stages.

- **Post-deployment validation**: Use Azure Monitor to validate the health and performance of the deployed infrastructure.

IaC tools for infrastructure security and compliance

Infrastructure security is a priority when using IaC. Solutions architects should be familiar with tools and techniques to secure IaC templates and maintain compliance.

The following table provides a list of security tools and example use cases to consider:

Security tool	Purpose	Example use case
Checkov	IaC security scanning	Detect misconfigurations in Terraform, CloudFormation, and ARM
Terraform sentinel	Policy as code for security and compliance	Enforce security policies during Terraform plan and apply
Azure policy	Enforce organizational standards in Azure	Ensure that only specific VM sizes can be deployed in production
ARM template test tool kit (TTK)	Testing ARM templates for security compliance	Validate templates against best practices
AWS Config Rules	Track resource compliance in AWS environments	Check for public S3 buckets or unrestricted security groups
OPA	General-purpose policy enforcement for IaC	Apply fine-grained access controls to Kubernetes and Terraform

Table 8.2: Tools for infrastructure security

While IaC focuses on defining and managing infrastructure in a repeatable, automated manner, its true power is unlocked when integrated into CI/CD pipelines. By incorporating IaC into CI/CD, organizations can automate the provisioning, configuration, and deployment of infrastructure alongside application code, ensuring consistency across environments.

In the next section, we will take a loot at the CI/CD process, highlighting how IaC plays a pivotal role in streamlining deployments, minimizing human intervention, and maintaining system reliability throughout the software delivery lifecycle.

Continuous integration and continuous deployment

CI/CD is a set of practices designed to enable faster, safer, and more reliable software delivery. For solutions architects, CI/CD is more than just a technical implementation; it is a strategy to streamline development, testing, and deployment processes. A well-designed CI/CD pipeline ensures that code changes are integrated, validated, and deployed seamlessly across various environments with minimal manual intervention. This section talks about how solutions architects can leverage CI/CD to architect resilient systems, optimize release cycles, and maintain high availability and security.

A typical CI/CD pipeline, as represented in *Figure 8.2*, consists of several stages that automate the process from code commit to deployment, incorporating checks and balances to ensure high-quality software delivery:

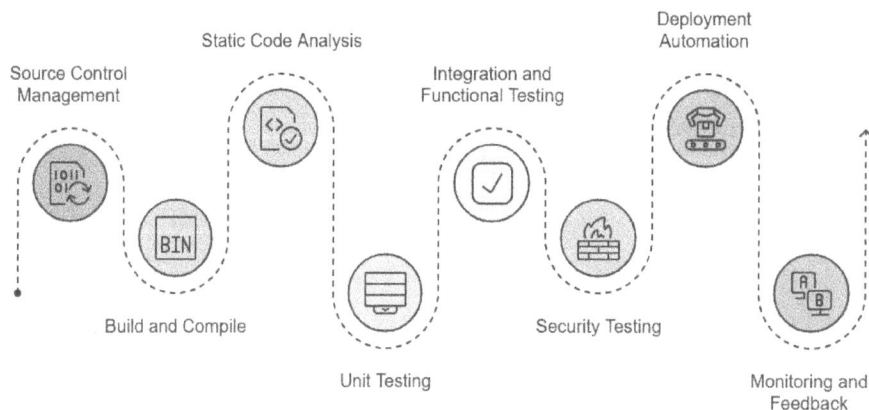

Figure 8.2: End to End CI/CD pipeline stages

The following is a breakdown of each component of the pipeline and shows how a solutions architect should approach designing each stage, in a table:

Stages in CI/CD pipeline	Purpose	Key tools
Source control management	Solutions architects should ensure that all code, configuration, and infrastructure scripts are version-controlled. Implement branch strategies, for example, feature branches, development, staging, and production branches, to maintain code integrity and facilitate smooth collaboration.	GitHub, GitLab, Bitbucket, Azure Repos.
Build and compile	The build stage compiles the code, resolves dependencies, and packages it for deployment. As an architect, ensure the pipeline is designed to support incremental builds and parallelization to reduce build time.	Jenkins, Azure Pipelines, GitLab CI/CD, GitHub Actions, CircleCI.
Static code analysis	Use static code analysis to catch bugs, code smells, and security vulnerabilities early. Incorporate automated tools in your pipeline to enforce coding standards, maintain code quality, and ensure compliance with security guidelines.	SonarQube, Mend, Checkmarx, Snyk.
Unit testing	Unit tests are executed to validate the functionality of individual components. As an architect, emphasize high code coverage and ensure that tests are modular and independent. Unit testing should be quick to provide fast feedback to developers.	JUnit, NUnit, pytest, Mocha.
Integration and functional testing	Integration testing validates that various modules work together as expected. For complex architectures, consider using test automation frameworks to handle API, UI, and system testing.	Selenium, Postman, Cypress.
Security testing	Security is a critical aspect of CI/CD pipelines. Automate security testing using tools that perform vulnerability scans, secret management, and penetration testing.	Veracode, Qualys, OWASP ZAP, Aqua Security, Blackduck.
Deployment automation	Automate deployment processes using scripts or dedicated deployment tools. Choose deployment strategies like blue-green or canary deployments to minimize downtime and ensure safe releases.	Spinnaker, Octopus Deploy, Azure DevOps.
Monitoring and feedback	Implement monitoring at every stage to capture metrics like build failures, deployment success rates, and performance KPIs. Use dashboards to visualize pipeline health and set up alerts for failures or anomalies.	Dynatrace, Elastic Stack, Prometheus, Grafana, Azure Monitor.

Table 8.3: CI/CD pipeline stages

Consider an example of a CI/CD pipeline using Azure DevOps. Azure DevOps is a powerful platform that provides end-to-end DevOps capabilities, making it an ideal choice for implementing CI/CD pipelines.

The following are the steps to set up a CI/CD pipeline for a web application using Azure DevOps:

1. **Set up Azure Repos**:
   - Store your application's source code in Azure Repos.
   - Define branching strategies such as feature, development, and main branches to organize your source code and control the flow of changes.

2. **Create a build Pipeline**:
   - Use Azure Pipelines to define the build process using a YAML file. For example:
     ```
     trigger:
       branches:
     ```

```
            include:
              - main
        pool:
          vmImage: 'ubuntu-latest'
        steps:
          - script: npm install
            displayName: 'Install Dependencies'
          - script: npm run build
            displayName: 'Build the Application'
```

- Add tasks for static code analysis using SonarQube and security scans using OWASP ZAP.

3. **Automate testing**:

   - Integrate unit and integration testing into the pipeline. Use Azure Test Plans to manage test cases and track test results.

   - Configure automated test scripts to run after the build stage completes successfully.

4. **Implement deployment pipeline**:

   - Use Azure Pipelines for deployment. Set up multiple stages for different environments, for example, dev, QA, prod.

   - Implement blue-green deployment to minimize downtime:

```
        jobs:
          - deployment: DeployApp
            environment: 'production'
            strategy:
              blueGreen:
                swapStrategy: 'auto'
                blue:
                  steps:
                    - script: echo 'Deploying to blue environment...'
                green:
                  steps:
                    - script: echo 'Swapping to green environment...'
```

5. **Monitoring and alerting**:

   - Implement Azure Monitor and Log Analytics to capture deployment metrics and set up alerts for any anomalies.

   - Use Application Insights to track performance and monitor end-user experience.

Comparison of CI/CD tools

Selecting the right CI/CD tool is critical for effective pipeline design. The following is a comparison grid of popular CI/CD tools based on features, scalability, and ideal use cases:

Tool	Key features	Ideal use case	Scalability	Integration capabilities
Azure DevOps	End-to-end DevOps, integration with Azure Services	Best for Azure-centric environments	High	Seamless with Azure, GitHub, and other tools
Jenkins	Highly extensible with plugins, customizable pipelines	Suitable for complex, large-scale CI/ CD needs	High	Wide range of integrations
GitLab CI/ CD	Integrated with GitLab, CI/CD, security, and monitoring	Best for teams using GitLab for source control	Medium	GitHub, Docker, Kubernetes
GitHub Actions	Native CI/CD within GitHub, supports event-driven workflows, and easy setup	Ideal for GitHub based repositories	High	Integrates with AWS, Azure, GCP, and Docker
Hyperscaler native tools	Native CI/CD services (AWS CodePipelines, Azure Pipelines, Google Cloud Build)	Best for cloud-native and hybrid cloud environments	Very high	Seamless integration with respective cloud ecosystems

Table 8.4: CI/CD tools comparison

The following are the key architectural considerations for designing CI/CD pipelines:

- **Separation of environments**: Maintain separate pipelines for development, staging, and production environments. Each environment should be isolated to prevent issues in one environment from affecting others.

- **Automated rollback strategies**: Implement automated rollback strategies in the event of a failed deployment. For example, use Azure DevOps to define conditions that trigger rollback to a previous stable version if certain KPIs, for example, CPU usage or response time) are breached.

- **Design for scalability**: Design pipelines that can handle high volumes of changes and builds. Consider using cloud-native services like AWS Code Pipeline or Azure Pipelines that automatically scale based on the workload.

- **Security integration**: Incorporate security testing, for example, SAST, DAST, at various stages of the pipeline. Implement tools like Snyk or Aqua Security to scan container images and IaC templates for vulnerabilities.

- **Implementing feature flags**: Use feature flags to control the release of new features. This allows you to enable or disable features dynamically without redeploying the application.

- **Disaster recovery (DR) and rollback strategies**: Disaster recovery and rollback strategies are critical for maintaining business continuity and minimizing downtime. In a DevOps context, these strategies must be automated to ensure rapid recovery and prevent manual errors.

    o **Rollback strategies**:

        ▪ **Blue-green deployments**: Maintain two identical environments (blue for production and green for testing). In case of failure, traffic can quickly switch back to the blue environment.

        ▪ **Canary releases**: Gradually release changes to a subset of users. If an issue arises, revert to the previous stable version.

        ▪ **Automated rollbacks**: Integrate rollback mechanisms in CI/CD pipelines using tools like Spinnaker or Azure Pipelines.

    o **DR**:

        ▪ **Data backup and restore**: Implement automated backups of critical data and configurations using cloud-native tools like Azure Backup or AWS Backup.

- **Chaos engineering**: Test DR mechanisms by simulating failures using tools like Gremlin or Chaos Monkey.

- **Geographically distributed deployments**: Deploy applications across multiple regions to ensure failover in case of a regional outage.

By incorporating these best practices and tools, solutions architects can ensure that their CI/CD pipelines are not only efficient and scalable but also secure and aligned with the organization's business objectives. Proper implementation of CI/CD enables faster delivery cycles, improved code quality, and a more streamlined development process that reduces risks and boosts productivity across teams.

While CI/CD pipelines automate the process of building, testing, and deploying applications, they often rely on scripts and configurations managed independently of the source control system. This is where GitOps steps in, enhancing the CI/CD approach by treating Git as the single source of truth for both application and infrastructure configurations.

In the following section, we will explore how GitOps builds on CI/CD principles to ensure version-controlled, auditable, and automated deployments.

GitOps

Building on the principles of IaC and CI/CD, modern DevOps practices are increasingly leveraging GitOps for managing application and infrastructure configurations. This approach ensures a streamlined, automated, and version-controlled pipeline, enabling rapid and reliable deployments across environments.

GitOps is an advanced CI/CD practice that uses Git as the single source of truth for both infrastructure and application configurations. By leveraging Git repositories, GitOps ensures that every change in the system is version-controlled and auditable. Tools like ArgoCD and FluxCD automate the process of syncing the desired state stored in Git with the actual state in the environment.

The following are the key benefits of GitOps:

- **Version control**: Every infrastructure change is recorded, providing a clear audit trail.

- **Automated rollbacks**: Reverting to a previous state is as simple as rolling back to a previous Git commit.

- **Consistency**: Ensures that environments remain consistent and free from configuration drift.

Common DevOps anti-patterns

While best practices in DevOps enable efficient, secure, and scalable pipelines, understanding common anti-patterns is equally important for solutions architects. Anti-patterns represent poor practices or design flaws that hinder the effectiveness of DevOps processes. Identifying and avoiding these pitfalls is critical to ensuring smooth operations and achieving the desired outcomes.

The following are the key DevOps anti-patterns:

- **Lack of automated testing**:
  - **Observation**: Relying solely on manual testing can lead to inconsistent results, longer feedback loops, and increased risk of introducing bugs into production.
  - **Impact**: Slower release cycles and reduced software quality.
  - **Solution**: Implement automated unit, integration, and regression tests as part of the CI/CD pipeline to ensure rapid and reliable feedback.

- **Hardcoding configurations**:
  - ○ **Observation**: Embedding environment-specific configurations directly into code or scripts leads to inflexibility and security risks.
  - ○ **Impact**: Difficulties in scaling or migrating applications, increased risk of exposing sensitive information.
  - ○ **Solution**: Use environment variables or configuration management tools like Vault, AWS Parameter Store, or Azure App Configuration to manage configurations securely and dynamically.

- **Over-reliance on manual approvals in CI/CD**:
  - ○ **Observation**: Requiring excessive manual approvals for every stage of the pipeline can bottleneck the deployment process.
  - ○ **Impact**: Delayed releases and reduced agility, defeating the purpose of CI/CD.
  - ○ **Solution**: Automate approvals for non-critical environments and implement policy as code solutions for enforcing compliance in production environments. Use tools like Azure Pipelines, GitHub Actions, or Spinnaker to streamline approvals based on pre-defined rules.

By recognizing and addressing these anti-patterns, solutions architects can ensure that their DevOps pipelines remain efficient, scalable, and secure, fostering a culture of continuous improvement.

Hybrid and multi-cloud DevOps

In today's enterprise IT landscape, leveraging hybrid and multi-cloud environments has become a strategic necessity for achieving flexibility, scalability, and resilience. However, managing DevOps practices across such diverse infrastructures introduces unique challenges that require specialized strategies and tools.

To bridge the gap between challenges and strategies, it is essential to recognize that overcoming these hurdles requires a combination of cloud-agnostic tools, standardized practices, and a robust architectural approach. In the following sub-section, we explore specific strategies to address the complexities of hybrid and multi-cloud DevOps.

Challenges and strategies

In modern enterprises, hybrid and multi-cloud environments are becoming the norm. These environments combine on-premises infrastructure with multiple cloud platforms (AWS, Azure, GCP). While this offers flexibility and resilience, it introduces complexities in managing CI/CD pipelines, consistent configurations, and security policies across diverse environments.

Solutions architects must navigate several hurdles when designing DevOps practices for hybrid and multi-cloud setups, some of which are mentioned as follows:

- **Inconsistent tooling**: Different cloud providers have varying CI/CD tools and processes, leading to operational silos.
- **Cross-cloud security**: Ensuring secure communication and consistent IAM policies across clouds.
- **Complex state management**: Managing infrastructure state in a distributed, multi-cloud environment.

To overcome these challenges and ensure efficiency, scalability, and security across platforms, consider the following approaches:

- **Use cloud-agnostic tools**: Tools like Spinnaker for multi-cloud CI/CD orchestration and Terraform for IaC ensure consistent deployments across providers.
- **Centralized logging and monitoring**: Employ tools like ELK Stack, Prometheus, or Datadog for unified observability.

- **Service meshes**: Use Istio or Linkerd to standardize service discovery, security, and communication across hybrid environments.

Monitoring and logging

Effective monitoring and logging are foundational for maintaining the performance, reliability, and security of software solutions. However, achieving observability, which is the ability to infer the internal state of a system from its outputs, requires integrating monitoring, logging, and tracing. As a solutions architect, your goal is to embed observability into every layer of the application and infrastructure stack. This ensures that issues are not only detected early but also understood and resolved swiftly. Observability empowers teams to continuously optimize system behavior, drive innovation, and enhance system uptime.

Observability is built on three key pillars, as follows:

- **Metrics**: Quantifiable data points (e.g., CPU usage, request latency).

- **Logs**: Detailed records of system events.

- **Traces**: Distributed tracing to track the flow of requests across services.

OpenTelemetry is a vendor-neutral framework for collecting, processing, and exporting telemetry data across different observability tools, ensuring a standardized approach.

Monitoring covers a wide spectrum of components and activities, including application performance, infrastructure health, network traffic, database usage, and security events. A robust monitoring and logging strategy will enable proactive issue detection, capacity planning, and compliance auditing.

Solutions architects should ensure that the following areas are monitored and logged:

- **Application performance**: Response times, request rates, error rates, and transaction latencies.

- **Infrastructure health**: CPU usage, memory usage, disk I/O, and network traffic for VMs, containers, and serverless components.

- **Database metrics**: Query performance, connection pool utilization, and read/write latencies.

- **Security events**: User authentication attempts, permission changes, and API access patterns.

- **Network traffic**: Throughput, packet loss, latency, and firewall activity.

- **Custom business metrics**: User engagement, purchase transactions, and feature usage patterns.

- **CI/CD pipeline health**: Build statuses, deployment times, and integration failures.

The following are the key considerations for solutions architects:

- **Define a comprehensive monitoring strategy**: Identify the key metrics and logs that are critical for the business and technical requirements of your application. Establish SLOs for performance, reliability, and security.

- **Implement centralized logging**: Use centralized logging solutions to aggregate and analyze logs from different sources. This ensures that logs are easily searchable and correlated across the entire application stack.

- **Enable distributed tracing**: For microservices-based architectures, enable distributed tracing to track requests across multiple services and identify bottlenecks.

- **Design alerts and dashboards**: Create alerting rules with appropriate thresholds for each metric. Use dynamic dashboards to visualize system health and present insights to stakeholders. ·

- **Automate monitoring as part of CI/CD pipelines**: Integrate monitoring configurations and alert setups as part of your CI/CD pipeline to ensure consistency across environments.

The following are the tools for monitoring and logging:

Category	Tools	Description
Application monitoring	Azure Monitor, Dynatrace, New Relic, AppDynamics	Monitor application performance, request rates, and latency. Track dependencies and bottlenecks.
Infrastructure monitoring	Prometheus, Datadog, Nagios, CloudWatch (AWS), Stackdriver (GCP)	Monitor VMs, containers, and serverless components for CPU, memory, and network usage.
Centralized logging	ELK Stack (Elasticsearch, Logstash, Kibana), Splunk, Azure Log Analytics, Fluentd, Google Cloud Logging	Aggregate logs from various sources and perform in-depth log analysis using powerful search queries.
Distributed tracing	Jaeger, Zipkin, OpenTelemetry, AWS X-Ray, Azure Application Insights	Trace requests across microservices to identify bottlenecks and visualize service dependencies.
Database monitoring	Azure SQL Analytics, Datadog DBM, New Relic	Monitor query performance, connection pools, and read/write latencies for relational and NoSQL databases.
Network monitoring	Wireshark, Nagios, SolarWinds, ThousandEyes	Monitor network traffic, latency, packet loss, and firewall activities.
Security monitoring	Azure Security Center, Qualys, Snyk, Splunk	Monitor and audit security events, track vulnerabilities, and ensure compliance with security policies.

Table 8.5: Monitoring tools comparison

The following are the ways for designing a monitoring and logging strategy as a solutions architect:

- **Start with a requirements assessment**: Identify the key metrics and logs for performance, security, and business insights.

- **Establish a data strategy**: Define data retention policies, log rotation schedules, and access controls for logs and metrics.

- **Implement across environments**: Ensure consistent monitoring and logging across development, testing, and production environments.

- **Use the right tools**: Choose tools based on integration requirements, scalability, and the specific needs of your application stack.

- **Design proactive alerts**: Set up alerting mechanisms to notify relevant teams before minor issues escalate into critical problems.

- **Review and optimize regularly**: Continuously refine the monitoring strategy based on feedback, changing business requirements, and new tool capabilities.

By adopting a comprehensive monitoring and logging approach, solutions architects can ensure that systems remain reliable, scalable, and secure while also enabling deep visibility into all layers of the technology stack.

While traditional monitoring tools provide visibility into system performance, the complexity of modern applications requires a more intelligent approach. This is where AIOps steps in, leveraging machine learning to predict issues, automate responses, and enhance operational efficiency. Let us examine how AIOps transforms IT operations by offering predictive and automated solutions to manage large-scale environments.

AIOps

As systems grow more complex, traditional monitoring and manual intervention are no longer sufficient to manage operational challenges. This is where AIOps comes into play. By applying AI and machine learning,

AIOps enhances DevOps by proactively identifying, predicting, and resolving issues, ensuring smoother operations and higher system reliability.

AIOps leverages machine learning and data analytics to enhance DevOps practices. By analysing vast amounts of operational data, AIOps can predict and prevent potential system failures before they occur.

The following are the key roles of AIOps in DevOps:

- **Predictive analysis**: Identify patterns and anomalies to foresee issues.

- **Incident management**: Automate root cause analysis and suggest fixes.

- **Resource optimization**: Optimize infrastructure usage based on predictive workloads.

Popular AIOps tools include Dynatrace, Splunk AIOps, and New Relic AI.

As AIOps focuses on optimizing system performance and reliability, another critical area for optimization is cloud spending. FinOps addresses this by ensuring cost efficiency while maintaining operational effectiveness. By integrating financial management practices into DevOps workflows, organizations can gain visibility into cloud expenditures and implement strategies for cost control. Let us look at how FinOps can help achieve financial accountability in cloud environments.

FinOps in DevOps

FinOps (cloud financial management) is an emerging discipline aimed at optimizing cloud spending without compromising performance. As DevOps accelerates deployments, managing costs effectively becomes a shared responsibility.

FinOps introduces a structured approach to cloud cost management, focusing on the following principles:

- **Cost visibility**: Track real-time costs associated with cloud resources across environments.

- **Budgets and alerts**: Set cost thresholds and receive alerts when nearing budget limits.

- **Optimization practices**: Identify underutilized resources, optimize instance sizes, and leverage savings plans or reserved instances.

The following are the FinOps tools:

Effective FinOps relies on leveraging the right tools to monitor, analyze, and optimize cloud costs. These tools provide visibility, enforce budget controls, and offer actionable insights to align financial management with DevOps practices.

- **AWS Cost Explorer** , **Azure Cost Management** , **Google Cloud Billing**: For real-time cost analysis and forecasting.

- **Kubecost**: Optimize Kubernetes-based workloads.

- **CloudHealth by VMware**: Multi-cloud cost optimization and governance.

While cost optimization and operational efficiency are crucial, security remains a cornerstone of any robust DevOps strategy. DevSecOps emphasizes the integration of security practices throughout the CI/CD pipeline, ensuring that systems are not only efficient but also secure and compliant. In the next section, we will explore how security can be seamlessly embedded into DevOps workflows.

Security in DevOps

As software delivery cycles continue to shorten, integrating security into every stage of the development lifecycle is no longer optional, it is a necessity. This is where DevSecOps comes into play. DevSecOps extends the DevOps philosophy by embedding security practices and considerations into the CI/CD pipeline. For solutions architects, the challenge is not just to design scalable and performant architectures but also to ensure that every component is secure and resistant to vulnerabilities.

During a solutions architect interview, you will likely encounter questions that test your understanding of DevSecOps principles, how you integrate security in various phases of the development lifecycle, and your approach to balancing security with speed and agility. This section aims to equip you with the knowledge to respond to such questions confidently and to demonstrate your ability to build secure, compliant pipelines that meet organizational and regulatory standards.

DevSecOps

DevSecOps is the practice of incorporating security principles, tools, and processes throughout the software development lifecycle, from coding to production deployment. Unlike traditional security practices, which are often applied as a final step, DevSecOps ensures that security is built into every stage of development, making it an integral part of the CI/CD pipeline. This proactive approach minimizes vulnerabilities and enhances the overall security posture of the application.

Solutions architects need to prioritize security for the following reasons:

For solutions architects, security is a non-negotiable design principle. During the interview, you may be asked how you will approach security considerations when designing architectures. Strong answers will cover topics such as secure coding practices, IAM policy enforcement, and compliance management. You should emphasize your understanding of security as a shared responsibility and your role in creating secure, compliant, and resilient architectures.

Static code analysis, dynamic analysis, and vulnerability scanning

Integrating security into CI/CD pipelines involves the use of tools and practices that continuously test code for vulnerabilities and enforce security standards before deployment. Solutions architects should be familiar with how to design these pipelines to include security gates, ensuring that insecure code is detected and remediated early in the lifecycle.

The following table outlines key security stages, their purposes, and the tools that can be used to enhance security throughout the software development lifecycle:

Security stage	Purpose	Tools	Example use case
Static code analysis	Analyzes the source code for potential vulnerabilities without executing the program.	SonarQube, Mend, Snyk, Checkmarx.	Checking for SQL injection vulnerabilities or insecure coding patterns in Java or .NET applications.
Dynamic analysis	Tests the running application in a runtime environment.	Veracode, Qualys, OWASP ZAP, Burp Suite	Identifying issues like **cross-site scripting** (**XSS**) or SQL injection that manifest only when the application is executed.
Vulnerability scanning	Scans code, containers, and infrastructure for known vulnerabilities	Aqua Security, Anchore, Twistlock	Scanning Docker images to ensure they do not include outdated libraries with known security flaws.

Table 8.6: Security scanning in CI/CD pipelines

Prepare to discuss scenarios where you have used these tools and how you would implement them in a CI/CD pipeline, ensuring that security testing does not delay deployments unnecessarily.

The following are the industry leading tools (there are many other tools available) for securing pipelines:

- SonarQube
- Veracode
- Aqua security

DevSecOps relies on a diverse set of tools that integrate directly into CI/CD pipelines to automate security testing. Solutions architects need to be well-versed in these tools, understanding their strengths, limitations, and where they fit into the development workflow.

The following are some commonly used tools:

Static code analysis	SonarQube, Mend, Snyk, Checkmarx, Fortify.
Dynamic application security testing (DAST)	OWASP ZAP, Burp Suite.
Vulnerability scanning	Veracode, Aqua Security, Qualys.
Secrets management	HashiCorp Vault, AWS Secrets Manager, Azure Key Vault.

Table 8.7: DevSecOps tools

IAM, policies, and compliance

Identity and access management (IAM) is the backbone of security in any architecture. For DevSecOps, IAM policies should be enforced for every pipeline stage to restrict access to sensitive operations. Solutions architects must design IAM policies that align with the principle of least privilege and implement RBAC to limit permissions based on the user's role.

Let us consider an example. In Azure DevOps, ensure that each build agent only has permissions to access the resources it needs, and use service principals for deployments rather than personal accounts.

Let us look at the ways for managing compliance like **General Data Protection Regulation** (GDPR) and **Health Insurance Portability and Accountability Act** (HIPAA) in DevOps pipelines. Security in DevOps is not just about protecting the application; it is also about ensuring compliance with industry regulations. Solutions architects should be able to design pipelines that enforce compliance requirements, such as encryption, data masking, and access logging, to meet standards like GDPR and HIPAA.

Designing a secure DevOps pipeline is a multi-step process that starts from code development and ends with deployment and production monitoring. Solutions architects should use the following best practices:

- **Shift left security**: Move security testing earlier in the development lifecycle.
- **Secure coding practices**: Implement OWASP recommendations for secure coding.
- **Container security**: Ensure containers are built from secure base images and scanned for vulnerabilities.

The following are the steps for implementing DevSecOps in an Azure CI/CD pipeline:

1. **Set up a CI/CD pipeline**: Use Azure Pipelines to automate builds, tests, and deployments.
2. **Integrate static code analysis**: Add a SonarQube task to the pipeline for static code analysis.
3. **Implement secrets management**: Use Azure Key Vault to securely store and retrieve secrets during the build and deployment stages.
4. **Enable vulnerability scanning**: Use Aqua Security to scan Docker images for vulnerabilities before deploying to **Azure Kubernetes Service** (AKS).
5. **Monitor and enforce compliance**: Use Azure Security Center to monitor compliance and generate alerts for any deviations from predefined policies.

Security compliance automation

In highly regulated industries such as finance, healthcare, and government, ensuring that infrastructure and application configurations comply with industry standards is not just a best practice; it is a mandate. Manual compliance checks can be time-consuming and prone to human error, which is where security compliance automation becomes essential. Automating compliance enables organizations to continuously enforce security and governance policies across all stages of the software delivery lifecycle, reducing risks and ensuring adherence to regulatory requirements.

Solutions architects must be familiar with various tools that facilitate automated compliance in DevOps pipelines. These policy enforcement tools help enforce policies as code, ensuring that security and compliance requirements are embedded into every stage of development and deployment. The tools are as follows:

- **HashiCorp Sentinel**: Sentinel is a policy as code framework that integrates seamlessly with Terraform. It allows organizations to define and enforce policies during the IaC deployment phase.

  For example, prevent the deployment of unencrypted storage or ensure that only specific VM sizes are used in production environments.

- **OPA**: OPA is a general-purpose policy engine that works with Kubernetes, Terraform, and CI/CD pipelines. It enables the enforcement of fine-grained policies, such as access control, resource quotas, and data encryption.

  For example, restrict public access to Kubernetes services or enforce mandatory encryption of data at rest.

- **Azure Policy and AWS Config**: These native cloud tools continuously monitor and enforce compliance within their respective ecosystems. They ensure that resources meet organizational policies and regulatory requirements.

  For example, Azure Policy can prevent the deployment of non-compliant resources, such as VMs without approved images, while AWS Config tracks resource changes and alerts on non-compliance with predefined rules.

Let us consider a use case example. In a healthcare application, compliance with HIPAA regulations is critical. By integrating OPA within the Kubernetes ecosystem, you can automate the enforcement of data encryption and logging policies. For instance:

- **Data encryption**: OPA ensures that all sensitive data stored in persistent volumes is encrypted.
- **Audit logging**: It mandates that logs capturing user activity and system events are retained for the required period, helping meet HIPAA audit requirements.

Automating these compliance tasks reduces the manual effort needed for audits and ensures that systems remain compliant, even as they evolve.

This structured approach ensures that you are able to articulate how security is woven into the fabric of the pipeline, making it easier to showcase your ability to design robust, secure solutions during the interview.

A secure pipeline sets the stage for delivering high-quality software, but ensuring this quality requires rigorous testing at every stage of the development lifecycle. **Quality assurance** (**QA**) and testing play a pivotal role in maintaining the reliability, performance, and functionality of applications. Let us dive into how automated testing strategies can be integrated into DevOps pipelines to guarantee continuous delivery of high-quality software.

QA and testing

In a DevOps environment, QA is not an isolated phase but an integral part of the entire software delivery lifecycle. For a solutions architect, it is imperative to ensure that testing practices are embedded at every stage of the CI/CD pipeline. This approach shifts the traditional concept of quality assurance from a final checkpoint to a continuous activity that runs in parallel with development, ensuring defects are identified and resolved early in the process.

Solutions architects are not just responsible for selecting the appropriate tools but also for designing systems that support robust automated testing, seamless QA integration, and alignment with business goals. This section will help you understand how to architect QA in DevOps pipelines, choose the right tools, and implement strategies to maintain high standards of software quality throughout the development process.

QA essential for solutions architects

The ability to build quality into software from the ground up is critical to the success of any DevOps initiative. As a solutions architect, your designs should enable rapid feedback loops, continuous testing, and easy integration of testing into automated pipelines. This ensures that the end product is not only delivered quickly but also meets the required quality and performance standards. In interviews, showing a deep understanding of QA integration in DevOps reflects your ability to design resilient pipelines and deliver scalable, high-quality software solutions.

QA practices in DevOps

Solutions architects must champion the following testing practices to ensure that quality is a built-in attribute of the system:

- **Automated testing**: Automated testing should be the backbone of a DevOps testing strategy. By automating unit, integration, and functional tests, teams can speed up the feedback loop, detect bugs early, and reduce manual testing efforts. As a solutions architect, you should design CI/CD pipelines to automatically trigger these tests upon every code change, ensuring that defects are caught as soon as possible.

- **Regression testing**: Regression testing is crucial in a continuous deployment environment where code changes are frequent. Implement automated regression tests to verify that new changes do not adversely affect existing functionality. This is vital for maintaining system stability and ensuring business continuity.

- **Exploratory testing**: While automation covers most of the testing needs, exploratory testing is essential for complex workflows and edge cases that are hard to capture through automation. Solutions architects should ensure that the system supports manual exploratory testing without impacting automated pipelines.

- **Performance and load testing**: Performance testing ensures that the application can handle the expected load and performs well under stress. Incorporating performance testing as part of the CI/CD pipeline helps identify bottlenecks and resolve them before going live.

- **Security testing**: With the rise of DevSecOps, integrating security testing into the pipeline is critical. Use automated tools for static code analysis, dependency scanning, and runtime security checks to identify vulnerabilities as early as possible.

Tools for testing in a DevOps environment

Selecting the right tools is key to implementing an effective QA strategy in DevOps. The following is a list of recommended tools based on the type of testing needed:

Testing type	Recommended tools	Purpose
Unit testing	Junit, NUnit, PyTest	Validate individual units of code. It is based on the technology stack. Junit for Java, NUnit for .NET, PyTest for Python
API testing	Postman, SoapUI	Verify API responses and behaviour
UI testing	Selenium, AccelQ	Automate Browser interactions for UI validation

Testing type	Recommended tools	Purpose
Performance testing	JMeter, LoadRunner	Simulate load and stress scenarios
Security testing	OWASP ZAP, Veracode, Checkmarx	Scan for vulnerabilities and compliance issues
Test management	Azure Test Plans	Manage test cases, executions, defects, and reports
BDD testing	Cucumber, SpecFlow	Behavior driven testing to cover the testing based on user stories

Table 8.8: Testing tools for DevOps

For a practical implementation of QA in DevOps, consider the following example of an Azure DevOps pipeline:

- **Code commit**: Developers commit code changes, triggering the pipeline.
- **Build**: The pipeline builds the application, and static code analysis (e.g., SonarQube) is performed.
- **Unit testing**: Automated unit tests validate the integrity of the code.
- **Integration testing**: The code is deployed to a test environment, and integration tests are run using Postman.
- **Security testing**: OWASP ZAP scans the application for security vulnerabilities.
- **Performance testing**: JMeter is used to simulate load and stress-test the system.
- **Manual QA**: Azure Test Plans executes manual test cases for complex workflows.
- **Approval gate**: Stakeholders review test results and approve the deployment to production.

Architectural considerations for QA in DevOps

A solutions architect needs to design architectures that are not only scalable and performant but also testable.

The following architectural considerations can help achieve this goal:

- **Design for testability**: Modular components that can be tested independently are a cornerstone of a testable architecture. Solutions architects should design systems with clearly defined modules, each with specific responsibilities and well-defined interfaces, enabling the use of stubs and mocks to isolate components for effective testing.

- **Parallel testing**: Support parallel test execution by architecting the system to dynamically provision environments using containerization (e.g., Docker) or cloud services for example, Azure DevTest Labs. Parallel testing helps reduce the overall testing time and speeds up the feedback loop.

- **Feature flags and toggle management**: Feature flags allow teams to safely test new features in production by toggling them on or off. This enables continuous testing without risking the stability of the live environment. Solutions architects should design pipelines that leverage feature flags for safe rollouts and A/B testing.

- **Test data management**: Managing test data is crucial for stable and repeatable test results. Ensure that test data is isolated, versioned, and refreshed regularly. Use IaC tools like Terraform or ARM templates to automate test environment provisioning.

- **Continuous feedback**: Build monitoring and alerting mechanisms into the architecture to provide continuous feedback to development teams. This includes setting up dashboards for real-time visibility into test results and system performance.

The following are the best practices for QA in DevOps:

- **Shift left testing**: Begin testing as early as possible in the development cycle to catch defects when they are cheaper to fix.

- **Embed quality in every stage**: Make quality a shared responsibility of developers, testers, and operations teams.

- **Use CI/CD pipelines effectively**: Automate as much as possible and ensure that pipelines are optimized for fast feedback.

- **Promote a culture of continuous improvement**: Learn from defects and incidents to continually enhance the quality strategy.

- **Test data management**: Automate the creation, refresh, and teardown of test data across environments to ensure consistent and reliable test results.

As a solutions architect, your focus should be on architecting systems that facilitate seamless QA integration, enable automated testing at every stage, and support a culture of continuous testing and delivery. By doing so, you not only ensure the delivery of high-quality software but also enhance the agility and resilience of your development teams.

Conclusion

DevOps has become an indispensable discipline in modern software development, particularly for solutions architects tasked with designing scalable, secure, and high-performing systems. This chapter emphasized that DevOps is more than a collection of tools; it is a culture and mindset that drives collaboration, automation, continuous delivery, and rapid feedback. For a solutions architect, embedding DevOps practices into architectural thinking ensures that solutions are not only technically sound but also operationally resilient and adaptable to change.

We explored core DevOps principles, platform engineering, IaC, and the full CI/CD lifecycle, including security (DevSecOps), monitoring, testing, cost management (FinOps), and emerging practices like GitOps and AIOps. We also addressed how architects can extend DevOps into hybrid and multi-cloud environments while maintaining governance, compliance, and performance visibility across distributed systems.

By mastering DevOps strategies, tools, and patterns, solutions architects can significantly reduce lead time, improve release quality, ensure system reliability, and align technology delivery with business objectives. These capabilities not only prepare you for interviews but also empower you to lead transformation initiatives in enterprise environments.

As you apply DevOps principles to streamline delivery, the next critical focus area is ensuring performance and scalability in real-world deployments. In the upcoming *Chapter 9, Performance and Scalability*, we will explore how architects can design systems that handle increasing workloads, maintain responsiveness, and deliver consistent user experiences, an essential competency in today's cloud-native, user-driven digital landscape.

Key takeaways

The takeaways are as follows:

- **DevOps is a cultural and technical shift** that promotes collaboration between development and operations teams, driving faster, more reliable software delivery.

- **Platform engineering standardizes environments** and empowers developers with self-service capabilities, improving developer productivity and deployment velocity.

- **IaC** ensures consistent, repeatable, and automated infrastructure management, with tools like Terraform, Pulumi, and ARM Templates enabling version-controlled deployments.

- **CI/CD pipelines streamline software delivery**, integrating automated testing, static code analysis, security scans, and deployment strategies like blue-green and canary releases.

- **GitOps extends CI/CD** by using Git as the single source of truth, enabling version-controlled and declarative infrastructure and application delivery.

- **Monitoring, logging, and observability** are essential for proactive system health checks and root cause analysis, with tools like Azure Monitor, Prometheus, and ELK Stack providing deep visibility.

- **AIOps enhances operations with intelligence**, using machine learning to predict issues and automate responses, improving performance and uptime.

- **FinOps integrates financial accountability into DevOps**, helping manage cloud costs with tools like Azure Cost Management , Kubecost, and CloudHealth.

- **DevSecOps embeds security into the DevOps lifecycle**, enforcing secure coding, vulnerability scanning, IAM, and policy as code across pipelines.

- **QA and testing must be automated and continuous**, with emphasis on unit, integration, performance, and security testing to maintain software quality at scale.

- **Anti-patterns such as hardcoded configs, lack of automation, and manual approvals** should be avoided to maintain DevOps maturity and velocity.

- **Multi-cloud and hybrid DevOps** strategies must address tooling, observability, and consistent security through cloud-agnostic and centralized solutions.

Model interview questions and answers

1. **As a solutions architect, how do you approach designing a CI/CD pipeline for complex, multi-tier applications?**

    Model answer:

    - Start by analyzing the application's architecture and identifying dependencies for each tier.

    - Separate pipelines for frontend, backend, and database to allow independent deployments and avoid bottlenecks.

    - Use gated stages for build, test, and deployment across dev, QA, staging, and production environments.

    - Choose deployment strategies like blue-green, canary, or rolling based on SLAs and risk tolerance.

    - Incorporate automated security checks, unit tests, integration tests, and infrastructure provisioning for example, Terraform.

    - This approach minimizes deployment risks and supports Agile release cycles.

2. **What considerations are taken into account when implementing DevSecOps in a cloud-native application?**

    Model answer:

    - Security is embedded into the pipeline using automated tools like SonarQube for static code analysis and Aqua Security for container security.

    - IAM policies are established to define role-based access, and secret management is handled through Azure Key Vault or AWS Secrets Manager.

    - Compliance with governance frameworks like Azure Policy or AWS Config is enforced to monitor configuration drift.

- Security checks are integrated into each build stage, ensuring sensitive information remains secure throughout the pipeline.

3. **How is state management for Terraform handled in a multi-cloud deployment?**

Model answer:

- Use remote state backends for each cloud provider (Azure Blob for Azure, S3 for AWS) to manage state independently.
- Ensure encryption and enforce access control policies to secure state files.
- State locking and versioning with Terraform are used to prevent conflicting changes.
- Service principals or IAM roles are employed to automate state management and enforce security policies.
- This approach secures state management and minimizes risks in multi-cloud environments.

4. **How are CI/CD pipelines optimized for microservices architecture?**

Model answer:

- Design modular pipeline structures allowing each microservice to be built, tested, and deployed independently.
- Implement dynamic environment creation with IaC tools like ARM templates or Terraform.
- Use containerization with Docker and Kubernetes for effective microservice management.
- Service discovery and versioned APIs ensure minimal impact on other services during updates.
- Feature toggles and canary releases allow gradual rollouts, reducing risks and enabling flexible testing.

5. **What is the approach to multi-environment deployment strategies using Azure DevOps?**

Model answer:

- Azure Pipelines is leveraged to define deployment stages for development, QA, staging, and production environments.
- Environment variables and separate configuration files are used to manage environment-specific settings.
- Security is maintained through approval gates, with deployment strategies like blue-green or canary releases minimizing downtime.
- Infrastructure is provisioned automatically using ARM templates or Terraform, with automated rollback mechanisms in case of failures.
- This ensures consistency and repeatability across all environments.

6. **How is observability implemented in large-scale applications?**

Model answer:

- Start by defining key metrics, logs, and traces that provide visibility into the application's health.
- Integrate monitoring tools like Azure Monitor, AWS CloudWatch, or Prometheus to track critical performance metrics.
- Set up centralized logging using systems like ELK or Azure Log Analytics.
- Use distributed tracing tools like Jaeger or AWS X-Ray to track requests across microservices and identify bottlenecks.
- This approach ensures optimal performance and proactive issue resolution.

7. **Describe a scenario where compliance was ensured using DevOps tools.**

   Model answer:

   - A solution using Azure Policy enforced compliance across multiple subscriptions by checking each resource deployment against predefined policies (e.g., PCI-DSS standards).

   - Continuous monitoring with Azure Security Center provided alerts on any deviations.

   - Third-party tools like Checkov and Conftest were integrated into the CI/CD pipeline to validate IaC templates against compliance rules before deployment.

8. **How do you manage blue-green or canary deployments at scale?**

   Model answer:

   - **Start by leveraging orchestration tools**: Use tools like Kubernetes, Spinnaker, or ArgoCD to manage blue-green and canary deployments at scale.

   - **Automate environment setup**: Blue-green deployments require two identical environments (blue for current production and green for new deployment). Canary deployments introduce changes to a small subset of users first. Automate the creation and teardown of these environments using **IaC tools** like Terraform or Helm for Kubernetes.

   - **Use traffic management tools**: Leverage tools such as Istio, NGINX, or AWS App Mesh to dynamically route traffic between environments during the deployment.

   - **Monitor metrics in real-time**: Integrate with Prometheus, Datadog, or CloudWatch to monitor error rates, latency, and user feedback.

   - **Set rollback triggers**: Define automated rollback conditions in your pipeline to revert traffic to the previous stable environment if KPIs fall below defined thresholds.

9. **How are DevOps tools selected for a large enterprise deployment?**

   Model answer:

   - Consider scalability, integration with existing systems, security, and ease of use.

   - For enterprises heavily invested in Microsoft technologies, Azure DevOps is prioritized for tight integration with Azure services and seamless CI/CD support.

   - For hybrid cloud environments, Jenkins or GitHub Actions may be evaluated for flexibility, with Terraform chosen for IaC.

   - The goal is to create a cohesive toolchain that aligns with the enterprise's operational needs and minimizes complexity in managing multiple tools.

10. **How would you implement GitOps in a CI/CD pipeline?**

    Model answer:

    - **Adopt a declarative approach**: GitOps relies on a declarative model where the desired state of infrastructure and applications is stored in a Git repository. Tools like FluxCD or ArgoCD monitor the Git repository and ensure that the cluster's state matches the desired state.

    - **Set up automated sync**: Changes to the infrastructure or application configurations are automatically applied when a commit is made to the Git repository. This ensures the CI/CD pipeline remains aligned with Git.

    - **Pipeline integration**: Integrate GitOps tools with CI/CD pipelines for automated testing and validation. For example, upon a commit to Git, run automated tests and security scans before syncing changes to the cluster.

- **Implement RBAC and approvals**: Use GitHub Actions or Azure DevOps to enforce branch protection and approval workflows to ensure only reviewed changes make it to the repository.

- **Monitor and observe drift**: Use tools like Prometheus and Grafana to detect and alert on drift between the desired state in Git and the actual state in the cluster.

    GitOps promotes a single source of truth and makes deployments predictable and repeatable.

11. **What is the difference between monitoring and observability, and how do you design for each?**

    Model answer:

    - **Monitoring**:

        o Monitoring is about collecting predefined metrics, logs, and events to track the health and performance of systems.

        o **Design**: Use tools like Prometheus, Nagios, or Azure Monitor to track KPIs such as CPU usage, response times, error rates, and availability.

        o Set up dashboards and alerts to notify teams when metrics breach defined thresholds.

    - **Observability**:

        o Observability focuses on understanding the internal state of systems based on external outputs (logs, metrics, and traces).

        o **Design**: Implement distributed tracing with tools like Jaeger, Zipkin, or AWS X-Ray to trace requests across microservices.

        o Use log aggregation tools such as ELK Stack or Splunk to correlate logs across the system and enable root cause analysis.

A well-observed system enables proactive issue resolution and provides deep insights into system behavior.

12. **Explain your approach to designing secure pipelines for a highly regulated industry (e.g., finance or healthcare).**

    Model answer:

    - **Secure code practices**: Begin by enforcing secure coding standards through automated **static application security testing** (**SAST**) tools like SonarQube or Checkmarx in the CI/CD pipeline.

    - **Secrets management**: Use tools like HashiCorp Vault, AWS Secrets Manager, or Azure Key Vault to securely store and access secrets during builds and deployments.

    - **IAM and RBAC Policies**: Implement RBAC and least privilege policies to restrict who can trigger builds, access pipelines, or deploy to production.

    - **Compliance checks**: Automate compliance checks (e.g., HIPAA, PCI-DSS) with tools like Terraform Sentinel, OPA, or Azure Policy to ensure that every deployment meets regulatory standards.

    - **Audit and logging**: Ensure all pipeline activities are logged and auditable. Use centralized logging solutions like Splunk or Azure Log Analytics for traceability and regulatory reporting.

    - **Continuous security testing**: Include DAST tools like OWASP ZAP or Burp Suite for runtime vulnerability scanning and penetration testing before deployment.

        This approach ensures compliance while maintaining a robust security posture throughout the CI/CD process.

CHAPTER 9

Performance and Scalability

Introduction

Enterprises develop applications with their users in mind. One of the qualities that users look for in an application is its usability. Usability is not just about sophisticated features rolled out or the navigational ease built into the application. Application performance is one of the key attributes that contribute to the usability of the application. A lot of enterprises spend millions of dollars every year to ensure that their applications are performant, and performance issues do not become a reason for their loss of business. With the attention span of users decreasing by the day, application performance must match the expectations of the user. Observability of systems in production has become one of the key activities to which enterprises give a lot of importance, and equip their development and performance test teams with state-of-the-art performance testing and monitoring tools. With so much significance being given to application performance, scalability is one lever that is normally used to ensure the performance of applications and give users a compelling user experience. Application performance and scalability are often discussed hand in hand when it comes to meeting the agreed performance metrics with different stakeholders of the system.

Structure

This chapter covers the following topics:

- Performance and scalability overview
- Performance strategies for solutions architects
- Application performance
- Scalability
- Application scalability strategies for solutions architects
- Performance and scalability on the cloud
- Artificial intelligence for performance and scalability

Objectives

In this chapter, readers will understand the basic concepts related to the performance and scalability of applications. The solutions architect will learn the strategies to apply to ensure the performance of applications, right from the blueprinting stage of the application. The reader will learn about the types of performance testing carried out in an enterprise. We will also discuss in detail the list of steps carried out in loading testing applications to ensure that the defined service level objectives of the applications are met. We will discuss application performance monitoring and key performance indicators used to measure application performance. The solutions architect will also learn about the different strategies available, to ensure application scalability. We will later discuss the support that major cloud providers offer, like content delivery networks and edge computing, to ensure application performance and scalability. We will finally discuss how **Artificial intelligence** (**AI**) and **machine learning** (**ML**) have redefined the performance engineering space and help architects and developers to optimize resources and reduce costs for the enterprise.

Performance and scalability overview

Performance and scalability are the drivers that have become the mainstay of any modern-day software application. These two qualities of service are discussed and debated in detail from the architectural blue printing stage of applications, and long after the applications are deployed into production. Architectural patterns that lend themselves to scalability and are inherently performant are chosen over others, keeping in mind the short and long-term benefits they shower on enterprises to realize their business goals. Performance and scalability determine all the aspects of software development, from architecture, design, infrastructure provisioning, team composition, and, more importantly, the cost budget of the project. It is imperative to assess the required performance and scalability aspects of the application to ensure that they are properly accounted for in terms of capacity, and there are mechanisms in place to continuously monitor and optimize them as the application is developed and deployed in production.

Performance

Performance is the ability of the application to process transactions within an accepted timeframe, which is measured as the response time for the transaction. Applications must respond to users as they interact with applications in the most efficient manner. The workload of an application could vary depending on the functionality being addressed within the application. For example, there could be a payment processing transaction that needs to respond to the user with a success or failure acknowledgement within two seconds. There could be a batch job that sends eligible offers to customers through emails, which needs to be completed within a given time window of three hours. Though performance at the outset is viewed as the time at which the users are responded to, it needs to be ensured that the application does this in the most reliable manner. It should not overwhelm the resources of the application infrastructure. Performance is therefore measured as a totality of how the application works in conjunction with the software platform on which it runs and the underlying hardware.

Development teams use specialized skills and monitoring tools to specifically measure the performance of applications. They measure performance in terms of transactions per second and response time. Additionally, they look at how the other parameters behave, such as the CPU and memory usage. Exceptions generated during the processing of those transactions by the application are also checked.

Scalability

Scalability is the ability of the system to seamlessly expand or shrink based on the workload imposed on the system. The load on the application deployed to production does not stay constant. The application is built, configured, and deployed for a known workload based on the total and the concurrent number of users. There will be spikes in the application depending on situational factors quite often. For instance, a hospital portal might experience additional load during a period of pandemic spread. The application should be architected and designed to support the required expansions based on these kinds of factors.

Scalability is a very important factor for a business to grow. If the application can be scaled without having to be redesigned for any functionality, it can easily be deployed to any data center or the cloud that is closer to the region in which the business wants to expand its operations. Scalability should also be achieved in a way that does not increase the total cost of ownership of the enterprise. Loosely coupled architectures enable scaling of independent components without the enterprise having to scale the entire application. This helps to address additional load only on a particular component (feature) within the application. Like performance, scalability is another quality of service that needs to be thought about right from the blueprinting of the solution. It should also be looked at during the design and development of the application. Solutions architects should always be conversant with the architectural and design principles that promote scalability and apply them consciously while crafting solutions for complex applications.

Performance strategies for a solutions architect

Application performance is an aspect that needs to be addressed right from the blueprinting stage of a software project. The solutions architect needs to explicitly capture the nonfunctional requirements with regard to the application performance of different transactions within the application. These requirements can be captured as user stories in an Agile setting and can be tracked and built during the software development lifecycle. Performance is not just for the online transactions that users might perform, but also for other offline jobs like batch jobs and those including loading of data into data warehouses or data lakes, for instance.

Let us discuss the strategies available to solutions architects to ensure that application performance as part of the solution blueprinting and design exercise.

Architecture and design

Choosing the right architecture is one of the easiest and best starting points to address the performance of the application landscape. There are architecture patterns that naturally lend themselves to building performant applications. Solutions architects should carefully study the performance requirements of the application and choose architectures and apply design patterns that enhance the performance of the application. Any architecture that promotes loose coupling is one of the ideal candidates to ensure and control the performance of the required scale.

Communication patterns and protocols used between components also play a key role in ensuring the performance of applications. For instance, **Google RPC (gRPC)** could be used to ensure inter services communication between microservices, which offers exchange of payloads using a binary format. Architectural patterns like event-driven architecture warrant asynchronous communication and enable components to be decoupled. In such architectures, messages exchanged through a service bus offer better performance by processing payloads by interested components in parallel. Design patterns like a circuit breaker prevent requests from being sent to unavailable services and avoid waiting time till the request to the failed component times out.

Caching

Cache is a high-speed data storage device. Caching of data that is being referred to by the application is one of the most effective ways to improve performance. Caching also reduces the load on the actual back-end systems. Master data used for reference by the applications to enable feature functionality is one of the primary candidates for caching. Apart from master data caching, many applications also consider caching transactional data that is very frequently accessed to provide the required performance. However, a caching strategy needs to carefully assess the type of data being cached. Data that gets frequently updated may not be the right candidate for caching, as it will end in stale data being served to the application users.

Choosing the keys to cache data is also one of the important criteria that designers need to be aware of. Dynamic keys may not be the right ones to store and retrieve data in a cache. Apart from the keys, the retention of data in the cache also needs to be carefully thought about. A frequent data refresh in the cache might degrade the performance of the solution, and a prolonged refresh might end up in the cache being left with stale data.

Load balancing

Load balancing is a technique of distributing the load among the available application resources to strike a balance in load among those resources. A resource could be an application server, a storage device, or a database used by an application. An application deployed across two data centers in an active-active mode or across two availability zones in a cloud region takes an equal amount of load(number of requests), thereby not overwhelming any instance of the resource. By splitting the load among resources, the hardware and the software platform function optimally without any spike in computational power or memory usage. This results in an improved response time for the users of the application. Load balancing can be dynamic or static. Static load balancing routes requests to server resources based on fixed rules and does not consider the current state of the server that hosts the application. Round robin and resource based allocation methods are examples of static load balancing. A dynamic load balancer takes into account the current state of the server in terms of the load handled by it and accordingly routes the request to the server with the least load. Least connection and least response time are some of the algorithms used for dynamic load balancing.

Data partitioning

Data partitioning is a strategy adopted to improve the performance of database systems. Like the way in which the application user load is spread across multiple data centres or availability zones, data stored can be partitioned across multiple servers to improve the read and write of a data store. Data partition improves performance by reducing contention among the partitions. This reduces the load on the infrastructure in terms of memory and computing power while the data is being scanned during query execution. Performance is also improved by segregating frequently accessed data from infrequently accessed data. When the data is split into multiple partitions, any query operation requiring access to the entire dataset may do so in parallel, and the result is collated into a single dataset using the results of those parallel executions. Data partition could be horizontal, vertical, or a functional partition. In a horizontal partition, the whole data set is divided into multiple partitions. In vertical partitioning, each partition has the total dataset, but for a set of attributes. Functional partitions contain data pertaining to a certain group of functions in an application.

Concurrency within applications

Concurrency within applications plays a key role in improving the performance of applications. While designing applications, tasks that can run concurrently need to be identified and should be executed in parallel. Applications can make optimum use of the hardware by running their tasks in parallel. With modern-day applications being supported by a large amount of primary memory and servers with multiple CPU cores, it becomes easier to design applications that make use of concurrency and parallelism. Software platforms like Java and .NET provide libraries to achieve parallelism out of the box for applications that run on them. For instance, in a batch processing of payments submitted by a merchant at the end of the day, a payment processing application can spawn multiple threads to execute each one of the payments in parallel. Concurrency not only helps to reduce response time by executing tasks in parallel, but it also helps to utilize the server resources like CPU and memory in the most optimal way.

Technology choices

Choosing the appropriate technology stack to build application components is key to ensuring the required performance levels. Low latency applications would require languages that can provide optimized interactions with the hardware components and network. For example, C and C++ would be better choices for low latency applications as they directly compile to the code to be executed on the processor, unlike Java, which compiles to an intermediate bytecode format. In the same way, an application in which tasks can be performed in an asynchronous fashion can choose a programming language like Node.js that lends itself to such a programming style. Third party libraries used by applications for database manipulation, message parsing, and connections to third party services with specific protocols must be carefully assessed for performance using a proof-of-concept exercise before they are used for mainstream application development. In the same way, JavaScript libraries that offer superior performance must be chosen for front end development over their features to ensure that the front-end lag does not hamper the overall user experience.

Application performance

Performance, being one of the key criteria for success in modern day software applications, is being addressed right from the requirement stage. Different stakeholders are consulted to understand the number of transactions required to be executed, along with the corresponding response time of the transaction. Enterprises also want to ensure that there is very minimal disruption or downtime for their applications and devise strategies to ensure the availability and performance efficiency of the application.

With most of the applications making use of DevOps principles and CI/CD pipelines throughout the development lifecycle, performance testing is no longer an isolated activity. It is ingrained as part of the regular build and testing process of the application. Solutions architects and project managers do not certify builds for user acceptance or production deploys if the application does not meet the performance service level agreements.

In this section, we will discuss the types of performance testing being done and, more specifically, the sequence of steps in load testing, which is very critical for ensuring application performance. We will further discuss performance monitoring and look at some of the key metrics that should be measured to fine tune application performance.

Types of application performance testing

There are different types of performance testing done to ensure the performance efficiency of the application. These kinds of tests measure the transaction processing time. They also check the quality of code to identify performance bottlenecks to assess the behavior of the application when it is subjected to constant load over a period. *Figure 9.1* depicts the most common type of performance tests carried out to measure and fine tune performance of applications:

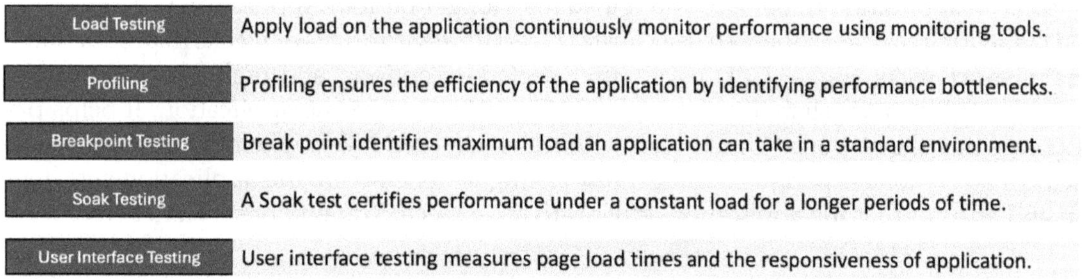

Load Testing	Apply load on the application continuously monitor performance using monitoring tools.
Profiling	Profiling ensures the efficiency of the application by identifying performance bottlenecks.
Breakpoint Testing	Break point identifies maximum load an application can take in a standard environment.
Soak Testing	A Soak test certifies performance under a constant load for a longer periods of time.
User Interface Testing	User interface testing measures page load times and the responsiveness of application.

Figure 9.1: Types of performance testing

Load testing

Load testing of an application is carried out by applying a specific load on the application, and the performance of the application is continuously monitored using **application performance monitoring (APM)** tools. Performance is measured in terms of the response time taken for a specific number of transactions executed. For example, if two transactions get completed in a second, then the response time of a transaction is half a second. So, the tools measure if a specific number of transactions of a particular functionality get completed within the agreed response time within the application. Apart from the response time of transactions, other parameters like the number of slow and stalled transactions, the CPU and memory usage during the execution of the load test, and the number of errors produced are all measured and documented. The values of these parameters are compared in a correlated manner, and it is understood if the performance of the application is within the accepted levels.

Profiling

Application profiling is done to ensure the efficiency of the application and that there are no resource leaks introduced by the application. It is also done to measure the time taken by each of the methods in the code and provides valuable information to the developers to improve efficiency by optimizing the code. Application profiling provides data related to memory and CPU usage, hanging threads, and resources left open after usage. For instance, application profiling can help developers find unclosed connections and open file handles within the code. Profiling can be done with a single user, and the memory snapshot captured for analysis to identify and fix issues in the code. Profiling can also help to find the size of objects in the heap, which can proliferate as the load increases and potentially cause out of memory issues.

Break point testing

Break point testing of an application component is carried out to find the maximum load that a single instance of the component can support. The component is deployed in a standard configuration of hardware infrastructure and tested. This test is normally conducted to baseline performance of an application or a service. Hardware infrastructure is provisioned with a set of memory and CPU cores, along with other required software dependencies deployed. The application is continuously tested by applying a load that constantly increases in a set time frame. For example, a break point test may start with a load of five transactions, and the test is incremented by five more transactions every 15 minutes. The response time and other performance parameters like CPU usage, memory usage, and error rates are continuously observed. When the test goes on, a point is marked in the test where the response time continues to be constant, and the error rates, CPU, and memory usage remain stable. The number of transactions, along with the response time, gives the benchmark of the application performance in the configured hardware and the software platform. If a better response time is required, the developer can reduce the number of transactions to start with in the break point test. The developer can also scale the hardware infrastructure vertically and repeat the test.

Soak testing

A soak test runs an application under a constant load for a longer period. Applications, at times, might exhibit unexpected behavior if they are subjected to a constant load for several days or weeks in production. This could manifest as memory leaks, higher CPU usage, unexpected exceptions, and higher error rates. Soak testing ensures system stability and reliability apart from the performance of the application. It helps performance engineers ensure that the response time is well within the accepted levels when the application continues to take a specific load for longer periods of time. Soak testing is done before the application gets deployed into production and ensures that the application adheres to the expected quality of services before it is rolled out to users.

User interface testing

User interface testing involves measuring page load times and the responsiveness of different user interface elements within the browser application. Modern browsers provide the required developer tools to measure UI performance by estimating network performance, memory usage, and UI components' responsiveness. Enabling caching of images and JavaScript files is one of the easiest and effective ways to ensure faster page load times. User interface profiling can also be done to understand elements that take time to load within the browser. Tools like Chrome developer tools and Apple Safari web inspector help to analyze inefficient memory usage, time taken to load images, and execution of JavaScript code within the browser application.

Task sequence in application performance testing

The following is the sequence of tasks carried out by a performance engineer to certify if an application or an application component (like a microservice) is performant. Its sequence is as follows:

- **Collect nonfunctional requirements**: This is the phase in which the requirements for application performance are discussed with the stakeholders and then documented. Service level agreements for metrics like **transactions per second** (**TPS**) and response time for various transactions within the application are agreed upon.

- **Create performance test scripts**: This step focuses on writing the performance test scripts for the test to be executed. Scripting syntax is provided by the load test tools using popular languages like C language (for load runner) and JMeter scripting (XML based) for Apache JMeter. This step can be automated using APIs provided by the tool provider.

- **Configure a performance test**: Once the script is ready, the test needs to be configured within the performance test tool environment for the load to be applied. This requires configuration like the number of virtual users, thresholds for parameters like CPU and memory usage.

- **Execute the test**: In this step, the test is executed by the performance test tool, which internally uses the performance test script and other configured parameters from the previous step. The execution of the test can also be automated using the APIs provided by the performance test tool.

- **Monitor the performance test**: As stated in the subsection *Load testing* before, performance tests are run for many hours. During the test execution, the status of the test is continuously monitored using application performance monitoring tools, and it is ensured that the values of performance metrics like TPS and response time are within the desired levels and there are no major errors reported.

- **Collect test results**: In this step, the results are collected from different tools that were used for load testing and monitoring. For instance, the performance engineer collects the load test results pertaining to transactions executed and response time from LoadRunner. Data points pertaining to memory, CPU usage, and threads could be gathered from AppDynamics. Data related to the number of errors and exceptions is collected from the log management tools like Splunk.

- **Interpret the test results**: This step is about analyzing the results collected in the previous step and certifying the performance of the application. The results are viewed in conjunction with each other and the required service level agreements.

- **Certify the test**: Based on analysis, the component is certified to be performant and ready to be deployed to production. If the test is not certified, the performance engineer executes the test again by adjusting the load and other parameters like CPU and memory usage thresholds.

Application performance monitoring

APM is a set of activities supported by tools to ensure the optimum performance of the application to users. Performance engineers use APM tools to collect telemetry data from the application environment to constantly monitor it and identify any deviations from set thresholds. As examples, AppDynamics and Dynatrace are two of the popular tools that a performance engineer can use to monitor performance.

Application performance monitoring deals with the following three types of resources:

- Infrastructure monitoring
- Application platform monitoring
- Application monitoring

Infrastructure monitoring involves measuring the usage of CPU and memory so that they do not cross the set thresholds and slow down the application. Network monitoring is also a key activity to ensure that data packets do not get dropped during round trips between the client and server. In case of read-write intensive applications, a number of reads and writes per minute and the average time taken for them are constantly measured and ensured they are within acceptable limits. Applications use **Redundant Array of Independent Disks (RAID)** configuration and opt for **solid state drives (SSD)** over **hard disk drives (HDD)** to improve the performance of input/output intensive applications.

Application platform monitoring focuses on the platforms where the applications are deployed for their run time and database systems that house the application's data. This helps to keep track of the hosting platform's health and ensures that they are active in supporting the applications to operate in the most efficient way. For example, in a microservices application deployed on Kubernetes, the control plane keeps monitoring the desired number of containers required for a particular microservice and instantiates a new container if any of the active container gets terminated. Similarly, when a read replica is set up to serve application reads, the database management system should ensure that the data is effectively replicated to the read replica as configured to ensure that the read and write instances are in sync.

Application performance monitoring deals with the application's usage of memory and computing resources. During a load test, an application's usage of the heap allocated to it is constantly monitored to ensure that it does not fill up very quickly with objects, causing out of memory issues. Another option could be for the application to make use of multiple cores in the server by creating threads to enable the processing of applicable tasks in parallel. Application monitoring also deals with monitoring the proper closure of resources for use by other threads or application components and ensures that there are no resource leaks. For instance, unclosed database connections will result in the connection pool running out of connections for newer requests to the application.

Key performance metrics

A solutions architect should be aware of key performance metrics to measure and fine tune performance of an application. They are as follows:

- **Response time**: This is the time taken by an application or a component to process one transaction. For example, if the application can perform four transactions per second, the response time is .25 seconds (250 milliseconds) per transaction.

- **Throughput**: This represents the number of transactions or tasks performed in unit time. It can also be the time taken to execute a query by a database in unit time. If a transaction takes two seconds to get completed, the throughput of the application will be .5.

- **CPU usage**: The amount of CPU used by the application while processing transactions in unit time. This is measured in percentage and in conjunction with the total amount of computing power available to the application.

- **Memory usage**: This is the total amount of memory used by the application as opposed to the memory allocated. This is measured in percentage in conjunction with the total amount of memory available to the application. For example, some applications have a threshold set to fifty percent.

- **Number of slow transactions**: In a load test, these are the transactions that have taken more time than the average or the desired transaction response time. The CPU and memory are adjusted to reduce the number of slow transactions. On the other hand, more instances can be added to reduce the number of transactions processed by the server or the node.

- **Number of failed transactions**: During the load test, this is the number of transactions that failed out of all the transactions that were triggered by the load testing tool. If the number of failed transactions is more, root cause analysis is done, and the cause is fixed.

- **Error rate**: The error rates are also monitored during the load test. Even though the response time might be within limits for the required number of transactions during the load test, the number of errors or exceptions reported should be at a minimum during a load test.

- **Number of major garbage collections**: Major **garbage collection (GC)** is one of the deterrents for efficient performance of applications. This means that the memory allocated is quickly getting filled and is to be recovered. The major GC must be within prescribed limits. For example, solutions architects may not certify a test if the number of major GC is more than one per hour during the entire duration of the performance test running for several hours.

Scalability

Scalability is an important quality of service that supports other qualities of service like performance, reliability, and availability. Scalability is not only about expansion of the application in case it is required, but also about shrinking just in case the load on the application decreases.

Scalability of applications has become very significant due to the following reasons:

- **Realize business goals**: Scalability helps to future-proof businesses for any expansion being planned and helps enterprises to achieve their business goals. An application built for scalability can be deployed in any part of the globe with minimum changes to the configuration.

- **Optimizing total cost of ownership**: Scalability helps enterprises to scale in and scale out hardware infrastructure based on the workloads at a given point in time. This adjustment of infrastructure based on load helps organizations reduce costs.

- **Improved performance**: Scalability helps applications improve performance of applications. Development teams can move applications to specific types of hardware based on application non-functional requirements that help to optimize cost.

- **Compelling user experience**: Compelling user experience determines the success of modern-day enterprises. With the reduced attention span of users, slow applications and websites are very quickly shunned by users, resulting in business reputation and monetary loss. Scalability ensures that there is enough capacity to serve the number of users as planned. The infrastructure also adjusts itself to any increase or decrease in the user count accessing the application.

- **Increased reliability**: Application reliability is about the ability of the system to behave predictably and provide the expected results in a performant way. In situations where there is a sudden unexpected load increase on the application, performance and reliability take a hit. Scalability can help to resolve issues arising from such situations by creating the required redundant nodes and spreading the load for a reliable functioning of the system.

- **Zero downtime**: Scalability creates redundancy of applications and components. This ensures that there is no single point of failure, and the application has the backup to process requests even if the primary application is down. This kind of availability is even more important for applications like health care and banks, which require a 24*7 availability.

Types of scaling

Solutions architects can make use of different options for increasing the scalability of applications. This includes scaling different layers of the application independently based on the load on the specific layer. For instance, the business logic layer can be scaled based on the number of users that need to be supported concurrently. Similarly, the database layer can be scaled depending on the read and write operations that need to be supported at the given point in time. There are options ranging from scaling the independent nodes to adding infrastructure for the application layer to overcome performance concerns and availability challenges.

Different types of scalability options available for the application layer are as follows:

- **Vertical scaling**: In this type of scaling, the server hardware is upgraded by adding more memory or computing power. This scaling option suits applications or services that need intense computing power or more memory for performing the required number of transactions per second. This is an easier option that helps applications scale up and perform well. However, this option does not improve the availability of the application, as this type of scaling is still prone to a single point of failure. This may not be the best option to scale mission critical applications to support larger workloads.

- **Horizontal scaling**: In horizontal scaling, more application nodes are added to spread the load across multiple nodes of the cluster. This type of scaling is ideal for mission critical applications as it provides the required availability, since there is redundancy of nodes even if one of the nodes goes down. However, solutions architects need to note that the application has to be designed in a stateless manner for an easier adoption of this scaling model. Otherwise, additional logic needs to be written in the code to persist application state outside of the node hosting the application, like a database or a cache. This type of scalability is provided by modern container management platforms like Kubernetes to avoid failures. The routing logic between the nodes in a cluster needs to be addressed carefully in this option. This is the option that is mostly adopted for applications using the event driven and microservices architectural patterns.

- **Task based scaling**: This type of scaling is more relevant to applications using message-based communication patterns between components. In applications where there are producers placing messages in a queue and consumers that process them, the consumers can be scaled based on the number of messages arriving at the queue (queue depth). This type of scaling can be done for independent sets of producers and consumers using a queue between them for processing a specific type of transaction. Task based scaling is applicable for event driven and microservices architectural patterns. For example, if an order queue is getting filled with many orders during a special sale event, the order processing microservice can be scaled independently based on the rate of message arrival in the order queue.

Scaling of the database layer is also very common in improving the overall performance of the application.

Common types of scaling that are particularly applicable to databases to improve their efficiency are as follows:

- **Partitioning**: This type of scaling is splitting the table into smaller chunks for easy manageability of data. This type of partitioning is divided into horizontal partitioning and vertical partitioning. Horizontal partitioning, which is also called sharding, is a technique in which the table is divided into multiple partitions, with each partition containing a subset of the entire set of records. In a vertical partition, the columns of a table are split between different partitions, with each partition storing a set of columns with all the table data in them. In range partitioning, each partition stores the data for a range of values of a specific key (column). For instance, a sales database table can be partitioned based on the revenue made each month. Some of the databases support a type called list partition, in which each partition stores data for a list of values. For example, each partition can store data pertaining to eligible voters for a set (list) of states in India.

- **Replication**: This is a technique in which multiple copies of the database are maintained, typically as a master for the write operations and its replicas for read operations. The database management system upgrades one of the read replicas as a write database, just in case the master or the write database goes down. This strategy to maintain read replicas helps to split the load between read and write operations within the application, which adds to the efficiency of processing the queries.

Having seen the types of scaling, we will discuss the application scalability strategies available to the solutions architects in the next section.

Application scalability strategies for solutions architects

Application scalability is an aspect that needs to be paid attention to, right from the conception of the solution by the solutions architect. The architected application should ensure that lends itself well to easier scalability without having to make any changes once it has been deployed to production, and at the same time, should take care of resource optimization and minimize cost to the enterprise.

Architectural patterns

The scalability of applications must be addressed right from the stage of solution blueprinting. Some of the ways to achieve application scalability by a proper choice of architectural patterns and design principles are as follows:

- **Loose coupling**: Any architectural pattern that promotes loose coupling of components lends itself well to scalability. In a loosely coupled architecture, the feature functionality is implemented as separate components, with each component communicating with others either directly or through a service bus. This enables each component to be deployed redundantly based on the load it is supposed to take and the performance considerations for the component. Event-driven architecture is one example of architectural patterns that promote loose coupling of components. Please refer to *Chapter 3, Technical Proficiency Essential Knowledge,* for an extensive study of the popular architectural and design patterns.

- **Microservices**: Microservices architecture is a popular case in point for a loosely coupled architecture. This distributed architecture enables each of the microservice components to be deployed and scaled independently. The decoupled microservices can communicate with each other asynchronously using a message queue or using protocols like gRPC.

- **Layered architecture**: A layered architecture enables the splitting up of different layers of the application, like user interface, backend logic, and database. This kind of architectural pattern promotes the scalability of the individual layers without affecting one another. For instance, the business logic layer or the backend logic can be independently scaled from the user interface. However, this architecture provides limited flexibility when compared to an architecture like microservices, where each component (feature functionality) can be scaled independently of other microservices.

Design principles

The following are the design principles that can be applied to ensure the scalability of applications being built:

- **Statelessness of applications**: The principle of statelessness advocates that the service or the API being called does not store any state with respect to the caller's request. Many times, the service of the API stores the state to be used in a subsequent request by the caller during the session. Storing the state adds extra complexity to scalability. When a service receives a spike of requests, being stateless enables the service to scale without having to worry about any stateful data it is holding on behalf of the client. Statelessness is one of the important design characteristics of application components to scale freely and be performant.

- **Idempotency of services**: Idempotency is an application characteristic in which the same type of requests passed to the services are treated the same way. Idempotency can be thought of as a corollary to the design principle of being stateless. This characteristic ensures that there can be redundant instances of the same service that can take up requests in parallel, execute them without causing any inconsistency or side effects, and leave the system in a state of equilibrium post the transaction.

- **Communication patterns**: Asynchronous communication patterns promote a loose coupling of components and thereby help them to scale very well. Any component-based design can make use of asynchronous communication patterns to let the components scale independently. Asynchronous communication also helps to separate out the producer and receiver, thereby providing flexibility to scale independently the producer and the receiver based on the load. Asynchronous communication also requires the use of a message service bus that acts as a layer between to hold messages and release them in chunks based on a delay configuration that creates a balance between the sender and receiver of messages.

Performance and scalability on the cloud

Applications deployed on the cloud have multiple avenues to ensure application scalability and the required levels of performance. With the ability to expand hardware to choose the required input/output operations per second, the cloud can boost the application's scalability and performance without any major changes to the application itself. The following are some of the options available to cloud deployed and cloud-native applications to ensure scalability and achieve the required levels of performance. They will be discussed in greater detail in *Chapter 22, Cloud-native Architectural and Design*.

The following are the options available as computing models and services on the cloud to ensure the performance and scalability of applications:

- **Content delivery network (CDN)**: CDN offers the application content to be deployed across multiple points of presence across the globe. This helps the application to serve customers from geographic locations that are closer to them. CDN also reduces the load on the actual backends and provides features to define different types of keys based on which the content can be cached and served.

- **Serverless computing**: Serverless computing model is one in which the cloud provider takes responsibility for the hardware and software platforms required for application deployment. Developers can directly run their code in a serverless mode, thereby moving the scalability concerns to the cloud provider. Developers can also configure the amount of memory and computing power to ensure the required performance levels in this option.

- **Edge computing**: Edge computing is a model offered by cloud providers to move the required infrastructure closer to the location of the application and the sources of data. This option helps to minimize the latency for applications that produce huge amounts of data that need to be processed and analyzed in real time. This model boosts the performance of such applications and provides the required scalability at the same time.

- **Auto scaling at work**: Autoscaling is one of the inherent and important features offered by the cloud. Autoscaling provides the required elasticity to expand the infrastructure within seconds, providing virtually infinite scalability on the cloud. The application owner can also choose from different types of hardware available and **input/output operations per second** (IOPS) required based on the workload deployed on the cloud, thereby getting the required scalability and performance.

Having discussed scalability and performance on the cloud, we will now discuss how artificial intelligence and machine learning are enabling applications to scale better and proactively manage performance.

Artificial intelligence in performance and scalability

AI and ML continue to disrupt all the phases of the software development lifecycle. All contemporary performance monitoring tools include AI-based features that can be used not only to analyze huge amounts of data coming out of these tools but also to forecast any deviations that might occur anytime soon. Solutions architects and developers also make use of machine learning algorithms to train models on the data to proactively monitor and act based on any contingency expected in the normal functioning of the applications in production. The following are some of the ways in which AI and ML are being used to ensure application scalability and performance of applications rolled out to users:

- **Anomaly detection**: AI models are trained on past data generated during application usage and can detect any deviations from normal patterns in the incoming traffic. AI models analyze data points coming out of the application performance monitoring tools and the log content generated by applications to quickly identify bottlenecks and trigger corrective actions. They also sieve huge amounts of data to cluster exceptions and single out the ones that cause performance deterioration and can result in failures if left unattended.

- **Proactive monitoring**: Models trained on past data can forecast events that can result in the deterioration of performance within applications. Models based on algorithms like auto regression and moving averages can forecast spikes in response times or spikes in major garbage collection that are potential situations for the application performance to deteriorate. Based on the forecast, the model can trigger the development teams to identify the possible causes that could result in the forecasted event and take corrective action to prevent performance degradation and even application downtime.

- **Predictive autoscaling**: AI and ML algorithms can continuously monitor the performance of the infrastructure, software platforms, and applications, and auto-scale the infrastructure based on the load to the system. This applies to both scaling out and scaling in, which results in an optimized use of the infrastructure. AI can understand patterns of usage of the application over a period and suggest plans to allocate desired capacity that can help the enterprise to optimize the overall cost of ownership as well.

- **Dynamic configuration management**: AI can be used to trigger actions that adjust the configuration parameters of platforms to ensure the scalability and performance of applications. AI can adjust application configuration to switch on the caching layer just in case there is a heavy load on the backend operational systems. AI can adjust the number of threads used by the application based on the incoming traffic. AI can also suggest database configurations like connection pooling and indexing based on the number of active connections and query complexity, respectively.

Having covered the essentials of application performance and scalability so far, the solutions architect needs to know the types of performance testing being done and strategies available for making the application scalable and improving performance, reliability, and availability. The solutions architect should also be conversant about the size and the capacity required for applications.

Conclusion

In this chapter, we looked at different aspects of application performance and scalability. These are two important areas that architects and developers should pay attention to, right from the software blueprinting stage to development and even after the application is moved to production. The knowledge of these areas helps the solutions architect to ensure that scalability and performance are built into the architecture and design, and a proper strategy is devised for testing the performance of applications.

In the next chapter, we will discuss data management and analytics, which are crucial areas for modern enterprises and form the backbone for making informed business decisions.

Takeaways

The takeaways are as follows:

- **Performance and scalability overview**: Understand what performance and scalability quality of services are and why they are important for an application.

- **Performance strategies for a solutions architect**: Understand the different strategies, like caching, load balancing, data partitioning, concurrency, and technology choices, for enhancing the performance of an application. Also, leverage architectural patterns and design principles to make an application performant.

- **Deep dive into application performance**: Learn the different important types of performance testing like load testing, break point testing, profiling, and soak testing. Also, learn the steps a performance engineer executes to certify an application or a service to be performant. Learn the important metrics used to measure and fine tune performance.

- **Application scalability strategies for a solutions architect**: Learn how architectural patterns like event-driven microservices and design principles like statelessness and idempotency that a solutions architect can use to enhance the scalability of applications.

- **Performance and scalability on the cloud**: Understand how the cloud supports higher performance with its services, like content delivery network and edge computing. Also, learn how the cloud naturally is a platform for scalability.

- **Performance and scalability with AI**: Understand how AI and ML is disrupting the performance and scalability quality of services of applications. Learn about using ML models to proactively monitor the performance of applications and use them to scale the application when required.

Model interview questions and answers

1. **What are the different types of testing done to improve the performance of applications?**

   Model answer:

   - Break point testing is done to baseline performance metrics like transactions per second and response time in a standard hardware configuration.

   - Load testing is done to assess the performance of applications and components in a lab environment that simulates a production setup.

   - Profiling of the application is done to understand the memory and computing power usage by an application and identify performance bottlenecks, open resource handles in the code.

   - Soak testing is done for many hours or even days with a specific load to ensure that the application is stable and performs within the accepted levels.

2. **What is break point testing, and how is it done?**

   Model answer:

   - Break point testing is done to assess the performance of a single component on a standardized hardware configuration.

   - This is to assess the number of transactions that can be executed in unit time and the associated performance parameters such as response time, memory, and CPU usage.

   - Once the break point test is completed, the results can be extrapolated and used to plan the capacity of the required servers to support the required TPS in production.

3. **How will you come up with the optimum size of containers required for a microservice in production? Can you explain with an example?**

   Model answer:

   - You will perform a break point test on standard hardware running a single instance of microservices.

   - You will slowly increase the load every fifteen minutes, and the test will run for about three hours.

   - You will measure the number of transactions that can be supported in this standard hardware configuration within the response time that you need.

   - You will recommend a capacity based on the TPS needed in production.

   - For example, if the TPS required in production is 100 and 2 seconds the response time, and the breakpoint test suggest a maximum TPS of 20 with a response time of 2 seconds in this standard hardware, you will suggest provisioning five instances of the microservice with each running on separate nodes with the specified hardware configuration.

4. **What are the different application performance strategies available from a solutions architecture standpoint?**

   Model answer:

   - You can include a caching layer for the frequently referenced data in the application.

- You can also configure multiple instances with a load balancer to split the load across instances.

- You will also ensure concurrency within the application, if tasks can be performed in parallel.

- For the database, you will implement data partitioning to split the load across multiple partitions.

5. **As a solutions architect, how will you ensure that the application you design is scalable?**

   Model answer:

   - You will make sure that the application component is designed to be stateless so that it can be scaled quickly without any concerns about transferring state.

   - You will ensure that the application components are designed to be idempotent.

   - You will ensure that the components communicate with each other in an asynchronous manner to ensure that the individual components can easily be scaled.

6. **What role do AI and ML play in ensuring application performance?**

   Model answer:

   - AI models are trained on past data generated in the course of application usage and can detect any deviations from normal patterns in the incoming traffic.

   - Models trained on past data can forecast events that can result in the deterioration of performance within applications.

   - AI and ML algorithms can continuously monitor the performance of the infrastructure, software platforms, and applications, and auto-scale the infrastructure based on the load on the system.

   - AI can be used to trigger actions that adjust the configuration parameters of platforms to ensure the scalability and performance of applications.

7. **What are the different performance metrics that you measure in your project?**

   Model answer:

   - You measure response time, which is the time taken by an application or a component to process one transaction.

   - You measure throughput, which represents the number of transactions or tasks performed in unit time.

   - You measure the amount of CPU and memory used by the application while processing transactions in unit time.

   - You also measure the number of major GCs happening during a load test and fine tune the code and infrastructure to keep it to a minimum.

8. **How can a solutions architect ensure performance and scalability of an application while blueprinting a solution?**

   Model answer:

   - The architect can recommend an event-driven architecture in which each component can be scaled independently of each other.

   - Distributed architectures like microservices lend themselves to superior performance and scalability by their nature of being independently deployable.

   - A layered architecture can also help to scale the layers of the application independently of each other.

Join our Discord space

Join our Discord workspace for latest updates, offers, tech happenings around the world, new releases, and sessions with the authors:

https://discord.bpbonline.com

Chapter 10

Data Management and Analytics

Introduction

Data management and analytics are crucial components of modern enterprise solutions, forming the backbone of informed business decisions and digital transformation initiatives. For solutions architects, a strong grasp of data strategies is essential to designing scalable, secure, and effective data architectures that drive value. This chapter gets into the core aspects of data management, covering data architecture design, integration strategies, big data solutions, and analytics. With the ever-increasing volume, variety, and velocity of data, solutions architects must be equipped to handle complex data environments across hybrid and multi-cloud setups.

Structure

This chapter covers the following topics:

- Data architecture design
- Real-world scenarios
- Data integration and management
- Big data solutions
- Leveraging analytics for business insights

Objectives

By the end of this chapter, readers will have a comprehensive understanding of designing scalable and compliant data architectures using industry best practices. They will be equipped to select appropriate tools and technologies for data integration and management, ensuring seamless and efficient data flows across different systems. Additionally, readers will gain insights into evaluating and implementing big data solutions across leading cloud platforms like Azure, AWS, and Google Cloud, making informed decisions on when to use data lakes, data warehouses, or lakehouses. Furthermore, they will learn how to leverage analytics to drive valuable business insights, supporting strategic decision-making within their organizations. Ultimately, readers will be well-prepared to showcase their knowledge of data management principles and demonstrate their ability to design efficient and impactful data-driven systems during interviews.

Data architecture design

Solutions architects are responsible for aligning data architecture with business objectives. They collaborate with stakeholders to design and implement data storage, processing, and retrieval systems that cater to various business functions. Their role extends beyond selecting technologies, they must ensure that these systems meet organizational goals related to scalability, security, and compliance.

By implementing robust data architectures, solutions architects guarantee that enterprise data remains accessible, reliable, and governed according to regulatory and business standards. Their designs consider present requirements while allowing room for future growth and technological advancements.

Defining data architecture

Data architecture refers to the structure and organization of an enterprise's data assets and data management resources. It is a blueprint that outlines how data is collected, stored, managed, and used across systems, ensuring that the data is readily available, consistent, and secure for business operations and decision-making.

For solutions architects, data architecture plays a pivotal role in ensuring that enterprise systems are designed to meet both present and future data needs. By designing efficient data architectures, solutions architects ensure that business data is not only accessible but also structured in a way that supports scalability, security, and governance.

Role of a solutions architect

Solutions architects are responsible for aligning data architecture with business goals. They work closely with stakeholders to design and implement data storage and processing systems that cater to various business functions. Their role encompasses evaluating different architectural patterns, selecting appropriate data storage mechanisms, and ensuring data compliance with relevant regulations.

Solutions architect must understand the intricacies of data management to make decisions about how data is ingested, processed, stored, and secured. They need to weigh factors like scalability, performance, and governance to design systems that can grow with the business.

Types of data architectures

Data architecture can take on several forms depending on the nature of the data and the business objectives. The four most common architectures are as follows:

- **Data warehouses**: Optimized for structured data, often used for reporting and business intelligence.

- **Data lakes**: Capable of handling unstructured, semi-structured, and structured data, suitable for big data analytics and machine learning.

- **Data mesh**: A decentralized approach, where domain-specific teams manage their data as products, promoting scalability and agility.

- **Hybrid models**: Combining elements of both data lakes and warehouses, these models offer flexibility for businesses that need the capabilities of both.

Each of these architectures has distinct advantages depending on the use case, scalability requirements, and governance models.

The following table provides a comparative view of the key attributes of data warehouses, data lakes, data mesh, and hybrid models:

Aspect	Data warehouses	Data lakes	Data mesh	Hybrid models
Primary use case	Structured data for reporting and analytics	Unstructured and semi-structured data for big data and analytics	Domain-specific data management with decentralized governance	Combines the strengths of data lakes and data warehouses
Data type	Structured	Unstructured, semi-structured, and structured	Structured, semi-structured, unstructured	Structured and unstructured
Scalability	Moderate to high, depending on traditional scaling approaches	Very high, built to store massive amounts of data	High, domain-oriented scalability	Flexible, both warehouse and lake scalability
Data processing	Batch processing, typically OLAP	Batch and real-time processing	Distributed data product teams managing data as a product	Combination of batch, real-time, OLAP, and big data processing
Governance	Centralized governance	Less rigid governance, must be managed to avoid data swamps	Decentralized governance with centralized standards	Combines both centralized and decentralized governance models
Tools	Azure Synapse, AWS Redshift, Google BigQuery	Azure data lake, AWS S3, Google Cloud Storage	Data mesh architecture tools like Dremio, Starburst	Lakehouse tools like Databricks, Delta Lake, Snowflake

Table 10.1: Overview of data architectures

The table highlights the strengths and unique attributes of each data architecture model, helping solutions architects make informed decisions based on their organization's data needs. For instance, **data warehouses** are ideal for structured data that requires fast and reliable reporting, while **data lakes** provide a more flexible approach to managing large-scale unstructured or semi-structured data. **Data mesh** offers a modern, decentralized approach that allows teams to manage data within their own domains, providing agility and scalability. Lastly, **hybrid models** combine the best of both worlds, allowing organizations to balance traditional analytics needs with the flexibility of big data.

As a solutions architect, understanding these architectures enables you to align data strategies with business objectives, ensuring the systems are scalable, efficient, and secure.

Once the foundational structure of data architecture is defined, it is crucial to incorporate core principles that ensure the architecture is scalable, secure, and aligned with business objectives. In this subsection, we will get into the essential principles that guide data availability, scalability, and security, which are the cornerstones of an efficient data architecture.

Core data architecture principles

A solid understanding of core data architecture principles is essential for solutions architects, as these principles form the foundation for building reliable, scalable, and secure data systems. This section covers critical areas, that is, data availability, scalability, security, data governance and compliance, and data provenance and lineage. Each of these plays a key role in ensuring the smooth operation and management of data within an organization.

Data availability

Data availability refers to the system's **ability to provide continuous access to data** without interruptions, ensuring that data is accessible whenever needed by business processes or applications. Solution architects must design architectures that minimize downtime and maintain high availability, even during system failures or peak usage times.

Key strategies for ensuring data availability are as follows:

- **Redundancy**: Storing data copies across multiple servers, regions, or data centres to prevent single points of failure.

- **Failover mechanisms**: Automatically switching to backup systems or databases in case of an outage.

- **Distributed databases**: Ensuring that data is distributed across multiple nodes, which allows systems to handle high demand and recover from failures quickly.

Data scalability

Scalability refers to the **ability of the system to handle increasing amounts of data** or traffic without sacrificing performance. Solution architects need to design data architectures that can scale horizontally (adding more servers or nodes) or vertically (increasing the capacity of existing servers) as data demands grow. The following are some strategies to ensure scalability:

- **Sharding**: Splitting data across multiple databases to spread the load and improve query performance.

- **Partitioning**: Dividing a large dataset into smaller, more manageable pieces, often based on time or key values, to improve read or write performance.

- **Elastic cloud Services**: Using cloud services such as AWS, Azure, or Google Cloud, which allow systems to dynamically scale resources up or down depending on the load.

Data security

Data security is paramount in any data architecture to **protect sensitive information** from unauthorized access, breaches, or loss. Solution architects must implement a variety of security measures, both at the infrastructure and application layers, to safeguard data.

Security practices are as follows:

- **Encryption**: Encrypting data **both at rest** (on storage devices) and **in transit** (while being transmitted over networks).

- **Access control**: Implementing RBAC to limit access to data based on the user's role within the organization.

- **Auditing and monitoring**: Continuously tracking access to data, maintaining logs, and monitoring for suspicious activities that may indicate a security breach.

Principles of data governance

Data governance refers to the set of processes, policies, and standards that dictate how data is managed, used, and secured within an organization. Solutions architects must design systems that ensure data is trustworthy, well-managed, and aligned with business objectives. Key components of data governance are as follows:

- **Data ownership and stewardship**: Assigning clear responsibilities for managing specific datasets to ensure accountability and proper data handling.

- **Data quality management**: Implementing tools and processes to continuously monitor, validate, and cleanse data to maintain high data quality across the organization.

- **Policy enforcement**: Ensuring adherence to data policies related to data privacy, retention, and usage through automated systems and manual oversight.

Principles of compliance

Compliance refers to adhering to legal, regulatory, and industry standards for data management. Solutions architects must design architectures that meet specific compliance requirements, such as GDPR, HIPAA, and **Payment Card Industry Data Security Standard** (**PCI-DSS**).

Key practices for ensuring compliance are as follows:

- **Data encryption and anonymization**: Encrypting sensitive data and using anonymization techniques to protect PII.

- **Data retention policies**: Implementing policies that dictate how long data should be retained and when it should be deleted, based on legal and business requirements.

- **Compliance auditing**: Ensuring that systems are regularly audited to demonstrate compliance with relevant regulations and industry standards.

Data provenance

Data provenance refers to the documentation of where data originates, how it moves through the system, and how it changes over time. Tracking the origin and transformation of data is essential for understanding data quality, verifying its accuracy, and maintaining trust in the data. Solutions architects must design systems that allow for detailed tracking of data provenance to support auditing, troubleshooting, and data quality efforts as follows:

- **Source tracking**: Keeping detailed records of where data was collected or ingested from, for example, system logs, databases, and external APIs.

- **Transformation logging**: Documenting any transformations applied to data during its lifecycle, such as data cleaning, aggregation, or enrichment.

- **Verification**: Ensuring that the provenance of data can be traced to verify its accuracy and authenticity, particularly in sensitive or regulated environments.

Data lineage

Data lineage refers to the ability to trace the flow of data from its source to its final destination. It provides visibility into how data moves across systems, how it is transformed, and where it is consumed. Solutions architects must design data architectures with robust data lineage capabilities to support transparency, compliance, and troubleshooting. Data lineage also helps track the dependencies between different datasets and systems, ensuring that changes to one component do not inadvertently affect others as follows:

- **End-to-end visibility**: Providing a clear map of how data flows from its source through pipelines, transformations, and into end-user applications or analytics tools.

- **Impact analysis**: Assessing the impact of changes to data sources, processing logic, or storage on downstream systems and applications.

- **Auditability**: Ensuring that data lineage is documented and auditable to support compliance with regulations like GDPR and HIPAA.

By adhering to these core data architecture principles, solutions architects can design systems that not only perform efficiently but also meet business, security, and compliance objectives, while ensuring the integrity and trustworthiness of the data.

With a firm understanding of the principles governing data architecture, the next step is to determine how to store and model data in a way that optimizes performance and flexibility. In the following subsection, we will explore the different techniques for storing and modeling data, focusing on balancing the needs for structured and unstructured data.

Data storage and modeling techniques

Effective data storage and modeling are crucial in designing systems that meet performance, scalability, and flexibility requirements. Solutions architects must evaluate different storage options based on the type of data being handled (structured, semi-structured, or unstructured) and choose the right data modeling techniques to optimize for performance. In this section, we will explore the distinctions between relational and non-relational databases, various types of data formats, and strategies for optimizing read or write performance.

Relational versus non-relational storage

Data storage can broadly be categorized into relational (SQL) and non-relational (NoSQL) databases, each serving different needs depending on the data's structure and the application's requirements.

Table 10.2 compares relational and non-relational databases, providing a clear distinction between their features, use cases, and scalability strategies. Relational databases are ideal for structured, transactional data, while non-relational databases offer flexibility and scalability for handling large-scale, unstructured or semi-structured data.

Criteria	Relational databases (SQL)	Non-relational databases (NoSQL)
Data structure	Structured (tables, rows, columns)	Flexible (documents, key-value, graphs)
Schema	Predefined, rigid schema	Dynamic, flexible schema
Consistency	High **atomicity, consistency, isolation, durability** (**ACID**) compliance	Eventual consistency **consistency, availability, partition** (**CAP**) tolerance
Query language	SQL	NoSQL (Varying APIs: JSON, Key-Value)
Scalability	Vertical (Adding more CPU or memory)	Horizontal (sharding, partitioning)
Use cases	Financial systems, CRM, ERP	Real-time analytics, IoT, social networks
Examples	MySQL, PostgreSQL, Oracle, SQL server	MongoDB, Cassandra, Redis, Neo4j

Table 10.2: Relational versus non-relational databases

Structured, semi-structured, and unstructured data

Data comes in various forms, such as structured, semi-structured, and unstructured. Each type requires different storage and processing techniques as follows:

- **Structured data**: It is highly organized and easily searchable in tables with rows and columns, like SQL databases.

- **Semi-structured data**: It includes elements like tags, for example, JSON, XML, which make it somewhat organized but still flexible.

- **Unstructured data**: It lacks a predefined format, such as images, videos, or social media content.

The following table outlines these data types, their descriptions, examples, and the most suitable storage options for each:

Data type	Description	Example	Storage options
Structured data	Organized in rows and columns for example SQL	Financial data, ERP records	SQL databases (MySQL, PostgreSQL)
Semi-structured	Partially organized for example, JSON, XML	Log files, Web data, API responses	NoSQL Databases (MongoDB, Couchbase)
Unstructured data	No predefined structure, for example, images, videos, text	Multimedia, social media content	Object storage (Amazon S3, Azure Blob Storage)

Table 10.3: Data types and their suitable storage options

Structured data fits well in relational databases, while semi-structured and unstructured data require more flexible, non-relational or object storage systems.

Designing data models

Optimizing data models for read and write operations is essential to ensure application performance and scalability. Solutions architects must carefully choose strategies like indexing, denormalization, and caching to achieve this balance.

The following table outlines key strategies and their effects on read and write performance:

Optimization strategy	Read performance	Write performance
Indexing	Speeds up query lookups on indexed fields	Adds overhead on write operations due to index updates
Denormalization	Reduces JOINs by storing redundant data	Increases complexity in maintaining data consistency
Caching	Stores frequently accessed data in memory	N/A (Caching typically focuses on read optimization)
Batch processing	N/A (Focused on optimizing writes)	Reduces write overhead by processing data in batches
Asynchronous writes	N/A	Decouples write operations, increasing performance
Partitioning or sharding	Improves query performance by distributing data	Distributes write load across multiple shards
Trade-off consideration	OLAP systems often favor read performance for example, reporting	OLTP systems focus on high-frequency transactions

Table 10.4: Performance optimization techniques

This table outlines various techniques for optimizing read or write performance. Indexing and caching favor faster read times, while strategies like denormalization and sharding can improve both read and write performance depending on the system's use case.

Data modeling for performance optimization

When designing data models, solutions architects must consider the trade-offs between optimizing for read or write performance, depending on the nature of the application. For example, an OLTP might prioritize write performance, while an OLAP focuses on read efficiency for reporting.

The following is a flowchart depicting how different optimization strategies fit into specific use cases:

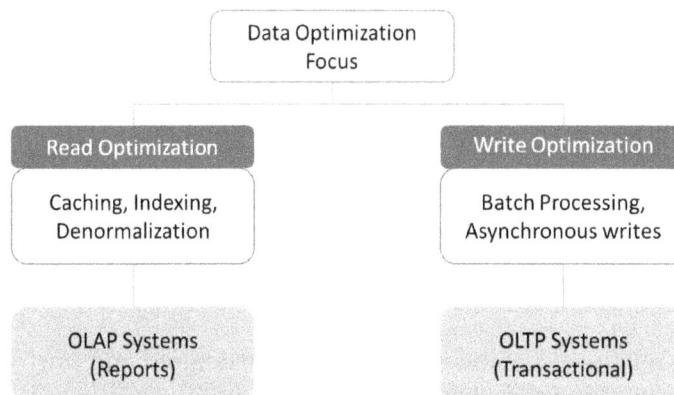

Figure 10.1: Performance optimization strategies with use cases

This flowchart illustrates how solutions architects can decide between read and write optimizations based on the system's needs. OLAP systems prioritize read performance for reporting, while OLTP systems focus on write-heavy operations like financial transactions.

After selecting the appropriate storage and modeling techniques, it is important to consider how your data architecture will scale to meet growing demands and ensure optimal performance.

Let us now discuss strategies for scaling and enhancing the performance of data systems in real-world scenarios.

Designing for scalability and performance

Designing data architectures that can scale efficiently and maintain high performance is essential for ensuring systems can handle increased demand over time. Solutions architects must consider how to scale data architectures both horizontally and vertically, implement techniques such as data partitioning, sharding, and caching, and apply these strategies to real-world use cases.

This section explores these methods and introduces practical strategies for building scalable data systems that can support enterprise workloads.

Strategies for scaling data architectures

As data volumes and traffic grow, it becomes crucial for organizations to ensure their systems can scale efficiently while maintaining performance and availability. Solutions architects must decide between two primary scaling approaches, vertical and horizontal, based on the system's requirements, anticipated growth, and budget constraints.

Each approach has distinct advantages and trade-offs, which are explored as follows:

- **Vertical scaling (scaling up)**: This approach involves adding more resources (CPU, memory, or storage) to a single machine or server. It is relatively easy to implement as it does not require significant architectural changes, but it has limitations because hardware improvements have an upper limit.

  The following are its key advantages, disadvantages, and typical use cases:

  - **Advantages**: Simple to implement, effective for smaller applications.
  - **Disadvantages**: Limited scalability and costly as system demand grows.
  - **Use case**: Suitable for smaller applications or environments with limited scaling needs, such as single-instance applications or small databases.

- **Horizontal scaling (scaling out)**: Horizontal scaling distributes the workload across multiple machines or nodes, improving the system's ability to handle large volumes of traffic and data.

  The following are its key advantages, disadvantages, and typical use cases:

  o **Advantages**: Highly scalable, offers fault tolerance, and can accommodate virtually unlimited growth.

  o **Disadvantages**: More complex architecture, requires careful management of distributed systems.

  o **Use case**: Ideal for large-scale systems with unpredictable growth patterns, such as e-commerce websites, global applications, or cloud-based solutions.

Implementing data partitioning, sharding and caching

As data systems scale, solutions architects must use intelligent data distribution and access optimization techniques to maintain performance, resilience, and manageability. Three foundational techniques, that are, partitioning, sharding, and caching, are commonly used to achieve this.

To make informed architectural decisions, it is essential to understand the specific benefits, trade-offs, and appropriate scenarios for each technique. The following outlines the key advantages, disadvantages, and typical use cases:

- **Data partitioning**: Partitioning breaks data into smaller, more manageable pieces. Vertical partitioning divides data based on columns, while horizontal partitioning divides data based on rows.

  The following are the key advantages, disadvantages, and typical use cases:

  o **Advantages**: Reduces the load on individual databases, increases performance, and improves query speed.

  o **Disadvantages**: Complexity in managing partitions and ensuring balanced data distribution.

  o **Use case**: Useful for managing large datasets, such as financial transactions, logs, or other high-volume databases.

- **Sharding**: Sharding is a form of horizontal partitioning where data is split across multiple databases, each holding a portion of the total dataset based on a shard key, for example, user ID.

  The following are the key advantages, disadvantages, and typical use cases:

  o **Advantages**: Balances database loads and provides better scalability for high-traffic applications.

  o **Disadvantages**: Complex implementation, requires careful planning for shard key selection.

  o **Use case**: High-traffic applications, such as social media platforms or large SaaS solutions that require the management of millions of user data points.

- **Caching**: Caching stores frequently accessed data in memory to speed up read operations. In-memory caching for example, using Redis or Memcached and edge caching for example, using a CDN are common techniques.

  Following are the key advantages, disadvantages, and typical use cases:

  o **Advantages**: Significantly faster data retrieval, reduces database load.

  o **Disadvantages**: Risk of stale or inconsistent data in caches, added complexity to ensure cache synchronization.

  o **Use case**: High-performance applications like news sites or e-commerce platforms where response time is critical.

Real-world scenarios

Consider the following scenarios:

- **E-commerce platform for Black Friday sales**: An e-commerce site experiences high demand during seasonal sales. Horizontal scaling is used to distribute traffic across multiple servers, and caching ensures that frequently accessed product data loads quickly.

  The following is the solution:

  Implement horizontal scaling with sharding to manage large volumes of transactional data, and use edge caching for faster product image loading.

- **Global social media platform**: A social media platform needs to manage millions of user interactions in real-time. Sharding helps distribute user data across multiple databases, and caching speeds up access to popular posts and comments.

  The following is the solution:

  Employ horizontal scaling with sharding based on user ID and in-memory caching to reduce database load.

- **Financial services application**: A financial services platform needs to process millions of transactions daily while maintaining historical data for auditing and compliance. Data partitioning allows for the separation of recent and historical data, and caching helps improve the performance of frequently accessed compliance reports.

  The following is the solution:

  Use horizontal partitioning to manage transactional data and implement caching for reports.

Data security and compliance

Data security and compliance are critical aspects of modern data architecture, ensuring that sensitive data is protected while meeting regulatory and legal requirements. Solutions architects play a key role in designing systems that not only support scalability and performance but also ensure the highest levels of security across on-premises, hybrid, and cloud environments. This section gets into the essential strategies for implementing robust security measures, complying with data protection laws, and addressing unique security concerns in different architectural models.

Table 10.5 provides a comparative overview of key security techniques, highlighting their use cases, advantages, and challenges across different deployment models (on-premises, hybrid, and cloud). Solutions architects can use the following table to determine the best approach for securing data in various environments:

Security technique	Description	Advantages	Challenges	Use case
Data encryption	Encrypts data at rest and in transit to prevent unauthorized access	Protects sensitive data, ensures compliance	Requires key management, potential performance impact	Healthcare apps storing patient data, financial services managing transactions
Data masking	Hides or anonymizes data to protect sensitive information while maintaining usability	Protects sensitive data in non-production environments	Ensuring that masked data remains useful for testing	Development and testing environments in retail or financial services
RBAC	Assigns access permissions based on user roles	Limits access to authorized users, enforces least privilege	Requires careful role design and maintenance	Large organizations with complex teams, such as hospitals or global enterprises

Security technique	Description	Advantages	Challenges	Use case
Compliance GDPR	Ensures personal data protection, requires consent management and data anonymization	Provides clear regulatory framework for data management	High fines for non-compliance, complex to implement in legacy systems	E-commerce, customer-facing apps that handle European data
Compliance HIPAA	Protects healthcare data with strict access, audit, and encryption requirements	Safeguards highly sensitive health data	Requires stringent policies, especially in hybrid architectures	Healthcare providers, insurance companies

Table 10.5: Security techniques

Table 10.5 helps solutions architects make informed decisions when integrating security and compliance into data architectures, ensuring that systems meet both regulatory requirements and business needs.

Practical decision-making frameworks

Solutions architects must choose the right data architecture based on business requirements, scalability needs, and specific data management scenarios. This section outlines the practical decision-making frameworks that help solutions architects navigate the complexities of modern data architectures. Whether selecting between data warehouses, data lakes, or data mesh, or evaluating cloud-native versus on-premises data solutions, using structured frameworks ensures that the right decisions are made for optimal performance and efficiency.

Each data architecture, data warehouses, data lakes, and data mesh has its strengths and weaknesses, making them suited for different business and technical needs. Solutions architects should understand these architectures and apply them based on the specific use case.

The following *Table 10.6* outlines how to choose between data warehouses, data lakes, and data mesh based on specific use cases:

Architecture	Best for	Examples	Limitations
Data warehouse	Structured data, centralized reporting	Financial reporting, business intelligence in retail, healthcare, finance	Less flexible for unstructured data, expensive for large-scale storage
Data lake	Unstructured, semi-structured, and large data	AI or ML workloads, data science, and analytics on big datasets for example, IoT data, logs, social media analytics	Can become a data swamp if not managed correctly
Data mesh	Decentralized, domain-driven data management	Large enterprises with multiple domains, microservices architectures for example, large retail or tech companies	Requires strong governance, complex to implement

Table 10.6: Use cases to choose data warehouse versus data lake versus data mesh

Selecting data storage and architecture patterns

To help select the appropriate data architecture, solutions architects can use decision trees and grids based on key factors such as data type, volume, processing needs, and use case complexity.

Table 10.7 is a simplified representation to assist solutions architects in choosing the right architecture based on the characteristics of their data and use case:

Criteria	Data warehouse	Data lake	Data mesh
Data type	Structured data	Structured, semi-structured, unstructured	Structured and unstructured, domain-specific
Query speed	Fast queries for structured data	Slower for complex, large datasets	Depends on the domain and setup
Data ownership	Centralized data ownership	Centralized, but supports multiple types	Decentralized, each domain owns its data
Processing needs	Real-time, transactional analysis	Batch processing, AI/ML workloads	Domain-level processing for specific use cases
Storage flexibility	Fixed schema, limited flexibility	High flexibility for raw data	Flexible, but needs strong governance
Scalability	Vertical scalability (upgrading servers)	Horizontal scalability (adding nodes)	Horizontally scalable across domains
Best use case	Real-time analytics, reporting	Data science, machine learning	Distributed organizations, complex ownership

Table 10.7: Decision tree for choosing data architecture patterns

Table 10.8 compares cloud-native and on-premises solutions across key decision factors for solutions architects:

Factor	Cloud-native	On-premises
Scalability	Highly scalable, on-demand	Limited by physical hardware
Cost model	Pay-as-you-go, operational expenses	High upfront capital expenditure
Data security	Shared responsibility, vendor-managed	Full control over security
Compliance	Must verify compliance with cloud provider	Easier to maintain strict compliance
Maintenance	Low, managed by cloud providers	High, internal IT responsibility
Integration with services	Seamless integration with AI, analytics, and other cloud services	Requires custom integrations

Table 10.8: Cloud-native versus on-premises

These practical decision-making frameworks empower solutions architects to make well-informed decisions when designing and implementing data architectures, ensuring that the chosen approach aligns with business goals, data characteristics, and technical requirements. Whether deciding between a data warehouse for real-time reporting or a data lake for machine learning, or choosing between cloud-native and on-premises solutions, these frameworks provide a structured approach to selecting the right architecture for the job.

Tools for data architecture design

Selecting the right tools for data architecture design is crucial for solutions architects as it ensures the scalability, efficiency, and reliability of data solutions. Various cloud platforms and third-party tools offer robust capabilities for designing, implementing, and managing modern data architectures.

Let us explore prominent tools such as Microsoft Fabric, Azure Synapse, AWS Redshift, and GCP BigQuery, as well as specialized data modeling tools like Erwin Data Modeler, dbt, and Lucidchart.

The following are the cloud-native data architecture tools:

- **Microsoft Fabric**: Microsoft Fabric is a unified platform that brings together various data management, integration, and analytics capabilities. It supports data engineering, data science, and real-time analytics while enabling seamless collaboration across teams. Microsoft Fabric is designed to provide end-to-end data architecture solutions, from data ingestion to advanced analytics.

The following are the use cases:

- o Fabric excels in environments where multiple teams are working on data pipelines, machine learning, and real-time reporting.
- o It integrates easily with other Microsoft services like Power BI for visualization and Azure Data Lake for storage.

The following are the advantages:

- o Strong integration with the Microsoft ecosystem.
- o Comprehensive features for data management and real-time analytics.
- o Ideal for enterprises leveraging Microsoft Azure and related services.

- **Azure Synapse Analytics**: Azure Synapse Analytics is a cloud-native, integrated analytics service that combines big data and data warehousing capabilities. It enables solutions architects to query data using both serverless and provisioned resources. Synapse supports various data processing needs, including ETL, real-time analytics, and advanced machine learning integration.

The following are the use cases:

- o Ideal for enterprises looking to analyze data from multiple sources, such as structured and unstructured data, Azure Synapse also provides tight integration with Power BI for visualization and Azure ML for predictive analytics.

The following are the advantages:

- o Flexibility to query data on-demand with serverless compute options.
- o Integrated with Azure's broader ecosystem for data lakes, machine learning, and IoT.
- o Optimized for hybrid data environments where organizations need to handle both big data and traditional BI workloads.

- **AWS Redshift**: Amazon Redshift is a cloud data warehouse that allows for fast, complex querying and analytics on massive datasets. It integrates seamlessly with other AWS services and is known for its ability to process petabytes of data quickly. Redshift Spectrum enables querying data stored in Amazon S3 without needing to load it into the warehouse, offering more flexibility.

The following are the use cases:

- o Redshift is often used for big data analytics, business intelligence reporting, and ETL pipelines in organizations with extensive AWS investments.

The following are the advantages:

- o Scalable architecture supporting massive data volumes.
- o Strong integration with AWS ecosystem tools like S3, Athena, and Glue.
- o Cost-effective due to its pay-per-query model and storage optimizations.

- **GCP BigQuery**: Google Cloud Platform's BigQuery is a fully managed, serverless data warehouse designed for fast SQL queries using massive processing power. It enables real-time analytics and integrates seamlessly with Google's Cloud services like Dataflow, Pub/Sub, and TensorFlow for ML.

The following are the use cases:

- o Best suited for organizations looking to analyze large datasets across distributed environments.
- o BigQuery supports multi-cloud analytics, allowing businesses to process data in Google Cloud alongside AWS or Azure data sources.

The following are the advantages:

- o Serverless model that eliminates infrastructure management.
- o Real-time, highly performant queries over massive datasets.
- o Supports multi-cloud data analytics, offering flexibility across platforms.

Data architecture design tools

In addition to cloud-native platforms, solutions architects need dedicated tools for designing data models, optimizing pipelines, and visualizing architecture.

The following tools are widely used for data architecture design, providing the necessary support for modeling, transformation, and collaboration:

- **Erwin Data Modeler**: Erwin Data Modeler is a widely used tool for visualizing and designing data models. It supports both physical and logical data modeling and offers integration with various databases, including SQL and NoSQL systems. It is ideal for maintaining data consistency, improving compliance, and managing data flow across the enterprise.

  The following are the use cases:

  - o Commonly used in large-scale enterprises, where managing complex data models and ensuring compliance are critical. It supports a wide range of database systems, making it versatile for organizations with hybrid or multi-cloud environments.

  The following are the advantages:

  - o Powerful visualization tools for both logical and physical data models.
  - o Integration with popular database platforms for easy deployment.
  - o Offers data lineage and governance features to ensure data integrity across systems.

- **Data build tool (dbt)**: dbt is a powerful transformation tool used to define and execute data transformations directly in the data warehouse. It focuses on the transformation in the ETL process, enabling teams to build modular, version-controlled data models using SQL. dbt integrates seamlessly with platforms like Snowflake, Redshift, and BigQuery.

  The following are the use cases:

  - o dbt is perfect for organizations that want to maintain control over their data transformations and adopt a more modular, code-driven approach to building data models.

  The following are the advantages:

  - o Promotes modular, reusable transformations that reduce redundancy.
  - o SQL-based approach makes it accessible for data teams.
  - o Integrated version control ensures data models remain maintainable and scalable.

- **Lucidchart**: Lucidchart is a cloud-based tool used for creating visual diagrams, flowcharts, and data models. It is highly versatile and often used for representing data architectures visually, helping teams collaborate on designing and documenting complex data systems.

  The following are the use cases:

  - o Lucidchart is ideal for visualizing data flow, integration architectures, and collaborative data modeling.
  - o Its ease of use and cloud-based nature make it a go-to tool for teams needing to quickly create and share visual data designs.

The following are the advantages:

- o Simple interface for creating complex diagrams, flowcharts, and models.
- o Enables real-time collaboration for distributed teams.
- o Integrates with other tools like Jira, Confluence, and Google Workspace.

These tools play a critical role in the design, implementation, and management of modern data architectures, providing solutions architects with the flexibility, power, and integration needed to build scalable and efficient data-driven solutions. The choice of tool should be aligned with the specific requirements of the project, including the size of the data, the complexity of the architecture, and the integration needs across platforms.

Now that we have established the fundamental principles of designing robust data architectures, the next critical step is ensuring seamless data flow across systems. In modern enterprises, data rarely resides in a single location, making data integration and management crucial for maintaining data quality, consistency, and accessibility.

Let us explore how to effectively integrate and manage data in diverse environments.

Data integration and management

Data integration is a critical aspect of modern enterprise systems. It involves combining data from different sources and making it accessible in a unified manner for analysis, reporting, and decision-making. solutions architects play a crucial role in designing and managing seamless data integration flows, ensuring data is transferred efficiently and accurately across various systems.

This section explores data integration scenarios, techniques, and best practices to equip solutions architects with the necessary tools and frameworks for successful data integration.

Understanding data integration needs

Data integration is essential for businesses to extract meaningful insights from their data, which often resides in multiple systems. The process of integrating data depends on several factors, such as the speed at which data needs to be transferred, the volume of data, and the business requirements for data freshness.

Key data integration scenarios are as follows:

- **Extract, transform, load (ETL)**: A traditional data integration approach where data is first extracted from various sources, transformed to fit the target schema, and then loaded into the destination system, such as a data warehouse. ETL is suitable for batch processing where real-time data is not a priority.

- **Extract, load, transform (ELT)**: A modern approach, often used in big data environments, where data is extracted and loaded into the target system first and then transformed. This is common in cloud data warehousing and Lakehouse architectures.

- **Real-time processing**: Data is ingested and processed as soon as it is generated. Real-time integration is necessary for applications such as monitoring systems, fraud detection, and real-time analytics.

- **Batch processing**: Data is collected over a period of time and processed in batches. Batch integration is useful for scenarios where real-time data is not critical, such as financial reporting at the end of the day.

As a solutions architect, ensuring seamless data flow across systems is key to maintaining business operations. They must design systems that handle various integration types, manage data latency, maintain quality, and ensure consistency. Solutions architects are responsible for selecting the right integration approach based on system needs, data volumes, and business requirements.

The following are the key considerations:

- **Latency**: The speed at which data is transferred and made available in the destination system.
- **Data quality**: Ensuring that the data being transferred is accurate, complete, and fit for analysis.
- **Consistency**: Data must remain consistent across systems, especially in real-time or event-driven architectures.
- **Synchronization**: Data updates must be synchronized across different systems to prevent data discrepancies.

With a clear understanding of the various scenarios where data integration is needed, it is important to explore the techniques that ensure data is seamlessly integrated across diverse systems.

Let us now take a look at the different methods for achieving efficient and reliable data integration.

Data integration techniques

Data integration involves several techniques, and solutions architects need to choose the right method based on the project requirements as follows:

- **ETL**: ETL is commonly used in traditional data warehouses and allows for comprehensive data transformations before loading into the destination. It is suitable for batch processing where transformations can be complex, and real-time updates are not necessary.

- **ELT**: ELT is more efficient for handling large volumes of data in big data architectures. The data is loaded first into the target system (often a cloud data warehouse), and transformations are performed within the target system using its processing power. ELT is commonly used in cloud-based systems where computing resources are elastic and scalable.

- **Data streaming and real-time integration**: Real-time data integration uses technologies like Apache Kafka, AWS Kinesis, and Azure Event Hubs to stream data continuously. This is ideal for systems that require immediate data availability, such as fraud detection, stock trading, or real-time monitoring systems.

- **Data virtualization**: Data virtualization enables real-time data access without the need for physically replicating data. Tools like Denodo and Tibco make it possible to query data from multiple systems in a unified view. This technique is ideal for organizations that need to integrate data from diverse systems without moving it.

Having explored the key techniques for data integration, we now turn our attention to more complex environments, such as hybrid and multi-cloud setups, which require advanced integration strategies to ensure smooth data flow between diverse systems.

Integration strategies for hybrid and multi-cloud

Modern enterprises often operate across on-premises, hybrid, and multi-cloud environments, making data integration more complex.

To address the challenges of integrating data across on-premises, hybrid, and multi-cloud environments, solutions architects can adopt several key strategies that ensure seamless and secure data flow.

The following are some common approaches:

- **Connecting on-premises systems with cloud services**: Many enterprises maintain legacy on-premises systems while adopting cloud solutions for scalability and agility. Solutions like Azure Data Factory, AWS Glue, and Google Cloud Dataflow help integrate on-premises databases and applications with cloud-based storage and services.

- **Managing data integration in multi-cloud deployments**: In multi-cloud environments, data resides in different cloud platforms, for example, AWS, Azure, and GCP. Integration tools that support multi-cloud data flows, like Talend, Informatica, and Apache NiFi, are essential for ensuring smooth and secure data transfers across platforms.

- **Using APIs, data gateways, and middleware**: APIs and data gateways are crucial for connecting disparate systems. Middleware solutions provide a bridge for applications to communicate across environments, ensuring data is passed securely and efficiently.

After reviewing the complexities of hybrid and multi-cloud integration strategies, it is essential to select the right tools and frameworks that can support these environments.

Tools and frameworks for data integration

Numerous tools are available to help solutions architects design, implement, and manage data integration solutions. Selecting the right tool depends on factors like data volume, real-time needs, complexity, and the existing technology stack are as follows:

- **Hyperscaler platforms**:

  - **Azure Data factory**: A fully managed cloud data integration service that orchestrates data movement and transformation between various data stores.

  - **AWS Glue**: A serverless ETL service from AWS that simplifies the process of preparing data for analysis. Glue integrates with other AWS services, such as Redshift, S3, and Athena.

  - **Google Cloud Dataflow**: A fully managed service for stream and batch processing that supports real-time data integration and transformation across cloud and on-premises systems.

- **Multi-platform industry-leading tools**:

  - **Talend**: Provides a unified platform for data integration and management, supporting ETL, real-time integration, and data governance.

  - **Informatica**: A robust enterprise-level data integration platform that supports multi-cloud and hybrid deployments.

  - **Apache NiFi**: An open-source tool designed for automating the flow of data between systems. NiFi excels in managing real-time, high-volume data flows.

The following table compares the previously mentioned data integration tools:

Tool	Platform	Key features	Best for
Azure Data Factory	Microsoft Azure	Managed service for orchestration, ETL, and ELT	Cloud-based data pipelines
AWS Glue	Amazon Web Services	Serverless ETL service, integrates with AWS services	Big data processing, ETL workflows
Google Cloud Dataflow	Google Cloud	Stream and batch processing for real-time data flows	Real-time analytics and transformations
Talend	Multi-platform	ETL, data integration, real-time processing	Hybrid and multi-cloud deployments
Informatica	Multi-platform	Comprehensive data integration, governance, and quality	Enterprise-grade integration
Apache NiFi	Open-source	Real-time data flow automation	High-volume, real-time data transfers

Table 10.9: Comparison of data integration tools

Selecting the right tools is just the beginning; ensuring that data management processes are efficient, reliable, and scalable is key to the success of any data integration strategy.

Best practices for data management

To ensure the reliability and accuracy of integrated data, solutions architects must follow best practices when managing data pipelines as follows:

- **Ensuring data consistency and quality**: It is crucial to monitor data consistency across systems, particularly in real-time integration scenarios. Using tools like Azure Data Quality Services or Informatica Data Quality, architects can ensure data is clean and accurate throughout the integration process.

- **Implementing error handling, retry mechanisms, and data audits**: Data pipelines should include mechanisms for handling errors and automatically retrying failed processes. Additionally, implementing audit trails helps monitor data flows and detect issues early.

- **Versioning and change management**: Proper versioning of data pipelines and integration scripts ensures that any changes can be tracked, tested, and rolled back if necessary. Solutions like Git for code management and Jenkins for continuous integration can automate change management in data integration processes.

Decision frameworks for data integration tool selection

Selecting the right data integration tool is critical for building efficient and scalable pipelines. Solutions architects can use decision frameworks based on data volume, processing speed, and business complexity to choose the best tool for their needs as follows:

- **Evaluating tools based on requirements**: Factors such as the volume of data, the complexity of transformations, and whether the data needs to be processed in real time or batch should guide tool selection.

- **Decision trees for integration**: A decision tree can be used to decide whether batch processing, real-time streaming, or event-driven architectures are appropriate based on the business requirements. For example, real-time data streaming tools like Kafka are ideal for high-frequency, low-latency applications, while batch processing with AWS Glue or Google Cloud Dataflow may be better for less time-sensitive data.

Let us take a look at tool recommendations, according to respective requirements:

Requirement	Tool recommendation
High-volume batch processing	AWS Glue, Google Cloud Dataflow
Real-time streaming	Apache Kafka, Azure Event Hubs
Multi-cloud environments	Talend, Informatica
Data governance and quality	Informatica, Azure Data Factory

Table 10.10: Decision framework for data integration tools

By following these frameworks, solutions architects can design and implement robust data integration solutions that meet the specific needs of their organization.

As data flows are managed and integrated across systems, enterprises face the challenge of handling increasingly large volumes of diverse data. This leads us into the realm of big data, where the sheer scale of information presents both opportunities and challenges. To effectively harness the power of big data, solutions architects must implement scalable architectures that can ingest, process, and analyze data in real-time.

Big data solutions

Big data has revolutionized the way organizations store, process, and analyze vast amounts of information. For solutions architects, understanding how to implement effective big data strategies is essential, as this enables businesses to extract meaningful insights from unstructured and structured data, address data governance concerns, and optimize operational efficiencies. This section gets into the key challenges of big data, the strategies for architecting scalable big data solutions, and the tools and frameworks required to manage and process big data in cloud-native environments.

Understanding big data challenges

Effectively managing big data requires solutions architects to address its unique challenges, which stem from the fundamental characteristics of big data. These challenges must be understood and addressed to build robust and scalable systems. The primary challenges are as follows:

- **Volume**: The sheer amount of data generated by enterprises is enormous and continuously growing. Data must be ingested, processed, and stored efficiently to maintain performance.

- **Velocity**: The speed at which data is generated and needs to be processed, especially with real-time applications such as IoT devices, financial markets, and social media, requires advanced streaming capabilities.

- **Variety**: The data comes in multiple formats, such as structured (relational databases), semi-structured (JSON, XML), and unstructured (videos, emails, and social media posts), which complicates the processing and analysis.

- **Big data in the context of enterprise architectures**: As organizations adopt cloud-native and hybrid architectures, managing the complexity of data becomes a top priority. Solutions architects must design systems that can scale dynamically, process large volumes of data in real-time or batches, and ensure data quality and consistency across distributed environments.

- **Role of solutions architects in implementing big data strategies**: Solutions architects play a crucial role in shaping the organization's big data strategy. This involves choosing the right storage, processing frameworks, and analytical tools while ensuring compliance with data governance policies. They must balance performance with cost-effectiveness and ensure that the architecture can scale with business needs.

Having identified the key challenges of big data, the next logical step is to explore how solutions architects can address these challenges by architecting scalable and efficient big data solutions. Let us examine the strategies that can help manage the volume, velocity, and variety of data in modern enterprises.

Architecting big data solutions

When architecting big data solutions, solutions architects must consider data ingestion, processing, and storage strategies that align with the business's goals and data use cases.

Data ingestion strategies

The following are a few data ingestion strategies:

- **Batch processing**: Suitable for scenarios where real-time data is not critical. Data is collected, processed, and moved in chunks, often at scheduled intervals, for example, nightly jobs.

- **Streaming**: Real-time data ingestion, where data is continuously captured and processed on-the-fly. Streaming solutions like Apache Kafka and AWS Kinesis are widely used in applications like fraud detection and real-time analytics.

- **Lambda architecture**: Combines batch and real-time processing, allowing for high-throughput and low-latency processing. This architecture is commonly used in large-scale data environments to process both real-time data streams and batch jobs.

Storage options for big data

The following are a few storage options for big data:

- **Data lakes**: A scalable storage solution for storing vast amounts of structured, semi-structured, and unstructured data in its raw form. Data lakes are highly flexible, enabling businesses to run different types of analytics on all their data.

- **Data warehouses**: A more structured storage option optimized for querying structured data and running complex analytical queries. Data warehouses, like AWS Redshift and Google BigQuery, are purpose-built for analytics at scale.

- **Lakehouses**: An emerging architectural pattern that combines the strengths of data lakes and data warehouses. Lakehouses provide the flexibility of a data lake with the data management and governance features of a data warehouse, using tools like Databricks or Delta Lake.

Implementing big data processing architectures

The following provides suggestions on how big data processing architectures can be implemented:

- **Lambda architecture**: Processes real-time and batch data streams, enabling low-latency querying and high-throughput operations. This architecture is suitable for workloads requiring both historical and real-time data analysis.

- **Kappa architecture**: A simplified version of Lambda that only processes data streams and removes batch layers, often used for real-time analytics where batch processing is not required.

- **Micro-batch processing**: This involves processing small batches of data in near real-time intervals, suitable for use cases where real-time precision is not required but faster processing than traditional batch methods is needed.

As organizations increasingly adopt cloud-native environments, it is critical to understand how big data architectures can be optimized using cloud-based solutions.

Cloud-native big data solutions

Cloud platforms provide a variety of managed services for big data solutions, which are highly scalable and can be easily integrated into enterprise environments.

The following are some cloud-native tools for processing and analyzing big data:

- **Microsoft Fabric, Azure HDInsight, Azure Databricks**: Azure offers managed services for big data, including Azure HDInsight, a fully-managed Hadoop and Spark service, and Azure Databricks, a collaborative analytics platform built on Apache Spark.

- **AWS Elastic MapReduce (EMR), AWS Redshift Spectrum**: AWS provides EMR, a managed cluster platform that simplifies running big data frameworks like Hadoop and Spark. AWS Redshift Spectrum enables querying data in S3 directly without having to load it into a Redshift data warehouse.

- **Google BigQuery, Google Cloud Dataproc**: BigQuery is a serverless, highly scalable data warehouse designed for analytics, while Google Cloud Dataproc offers a managed Hadoop and Spark environment for processing big data.

- **Decision-making framework for selecting cloud-native services**: Solutions architects should evaluate cloud services based on factors like data volume, real-time processing needs, and the nature of analytics. For instance, if real-time analytics is a priority, AWS Kinesis or Azure Event Hubs might be appropriate. For large-scale data processing, Google BigQuery or Azure Databricks would be more suited.

With a grasp of cloud-native big data solutions, it is also important to consider how enterprises can implement data lakes and lakehouses, which allow for more flexible storage and analytics capabilities. Let us now dive into the specifics of these storage architectures.

Implementing data lakes and lakehouses

Implementing the right data storage solutions, such as data lakes and lakehouses, is crucial for managing vast amounts of unstructured and structured data. These architectures provide the flexibility needed for advanced analytics and machine learning, while maintaining governance and performance standards to avoid common pitfalls like data swamps.

To harness the full potential of vast data repositories, solutions architects must implement storage architectures that balance flexibility, performance, and governance. Data lakes and lakehouses offer distinct advantages for handling both structured and unstructured data, supporting diverse analytics and machine learning workloads.

Key considerations are as follows:

- **Designing data lakes**: Data lakes store data in its raw form, which allows for flexibility in running analytics, machine learning, and other advanced data processing techniques. However, they require proper data governance and management to avoid becoming Data Swamps (unstructured and ungoverned storage).

- **Understanding the data lakehouse architecture**: Lakehouses combine the advantages of data lakes and data warehouses by providing transactional support, governance, and high performance. Tools like Databricks, Delta Lake, and Apache Hudi are designed to support lakehouse architectures, providing both flexibility and structure.

Tools for building data lakes are as follows:

- **Delta Lake**: An open-source storage layer that brings reliability to data lakes.
- **Apache Hudi**: Enables efficient ingestion, upserts, and incremental processing of data lakes.
- **Databricks**: A unified data analytics platform for data science, engineering, and machine learning.

After selecting the appropriate storage architecture, such as data lakes or lakehouses, implementing the right tools for big data analytics becomes the next priority.

Tools for big data analytics and processing

Various tools are available to help solutions architects implement big data analytics and processing frameworks as follows:

- **Apache Spark**: A fast, general-purpose cluster-computing framework for big data processing.

- **Presto**: A distributed SQL query engine optimized for running interactive analytic queries against data sources of all sizes.

- **Dremio**: A data lake engine built to simplify and accelerate analytics workflows.

- **Apache Flink**: A stream processing framework that supports event-driven applications and real-time analytics.

- **Real-time data processing**: Real-time data processing is essential for applications that require immediate insights and quick decision-making. These systems handle continuous data streams and process them as they arrive, enabling businesses to react to events in real time. The following tools are commonly used to implement real-time data processing:

- o **Kafka**: A distributed streaming platform for building real-time data pipelines.
- o **Apache Storm**: A real-time computation system for processing unbounded data streams.

With powerful tools for big data analytics in place, it is crucial to address data governance to ensure quality, compliance, and security across systems.

Data governance in big data architectures

With big data comes the challenge of governance. Solutions architects must ensure data is managed securely and remains compliant with industry regulations as follows:

- **Managing data governance**: Data governance involves ensuring data is accurate, accessible, consistent, and secure. In big data environments, this means managing data lineage, provenance, and compliance across large, distributed systems.

- **Implementing data lineage, provenance, and compliance**: Understanding where data comes from (provenance), how it is used, and ensuring it is traceable (lineage) are key aspects of big data governance. Compliance with regulations like GDPR and HIPAA.

The following are the governance tools:

- **Collibra**: A data governance and management platform that helps organizations manage their data governance policies.

- **Informatica Axon**: A data governance solution designed for tracking data lineage and enforcing governance policies.

- **AWS Lake Formation**: Simplifies the process of building, securing, and managing data lakes.

- **Microsoft Purview**: A unified data governance solution that enables organizations to manage and govern their on-premises, multi-cloud, and SaaS data.

By mastering these aspects of big data architecture, solutions architects can effectively design and manage scalable, secure, and compliant big data solutions.

With a solid framework in place for managing and processing large datasets, the final step is to convert this data into actionable insights that drive business decisions. Analytics bridges the gap between raw data and meaningful outcomes, enabling organizations to make data-driven decisions. In this final section, we will discuss how to architect analytics solutions and leverage advanced tools to extract business insights from data.

Leveraging analytics for business insights

In the modern data-driven landscape, businesses are increasingly relying on analytics to gain actionable insights and make informed decisions. As a solutions architect, understanding how to leverage analytics to provide business insights is a critical skill, particularly in designing scalable, secure, and impactful data architectures. This section will guide you through the key roles that analytics play in solutions architecture, the techniques and approaches used for effective analytics, and the best practices for designing scalable, high-performance analytics systems.

Role of analytics in solutions architecture

To fully harness the power of data, solutions architects must go beyond traditional data management by integrating advanced analytics strategies. This section explores how analytics transforms raw data into actionable insights, driving key business decisions.

Importance of data-driven decision-making

Analytics enables organizations to transform raw data into meaningful insights, allowing leaders to make better decisions. For solutions architects, this means designing systems that facilitate the seamless collection, analysis, and presentation of data. These systems not only need to handle vast amounts of data but must also ensure that the data is accurate, timely, and accessible to business users.

Solutions architect's role in enabling business insights through analytics

A solutions architect must ensure that the data infrastructure is optimized for analytics, from integrating the right tools and technologies to defining data pipelines. This involves choosing appropriate data storage solutions, designing data flows, and implementing systems that enable analytics to be performed efficiently and effectively.

Aligning analytics strategy with business goals

It is vital to ensure that the analytics strategy is closely aligned with business objectives. Whether it is improving customer engagement, optimizing supply chain operations, or identifying market trends, the solutions architect must work closely with business stakeholders to ensure the analytics platform supports the organization's strategic initiatives. Analytics should not just provide raw data but should offer clear, actionable insights that drive business value.

Understanding the role of analytics in enabling business insights is only the first step. Solutions architects must also be familiar with the techniques that drive value from data. Let us now explore the core analytics approaches that can help organizations make informed decisions.

Key analytics techniques and approaches

Once solutions architects have selected the appropriate analytics techniques, the next crucial step is ensuring that the analytics system can handle the data efficiently and scale as the business grows. Let us explore how to design scalable analytics architectures that prioritize both performance and reliability.

Descriptive, predictive, and prescriptive analytics

The following are the three primary categories of analytics that solutions architects need to design for:

- **Descriptive analytics**: It focuses on understanding what has happened by analyzing historical data. This often involves reporting, data visualization, and dashboarding.

- **Predictive analytics**: It uses statistical models and machine learning to predict future trends based on historical data.

- **Prescriptive analytics**: It goes one step further by suggesting actions based on predictive outcomes, using techniques like optimization and simulation to recommend the best course of action.

Real-time analytics, dashboarding, and visualization techniques

In many business scenarios, real-time data analytics is crucial, especially in industries like finance, retail, and healthcare. Real-time dashboards that display metrics and KPIs help business users make timely decisions. Solutions architects must integrate streaming data platforms and design real-time processing pipelines to support this need.

Using AI/ML models for advanced analytics

AI and ML are increasingly being leveraged for deeper insights and automation of decision-making. Solutions architects are responsible for integrating AI/ML models into the analytics infrastructure, using tools like Azure Machine Learning, Amazon SageMaker, or Google AI Platform. The use cases are as follows:

- **Deep learning**: It is for image and speech recognition.
- **Natural language processing (NLP)**: It is for text analytics and sentiment analysis.
- **Forecasting**: It models to predict sales, demand, or financial trends.

Once the right analytics techniques are chosen, it is vital to ensure that the underlying architecture can scale to meet the growing demands of data processing and analysis.

Designing scalable analytics architectures

Designing scalable analytics architectures ensures that data systems can handle growing volumes while maintaining performance and availability. Solutions architects must integrate tools and strategies that allow for flexible scaling, minimal latency, and seamless data processing across cloud-native environments.

Architecting analytics solutions for high availability and low latency

When designing analytics solutions, it is crucial to ensure that the architecture can handle large volumes of data while providing results with minimal latency. High availability ensures that analytics services are always accessible, even during peak loads or system failures. Solutions architects often use replication, load balancing, and failover mechanisms to achieve this.

Integrating analytics into cloud-native architectures using serverless and containerized approaches

Cloud-native solutions provide flexibility, scalability, and cost-efficiency. Using serverless architectures like AWS Lambda, Azure Functions, or Google Cloud Functions for running analytics workloads can eliminate the need to manage infrastructure, while containerized approaches like Kubernetes or Docker provide isolated environments for analytics services. Both approaches help ensure that analytics applications scale easily with demand.

Designing data pipelines for analytics using Azure Synapse, AWS Athena, Google Cloud BigQuery, and Databricks

Solutions architects need to design data pipelines that ETL data for analytics. Azure Synapse, AWS Athena, Google BigQuery, and Databricks are powerful tools that enable solutions architects to build scalable, high-performance analytics pipelines. These platforms support querying, processing, and analyzing large datasets across various environments.

As the architecture is designed for scalability and performance, the next step is selecting the right tools that can help visualize and communicate insights.

Tools for business analytics and visualization

Selecting the right tools for business analytics and visualization is key to delivering actionable insights. Solutions architects must choose platforms that balance ease of use with the capability to handle complex data and advanced visualizations.

Microsoft Power BI, AWS QuickSight, Google Data Studio, and Tableau

Selecting the right tools for business analytics is crucial for delivering insights that drive decision-making. Power BI, AWS QuickSight, Google Data Studio, and Tableau are some of the leading platforms for creating interactive dashboards and reports. These tools allow business users to visualize complex datasets and explore insights without needing advanced technical skills.

Implementing custom visualizations with D3.js, Plotly, and Highcharts

When pre-built visualization tools do not meet specific business requirements, Solutions architects may need to implement custom visualizations using libraries like D3.js, Plotly, or Highcharts. These tools provide more control over the appearance and interactivity of data visualizations and can be embedded into custom analytics applications.

Tool selection frameworks based on data volume, complexity, and business requirements

Choosing the right analytics tool depends on factors such as data volume, complexity, and the specific needs of the business. Solutions architects must evaluate whether a tool can handle the scale of data required, integrate with existing infrastructure, and provide the flexibility for advanced analytics and visualizations.

Having explored the tools for data visualization and business analytics, it is essential to ensure that these tools are implemented effectively.

Best practices for implementing business analytics

Implementing business analytics effectively requires adhering to best practices that ensure clarity, simplicity, and accessibility for all users. Solutions architects must design systems that empower users to gain insights independently while maintaining control over data quality and governance.

Designing dashboards for clarity, simplicity, and impact

A well-designed dashboard can transform data into actionable insights. Solutions architects should focus on creating dashboards that present key information clearly and concisely, avoiding information overload. Use color-coding, clear labels, and consistent layouts to ensure users can quickly understand the data presented.

Implementing self-service analytics for business users

Empowering business users to perform their own analytics without relying on IT is a growing trend. Self-service analytics platforms, such as Power BI or Tableau, allow users to build custom reports and dashboards. Solutions architects must design systems that balance user autonomy with data governance, ensuring users have access to the data they need while maintaining security and compliance.

Using KPIs and Metrics to drive actionable insights

KPIs and metrics are essential for tracking business performance. Solutions architects should work with stakeholders to define relevant KPIs and ensure that the analytics infrastructure provides real-time access to these metrics. This enables decision-makers to react to changes in business conditions quickly.

Data storytelling and communication

In today's data-driven world, conveying insights effectively through storytelling is essential for driving business outcomes. Solutions architects must focus on creating impactful data narratives that transform raw data into meaningful, actionable insights for decision-makers.

Importance of effective data storytelling in driving business outcomes

Data storytelling is the process of translating complex data into a compelling narrative that drives action. Solutions architects need to ensure that the analytics system not only provides accurate data but also enables users to create meaningful data stories that resonate with stakeholders.

Structuring data narratives to influence decision-making

A well-structured data narrative is key to making insights understandable and actionable. By highlighting trends, anomalies, and key takeaways, solutions architects can help business users grasp the implications of data and make informed decisions.

Tools and techniques for creating impactful data stories

Solutions architects can use tools like Narrative Science, Tableau Storytelling, and Power BI Dataflows to create dynamic, interactive data stories. These tools allow users to combine data visualizations with explanatory text, enabling them to present insights in a way that influences business decisions.

Conclusion

In this chapter, we explored the pivotal role that analytics plays in a solutions architect's responsibilities. Designing scalable, secure, and impactful analytics solutions is crucial for enabling data-driven decision-making. By understanding key analytics techniques, leveraging cloud-native tools, and ensuring that the architecture supports both business insights and real-time analytics, solutions architects can drive value across the organization. Whether implementing AI/ML models or designing effective dashboards, the ability to align analytics strategy with business goals ensures that data delivers actionable insights that enhance business performance.

In the next chapter, we will get into how user-centric design principles can enhance the effectiveness of solutions architecture. This chapter will equip solutions architects with the skills needed to create solutions that are not only technically robust but also user-friendly and accessible, ensuring a seamless user experience across all stakeholders.

Key takeaways

The takeaways are as follows:

- **Data-driven decision-making**: Solutions architects play a crucial role in enabling data-driven decision-making by designing analytics systems that provide actionable insights aligned with business goals.

- **Analytics techniques**: Understanding the different types of analytics, that is, descriptive, predictive, and prescriptive, is the key to building solutions that address current performance and future trends.

- **Scalable analytics architectures**: Architecting solutions for high availability, low latency, and real-time analytics is essential in large-scale, data-driven organizations.

- **Cloud-native analytics**: Leveraging cloud-native services like Azure Synapse, AWS Athena, and Google BigQuery can provide scalable and cost-effective analytics platforms.

- **Visualization tools**: Choosing the right business analytics tools, like Power BI, AWS QuickSight, and Tableau, ensures that decision-makers can interact with data meaningfully and effectively.

- **Data storytelling**: Effective data storytelling and communication transform raw data into impactful narratives that drive business outcomes and influence decision-making.

Model interview questions and answers

1. **How do you design a scalable analytics architecture for large enterprises?**

   Model answer:

   - Well, when it comes to scalability, it is all about building for growth. You typically start by focusing on cloud-native services like Azure Synapse, AWS Redshift, or Google BigQuery because they are built to scale without too much overhead on infrastructure management. These services handle massive datasets efficiently and allow us to focus more on the analytics side.

   - For self-service analytics, enabling business users to explore data on their own is key. You ensure that dashboards and data visualization tools, like Power BI or Tableau, are tightly integrated.

   - To make sure the system is highly available, you set up redundancy and failover mechanisms. After all, availability is critical, especially in real-time analytics scenarios like fraud detection.

2. **How do you decide between using a data warehouse, data lake, or data mesh for a given architecture?**

   Model answer:

   - It depends on the nature of the data and the organization's structure. If the data is highly structured and mainly used for reporting or BI, you lean towards a data warehouse, it is optimized for OLAP-style queries and business intelligence.

   - For unstructured or semi-structured data, where you need flexibility for AI or machine learning workloads, data lakes are fantastic. They give the ability to store raw data and process it later, and cloud platforms like Azure Data Lake or AWS S3 make this really easy.

   - When dealing with large, distributed teams, particularly in larger enterprises where different departments own their data, data mesh becomes valuable. It decentralizes data ownership but requires strong governance. It is a newer approach, but you have seen it work well in organizations that prioritize autonomy.

3. **When would you recommend using real-time data integration, and how would you design it?**

   Model answer:

   - Real-time data integration makes sense when businesses need to react immediately to incoming data like fraud detection, stock trading, or monitoring applications. In these cases, low latency is everything.

   - You usually go with a streaming platform like Apache Kafka, AWS Kinesis, or Azure Event Hubs for continuous data flow. The goal is to ensure data arrives in real-time, so you focus on minimizing delays by setting up data pipelines with minimal hops.

   - The key is to balance speed with data accuracy. You also set up checkpoints and validation mechanisms in the pipeline to handle any inconsistencies that might come with fast data movement.

4. **What are the key differences between ETL and ELT, and when would you choose one over the other?**

   Model answer:

   - ETL is all about transforming data before loading it into the target system, usually when dealing with highly structured data environments like data warehouses. The transformation happens on the go, so by the time the data lands, it is ready for use.

   - On the flip side, ELT loads the raw data first, then performs transformations within the target environment, which works well in big data environments or data lakes. With ELT, you have the flexibility to process massive amounts of raw data at a later stage using the processing power of the cloud.

   - You usually opt for ETL if you need immediate reporting or when data needs heavy transformation upfront. For large-scale, raw data where transformation can wait, ELT is much more efficient.

5. **How would you ensure data security and compliance when designing data architectures?**

   Model answer:

   - For security, encryption is non-negotiable, both at rest and in transit. Tools like AWS KMS or Azure Key Vault make it easy to manage encryption keys and ensure that sensitive data is protected.

   - You also implement RBAC to make sure only the right people can access sensitive data. Compliance with GDPR and HIPAA or other regulations is often a challenge, so you use automated tools for data masking and anonymization, this ensures PII is protected.

   - Regular auditing is also key. You set up monitoring systems that log all data access and changes. This keeps everything above board and helps prevent issues before they become a problem.

6. **Scenario-based: You are tasked with integrating on-premises systems with cloud services for a hybrid cloud environment. What would your approach be?**

   Model answer:

   - In a hybrid setup, your first priority is secure connectivity between the on-prem systems and the cloud. This usually means VPNs or private links to ensure data moves securely.

   - For data movement, you would use tools like Azure Data Factory or AWS Glue. These allow you to automate and orchestrate the data flow between on-prem systems and the cloud, handling large volumes with ease.

   - Since latency is often a concern, especially in a hybrid setup, you would prioritize caching where appropriate and use event-driven architectures to keep everything in sync without creating bottlenecks. It is also critical to build in redundancy for failover in case the connection drops.

7. **What are some key considerations when architecting big data solutions in the cloud?**

   Model answer:

   - It always comes down to the three Vs as Volume, Velocity, and Variety. With large datasets, you need to design for horizontal scalability from day one. This is where tools like Azure Databricks or AWS EMR come into play; they handle distributed processing well.

   - For data ingestion, streaming and batch processing need to work in harmony. For real-time processing, you typically use Apache Kafka or Kinesis, while batch workloads are handled with Dataflow or Azure Data Factory.

- Security and data governance are top priorities as well, especially for sensitive data. You need to make sure we have proper data lineage and provenance in place to track where data is coming from and how it is being processed.

8. **How would you ensure effective data governance in a distributed big data environment?**

   Model answer:

   - Governance starts with data lineage, knowing where the data is coming from, how it is being processed, and where it is going. Tools like Collibra or AWS Lake Formation are excellent for this, especially when dealing with complex pipelines.

   - You set up centralized governance policies but also ensure domain-specific teams have some control over their data with role-based access and data ownership models. It is a balancing act between control and flexibility.

   - Compliance is also huge here. We make sure that everything adheres to regulations like GDPR and HIPAA, and this is where automated audit logs and encryption practices come into play. Having those tools in place ensures compliance across distributed environments.

9. **What cloud-native tools do you recommend for big data processing, and how do they differ?**

   Model answer:

   - Azure Databricks and AWS EMR are great for big data processing. They both handle distributed computing exceptionally well, but you choose Azure Databricks when you need deep integration with Azure services and EMR for AWS-heavy workloads.

   - Google BigQuery stands out for its serverless approach to large-scale data querying. It is super powerful for real-time analytics at scale without managing infrastructure.

   - When it comes to cost and performance, the decision depends on the volume of data and how often you will need to access it. BigQuery's pay-as-you-go model is ideal for ad-hoc querying, while EMR is great when you need heavy, continuous processing.

10. **How do you design analytics architectures that balance high availability and low latency?**

    Model answer:

    - High availability requires replication and redundancy, so you usually set up data replication across multiple regions or availability zones. In cloud-native solutions like AWS or Azure, this is straightforward with tools like DynamoDB or Azure Cosmos DB.

    - For low-latency access, you use in-memory caching with Redis or Memcached. This is crucial for applications that need fast access to frequently queried data.

    - You also architect for auto-scaling so the system can handle spikes in data usage. This is where serverless functions like AWS Lambda or Azure Functions can be very effective; they spin up resources only when needed, ensuring both performance and cost-efficiency.

11. **How would you approach multi-cloud data integration, and what are the challenges?**

    Model answer:

    - Multi-cloud comes with challenges, mainly around keeping security, monitoring, and APIs consistent across different platforms. You use cloud-agnostic tools like Apache NiFi or Terraform to ensure that our infrastructure can communicate between AWS, Azure, and other platforms.

    - One of the biggest challenges is latency, so you implement data gateways and ensure secure communication between clouds through VPNs or private links.

    - Monitoring is also critical. You centralize logging and monitoring with a tool like ELK Stack to keep track of data flows across multiple clouds, so there are no blind spots.

12. **What are your strategies for balancing read/write performance in data modeling?**

Model answer:

- Indexing is the first place to start for optimizing read performance, it speeds up queries but can slow down writes, so you try to balance how many indexes we create.

- In some cases, denormalization is a good option, especially if the system is read-heavy, like an analytics platform. However, you make sure the data is still manageable and consistency can be maintained.

- Sharding is another go-to when we need to distribute data across multiple databases, which balances the load and improves both read and write performance in a high-scale environment.

13. **How do you ensure that analytics align with business goals in an organization?**

Model answer:

- The first step is to work closely with business stakeholders to understand what their KPIs and strategic goals are. From there, you make sure that the data pipelines and analytics tools we implement can provide the insights they need in real time.

- You set up dashboards that are not just visually appealing but actionable, so stakeholders can make informed decisions based on real-time data.

- Additionally, you push for self-service analytics so that business users have more control and flexibility to dive into the data themselves without having to rely on IT every time.

14. **How do you implement AI or ML models for advanced analytics in business use cases?**

Model answer:

- You start by identifying the business use cases, whether it is predictive analytics for sales forecasts or deep learning models for image recognition. Then you use platforms like Azure ML, AWS SageMaker, or Google AI Platform to train, deploy, and manage these models.

- The key is integrating these AI or ML models into the data pipeline seamlessly so that the insights generated are actionable and real-time. For example, integrating NLP models into customer support data streams helps analyze sentiment in real-time.

- You also prioritize model monitoring and retraining, ensuring that the models evolve and adapt as the data changes, which is critical for long-term success.

15. **What is your approach to designing self-service analytics for business users?**

Model answer:

- It starts with giving business users access to the right tools like Power BI or Tableau are great for this. You make sure these platforms are integrated with the data warehouse or data lake so they can explore the data independently.

- Data governance is key here. You make sure there is proper role-based access control in place, so users can access only the data they need without compromising security.

- You focus on creating pre-built dashboards and templates that are easy to use but customizable, allowing business users to tweak them according to their needs.

CHAPTER 11

User Experience Considerations

Introduction

User experience (**UX**) has become a fundamental aspect of modern solutions architecture, where creating systems that not only perform well but are also intuitive and user-friendly is critical. Solutions architects play a key role in balancing technical requirements with the needs and behavior of end-users. Incorporating UX principles into architecture design ensures that solutions are effective, accessible, and engaging across various platforms and devices. This chapter gets into the importance of UX in the realm of solutions architecture, exploring how **human-centered design** (**HCD**), accessibility, and best practices can be applied to build systems that enhance user satisfaction while meeting business goals.

Throughout the chapter, we will cover essential UX strategies that help architects make informed decisions on usability, accessibility, and user engagement. With the increasing importance of creating seamless, inclusive digital experiences, understanding and implementing UX best practices is critical for delivering solutions that resonate with end-users. As we explore the core principles, tools, and advanced UX concepts, this chapter will equip you with the knowledge to design architectures that prioritize users while maintaining technical excellence.

As we move forward, it is essential to explore how solutions architects can effectively incorporate UX principles into architecture and design. This ensures that the systems they build are not only technically sound but also user-friendly.

Structure

This chapter covers the following topics:

- Incorporating UX into architecture and design
- Balancing technical excellence with user needs
- Designing for accessibility and usability
- UX best practices in solutions architecture
- Ethical and global considerations in UX design
- Advanced UX concepts for modern solutions architects

Objectives

By the end of this chapter, readers will gain a comprehensive understanding of how to seamlessly integrate UX principles into their architectural designs. They will be equipped to apply HCD and design thinking methodologies in their architectural approach, ensuring that solutions are built around the needs of users while meeting business objectives. Readers will learn how to balance user-centric requirements with technical and business goals, creating impactful solutions that prioritize accessibility, usability, and inclusivity. Additionally, this chapter will enable readers to utilize key UX tools and techniques, such as gamification, heuristics, and prototyping, to optimize user engagement.

Moreover, they will understand how to incorporate regulatory compliance, including **Americans with Disabilities Act** (**ADA**), GDPR, and industry-specific standards, into UX design. The chapter will also emphasize the importance of cross-platform UX, enabling architects to evaluate and improve experiences across various devices. Readers will learn to integrate performance metrics and feedback loops into UX designs, fostering continuous improvement. Ethical design will also be highlighted, ensuring systems are transparent, avoid dark patterns, and prioritize user trust. Lastly, readers will gain insights into the complexities of internationalization and localization in UX design, equipping them to create solutions for a global audience.

Incorporating UX into architecture and design

Incorporating UX in architecture and design is essential for ensuring that systems not only meet technical requirements but also provide intuitive, seamless, and satisfying interactions for users. Solutions architects play a critical role in balancing technical functionality with user needs, making UX a key consideration in modern system architecture. This section explores how UX principles align with architectural goals, emphasizing the value of HCD and design thinking, as well as the importance of collaboration between architects and UX teams.

Role of UX in solutions architecture

In today's fast-paced digital environment, UX is no longer an afterthought; it is a core element of any successful architecture. Solutions architects must understand how to integrate UX into the foundation of system design, balancing the technical rigor required for performance with the ease of use necessary for user adoption.

Defining UX from an architectural standpoint

From an architectural perspective, UX refers to the overall experience users have while interacting with a system, encompassing everything from the system's responsiveness and efficiency to its aesthetic appeal and accessibility. Solutions architects need to think beyond technical specifications and ensure that their design enhances user satisfaction, ease of navigation, and overall usability. This requires a careful balance between technical robustness and user-centric features.

Solutions architects and advocating for UX best practices

Solutions architects are uniquely positioned to advocate for UX best practices across project teams, ensuring that UX considerations are included in the design, development, and deployment phases. By championing user-centric design approaches early in the process, solutions architects can ensure that technical decisions, such as system workflows, data architecture, and interface components, do not inadvertently compromise usability. They should work closely with UX designers, product managers, and stakeholders to align the architecture with the overall user journey, ensuring that technical choices do not create friction for users.

Once solutions architects understand the pivotal role of UX in system design, they can take this a step further by embedding HCD principles into the process. Let us now explore how these principles help architects keep the user at the forefront of their design decisions.

Human-centered design in architecture

HCD focuses on putting users at the heart of the design process, ensuring that systems are created with their needs, preferences, and behaviors in mind. For solutions architects, integrating HCD into architecture design ensures that solutions are not only functional but are also adaptable and user-friendly.

Human-centered design principles

HCD revolves around understanding the user's problems, needs, and desires, and creating systems that cater to those needs while being scalable, reliable, and performant. Solutions architects must ensure that the system architecture aligns with these principles to build applications that are intuitive and efficient for users, regardless of the complexity of the back-end systems.

Stages of human-centered design

Figure 11.1 illustrates the key stages of HCD, providing a structured approach to developing user-focused solutions. Each stage, i.e., empathize, define, ideate, prototype, and test, plays a crucial role in ensuring that system architectures align with user needs while maintaining scalability and efficiency. This visual representation helps solutions architects integrate HCD principles into their design process, fostering intuitive, adaptable, and high-performing systems.

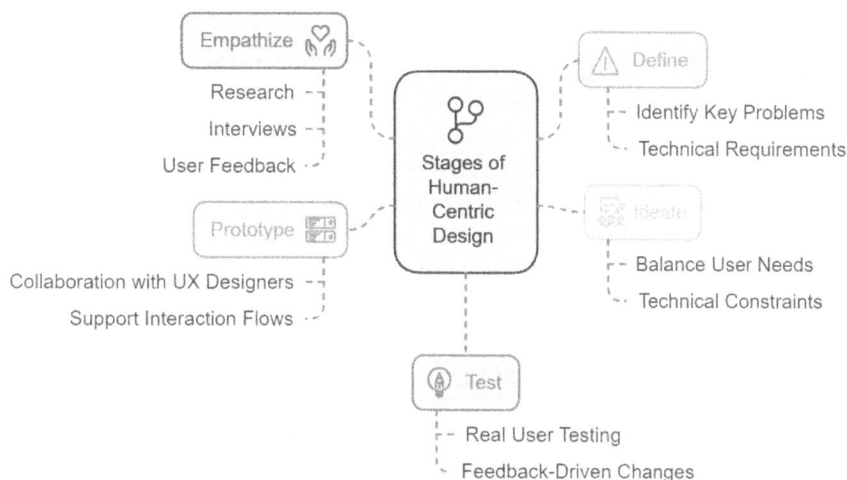

Figure 11.1: *Stages of human-centered design*

Let us understand these stages in more detail:

- **Empathize**: Solutions architects must begin by understanding the end-users' pain points, typically through research, interviews, and user feedback sessions. This insight guides critical architectural decisions.

- **Define**: Once user needs are understood, the next step is defining the key problems the system will solve. Architects must translate these problems into technical requirements that guide the development of system components.

- **Ideate**: At this stage, solutions architects and UX designers brainstorm possible solutions. Here, the challenge is to balance user needs with the technical constraints of the system. Architects must ensure that the proposed solutions are feasible from a scalability and performance perspective while satisfying user expectations.

- **Prototype**: Solutions architects collaborate with UX designers to develop prototypes that help visualize the architecture's interaction elements. While UX teams may focus on visual designs, architects ensure that the system's structure supports interaction flows.

- **Test**: Testing prototypes with real users allows the team to validate their assumptions and refine both the UX and technical aspects of the design. Solutions architects need to ensure that the system can handle feedback-driven changes efficiently without significant re-engineering.

While HCD focuses on ensuring systems are user-friendly, solutions architects must also apply structured problem-solving methods like design thinking to address complex architectural challenges. Furthermore, design thinking refines the architecture process.

Design thinking in solutions architecture

Design thinking is a problem-solving methodology that helps solutions architects approach complex challenges by centering solutions around user needs while considering technical and business constraints.

Design thinking as a problem-solving methodology

Design thinking helps solutions architects break down complex problems into manageable stages. It encourages creative problem-solving and iterative improvements, ensuring that the user's experience remains central throughout the process. This methodology is especially useful in large-scale, multi-system architectures where balancing technical requirements with user needs can be challenging.

Stages of design thinking

The design thinking process is structured into distinct stages that guide solutions architects in developing user-centric, innovative, and technically sound solutions. Each stage plays a crucial role in ensuring that architectural decisions are aligned with both business objectives and user needs. By following this iterative approach, solutions architects can systematically refine their solutions, incorporating feedback at every step to enhance usability, scalability, and efficiency. The five key stages, i.e., empathize, define, ideate, prototype, and test, form a continuous cycle of improvement, allowing architects to create solutions that are both technically feasible and user-friendly. Let us take a closer look at these stages:

- **Empathize**: Understand the user experience deeply by putting yourself in their shoes.
- **Define**: Clearly define the problem you aim to solve, focusing on both user needs and technical constraints.
- **Ideate**: Brainstorm innovative solutions that address the user's problems without sacrificing technical excellence.
- **Prototype**: Develop quick prototypes that demonstrate potential solutions, allowing both UX designers and solutions architects to see how users interact with the system.
- **Test**: Test these prototypes with users, gathering feedback to refine both UX and technical components.

Solutions architects can apply these stages to manage complex technical scenarios, ensuring that the system's performance, scalability, and security requirements are met without compromising the user experience.

Decision tree for applying design thinking

Solutions architects often face the challenge of deciding when and how to implement different stages of design thinking. A decision tree can guide them through the process, showing when to focus on user research, ideation, or prototyping based on project requirements, available resources, and timelines.

Having explored the stages of design thinking, it is crucial to remember that solutions architects cannot work in isolation. Collaborating with UX designers and stakeholders ensures that both technical and user experience requirements are aligned. Let us look at how effective collaboration can lead to more cohesive designs.

Collaborating with UX designers and stakeholders

Collaboration between solutions architects and UX designers is essential for ensuring that both technical and user experience requirements are aligned from the beginning of the project. Effective communication and iterative feedback loops can prevent misunderstandings and reduce costly rework.

Importance of early collaboration with UX designers

Collaboration should begin during the requirements gathering phase to ensure that both the system's architecture and user experience evolve in tandem. This early alignment helps avoid situations where architecture decisions constrain UX possibilities or vice versa.

Techniques for effective communication and feedback loops

Solutions architects can use collaborative tools like Figma, Miro, or Sketch to maintain consistent communication with UX teams. These tools allow real-time feedback and enable architects to visualize how technical elements, such as data flows and API endpoints, support the user's journey.

After establishing a solid foundation of UX principles and HCD in architecture, solutions architects face the challenge of aligning these principles with the technical demands of modern systems. In the next section, we will explore how solutions architects can reconcile user needs with technical constraints, make informed trade-offs, and ensure continuous improvement through feedback loops, all while maintaining security and performance.

Balancing technical excellence with user needs

Incorporating UX into architecture and design requires solutions architects to continuously balance technical excellence with user needs. This section explores how architects can align UX and technical goals, manage trade-offs between performance and usability, implement continuous feedback loops, and balance security requirements with user experience. Achieving harmony between these competing priorities ensures that the final solution is robust, user-friendly, and meets business objectives.

Defining and reconciling technical and UX goals

For any project, it is essential to establish clear, measurable objectives for both UX and technical excellence. These goals ensure that the architecture not only meets functional requirements but also delivers an intuitive and seamless user experience. They are as follows:

- **Establishing measurable goals**: Solutions architects should work with stakeholders and UX designers to set tangible targets for both UX and technical performance. These could include specific metrics like system response time, uptime, user engagement levels, and task success rates.

  - **UX goals**: Objectives might involve minimizing cognitive load, optimizing task completion times, or improving accessibility features. For example, ensuring users can complete a specific task within two minutes or reducing the number of clicks needed to access a feature.

  - **Technical goals**: These include optimizing system performance, ensuring scalability, and maintaining security and compliance standards. Technical excellence might focus on maintaining 99.99% uptime or processing data within a set threshold.

- **Common conflicts between UX and technical constraints**: Solutions architects often encounter conflicts between UX aspirations and technical constraints. For instance, a highly interactive feature might improve usability but could negatively impact load times or resource consumption. Similarly, technical constraints like security requirements or backend complexity may restrict how simple the user interface can be.

For example, an e-commerce platform wants to implement real-time recommendations based on user behavior, which can enhance the user experience. However, real-time data processing requires significant server resources, leading to higher costs and potential delays in system performance.

- **Resolving conflicts**: Architects can resolve these conflicts by prioritizing user-centred design while working within technical limitations. Collaborating early in the process with both UX and technical teams ensures that each side understands the other's needs and constraints. Compromise may involve refining the UX to reduce system load or optimizing the back-end infrastructure to handle more intensive user interactions without sacrificing performance.

With clear goals defined, architects often face trade-offs between performance, scalability, and usability. The next step is learning how to evaluate these trade-offs and choose the most effective solutions.

Implementing design trade-offs

In architecture design, trade-offs between competing priorities are inevitable. Solutions architects must find ways to maintain both usability and performance, ensuring that neither aspect is compromised beyond acceptable limits. The ways are as follows:

- **Strategies for trade-offs**: Solutions architects need to employ strategies that strike a balance between user experience and technical constraints. This could involve simplifying the user interface to improve performance or leveraging advanced technologies to maintain usability while optimizing resource consumption.

    o **Prioritization**: Identify which aspects of the user experience are most critical to business success and focus resources on maintaining those. For example, prioritizing quick page load times over advanced animation features.

    o **Incremental enhancement**: Roll out complex features in phases, starting with the simplest version. As the technical infrastructure improves, additional UX features can be added without overwhelming the system.

- **Frameworks for evaluating trade-offs**: Using decision frameworks helps solutions architects assess the impact of various trade-offs and how they align with project objectives. Some frameworks to consider include:

    o **Impact versus effort matrix**: This framework helps evaluate the potential impact of a feature on user experience against the technical effort required to implement it. Low-effort, high-impact features should be prioritized.

    o **Risk-reward analysis**: Architects can evaluate the risks of sacrificing performance for user experience or vice versa and determine whether the benefits outweigh the risks. For example, reducing page load times might involve simplifying the interface, but the risk of user frustration is low if the feature is less frequently used.

After trade-offs are implemented, it is crucial to monitor how these decisions impact users. Feedback loops allow for continuous evaluation and refinement of the design to meet evolving user needs.

Feedback loop for continuous improvement

Designing with the user in mind does not end when the system goes live. Solutions architects need to establish methods for gathering feedback from users and iterating on the design to ensure continuous improvement. The methods are as follows:

- **Gathering user feedback post-deployment**: Once the solution is in production, gathering user feedback is essential for refining both the user experience and the technical performance. Solutions architects can use the following methods:

- o **Surveys and user testing**: Direct feedback from users through surveys or usability tests helps identify areas where the system may not be performing as expected.

- o **Usage analytics**: Monitoring user behavior through analytics tools like Google Analytics or Hotjar provides insights into how users interact with the system, where they encounter difficulties, and which features are most valuable.

- o **Heatmaps**: Tools that generate heatmaps show where users are focusing their attention on the screen, helping to identify confusing or underutilized features.

- **Agile frameworks for UX adjustments**: Agile development methodologies provide the flexibility to continuously refine UX based on user feedback. Solutions architects can integrate feedback into Agile sprints to make rapid, iterative improvements to the system.

- o **Sprint reviews**: In each sprint, review user feedback and prioritize UX improvements that will have the highest impact on user satisfaction.

- o **Continuous delivery**: With continuous delivery pipelines, small adjustments to the user interface can be tested and deployed frequently, ensuring that feedback is incorporated quickly without waiting for major release cycles.

An essential part of balancing technical excellence with user needs involves security, particularly in environments where sensitive data is handled. The next section explores how to balance robust security with a seamless user experience.

Example of balancing security with usability

Security and usability are often seen as competing priorities, especially in systems where sensitive information is involved. Solutions architects must find ways to ensure the system is secure without compromising the user experience. They are as follows:

- **Designing secure yet user-friendly systems**: Security measures such as **multi-factor authentication** (**MFA**) or complex password requirements can improve system security, but may frustrate users. To maintain a user-friendly experience, solutions architects should:

- o **Minimize friction**: Use techniques like **single sign-on** (**SSO**) to streamline the login process while maintaining security.

- o **Contextual authentication**: Implement risk-based authentication methods where additional security measures are triggered only under suspicious circumstances (e.g., logging in from a new device or location).

- **Best practices for integrating MFA**: MFA is critical for securing systems but can introduce friction into the user experience. Solutions architects can implement MFA without compromising usability by:

- o **Offering multiple MFA options**: Allow users to choose from different authentication methods (e.g., biometric, SMS, email) to enhance usability.

- o **Remembering trusted devices**: After successful MFA on a trusted device, allow users to skip MFA for future logins, reducing unnecessary friction.

As we strive to balance user experience with technical constraints, it is essential to ensure that these systems are accessible and usable for all, including users with diverse abilities. The next section explores how to integrate accessibility as a core part of your design strategy.

Designing for accessibility and usability

In modern solutions architecture, designing for accessibility and usability is critical to ensuring that digital systems and interfaces are inclusive, easy to navigate, and functional for all users, including those with diverse abilities. This section gets into the foundational aspects of accessibility standards, the importance of compliance, and practical strategies for creating user-friendly designs that meet legal and regulatory requirements.

Understanding accessibility and compliance requirements

Designing accessible systems is not only a moral responsibility but also a legal one. Solutions architects must understand and incorporate key accessibility standards to ensure that systems are usable for individuals with varying abilities. Some of the key standards include:

- **Web content accessibility guidelines (WCAG 2.1)**: These guidelines are developed through the W3C process to ensure web content is accessible to individuals with diverse abilities. They are categorized into four principles: **Perceivable, Operable, Understandable, and Robust** (**POUR**).

- **Americans with Disabilities Act**: This US law prohibits discrimination based on diverse ability and includes digital accessibility as part of its broader mandate. Websites and applications must meet specific ADA guidelines to be compliant.

- **Section 508**: This US government regulation requires federal agencies to make their electronic and information technology accessible to people with diverse abilities. Solutions architects working on government contracts or digital services should ensure their systems are Section 508 compliant.

Non-compliance with these regulations can lead to lawsuits, hefty fines, and damaged reputations. Solutions architects have a responsibility to ensure that systems meet these standards, not just to avoid legal consequences but to make systems more usable for everyone. The role of the architect is to embed accessibility from the beginning of the design process, rather than adding it as an afterthought.

The compliance checklist is as follows:

- Adherence to **WCAG 2.1** principles.

- Ensure all interfaces meet **ADA** guidelines for accessibility.

- Confirm that government-facing systems comply with **Section 508**.

- Evaluate system interfaces against key compliance metrics for accessibility.

Now that we have explored the key accessibility standards and the legal impacts of non-compliance, let us discuss how to create inclusive design solutions that ensure your systems are usable by everyone.

Creating inclusive design solutions

Inclusive design ensures that digital systems are accessible and usable by everyone, regardless of ability. Solutions architects must go beyond compliance and consider the diverse range of user abilities and preferences. This involves incorporating specific accessibility features such as:

- **Alternative text (Alt Text)**: Provide descriptive text for images and non-text elements so that users relying on screen readers can understand the content.

- **Keyboard navigation**: Ensure that all interactive elements of the system can be accessed and navigated through keyboard shortcuts. This is crucial for users who cannot use a mouse.

- **Screen reader support**: Test and implement compatibility with screen readers to ensure that visually impaired users can interact with the content.

Once inclusive design solutions have been implemented, it is necessary to evaluate their effectiveness. Automated testing tools and usability evaluations help Solutions architects assess and improve accessibility.

Evaluating accessibility and usability

Evaluation is a critical step in ensuring that systems meet accessibility and usability goals. Solutions architects can leverage various tools to automate testing and improve the accessibility of digital systems:

- **Axe**: A popular open-source tool used to automate accessibility testing, identifying areas that do not meet WCAG standards.

- **Web accessibility evaluation tool (WAVE)**: This tool provides visual feedback on accessibility issues directly on the webpage. It is particularly useful for identifying areas where improvements are needed.

- **SiteImprove**: This comprehensive tool analyses web content for accessibility, quality, and SEO, offering actionable insights for architects to improve user experience.

In addition to automated tools, **heuristic evaluations** and **cognitive walkthroughs** are valuable techniques that involve manually reviewing a system's interface to identify usability and accessibility issues. Solutions architects should perform these evaluations regularly to ensure continuous improvement in design and accessibility.

While accessibility is critical, user engagement is also essential to a system's success. Using gamification techniques can help make systems more interactive and enjoyable for users, boosting engagement.

Using gamification techniques for engagement

Gamification refers to the application of game-design elements in non-game contexts to enhance user engagement. Solutions architects can use gamification to improve the user experience by making systems more interactive and enjoyable. Examples of gamification techniques include:

- **Badges and rewards**: Offer users badges or rewards for completing tasks, such as filling out a profile or achieving milestones within the system.

- **Progress bars**: Show progress indicators that encourage users to complete certain steps or processes.

- **Leaderboards and challenges**: For enterprise applications, gamification can create healthy competition, which may drive productivity and engagement.

Gamification can be particularly effective in enterprise applications by motivating users to interact more deeply with the system. Solutions architects can explore opportunities to introduce game-like elements into everyday tasks to improve engagement and productivity.

Although engaging users is important, it is equally important to ensure that systems comply with industry-specific regulations. Let us now examine how solutions architects can incorporate compliance requirements into UX design.

Regulatory compliance in UX design

Compliance with accessibility regulations is critical, but solutions architects must also consider industry-specific standards. For example:

- **HIPAA**: This US regulation governs the handling of healthcare information. Solutions architects working in healthcare must ensure that digital interfaces protect patient data and are accessible to all users, including those with diverse abilities.

- **GDPR**: In the EU, GDPR governs how personal data is collected, stored, and used. Solutions architects must ensure that systems handling personal data comply with GDPR requirements while remaining accessible and usable.

Incorporating compliance into UX design documentation ensures that accessibility and data protection are considered at every stage of development. Solutions architects should also establish ongoing compliance checks to ensure that systems remain up to date with evolving regulations.

Designing for accessibility and usability is part of a larger set of UX best practices that Solutions architects must follow. By applying these practices, you can ensure that systems are intuitive, scalable, and aligned with user needs.

UX best practices in solutions architecture

Incorporating best practices in UX design is essential for solutions architects, as it ensures that systems are user-centric, functional, and scalable. This section covers key UX methodologies and techniques, providing practical insights that can help solutions architects improve the overall user experience while maintaining consistency and addressing user needs.

Figure 11.2 visually represents key methodologies, including **user-centered design** (**UCD**), prototyping techniques, consistency in UX patterns, heuristic evaluation, and data-driven decision-making. By integrating these principles, architects can enhance usability, streamline workflows, and create seamless digital experiences that balance technical feasibility with user needs.

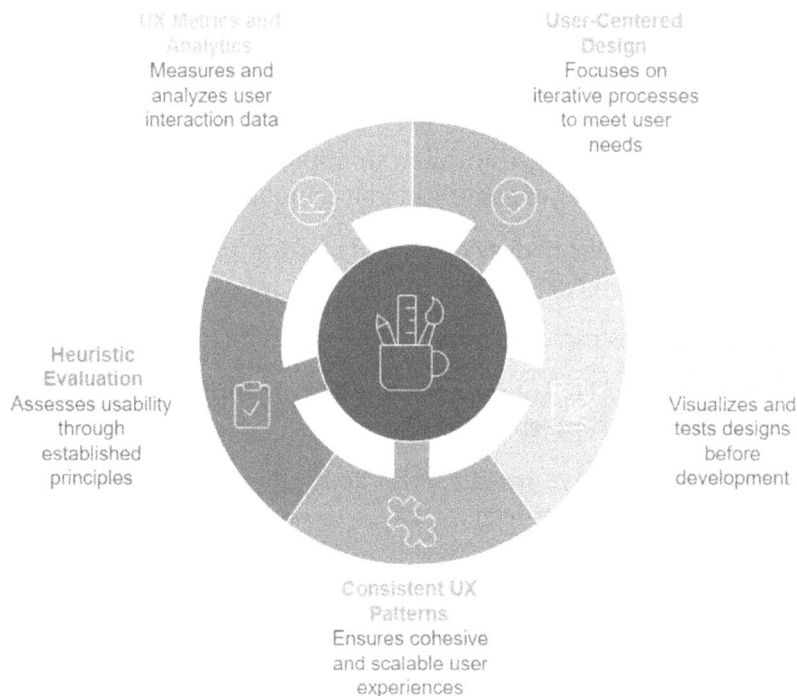

Figure 11.2: UX best practices

Applying user-centered design approach

The UCD approach places the user at the center of the design process, ensuring that the final product meets the user's needs and expectations. UCD is an iterative process that involves four key stages: research, design, testing, and implementation.

The details are as follows:

- **Research**: This stage involves gathering data on user needs, behaviors, and pain points through methods such as user interviews, surveys, and observations. Solutions architects must collaborate with UX designers to understand user expectations and technical constraints.

- **Design**: In this phase, solutions architects work closely with designers to create wireframes, prototypes, and mock-ups that align with both user requirements and business objectives. It is important to ensure the designs reflect user feedback while being feasible to implement.

- **Testing**: Prototypes are tested with real users to gather feedback and identify usability issues. Solutions architects should focus on how the system performs under different conditions and whether it meets the established goals.

- **Implementation**: Once the design is finalized and tested, the architecture is implemented, keeping the user experience intact while ensuring that technical requirements are met.

Techniques for building user personas, empathy maps, and journey maps are critical to the success of UCD:

- **User personas**: Create profiles representing typical users, capturing demographics, behaviors, goals, and challenges. This helps in tailoring solutions to different user segments.

- **Empathy maps**: Visual tools that allow teams to gain a deeper understanding of user emotions, thoughts, and actions.

- **Journey maps**: Visual representations of a user's interaction with the system, highlighting pain points and areas for improvement.

By employing these techniques, solutions architects can ensure that their designs are not only functional but also intuitive and user-friendly.

While UCD ensures that systems are designed around user needs, prototyping is key to refining those designs before full-scale development begins. Let us explore the different types of prototyping techniques and their effectiveness.

Prototyping techniques and their effectiveness

Prototyping is an essential step in the design process that allows stakeholders to visualize and interact with a system before full-scale development begins. Various prototyping techniques can be used, depending on the project phase and complexity, and they are as follows:

- **Low-fidelity wireframes**: These are simple, static sketches or digital drawings that represent the basic structure of the system. They are ideal for early-stage discussions and rapid iterations.

- **High-fidelity prototypes**: These are more detailed representations of the system, including interactive elements and closer to the final design in terms of layout, colour schemes, and user interactions. High-fidelity prototypes are suitable for more refined feedback from stakeholders or for usability testing.

- **Interactive mockups**: These prototypes offer near-complete functionality, allowing users to interact with the system as if it were fully developed. Interactive mockups are useful for gathering user feedback on detailed interactions, workflows, and interface elements.

Best practices for selecting the appropriate technique are as follows:

- Use **low-fidelity wireframes** for early brainstorming and gathering initial feedback.

- Switch to **high-fidelity prototypes** as the project matures, when detailed user feedback is required.

- **Interactive mockups** should be reserved for the final stages, where the user experience needs to be thoroughly tested before development.

Tools for prototyping include the following:

- **Figma**: A collaborative design tool for creating interactive prototypes.

- **Balsamiq**: Best for low-fidelity wireframes and early-stage design iterations.

- **InVision**: Allows for the creation of clickable prototypes with interactive features, useful for stakeholder presentations.

As the design progresses, maintaining consistency across the system becomes essential. Implementing scalable UX patterns helps ensure a cohesive user experience, no matter the complexity of the system.

Creating consistent and scalable UX patterns

Consistency in UX patterns is crucial for creating intuitive systems that are easy to navigate and scale. Solutions architects should focus on ensuring that design patterns, navigation elements, and interaction methods remain consistent across all parts of the system.

Material design (Google) and **Fluent UI** (Microsoft) are two widely used design systems that provide ready-made components and patterns to ensure consistency in look, feel, and interaction. By implementing these design systems, solutions architects can ensure a cohesive experience across multiple platforms and devices, reducing the learning curve for users and making systems easier to scale.

Maintaining consistency is especially important in enterprise systems, where users may need to interact with different components of the system frequently. A consistent UX pattern helps improve usability, reduces errors, and enhances user satisfaction.

Consistency is key, but evaluating the effectiveness of your design is just as important. Let us dive into heuristic evaluation techniques to assess how well a website or application adheres to UX best practices.

Assessing a website using heuristic evaluation

Heuristic evaluation is a usability inspection method that helps identify usability issues in a system's user interface. Solutions architects can apply **Jakob Nielsen's 10 Heuristics** for usability evaluation, which include:

- **Visibility of system status**: Keep users informed about what is going on through appropriate feedback within a reasonable time.

- **Match between system and the real world**: Ensure the system speaks the users' language with familiar terms and concepts.

- **User control and freedom**: Provide easy exits for users, allowing them to undo and redo actions.

- **Consistency and standards**: Maintain consistency across design patterns and system behavior.

- **Error prevention**: Design systems that minimize the likelihood of user errors.

- **Recognition rather than recall**: Reduce the memory load by making actions, options, and information easily visible.

- **Flexibility and efficiency of use**: Design interfaces to accommodate both novice and expert users.

- **Aesthetic and minimalist design**: Avoid unnecessary elements that do not add value to the user's experience.

- **Help users recognize, diagnose, and recover from errors**: Provide meaningful error messages.

- **Help and documentation**: Ensure users have access to clear and easy-to-find help resources.

Solutions architects should create a heuristic evaluation checklist based on these principles to assess and improve website or application usability, especially during the pre-launch phase.

For example, if heuristic evaluation reveals that users experience delays due to complex navigation paths, solutions architects can streamline the backend data flow or implement efficient caching strategies to improve responsiveness.

After assessing your design using heuristics, it is crucial to track key metrics and analytics to measure the success of the user experience. This data-driven approach allows solutions architects to continuously refine and optimize the design.

UX metrics and analytics for solutions architects

Measuring the effectiveness of UX is crucial for ensuring that design decisions have a positive impact. Solutions architects can leverage UX metrics to assess user satisfaction and identify areas for improvement:

- **Task success rate**: Measures the percentage of users who can complete a task successfully without errors. This helps assess the system's usability and efficiency.

- **Time on task**: Tracks how long users take to complete a specific task. Longer times may indicate complexity or inefficiency in the design.

- **Net promoter score (NPS)**: Gauges user satisfaction and their likelihood to recommend the system to others.

Incorporating analytics tools like Google Analytics and Hotjar provides insights into user behavior, revealing where users may struggle and offering data-driven opportunities to optimize the UX design.

By analyzing these metrics, solutions architects can identify specific areas where the architecture may be adjusted to enhance responsiveness, improve data handling, or refine performance thresholds, creating a more seamless experience for end-users.

As we have seen, adhering to UX best practices is critical for system design. However, solutions architects must also consider ethical responsibilities and global user needs when designing systems.

Ethical and global considerations in UX design

As digital experiences become more integrated into our daily lives, designing for ethics, trust, and global inclusivity has never been more critical. Solutions architects must ensure that the systems they design not only meet technical and business requirements but also prioritize the well-being of users. This section explores the ethical responsibilities of solutions architects, including fostering trust through transparent design and addressing the challenges of designing for a global audience through internationalization and localization.

Figure 11.3 illustrates the core principles of ethical design, including transparency, user autonomy, and fairness, alongside global UX considerations such as internationalization and localization:

Figure 11.3: *Ethical and global UX design*

Designing for user trust and transparency

Building and maintaining user trust is a fundamental aspect of UX design, especially as users become more aware of how their personal data is collected, stored, and used. Ethical UX design prioritizes transparency and respect for user autonomy, which not only enhances trust but also supports long-term engagement with a product or service. The factors are as follows:

- **Techniques for building trust through transparent UX design**: Trust is a key factor in user engagement and retention. When users feel that a system respects their privacy, communicates clearly, and empowers them with control, they are more likely to interact with it confidently. Solutions architects play a crucial role in ensuring that transparency is embedded in the design process. By implementing clear data privacy notices, eliminating deceptive design patterns, and providing users with control over their personal data, architects can create ethical and user-friendly systems that foster long-term trust and compliance with global regulations.

- o **Clear data privacy notices**: One of the most effective ways to build trust is to be transparent about how user data is handled. Solutions architects should work with UX teams to ensure that privacy policies and consent forms are easy to understand and accessible. This involves avoiding complex legal jargon and presenting information in a way that users can easily comprehend.

- o **Avoiding dark patterns**: Dark patterns are deceptive design techniques that manipulate users into taking actions they may not fully understand or intend. Examples include hiding subscription cancellations, sneaky opt-ins, and using misleading language. Solutions architects have an ethical responsibility to advocate against the use of dark patterns and ensure that the systems they design are transparent and user-friendly.

- o **User control over data**: Giving users control over their data builds trust. Solutions architects should ensure that users can easily manage their privacy settings, review what data is being collected, and have the option to delete their data. This practice aligns with regulatory standards like GDPR and **California Consumer Privacy Act (CCPA)**.

- **The role of solutions architects in fostering ethical design**:

  - o Solutions architects act as a bridge between technical teams and end-users. They must advocate for ethical considerations in design during every stage of development, from system architecture to user interface decisions.

  - o Solutions architects should implement design principles that support transparency, consent, and user autonomy. This includes advising on features like cookie consent banners, data anonymization, and user-friendly opt-out mechanisms.

  - o In practice, this might mean ensuring that user flows are designed in a way that empowers users to make informed decisions without feeling pressured or misled. For example, when designing an e-commerce checkout flow, ensuring that additional charges or subscriptions are not pre-selected by default promotes transparency and trust.

By embedding ethical considerations into the architectural design, solutions architects play a key role in shaping user experiences that are not only functional but also honest and trustworthy.

While transparency and trust are important for all users, solutions architects must also consider the unique needs of global audiences. Internationalization and localization ensure that systems are adaptable to different cultural and linguistic contexts.

Internationalization and localization

As businesses expand globally, designing systems that cater to diverse cultural and linguistic audiences becomes essential. Solutions architects must consider internationalization and localization as critical components of UX design, ensuring that systems are adaptable to different regions while maintaining a consistent user experience. The following should be kept in mind:

- **Addressing UX for global audiences**:

  - o **Language support**: One of the primary challenges of designing for global audiences is providing seamless language support. Solutions architects must ensure that systems can support multiple languages, including languages that read from right to left (e.g., Arabic, Hebrew), and that user interfaces can adapt to different text lengths and formats.

  - o **Cultural adaptations**: Beyond language, UX design must account for cultural differences in how users interact with systems. For example, colour schemes, symbols, and navigation patterns may have different connotations in various cultures. Solutions architects need to work with UX designers to research and implement designs that are culturally appropriate while maintaining overall system coherence.

- **Date, time, and currency formats**: Systems must be flexible enough to handle various local formats for dates, times, and currencies. A seamless UX experience requires that these elements are automatically adjusted based on the user's location or selected preferences.

- **Tools and best practices for localizing UX across different regions**:

  - **Translation management tools**: Tools such as Transifex, Smartling, and Phrase allow developers and UX teams to manage translations efficiently across different languages. These tools integrate directly with design and development workflows, ensuring that updates to the system are reflected in all localized versions.

  - **Responsive design and layout adaptation**: Solutions architects must ensure that layouts are responsive and adaptable to different languages, text lengths, and character sets. This is particularly important when dealing with languages that expand the length of text significantly, such as German, or those that use characters from different scripts, like Chinese.

  - **Internationalization frameworks**: Solutions architects can leverage **internationalization (i18n)** frameworks that automatically adjust the system based on the user's region or language. Popular frameworks like React-i18next and Angular i18n offer built-in localization support for web applications.

  - **Testing for localization**: Conducting usability testing in different regions helps identify cultural or language-specific issues that may not be apparent during the design phase. Solutions architects should work with testing teams to ensure that localized versions of the system are as user-friendly as the original.

Localizing a system's UX goes beyond just translating text; it involves adapting the design to meet the cultural, linguistic, and functional needs of users around the world. By employing the right tools and frameworks, solutions architects can ensure that their systems provide a seamless experience for all users, regardless of location.

With the foundations of ethical and global UX design in place, let us look ahead to the future. Modern UX concepts such as cognitive psychology, AI-driven personalization, and AR/VR are becoming increasingly important for solutions architects.

Advanced UX concepts for modern solutions architects

As the digital landscape continues to evolve, solutions architects must stay ahead of the curve by incorporating advanced UX concepts into their designs. Modern UX goes beyond aesthetics and usability; it gets into understanding user psychology, leveraging AI for personalization, and embracing future-forward trends like voice interfaces, **augmented reality (AR)** and **virtual reality (VR)**. This section explores these advanced concepts and highlights their implications for solutions architects.

The following figure illustrates key advanced UX concepts and their impact on modern system design:

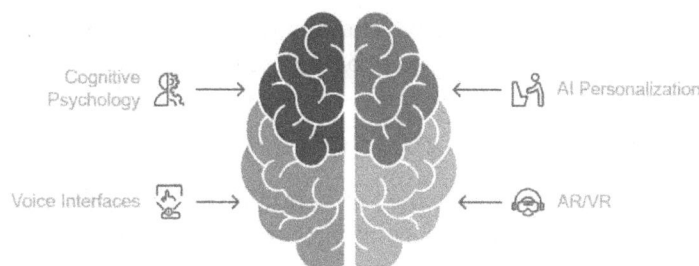

Figure 11.4: *Advanced UX concepts*

Psychology in UX design

Understanding the cognitive psychology that drives user behavior is crucial for creating intuitive and effective interfaces. Solutions architects, while designing systems and workflows, must consider how users think, process information, and make decisions. Two key psychological principles often applied in UX design are **Hick's Law** and **Fitts' Law**, both of which have significant implications for the layout and functionality of interfaces.

Cognitive psychology influences user behavior and design choices

Cognitive psychology plays a fundamental role in shaping user experience by helping solutions architects design systems that align with human decision-making processes. Understanding how users perceive, process, and interact with digital interfaces allows architects to create intuitive, user-friendly, and efficient systems. By leveraging cognitive principles such as cognitive load, choice overload, Hick's Law, and Fitts' Law, architects can optimize design choices to reduce friction, enhance usability, and improve overall engagement. The following sections explore key cognitive psychology concepts and their practical applications in UX design:

- **Cognitive load**: Cognitive load refers to the amount of mental effort required for a user to interact with a system. Solutions architects must design interfaces that reduce unnecessary complexity, helping users focus on their tasks without feeling overwhelmed. Simple, intuitive designs lead to a better user experience.

- **Choice overload**: Too many choices can overwhelm users, leading to decision fatigue. Streamlining options in key decision-making points, such as checkout pages or settings menus, can improve usability and reduce abandonment rates.

Applying Hick's Law in interface design

Hick's Law posits that the time it takes for a person to make a decision increases with the number of options available. In the context of UX design, this means that as the number of buttons, links, or menu items increases, users will take longer to make a selection. Solutions architects should aim to simplify complex systems by reducing the number of options presented at any given point.

Let us consider a practical example. Instead of overwhelming users with a sprawling navigation menu, implementing a hierarchical structure with dropdowns or filters can help guide users through their options without causing delays.

Applying Fitts' Law in interface design

Fitts' Law states that the time to acquire a target (like a button or icon) is a function of the distance to the target and the size of the target. In practical terms, larger buttons that are closer to the user's cursor or touchpoint are easier and quicker to interact with. Solutions architects must apply this principle when designing key interface elements, such as call-to-action buttons or navigation links.

Let us consider a practical example. In mobile applications, where screen space is limited, placing frequently used actions at the bottom of the screen (within easy reach of thumbs) and increasing the size of touchpoints improves user efficiency and satisfaction.

Understanding user behavior through cognitive psychology can improve UX design, but solutions architects can also leverage AI and ML to create personalized experiences that adapt to individual user preferences.

Leveraging AI and ML for personalization

As AI and ML technologies continue to advance, they offer immense potential for creating more personalized, engaging user experiences. For solutions architects, integrating AI-driven personalization into their designs is becoming increasingly important, as users expect systems to adapt to their preferences and behaviors in real-time.

Using AI to create personalized experiences based on user behavior

AI and ML can analyse user data to predict preferences and behaviors, enabling systems to offer customized content, recommendations, and interfaces. Solutions architects need to design systems that collect, analyze, and apply user data in a way that enhances personalization while respecting privacy.

Let us consider a practical example. In e-commerce platforms, AI can analyse browsing and purchase history to offer personalized product recommendations, dynamically tailoring the interface to suit each user's needs.

Recommendation engines and adaptive interfaces

Let us take a look at recommendation engines and adaptive interfaces:

- **Recommendation engines**: These AI-driven systems analyze user data to provide personalized suggestions, from movies to products to news articles. Solutions architects must ensure these engines are integrated into the architecture in a way that balances computational efficiency with user value.

- **Adaptive interfaces**: AI can also drive adaptive interfaces that change dynamically based on user preferences or behaviors. For example, an AI-driven dashboard might rearrange itself to prioritize the metrics most important to each individual user. Solutions architects must ensure that these adaptive systems are scalable and maintainable across various user personas and behaviors.

Challenges and considerations

Let us take a look at the following challenges and considerations:

- **Data privacy**: Personalization relies heavily on data collection. Solutions architects must design systems that comply with data privacy regulations like GDPR and CCPA ensuring that user consent and data anonymization practices are in place.

- **Bias in AI**: AI systems must be designed carefully to avoid introducing biases into personalization algorithms. Solutions architects need to work closely with data scientists and UX teams to ensure that AI-driven features are fair, transparent, and unbiased.

  As AI transforms how we personalize user experiences, it is important to stay ahead of emerging trends. Voice-based interfaces, augmented reality, and virtual reality offer exciting opportunities for solutions architects to design the future of user experiences.

Future trends in UX for solutions architects

As technology advances, new interaction paradigms are emerging, including voice-based UX, AR, and VR. These trends are shaping the future of user interfaces and pose exciting challenges and opportunities for solutions architects. They are as follows:

- **Voice-based UX**:
  - **Voice interfaces** (e.g., Alexa, Google Assistant) are becoming more prevalent as users increasingly prefer hands-free interactions. Designing systems that can handle NLP and voice-based commands opens up new possibilities for user interaction.
  - **Challenges**: Voice interfaces present unique challenges, such as ensuring accuracy in voice recognition, providing meaningful feedback in the absence of visual cues, and supporting multi-language voice interactions. Solutions architects must ensure that backend systems can efficiently handle voice data and integrate it seamlessly into the overall architecture.
  - **Opportunities**: In industries like healthcare and automotive, voice-based interfaces can offer hands-free convenience, enhancing accessibility and productivity.

- **AR and VR**:

  o AR superimposes digital elements onto the physical world, while VR creates immersive digital environments. Both technologies are growing rapidly, particularly in fields such as gaming, education, and industrial design. Solutions architects need to consider how these technologies can be integrated into traditional systems to enhance user experience.

  o **Challenges**: Designing for AR/VR involves unique challenges, including hardware limitations, user comfort, and spatial design. Solutions architects must work with UX designers and developers to ensure that AR/VR experiences are smooth, intuitive, and accessible.

  o **Opportunities**: AR/VR opens new possibilities for interactive learning, remote collaboration, and customer engagement. For instance, retailers can use AR to let customers *try on* products virtually, while VR can enable virtual meetings or training sessions in lifelike settings.

Conclusion

In this chapter, we explored the critical role of UX in solutions architecture, focusing on how architects can integrate UX principles into the design of scalable, efficient, and user-centered systems. From understanding the balance between technical excellence and user needs to implementing accessible and inclusive designs, solutions architects are tasked with ensuring that every solution delivers high usability while meeting business objectives. We also covered advanced topics such as HCD, design thinking, ethical considerations, and internationalization, providing insights into how modern solutions architects can create responsive, ethical, and globally adaptable experiences. As the demand for intuitive digital experiences continues to rise, solutions architects who incorporate these principles will be well-equipped to deliver systems that users trust and enjoy.

In the next chapter, we will discuss **disaster recovery** (**DR**) and **business continuity planning** (**BCP**), which are critical components of resilient architecture that ensure system availability, data integrity, and business operations remain uninterrupted in the face of disruptions.

Key takeaways

UX plays a crucial role in modern architectural design, ensuring that technical solutions align with user needs and business goals. Solutions architects must integrate UX best practices into their workflows to enhance usability, engagement, and accessibility while balancing technical constraints. The following takeaways highlight essential considerations for incorporating UX into architectural decisions:

- **Incorporating UX in architecture**: Solutions architects must balance technical requirements with user-centric goals, integrating HCD and design thinking methodologies to build intuitive systems.

- **Balancing technical and UX goals**: Trade-offs between technical constraints and UX should be strategically evaluated to ensure both usability and system performance.

- **Accessibility and usability**: Adherence to WCAG 2.1, ADA, and Section 508 standards is critical to ensure accessibility for all users, alongside incorporating inclusive design solutions.

- **Gamification and engagement**: Techniques like gamification can enhance user engagement, particularly in enterprise applications, by offering rewards, badges, or progress tracking.

- **UX best practices**: Prototyping, consistent UX patterns, and heuristic evaluation should be part of the design process to ensure seamless user experiences across platforms.

- **Globalization and localization**: Adapting designs for international users by addressing language and cultural differences is essential for global scalability.

- **Advanced UX concepts**: Leveraging cognitive psychology and AI-driven **personalization** can optimize user behavior and experiences in modern applications.

- **Ethical considerations**: Transparency, avoiding dark patterns, and ensuring user trust should be central to ethical UX design.

Model interview questions and answers

1. **What role does UX play in solutions architecture?**

    Model answer:
    - UX ensures systems are designed with the end user in mind, balancing functionality with ease of use.
    - As a solutions architect, you advocate for UX from the planning phase, ensuring that technical solutions align with user needs.
    - Incorporating UX early in the architecture process reduces rework and enhances user satisfaction.

2. **How do you balance technical excellence with user needs in system design?**

    Model answer:
    - It is about defining measurable technical and UX goals upfront.
    - You use frameworks like **Must Have, Should Have, Could Have, Won't Have (MoSCoW)** to prioritize features that matter to users without compromising system performance.
    - For example, you once had to optimize database performance while maintaining an intuitive interface; this required you to design intelligent caching without sacrificing UX responsiveness.

3. **Can you explain the concept of HCD in architecture?**

    Model answer:
    - HCD puts the user at the core of the design process, focusing on empathy, define, ideate, prototype, and test stages.
    - You applied this approach in an enterprise CRM project where you started with user interviews to define pain points, then iterated prototypes based on continuous feedback.
    - This iterative design ensured the final product met both business objectives and user expectations.

4. **What strategies do you use for reconciling technical and UX conflicts?**

    Model answer:
    - You work with cross-functional teams to identify areas where user experience could be impacted by technical constraints, using data to make informed trade-offs.
    - One strategy is to build performance benchmarks alongside usability tests to quantify the impact on both.
    - In a project involving real-time data processing, you balanced backend performance with a responsive frontend by offloading some tasks to background processing.

5. **How do you ensure accessibility and inclusivity in your solutions?**

    Model answer:
    - You adhere to standards like WCAG 2.1 and Section 508 to ensure accessibility is built into the design from the ground up.
    - You recently implemented keyboard navigation and screen reader compatibility for a public-facing app, ensuring it was accessible to users with diverse abilities.
    - Tools like Axe and WAVE are part of your QA process to ensure ongoing compliance.

6. **What UX metrics do you track to measure the success of a design?**

   Model answer:

   - You track metrics like task success rate, time on task, and **net promoter score (NPS)** to quantify the effectiveness of a UX design.

   - In a previous project, you used Google Analytics and Hotjar to monitor drop-off points and fine-tune the user flow, which improved your task completion rates by 20%.

   - By analyzing these metrics, solutions architects can identify specific areas where the architecture may be adjusted to enhance responsiveness, improve data handling, or refine performance thresholds, creating a more seamless experience for end-users.

7. **Can you give an example of using gamification in UX design?**

   Model answer:

   - Gamification adds elements like rewards or progress bars to enhance user engagement.

   - For an internal training platform, you introduced badges and progress tracking to motivate employees to complete courses. This resulted in a 35% increase in course completion rates.

   - The key is balancing fun elements with core functionality to avoid distracting from the main user tasks.

8. **How do you incorporate design thinking into solutions architecture?**

   Model answer:

   - Design thinking allows you to tackle complex problems by iterating solutions through empathy, ideation, and testing.

   - You used design thinking in a healthcare application to identify user frustrations during patient intake and redesigned the interface to simplify data entry, cutting input time in half.

   - This method helps prioritize user needs while developing scalable, technical solutions.

9. **How do you evaluate the effectiveness of accessibility solutions in your architecture?**

   Model answer:

   - You use automated tools like SiteImprove alongside manual cognitive walkthroughs to ensure that accessibility measures are fully implemented.

   - In a government project, you regularly ran accessibility checks to ensure compliance with WCAG 2.1, addressing any issues before each release.

   - Continuous testing with real users who have accessibility needs is also crucial for validation.

10. **How do you ensure that your UX design supports global audiences?**

    Model answer:

    - You plan for internationalization early, ensuring that designs can accommodate multiple languages and cultural nuances.

    - Recently, you localized a financial application for three markets, adapting not just the language but also the workflow to meet regional preferences.

    - Tools like Transifex help in managing translations efficiently while ensuring a consistent UX.

11. **What is the role of cognitive psychology in UX design?**

Model answer:

- Cognitive psychology helps us predict how users interact with systems. Concepts like Hick's Law and Fitts' Law guide interface design to reduce cognitive load and streamline interactions.

- You applied Hick's Law to simplify a navigation menu by reducing the number of choices presented to users, improving their decision-making speed.

- These principles ensure that UX decisions are backed by scientific understanding of user behavior.

12. **How do you use AI and machine learning to enhance user experiences?**

Model answer:

- AI and machine learning allow us to tailor experiences to individual users through recommendation engines or adaptive interfaces.

- In an e-commerce app, we implemented a recommendation engine that suggested products based on user history, leading to a 15% increase in cross-sells.

- Personalization driven by AI keeps users engaged while reducing their effort in finding relevant content.

13. **How do you handle UX for secure systems without compromising usability?**

Model answer:

- Balancing security with usability is key, especially in systems requiring MFA or encryption.

- For a recent banking app, we integrated MFA via push notifications, offering a seamless yet secure experience. This approach avoided complex login steps while ensuring data protection.

- By designing intuitive security flows, you ensure that users are not overwhelmed by technical safeguards.

14. **What are the challenges in implementing UX for AR/VR interfaces?**

Model answer:

- Designing for AR/VR brings unique challenges like spatial navigation and maintaining high performance.

- You developed a VR training app where users had to interact with virtual controls, and we had to ensure that the interface was intuitive even in 3D space.

- The challenge is making the experience seamless without causing user disorientation or lag.

15. **How do you integrate performance metrics into UX design?**

Model answer:

- You integrate load time and response metrics into the UX evaluation to ensure fast, responsive experiences.

- In a SaaS platform, you monitored response time after every update using a tool like Google Lighthouse, making iterative improvements to reduce delays by 30%.

- Tracking these metrics ensures that the design is not just aesthetically pleasing but also performs efficiently.

Join our Discord space

Join our Discord workspace for latest updates, offers, tech happenings around the world, new releases, and sessions with the authors:

https://discord.bpbonline.com

CHAPTER 12
Disaster Recovery and Business Continuity

Introduction

Disaster recovery (DR) and **business continuity (BC)** are essential elements of today's applications, ensuring that systems remain operational for end users even when disruptions such as system failures, cyberattacks, or natural disasters occur. Therefore, designing systems that minimize downtime but have continuous availability of business service is extremely important. Solutions architects play crucial roles in providing such applications. DR and BC are integrated into architecture design so that businesses recover as soon as possible and remain stable during adverse situations. This chapter discusses the relevance of DR and BC in solutions architecture by discussing how strategic planning, robust backup solutions, and high-availability designs can prepare systems to face disruption while meeting business objectives.

We will cover DR and BC concepts with terms like **recovery time objective (RTO)**, **recovery point objective (RPO)**, and solutions including **infrastructure as code (IaC)** and **policy as code (PaC)** for automated processes through recovery throughout the chapter.

This chapter will prepare you to design architectures that put operational continuity and disaster readiness first by exploring real-world scenarios, failover strategies, and proactive testing techniques such as **chaos engineering**. In our discussion going forward, we should consider how solutions architects can embed DR and BC principles into architecture and design to build systems that are not only robust but also resilient against challenges.

Structure

This chapter covers the following topics:

- Introduction to DR and BC
- DR planning
- Implementing effective backup solutions
- DR architectures and failover strategies
- BC planning for high availability

- Testing and validating DR plans
- Practical DR and continuity scenarios

Objectives

This chapter will prepare readers with the knowledge they need to effectively design disruption-resilient systems able to survive and thrive after events. They will be capable of developing DR and BC plans tailored to the objectives of a business, identifying risks to make risk-based decisions, and selecting priority recovery for critical systems. Readers will learn to implement effective disaster recoveries and failovers along with infrastructure as code, policy as code, with the use of automation by IaC and PaC.

Additionally, this chapter will allow readers to learn critical DR and BC concepts, such as RTO and RPO, and apply these metrics for proper recovery strategies. It shall also give readers practical insights into Active-Active and Active-Passive architecture, real-time replication, and high-availability designs so that they may well design architectures that keep operations up even during disaster scenarios. It also includes advanced testing methods such as chaos engineering for validation and strengthening of the reader's DR plans.

Finally, the chapter will equip the reader with the confidence to answer questions on disaster recovery and business continuity and to demonstrate capability in designing systems that are resilient, continuous, and compliant in dynamic, real-world environments.

Introduction to DR and BC

In today's digital world, businesses rely heavily on IT systems and digital assets, so resilience planning forms a very important part of any organization's operational strategy. For solutions architects, understanding DR and BC is, therefore, very important to design robust architectures that assure system availability and data integrity during an unexpected disruption. This knowledge becomes highly valuable in scenarios in which an event such as system failure, data loss, or cyber-attack could pose serious business impacts. As part of the interview preparation, solutions architects should clearly explain the difference, the relevance, and how DR and BC strategies are implemented within enterprise environments, as well as a clear comprehension of industrial standards and best practices.

Figure 12.1 illustrates the key elements of business resilience, highlighting critical components such as RTO, RPO, BC, DR, and continuity plans. These elements collectively form the foundation for building highly available, fault-tolerant, and recoverable architectures, enabling businesses to navigate unforeseen disruptions with minimal impact.

The key elements of business resilience are shown in the following figure:

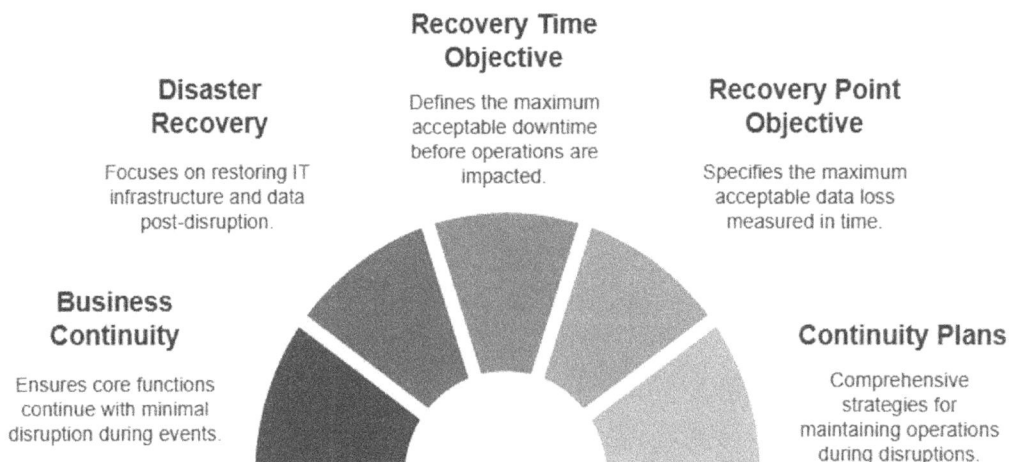

Fig 12.1: *Key elements of business resilience*

Importance of BC/DR in solutions architecture

The role of solutions architects is to design systems that not only meet functional requirements but are also resilient and capable of recovering from interruptions.

BC is the ability that continues critical operations with minimal losses during a disruption, protecting the core services of an organization and allowing for an appropriate recovery.

DR deals with the restoration of information technology infrastructure, applications, and data to a recovered state after an incident; risk management for solutions architects also involves designing for BC/DR.

In interviews, solutions architects should be able to explain why BC and DR are integral components of their design methodology. They should be well-equipped to speak about industries where business resilience is highly critical, such as financial services, healthcare, and the e-commerce sectors, because prolonged downtime or data loss will have financial, reputational, and regulatory consequences of significant magnitude.

Difference between DR and BC

While often discussed together, DR and BC serve distinct functions in an organization's resilience strategy:

- **Business continuity** is the overarching strategy whereby core functions and services for a company continue to work during these unpredictable events, such as a power outage, failure in networks, or natural calamity. BC focuses on continuation and sustaining operations and services in terms of clients, enabling an organization to work or continue at a diminished rate of capacity until recovery in full is attained.

- **Disaster recovery** refers to the restoration of IT infrastructure, applications, and data after disruption; BC is a subset of it, relating to technical recovery efforts in terms of restoring data from backups, failover mechanisms, and re-established network connectivity.

Here, while BC is concerned with keeping operations running, DR concerns the restoration of the technological assets supporting those operations.

It is important in a solutions architect interview to clearly differentiate BC and DR. The candidate should indicate that both are meant to provide business resilience, but while BC is more of an overall organizational strategy to ensure continuity, DR is a tactical approach aimed at restoring IT.

Key concepts

A strong understanding of RTO, RPO, **disaster recovery plan** (**DRP**), and **business continuity plan** (**BCP**) is vital to solutions architects designing resilient architectures:

- **Recovery time objective**: RTO is the maximum acceptable period for a system, application, or function to be unavailable in case of disaster or interruption, after which business processes would be affected. An RTO guides how long it will take to return systems to their normal running state to prevent severe financial and operational impact. In the interview, solutions architects should be able to elucidate how RTO goes into the design of restore and recovery processes.

- **Recovery point objective**: RPO describes the maximum acceptable amount of data loss in terms of time. For instance, an RPO of one hour would mean that in case of failure, the system should not lose more than an hour's worth of data. Solutions architects should be able to discuss how they set RPO based on the criticality of data and incorporate it into backup frequency and replication strategies.

- **Disaster recovery plan**: A DRP is an elaborated, documented methodology of what should be done to restore IT infrastructure and services after a disruption has occurred. DRPs contain data recovery procedures, the re-configuration of infrastructures, and roles and responsibilities. Solutions architects interviewed for such positions should illustrate an awareness of how DRPs are developed, in both the strategic, high level and technical aspects.

- **Business continuity plan**: This is a plan that includes a broader scope of continuous critical business functions and services. Here, an organization will discuss how to keep operations alive and running during and post-disruption for clients. A well-thought-out BCP would include a list of emergency contacts, contingency plans, and more resources that could be applied to maintaining continuity. The solutions architect should explain how BCPS ties in with their design to maintain continuity even beyond the prolonged outages.

The ability to express these concepts in an interview is essential for solutions architects; it will indicate that the architect knows how to design solutions, which are minimizing downtime while preserving data integrity and offering operational resilience. Being good at BC and DR ideas will inform the employer of the architect's ability to develop solutions to mitigate the risk and safeguard business processes and prepare organizations to meet potential crises effectively.

Having laid the groundwork on what DR and BC are, we can discuss in depth how planning should work to prepare systems for interruptions. The next section addresses more critical steps that solutions architects need to take regarding priority in recovery efforts, evaluation of risk, and strategic automation to enhance disaster recovery.

DR planning

DR planning is part of solutions architecture, mainly when one thinks about the resiliency of the IT infrastructure of an organization. Solutions architects design systems that can recover quickly in case of disruptions, hence minimizing downtime and preserving data integrity. This section explores the key elements of DR planning, including assessing risks, identifying critical systems, implementing IaC for recovery automation, and structuring a DRP with essential components.

Every element has its importance to make the architecture resilient for continuous delivery with rapid recovery from interruptions. These elements work together to build resilient architectures that support rapid restoration, data integrity, and high availability in the face of unexpected disruptions. The following figure outlines the key elements of DRP, emphasizing essential steps such as risk assessment, identifying critical systems, IaC, and core components of the DRP:

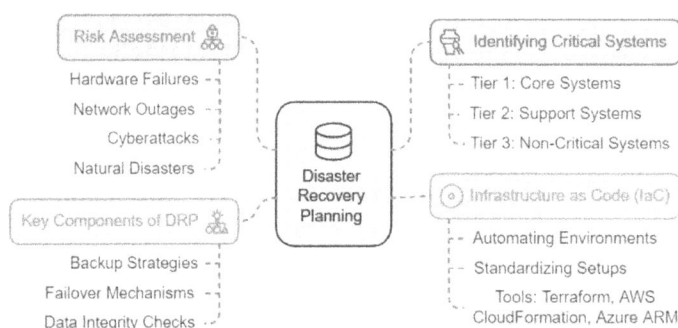

Figure 12.2: Key elements of disaster recovery planning

Understanding risk assessment in DR

Risk assessment is the foundation of any DR plan. For solutions architects, conducting a comprehensive risk assessment means that they have the identification of potential vulnerabilities to the system and applications through which such disruptions may manifest themselves, such as hardware failures, network outages, cyber-attacks, or natural disasters, for each one, to understand the possibility and impact they might cause on the activities of the organization. High-impact, high-probability risks should be focused within the DR strategy to ensure that their recovery efforts are directed towards areas of highest criticality. Questions during interviews could focus on risk assessment techniques, to demonstrate how a solutions architect is going to prioritize the risk identified based on the needs of the organization and dependencies for the system.

Identifying critical systems and prioritizing recovery

In any disaster, not all systems and services have equal priority. Part of the role for the solutions architect is determining what level of service impacts business in the event of an interruption, which in turn informs critical recovery tasks. These system tiers are generally identified. For instance, critical systems must be restored at Tier 1. Thus, these are critical for ensuring that an organization minimizes disruption. Systems can be prioritized in the following manner:

- **Tier 1**: Core systems that must function to operate a business, including customer-facing applications, payment processing, and order management.

- **Tier 2**: Support systems, though important, that would not cause immediate critical operations disruption, such as data analytics and reporting.

- **Tier 3**: Non-critical systems, which could be brought back online later, including development and testing environments.

With such categorization, solutions architects can outline a road recovery map that optimizes the assignment of resources when a disaster is declared. Indeed, the priority skills often put candidates on the spot as they must determine the way limited resources will be assigned to meet a particular disaster recovery objective in interviews.

Infrastructure as code for disaster recovery

IaC, is a practice using which solutions architects can create the infrastructure, instead of the tedious process of manually doing so, using code. IaC helps significantly in disaster recovery since architects can standardize their recovery environments and deploy infrastructure very quickly if something happens to disrupt their normal systems. Let us take a closer look:

- **Automating DR environments**: IaC enables automated setup of disaster recovery environments, reducing the time needed to provision and configure resources. With IaC tools like Terraform, AWS CloudFormation, and Azure ARM Templates, solutions architects can predefine infrastructure configurations for recovery environments, making them readily available and consistent across different locations.

- **Standardization of recovery configurations**: IaC enables Solutions architects to standardize recovery configurations across all environments. Through standardization, they ensure that the DR environments replicate the production setups, which reduces the likelihood of configuration drifts that may result in failures during recovery. Solutions architects should be able to discuss IaC tools and the benefits they bring in DR during interviews, as this approach accelerates and standardizes speed in disaster recovery scenarios.

Key components of a disaster recovery plan

A DRP is a documented approach indicating how IT services and infrastructures will be restored after disruptions. The structured DRP will comprise the following major elements:

- **Backup strategies**: Effective backup strategies are crucial for data recovery in disaster scenarios. Solutions architects should implement a layered backup approach, using full, incremental, and differential backups to balance recovery speed and storage efficiency. The backup frequency should align with the RPO, ensuring minimal data loss based on the business's tolerance levels.

- **Failover mechanisms**: Failover mechanisms automatically or manually transfer to a standby system in case the primary system crashes. Solutions architects make the most of techniques such as Active-Active and Active-Passive configurations to achieve failover. In the Active-Active configuration, both systems run in parallel, each handling its workload, so that the high availability provides instant failover. In contrast to this, in the case of an Active-Passive configuration, a secondary system is kept in standby till the primary system fails, then it is activated. How to use each kind of Failover architecture is imperative knowledge for solutions architects in preparing effective DR solutions.

- **Data integrity checks**: Disaster recovery relies on the integrity of data, since damaged data can destroy recovery processes. Solutions architects should include periodic integrity checks of data integrity that include checksum verifications and data comparison routines in the process of recovery. Such integrity checks ensure that any corrupted data is not restored, which would again destabilize business operations. Solutions architects should be aware of such checks and prepared to describe their importance in ensuring the reliability of data during an interview.

Through comprehensive DR planning, solutions architects can make their systems resilient, recoverable, and aligned with business continuity objectives. The practices covered in this section equip architects with the tactics for assessing risks, making priorities in recovery, IaC automation in the DR environment, and design of DR plans in protecting data integrity and its availability during adverse events.

One of the most important components in any disaster recovery plan is good, reliable backup solutions that match the priorities of recovery. Having done risk assessment and system prioritization, let us proceed to discuss the types of backup strategies in the following section, which solutions architects can implement to ensure consistency in data availability and recovery.

Implementing effective backup solutions

Disaster recovery is all about having a backup solution to restore data and continue operations after disruptions. Solutions architects need to understand various backup strategies and design systems that balance data recovery speed, cost, and reliability. This section explores the essentials of backup strategies, immutable backups, comparisons between cloud and on-premises solutions, best practices for redundancy and data integrity, the role of PaC, and considerations for hybrid and multi-cloud environments.

The following figure provides the complete overview of effective backup solutions which includes types of backups, immutable backups, cloud and hybrid environments solutions, PaC:

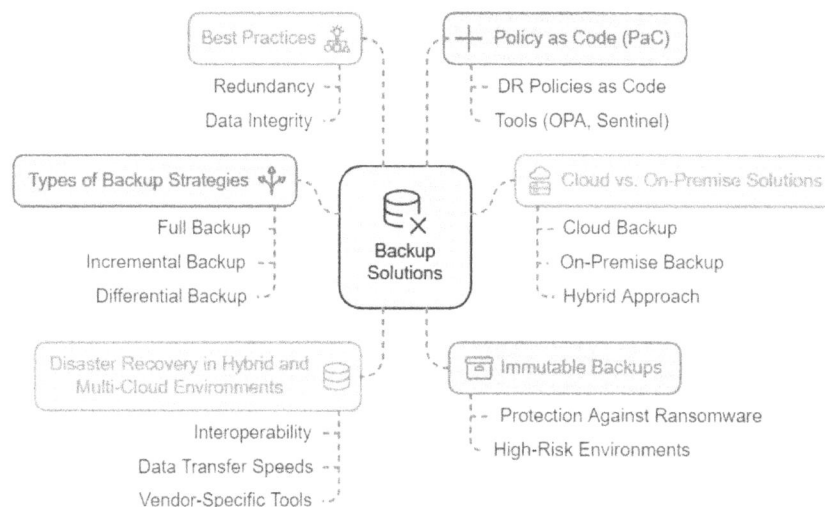

Figure 12.3: Overview of backup solutions implementation

Types of backup strategies

Selecting the right backup strategy is critical for ensuring data availability and quick recovery in the event of a failure. Solutions architects must design optimized backup solutions that balance storage efficiency, recovery speed, and data integrity based on an organization's **recovery time objective (RTO)** and **recovery point**

objective (RPO). The following backup strategies offer different trade-offs between storage requirements and restoration speed:

- Full backup
- Incremental backup
- Differential backup

Full backup

All data in a system is copied to a different storage location, thus a complete snapshot of the system is obtained. Full backups are thorough but time consuming and require more storage; hence, they are best utilized during periodic use rather than for daily updates. Incremental or differential backup solutions architectures should utilize full backups along with them for optimal performance.

Incremental backup

Incremental backup copies only the changed data since the last performed backup, thus reducing storage space and time spent making a backup. Still, restoring from incremental backup requires applying several backups sequentially; this slows down the process of recovery. Differential backups are ideal for everyday backup in systems where there is a need for minimal interruption.

Differential backup

Differential backups copy all changes made since the last full backup, and thus the restoration process is quicker than that of incremental ones because only two files (the last full and differential backup) are required. Solutions architects must consider whether the extra storage requirements for differential backups offset the potential for faster restoration to help an organization meet its recovery time objectives.

Immutable backups

Immutable backups are immutable by design once they have been created. It means critical protection from ransomware attacks and unauthorized access to data. With the added security of making sure the backup files cannot be altered, deleted, or encrypted by malicious users, this is a powerful addition to DR strategies. Implementing immutable backups is especially important in high-risk environments, and it can be set up using certain storage solutions for cloud and on-premise environments.

Cloud versus on-premise backup solutions

When it comes to choosing between cloud and on-premise backups, solutions architects must consider such factors as scalability, accessibility, compliance, and cost.

Cloud backup

Cloud storage has high scalability, global accessibility, and lower upfront costs because the hardware is eliminated from the on-premise hardware. Cloud backups may be a source of concern when it comes to data sovereignty, latency, and long-term costs in case large volumes of data are involved.

On-premise backup

On-premise backups provide better control, low latency, and meet strict compliance standards. They may, however, have higher capital expenditure and can be less scalable compared to cloud solutions.

A hybrid approach that combines both options allows organizations to maintain on-premise control for critical data while using cloud storage for scalability and cost-efficiency.

Best practices for redundancy and data integrity

The importance of a good backup strategy lies in redundancy and integrity of the data, which can serve as a dependable access in times of disaster.

Redundancy

By making redundant backup copies stored at geographically dispersed sites, it could minimize localized disaster-induced loss of data. Solution architects shall take care to maintain a **3-2-1 rule** that maintains three copies of data on two types of storage with one copy maintained offsite.

Data integrity

Regular integrity checks assure the backup files are both accurate and complete, preventing data corruption. Automated integrity validation tools would make the process easier in terms of verifying data reliability, without necessarily requiring manual intervention.

Policy as code for disaster recovery automation

PaC allows the definition of DR policies, including all backup and security standards as code to enable automated governance in CI/CD pipelines.

PaC overview

With PaC, DR policies, such as backup encryption, replication requirements, and retention periods, are set in machine-readable code. This will ensure uniformity across environments and cut down on human error.

PaC for disaster recovery

PaC ensures that the DR policies are applied automatically on all backup processes. Popular tools that enforce backup policies on CI/CD pipelines include **Open Policy Agent** (**OPA**) and HashiCorp Sentinel, which ensure that each backup adheres to the standards set by the organization.

Disaster recovery in hybrid and multi-cloud environments

Disaster recovery strategies must account for the diversified infrastructure and storage needs of hybrid and multi-cloud environments. Interoperability, data transfer speeds, and vendor-specific DR tools will need to be considered in designing cross-platform backup and recovery processes by solutions architects. It will help streamline cross-platform recovery if the DR strategy is aligned with each environment's capabilities, perhaps leveraging cloud-native tools on AWS and Azure, among others.

By mastering these backup strategies and practices, solutions architects can effectively design DR frameworks that ensure quick data recovery, maintain integrity, and meet compliance requirements across various environments.

While backup solutions provide data recovery capabilities, it is also essential to design system architectures that can handle failover smoothly and ensure high availability. In the next section, we will look at disaster recovery architectures and failover strategies that support continuity during failures.

DR architectures and failover strategies

Designing DR architectures and failover strategies is the most important task for solutions architects to ensure that critical systems remain operational during disruptions. Solutions architects should consider architectures and strategies that balance performance, resilience, and speed of recovery.

Active-Active and Active-Passive architectures

Designing a high-availability architecture requires choosing between Active-Active and Active-Passive configurations, each with its own trade-offs in downtime, cost, and complexity. Solutions architects must align these strategies with business continuity requirements to ensure system resilience, fast failover, and optimal resource utilization.

Active-Active architecture

An Active-Active setup ensures continuous availability by distributing real-time traffic across multiple active nodes or data centers. This approach minimizes downtime and enhances scalability, making it ideal for mission-critical applications that require uninterrupted service.

This setup is ideal for systems requiring high availability and seamless failovers. By spreading workloads across multiple systems, Active-Active architecture reduces the likelihood of downtime and provides a backup that's always ready to take over.

Let us consider an example. Two data centers, each capable of processing user requests, are used for a large-scale e-commerce platform. In the event of a data center failure, the remaining data center continues serving requests without interruption.

Active-Passive architecture

An Active-Passive setup relies on a standby system that remains idle until the primary system fails. While this approach reduces costs compared to Active-Active, it introduces slight downtime during failover. It is well-suited for cost-sensitive environments where immediate failover is not mandatory but still ensures high availability.

Let us consider an example. A high-availability payroll system might use Active-Passive configuration where the active system processes payments, and the passive waits in a standby mode. Once the active system fails, the passive system becomes active.

Selecting the right high-availability strategy depends on factors such as downtime tolerance, cost, and complexity. *Table 12.1* compares Active-Active and Active-Passive architectures to help solutions architects determine the most suitable option based on business needs:

Architecture	Downtime	Cost	Complexity	Use case
Active-Active	Minimal	High	High	Critical apps needing 24/7 uptime
Active-Passive	Low	Medium	Moderate	Cost-conscious environments

Table 12.1: Comparison of high-availability and disaster recovery architectures

Real-time data replication

Data replication mechanisms are very important in DR architectures to ensure that the systems can recover with zero data loss and zero-time loss.

Synchronous replication

It ensures that data is written to both primary and secondary systems simultaneously. It guarantees data consistency but may increase latency.

Asynchronous replication

Replication occurs at intervals, thus providing lower latency but risking data loss between replication events.

Architects should consider factors such as network bandwidth, data criticality, and recovery objectives when choosing a replication strategy. Synchronous replication is often preferred for applications that have low tolerance for data loss, whereas asynchronous replication is effective for systems that have performance as a priority.

DR and failover strategies for critical systems

The following figure gives an overview of the various DR strategies for critical systems:

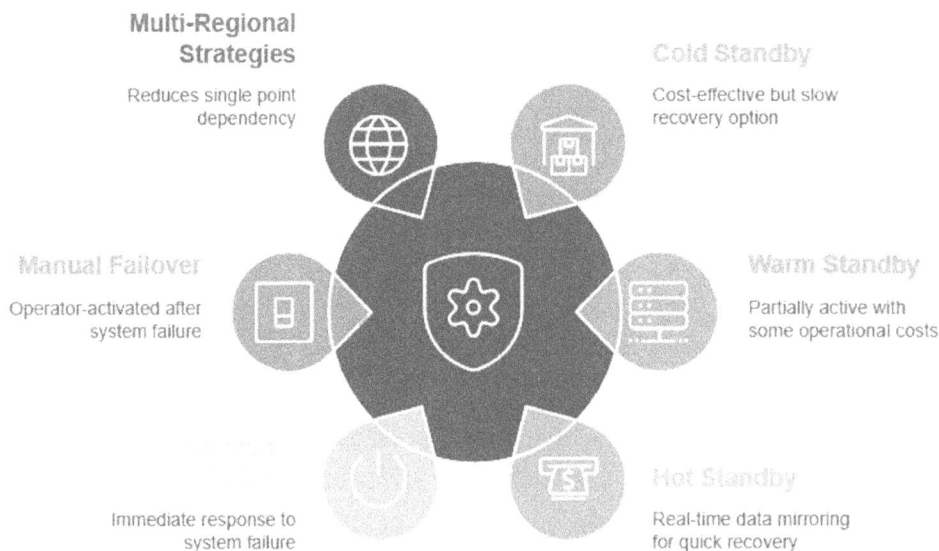

Figure 12.4: Strategies for disaster recovery

Cold, warm, and hot standby

Standby strategies determine the speed and efficiency of recovery, balancing cost, downtime, and operational readiness. Solutions architects can choose from cold, warm, or hot standby, depending on their recovery time objectives and budget constraints. These concepts are explained as follows:

- **Cold standby**: This takes the longest period to recover. A secondary system is kept totally off until required, which reduces costs but increases the time for recovery.

- **Warm standby**: The backup is partially active as key applications are pre-installed. This reduces the period of recovery from cold standby, but there is some ongoing operational cost.

- **Hot standby**: Mirrors the primary, constantly synchronizing with real-time information. This method is quicker but more expensive.

Automated versus manual failover

Failover mechanisms define how quickly and efficiently a system can recover from failures, with automation offering rapid response and manual failover providing controlled recovery. Depending on system criticality, businesses can implement automated or manual failover strategies to ensure seamless continuity. Let us take a closer look:

- **Automated failover**: Triggers as soon as a system crashes; ideal for applications requiring seamless access.

- **Manual failover**: Initiated by operators upon system failure; typically reserved for critical or intricate applications for which automated failover poses too great a risk.

Ensuring DR across distributed architectures

Disasters can be particularly challenging in distributed systems due to the interdependence of networked components. The architect should:

- Implement multi-regional or multi-availability zone strategies to reduce dependency on a point.

- Use load balancers to distribute traffic and provide failover solutions, probably across regions or availability zones.

- Provide cross-cloud redundancy for defenses against cloud provider outages.

Case study: Real-world examples of DR architectures

Suppose a financial institution globally needs continuous operations and solid DR strategies. Let us take a look at the scenario, and the approach that can be followed.

Scenario: The institution employs an active-active architecture across the *New York* and *London* data centers. The data centers both operate in synchronous replication so that there is data consistency. In the event of failure, the traffic will be redirected immediately to the remaining data center, which means no stoppage in service.

Approach: The architecture entails load balancing, automated failover mechanisms, and multi-cloud redundancy for critical services.

This is how the existence of redundancy, real-time replication, and cross-regional failover impacts business continuity for high stake industries.

The article sets foundational grounding for a solutions architect's role in determining robust DR strategies to have standby readiness for the worst that might happen and increases their resilience factor.

Besides the architectural strategies for disaster recovery, solutions architects should consider broader business continuity planning to maintain high availability in several failure scenarios. This next section addresses how to incorporate continuity planning for a resilient system design.

BC planning for high availability

BCP involves the ability of systems and services to continue working with no interruption in case of a sudden disruption. Solutions architects should design architectures that can respond to different failure scenarios to ensure availability and operational integrity.

Differences between high availability and DR

Although the two are related, **high availability** (**HA**) and DR are used for different purposes in resilience planning:

- HA is minimizing the downtime during normal operation, distributing workloads, and making use of redundant components. HA architectures are about having systems running continuously, even under minimal disruptions.

- DR is about getting out of a major system failure or disaster. DR usually involves restoring data, restarting services, and then re-establishing operations from backup locations after some sort of unexpected event.

Understanding these differences enables solutions architects to focus BCP elements on system requirements with short-term operational continuity (HA) and longer-term recovery (DR).

Service level agreements and BC needs

Service level agreements (**SLAs**) set certain uptime and performance standards, which typically dictate BCP objectives:

- **Setting SLAs**: Organizations set SLAs to achieve business continuity goals that encompass allowable downtime, response time, and recovery criteria.

- **Mapping SLAs to continuity requirements**: Solutions architects should ensure that the business needs and technical capabilities align. They should see that architectures meet or surpass the defined SLAs. In this case, a 99.99% uptime SLA could require failover across multiple availability zones or regions.

The inclusion of HA features and robust continuity solutions ensures that operations are kept at agreed performance levels, thus meeting the SLAs.

Building BC into your architecture

To build resilient systems, solutions architects should consider multiple strategies for maintaining continuity in various failure scenarios. Let us take a look at the key areas to address.

Ensuring operations during cyber attacks

Cyber threats are a significant risk to business continuity, requiring proactive security measures to ensure systems remain operational during an attack. Implementing redundancy, network isolation, Zero Trust principles, and multi-factor authentication, data encryption can help mitigate risks and maintain service availability, which has been further explained as follows:

- **Implement redundancy and isolation**: Use network segmentation and redundancy to contain cyber threats, allowing unaffected parts of the system to continue operating.

- **Zero Trust Architecture**: A Zero Trust approach is one where all users, inside or outside the network, are authenticated and authorized in real-time, thus limiting unauthorized access during attacks.

- **Multi-factor authentication and data encryption**: Implementing MFA and data encryption offers layers of security, therefore preventing data breaches and system outages.

Continuity during power outages

Power disruptions can severely impact critical operations, making it essential to have backup power solutions and redundancy mechanisms in place. Solutions architects should design architectures that leverage **uninterruptible power supply** (**UPS**) systems, geographical redundancy, and hybrid cloud solutions to maintain availability. The details are as follows:

- **UPS systems**: Implement UPS systems to maintain short-term power in case of outages, thereby reducing the risk of data loss and allowing time for systems to failover.

- **Geographical redundancy**: Host critical applications in multiple regions or data centers to ensure continuity if one location experiences a power disruption.

- **Cloud and on-premise hybrid solutions**: Combine on-premise resilience with cloud redundancy to ensure continuity during outages, with cloud services providing instant failover capabilities.

Natural disasters and system failures

Disruptions caused by natural disasters or infrastructure failures require robust failover strategies to minimize downtime. By implementing regional failover plans, load balancing, and automated failover mechanisms, organizations can ensure resilience against large-scale disruptions, as follows:

- **Regional failover plans**: Critical systems are dispersed geographically to prevent the impacts of regional disasters. Where one location is down, systems are available elsewhere.

- **Load balancing and traffic management**: Employing load balancers and global traffic managers to send the traffic to available resources during a regional disaster. During such an outage, traffic can be redirected to unaffected regions without a single degradation in system performance.

- **Automated failover mechanisms**: Utilize cloud-native services such as AWS Route 53, Azure Traffic Manager, among others, for automation of fails processes so that rerouting of users to the backup sites is done efficiently when a failure occurs.

Solutions architects must design BCP measures that address both huge-scale and localized disruptions, such that they are aligned with the SLAs and all critical systems are resilient and survive any event.

Designing a strong continuity and disaster recovery strategy is half the solution. Testing and validation, however, are required to ensure these plans will work as envisioned. The following section discusses methods of testing, including simulation and proactive techniques like chaos engineering.

Testing and validating DR plans

For adequate preparedness and avoiding longer downtime during disruptions, the DR plans must undergo regular testing and validation. For solutions architects, proper testing practices must be applied for the verification of recovery strategies against the expected performance or real-world scenarios to meet specific recovery objectives.

Importance of regular testing and simulations

Testing DR plans is essential for finding out the weaknesses and preparing to improve them before a real disaster hits. Periodic simulations assist with:

- **Recovery strategy validation**: The strategy implemented in the plan meets the RTOs and RPOs.

- **Identification and filling of gaps**: Testing will reveal where the plan is weak, thereby filling those gaps.

- **Improving team readiness**: Teams can get advanced preparation on DR procedures, which would minimize response time at the event.

Tests should be scheduled to be held quarterly or semiannually, and after important infrastructure or application changes, the test should be performed.

How to design DR simulations

Designing a valid DR simulation requires mimicking disaster conditions to test for responses from the system:

- **Define scenarios**: Some of the possible disasters included data center outages, network failures, and cyberattacks.

- **Define clear goals**: To prove that a failover does happen within an RTO, or data loss is minimized according to the RPO.

- **Execute tests gradually**: Start with low-risk components before scaling up to full-scale simulations.

- **Document results and lessons learned**: Review results to identify actionable improvements, documenting lessons learned for future testing.

Chaos engineering for proactive DR testing

Chaos engineering is a new type of DR strategy testing in which failure is deliberately injected into systems to observe how they respond. Let us take a closer look:

- **Chaos engineering**: Chaos engineering is the process by which one tests the resilience of systems through controlled failures. It is a way of testing the systems under stressful and unpredictable conditions so that solution architects can test the robustness of DR plans.

- **Applying chaos engineering to DR testing**: Simulating real-world failures such as database downtime or network interruptions, chaos engineering tests if systems can auto-recover from these failures. The injection of failures, including disabling certain nodes or throttling network speeds, shows vulnerabilities that might not occur in the course of testing with other tools.

- **Tools for chaos engineering**:

    o **Gremlin**: Allows engineers to simulate different failure scenarios, from CPU spikes to network outages, and analyse recovery responses.

    o **Chaos monkey**: Part of Netflix's Simian Army, Chaos Monkey randomly disables production instances to test failover mechanisms.

    o **AWS fault injection simulator**: Enables engineers to test how AWS environments respond to faults, like latency or system crashes.

- **Benefits of chaos engineering in DR and BC plans**:

    o **Proactive vulnerability detection**: Chaos engineering helps identify issues in system resilience proactively, minimizing the risk of unexpected failures.

    o **Improved confidence in DR**: Frequent testing under real-world conditions increases confidence that DR plans will work during an actual disaster.

    o **Enhanced system stability**: By constantly challenging systems, architects can design more stable, resilient architectures.

Common pitfalls in DR testing

Common mistakes in DR testing can render plans ineffective when needed most:

- **Incomplete test coverage**: Testing only specific components rather than the full architecture can overlook critical interdependencies.

- **Lack of documentation**: Failing to document procedures and results may cause teams to repeat mistakes or overlook essential lessons.

- **Untrained personnel**: Testing often involves only the IT team, but DR events impact multiple departments. Including cross-functional teams ensures everyone knows their role.

- **Overlooking non-IT dependencies**: DR plans must consider dependencies beyond IT, such as power and logistics, to ensure a comprehensive recovery approach.

Real-world example: DR testing in large enterprises

Consider a multinational bank that performs quarterly DR simulations across its global data centres. The testing involves:

- **Simulating regional failures**: By creating scenarios that take entire regions offline, the bank verifies its failover across multiple geographies, ensuring customer services remain available.
- **Cross-functional collaboration**: Teams from IT, operations, and compliance collaborate in testing, ensuring that all business aspects remain operational.
- **Using chaos engineering tools**: The bank utilizes tools like Gremlin to simulate database outages and load balancing failures, strengthening its DR posture and verifying recovery times.

This approach not only prepares the bank for actual disruptions but also strengthens its overall resilience by regularly identifying and addressing potential weak points.

With a strong understanding of testing and validating DR plans, it is helpful to apply these concepts to real-world scenarios.

The role of SRE in enhancing DR and BC

Site reliability engineering (SRE) is a discipline that combines software engineering principles with IT operations to ensure system reliability, scalability, and performance. In the context of DR and BC, SRE focuses on proactive measures to minimize downtime, automate recovery processes, and enhance system resilience. By embedding reliability practices into the development lifecycle, SRE teams help ensure that architectures meet RTOs and RPOs.

Core SRE practices for BC/DR

SRE applies engineering principles to enhance disaster recovery and business continuity by defining clear objectives, managing error budgets, streamlining incident response, and leveraging automation to minimize downtime and improve system resilience. The following list provides more details:

- **Service level objectives (SLOs)**:
  - SRE emphasizes setting clear SLOs, which define measurable targets for availability and performance.
  - SLOs align with RTO and RPO goals, ensuring that disaster recovery plans meet business and operational needs.

- **Error budgets**:
  - Error budgets provide a quantified allowance for downtime, balancing reliability and innovation. SRE uses error budgets to prioritize recovery efforts and justify investments in DR and BC strategies.

- **Incident response and post-mortems**:
  - SRE practices involve structured incident response plans, including detailed runbooks for handling outages.
  - Post-mortems analyse the root cause of failures, ensuring lessons learned improve DR and BC strategies.

- **Automation and tooling**:
  - SRE leverages automation to streamline failover, backup testing, and recovery processes, reducing manual intervention during incidents.

SRE's contribution towards resilience

The following mentions SRE's contribution towards resilience:

- Principles of SRE leverage the culture of DR/BC with prevention, reduction of mean time to recovery, and improvement.

- Proactive testing, such as chaos engineering, in the service of SRE, to fit the intent for the resiliency of a system under test.

Combining SRE with solutions architecture

Solution architects work closely with SREs to create architectures that best balance performance, cost, and reliability. Though the solution architect is the system designer and planner, the SRE ensures the design is operationally valid and can handle real-world stressors.

The following section considers some of the more typical disaster recovery and continuity scenarios (from data center collapse through to ransomware attack and cloud outage) and what the solution architect can do for each.

Practical DR and continuity scenarios

Solutions architects need to be ready to answer scenario-based questions on DR and BC strategies. In the following examples, we cover common scenarios and how architectures need to be designed to address each of these situations effectively.

Example scenarios

Disaster recovery and business continuity require well-defined strategies tailored to specific failure scenarios. Solutions architects must be prepared to design architectures that ensure minimal downtime, quick recovery, and resilience against various disruptions. The following real-world scenarios highlight how DR and BC strategies can be implemented to mitigate risks and maintain operational stability.

Data center failure

In case of failure at a data center:

- It is important that DR architecture makes critical services accessible while automatically redirecting the workloads to other locations.
- **Recommended solution**: Deploy the multi-regional architecture having the load balancer distribution across multiple data centers. Data should be replicated in real-time so that there is continuity, and applications should either be stateless or use distributed databases, so that failover is possible without losing data.

Cloud provider outage

Cloud provider outages can affect many services across regions. In such a case:

- Critical applications should be planned for cloud redundancy.
- **Recommended solution**: Implement a multi-cloud strategy to diversify dependencies and avoid single points of failure. Architect the applications to be cloud-agnostic where possible, using containers and orchestration tools (e.g., Kubernetes) to facilitate portability across cloud providers. Alternatively, design for cross-region replication within the same cloud provider, ensuring failover within unaffected regions.

Ransomware attack recovery

A ransomware attack:

- Can freeze essential systems and data, causing quite a disruption to business activity.
- **Recommended solution**: Harness immutable backups and data snapshots that cannot be changed even after they have been written, thus being ransomware encryption-proof. Implement a rapid

backup restore process using isolated recovery zones to quickly access clean data copies. Regularly test backups to ensure they are uncompromised, and consider using tools that detect unusual file activity or access patterns as early indicators of potential ransomware.

It helps to overcome known risks through practical scenario implementation; however, it introduces yet another layer of resilience because policy as a service enforces policies in real time to support dynamic ongoing compliance and business continuity across the environments.

Policy as a service for business continuity

Policy as a service helps to enforce policies across systems in real time, ensuring continuity with the agreed-to DR and BC standards. Policies like data replication or failover rules are coded, thus allowing dynamic and consistent governance across environments. These concepts are explained in more detail, as follows:

- **In BCP, policy as a service provides for continuous policy compliance**: Defining DR and BC policies as code, policy as a service continuously evaluates systems to be compliant with established standards, meaning systems will meet the criteria for high availability and security even as applications update or environments change.

- **Practical example**: Assume a system configured with policy as a service for regional availability monitoring. When an availability zone goes down, policy as a service will automatically enforce a failover policy, initiate data replication, and redirect traffic to a working zone without requiring manual intervention.

- **Business continuity through automatic policy enforcement**: With policy as a service, business continuity can be achieved through automatic load distribution and failover. Thus, in case of disruption, the system would ensure a smooth transition. For example, policies can enforce redundant storage configurations so that data is always available, and services are not interrupted.

How to design DR/BC architectures for common scenarios

Designing resilient DR/BC architectures for particular scenarios requires a customized approach:

- **For data center failures**:
  - o Design a multi-region architecture with Active-Active or Active-Passive failover between data centres.
  - o Utilize synchronous replication to ensure data consistency across locations, with load balancers distributing traffic.
  - o Periodically test failover to ensure RTO and RPO compliance.

- **For cloud provider outages**:
  - o Employ a multi-cloud strategy or regional redundancy in the same provider to maintain flexibility.
  - o Cloud-agnostic components such as containers and orchestration tools to make it easy to migrate.
  - o Use multi-cloud backup and storage solutions that make rapid recovery possible if one provider fails.

- **For ransomware attacks**:
  - o Immutable backups and enabling regular data snapshots.
  - o Security policies for the early detection of unusual behavior by integrating them into your DR framework to trigger immediate isolation of affected systems.
  - o Design isolated recovery environments that will restore backups without cross-contamination.

Conclusion

In this chapter, we explored the key role that DR and BC play in solutions architecture and how architects design systems to survive disruptions and stay up and running. From knowing what RTO and RPO are and how to implement backup solutions and failover mechanisms to IaC, this chapter provided an overview of resilient architectures.

We also explored policy as code and policy as a service, which dynamically enforce continuity and compliance standards, thus making it possible to adapt in real-time in the face of potential failures. Practical examples and scenario-based insights helped us understand how to respond to data center failures, cloud provider outages, and cybersecurity threats.

As a solutions architect, mastering DR and BC involves not only designing for continuity but also consistently testing these designs to ensure their effectiveness. Techniques such as chaos engineering expose weaknesses proactively, so that architects fine-tune their DR plans to meet the very highest standards of resilience. Integrated with such strategies, solutions architects will be perfectly equipped to address all interview scenarios and real-world challenges, leading to the delivery of systems that safeguard business operations and generate user trust by dependable availability.

While designing resilient architectures is crucial for maintaining operations during disruptions, governance and compliance play an equally vital role in ensuring that these architectures adhere to regulatory and organizational policies. In the next chapter, we will explore how governance frameworks and compliance regulations influence architectural decisions. We will discuss how solutions architects can design secure, audit-ready systems while balancing regulatory requirements with business innovation.

In the next chapter, we will learn about governance and compliance and how they are the backbone of enterprise level applications.

Key takeaways

Designing resilient and recoverable systems is a critical responsibility for solutions architects, ensuring that businesses can withstand disruptions and maintain continuity. This section summarizes the essential principles, best practices, and proactive strategies that drive effective DR and BC planning. From defining RTO and RPO to leveraging IaC, PaC, and automated failover mechanisms, these takeaways equip architects with the necessary tools to build robust, compliant, and highly available architectures:

- **Core DR and BC strategies**: Solutions architects must design systems with robust DR and BC plans to maintain resilience and recoverability.

- **Setting RTO and RPO**: Define RTO and RPO to guide replication and backup strategies effectively.

- **Effective backup and automation**: Use automated backups and IaC to standardize recovery, ensure consistency, and reduce downtime.

- **Active-Active vs. Active-Passive**: Choose Active-Active for high availability with low downtime or Active-Passive for cost-effective recovery.

- **Policy as code**: Enforce DR compliance with automated policy checks, ensuring recovery standards are continuously met.

- **Chaos engineering for resilience**: Use tools like Gremlin and Chaos Monkey to test and strengthen system resilience proactively.

- **Immutable backups for security**: Protect against ransomware with immutable backups, providing clean data for recovery.

- **Multi-cloud and hybrid DR**: Multi-cloud or hybrid solutions reduce reliance on a single provider, enhancing overall resilience.

- **Policy as a service**: Automate continuity policies with policy as a service for real-time failover and recovery.

- **Regular testing and simulations**: Routine DR testing and simulations prepare systems and teams for real-world scenarios.

Model interview questions and answers

1. **How do you decide between synchronous and asynchronous data replication for disaster recovery?**

   Model answer:

   - **Synchronous replication:**

     o Ensures data consistency across locations, minimizing the risk of data loss.

     o Involves higher latency, making it suitable for applications needing strong data integrity.

     o Used in cases where RTO and RPO are low (e.g., financial applications).

   - **Asynchronous replication:**

     o Offers faster performance with reduced latency.

     o Allows minor data loss, making it ideal for applications that can tolerate slight discrepancies.

     o Applied in applications prioritizing speed and less-critical data requirements.

     o **Example**: For a financial client, you implemented synchronous replication between data centres to achieve near-zero data loss, while using asynchronous replication for less critical services.

2. **Describe a scenario where you used IaC for rapid disaster recovery and how it improved your DR plan.**

   Model answer:

   - IaC (e.g., Terraform or CloudFormation) automates environment creation, ensuring consistency.

   - Eliminates manual steps, reducing setup and failover time.

   - Improves recovery reliability by removing human error from configuration.

   - **Example**: For an e-commerce client, you used IaC to deploy mirrored infrastructure in a backup region. During DR testing, the automated setup allowed you to meet RTO targets, restoring the environment in minutes.

3. **How do you manage compliance in disaster recovery planning, especially in regulated industries like healthcare or finance?**

   Model answer:

   - Use policy as code to enforce compliance on backup encryption, data retention, and residency.

   - Implement automated checks with tools like HashiCorp Sentinel or Open Policy Agent to verify policy adherence.

   - Regularly test DR processes against compliance standards to address regulatory audits.

   - **Example**: In a healthcare project, you automated PaC checks for encryption and data location, ensuring that all backups were securely stored within the required regions.

4. **Explain how you would design a disaster recovery architecture for a critical application that must have minimal downtime.**

   Model answer:

   - Use an Active-Active architecture for seamless failover and load balancing.

   - Employ real-time data replication to keep data synchronized across regions.

   - Implement automated failover mechanisms with health checks to redirect traffic instantly upon failure.

   - **Example:** For a global payment system, you configured two data centres in an Active-Active setup. Real-time replication and load balancing ensured continuous availability, allowing near-zero downtime during regional disruptions.

5. **What steps do you take to regularly test and validate disaster recovery plans?**

   Model answer:

   - Schedule quarterly DR simulations covering various failure scenarios.

   - Include cross-functional teams (IT, operations, security) to ensure all stakeholders are prepared.

   - Document and review outcomes to identify gaps or areas for improvement.

   - **Example:** For a finance client, you ran annual simulations simulating regional failures, training teams and refining recovery processes based on results.

6. **How would you implement chaos engineering to test disaster recovery strategies effectively?**

   Model answer:

   - Use tools like Gremlin or Chaos Monkey to simulate failures such as network latency or service unavailability.

   - Focus on critical components (e.g., databases, load balancers) to test system resilience.

   - Monitor and adjust DR strategies based on failure responses to improve reliability.

   - **Example:** In a distributed system, you used chaos engineering to simulate network outages, validating your load balancer's failover capabilities and adjusting to improve recovery.

7. **Can you discuss the role of immutable backups in ransomware recovery?**

   Model answer:

   - Immutable backups prevent modification, making them resistant to ransomware attacks.

   - Use **write-once-read-many** (**WORM**) storage to create secure backup copies.

   - Store immutable backups in isolated environments for rapid recovery.

   - **Example:** For a healthcare project, you stored immutable backups offsite with strict access controls, ensuring clean recovery copies even during a ransomware event.

8. **How do you design DR for multi-cloud environments to handle cloud provider outages?**

   Model answer:

   - Implement redundancy across multiple cloud providers for critical services.

   - Use cloud-agnostic tools (e.g., Kubernetes) to facilitate portability.

   - Regularly test failover to ensure applications can switch providers seamlessly.

   - **Example:** For a SaaS product, you set up parallel deployments in AWS and Azure, ensuring failover between clouds for continuous service during outages.

9. **What are the key considerations for disaster recovery in a hybrid cloud setup?**

   Model answer:

   - Ensure network connectivity and security controls between on-premises and cloud environments.

   - Use compatible backup and storage solutions across both environments.

   - Implement cross-environment failover strategies to handle data recovery.

   - **Example:** For a manufacturing client, you designed a DR plan with synchronized backups across on-premises and cloud systems, enabling a quick switch to cloud-based systems during local outages.

10. **How do you evaluate the effectiveness of disaster recovery policies using policy as a service?**

    Model answer:

    - Configure PaaS to apply policies dynamically, triggering actions like failover based on real-time monitoring.

    - Define DR policies as code to ensure continuous enforcement across environments.

    - Regularly review and test policies with scenarios like regional outages.

    - **Example:** For a financial app, you used PaaS to enforce cross-region failover policies, allowing the system to redirect traffic automatically when an availability zone went down.

11. **What are the advantages of Active-Active over Active-Passive architectures for disaster recovery?**

    Model answer:

    - Active-Active offers real-time load sharing, minimizing downtime during failover.

    - Provides immediate backup as all nodes are live and accessible.

    - Active-Passive, while cost-effective, involves slight downtime as backup systems must activate.

    - **Example:** For a high-availability e-commerce app, you implemented an Active-Active setup, distributing traffic between regions to ensure continuous service even if one region experienced issues.

12. **How do you ensure data integrity in backup and disaster recovery processes?**

    Model answer:

    - Use hash verification or checksums to confirm data integrity.

    - Schedule automated checks on backup data to catch discrepancies early.

    - Regularly audit data recovery tests to verify data accuracy.

    - **Example:** In a banking environment, you implemented nightly hash checks on backups, catching any integrity issues before backups were moved to storage.

13. **Describe your approach to designing a ransomware-resilient architecture.**

    Model answer:

    - Implement layered security with immutable backups and network segmentation.

    - Store backups offline or in isolated environments to prevent tampering.

    - Use advanced monitoring tools to detect unusual access or encryption patterns.

    - **Example:** For a legal client, you designed a segmented network with offsite immutable backups, which allowed you to quickly recover unaffected data after a ransomware incident.

14. **How do you ensure business continuity during a regional disaster affecting primary operations?**

    Model answer:

    - Utilize geographically dispersed data centres for primary and backup locations.

    - Automate traffic routing through DNS services (e.g., AWS Route 53, Azure Traffic Manager) to unaffected regions.

    - Regularly test regional failover to validate continuity plans.

    - **Example**: For a telecom client, you implemented regional failover across data centres in separate geographic zones, maintaining service during a regional outage.

15. **What are the common pitfalls in disaster recovery testing, and how do you avoid them?**

    Model answer:

    - Pitfalls include inadequate testing frequency, missing critical components, and untrained personnel.

    - Avoid these by:

        o Scheduling regular tests and covering both planned and spontaneous simulations.

        o Testing all critical infrastructure, including dependencies.

        o Including cross-functional teams in simulations.

    - **Example**: For an enterprise client, you scheduled quarterly DR tests, including cross-departmental roles, ensuring all stakeholders understood recovery processes and were prepared for real incidents.

Join our Discord space

Join our Discord workspace for latest updates, offers, tech happenings around the world, new releases, and sessions with the authors:

https://discord.bpbonline.com

CHAPTER 13
Governance and Compliance

Introduction

Governance and compliance are the backbone for enterprise-level applications. Regulations are becoming more stringent, business environments are changing, and security threats are increasing. In such a scenario, solutions architects need to design systems that are innovative yet accountable and regulatorily compliant. Governance is ensuring that architectural decisions align with organizational objectives, whereas compliance ensures legal and regulatory requirements are met.

Good governance frameworks guide to make the right kind of decisions, ensure accountability, and reduce risks within the organization. Compliance is very different from this, and it specifically refers to standards like GDPR, HIPAA, PCI DSS, and SOX standards, and how systems are designed safely, ethically, and are sound for audits. Together, these define a solid foundation of offering secure, scalable, and dependable solutions.

In this chapter, we provide insights on how solutions architects can embed governance and compliance practices into their design. Learn action-oriented strategies for implementing governance frameworks to manage regulatory requirements, risk, and innovation. Understand how automation, with technologies like **policy as code** (**PaC**) and PaaS, helps streamline governance and keeps your systems audit-ready and secure over time.

At the end of this chapter, you will have learned how to design solutions that are governed and compliant, how to manage risks in a proactive way, and how to respond to the evolving legal and business environments. You might be trying to address compliance challenges in a multi-cloud environment, architect for GDPR, or implement governance in a distributed system; at the end of this chapter, you will have practical strategies that help you achieve operational excellence with accountability.

Structure

This chapter covers the following topics:

- Introduction to governance and compliance
- Understanding governance frameworks
- Establishing effective governance policies and procedures

- Adhering to compliance requirements
- Designing architectures for compliance
- Risk management in governance and compliance
- Governance and emerging technologies
- Practical case studies and governance scenarios

Objectives

This chapter will enable readers to know how to design governance and compliance-focused systems that will meet regulatory demands, mitigate risks, and make stakeholders accountable. The reader will be well-equipped to set up governance frameworks, develop compliance practices, and address the issues of regulation versus innovation.

These are the principles mastered in reading, mapping compliance standards such as **General Data Protection Regulation (GDPR)**, **Health Insurance Portability and Accountability Act (HIPAA)**, and **Payment Card Industry Data Security Standard (PCI DSS)** to architectural designs and enforcing governance policies using automated tools like PaC and PaaS. They will also be exposed to strategies as to how governance and compliance can be fluidly integrated with Agile and DevOps practice so that systems remain compliant throughout their lifecycle.

In addition, it will get readers familiar with governance frameworks such as *Control Objectives for Information and Related Technologies*, *The Open Group Architecture Framework*, and *Information Technology Infrastructure Library*, with actual examples about how it is applied to the real world. It will disclose designing for compliance with Privacy by Design, checking on compliance as part of continuous integration/continuous delivery pipelines, and guaranteeing security with security as code.

Finally, by the end of this chapter, readers will be confident in their ability to navigate complex governance and compliance requirements, solve real case studies, and prepare them for interview questions. By the end of this chapter, readers will be well equipped to design solutions that are secure, resilient, and compliant, but also foster innovation in dynamic environments.

Introduction to governance and compliance

Governance and compliance are at the heart of building resilient and reliable systems that align with the organizational goals and regulatory mandates. Their role in solutions architecture is very important to ensure that designs are innovative as well as responsible, balancing technical capabilities with accountability.

The key elements of governance and compliance are shown in the following figure:

Figure 13.1: Key elements of governance and compliance

Importance of governance in solutions architecture

An effective governance in solutions architecture will ensure that systems design, implementation, and management are done in alignment with an organization's strategic objectives, regulatory needs, and its operational policies. Hence, governance will structure decision-making for accountability, transparency, and consistency both within the team as well as other stakeholders. Key aspects of governance include:

- **Decision-making frameworks**: They define who may make decisions and how well those decisions align with policy.

- **Policy enforcement**: Architecture, security, and compliance policies are created and enforced to prevent them from being violated.

- **Alignment with the business objectives**: Technological solutions need to support major organizational strategies.

- **Cost optimization**: Resource management as it enforces guardrails on the cost and resource utilization.

Compliance

Compliance involves the observance of the rules governing the protection of data and other operations. Solutions architecture complies with the established regulations while not losing innovative power and agility.

Organizations suffer due to non-compliance with various standards of implementation. Penalties and fines may come through litigation, loss of revenue, and reputation. Different industry standards are developed while upholding common values that encompass the protection of data, respect for personal privacy, and liability accountability.

Let us consider a few examples:

- **Healthcare**: HIPAA controls access and protects patient data and privacy.

- **Finance**: PCI DSS ensures safe payment card information handling.

- **Global**: GDPR imposes severe data-privacy regulations for citizens in the EU and has business implications across the globe.

Balancing innovation and compliance requires solutions architects to:

- Build systems with compliance requirements from the beginning (for example, Privacy by Design).

- Leverage tools like PaC and automation to enforce compliance without hindering innovation cycles.

- Collaborate with stakeholders, such as legal, IT, and business teams, to ensure that innovative solutions are developed in conjunction with regulatory requirements.

Governance frameworks and compliance standards bring structured guidelines to the management of risk, accountability, and assurance of system integrity. Using such frameworks, solutions architects define best practices and come up with systems that may meet the organizational and regulatory expectations.

This section is more of a basis for further reading of governance frameworks, compliance requirements, and approaches in their implementation in solution architecture.

Understanding governance frameworks

Governance frameworks provide structured approaches for managing systems, processes, and teams within organizations, ensuring they align with strategic goals and regulatory requirements. Solutions architects must understand these frameworks to design systems that adhere to best practices, maintain compliance, and enable effective decision-making. *Figure 13.2* shows the overview of governance and compliance:

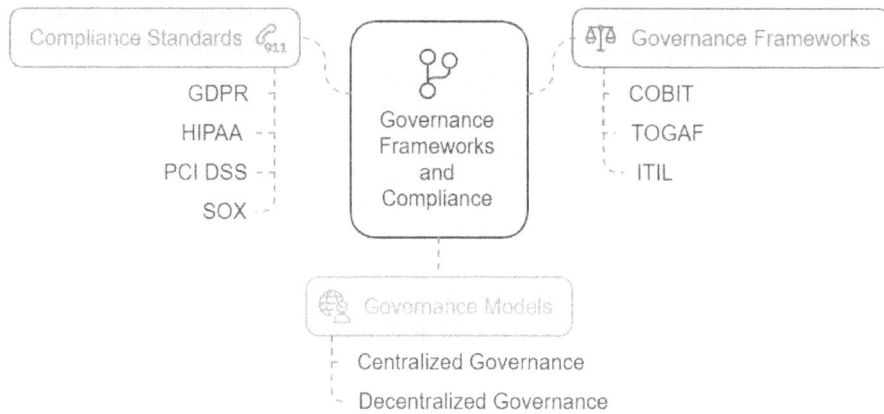

Figure 13.2: Overview of governance and compliance standards, frameworks

Overview of popular governance frameworks

Popular governance frameworks offer guidelines and methodologies for implementing robust governance practices in organizations. We will look at three key frameworks in more detail.

Control Objectives for Information and Related Technologies

Control Objectives for Information and Related Technologies (COBIT) is a framework focused on aligning IT governance with business objectives. It puts forward processes such as risk management, compliance, and performance monitoring. Solutions architects can apply COBIT to build controls that will ensure accountability and alignment with organizational objectives.

The Open Group Architecture Framework

The Open Group Architecture Framework (TOGAF) offers a holistic approach to designing, planning, implementing, and governing enterprise architecture. Solutions architects apply TOGAF to ensure that architectural designs are in line with business strategies and scalable, reliable, and compliant.

Information Technology Infrastructure Library

Information Technology Infrastructure Library (ITIL) is an IT service management framework that provides best practices for delivering high-quality IT services. Solutions architects can apply ITIL to integrate governance principles into service design and operations, ensuring smooth delivery and compliance.

Each framework has its peculiar strengths and applicability. Understanding these frameworks will assist solutions architects in choosing and applying the most appropriate framework for their organizational context.

Centralized versus decentralized governance

Enterprises must decide between centralized and decentralized governance models based on their size, structure, and strategic objectives.

Centralized governance

In this model, decision-making authority is concentrated within a single governing body or team. It is ideal for organizations requiring uniform policies, strong oversight, and centralized risk management. For example, financial institutions often use centralized governance to meet stringent regulatory requirements.

Decentralized governance

This model spreads governance decision-making among several teams or units, thus fostering agility and innovation. It is perfectly applicable to large, fast-paced organizations with diverse requirements of operations, such as multinational businesses. Decentralized governance enables teams to make proper decisions within the boundaries defined by overall policies.

In order to suggest the ideal governance model that ensures not only efficiency and compliance with rules but also support for business goals, solution architects must analyze the business structure and goals.

Establishing governance policies

Setting governance policies is one of the most critical tasks that solutions architects should perform because such policies establish the rules, processes, and roles to maintain accountability and compliance. The key features are as follows:

- **Roles and responsibilities**: Establish clear governance responsibilities for all stakeholders involved, including architects, developers, and business leaders. This ensures accountability and alignment among teams.

- **Policy development**: Develop comprehensive governance policies in areas such as security of data, access, and regulatory compliance. All policies should be actionable in the direction of the business objectives.

- **Automated enforcing**: Apply tools such as PaC to enforce automated governance in CI/CD pipelines. Automating your policies eliminates human errors during their lifecycle and maintains their compliance.

- **Continual monitoring and auditing**: Implement monitoring tools to track adherence to governance policies and conduct regular audits to identify gaps. Continuous oversight strengthens governance and ensures compliance with evolving standards.

Having a clear understanding of governance frameworks is a basis for solutions architects' design of systems that not only clearly meet technical and business objectives but also maintain compliance and accountability in dynamic, real-world environments. Having contextualized the theoretical basis of popular governance frameworks, the task then shifts towards translating these principles into actionable policies specific to organizational needs, as discussed in the subsequent section.

Establishing effective governance policies and procedures

In large organizations, effective governance requires a structured approach to defining roles, implementing processes, and leveraging tools for monitoring and enforcement. The solutions architect is instrumental in setting up a governance framework that aligns with technical solutions for organizational objectives and regulatory requirements.

Roles and responsibilities in governance

Clear delineation of roles and responsibilities is important for effective governance. *Figure 13.3* provides the roles and responsibilities in governance, highlighting the key roles:

Governance Framework

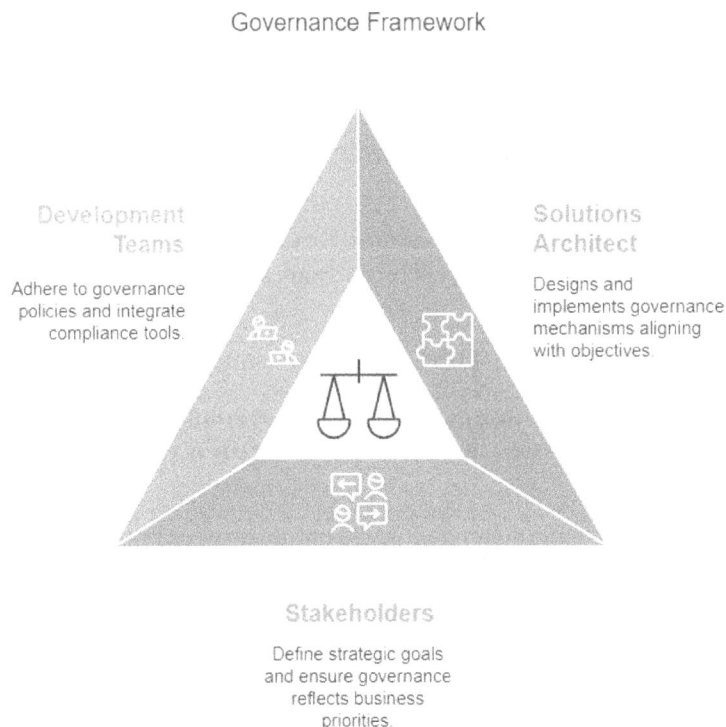

Figure 13.3: Roles and responsibilities in governance

Key roles include:

- **Solutions architect**: Solutions architects are responsible for designing and implementing governance mechanisms that align with both technical and business objectives. They ensure that architectures comply with regulatory requirements, enforce governance policies, and integrate governance tools into the system lifecycle.

- **Stakeholders**: Stakeholders, including business leaders, compliance officers, and IT managers, define the organization's strategic goals, risk appetite, and compliance requirements. Their input ensures governance policies reflect in business priorities.

- **Development teams**: Development teams are responsible for adhering to governance policies during the design, development, and deployment of systems. They integrate tools and practices, such as PaC, into their workflows to maintain compliance and reduce risks.

Establishing clear roles fosters accountability, ensures alignment across teams, and simplifies the implementation of governance policies.

Monitoring and auditing tools for governance

Governance is a continuous process that must be monitored continuously. With monitoring and auditing tools, organizations can track compliance and identify risks to proactively address potential gaps. The most important practices are as follows:

- **Automated monitoring**: Use tools such as AWS Config, Azure Policy, or HashiCorp Sentinel to monitor system configurations, detect non-compliance, and enforce corrective actions automatically.

- **Real-time auditing**: Solutions like Splunk or Elastic Security enable real-time auditing of system and user activity logs, enabling organizations to instantly respond to potential violations or breaches.

- **Reporting and dashboards**: You install reporting tools which offer insight into compliance metrics, such as adherence to access controls, encryption policies, among others. Dashboards assist stakeholders in making well-informed decisions based on current data.

Continuous monitoring and auditing ensure that governance policies are effective, even as systems evolve and organizational needs change.

Governance integrating with Agile and DevOps

Agile and DevOps methods emphasize speed and flexibility. In some cases, it becomes a tension point between the traditional governance and results in innovation at the cost of compliance. Integrating governance into these workflows ensures innovation without a cost for compliance.

Governance in Agile

In Agile, governance policies should be part of iterative processes. This should include defining *Definition of Done* criteria that must include compliance checks to ensure that every sprint delivers solutions that are not only functional but also compliant.

Governance in DevOps

DevOps emphasizes automation, making it the perfect environment for embedding governance practices into CI/CD pipelines. Governance in DevOps ensures that every code deployment undergoes compliance checks and aligns with organizational policies before release.

Policy as code for governance and compliance

Again, PaC, which we discussed in *Chapter 12, Disaster Recovery and Business Continuity* for DR and BCP, comes to enable the governance and compliance here.

Policy as code

PaC is the practice of codifying governance and compliance policies into machine-readable formats. This enables automated enforcement of policies in CI/CD pipelines, reducing manual effort and ensuring consistent compliance. Features of PaC work in governance are mentioned as follows:

- **Automated enforcement**: PaC tools, such as OPA or HashiCorp Sentinel, automatically evaluate infrastructure configurations, deployment processes, and application behaviors against predefined policies.

- **Continuous validation**: PaC ensures that systems remain compliant throughout their lifecycle by continuously validating configurations against regulatory and organizational standards.

- **Risk mitigation**: PaC identifies non-compliance issues early in the development cycle, reducing the risk of costly remediations or regulatory penalties post-deployment.

Let us look at a few examples of PaC in action:

- **GDPR compliance**: A PaC rule might enforce data encryption for all personal data stored in cloud environments, ensuring compliance with GDPR requirements.

- **PCI DSS compliance**: PaC can validate that firewall configurations adhere to PCI DSS standards, automatically rejecting deployments with non-compliant settings.

The benefits of PaC in governance are as follows:

- **Scalability**: PaC scales easily across large, complex systems, ensuring consistent enforcement across diverse environments.

- **Efficiency**: Automation eliminates manual compliance checks, speeding up deployment processes without compromising governance.

- **Proactivity**: PaC enforces governance policies in real time, reducing the likelihood of compliance violations.

Using PaC, solutions architects can seamlessly integrate governance and compliance into modern development workflows, ensuring systems stay compliant and secure without stifling innovation.

Establishing effective governance policies and procedures requires clear roles, robust tools, and integration with Agile and DevOps practices. With this, continuous monitoring, automatic enforcement, and practices such as PaC will ensure that solutions architects ensure governance is not just effective but also adaptive to the demands of modern development and operational environments.

Even as PaC automates governance enforcement, integration with Agile and DevOps makes it even more effective through the embedding of compliance checks into rapid development cycles.

Adhering to compliance requirements

Adherence to the compliance requirements is one of the critical components of solution architecture, particularly in industries that include finance, healthcare, and government. Such sectors adhere to the regulatory standards for data handling, security, and privacy. Solution architects, therefore, design systems not just to meet functional requirements but also stringent compliance mandates as a means of risk avoidance and accountability. The chapter discusses key considerations on solutions architecture related to addressing challenges in compliance.

Overview of compliance standards

Compliance standards provide frameworks and guidelines that organizations must follow to ensure data protection, privacy, and operational integrity. Common standards include:

- **GDPR**: Focuses on protecting the personal data of EU citizens, requiring strict data handling policies, consent management, and the *right to be forgotten*.
- **HIPAA**: Mandates safeguards for sensitive healthcare information, including encryption, access controls, and audit trails.
- **PCI DSS**: Ensures the secure processing, storage, and transmission of payment card information.
- **Sarbanes-Oxley Act**: Establishes financial reporting and data integrity standards, requiring organizations to maintain accurate records and audit trails.

Understanding these standards is vital for solutions architects to design compliant systems tailored to organizational and industry requirements.

Design for compliance

Compliance-centric design is about embedding the core security and privacy principles into system architectures:

- **Data privacy**: Implement Privacy by Design principles by limiting data collection, anonymizing sensitive information, and providing users with control over their data (e.g., consent mechanisms and opt-out options).
- **Encryption**: Ensure end-to-end encryption for data both in transit and at rest using strong encryption algorithms, like AES-256. In addition, solutions should support **key management services** (**KMS**) that ensure encryption keys are secure as well as compliant with the requirements for compliance.
- **Access controls**: Implement granular access controls by using **role-based access control** (**RBAC**) or **attribute-based access control** (**ABAC**). Implement **multi-factor authentication** (**MFA**) to reduce risk from unauthorized access.

By combining these elements, solutions architects can develop architectures that inherently support compliance requirements.

Compliance mapping in architecture design

Mapping compliance requirements to architectural components ensures that regulatory standards are met throughout the system lifecycle:

- **Identify regulatory requirements**: Determine specific compliance requirements relevant to the organization, such as data residency, encryption standards, or breach notification timelines.

- **Align with architectural layers**: Map each requirement to specific architectural components. For instance, data encryption policies map to database configurations, while breach notification requirements map to monitoring and alerting systems.

- **Automate compliance checks**: Implement automated validation to ensure that systems consistently meet mapped compliance requirements. For example, use CI/CD pipeline checks to verify encryption configurations before deployment.

This systematic approach ensures that compliance is not an afterthought but a foundational element of the architecture.

Policy as a service for regulatory compliance

Policy as a service is a governance model where compliance policies are enforced dynamically across systems in real time. By continuously monitoring system configurations and behaviors, PaaS ensures ongoing adherence to regulatory requirements.

Let us look at how PaaS supports compliance:

- **Automatic enforcement**: PaaS frameworks automatically enforce compliance policies, such as requiring encrypted connections, validating firewall rules, or ensuring proper access controls.

- **Alerting and auto-remediation**: PaaS triggers alerts or auto-remediation actions when configurations deviate from compliance standards. For example, if a firewall rule is misconfigured, PaaS can either notify the administrator or automatically correct the rule.

- **Runtime validation**: PaaS validates compliance policies during system runtime, making architectures resilient to configuration drift and ensuring readiness for regulatory audits.

The following are the benefits of PaaS for compliance:

- **Consistency**: Ensures policies are uniformly applied across infrastructure, applications, and workflows.

- **Efficiency**: Reduces the manual effort required for compliance checks.

- **Audit readiness**: Continuously monitors systems, simplifying the process of demonstrating compliance during regulatory audits.

By leveraging PaaS, solutions architects can create systems that are both compliant and adaptive to evolving regulatory landscapes.

Compliance in cloud and multi-cloud environments

Compliance in cloud and multi-cloud environments introduces additional complexity due to diverse infrastructure, vendor policies, and shared responsibility models. Solutions architects must consider:

- **Data residency and sovereignty**: Ensure that data is stored and processed in regions that comply with local regulations (e.g., GDPR mandates data storage within the EU).

- **Vendor-specific compliance tools**: Utilize cloud-native compliance tools like AWS Config, Azure Policy, or Google Cloud Security Command Center to monitor and enforce compliance within specific cloud environments.

- **Interoperability across clouds**: Implement policies that apply consistently across multiple cloud providers. For instance, use tools like Terraform or Kubernetes for unified configuration management.

- **Shared responsibility model**: Clearly define responsibilities between the organization and cloud providers to ensure that all compliance requirements are met without gaps.

By addressing these considerations, solutions architects can ensure that compliance is maintained even in complex, multi-cloud deployments.

Adhering to compliance requirements involves a comprehensive approach that integrates regulatory standards, robust design principles, and modern governance tools like PaaS. By understanding compliance frameworks, designing architectures with privacy and security in mind, and leveraging automation, solutions architects can create systems that not only meet regulatory demands but also foster trust and accountability. These practices prepare architects to navigate real-world challenges and excel in compliance-focused roles.

Compliance standards establish the rules, but translating these rules into architectural design is where solutions architects truly add value.

Designing architectures for compliance

Designing architectures for compliance requires a proactive approach to embedding regulatory adherence, security, and governance throughout the lifecycle of a system. For solutions architects, this involves integrating compliance from the initial design stages and maintaining it through automation, security practices, and continuous validation. This section explores practical strategies for achieving compliant architectures, which can also be effectively discussed in interviews to showcase expertise.

The building blocks of compliance architecture are shown in the following figure:

Building Blocks of Compliant Architectures

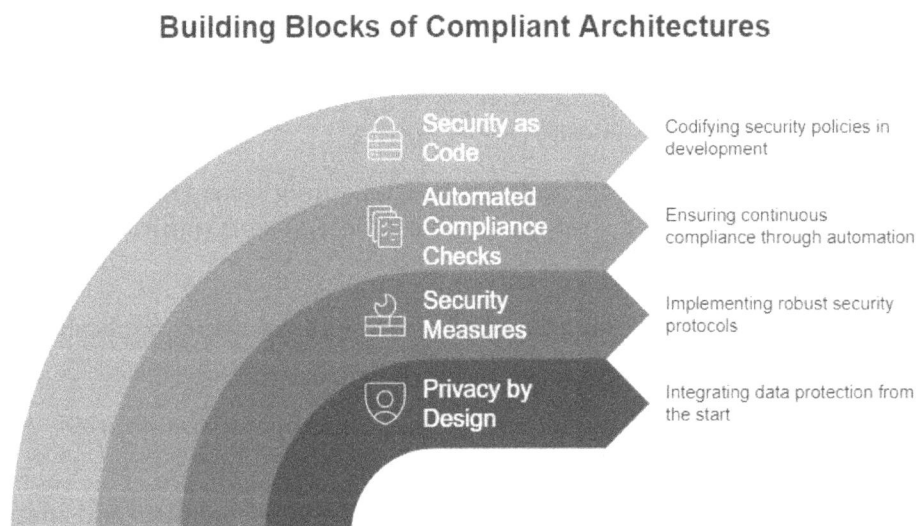

- **Security as Code** — Codifying security policies in development
- **Automated Compliance Checks** — Ensuring continuous compliance through automation
- **Security Measures** — Implementing robust security protocols
- **Privacy by Design** — Integrating data protection from the start

Figure 13.4: Building blocks of compliance architectures

Privacy by Design, integrating compliance

Privacy by Design (**PbD**) is a framework for ensuring that privacy and data protection are embedded into the design and operation of systems from the outset. Let us learn more about PbD:

- **Key principles of PbD**:
  - **Data minimization**: Collect only the data necessary for system functionality.
  - **Transparency**: Ensure clear communication with users about how their data is collected, stored, and used.

- o **Default privacy**: Configure systems to provide maximum privacy protection by default (e.g., opt-in settings for data sharing).

- **Implementation in architecture design**: Solutions architects can apply PbD by implementing features such as pseudonymization, data masking, and secure access controls to protect user data from unauthorized access. For instance, in an e-commerce platform, PbD can ensure that sensitive customer data is encrypted at rest and in transit, and access is limited to authorized personnel only.

Integrating PbD principles builds trust with stakeholders and ensures that systems align with regulations such as GDPR and HIPAA.

Ensuring security and data protection in architecture

Compliant architectures are primarily concerned with security and data protection. Solutions architects should implement strong security mechanisms that protect systems and conform to regulations. The details are as follows:

- **Encryption standards**: Use strong encryption protocols, such as AES-256, to encrypt data while in transit and at rest. Implement KMSs for secure handling of encryption keys.

- **Access controls**: Implement fine-grained access controls using RBAC or ABAC. Use MFA to add security.

- **Data segregation**: Segregate sensitive data from non-sensitive data so that exposure in case of a breach is minimized. For example, maintain PII in one database and transaction logs in another.

These steps are not only compliant but also strengthen the security posture of the architecture.

Automated compliance checks: Integrations of CI/CD pipelines

Automated compliance checks will ensure that the systems remain compliant throughout the lifecycle of development and deployment. Compliance validations, therefore, need to be integrated into CI/CD pipelines so that non-compliant configurations are not deployed into production by solutions architects.

Continuous security and compliance monitoring

Tools such as AWS Config, Azure Policy, and Google Cloud Security Command Center are checking infrastructure and applications for compliance violations in real-time. The real-time assessments are coupled with actionable insights for remediation.

Ensuring post-deployment compliance

Automated checks in CI/CD pipelines can validate configurations such as encryption settings, firewall rules, and data residency requirements before deployment. For example, a pipeline step could automatically reject any deployment that fails to meet encryption standards mandated by PCI DSS.

Automated compliance checks reduce manual errors, improve efficiency, and ensure adherence to regulatory standards.

Security as code for compliance and governance

Security as code (SaC) is the process of codifying security practices and policies into development pipelines so that compliance and governance can be enforced automatically.

Integrating security policies directly into the development lifecycle:

- Codify security rules as code with Terraform, AWS IAM Policies, or Azure Blueprints.
- Incorporate these rules into CI/CD pipelines to enforce security standards.

Providing governance, compliance, and security: SaC automates the enforcement of policies, including access restrictions, encryption requirements, and data retention standards. For example, if a developer tries to deploy a resource without enabling encryption, SaC policies in the pipeline will block the deployment and notify the team.

By adopting SaC, solutions architects can ensure that systems remain secure and compliant even as they scale or evolve.

Case study: Architecting for compliance in healthcare and finance

Compliance in highly regulated industries like healthcare and finance requires meticulous architectural planning to ensure data security, privacy, and regulatory adherence. This case study highlights how solutions architects can design robust, compliant systems that align with industry standards such as HIPAA and PCI DSS while maintaining scalability and operational efficiency. Let us take a look at a few scenarios and solutions for those scenarios:

- **Scenario 1: Compliance in healthcare (HIPAA)**
  - **Challenge**: Design a healthcare system that processes and stores sensitive patient data while adhering to HIPAA regulations.
  - **Solution**:
    - Implement end-to-end encryption for all patient data.
    - Use IAM policies to restrict data access based on roles, for example, only doctors can access specific patient records.
    - Utilize automated compliance tools like AWS Config to monitor system configurations for HIPAA compliance.
- **Scenario 2: Compliance in finance (PCI DSS)**
  - **Challenge**: Building a payment processing system that processes credit card transactions and is in line with the PCI DSS.
  - **Solution**:
    - Tokenize credit card numbers to have unique tokens and reduce sensitive data exposure.
    - Establish periodic vulnerability scans as well as penetration testing of systems for detection of security loopholes.
    - Use audit trails of all access as well as all transactions as transparency measures during compliance audit.

The case studies show how compliance requirements affect the architecture design and how solution architects can better handle it during real-world implementation.

Designing compliant architectures requires a balance of technical acumen, regulatory expertise, and forward-looking approaches. Solutions architects can create systems that are secure, scalable, and aligned with the regulations by embedding Privacy by Design principles, robust security controls, automated compliance checks, and SaC. Real-world application of these principles is demonstrated through practical examples and case studies, making it easier for architects to have confidence in compliance and be successful in interviews.

Proactive risk management is incomplete without effective governance. It means identifying potential vulnerabilities and implementing strategies to mitigate them across diverse architectures.

Risk management in governance and compliance

In solutions architecture, risk management is a critical component of governance and compliance, ensuring that systems remain secure, regulatory requirements are met, and vulnerabilities are proactively addressed. The growing adoption of hybrid and multi-cloud systems introduces additional layers of complexity, requiring solutions architects to employ robust risk management strategies. This section explores how to identify, assess, and mitigate risks in governance and compliance across diverse environments.

The following figure illustrates key aspects of risk management in governance and compliance, covering risk identification, mitigation strategies, and governance approaches for cloud, hybrid, and multi-cloud environments:

Figure 13.5: Risk management in governance and compliance

Identifying and mitigating governance and compliance risks

Effective risk management begins with a comprehensive understanding of potential vulnerabilities and the implementation of strategies to mitigate them.

Risk identification

Identifying potential vulnerabilities early helps organizations prevent compliance failures and security breaches. A structured risk assessment ensures that governance gaps are detected and addressed proactively. The details are as follows:

- **Assessment of vulnerabilities**: Identify potential weak points in systems that could lead to regulatory breaches. Examples include unencrypted sensitive data, misconfigured access controls, and inadequate logging mechanisms.

- **Compliance gap analysis**: Perform detailed evaluations to identify gaps in meeting standards such as GDPR, HIPAA, PCI DSS, and SOX. This analysis should begin during the design phase to embed compliance into the architecture at the outset.

- **Risk matrices**: Utilize tools like risk matrices to assess risks based on their likelihood and potential impact. These matrices help prioritize focus areas, ensuring that high-risk vulnerabilities are addressed promptly.

Mitigation strategies

Implementing preventive measures, clear policies, and continuous monitoring helps minimize compliance risks, strengthen governance, and ensure regulatory adherence. The details are as follows:

- **Preventive measures**:
  - Encrypt sensitive data at rest and in transit to prevent unauthorized access.
  - Enforce RBAC to limit access to critical resources based on user roles.
  - Use continuous compliance monitoring tools to detect non-compliance in real-time.
- **Clear policies and guidelines**: Codify governance practices in well-documented policies that are understandable and actionable by all stakeholders, from development teams to executives.
- **Regular audits**: Conduct periodic internal audits to ensure ongoing adherence to governance and compliance standards. Audit outcomes should inform iterative improvements to systems and policies.

Ensuring compliance with cloud providers

Cloud architectures function on a shared responsibility model, which splits security and compliance responsibilities between the cloud provider and the organization. Solutions architects need to understand and navigate this model to ensure comprehensive governance.

Shared responsibility model

Cloud security and compliance are a shared responsibility between cloud providers and organizations. While providers ensure the security of the cloud infrastructure, organizations must safeguard their data, applications, and user access. Solutions architects must clearly define these responsibilities to prevent compliance gaps and security risks. Further details are as follows:

- **Cloud provider responsibilities**: Infrastructure security, physical data center security, and certain compliance certifications.
- **Organization responsibilities**: Data protection, application security, and user access management.

Compliance mapping

To maintain regulatory compliance across cloud environments, organizations should leverage provider-specific compliance tools and frameworks. Mapping compliance requirements to cloud-native services helps automate validation, streamline audits, and ensure continuous adherence to industry standards. Let us take a look at provider-specific tools:

- **AWS Audit Manager**: automates evidence gathering for audits.
- **Azure Security Center**: facilitates compliance checks and recommendations on the Azure environment.

Service level agreements

Critical SLAs with cloud providers, which one should establish to define governance expectations, particularly:

- Data sovereignty and residency.
- Encryption protocols and standards.
- Guarantees of disaster recovery and failover.

Governance implementation on hybrid and multi-cloud systems

Managing governance in hybrid and multi-cloud environments presents unique challenges due to varying platform policies, compliance requirements, and security controls. Solutions architects must establish consistent governance frameworks that ensure policy enforcement, data security, and risk management across all cloud and on-premise environments. The following strategies help maintain governance uniformity and compliance across diverse infrastructures. The details are as follows:

- **Unified governance framework**: Establishing a consistent governance framework across hybrid and multi-cloud environments ensures uniform policy enforcement, security, and compliance.

    o Make use of tools such as HashiCorp Terraform or Kubernetes for uniformity in terms of infrastructure and policies both at cloud and on-prem systems.

    o Use a single governance monitoring tool like Azure Arc or Google Anthos that brings together the management of many different environments.

- **Data locality and sovereignty**: Ensuring compliance with regional regulations requires defining policies for data storage, residency, and processing locations.

    o Choose data centers with the local data residency law in place (for example, GDPR requirements in the EU).

    o Define and implement a policy for where and how data is stored and processed.

- **Cross-platform risk management**: Implementing governance tools and automated monitoring helps detect and mitigate compliance risks across multiple cloud platforms.

    o Use multi-platform governance tools like Prisma Cloud or IBM Cloud Pak for Security to maintain visibility and control across different environments.

    o Implement automated alerts that flag non-compliance in real-time to be brought to immediate attention for risks.

Real-world examples: Risk management practices

Effective risk management is crucial for maintaining compliance and protecting sensitive data in highly regulated industries like healthcare and finance. By implementing encryption, access controls, and continuous monitoring, solutions architects can mitigate security risks while ensuring adherence to compliance standards such as HIPAA and PCI DSS. The following case studies illustrate how organizations apply risk management strategies to safeguard data and enhance system resilience.

Healthcare provider

The details are as follows:

- **Risk**: Incidences of data breaches through poor encryption.
- **Solution**: Employ end-to-end encryption on patient records, enforces access controls on users by limiting access to specific user permissions, and finally use HIPAA compliant tools like AWS Health Lake for safe storage and process sensitive data.

Financial institution

The details are as follows:

- **Risk**: Access to payment systems with possible exposure to customer data.

- **Solution**: Employ tokenization; replacement of sensitive data of payments with non-sensitive tokens.

  o Implement multi-factor authentication for all user access to payment systems.

  o Deploy real-time compliance monitoring tools to continuously audit payment systems for adherence to PCI DSS standards.

With these approaches, solutions architects can have assured effective governance and compliance even in the most complex hybrid and multi-cloud environments. Proactive risk management helps protect systems from breaches in regulatory requirements but also makes them stronger and more robust in terms of their operational integrity.

Governance and emerging technologies

As technology evolves, governance must evolve with it to address the new challenges that emerging technologies and methodologies bring. Solutions architects have a significant role in implementing governance in systems that make use of AI, ML, cloud-native architectures, and Agile development practices. The following section discusses governance for these innovations, with risk management, accountability, and compliance in fast-changing environments.

Governance for AI, ML, and cloud-native systems

AI, ML, and cloud-native systems introduce unique governance considerations due to their dynamic, data-intensive, and distributed nature.

AI and ML governance

Governance in AI and ML systems is essential to ensure ethical use, data integrity, and regulatory compliance. Solutions architects must implement policies that address bias mitigation, transparency, and model lifecycle management, ensuring AI-driven decisions are fair, accountable, and secure. Here are some attributes that the readers should remember:

- **Ethical AI practices**:

  Ensure algorithms are designed and trained in a manner that avoids bias and promotes fairness. Establish policies for ethical AI usage, including guidelines for transparency and explainability.

- **Data governance for AI and ML**:

  o Sophisticated data management practices ensuring data quality and integrity.

  o Use techniques of anonymization to maintain sensitive data in training as well as testing.

  o Monitor adherence to data privacy regulations, such as GDPR and HIPAA.

- **Model lifecycle management**:

  o Establish governance policies for all the AI/ML lifecycle, including model development, deployment, monitoring, and retirement.

  o Utilize ModelOps to enforce consistent governance practices for model management.

Cloud-native systems governance

Cloud-native environments require governance strategies that adapt to dynamic workloads, containerized applications, and infrastructure automation. Solutions architects must enforce policies for resource allocation, security, and configuration management, ensuring compliance and operational consistency across cloud platforms. The details are as follows:

- **Dynamic workloads and elasticity**: Govern dynamic cloud-native workloads with policies related to resource allocation, cost optimization, and scaling.
- **Container security**:
  - Apply governance policies in containerized workloads by means of tools like Kubernetes and Docker.
  - Schedule audit of images in containers for vulnerabilities and be sure to meet security requirements.
- **Configuration management**: Utilize IaC in the area of infrastructure configurations. Thereby, the misconfiguration risks are minimized, thus bringing order in infrastructure setups.

Governance in DevOps and Agile development

Agile and DevOps value speed and flexibility, though these are the same attributes that can generate risk when governance is left out of the workflow.

Agile governance principles

In Agile and DevOps environments, governance must strike a balance between enabling innovation and ensuring compliance, security, and accountability. Traditional governance models often introduce overhead and friction, which can hinder the agility and speed that modern development practices demand. Therefore, Agile governance emphasizes adaptability, transparency, and collaboration. The following are the core principles that guide effective governance in Agile settings:

- **Lightweight policies**: Implement very minimal governance policies that also follow the iterative nature of development in Agile.
- **Stakeholder alignment**: Involve cross-functional teams in governance discussions to ensure accountability and adherence to policies without slowing development cycles.

Governance for distributed architectures and microservices

Distributed architectures and microservices offer scalability and flexibility but pose unique governance challenges due to their decentralized nature.

Service-level governance

In distributed architectures and microservices, governance must ensure consistency, security, and compliance across independent services. Service-level governance defines policies for performance, inter-service communication, and change management, enabling seamless operations while maintaining regulatory and business standards. Let us take a closer look:

- **Service contracts**: Define and enforce SLAs for individual microservices to ensure consistent performance, security, and compliance.
- **Inter-service communication policies**: Establish governance policies for secure and reliable communication between services, including secure protocols like TLS, authentication, authorization, and data integrity.
- **Monitoring and observability**: Use tools like Prometheus, Grafana, or OpenTelemetry to ensure visibility across distributed systems. Governance policies should include requirements for logging, tracing, and monitoring to maintain accountability.
- **Change management in distributed systems**: Enforce version control and change management practices to minimize disruptions caused by frequent updates or new deployments.

Implement canary deployments or blue-green deployment strategies to test changes in controlled environments before full-scale implementation.

Governance in emerging technologies must be very adaptable and proactive. Whether that's managing ethical issues in AI, securing architectures in a cloud-native context, or controlling DevOps and microservices, solutions architects must get governance practices established that nurture innovation while making sure those are compliant, secure, and operationally excellent systems. By embedding governance into these technology lifecycles, architects can develop resilient systems that are compliant and keep working in highly dynamic environments.

Practical case studies and governance scenarios

Practical case studies and scenarios enable solutions architects to visualize how governance and compliance strategies are applied in real systems. This section discusses important governance models, examples of architectures driven by compliance, and strategies for implementing governance in complex systems. These practical examples help architects solve governance-related challenges during interviews and in professional practice.

Zero Trust Architecture for compliance and governance

Zero Trust Architecture (**ZTA**) emphasizes the principle of *never trust, always verify*. This model enforces very strict access controls and continuously verifies all users and devices, regardless of where they are located, thus boosting governance and compliance. Let us take a closer look:

- **Components of Zero Trust for governance**:
    - **Identity and access management** (**IAM**): Enforce strong identity verification, MFA, and least privilege access controls to govern the access of users.
    - **Micro-segmentation**: Divide networks into smaller segments to contain potential breaches and enforce governance policies for intersegment communication.
    - **Continuous monitoring and analytics**: Use real-time monitoring tools to assess user behaviour, detect anomalies, and ensure compliance with governance policies.
- **Compliance benefits**:
    - Ensures adherence to GDPR, HIPAA, and PCI DSS by restricting access to sensitive data and continuously verifying compliance with data protection policies.
    - Reduces risk exposure by isolating critical resources and limiting unauthorized access.

Real-world case studies

Implementing governance and compliance frameworks in real-world scenarios ensures organizations meet regulatory standards, mitigate risks, and enhance security. These case studies demonstrate how structured governance strategies help industries such as finance, healthcare, and government achieve compliance while maintaining operational efficiency.

PCI DSS-compliant architecture

The details are as follows:

- **Scenario**: A bank needs to ensure that the payment processing system of its financial institution complies with the PCI DSS requirements, as it calls for strict security controls over cardholder data.

- **Challenges**:
    - Protect sensitive payment data during its transmission and storage.
    - Maintain real-time compliance monitoring.
    - Ensure that all systems get regular audits and vulnerability assessment.
- **Solution**:
    - **Encryption and tokenization**: Encrypting payment data in transit and at rest and replacing sensitive information with tokens in the processing systems.
    - **Access controls**: Utilize IAM and MFA to restrict access to payment systems.
    - **Monitoring and auditing**: Utilize tools such as Splunk or AWS Security Hub for real-time checks of compliance and log monitoring.
    - **Automated compliance validation**: Integrate automated scripts into CI/CD pipelines to validate compliance before deployment.
- **Result**: The institution was able to attain PCI DSS compliance with reduced audit overhead and increased confidence in the security of its payment systems.

Government agency systems governance

Government agencies handle vast amounts of sensitive citizen data, making strong governance essential to ensure data privacy, compliance, and operational transparency. With stringent data residency laws, inter-agency data sharing requirements, and accountability challenges, agencies must implement standardized governance models that enforce policies consistently across departments.

By leveraging unified governance frameworks, data classification, PaC, and continuous auditing, agencies can streamline compliance, minimize data breach risks, and enhance transparency. This case study highlights how structured governance ensures regulatory adherence while maintaining efficiency in public sector operations.

The details are as follows:

- **Case study**: A government agency needs strong governance to meet data privacy standards, remain transparent, and protect citizen data.
- **Challenges**:
    - Strict data residency is a requirement.
    - Data should be shared across agencies while not revealing sensitive information.
    - There is a lack of accountability in the dispersed teams.
- **Solutions**:
    - **Unified governance model**: Implement an overarching governance model that makes the policies uniform for the agencies
    - **Data classification**: Employ data classification mechanisms to tag and govern the sensitive data based on their criticality.
    - **Policy as code**: Enforce governance policy through PaC to hold the infrastructure and workflows liable to compliance requirements.
    - **Audit/reporting**: Continuous auditing technologies should be in place. They should be able to provide real-time compliance report to regulatory reviews.

- **Result**:
  - Compliance was streamlined.
  - The risk of data breach reduced.
  - Transparency on the operations was maintained.

Implement governance in complex systems

As organizations scale, governance must remain scalable, enforceable, and adaptable. Solutions architects ensure compliance by integrating PaC, IaC, and centralized governance tools while fostering cross-team collaboration.

By defining clear governance objectives, automating enforcement, and conducting regular reviews, architects maintain consistency across multi-team, multi-cloud environments. These strategies enable solutions architects to design secure, compliant, and efficient systems in complex enterprise landscapes.

Role of solutions architect

In complex systems, solutions architects must:

- Design scalable governance models that address multi-team, multi-region, and multi-cloud environments.
- Integrate governance into every phase of the **software development lifecycle** (**SDLC**), from planning to deployment.
- Balance innovation with compliance, ensuring systems remain Agile while adhering to regulatory standards.

Strategies for implementing governance in complex systems include:

- **Define governance objectives**: Define key compliance standards, operational goals, and accountability metrics aligned to system needs.
- **Use centralized governance tools**: Implement via mechanisms like ServiceNow **Governance, Risk, and Compliance** (**GRC**) or CloudHealth, an integrated view of compliance and governance activities.
- **Utilize automation**: Apply governance policies across teams and environments using IaC and PaC.
- **Develop cross-team collaboration**: Align through governance committees that have representation from both IT, legal, security, and operations teams.
- **Governance review**: Review governance periodically and change policies as required by the dynamic needs of the business, changing regulatory environment, and advances in technology.

Real-life governance scenarios and case studies illustrate how solutions architects can create systems that are not only compliant but also efficient and scalable. With principles from Zero Trust, challenges such as PCI DSS compliance, and the addition of governance in complex systems, architects can be confident that their solutions are responsive to organizational and regulatory demands while instilling trust and accountability.

Conclusion

Governance and compliance are cornerstones of robust and scalable solutions architecture. This chapter emphasized the importance of integrating governance frameworks and compliance standards into the design and operation of modern systems. Solutions architects are tasked with balancing innovation with regulatory adherence, ensuring that systems not only meet business objectives but also withstand scrutiny from stakeholders and regulatory bodies.

From understanding the governance frameworks, such as TOGAF, COBIT, and ITIL; adherence to compliance standards, such as GDPR, HIPAA, and PCI DSS, and more, this chapter puts into practice action strategies as well as tools to cope with real-world challenges. Therefore, automation is a must for this continuous compliance and governance in dynamic and multi-cloud, distributed environments, which would be the role, like PaC and PaaS.

With practical insights into Zero Trust Architecture, real-world case studies, and emerging technologies, solutions architects are now better positioned to design systems that are secure, compliant, and resilient. This chapter ensures that you are prepared to navigate governance and compliance requirements, answer challenging interview questions, and implement scalable solutions that foster accountability and innovation.

However, governance and compliance are not just about policies and automation; effective communication and collaboration are equally vital. Solutions architects must work with diverse stakeholders, align technical and business priorities, and convey complex solutions clearly. The next chapter explores the critical soft skills needed for success, including stakeholder communication, documentation, presentation skills, and leading cross-functional teams. Mastering these skills ensures that solutions architects can translate governance and compliance strategies into actionable, well-aligned solutions across an organization.

In the next chapter, we will study communication and collaboration, which are the foundation of a solutions architect's role.

Key takeaways

The takeaways are as follows:

- **Governance and compliance**: They are critical for secure and scalable architectures. This chapter covered key frameworks, automation strategies like PaC and SaC, and Zero Trust principles to enforce compliance dynamically. Real-world case studies illustrate how architects can integrate governance without hindering innovation, ensuring resilience, risk mitigation, and readiness for regulatory challenges.

- **Governance frameworks**: TOGAF, COBIT, ITIL to be used by solution architects to align architectures towards organizational goals and regulatory standards.

- **Compliance integration**: Design systems and incorporate compliance through design, Privacy by Design. Implement data encryption and appropriate controls toward maintaining standards such as GDPR, HIPAA, or PCI DSS.

- **Governance through automation**: Use PaC and SaC for dynamic enforcement of governance and compliance across CI/CD pipelines and runtime environments.

- **Risk management**: Implement proactive risk management in order to identify vulnerability and mitigate compliance risks that add to the system's resilience within hybrid and multi-cloud architectures.

- **Zero Trust Architecture**: Apply the Zero Trust principles for continuous verification, secure access, and adherence to data protection policies.

- **Emerging technologies**: Adopt governance practices to innovations like AI, ML, cloud-native systems, and distributed architectures, ensuring agility with compliance.

- **Practical applications**: Case studies in the healthcare, finance, and government sectors showcase how governance and compliance strategies are effectively implemented.

- **Interview preparation**: Prepare to respond to governance and compliance scenarios and explain the rationale for decisions. Show your expertise on tools and frameworks.

Model interview questions and answers

1. **What is the role of governance in solutions architecture?**

   Model answer:

   - Governance is a process that ensures that systems are delivered within organizational objectives, regulatory requirements, and operational guidelines.

   - It includes structures that define decision-making, ensure compliance with policy, and check balances to avoid mismatches, security breaches, and inefficiencies.

   - Governance structures like TOGAF ensure that architectures are scalable, but business imperatives are aligned.

2. **Describe how you would design such a system to be GDPR compliant.**

   Model answer:

   - **Data privacy**: Apply the principles of Privacy by Design, including data limitation collection and user control over personal information.

   - **Data encryption**: Use strong encryption for rest and in-transit.

   - **Consent management**: Ensure explicit user consent for data processing activities.

   - **Data residency**: Store data within the European Union as required by residency.

   - **Monitoring and auditing**: Use something like AWS Config to watch for non-compliance continuously.

3. **What is policy as code, and how does it help governance and compliance?**

   Model answer:

   - Policy as code takes the policies of governance and compliance and turns them into something machine-readable, so they can automate enforcement in CI/CD pipelines. For example:

     o **Compliance validation**: PaC will always ensure that any deployment done is always GDPR or PCI DSS compliant.

     o **Automation**: Prevents human error when non-compliant configurations will automatically get rejected.

     o **Tools**: OPA will enforce policies like data encryption or role-based access.

4. **Describe the centralized versus decentralized governance difference.**

   Model answer:

   - **Centralized governance**: All decisions are taken with a high level of centralization and strict uniform policies are in place along with strict oversight. Ideally suited for industry sectors like finance, where rules and regulation are highly rigorous.

   - **Decentralized governance**: It spreads out responsibilities, hence encouraging agility and innovation. It suits dynamic organizations like multinational corporations where teams need autonomy within a governance framework.

5. **How would you enforce compliance in a hybrid or multi-cloud environment?**

   Model answer:

   - **Unified governance framework**: Apply tools such as Terraform or Azure Arc to ensure consistency in policy implementation across platforms.

   - **Data residency**: Ensure that data complies with the local laws through strategic choice of compliant data centers.

- **Monitoring and alerts**: Tools like Prisma Cloud for the real-time detection and remediation of non-compliance.

6. **Describe a scenario that illustrates how Zero Trust Architecture provides compliance.**

   Model answer:

   - **Scenario**: A healthcare application that needs HIPAA, where Zero Trust Architecture provides-

     o **IAM and MFA**: Only the authorized will get access to sensitive data.

     o **Micro-segmentation**: Patient records are segregated by department so that no lateral breach is possible.

     o **Continuous monitoring**: Tools will detect and report the unauthorized accesses in real-time.

7. **How does SaC facilitate compliance?**

   Model answer:

   - SaC can integrate security policies into the development lifecycle and then automatically enforce in CI/CD pipelines. Some examples are as follows:

     o **Access control policies**: Enforce role-based access using IAM rules.

     o **Encryption standards**: Automatically check for proper encryption settings while deploying.

     o **Compliance assurance**: HashiCorp Sentinel ensures consistency in security practice between environments.

Join our Discord space

Join our Discord workspace for latest updates, offers, tech happenings around the world, new releases, and sessions with the authors:

https://discord.bpbonline.com

CHAPTER 14

Communication and Collaboration

Introduction

Communication and collaboration are the foundations of a successful solutions architect's role. It is often the case that, beyond technical skills, an architect's ability to connect well with stakeholders, align different teams, and present ideas confidently determines project success and stakeholder satisfaction. These soft skills are essential for transforming technical designs or solutions into actionable, impactful outcomes.

The role of a solutions architect is not without challenges. Solutions architects must navigate and negotiate competing priorities, bridge gaps between technical and non-technical stakeholders, and guide cross-functional teams toward shared goals. With the increasing prevalence of hybrid and distributed teams, mastering these skills requires not just technical acumen but also emotional intelligence, adaptability, and clarity of communication.

This chapter discusses the key communication and collaboration skills that are required to succeed as a solutions architect. It underlines the need for building trust, effective documentation, confidence in presenting ideas, and achieving team alignment. By mastering these techniques, you will not only enhance your professional capabilities but also position yourself as a leader who advocates impactful solutions in any organization.

Structure

This chapter covers the following topics:

- Communicating with stakeholders
- Creating clear and concise documentation
- Presentation skills for solutions architects
- Leading cross-functional teams
- Advanced techniques for communication and collaboration

Objectives

By the end of this chapter, readers will have a comprehensive understanding of the critical communication and collaboration skills that contribute to the success of a solutions architect. They will gain valuable insights into how effective communication drives stakeholder satisfaction, aligns team efforts, and ensures successful project outcomes.

Readers will learn practical strategies for communicating with diverse stakeholders, crafting clear and concise documentation, delivering impactful presentations, and leading cross-functional teams with confidence and empathy.

This chapter also emphasizes overcoming challenges such as misaligned expectations, remote or hybrid team dynamics, and conflicts in stakeholder priorities. Practical tools, frameworks, and real-life examples are provided to enhance the understanding and application of these skills.

By the end of this chapter, readers will be well-prepared to demonstrate strong communication and collaboration skills in professional settings and interviews, positioning themselves as influential and effective solutions architects.

Communicating with stakeholders

For a solutions architect, the ability to communicate effectively with stakeholders is as important as technical expertise. Stakeholders are often the drivers of project requirements and success metrics. However, they come from diverse domains, each with unique expectations and communication needs. Bridging these gaps is critical to ensuring project alignment, fostering trust, and delivering value. This section explores how to identify stakeholder types, build rapport, and tailor communication to meet their expectations.

Introduction to stakeholder communication

Effective communication with stakeholders is very important for successful project management and solution architecture.

Types of stakeholders and their expectations

Understanding the different types of stakeholders you need to engage with is the first step towards effective communication. Each group has distinct priorities, and addressing these appropriately can make the difference between a successful project and misaligned expectations.

Stakeholders often have varying expectations based on their roles, as noted in *Table 14.1*:

Stakeholder type	Expectations	Communication style
Business stakeholders	Clear explanations of how the solution addresses business needs, improves workflows, and delivers ROI.	High-level overviews with a focus on usability and cost-benefit analysis.
Technical stakeholders	Detailed architectural diagrams, technical specifications, and insights into scalability and performance.	Technical depth, industry terminology, and integration details.
Executive stakeholders	High-level summaries of strategic alignment, risks, and benefits supported by data-driven insights.	Concise, outcome-focused presentations using visuals like dashboards or summary charts.

Table 14.1: Types of stakeholders and communication style

Understanding these stakeholder types and tailoring your communication accordingly is vital for engagement and alignment.

After identifying stakeholder types, the next step is to build strong relationships. This involves understanding their expectations, concerns, and priorities through active listening and empathy.

Building rapport and understanding needs

Strong relationships with stakeholders are built on trust and mutual understanding. Employing active listening, empathy, and targeted questioning ensures you address their concerns effectively.

Active listening techniques

Active listening demonstrates respect for stakeholders' perspectives and helps you accurately capture their needs. *Table 14.2* provides the key techniques for active listening along with examples which helps in effective communication:

Technique	Description	Example
Paraphrasing	Reiterate stakeholders' concerns to confirm understanding.	*So, if I understand correctly, is your concern about the impact on existing workflows?*
Summarizing	Provide concise recaps of key points to validate alignment.	*To summarize, your priorities are scalability and improved user experience.*
Reflecting	Acknowledge stakeholders' emotions or concerns to build rapport.	*I see how tight deadlines are creating challenges for your team.*

Table 14.2: Listening techniques

Using empathy to uncover priorities

Empathy allows you to uncover stakeholders' implicit priorities and concerns.

Practical applications include:

- Using open-ended questions to explore their needs.

  Example: *What challenges are you facing that this project could address?*

- Observe non-verbal cues during discussions, such as hesitation or tone, to identify underlying concerns.

Building rapport is essential, but it is equally important to ask the right questions to uncover hidden requirements and ensure nothing is overlooked.

Asking the right questions to identify hidden requirements

Stakeholders often focus on immediate needs, leaving implicit requirements unspoken. Proactively uncovering these needs ensures that the solution is comprehensive and future-proof.

Insightful questions can surface unstated requirements:

- **The five whys**: Repeatedly ask *Why?* to identify the root of a requirement.

  Example: *Why is real-time reporting important? Because decisions rely on immediate data.*

- **Scenario-based questions**: Use *What if?* scenarios to explore potential needs.

  Example: *What if the user base doubles in six months? How would that affect your expectations?*

Once you have identified stakeholder needs, adapting your communication style to their preferences ensures clarity and engagement.

Tailoring communication styles

Effective communication requires adjusting your approach based on the audience, whether they are technical, non-technical, or executives.

Adapting to technical and non-technical audiences

Effective communication requires tailoring your message to the audience's level of understanding. Here is how to adjust your approach for different stakeholders:

- **Technical stakeholders**: Dive into technical details, using precise language and industry terminology.

  Example: Presenting API specifications with sequence diagrams.

- **Non-technical stakeholders**: Simplify complex concepts using analogies and plain language.

  Example: *This data pipeline works like a conveyor belt, moving information from one point to another smoothly.*

Simplifying jargon for non-technical stakeholders

Avoid unnecessary jargon with non-technical stakeholders. Instead, explain technical terms in relatable ways. Explain technical terms in relatable ways:

- **Instead of:** *We will deploy a Kubernetes cluster.*
  - ○ **Say:** *We will set up a system to automatically manage and scale your applications.*

Presenting data-driven insights to executives

Executives value concise, outcome-focused communication.

Here are the key elements:

- **Business impact**: Highlight measurable outcomes, like increased efficiency or revenue.

  Example: *By automating data ingestion, we can save 200 staff-hours monthly.*

- **ROI analysis**: Use visual aids (e.g., graphs, dashboards) to present cost-benefit comparisons succinctly.

  Example: *Here is a chart showing a 30% reduction in operational costs after implementation.*

Communication is not just about sharing information; it is also about managing conflicts when priorities clash. Let us discuss some strategies to address these challenges.

Conflict management in communication

Conflicts may arise from differing priorities, resource limitations, or misunderstandings. Solutions architects must manage these conflicts tactfully to maintain alignment.

Root cause identification and alignment strategies

To resolve conflicts effectively, it is crucial to understand the underlying issues and find common ground. Here are key strategies to achieve alignment:

1. **Identify root causes**: Ask open-ended questions to uncover underlying issues.

   Example: *Can you elaborate on why this timeline feels unmanageable?*

2. **Align interests**: Focus on shared goals, such as customer satisfaction or cost savings.

   Example: *Both teams want a secure solution, so let us prioritize features that address those concerns first.*

Techniques like interest-based negotiation and I statements

Constructive communication techniques help navigate conflicts while preserving collaboration. Consider these approaches:

- **Interest-based negotiation**: Collaboratively explore options that satisfy all parties.

  Example: *Let us find a way to meet the timeline without compromising data security.*

- **Using I statements**: Express concerns constructively to avoid blame.

  Example: *I feel concerned about the performance implications of removing this feature.*

With remote work becoming the norm, adapting these strategies to virtual and hybrid environments is essential for maintaining engagement and effectiveness.

Addressing virtual and hybrid environments

Effective communication in remote or hybrid settings requires intentional effort to overcome physical and technological barriers.

Effective communication strategies for remote and hybrid teams

In distributed work environments, maintaining clarity and alignment requires structured communication. Here are key strategies to keep teams connected:

- **Regular check-ins**: Schedule consistent sync-ups to align on goals and progress.

  Example: Weekly video calls to review milestones.

- **Clear agendas**: Share detailed agendas before meetings to maintain focus.

  Example: Include specific discussion points and time allocations.

Building rapport in virtual settings

Fostering personal connections in remote settings helps build trust and collaboration. Consider these approaches to strengthen team bonds:

- **Icebreakers**: Start meetings with casual conversation or shared experiences.

  Example: *What is one highlight from your week?*

- **Use video**: Turn on cameras during calls to foster a personal connection.

Leveraging virtual tools for engagement

The right tools can bridge communication gaps and enhance collaboration. Here are some effective digital solutions:

- **Collaboration platforms**:
  - **Slack**: Quick updates and discussions.
  - **Microsoft Teams**: Persistent chat channels for ongoing communication.
- **Interactive tools**:
  - **Polls or surveys**: Gather input or preferences quickly during meetings.

    For example, use Zoom polls to prioritize features during virtual workshops.

Adapting communication strategies to virtual and hybrid environments ensures effective collaboration despite physical distance and technological barriers. However, the success of these strategies often hinges on the tools we use. In the next section, we will explore practical communication tools and frameworks that can streamline interactions, enhance clarity, and foster collaboration across teams, both in-person and remote.

Practical tools for communication

In a solutions architect's role, communication tools are essential for streamlining interactions, ensuring clarity, and fostering collaboration across teams. Selecting the right tools and using them effectively can make the difference between smooth project execution and misaligned expectations. This section explores practical tools and frameworks that can enhance communication in a variety of contexts.

Table 14.3 summarizes key communication tools and frameworks, providing their purpose, best practices, and practical examples for effective use:

Tool or Framework	Purpose	Key features or steps	Example
Slack or Microsoft Teams	Real-time updates, group discussions, and file sharing.	Create dedicated channels for projects or teams. Use @mentions for critical updates. Integrate with tools like Jira or Confluence.	Use a *CRM Migration Updates* channel for focused discussions on tasks and blockers.
Email best practices	Professional communication via email.	Concise subject lines (e.g., *API Integration Update, Immediate Action*). Use bullet points for clarity. Clear next steps.	*Please review the attached spec and share feedback by EOD Friday.*
Situation, Background, Assessment, and Recommendation (SBAR) framework	Structured approach for sharing critical information.	**S**: State the issue. **B**: Provide context. **A**: Highlight the impact. **R**: Suggest next steps.	**S**: API integration delayed. **B**: Vendor endpoint changes. **A**: Potential 2-week delay. **R**: Allocate additional resources.

Table 14.3: Tools for communication

Effective communication with stakeholders lays the foundation for project success, but it is only part of the equation. To ensure alignment across teams and maintain clarity throughout the project lifecycle, documentation becomes equally critical. The next section gets into the art of creating clear and concise documentation, which is a skill that transforms complex ideas into actionable blueprints for both technical and non-technical audiences.

Creating clear and concise documentation

Effective documentation is another key aspect of successful solution architecture. It provides a clear blueprint for implementation, aligns stakeholders, and ensures that both functional and non-functional requirements are met. However, creating documentation that is both comprehensive and accessible requires thoughtful planning and execution.

Types of documentation

Effective documentation is the backbone of successful solution design and implementation. By categorizing documentation into **High-Level Design (HLD)**, **Low-Level Design (LLD)**, **Architectural Decision Logs (ADL)**, and requirements documentation, solutions architects can address the diverse needs of stakeholders and teams.

Figure 14.1 illustrates the four primary documentation types (HLD, LLD, ADL, and Requirements documentation) along with their key components and target audiences:

System Documentation

Low-Level
Design

Provides detailed
technical specifications
for implementation.

Architectural
Decision Logs

Captures reasoning
behind key design
decisions and trade-offs.

High-Level
Design

Outlines system
architecture and key
components for broad
understanding.

Requirements

Defines functional and
non-functional
expectations for the
system.

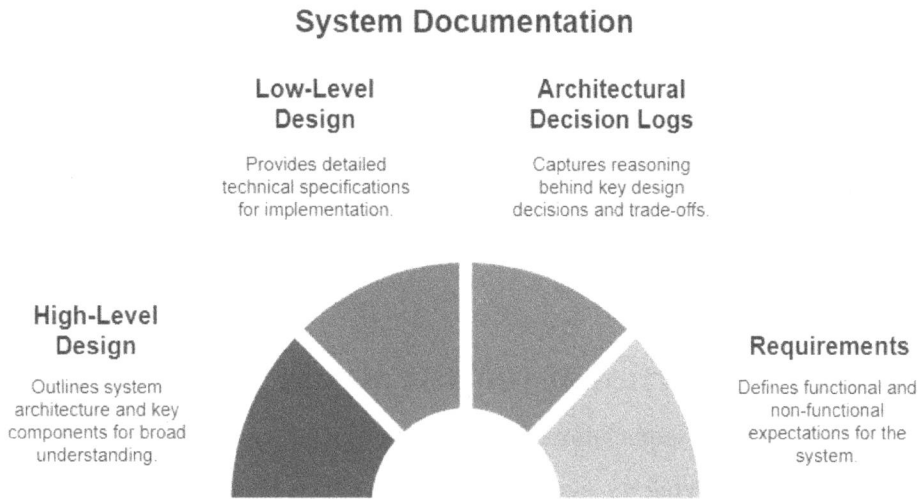

Figure 14.1: Overview of documentation types

High-level design

The HLD document outlines the overall system architecture and key components. It is aimed at non-technical and technical stakeholders alike to provide a broad understanding of the solution. Let us take a closer look:

- **Key components** include, but are not limited to, the following sections:
  - System overview and purpose.
  - Architectural diagram (Business, Application, Infrastructure) showing system components and their interactions.
  - Technology stack used in the solution.
  - High-level data flow and integration points.
  - Disaster recovery, BCP strategy.
- **Audience**: Business stakeholders, project managers, and executives.

A sample document template (software vision document/HLD) has been provided as part of *Chapter 25, Appendix,* under the *Software system vision document* section to cover all essential sections.

Low-level design

LLD document dives into detailed technical specifications required for implementation. It serves as a guide for developers, system administrators, and other technical teams. Let us take a closer look:

- **Key components**:
  - Detailed data flow diagrams and sequence diagrams.
  - Database schema designs and configurations.
  - API specifications, including endpoints, parameters, and expected outputs.
  - Security configurations, including encryption and access control details.
  - Error handling and logging mechanisms.
- **Audience**: Developers, IT staff, and technical leads.

Architectural decision logs and diagrams

ADLs capture the reasoning behind key design decisions, including trade-offs considered and alternatives evaluated. Its key components include:

- Problem statement.
- Options considered and their pros and cons.
- Final decision and rationale.
- Impact of the decision on the project.

Functional and non-functional requirements

These documents define the specific expectations for the system:

- **Functional requirements**: What the system must do.

  Example: *The system should support user authentication via email and social login.*

- **Non-functional requirements**: How the system performs its functions.

  Example: *The system must handle 10,000 concurrent users with a response time under 200ms.*

Having explored the different types of documentation, it is clear that each serves a specific purpose and audience. However, the effectiveness of these documents depends on how well they are structured, presented, and maintained. This brings us to the best practices that can elevate your documentation from merely functional to highly impactful.

Best practices for documentation

The best practices for documentation ensure clarity, consistency, and accessibility. By adopting these strategies, solutions architects can create documentation that effectively communicates ideas, aligns stakeholders, and streamlines implementation.

Structuring content

Organizing documentation effectively ensures that readers can easily find the information they need:

- **Headers and sub-headers**: Use descriptive headings to break content into logical sections.
- **Bullet points**: Highlight key points for quick readability.
- **Summaries**: Include a brief summary at the beginning of the document.

For example, an HLD document might have sections titled *System Overview*, *Key Components*, and *Technology Stack*.

Using visuals

Visual aids make complex ideas more accessible and engaging. Some of their examples are as follows:

- **Flowcharts**: Represent workflows or processes.

  For example, a flowchart showing the steps in a customer purchase process.

- **Sequence diagrams**: Illustrate interactions between system components.

  For example, a diagram showing API calls between a client application and a server.

- **Tables**: Compare options or summarize configurations.

  For example, a table comparing database solutions for scalability, cost, and performance.

Maintaining version control and template consistency

Version control ensures that all stakeholders work with the latest document iteration, while templates promote consistency:

- **Version control**:
  - Use tools like Git or SharePoint for tracking changes.
  - Include a version history table in documents.

- **Templates**:
  - Develop standardized templates for HLD, LLD, and ADL documents.
  - Include placeholders for key sections to maintain uniformity.

While following best practices helps create strong documentation, it is equally important to be mindful of common mistakes that can undermine its value. Understanding these pitfalls allows you to proactively address issues and ensure that your documentation remains effective and user-friendly.

Common pitfalls in documentation

Even the most well-intentioned documentation efforts can fall short if they fail to consider the audience's ability to quickly comprehend and act on the information provided. Poorly structured or overly detailed documents can lead to misinterpretations, confusion, or disengagement among stakeholders. Recognizing and addressing these common pitfalls, like those mentioned as follows, ensures that your documentation remains a valuable resource throughout the project lifecycle:

- **Overloading with unnecessary details**: Including excessive detail can overwhelm readers and obscure critical points. Prioritize information relevant to the audience. The solution is to use appendices for supplementary details.

- **Ambiguity and misinterpretation**: Unclear language can lead to misunderstandings. The solution is to use precise language and avoid jargon unless defined. Include examples to clarify abstract concepts.

- **Lack of visuals for complex ideas**: Text-heavy documentation can make it difficult to grasp intricate concepts. The solution is to incorporate visuals wherever possible, ensuring they are labelled and integrated seamlessly with the text.

Avoiding these pitfalls is easier when you leverage the right tools to create and manage your documentation. From collaborative platforms to visual design software, these tools enable solutions architects to produce clear, concise, and visually engaging documents that enhance stakeholder understanding. Let us explore some of the most effective tools for this purpose.

Expanding tools for documentation

In solution architecture, effective documentation is only as strong as the tools used to create and maintain it. The right tools streamline collaboration, ensure clarity, and enable teams to maintain consistency across all project documentation. From drafting detailed architectural designs to creating visual aids and maintaining version control, these tools enhance the efficiency and accessibility of your documentation efforts.

Table 14.4 highlights key documentation tools, their purposes, features, and practical applications to ensure your documentation is comprehensive, accessible, and professional:

Tool	Purpose	Features	Use case
Confluence	An excellent tool for collaborative documentation with support for versioning and rich formatting.	Version control, templates, and rich formatting support.	Documenting HLDs, LLDs, and maintaining ADLs.
Lucidchart	Perfect for creating architectural diagrams, flowcharts, and data models.	Drag-and-drop interface, pre-built templates.	Visualizing system designs and workflows.
Microsoft word	A versatile tool for creating text-heavy documents with built-in templates and styling options.	Custom templates, styling options, and integration with version control systems.	Drafting comprehensive, text-heavy documents like functional or non-functional requirements.
Figma	Ideal for UX discussions, enabling teams to design and review user interfaces collaboratively.	Real-time collaboration, feedback tools.	Prototyping user interfaces or visualizing front-end workflows.
Miro	A brainstorming tool that supports virtual whiteboarding and collaborative idea mapping.	Virtual whiteboards, sticky notes, and collaborative tools.	Mapping out early-stage ideas or engaging in collaborative decision-making during architecture discussions.

Table 14.4: Tools for documentation

By adhering to these practices and leveraging the right tools, solutions architects can create documentation that is not only comprehensive but also clear, concise, and actionable for all stakeholders.

While creating clear and concise documentation is essential for aligning teams and ensuring project clarity, effectively presenting these ideas to diverse stakeholders takes communication to the next level. Whether addressing technical teams, business executives, or cross-functional groups, presentation skills enable a solutions architect to transform complex concepts into engaging narratives that inspire confidence and drive decision-making. Let us see how to master the art of impactful presentations.

Presentation skills for solutions architects

Presentation skills are a critical aspect of a solutions architect's role. They enable architects to effectively communicate complex technical ideas, gain stakeholder buy-in, and ensure project alignment. Whether you are presenting to technical teams, business leaders, or external clients, the ability to craft and deliver impactful presentations can significantly influence the success of your solutions.

Importance of presentation skills

Strong presentation skills are essential for solutions architects to communicate complex ideas clearly, persuade stakeholders, and drive decision-making. A well-structured presentation ensures technical insights are effectively translated into actionable business strategies, fostering alignment across teams.

Explaining technical concepts to diverse audiences

Solutions architects often bridge the gap between technical and non-technical stakeholders. Presentations must convey intricate technical details in a way that is both accessible to business stakeholders and meaningful to technical teams.

For technical teams, focus on specifics like architecture diagrams, integration points, and security protocols.

For non-technical audiences, highlight business outcomes, user benefits, and ROI while simplifying technical jargon.

Consider an example. Explaining a data migration strategy might involve discussing database indexing techniques with developers and emphasizing cost savings and reduced downtime with executives.

Gaining buy-in from stakeholders and decision-makers

Stakeholders may have varied priorities, such as cost, time, scalability, or user experience. A well-structured presentation aligns these priorities with your proposed solution, ensuring stakeholders are engaged and convinced.

Use data-driven insights, such as cost analysis or performance metrics, to build trust and credibility.

Highlight alignment with organizational goals to address executive concerns.

Preparation for presentations

Effective presentations start with thorough preparation.

Understanding audience expectations

To deliver an effective presentation as a solutions architect, understanding your audience's expectations is crucial. By tailoring your content to meet their unique needs, you can ensure your message resonates and drives engagement. Consider these strategies:

- **Technical teams:** Expect in-depth details about system architecture, tools, and implementation processes.
- **Business stakeholders:** Focus on outcomes, risks, and benefits.
- **Executives:** Provide concise summaries with high-level insights supported by data.

Tip: **Pre-meeting discussions can help identify specific audience concerns or interests.**

Structuring presentations

A well-structured presentation is key to delivering your ideas clearly and persuasively. By following a logical flow, you can guide your audience through the content effectively, ensuring they stay engaged and retain key insights. Consider the following structure for impactful presentations:

- **Introduction**:
  - o Define the purpose of the presentation.
  - o Set expectations and provide a brief agenda.

Example: *Today, we will review the proposed cloud architecture for our CRM migration, focusing on scalability, cost-efficiency, and security.*

- **Key points**:
  - o Cover the main aspects of your proposal, using 2-4 major sections to maintain focus.
  - o Support key points with visuals like diagrams or charts.

For example, highlighting how the proposed architecture enhances uptime through load balancing.

- **Conclusion**:
  - o Summarize the presentation's key takeaways.
  - o Include a clear call to action, such as approving the next project phase.

Mastering the HERO storytelling framework

Storytelling creates a narrative that resonates with your audience. The HERO model is particularly effective:

- **Hero:** Introduce the business or user challenge as the hero's journey.
- **Obstacle:** Describe the problems or risks the hero faces (e.g., scalability issues or security vulnerabilities).
- **Resolution:** Present your solution as the key to overcoming these obstacles.
- **Outcome:** Highlight the benefits and success achieved through your approach.

  Example: *Our CRM migration will be the hero that overcomes downtime challenges, empowering our sales team with real-time data access.*

Delivering impactful presentations

Effective presentation skills are crucial for solutions architects, as clear communication ensures your ideas resonate with both technical and non-technical stakeholders. Mastering delivery techniques can enhance your credibility and influence.

Speaking clearly and confidently

Delivering your message with clarity and confidence not only enhances audience engagement but also establishes your credibility as a solutions architect. Consider these key techniques to improve your delivery style:

- **Pacing:** Speak at a steady pace, pausing to emphasize key points.
- **Tone:** Use a confident and enthusiastic tone to maintain interest.
- **Body language:** Make eye contact, use gestures purposefully, and stand tall to convey confidence.

Managing question and answer sessions effectively

Handling question and answer sessions with poise demonstrates your expertise and strengthens stakeholder trust. By preparing strategically and responding thoughtfully, you can turn question and answer interactions into valuable opportunities to reinforce your ideas. Here are some best practices to manage these sessions effectively:

- **Anticipate questions:** Prepare responses to likely questions in advance, particularly those around risks, costs, or alternatives.
- **Active listening:** Restate questions to confirm understanding before answering.
- **Bridging techniques:** If unsure of an answer, pivot to related points and commit to following up with specifics later.

Handling virtual presentations

In the era of hybrid and remote work, virtual presentations are increasingly common. Virtual presentations require a different approach than in-person interactions. Mastering the right tools, ensuring technical readiness, and actively engaging your audience are crucial for delivering impactful presentations in remote or hybrid environments. Let us look at key strategies to enhance your virtual presentation skills.

Tools: Zoom, Microsoft Teams, Webex

Familiarity with virtual tools ensures a smooth delivery. Features like screen sharing, breakout rooms, and real-time polls can enhance engagement.

Ensuring audio-visual clarity and audience engagement

The following factors will work well:

- **Audio-visual setup:** Use a high-quality microphone and ensure proper lighting.
- **Interactive elements:** Incorporate polls, Q&A features, and chat interactions to engage participants.
- **Camera presence:** Maintain eye contact with the camera to simulate in-person interaction.

For example, use a live poll to gauge stakeholder opinions on different deployment strategies.

Common pitfalls in presentations

Avoiding common mistakes can significantly enhance the effectiveness of your presentations. Even well-prepared presentations can lose impact if common mistakes are overlooked. Being aware of these pitfalls allows you to refine your delivery, ensuring your message is clear, engaging, and memorable. Here are key pitfalls to avoid.

Avoiding information overload

Overloading your presentation with excessive text or data can overwhelm your audience, making it difficult for them to absorb key points. Follow these strategies to maintain clarity:

- Overloading slides with text or data can overwhelm your audience.
- Use the *6x6 Rule* says no more than six bullet points per slide, with six words per point.
- Provide supplementary material for detailed data, rather than cramming it into slides.

Ensuring visuals are engaging and not overly complex

Visual aids are powerful tools, but cluttered or confusing visuals can distract from your message. Use these tips to create clear, impactful visuals:

- Complicated diagrams or cluttered visuals can confuse your audience.
- Use color-coded, labelled diagrams for clarity.
- Simplify complex ideas by breaking them into smaller, digestible parts.

By honing your presentation skills, you can effectively communicate your ideas, inspire confidence among stakeholders, and drive project success.

In addition to strong presentation skills, solutions architects must demonstrate leadership to guide diverse teams and ensure alignment. The following section explores techniques for driving collaboration, resolving conflicts, and fostering trust among cross-functional teams.

Leading cross-functional teams

In a solutions architect role, success often depends not just on technical expertise but also on the ability to lead cross-functional teams effectively. This requires fostering collaboration, resolving conflicts, and aligning diverse priorities. The solutions architect acts as a bridge between business and technical teams, ensuring that all voices are heard and the project stays on track.

Role of a solutions architect as a leader

Solutions architect plays a pivotal role in bridging the gap between business and technical teams. By aligning technical solutions with business goals, they ensure both strategic objectives and implementation details are effectively communicated.

Facilitating collaboration between business and technical teams

As a solutions architect, one of your primary responsibilities is to ensure seamless collaboration between business stakeholders and technical teams:

- **Business teams**: Focus on strategic goals, timelines, and ROI. They need high-level overviews that connect technical solutions to business objectives.

- **Technical teams**: Concentrate on implementation details, such as system design, scalability, and security. They require precise technical requirements and integration strategies.

A solutions architect must act as a translator, breaking down complex technical concepts for business teams while providing the technical depth needed by engineering teams.

For example, explaining how a proposed API integration will streamline customer service workflows for business teams while detailing its implementation for developers.

Balancing competing priorities and driving alignment

Conflicting priorities are common in cross-functional teams. Solutions architects must mediate and prioritize effectively to keep the project aligned with organizational goals:

- **Example scenario**: The product team demands feature delivery by a tight deadline, while the engineering team requires more time for performance optimization.

- **Approach**:
  - Understand the criticality of each priority.
  - Propose a phased implementation where foundational features are delivered first, followed by performance enhancements.

Balancing these priorities ensures that stakeholder expectations are met without compromising the project's long-term success.

Fostering collaboration and trust

Building trust and encouraging open communication are key to fostering productive team dynamics. Solutions architects can promote collaboration by creating safe spaces for idea sharing and ensuring all voices are heard.

Encouraging open communication and idea sharing

Creating an environment where team members feel comfortable sharing their thoughts fosters innovation and strengthens collaboration:

- **Techniques**:
  - Hold regular brainstorming sessions to encourage creative input.
  - Use tools like Miro for collaborative whiteboarding during remote meetings.

For example, involving both business analysts and developers in a brainstorming session for optimizing customer onboarding workflows.

Recognizing and respecting diverse team contributions

Cross-functional teams often comprise individuals with diverse skills, perspectives, and cultural backgrounds. Recognizing and respecting these differences strengthens team cohesion:

- **Strategies**:
    - o Acknowledge individual achievements during team meetings.
    - o Rotate leadership roles in meetings to ensure equal participation.

Addressing cultural differences in communication styles

In global teams, cultural differences can affect communication styles and expectations:

- **Example scenario**: Some cultures value direct communication, while others prefer indirect approaches.
- **Solutions**:
    - o Use standardized communication frameworks, such as SBAR, to reduce ambiguity.
    - o Encourage cultural awareness training within the team.

Effective leadership often involves mediating between competing priorities or team disagreements. The following section explores proven techniques for resolving conflicts and aligning stakeholders to ensure project progress.

Conflict resolution strategies

Effective conflict resolution is essential for solutions architects to maintain team harmony and ensure project success. By adopting negotiation and mediation techniques, architects can turn conflicts into opportunities for collaboration and alignment.

Interest-based negotiation and active mediation techniques

Conflicts, while inevitable, can be opportunities to align teams around shared objectives:

- **Interest-based negotiation**:
    - o Focus on underlying interests rather than stated positions.

        For example, if a development team resists adding a new feature, explore their concerns (e.g., resource constraints) and propose solutions like resource reallocation.

- **Active mediation**:
    - o Act as a neutral party to facilitate constructive dialogue.

        For example, use mediation techniques to resolve disagreements over technology stack selection by focusing on project requirements rather than personal preferences.

Turning disagreements into opportunities for team alignment

Rather than viewing disagreements as obstacles, solutions architects can turn them into opportunities for innovation:

- **Approach**:
    - o Document the points of disagreement.
    - o Highlight areas of overlap and propose solutions that incorporate the best ideas from each side.

To keep teams motivated and aligned, solutions architects must proactively define shared goals and establish clear accountability frameworks. The following section outlines practical strategies for achieving team alignment and maintaining focus throughout the project lifecycle.

Driving alignment across teams

Ensuring alignment across teams is crucial for achieving project success. By setting clear goals, defining success metrics, and establishing accountability frameworks, solutions architects can foster collaboration, maintain focus, and drive impactful results.

Setting shared goals and success metrics

Shared goals provide a sense of purpose and direction for cross-functional teams. Consider the following examples:

- Define success metrics like reduced downtime, faster deployment cycles, or increased customer satisfaction.

- Use dashboards to track progress and keep all teams aligned.

Establishing accountability frameworks

Accountability ensures that everyone understands their role and responsibilities. The following are a few frameworks:

- Use **Responsible, Accountable, Consulted, Informed** (**RACI**) charts to clarify ownership of tasks.

- Hold regular progress reviews to ensure accountability and address blockers.

In addition to setting goals and resolving conflicts, solutions architects must leverage the right tools to streamline collaboration, manage tasks, and track progress. The following section highlights practical tools for enhancing team leadership and productivity.

Practical tools for team leadership

Effective leadership requires leveraging the right tools and techniques to guide teams, improve collaboration, and enhance productivity. Solutions architects can adopt practical strategies to ensure teams remain aligned and focused.

Collaboration platforms

Effective collaboration requires the right tools to manage tasks, track progress, and centralize knowledge sharing. Key platforms include:

- **Jira**: Manage tasks, track progress, and visualize workflows.
- **Trello**: Create simple, intuitive boards for task tracking.
- **Confluence**: Centralize documentation and promote knowledge sharing.

Agile techniques

Agile practices enhance team efficiency by promoting continuous improvement and adaptability. Essential techniques include:

- **Stand-ups**: Daily check-ins to address progress and roadblocks.
- **Retrospectives**: Reflect on completed work to identify areas for improvement.
- **Sprint planning**: Prioritize tasks for upcoming work cycles.

By mastering these leadership techniques, solutions architects can foster collaboration, resolve conflicts, and drive alignment across diverse teams, ensuring project success and stakeholder satisfaction.

While foundational communication and collaboration skills are essential, mastering advanced techniques can elevate your impact as a solutions architect. The following section introduces advanced strategies to foster inclusion, enhance presentations, and drive continuous improvement.

Advanced techniques for communication and collaboration

In today's dynamic and globalized workplace, communication and collaboration demand more than just basic skills. For a solutions architect, the ability to lead diverse teams, craft compelling narratives, and continuously refine these skills is crucial. This section explores advanced strategies to foster inclusive environments, deliver impactful presentations, and commit to continuous improvement in communication and collaboration.

Diversity and inclusion in collaboration

Embracing diversity and fostering inclusion is essential for solutions architects working with cross-functional and multicultural teams. Creating an environment where all voices are valued drives innovation, strengthens collaboration, and improves overall project outcomes.

Creating inclusive team environments

Solutions architects often work with cross-functional teams that span different disciplines, geographies, and cultural backgrounds. Fostering an inclusive environment ensures that every team member feels valued and heard, ultimately improving team cohesion and performance. Look at the following list for more details:

- **Recognize cultural differences**: Be aware of how cultural norms influence communication styles. For instance, some cultures may value directness, while others prefer more indirect approaches.

- **Create equal opportunities for contribution**: Encourage quieter team members to share their perspectives by inviting their input during meetings or using anonymous tools for idea sharing, such as online polls or brainstorming boards.

For example, in a project involving global stakeholders, a solutions architect can use structured meeting agendas and rotation of leadership roles to ensure every voice is heard, regardless of hierarchy or cultural differences.

Encouraging participation from all team members

Participation is critical for innovation and team success. To encourage active involvement:

- **Set expectations**: At the start of a project, clarify that every team member's input is valued and expected.

- **Leverage collaboration tools**: Use tools like Miro or Slack to provide multiple channels for engagement, accommodating diverse communication preferences.

- **Acknowledge contributions**: Publicly recognize team members for their ideas and efforts, reinforcing a culture of inclusion.

Advanced presentation techniques

Effective presentations go beyond conveying information; they engage the audience, simplify complex ideas, and inspire action. Leveraging storytelling frameworks and audience analysis can significantly enhance your message's clarity and impact.

Storytelling frameworks for impactful narratives

Storytelling is a powerful tool to engage audiences and convey complex ideas in an accessible manner. Frameworks like the HERO model can be particularly effective:

- **Hero**: Introduce the main character or entity (e.g., the organization or system).

- **Challenge**: Present the problem or obstacle faced.

- **Solution**: Describe how the proposed solution addresses the challenge.

- **Outcome**: Highlight the results and benefits achieved.

For example, when presenting a cloud migration strategy, frame the organization as the hero overcoming challenges like outdated systems and downtime, with the proposed migration as the transformative solution.

Using audience analysis to tailor presentations

Understanding your audience is crucial for tailoring presentations:

- **Technical audiences**: Focus on detailed designs, integration points, and technical feasibility.

- **Non-technical audiences**: Emphasize business outcomes, cost savings, and strategic alignment.

- **Mixed audiences**: Balance the presentation with technical depth and high-level insights, using visuals like diagrams to bridge gaps.

Let us consider a technique. Before a presentation, conduct a stakeholder analysis to identify the audience's knowledge level, concerns, and expectations. Tailor your message to address these aspects effectively.

Continuous improvement

Consistently refining communication and collaboration skills is vital for solutions architects. Regular self-assessment and reflection help identify strengths, address gaps, and foster continuous growth in these critical areas.

Self-assessment checklist for communication and collaboration skills

Regular self-assessment helps identify areas for growth. Consider using the following checklist:

- **Communication**:
    - Am I tailoring my message to the audience?
    - Do I use clear and concise language?
    - Am I actively listening and acknowledging feedback?

- **Collaboration**:
    - Do I foster open communication and inclusivity in my teams?
    - Am I addressing conflicts constructively?
    - Do I ensure shared accountability in team goals?

Reflecting on these questions after each project or interaction can help you identify patterns and areas for improvement.

Seeking feedback from stakeholders and teams

Constructive feedback is essential for growth. Solutions architects should proactively seek input from both stakeholders and team members:

- **Anonymous surveys**: Use tools like Google Forms or SurveyMonkey to gather honest feedback.

- **One-on-one discussions**: Schedule regular check-ins to discuss how your communication and collaboration strategies are perceived.

- **Feedback on presentations**: After presenting, ask for feedback on clarity, engagement, and overall impact.

For example, following a sprint review meeting, a solutions architect might ask the team for suggestions on improving future discussions or documentation clarity.

By fostering diversity and inclusion, leveraging advanced storytelling techniques, and committing to continuous self-improvement, solutions architects can master the art of effective communication and collaboration. These skills not only enhance individual performance but also contribute to the success of projects and the satisfaction of all stakeholders involved.

Conclusion

Communication and collaboration are the essential need for a solutions architect's success. Beyond technical expertise, the ability to connect with stakeholders, craft clear documentation, present ideas effectively, and lead diverse teams ensures that projects are not only delivered but thrive. This chapter has explored practical strategies and frameworks to build these essential soft skills, addressing real-world challenges and offering actionable insights.

As a solutions architect, mastering these skills equips you to align business and technical goals, drive stakeholder satisfaction, and foster team cohesion. Whether you are presenting a complex solution, resolving conflicts, or guiding a cross-functional team, your ability to communicate and collaborate effectively will set you apart as a trusted leader and problem-solver.

In interviews and professional practice, remember that showcasing your communication and collaboration capabilities demonstrates not only your technical acumen but also your ability to lead with influence and empathy. Continue to refine these skills through practice, feedback, and real-world application, ensuring your growth as a successful and impactful solutions architect.

Building upon the strong foundation of communication and collaboration, the next chapter gets into the critical analytical and creative skills needed to tackle the complex challenges inherent in solutions architecture. We will explore how to apply structured problem-solving techniques, foster innovation, manage risks, and leverage team dynamics to create robust and future-proof solutions.

Key takeaways

The key takeaways are as follows:

- **Adapt communication to stakeholders**: Tailor your communication style to align with the needs of diverse audiences, ensuring technical and non-technical stakeholders can clearly understand your vision and solutions.

- **Prioritize clarity in documentation**: Use well-structured, concise, and visually supported documentation to effectively communicate complex ideas and maintain alignment among all project contributors.

- **Engage through storytelling in presentations**: Leverage storytelling techniques and impactful visuals to capture attention and convey the value of your architectural solutions confidently and persuasively.

- **Foster collaboration in teams**: Cultivate a collaborative environment by encouraging open communication, aligning team goals, and respecting diverse perspectives in cross-functional settings.

- **Resolve conflicts proactively**: Address team and stakeholder conflicts with empathy and structured techniques, such as active listening and interest-based negotiation, to align competing priorities effectively.

- **Master virtual and hybrid communication**: Adapt strategies for remote and hybrid environments by leveraging collaboration tools and maintaining engagement through interactive and inclusive practices.

- **Practice continuous improvement**: Use feedback, self-assessments, and real-world applications to continuously enhance your communication, documentation, and leadership skills.

Model interview questions and scenarios

1. **How do you communicate with non-technical stakeholders during architecture reviews technical decision meetings?**

   Model answer:

   - To communicate effectively with non-technical stakeholders, you focus on aligning technical concepts with business goals.

   - For instance, during a cloud migration project, you worked with the finance team concerned about cost implications.

   - Instead of explaining infrastructure configurations, you used relatable examples, like comparing traditional on-premises servers to owning a fleet of cars and cloud services to a subscription-based ride-sharing model.

   - You supplemented this explanation with visual aids, such as a cost-benefit analysis graph, to simplify the trade-offs.

   - Regular check-ins and summaries ensured alignment throughout the project.

2. **Describe a time when you had to manage conflicting requirements from different stakeholders and how you dealt with it.**

   Model answer:

   - In a project to design an e-commerce platform, the marketing team wanted rapid deployment of new features to support a seasonal campaign, while the engineering team prioritized security and code quality.

   - You organized a joint workshop to allow both teams to voice their concerns and align priorities.

   - By presenting a phased deployment approach, prioritizing marketing's essential features with minimal security trade-offs, you created a roadmap that satisfied both teams.

   - The platform went live on schedule, and post-launch feedback showed no security incidents or user issues.

3. **What strategies do you use to gather requirements?**

   Model answer:

   - You employ a structured approach for gathering requirements:

     o **Stakeholder workshops:** You conduct initial workshops to understand high-level goals and key pain points. For example, in a logistics optimization project, you invited representatives from operations, IT, and sales to identify cross-departmental needs.

     o **User interviews:** You dive deeper into specific user needs through one-on-one discussions, which often reveal hidden pain points or missed opportunities.

- o **Process analysis and documentation:** You analyze existing workflows, using tools like process maps, to identify gaps or inefficiencies. During one project, this approach revealed that a sales team's repetitive manual data entry could be automated, resulting in a 20% productivity improvement.

4. **How do you handle communication during project changes or updates?**

   Model answer:

   - Transparency is critical when managing project changes.

   - During a system redesign, a last-minute vendor API deprecation required a significant shift in the delivery timeline.

   - You quickly informed stakeholders through a detailed email outlining:

     - o The nature of the issue and its impact on the timeline.

     - o Proposed alternatives and their respective trade-offs.

     - o A revised roadmap with new milestones. You then scheduled a meeting to address concerns and answer questions. By providing clear updates and involving stakeholders in the decision-making process, you maintained trust and avoided project derailment.

5. **Describe your approach to presenting architectural designs to stakeholders.**

   Model answer:

   - The approach is to structure presentations in three stages:

     - o **Context setting:** Start by outlining the problem statement and objectives, ensuring all stakeholders understand the business context. For example, in a data warehousing project, you began by presenting data fragmentation challenges and their impact on reporting.

     - o **Solution overview:** Use diagrams and visual aids to explain the architecture, focusing on how it solves the stated problem. For instance, you used a flowchart to show how the proposed ETL pipeline would streamline data integration.

     - o **Business impact:** Conclude with measurable outcomes, like improved reporting speeds or cost savings. You also anticipate questions by preparing FAQs in advance to address potential concerns effectively. This structured approach consistently earns buy-in from stakeholders.

Join our Discord space

Join our Discord workspace for latest updates, offers, tech happenings around the world, new releases, and sessions with the authors:

https://discord.bpbonline.com

CHAPTER 15

Problem-solving and Innovation

Introduction

Problem-solving and innovation are necessary skills for a solutions architect in today's fast-evolving technological landscape. Solutions architects design and implement highly robust, scalable, and efficient systems that may not only solve current business problems but also help enterprises to adapt to future challenges. The ability to solve complex problems in conjunction with innovation ensures that solutions are not only functional but are aligned to strategic objectives that deliver value across technical and business domains.

Solutions architects typically operate at the intersection of technical complexity and business strategy. They need to deal with such issues as integrating legacy systems, performance optimization, and scalability while ensuring that costs, compliance, and stakeholder expectations are all balanced. Under such a dynamic environment, thinking critically, assessing risk, and being creative are important success factors.

Innovation complements problem-solving by pushing boundaries and finding new ways of delivering value. Whether it is using emerging technologies such as AI or cloud-native architectures or creating a culture of collaboration and creativity within teams, innovation enables architects to stay ahead in an increasingly competitive industry.

This chapter focuses on problem-solving and innovation and offers an analytical approach, real-world scenarios of problems to be solved, and risk management. With mastery over these skills, solutions architects will be equipped to tackle challenges of complexity while inspiring their team members to bring out solutions not only to cure immediate issues but to spur long-term business growth as well.

Structure

This chapter covers the following topics:

- Analytical thinking in architecture
- Real-world problem-solving scenarios
- Innovation in solutions architecture

- Risk management strategies
- Collaboration and team dynamics in problem-solving

Objectives

By the end of this chapter, readers will have a clear understanding of how to approach problem-solving and innovation, which are critical skills for solutions architects. Readers will learn how to apply techniques of analytical thinking in breaking down complex challenges and employ tools such as **root cause analysis** (**RCA**) and **strengths, weaknesses, opportunities, threats** (**SWOT**) frameworks in developing structured, effective solutions. The chapter will focus on solving real-world architectural problems by discussing case studies on how to succeed and what to learn from them. Readers will also learn about how to cultivate innovation in teams, how to leverage emerging technologies, and how to adopt forward-looking strategies in order to be competitive. In addition, the chapter will place importance on risk management, discussing practical techniques to identify, assess, and mitigate risks in architecture designs. By combining these skills, readers will be prepared to address the most diverse technical and business challenges while driving meaningful innovation in their projects.

Analytical thinking in architecture

Analytical thinking is one of the fundamental skills for solutions architects, allowing them to break down complex problems and create scalable and robust solutions. This way, decisions are not only well-informed but also in line with business objectives and technical constraints. In this section, we explore some of the important techniques and frameworks and their practical applications in architectural decision-making.

Definition and importance

Analytical thinking is the capability to analyze systematically and break problems into workable parts. It is essential for solutions architects to design systems, troubleshoot, and ensure alignment of solutions to organizational goals. The key benefits are as follows:

- **Better decision-making**: Enabling data-driven decisions in a trade-off.
- **Problem-solving precision**: Determining the source of problems and not the symptoms.
- **Scalable solutions**: Ensuring solutions are suitable for long-term growth and adaptability.

  For example, during the migration of a legacy system into the cloud environment which is covered in the *Chapter 7, Legacy Modernization and Migration Strategies*, using analytical skills, technical and cost-related constraints that arise can be evaluated to produce an optimal migration strategy.

Techniques and frameworks

To tackle architectural challenges effectively, solutions architects rely on structured techniques and frameworks that offer clarity and precision in decision-making. These tools help break down complex problems, evaluate trade-offs, and align technical solutions with business goals. *Table 15.1* introduces some of the most impactful techniques, such as SWOT analysis, root cause analysis, and decision trees, highlighting their practical applications in solving real-world architectural problems. These frameworks serve as a blueprint for analyzing situations systematically and arriving at well-informed decisions.

Technique or framework	Description	Application	Example
SWOT analysis	Framework to evaluate strengths, weaknesses, opportunities, and threats.	Assess feasibility of architectural decisions.	**Cloud migration: Strengths**: Improved scalability. **Weaknesses**: High initial costs. Threats: Downtime.
Root cause analysis (RCA)	Method to identify and address underlying issues using tools like 5 Whys or Pareto Analysis.	Debugging and system diagnostics.	**Latency issue: Problem**: Increased API response times. **Cause**: Inefficient queries. Fix: Optimized caching.
Ishikawa diagram	Visualization tool to map cause-and-effect relationships.	Tackles multi-faceted issues.	**E-commerce UX issue: Causes**: Server downtimes, poor navigation. **Fixes**: Optimized UI/UX, load balancers.
Decision trees	Structured diagrams for comparing options and outcomes.	Simplifies decision-making processes.	**Cloud provider selection: Criteria**: Cost, scalability. **Outcome**: Provider A for cost efficiency.

Table 15.1: Analytical thinking, essential techniques and frameworks

Applications in solutions architecture

Once the techniques are understood, their value becomes evident through practical implementation. *Table 15.2* illustrates real-world applications of these techniques, showing how they enable solutions architects to address specific challenges, such as cloud migrations, system debugging, and UX optimizations:

Scenario	Technique used	Outcome
Migrating legacy system to cloud	SWOT analysis	Identified a phased migration strategy, balancing immediate ROI with risk mitigation.
Debugging latency in microservices	Root cause analysis	Optimized database indexing and reduced API response times by 90%.
Enhancing e-commerce platform UX	Ishikawa diagram	Improved load times by 40%, reduced bounce rates by 25%, and boosted sales by 15%.
Selecting a SaaS hosting platform	Decision trees	Chose a provider with the best combination of cost-efficiency, compliance adherence, and scalability for future growth.

Table 15.2: Applications of analytical thinking techniques

Together, *Table 15.1* and *Table 15.2* bridge theory and practice, providing a clear pathway for applying analytical thinking in architecture.

In the next section, we will get into practical scenarios where these skills are put into action, demonstrating their impact and relevance.

Real-world problem-solving scenarios

Solutions architects face a wide range of challenges that require not only technical expertise, but also strategic thinking, communication skills, and collaboration across teams. This section dives into common challenges, detailed case studies, and key lessons learned to prepare you for real-world scenarios and interviews.

Introduction to common challenges

Solutions architects are constantly navigating a landscape of technical complexity and business priorities. Some challenges recur across industries and require creative yet structured problem-solving approaches. The summary of common challenges solutions architects face, setting the stage for detailed case studies, is as follows:

Challenge	Description	Impact
Integration of legacy systems	Bridging outdated systems with modern platforms, often hampered by incompatibility and poor documentation.	Limits innovation and scalability; increases operational costs and security vulnerabilities.
Scalability bottlenecks	Handling sudden traffic surges or accommodating business growth without degrading performance.	Leads to downtime, poor user experiences, and revenue loss.
Cost optimization in cloud deployments	Managing unexpected expenses in pay-as-you-go cloud environments.	Erodes profit margins and creates inefficiencies.
Security in distributed architectures	Ensuring compliance and data protection in hybrid or microservices-based architectures.	Risk of breaches, fines, and reputational damage.
Team conflicts over technology choices	Aligning differing priorities of development, operations, and business teams.	Delays decisions and increases implementation risks.
Managing stakeholder expectations	Balancing competing priorities like speed-to-market and long-term scalability.	Creates misalignment, delays, or resource mismanagement.

Table 15.3: Summary of challenges

By understanding these challenges, solutions architects can better anticipate potential roadblocks and devise targeted solutions. The following case studies illustrate how these challenges were tackled in real-world scenarios.

Detailed case studies

These case studies illustrate real-world scenarios, highlighting the processes of diagnosing issues, implementing solutions, and achieving impactful outcomes. These examples offer valuable insights into tackling systemic problems, ensuring alignment with business goals, and driving operational excellence.

Scenario 1: Optimizing API traffic in e-commerce

A global e-commerce platform struggled to maintain API reliability during peak sales events like Black Friday, impacting user experience and causing significant revenue loss. The platform lacked proper traffic management mechanisms, making it vulnerable to traffic surges that overwhelmed backend systems.

Let us look at it in more detail:

- **Problem**:
    - o Repeated API failures due to unregulated request surges.
    - o Backend systems slowed by synchronous dependencies and lack of caching.
    - o Poor user experience led to abandoned transactions and reduced customer trust.
- **Analysis**:
    - o **Traffic analysis**: Spikes exceeded the system's throughput capacity.
    - o **Architecture gaps**:
        - No API gateway in place to manage or throttle requests.
        - Heavy reliance on synchronous services increased latency.
        - Frequently requested data required multiple backend calls, adding unnecessary load.

- **Solution**:
    - o **Implemented API gateway**: Introduced rate-limiting to throttle excessive requests and prevent backend overload.
    - o **Asynchronous processing**: Shifted non-critical API calls to asynchronous queues, reducing real-time pressure on backend systems.
    - o **Caching layer**: Deployed a caching solution at the API level to serve frequent requests without querying backend systems repeatedly.

- **Outcomes**:
    - o API failures reduced, ensuring better availability during high-traffic events.
    - o Customer satisfaction scores improved, leading to increased sales and customer loyalty.
    - o Operational efficiency increased as backend systems remained stable even during peak traffic.

- **Key lesson**:
    - o Proactively preparing for traffic surges by analyzing patterns and implementing scalable architecture ensures seamless user experiences during critical business events.

Scenario 2: Optimizing data pipelines for real-time analytics

A logistics company relied on real-time shipment tracking to provide timely updates to customers and optimize delivery routes. However, delays in the data pipeline led to outdated information, impacting both customer experience and operational decision-making.

Let us look at it in more detail:

- **Problem**:
    - o Shipment tracking data experienced delays.
    - o Batch-based ETL processes were unable to handle the growing volume of data.
    - o Message queues faced bottlenecks, and the data processing framework lacked scalability.

- **Analysis**:
    - o **Pipeline evaluation**: Identified inefficient ETL processes and message queue saturation as primary bottlenecks.
    - o **Scalability issues**: A monolithic data processing framework hindered horizontal scaling.
    - o **Data duplication**: Redundant data inflows further increased processing time.

- **Applied framework**:
    - o **Root cause analysis**: Used RCA to pinpoint inefficiencies in the ETL and data ingestion stages.
    - o **Performance testing**: Simulated traffic patterns to understand system behaviour under peak load.

- **Implementation**:
    - o **Streaming framework**: Replaced batch-based ETL with Apache Kafka for real-time data streaming.
    - o **Horizontal scaling**: Sharded processing nodes to distribute load effectively.
    - o **Data deduplication**: Reduced redundancy at the ingestion point, optimizing processing time.

- **Results**:
    - o **Reduction in delays**: Data latency dropped, enabling real-time analytics.

- o **Enhanced customer experience**: Customers received accurate updates in real time, boosting satisfaction.

- o **Improved decision-making**: Operations benefited from up-to-date data, allowing proactive route optimization.

- **Key lesson**:

  - o Investing in modern streaming architectures and horizontal scaling unlocks real-time insights and operational efficiency, essential for dynamic and data-driven industries.

Transitioning to actionable insights

The case studies demonstrate that structured problem-solving, modern architectural practices, and collaboration across teams are crucial to addressing complex challenges. The lessons learned from these examples can guide solutions architects in designing robust, scalable, and innovative solutions that align with organizational goals.

This structured flow reduces redundancy, keeps the content focused, and ties the challenges directly into actionable case studies, making it practical and insightful for interview preparation or real-world application.

As problem-solving addresses immediate challenges, innovation takes us further by anticipating future needs and exploring novel approaches. Let us move from reactive solutions to proactive innovation, examining how solutions architects can foster creativity and leverage emerging technologies.

Innovation in solutions architecture

Innovation is the backbone of solutions architecture, enabling organizations to adapt to evolving market needs and maintain a competitive edge. For solutions architects, innovation means more than adopting new technologies. It involves fostering a mindset of creativity, structured problem-solving, and alignment with business goals. This section explores actionable strategies, proven frameworks, and practical scenarios to prepare you for challenges in the real world and interviews.

Encouraging a culture of innovation

Fostering innovation requires creating an environment where creativity thrives, team members feel empowered, and continuous learning is a priority. These strategies discussed in this section inspire groundbreaking ideas and collaborative problem-solving:

- **Create a safe environment**: Encourage sharing of ideas without fear of criticism or failure.

  For example, establish a no-bad-ideas rule in brainstorming sessions to unlock team creativity.

- **Incentivize innovation**: Recognize contributions to encourage participation.

  For example, introduce awards like Innovation of the Month to highlight impactful ideas.

- **Promote continuous learning**: Provide access to training and workshops on emerging technologies.

  For example, sponsor team members for courses on generative AI or blockchain.

Frameworks for driving innovation

Figure 15.1 illustrates three prominent frameworks for fostering innovation in solutions architecture: Design Thinking, Lean Startup Methodology, and **Theory of Inventive Problem Solving (TRIZ)**:

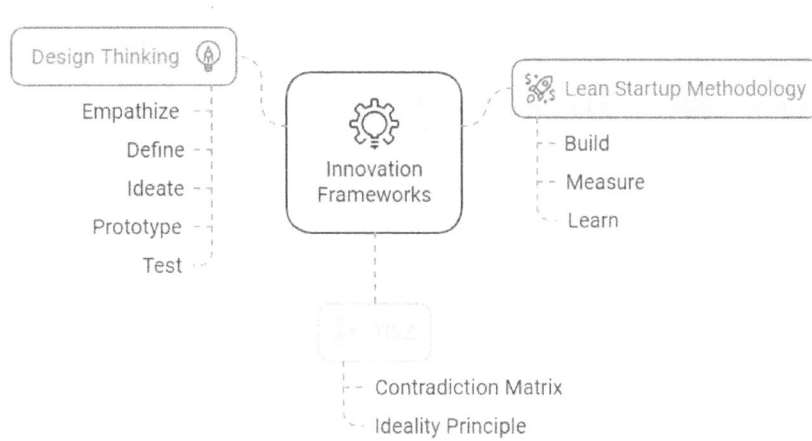

Figure 15.1: Frameworks for innovation

Each framework represents a distinct approach to problem-solving, with its own unique focus, steps, and techniques as represented in *Table 15.4*. This table simplifies complex frameworks into actionable insights, helping solutions architects understand their utility and apply them effectively in real-world scenarios:

Framework	What it is	Steps or key techniques	Example
Design thinking	A user-centric, iterative process for solving problems.	**Steps**: Empathize ǀ Define ǀ Ideate ǀ Prototype ǀ Test	Designing a rural banking app by conducting interviews during the Empathize phase to incorporate offline features.
Lean startup methodology	Rapid prototyping to test and refine solutions, minimizing waste.	**Steps**: Build ǀ Measure ǀ Learn	A SaaS startup launches a beta analytics dashboard, gathers feedback, and iterates before scaling up.
TRIZ	A structured approach to resolve technical contradictions by analyzing problem patterns and solutions.	**Key techniques**: **Contradiction matrix**: Balances conflicting requirements like cost vs. performance. **Ideality principle**: Maximizes benefits with minimal resources.	Optimizing data center efficiency by provisioning servers that maintain performance while reducing energy consumption.

Table 15.4: Frameworks for innovation

Innovation in solutions architecture requires a blend of technical expertise, creativity, and structured problem-solving approaches. By fostering a culture of collaboration, leveraging diverse frameworks, and staying ahead of emerging technologies, solutions architects can design systems that not only meet present needs but also anticipate future challenges. As you prepare for interviews, think beyond technology. Focus on your ability to align innovative ideas with strategic goals and drive tangible results.

While innovation pushes boundaries, it also introduces uncertainties and challenges. Risk management is essential to ensure that innovative solutions are viable, sustainable, and aligned with organizational objectives. The next section gets into practical strategies for identifying, assessing, and mitigating risks in architectural decisions.

Risk management strategies

Risk management is a cornerstone of effective solutions architecture. It ensures architectural decisions are robust, adaptable, and aligned with business goals by proactively identifying, assessing, and mitigating risks. This section focuses on practical, actionable strategies that solutions architects can apply to navigate complex projects, ensuring both technical success and stakeholder confidence.

Understanding risks in architectural decisions

Every architecture decision carries inherent risks, whether technical, operational, compliance-related, or financial. By understanding these risks, solutions architects can address vulnerabilities before they escalate, safeguarding project success and organizational goals.

Solutions architects encounter diverse risks. Some of them that require tailored strategies for mitigation are mentioned in the following table:

Risk type	Description	Example
Technical risks	Arise from design flaws, outdated technologies, or scalability issues.	A database system fails under high traffic due to inadequate capacity planning, causing downtime.
Operational risks	Stem from resource constraints, inefficiencies, or downtime scenarios.	A critical application becomes unavailable due to insufficient failover mechanisms.
Compliance risks	Relate to failure to meet regulatory standards or governance policies.	Storing customer data in non-compliant regions, resulting in legal penalties and reputational damage.
Financial risks	Involve budget overruns, misestimate costs, or poor ROI.	Underestimating costs during a cloud migration, leading to project delays or cancellations.

Table 15.5: Typical risks encountered in projects

Identifying risks is only the first step. The next section explores practical techniques to assess and prioritize these risks effectively.

Practical risk assessment techniques

Proactively assessing risks helps solutions architects focus on the most critical vulnerabilities, enabling informed decisions and efficient allocation of resources.

Risk matrices

The details are as follows:

- **What it is**: A visual tool to prioritize risks based on likelihood and impact.
- **How it works**:
    - Categorize risks (e.g., technical, operational).
    - Assign likelihood (low, medium, high) and impact (minor, moderate, critical) scores.
    - Plot risks on a matrix to identify high-priority areas.
- **Example**: A database crash during peak traffic is classified as high impact and medium likelihood, prompting immediate mitigation strategies like replication and backups.

Scenario analysis

The details are as follows:

- **What it is**: Evaluates potential outcomes of identified risks, preparing for best-case, worst-case, and most-likely scenarios.
- **How it works**:
    - Identify risks and define outcomes.
    - Assess implications of each scenario.

- o   Develop mitigation plans for high-risk scenarios.
- **Example**: Assessing server downtime scenarios (1 hour, 6 hours, 24 hours) to design contingency plans that protect e-commerce revenue during outages.

Redundancy planning

The details are as follows:

- **What it is**: Building fail-safes to ensure system continuity during failures.
- **How it works**:
  - o   Deploy load balancers and redundant servers.
  - o   Use geo-redundant databases and failover mechanisms.
- **Example**: A banking application implements Active-Passive failover systems to ensure uninterrupted transaction processing during regional outages.

Once risks are assessed, solutions architects need effective mitigation strategies to minimize their impact and ensure project continuity.

Streamlined risk mitigation strategies

Mitigation strategies are essential for minimizing the likelihood or impact of risks. By proactively planning, monitoring, and iterating, solutions architects can ensure that risks are addressed without disrupting project objectives.

Proactive risk planning

The details are as follows:

- **Definition**: Allocate resources (budget, time, infrastructure) to address unforeseen risks.
- **Practical tip**: Reserve 10 to 15% of the project budget for risk management activities.
- **Example**: During cloud migration, contingency funds addressed unexpected storage and licensing costs.

Continuous monitoring

The details are as follows:

- **Definition**: Use monitoring tools to detect anomalies and mitigate risks in real time.
- **Tools**:
  - o   AWS CloudWatch, Azure Monitor for infrastructure health.
  - o   PagerDuty for automated incident alerts.
- **Example**: Monitoring flagged sudden CPU spikes, allowing the team to scale resources dynamically and prevent downtime.

Incremental implementation

The details are as follows:

- **Definition**: Adopt phased rollouts or **proof of concept** (**POC**) approaches to validate solutions.
- **Example**: Migrating non-critical components of a system first to test functionality and address risks without affecting core operations.

With these mitigation strategies in place, let us understand how they apply to real-world scenarios for better understanding and practical implementation.

Example of real-world risk management scenario

Multi-cloud strategies introduce flexibility but also dependency risks. This scenario demonstrates how proactive planning and redundancy can safeguard operations during vendor-related disruptions.

Let us consider the following scenario:

- **Problem**: An insurance company's claims processing system relied heavily on a vendor API. A sudden vendor outage disrupted workflows, causing delays and risking customer dissatisfaction.

- **Solution**:
  o **Redundancy planning**: Integrated an alternate vendor for critical APIs to ensure continuity.
  o **Enhanced SLAs**: Negotiated stricter service-level agreements to hold vendors accountable.
  o **Real-time monitoring**: Deployed monitoring tools to detect and automatically switch to the alternate vendor during outages.

- **Outcome**:
  o Downtime was reduced during future outages.
  o Business continuity was preserved, maintaining customer trust and operational efficiency.

Risk management is most effective when paired with collaboration and innovation, ensuring that solutions are both robust and forward-looking.

Key lessons

Risk management is not just about addressing issues but ensuring long-term resilience and adaptability. These takeaways consolidate the section's insights:

- **Prioritize risks**: Use tools like risk matrices to focus on high-priority issues.
- **Build resilience**: Plan redundancies and failover mechanisms to minimize operational risks.
- **Stay proactive**: Continuous monitoring ensures early detection and mitigation.
- **Iterate for success**: Incremental rollouts reduce risks and align solutions with business needs.

By mastering these risk management strategies, solutions architects can create resilient systems, align technical decisions with business goals, and safeguard projects against unforeseen challenges.

Risk management is not a solitary task; it requires collaboration across teams to identify, assess, and mitigate risks effectively. By fostering open communication and leveraging diverse perspectives, solutions architects can ensure robust risk mitigation while aligning technical decisions with business goals. In the next section, we explore how collaboration and team dynamics play a pivotal role in solving complex architectural challenges.

Collaboration and team dynamics in problem-solving

Effective collaboration and team dynamics are critical to tackling complex challenges in solutions architecture. As a solutions architect, your role often involves mediating between diverse teams, fostering innovation, and ensuring alignment with business objectives. This section explores how structured collaboration and real-world teamwork can drive impactful results.

The role of collaboration in problem-solving

Collaboration is essential for addressing multifaceted architectural challenges. By leveraging the expertise and perspectives of diverse teams, solutions architects can generate innovative solutions, resolve conflicts, and align technical implementations with business goals.

Tools for collaboration

While tools play a vital role in fostering collaboration, the focus should remain on how they enable teamwork and enhance problem-solving rather than the tools themselves. In the following table, some of the prominent tools for collaboration are noted:

Tool	Purpose	Role in collaboration
Confluence	Content sharing and documentation.	Centralized repository for project documentation, design specs, and meeting notes, enabling seamless access and collaboration.
Miro	Virtual whiteboarding and real-time brainstorming.	Facilitates visualization of workflows, architectural diagrams, and team brainstorming sessions.
Slack	Real-time communication with integration capabilities.	Supports team coordination and quick resolution of queries while integrating with tools like Jira or Confluence for efficient project tracking.

Table 15.6: Tools for collaboration

Techniques for fostering team innovation

Beyond tools, fostering a culture of open communication and creativity is essential for collaboration. Structured techniques can unlock innovative solutions while ensuring alignment across teams.

The details are as follows:

- **Brainwriting**: Instead of verbal brainstorming, team members anonymously submit written ideas, reducing bias and encouraging creativity.

  For example, when brainstorming solutions for a cloud migration, the team submitted ideas for cost optimization and scalability enhancements.

- **Substitute, Combine, Adapt, Modify, Put to another use, Eliminate, Reverse (SCAMPER) method**: Prompts like *Substitute*, *Combine*, and *Modify* are used to rethink existing solutions.

  For example, a team reimagined an outdated microservices architecture by substituting synchronous APIs with asynchronous messaging.

- **Cross-functional workshops**: Involve diverse stakeholders, such as developers, designers, and business analysts, to ensure well-rounded solutions.

  For example, during a project to integrate a payment gateway, the team mapped workflows collaboratively to align technical design with user expectations.

Key lessons from collaborative problem-solving

Collaboration is more than just teamwork. It is about leveraging diverse perspectives to achieve innovation and alignment. These lessons summarize best practices for solutions architects:

- **Encourage open communication**: Foster an environment where all voices are heard, ensuring well-rounded solutions.

- **Use structured techniques**: Techniques like brainwriting and cross-functional workshops reduce bias and encourage creativity.

- **Prioritize iterative improvements**: Phased approaches strike a balance between short-term needs and long-term goals.

- **Act as a mediator**: Solutions architects must bridge technical and business priorities, ensuring alignment across stakeholders.

- **Document and share learnings**: Collaborative post-mortems and retrospectives improve future projects by capturing lessons learned.

While collaboration fosters innovative problem-solving and team alignment, achieving project success also requires robust risk management to ensure resilience against disruptions and adaptability to changing conditions. The next section explores strategies for assessing, prioritizing, and mitigating risks to safeguard project outcomes.

Real-world applications of collaboration

Practical examples of collaboration in action illustrate how solutions architects bridge gaps, resolve conflicts, and deliver results. Let us consider a few scenarios.

Scenario 1: Scaling an e-commerce platform for peak traffic

It was late October, and the IT team of an e-commerce company was preparing for their annual Black Friday sale. The marketing team was all too confident about breaking sales records; the engineering team was not. Last year, their monolithic architecture had folded under the traffic, and the hours and revenue going lost were something they could hardly get out of their minds. Leadership this time put on more significant demands.

The challenge

The system response times had begun to slow during the moderate traffic tests, making the team nervous about its behaviour at peak loads. The aim was clear: the platform needed to be ensured to handle up to three times the usual traffic without compromising the performance or the user experience.

The collaboration

The details are as follows:

- **Development team**: They suggested breaking the monolithic application into microservices, starting with the most critical module, order processing.

- **Operations team**: They utilized proactive monitoring techniques, leveraging AI and ML to predict traffic surges and optimize resource allocation during high-peak hours.

- **Solutions architect**: The team acted as a mediator and strategist. After understanding what the business priorities are, the architect presented a hybrid approach. For all critical areas, microservices would be used, and for the overall modules, caching would relieve immediate load concerns.

Role of the solutions architect

The details are as follows:

- The architect led a series of brainstorming sessions, ensuring every stakeholder's input was heard. Developers raised concerns about the timeline for microservices implementation, while the operations team emphasized the risks of introducing caching without thorough testing.

- The architect translated technical discussions into business terms for the leadership team, aligning everyone on the need to prioritize long-term scalability over short-term fixes.

- A phased plan was devised. Within a week, the caching layers were deployed, and performance was enhanced. At the same time, the order processing module was migrated to a microservices architecture within a month.

Outcome

On Black Friday, the site withstood multiple times the traffic it would experience on a regular day. Its response time had improved. A combination of caching and microservices ensured a flawless user experience. By the end of the quarter, revenue had grown, and the engineering team had set up a fully scalable architecture.

Scenario 2: Enhancing customer portal usability

A major financial institution had recently launched a customer self-service portal. The technical team had delivered the product on time, but user adoption was very poor. Feedback indicated that navigation was poor and workflows were unclear, leaving users frustrated. The company was at a crossroads: continue iterating on the existing design or start from scratch.

The challenge

The primary complaint from customers was the difficulty in completing routine tasks like updating account information or viewing transaction history. Internal teams were divided; developers were reluctant to overhaul the portal, citing resource constraints, while the design team insisted on a fresh start to address foundational UX flaws.

The collaboration

The details are as follows:

- **Design team**: Conducted user interviews and created detailed personas highlighting pain points. They proposed a streamlined navigation structure and intuitive workflows.

- **Development team**: Pointed out how the innovation of a new design is complicated and suggested staggered changes.

- **Solutions architect**: Facilitated both teams' discussion, which mandated user needs should be balanced with technical feasibility.

Next steps

The details are as follows:

- The architect led a collaborative workshop in which designers presented their proposed workflows in Figma, and challenged their design and was allowed to revert their design to the respective implementation, which was complex and needed different design alternatives.

- A compromise was struck; a hybrid approach that maintained the existing portal's backend but introduced major frontend improvements based on user feedback. Key features, such as account updates and transaction views, were prioritized for redesign.

- The architect also involved the marketing and customer support teams in the design to ensure that the new design aligned with the broader business objectives and addressed the most frequent complaints from customers.

Outcome

The new portal was released in phases over a period of three months. Within the first month, customer satisfaction scores improved by 20%, and task completion rates increased by 30%. The incremental approach allowed the development team to meet deadlines without disturbing the backend infrastructure. Collaboration across teams not only delivered a better product but also improved interdepartmental trust and alignment.

Lessons from collaboration

Effective collaboration is key to overcoming technical and business challenges. These principles highlight how structured teamwork leads to scalable, efficient solutions while ensuring alignment across stakeholders.

The details are as follows:

- **Open communication**: Open discussion encourages all the perspectives; thus, solutions are well-balanced.

- **Structured decision-making**: Solutions architects are responsible for mediating discussions and bringing technical possibilities into alignment with business goals.

- **Iterative improvements**: Phased approaches usually find the right balance between short-term needs and long-term goals.

These examples underscore the transformative power of collaboration in solving complex challenges, emphasizing the solutions architect's critical role in guiding diverse teams toward shared success.

Conclusion

Problem-solving and innovation are the cornerstone of effective solutions architecture, thereby allowing architects to bridge business needs with technical possibilities. This chapter highlighted the importance of analytical thinking while providing tools and frameworks to tackle complex challenges in a methodical way. It has been explained through real-life scenarios and case studies how creative and structured problem-solving leads to impactful solutions.

The role of a solutions architect goes beyond the technical expertise of an individual and requires fostering innovation within teams, staying abreast of emerging technologies, and integrating new ideas into practical solutions. Equally, understanding and managing risks is vital to ensuring that innovative approaches remain viable and sustainable.

The future technology landscape will see the evolution of adaptability, innovation, and effective problem solving as the new hallmark of success for solutions architects. Apply what you have learned in this chapter to tackle architectural challenges with confidence, drive innovation, and add value to your organization and its stakeholders. Use these principles on your path toward becoming a trusted and visionary solutions architect.

Having explored the critical skills of problem-solving and innovation, the next chapter shifts our focus to the equally essential art of managing relationships. This chapter will equip you with the strategies and techniques needed to effectively collaborate with vendors and stakeholders, ensuring that projects are not only technically sound but also strategically aligned and successfully executed. You will learn how to navigate the complexities of vendor selection, negotiation, and integration, as well as how to build and maintain strong stakeholder relationships to drive project success.

Key takeaways

The takeaways are as follows:

- **Emphasize analytical thinking**: Approach architectural challenges systematically using proven techniques like root cause analysis, SWOT analysis, and data-driven decision-making.

- **Solve real-world problems**: Leverage case studies and past experiences to demonstrate practical problem-solving skills during interviews and professional practice.

- **Foster innovation**: Create a culture of innovation within teams by encouraging collaboration, embracing diverse perspectives, and iterating on experimental ideas.

- **Leverage emerging technologies**: Stay updated on trends like AI, cloud computing, and DevOps to develop forward-thinking, innovative solutions that align with business goals.

- **Understand risk management**: Identify, assess, and mitigate risks effectively using frameworks like risk matrices and impact analysis to ensure project success and stakeholder confidence.

- **Combine creativity with constraints**: Balance the need for innovation with real-world constraints like budgets, timelines, and resource availability.

- **Master collaboration for innovation**: Use design thinking workshops, brainstorming sessions, and prototyping to inspire team-driven creativity and solve complex problems.

- **Document lessons learned**: Use retrospective analyses of solved challenges to refine future approaches and build a repository of best practices.

- **Prepare for interview scenarios**: Develop stories and examples of past problem-solving and innovative projects, highlighting the process, results, and lessons learned.

Model interview questions and answers

1. **Can you describe a complex problem you encountered in a project and how you solved it?**

   Model answer:

   - In a previous project, the challenge was to integrate multiple legacy systems into a unified platform during a company merger.

   - These systems had incompatible data formats and APIs, making seamless integration a significant hurdle.

   - You conducted a root cause analysis to understand compatibility issues and proposed a middleware solution using an ESB.

   - This middleware normalized data formats and provided a centralized API gateway for consistent communication.

   - By implementing this solution iteratively, you minimized downtime and achieved integration within the stipulated timeline.

   - The key to solving this was stakeholder alignment and leveraging the ESB's flexibility.

2. **How do you approach fostering innovation within your team?**

   Model answer:

   - To foster innovation, you focus on creating an open and collaborative environment.

   - During a cloud migration project, you initiated *Innovation Sprints,* where team members could brainstorm ideas for optimizing migration paths.

   - You encouraged diverse perspectives by involving cross-functional teams and facilitated sessions using design thinking workshops.

   - By implementing ideas like automation scripts for repetitive tasks, you and your team reduced migration time by 25%.

   - You believe structured brainstorming, recognizing contributions, and iterating on small experiments cultivate a sustainable culture of innovation.

3. **What strategies do you use to assess and mitigate risks in a project?**

   Model answer:

   - Risk assessment starts with identifying potential risks using techniques like risk matrices and stakeholder interviews.

   - For example, in a microservices architecture project, you and your team identified potential latency risks due to inter-service communication.

- To mitigate this, you introduced caching layers and asynchronous messaging queues to optimize performance.

- Regular monitoring and simulation testing using chaos engineering tools further ensured system resilience.

- Documenting risks and communicating them transparently with stakeholders helped align expectations and create contingency plans.

4. **How do you balance the need for innovation with the constraints of timelines and budgets?**

   Model answer:

   - Balancing innovation with constraints requires a pragmatic approach.

   - In a data analytics project, the team wanted to use a cutting-edge but expensive data lake platform.

   - To balance cost and innovation, you proposed a phased adoption strategy: starting with an open-source data pipeline and gradually transitioning to the advanced platform after demonstrating ROI.

   - This approach allowed you to stay within budget while showcasing the platform's value.

   - Additionally, prioritizing features based on business impact ensured timely delivery.

5. **Can you give an example of how you leveraged emerging technologies to solve a business problem?**

   Model answer:

   - In a retail project, the business faced challenges with personalized customer engagement.

   - You proposed leveraging machine learning models to analyse customer purchasing patterns and recommend products in real time.

   - Using AWS Personalize, you integrated the ML solution into the e-commerce platform with minimal disruption.

   - The solution increased upselling opportunities by 15% and improved customer satisfaction scores.

   - Staying updated on technologies like AWS Personalize and implementing them thoughtfully was key to solving this problem effectively.

Join our Discord space

Join our Discord workspace for latest updates, offers, tech happenings around the world, new releases, and sessions with the authors:

https://discord.bpbonline.com

CHAPTER 16

Vendor and Stakeholder Management

Introduction

In solutions architecture, technical capabilities alone are insufficient for project success. Equally important is the ability to manage relationships with vendors and stakeholders; these partnerships lay the foundation for reliable, scalable, and cost-effective solutions. Vendors add specialized capabilities and external resources while stakeholders define vision, priorities, and success criteria that guide outcomes.

Solutions architects are likely to operate at a point where there exist diverse expectations, such as technical feasibility, organizational objectives, and harmonization of vendor solutions. This is undertaken through strategies that involve negotiation, clear communication, and monitoring of performance. For the stakeholders, effective engagement builds trust, resolves conflict, and aligns on project goals.

This chapter thus provides a practically applicable roadmap towards mastering vendor and stakeholder management. Mastering these skills shall ensure that a solutions architect provides efficiency in managing projects, lowers risks, and builds long-lasting partnerships.

Whether it is the intricacies of a vendor ecosystem or the priorities of stakeholders, the insights and techniques of this chapter are meant to prepare solutions architects for real-world challenges and interview success.

Structure

This chapter covers the following topics:

- Managing vendor relationships
- Selecting and managing third-party vendors
- Vendor negotiation and integration
- Stakeholder management techniques
- Collaboration between vendors and stakeholders

Objectives

The aim of this chapter is to equip readers with the necessary strategies and skills for the effective management of vendors and stakeholders in solutions architecture. Readers will learn how to build and maintain strong vendor relationships, select and integrate third-party vendors, and monitor their performance using defined metrics. The chapter will also focus on negotiation tactics for securing favorable contracts and handling integration challenges. Further, readers will learn techniques to identify, engage, and align diverse stakeholder groups in ways that are transparent and consensual through the project lifecycle. By mastering these approaches, solutions architects will be well-prepared to navigate the complexities of managing external and internal collaborators, driving project success, and fostering long-term partnerships.

Managing vendor relationships

A fundamental element of delivering solutions architecture is successful vendor management. Vendors are critical components because they bring the necessary services and expertise to the table that contribute to any project's success. Taking charge of these relationships requires all deliberate planning, open communication, and ongoing oversight to ensure that organizational goals and project objectives are correctly aligned.

Understanding vendor roles

Vendors provide the external resources, products, or specialized expertise necessary to support a project's goals. Their contributions vary in significance based on their role within the project.

Vendors can be defined as those that range from software license providers and hardware suppliers to consultants offering niche technical expertise. They are integral to achieving project objectives efficiently and cost-effectively.

The types of vendors are as follows:

- **Critical vendors**: Provide critical services or systems, which have an immediate impact on the project output (for instance, cloud providers, cybersecurity software).

- **Auxiliary vendors**: Offer supplementary capabilities, like training materials or adjunct tools, which add value to but do not directly affect project success.

The lesson learned is that making a distinction between critical and auxiliary vendors can identify where to spend time and effort.

Building and sustaining strong vendor partnerships

Collaborative vendor relationships help in ensuring alignment, avoiding conflicts, and creating long-term success. A partnership approach can spur mutual growth and operational efficiency.

Techniques for building trust and collaboration

Establishing a foundation of trust with vendors is essential for maintaining productive and mutually beneficial relationships. By fostering transparency, consistency, and recognition, solutions architects can create an environment where vendors feel valued and aligned with project objectives.

Here are some key techniques for building trust and collaboration with vendors:

- **Transparency**: Share project objectives, timelines, and challenges to build trust and ensure alignment.

- **Consistency**: Establish predictable interactions, such as regular updates and consistent messaging.

- **Celebrating success**: Recognize vendor contributions and celebrate milestones to encourage collaboration.

Setting up effective communication channels

Clear and reliable communication channels are the key to ensuring smooth coordination and accountability with vendors. Regular check-ins, digital collaboration tools, and performance dashboards enable timely updates and transparency across all stakeholders.

To establish effective communication channels, consider the following:

- **Regular check-ins**: Meet weekly or biweekly to track progress, troubleshoot, and align on what is next.

- **Digital collaboration platforms**: Utilize Microsoft Teams or Slack for quick communication and immediate resolution of questions.

- **Performance dashboards**: Share dashboards showing how things are tracking and **key performance indicators** (**KPIs**) to provide transparency and accountability.

Evaluating and monitoring vendor performance

Ongoing performance monitoring ensures vendors meet quality standards and deliverables align with project goals. Proactive evaluations using KPIs, as mentioned, help address performance gaps before they escalate, as shown in *Table 16.1*:

KPI	Metric	Example evaluation
Timeliness	Percentage of milestones on schedule	Vendor met 95% of deadlines in the last quarter.
Quality	Defects per deliverable	Two critical issues detected in 50 deliverables.
Responsiveness	Average query response time	Vendor resolved support tickets within 4 hours.
Cost effectiveness	Percentage deviation from budget	Vendor completed 5% over budget in recent projects.

Table 16.1: *KPIs for monitoring vendors*

Providing feedback and addressing performance gaps

Constructive feedback and proactive resolution of performance gaps are key to maintaining productive vendor relationships. Regular reviews and collaborative problem-solving ensure that issues are addressed promptly, fostering continuous improvement and alignment with project goals.

Here is how to effectively provide feedback and address performance gaps:

- **Structured reviews**: Conduct quarterly reviews to evaluate performance against KPIs and share actionable feedback.

- **Collaborative problem-solving**: Address performance issues collaboratively, focusing on solutions rather than blame.

- **Improvement plans**: Use **performance improvement plans** (**PIPs**) to set clear goals and timelines for underperforming vendors.

Tools for vendor performance management

Leveraging the right tools will help efficiently track and manage the performance of vendors. They provide deliverable visibility, monitor KPI progress, and maintain SLA compliance for agreed terms to allow solutions architects to keep accountability while ensuring streamlined collaboration.

Here are some key tools used for vendor performance management:

- **ServiceNow**: Vendor performance, SLA compliance, and issue resolution.
- **Jira**: Enables tracking of projects, vendor deliverables, and timelines.
- **Tableau**: Provides advanced analytics of trends in vendor performance.

Effective vendor relationship management involves strategic selection, transparent communication, and consistent performance monitoring. By fostering trust, collaboration, and accountability, solutions architects can ensure that vendors contribute meaningfully to the success of the project. Strong vendor partnerships not only improve immediate outcomes but also drive innovation and efficiency in the long term, creating a foundation for future collaboration.

Interview tip: **Be prepared to discuss specific strategies for managing vendor relationships and real-world examples of successful partnerships or performance improvement efforts.**

Selecting and managing third-party vendors

Selecting and effectively managing third-party vendors is a critical aspect of solutions architecture. Vendors provide specialized expertise, tools, and services that complement an organization's capabilities, ensuring project success. This process requires a structured approach to vendor evaluation, onboarding, and coordination, especially in complex multi-vendor environments.

Criteria for vendor selection

Choosing the right vendor is essential for achieving project goals efficiently and effectively. A thorough evaluation process ensures that vendors align with the organization's technical and business objectives.

Essential factors in vendor selection

The following table presents the key criteria for evaluating vendors in solutions architecture, providing a concise description of each factor along with practical examples to illustrate their application. *Table 16.2* serves as a quick reference to ensure alignment between vendor capabilities and project requirements:

Criteria	Description	Example
Expertise	Proficiency demonstrated through certifications, client testimonials, and experience.	Vendor A provides certified cloud experts with a strong track record.
Cost	Includes upfront fees, ongoing expenses, and hidden costs.	Vendor B offers competitive pricing with low annual maintenance costs.
Compliance	Adherence to regulations like GDPR or HIPAA.	Vendor C ensures full HIPAA compliance for healthcare data.
Scalability	Ability to scale solutions as project demands grow.	Vendor D provides flexible cloud storage that expands dynamically.
Innovation	Forward-thinking solutions and emerging technology expertise.	Vendor E integrates AI for predictive analytics.

Table 16.2: Factors for vendor selection

Utilizing scorecards, request for proposal (RFPs), and checklists for evaluation

To systematically evaluate and select the best vendor, consider these tools and methods:

- **Scorecards**: Create weighted scorecards to rank vendors based on key criteria. For instance:
  - **Expertise**: 30%

- o **Cost**: 25%
- o **Compliance**: 20%
- o **Scalability**: 15%
- o **Innovation**: 10%

- **RFPs**: Develop detailed RFPs outlining project requirements, deliverables, and expectations. Analyze vendor responses for clarity, feasibility, and alignment with project goals.

- **Checklists**: Use checklists to ensure all evaluation criteria are addressed during vendor selection.

Vendor onboarding and project integration

The onboarding process sets the foundation for a productive relationship between the organization and the vendor. Clear communication and alignment during onboarding mitigate potential misunderstandings and ensure smooth project execution.

Steps for effective onboarding

The steps for effective onboarding are as follows:

- **Define roles and responsibilities**: Clearly outline each party's duties, expectations, and ownership of deliverables.

- **Establish milestones**: Create a timeline with key milestones to monitor progress and maintain accountability.

- **Set up communication channels**: Determine preferred modes of communication (e.g., Slack, email) and establish regular meeting schedules.

- **Provide access and resources**: Ensure vendors have access to the necessary tools, platforms, and documentation to perform their tasks effectively.

Importance of service level agreements

Service level agreements (**SLAs**) define measurable performance standards, ensuring vendors meet project expectations.

The key elements include:

- **Scope**: Clearly delineate what the vendor will deliver.
- **Timelines**: Specify deadlines for milestones and deliverables.
- **Performance metrics**: Define KPIs, such as uptime guarantees, response times, and defect rates.
- **Remediation**: Outline penalties or corrective actions for SLA breaches.

Benefits of vendor alignment with project objectives

Aligning vendor goals with project outcomes fosters collaboration and ensures their contributions directly support organizational priorities.

For example, a vendor providing a cloud data storage solution is briefed on the organization's emphasis on data compliance and scalability, tailoring their services accordingly.

Balancing multi-vendor environments

In large-scale projects, managing multiple vendors is common but challenging. Effective coordination among vendors ensures seamless integration and prevents conflicts.

Strategies for managing coordination among multiple vendors

To effectively manage the complexities of multi-vendor environments, employ these coordination strategies:

- **Centralized coordination**: Assign a project lead or solutions architect to oversee all vendor interactions and maintain a unified vision.

- **Defined interfaces**: Clearly delineate responsibilities to avoid overlaps and conflicts. For example, one vendor handles infrastructure while another manages application-level services.

- **Periodic syncs**: Conduct joint meetings to align vendors on progress, dependencies, and upcoming milestones.

Tools for ensuring collaboration

To facilitate seamless collaboration across multiple vendors, utilize these tools:

- **Integrated dashboards**: Use tools like ServiceNow or Jira to track deliverables, deadlines, and issues across all vendors in one place.

- **Shared repositories**: Provide shared access to project documentation and resources through platforms like Confluence or GitHub.

- **Communication tools**: Establish multi-vendor Slack channels or Microsoft Teams groups to facilitate real-time collaboration.

Effective selection and management of third-party vendors are critical for delivering successful projects. By employing structured evaluation criteria, setting up robust onboarding processes, and fostering collaboration in multi-vendor environments, solutions architects can ensure that vendors become valuable partners in achieving project objectives. These practices reduce risks, enhance productivity, and drive project success in increasingly complex and dynamic technological landscapes.

Vendor negotiation and integration

Vendor negotiation and integration are pivotal aspects of solutions architecture, ensuring that external partnerships align with organizational goals and deliver tangible value. Effective negotiation establishes a strong foundation for collaboration, while seamless integration guarantees that vendor solutions function cohesively within the existing ecosystem. This section explores strategic negotiation techniques, contract management essentials, and practical strategies for overcoming integration challenges.

Strategic negotiation techniques

Negotiation with a vendor requires a structured approach and should balance the needs of the organization with the priorities of the vendor. The strategic tactics adopted by solutions architects can help ensure that the most favorable terms are achieved in order to meet the technical and business requirements.

Researching vendor strengths and priorities

Understanding a vendor's position is critical before entering negotiations. This allows for a more informed and strategic approach. To effectively prepare for vendor negotiations, start by:

- **Preparation**: Conduct research about the vendor's strengths, weaknesses, and standing in the market. Understand the priorities of the vendor, including gaining market share, increasing revenue, or achieving long-term relationships.

- **Alignment**: Emphasize mutual value creation, as the vendor has an opportunity to demonstrate their competency by delivering effective implementations.

Major negotiation techniques

Successful negotiation hinges on strategic tactics that balance your needs with the vendor's priorities. During the negotiation process, employ these key strategies:

- **Anchoring**: This gives the direction for negotiation in your favor. Start with a lower price point; the rest of the discussion should be around price effectiveness, keeping in mind an opening position.

- **Trade-offs**: Concessions on not-so-critical issues to bargain for the preferred terms on major areas of concern like cost, SLAs, or support services.

- **Competition**: Use competitive vendors' bids or proposals as a bargaining chip for better terms. Clearly communicating the alternatives can get vendors to agree to more competitive deals.

Contract management essentials

Contracts form the basis of the relationship with vendors and define expectations, deliverables, and recourse in case of deviations. Managing contracts properly helps reduce risks and ensures accountability.

Key components of contracts

Robust contract management is vital for maintaining clear expectations and mitigating risks in vendor relationships. To ensure clarity and alignment, contracts should include these key components:

- **Scope**: Clearly outline the services or products to be delivered, including specific technical and functional requirements.

- **Deliverables**: Outline the milestones, timelines, and quality standards for deliverables.

- **SLAs**: Outline performance metrics, such as uptime guarantees, response times, and issue resolution timelines.

- **Penalties**: Insert provisions for failure, including penalties related to breach of SLA and late milestone completions.

- **Exit clauses**: Include terms on contract termination and the implications in terms of minimally affecting an ongoing project.

Handling contract modifications and resolving disputes

Maintaining flexibility and addressing potential conflicts are essential aspects of contract management. When contract modifications or disputes arise, employ these techniques for effective resolution:

- **Contract modifications**:
  - Use structured change management processes to evaluate the impact of modifications on timelines and costs.
  - Ensure mutual agreement on changes, documenting them formally through addendums.

- **Resolving disputes**:
  - Use mediation or arbitration to address disagreements while maintaining professional relationships.
  - Keep communication transparent and focus on shared objectives to expedite resolutions.

Overcoming integration challenges

Integrating vendor solutions into existing systems often presents technical and operational roadblocks. Addressing these challenges proactively ensures seamless collaboration and successful outcomes.

Common roadblocks in integration

Integration projects often encounter unforeseen obstacles that can hinder progress and impact system stability.

Here is a look at the common challenges you might face:

- **Compatibility issues**: Vendor solutions may not align with the organization's existing technology stack.

- **Latency problems**: Integration with third-party tools can introduce delays, impacting system performance.

- **Data security concerns**: Vendors handling sensitive organizational data may not comply with internal security standards.

- **Insufficient documentation**: Lack of detailed documentation from vendors can slow down the integration process.

Frameworks for ensuring seamless integration

Overcoming integration challenges requires a structured approach to ensure smooth data flow and system compatibility.

Here is how to establish effective integration frameworks:

- **Middleware platforms**: Use middleware solutions to bridge incompatibilities between vendor tools and existing systems. Middleware acts as an intermediary layer, enabling seamless communication and data exchange.

- **API standardization**: Establish consistent API standards for all vendor integrations, ensuring uniformity in communication protocols and data formats.

- **Incremental rollouts**: Deploy vendor solutions in phases, starting with low-impact environments to identify and address potential issues early.

Effective negotiation and integration strategies are vital for establishing productive vendor relationships and maximizing the value of their solutions. By employing structured negotiation tactics, maintaining robust contract management practices, and proactively addressing integration challenges, solutions architects can build resilient systems that align with organizational objectives and deliver long-term success.

Stakeholder management techniques

Effective stakeholder management is crucial in solutions architecture, as stakeholders influence project success through their requirements, approvals, and ongoing support. This section outlines techniques for identifying and analyzing stakeholders, engaging them effectively, and managing their expectations while addressing conflicts.

Identifying and analyzing stakeholders

Understanding who your stakeholders are and analysing their influence and interests is the foundation of effective stakeholder management. This step ensures that all critical voices are heard, reducing the risk of misalignment or resistance during the project lifecycle.

Stakeholder mapping and influence-interest matrices

Effective stakeholder management begins with a clear understanding of who is involved and their potential impact on the project. Here is how to map and analyze stakeholders:

- **What it is**: A systematic approach to categorize stakeholders based on their level of influence over the project and their interest in its outcomes.

- **How it works**:
    - **High influence, high interest**: Engage regularly and keep informed about key decisions (e.g., executive sponsors).
    - **High influence, low interest**: Focus on specific aspects that align with their priorities (e.g., legal teams).
    - **Low influence, high interest**: Keep informed and gather feedback (e.g., end-users).
    - **Low influence, low interest**: Provide minimal but essential updates (e.g., peripheral stakeholders).

    For example, during the deployment of a new **customer relationship management (CRM)** system, a stakeholder matrix helped prioritize communication efforts, ensuring that executives received strategic updates while operational teams were involved in detailed discussions.

Techniques for understanding stakeholder needs and concerns

To effectively address stakeholder needs and ensure project alignment, it is crucial to gather detailed insights into their perspectives and concerns. Here are practical methods for understanding stakeholders' needs:

- **Interviews and surveys**: Direct conversations or structured questionnaires to gather input on expectations and apprehensions.
- **Workshops**: Collaborative sessions to uncover hidden requirements and align on objectives.
- **Observation**: Shadowing stakeholders in their work environments to understand pain points and workflow inefficiencies.

Effective engagement strategies

Engaging stakeholders effectively is vital to building trust, maintaining alignment, and ensuring their continued support throughout the project.

Building trust through transparency and regular updates

Maintaining stakeholder engagement is crucial for project success, fostering a collaborative environment, and ensuring alignment with project goals. Here is how to build trust and tailor communication:

- **Regular communication**: Establish recurring meetings or updates to keep stakeholders informed of progress and challenges.
- **Transparency**: Share risks, issues, and mitigation strategies openly to foster trust.

    For example, a weekly progress report highlighting milestones achieved and pending challenges ensured continued executive confidence during a data center migration.

Establishing stakeholder-specific communication plans

Effective communication is key to maintaining stakeholder alignment and support. Tailoring communication strategies to each stakeholder group ensures that information is relevant and impactful. Here is how to establish stakeholder-specific communication plans:

- **Customized plans**: Tailor communication frequency, detail, and format based on stakeholder roles.
    - **Executives**: High-level summaries focused on business impact.

- o **Technical teams**: Detailed technical updates and design reviews.
- o **End-users**: Updates on changes affecting workflows and training schedules.
- **Tools**: Use platforms like Microsoft Teams or Slack for real-time updates, supplemented by Confluence for comprehensive documentation.

  For example, during an ERP implementation, customized email summaries for executives complemented detailed Slack updates for project teams, ensuring all stakeholders were engaged appropriately.

Managing expectations and resolving conflicts

Balancing diverse stakeholder priorities is a common challenge in solutions architecture. Managing expectations and resolving conflicts effectively ensures project alignment and smooth execution.

Finding common ground through negotiation

Navigating conflicting stakeholder priorities requires a strategic approach that prioritizes shared objectives. Here is how to effectively negotiate and find common ground:

- **Principle**: Focus on shared goals rather than individual positions to find mutually beneficial solutions.
- **Steps**:
  - o Identify common objectives (e.g., system reliability, cost efficiency).
  - o Explore alternative solutions that address core concerns.
  - o Emphasize trade-offs and benefits transparently.

  For example, balancing cost constraints with scalability needs during a cloud migration by prioritizing a hybrid cloud model.

Techniques to handle conflicts

Conflict resolution is an essential skill for solutions architects, as misaligned priorities or misunderstandings can derail projects. The following techniques provide practical approaches to fostering collaboration, addressing concerns, and aligning stakeholders effectively.

- **Active listening**:
  - o Show empathy by acknowledging stakeholder concerns.
  - o Clarify misunderstandings by paraphrasing key points.
- **Mediation**:
  - o Act as a neutral facilitator to guide discussions toward constructive solutions.
  - o Use data or prototypes to validate proposed approaches.
- **Collaborative problem-solving**:
  - o Involve all parties in brainstorming solutions.
  - o Use tools like decision matrices to evaluate options objectively.

For example, resolving disagreements between developers advocating for rapid feature deployment and operations teams prioritizing stability by agreeing on phased rollouts.

Stakeholder management is as much about soft skills as it is about strategic planning. By identifying stakeholder needs, engaging them effectively, and proactively addressing conflicts, solutions architects can build trust, ensure alignment, and navigate complex projects successfully. These techniques not only enhance collaboration but also pave the way for delivering impactful, stakeholder-approved solutions.

Collaboration between vendors and stakeholders

Collaboration between vendors and stakeholders is vital for the success of solutions architecture projects. Effective synergy ensures that both groups work cohesively toward shared goals, minimizing friction and maximizing project outcomes. Solutions architects play a pivotal role in facilitating this collaboration, bridging gaps between technical feasibility and business objectives.

Creating synergy

In the complex landscape of solutions architecture, aligning the diverse goals of vendors and stakeholders is paramount. Vendors, driven by technical expertise, often focus on solution delivery, while stakeholders prioritize business objectives and outcomes. This divergence can lead to misinterpretations and inefficiencies if not properly managed. Creating synergy, therefore, involves establishing a cohesive environment where technical solutions directly support and enhance business goals. Importance of aligning vendor efforts with stakeholder expectations.

Vendors focus on delivering specific solutions, while stakeholders emphasize meeting business objectives. Misalignment can lead to delays, budget overruns, or suboptimal outcomes. Creating synergy involves ensuring that vendor deliverables are tightly aligned with stakeholder needs:

- **Joint goal setting**: Conducting workshops where both vendors and stakeholders outline shared objectives ensures that efforts are harmonized.
- **Collaborative problem-solving**: Encouraging open dialogue to address challenges fosters trust and commitment among all parties.

Joint workshops for alignment

Workshops provide a structured environment for vendors and stakeholders to collaborate, enabling alignment of priorities.

Consider a scenario where, during the deployment of a multi-cloud infrastructure, stakeholders expressed concerns about costs, while vendors focused on technical deployment. A joint workshop was organized to reconcile these priorities, resulting in a phased deployment strategy that balanced cost efficiency with scalability.

Technology as a bridge

In today's interconnected world, technology serves as the essential conduit for seamless collaboration. It breaks down communication barriers and facilitates real-time information sharing, thereby fostering a unified working environment between vendors and stakeholders.

Leveraging tools for communication

Modern tools are a bridge that can be used to streamline communication and collaboration between vendors and stakeholders:

- **Slack and Microsoft Teams**: Enables real-time communication, ensuring that queries and updates are resolved promptly.
- **Confluence**: A shared knowledge repository where both vendors and stakeholders can access project documentation, timelines, and deliverables.

For example, using integrated dashboards for real-time updates. Integrated dashboards provide a unified view of project progress, ensuring transparency and accountability.

Scenario: When a third-party API was being integrated, a shared dashboard was tracking key milestones that allowed stakeholders to track the progress and vendors to show what has been delivered. The dashboard prevented miscommunication and built trust.

Role of solutions architects in mediation

Effective collaboration between vendors and stakeholders is essential for delivering successful solutions. Solutions architects play a crucial role in bridging the gap, ensuring technical feasibility aligns with business goals while mitigating conflicts and fostering productive partnerships.

Acting as the intermediary

Acting as the intermediary, solutions architects play a pivotal role in ensuring seamless communication and alignment between technical teams and business stakeholders. Here is how they bridge the gap:

- **Key role**: Translating technical jargon into business language and vice versa, ensuring mutual understanding.

- **Scenario**: In a healthcare project, vendors proposed a complex data storage solution, while stakeholders prioritized patient data accessibility. The solutions architect mediated by suggesting a hybrid approach, balancing performance and usability.

Bridging tech and business needs

Aligning technical solutions with business objectives requires a nuanced approach that considers both feasibility and stakeholder priorities. Here are key techniques to achieve this balance:

- **Active listening**: Understanding concerns from both sides to propose balanced solutions.

- **Feasibility studies**: Evaluating vendor solutions against stakeholder priorities to ensure compatibility.

- **Iterative feedback loops**: Establishing checkpoints where stakeholders review vendor progress to maintain alignment.

Real-world impact of effective collaboration

When vendors and stakeholders work in harmony, the benefits are tangible and significant. Here is a look at the real-world impact of effective collaboration:

- **Enhanced efficiency**: Synergized efforts reduce redundancies and streamline workflows.

- **Increased trust**: Open communication builds confidence between stakeholders and vendors.

- **Improved outcomes**: Aligning technical deliverables with business goals ensures project success.

By fostering collaboration between vendors and stakeholders, solutions architects enable seamless execution of complex projects. Using a combination of structured workshops, advanced communication tools, and proactive mediation, they create an environment where both groups can thrive, ensuring the delivery of robust and business-aligned solutions.

Conclusion

Effective vendor and stakeholder management is crucial for the successful delivery of solutions architecture projects. This chapter covered key strategies for building strong vendor relationships, selecting and integrating third-party vendors, and maintaining alignment through structured performance monitoring. By fostering transparent communication, establishing well-defined SLAs, and leveraging collaborative problem-solving techniques, solutions architects can create long-term partnerships that enhance efficiency, drive innovation, and ensure business success.

However, the role of a solutions architect extends beyond vendor and stakeholder management. It requires continuous learning and adaptation in a rapidly evolving technological landscape. Mastering these skills is just one aspect of professional growth.

In the next chapter, we will explore the significance of continuous learning, industry certifications, and networking in maintaining a competitive edge. To stay relevant, solutions architects must not only deepen their technical expertise but also embrace a mindset of lifelong learning to navigate the ever-changing demands of the industry.

Key takeaways

The takeaways are as follows:

- **Vendor relationships are strategic assets**: Establishing trust and collaboration with vendors ensures long-term success and effective project execution.

- **Structured vendor selection is critical**: Use criteria like expertise, reliability, and cost to evaluate vendors and ensure alignment with project goals.

- **Negotiation requires balance**: Obtain favourable terms while preserving a good relationship by concentrating on shared goals and mutual benefits.

- **Stakeholder alignment leads to success**: Being in close contact and communicating openly with stakeholders is what aligns diverse priorities to achieve the desired results.

- **Proactive conflict escalation avoidance**: Tackle disagreement before it becomes a critical problem by proposing structured communication and focusing on the shared output.

- **Continuous monitoring of performance**: Utilize KPIs and feedback cycles to evaluate and enhance vendor and stakeholder performance continually.

- **More than an agreement**: Detailed contracts outlining deliverables, SLAs, and formal change management provisions protect against risks.

- **Collaboration tools increase efficiency**: Utilize tools, such as Slack, Miro, and Jira, to organize and ensure all stakeholders are aligned.

- **Stakeholder mapping is critical**: People need to be aware of stakeholder roles, influence, and interest to engage and manage expectations properly throughout the project life cycle.

- **Continuous improvement is important**: Document lessons learned to better refine vendor and stakeholder management strategies for future projects.

Model interview questions and answers

1. **How do you evaluate and select a third-party vendor for a critical project?**

   Model answer:

   When evaluating and selecting a third-party vendor, you use a structured approach to ensure alignment with project requirements. Key steps are as follows:

   - **Define criteria**: You establish criteria such as technical expertise, reliability, cost, compliance, and scalability.

- **Vendor evaluation**: You utilize a vendor scorecard or checklist to assess potential vendors, considering past performance, customer references, and certifications.

- **RFP**: You issue detailed RFPs to ensure the vendor understands the scope of the project and deliverables.

- **POC**: You often request a POC to validate the capabilities of the vendor in a controlled environment.

- **Stakeholder involvement**: You involve key stakeholders in the decision-making process to ensure consensus. For example, during a cloud migration project, you evaluated three vendors. After a thorough assessment and POC, we selected a vendor that offered the best mix of cost-efficiency and technical expertise, resulting in a smooth migration.

2. **How do you manage conflicts with vendors regarding project deliverables?**

Model answer:

Conflict management with the vendors begins with open communication and shared goals. The main steps include:

- **Understand the issue**: You ensure the problem is documented well and the parties understand what the scope of the conflict is.

- **Refer to the contract**: You refer to the terms of the contract and the SLAs of the contract that define the expectations of the obligations of the vendor.

- **Collaborative problem-solving**: You organize a meeting to discuss the issue and identify mutually acceptable solutions, focusing on the project's overall success.

- **Escalation**: If the issue does not get resolved, you escalate the issue through the appropriate channels that the contract specifies, such as legal or higher management. For example, once in a project, a vendor failed to deliver on time. After going through the SLA, you aligned the timeline along with penalties if the timelines further. So, it maintains the relationship with accountability.

3. **Can you describe a situation where stakeholder misalignment impacted a project, and how you addressed it?**

Model answer:

In a CRM system integration project, business stakeholders prioritized features that enhanced customer engagement, while IT stakeholders focused on minimizing disruption to existing systems. This misalignment caused delays in decision-making.

- **Stakeholder mapping**: You identified the key stakeholders and their priorities.

- **Communication facilitation**: You conducted workshops to align on a shared vision, ensuring all parties understood the project's business objectives and technical constraints.

- **Consensus building**: You created a roadmap that balanced immediate business needs with technical feasibility, prioritizing features in phases.

- **Outcome**: This approach reduced friction, and you successfully delivered a phased integration with minimal downtime and high user adoption.

4. **How would you negotiate better terms with a vendor while not losing the good relationship?**

Model answer:

A good negotiation looks for win-win. Your method is:

- **Preparation**: You do your research on the position of the vendor in the market, their competition, and common pricing models.

- **Understanding needs**: You make sure that both parties' needs are understood, such as long-term collaboration rather than short-term benefits.

- **Leveraging data**: You use benchmarking and data to support your argument for lower costs or other benefits.

- **Flexibility**: You find additional benefits such as extended warranties or extra support, creating value over cost.

- **Recording agreements**: All negotiated terms are documented in a clear and enforceable contract. For example, in a software procurement project, you were able to negotiate a 20% discount by agreeing to a multi-year contract and including the vendor in future RFPs, creating a long-term partnership.

5. **How do you ensure continuous engagement and communication with stakeholders throughout a project?**

   Model answer:

   Continuous engagement with stakeholders involves structured communication and transparency. Your approach includes:

   - **Stakeholder mapping**: You identify stakeholders early and understand their interests, influence, and preferred communication styles.

   - **Communication plan**: You create a plan outlining regular updates, meeting schedules, and escalation paths.

   - **Transparency**: Share progress updates and maintain communication open for feedback by using communication tools like Slack or Microsoft Teams for instant updates.

   - **Active problem prevention**: Tackle an issue before escalating by keeping stakeholders on board throughout key decisions to avoid derailment. For example, for a data migration project, weekly updates and hosting stakeholder workshops ensured alignment, reducing rework by 30% because of early feedback.

Join our Discord space

Join our Discord workspace for latest updates, offers, tech happenings around the world, new releases, and sessions with the authors:

https://discord.bpbonline.com

CHAPTER 17
Continuous Learning and Improvement

Introduction

In the rapidly evolving field of solutions architecture, staying relevant requires more than just technical expertise. It demands a commitment to continuous learning and professional development. With new technologies, methodologies, and industry trends emerging at an unprecedented pace, solutions architects must proactively adapt to meet the demands of modern enterprises. Continuous learning is no longer optional; it is a strategic necessity for those seeking to excel in this dynamic role.

This chapter focuses on the importance of cultivating a mindset of lifelong learning, providing practical strategies to help solutions architects remain competitive and innovative. From acquiring industry-recognized certifications to staying informed about emerging trends, this chapter highlights actionable ways to enhance both technical and interpersonal skills. It also underscores the value of building professional networks and engaging in knowledge-sharing practices, which are critical for career growth and staying ahead in a highly competitive market.

Whether you are an aspiring solutions architect or a seasoned professional looking to refine your skills, this chapter will equip you with the tools and strategies needed to thrive in a field that is defined by change and innovation.

Structure

This chapter covers the following topics:

- Importance of continuous learning
- Certifications for solutions architects
- Keeping up with industry trends
- Networking and knowledge sharing

Objectives

The objective of this chapter is to emphasize the significance of continuous learning and improvement as a cornerstone of success for solutions architects. It aims to equip readers with actionable strategies to stay relevant and competitive in an ever-evolving technological landscape. The chapter gets into the benefits of certifications, highlighting how they validate expertise and open doors to new opportunities. Readers will also gain insights into tracking and adapting industry trends, ensuring their architectural practices remain innovative and aligned with emerging technologies. Additionally, the chapter underscores the importance of building professional networks and engaging in knowledge-sharing practices, fostering a collaborative and growth-oriented mindset. By mastering these principles, solutions architects can not only enhance their technical and interpersonal skills but also position themselves as trusted advisors and leaders in their field.

Importance of continuous learning

In the rapidly evolving field of solutions architecture, where technological advancements and industry standards shift frequently, continuous learning is not a requirement, but a necessity. Solutions architects must adapt to emerging trends, integrate innovative technologies, and provide business-aligned, scalable solutions to remain relevant and effective. This section explores the concept of continuous learning, its benefits, and strategies for cultivating a growth-oriented learning mindset.

Defining continuous learning

Continuous learning refers to an ongoing, self-motivated pursuit of knowledge and skill development. For solutions architects, this involves staying updated with the latest advancements in cloud technologies, architectural frameworks, cybersecurity practices, and industry-specific solutions. Beyond technical expertise, continuous learning encompasses the enhancement of soft skills such as communication, collaboration, and leadership. Refer to the following list for more details:

- **Proactive skill development**: The role of proactive learning cannot be overstated. In an era marked by technological disruptions, from the rapid adoption of artificial intelligence to the shift toward serverless architectures, solutions architects must anticipate changes rather than react to them. Proactive skill development enables architects to:
    - Understand and address business challenges with up-to-date knowledge of industry regulations or new service offerings from cloud providers.
    - Align their solutions with evolving business and market demands.
- **Context in solutions architecture**: Continuous learning in this domain extends beyond acquiring certifications or attending workshops. It involves applying knowledge to design innovative and sustainable systems that align with business goals. For instance:
    - Adopting cloud-native design patterns in response to the growing demand for scalable and resilient architectures.
    - Leveraging new data analytics frameworks to enhance business decision-making processes.
    - Incorporating security-first principles to address the increasing importance of data protection and privacy.

Benefits of continuous learning

The advantages of committing to lifelong learning are profound, both for individual career growth and organizational success, and they are as follows:

- **Improved adaptability**: Continuous learners develop the agility to respond to emerging challenges. Whether integrating a disruptive technology like generative AI or addressing performance bottlenecks in complex systems, solutions architects who prioritize learning can adapt to evolving requirements more effectively. For example:

    o When a company transitions from on-premises infrastructure to a hybrid cloud model, a well-informed architect can guide the process seamlessly by leveraging knowledge of cloud migration strategies.

- **Enhanced career prospects**: Staying ahead of industry advancements positions solutions architects as valuable assets to their organizations. Professionals who pursue certifications, attend conferences, and contribute to industry discussions are more likely to:

    o Advance into leadership roles.

    o Command higher compensation due to their expertise and forward-thinking approach.

    o Be sought after for high-impact projects that require innovative architectural solutions.

- **Greater ability to innovate**: Continuous learners are better equipped to integrate innovative solutions into their designs. By staying informed about trends like edge computing, blockchain, and AI/ML integration, solutions architects can:

    o Develop cutting-edge systems that differentiate their organizations from competitors.

    o Solve complex problems with creative and efficient approaches.

    o Drive strategic initiatives that align with future industry directions.

With a solid understanding of the importance of continuous learning, the next step is to develop the right mindset for adopting new skills and embracing change.

Building a learning mindset

A sustainable learning mindset is the foundation of continuous improvement. Developing this mindset requires motivation, discipline, and the right tools. Refer to the following list of attributes that will help:

- **Strategies for self-motivation**:

    o **Set clear goals**: Define short-term and long-term learning objectives that align with career aspirations. For example, commit to completing an AWS Solutions architect certification within six months.

    o **Celebrate milestones**: Recognize and reward yourself for achieving learning goals, whether it is mastering a new framework or successfully implementing an innovative design.

    o **Seek inspiration**: Follow industry leaders, read success stories, and participate in online forums to stay motivated and engaged.

- **Consistency in learning**:

    o **Allocate time**: Dedicate a specific number of hours each week to learning new skills or exploring emerging trends.

    o **Create a routine**: Build a habit of reading industry blogs, listening to podcasts, or practicing hands-on labs daily or weekly.

- **Tools for self-assessment and goal-setting**:

    o **Learning platforms**: Use tools like Coursera, Pluralsight, and AWS Training to access structured learning paths.

    o **Knowledge checkpoints**: Regularly test your understanding through quizzes, mock exams, or practical challenges.

     o **Progress tracking**: Leverage productivity tools like Notion or Trello to document learning objectives, progress, and reflections.

By cultivating a learning mindset, solutions architects can not only enhance their own skill sets but also inspire their teams and contribute to a culture of continuous improvement within their organizations. This proactive approach ensures that architects remain indispensable in an ever-changing technological landscape.

Certifications for solutions architects

In the rapidly evolving field of solutions architecture, certifications are an essential way to validate your expertise and remain competitive. As technology continues to advance, employers increasingly value recognized certifications as they provide proof of your knowledge, technical proficiency, and ability to tackle real-world architectural challenges. This section provides an in-depth overview of key certifications for solutions architects, how to choose the right one for your career path, and how to effectively prepare and maintain them.

Overview of key certifications

Several well-respected certifications are available for solutions architects across various cloud platforms and architectural frameworks. These certifications demonstrate your competency in key areas such as cloud architecture, enterprise solutions, and design frameworks. Refer to the following list for more details:

- **AWS Certified Solutions architect (Associate and professional)**:
  - o **Focus areas**: AWS certification validates your ability to design distributed systems on AWS, ensuring reliability, scalability, and cost-efficiency. The certification covers aspects of AWS services such as EC2, S3, VPC, IAM, and RDS.
  - o **Prerequisites**: None for the associate level; however, it is recommended to have some hands-on experience with AWS services before attempting the exam. The professional level requires more in-depth knowledge and experience.
  - o **Benefits**: AWS is the market leader in cloud services, and this certification helps professionals stand out by demonstrating expertise in managing cloud architecture and deploying applications on AWS.

- **Microsoft Certified (Azure Solutions architect Expert)**:
  - o **Focus areas**: This certification focuses on the architecture of solutions on Microsoft Azure. It covers areas like virtual machines, Azure Active Directory, App Services, and storage solutions.
  - o **Prerequisites**: Candidates should have experience with Azure and its components, as well as familiarity with core Azure services and advanced networking, security, and data services.
  - o **Benefits**: Azure is the second largest cloud provider, and obtaining this certification can significantly boost your credibility, especially in enterprises heavily using the Microsoft ecosystem.

- **Google Cloud Professional Cloud Architect**:
  - o **Focus areas**: This certification assesses your ability to design, develop, and manage dynamic solutions using Google Cloud services, including Compute Engine, App Engine, Cloud Storage, and BigQuery.
  - o **Prerequisites**: Google recommends having at least three years of industry experience and one or more years of hands-on experience with Google Cloud before attempting this exam.
  - o **Benefits**: Google Cloud has gained significant market traction, and this certification opens doors for architects focusing on high-performance, data-driven solutions that require Google's scalable and innovative cloud services.

- **TOGAF certification for enterprise architecture**:
  - o **Focus areas**: **The Open Group Architecture Framework (TOGAF)** is an enterprise architecture methodology used to design, plan, implement, and govern an enterprise IT architecture. It emphasizes creating cohesive business strategies through standardized architecture processes.
  - o **Prerequisites**: No formal prerequisites, but experience in enterprise architecture practices is beneficial.
  - o **Benefits**: TOGAF certification is globally recognized and often required for roles in large organizations that manage complex, multi-faceted technology environments. It is highly beneficial for those working in enterprise-scale solutions and integrating business needs with technical strategies.

Choosing the right certification

Choosing the right certification depends on your current expertise, career aspirations, and the specific demands of the industry you work in. Certifications can serve different career goals, and the path you select should align with your skills, interests, and long-term objectives. Refer to the following list for more details:

- **Aligning certifications with career goals**:
  - o If your goal is to become proficient in cloud technologies and take on roles focused on cloud architecture, certifications like AWS, Azure, or Google Cloud Professional Cloud Architect are ideal. These certifications ensure you are well-versed in designing, implementing, and managing cloud-based systems.
  - o For those aspiring to work in enterprise architecture or business-driven IT strategy, the TOGAF certification provides a comprehensive framework for designing and governing enterprise IT systems. This is valuable for architects looking to make strategic decisions at an enterprise level.

- **Factors to consider when choosing certifications**:
  - o **Cost**: Certification exams and study materials can be costly. AWS, Azure, and Google Cloud certifications generally cost between $150 to $300 per exam. Consider your budget and whether your employer offers financial support for professional development.
  - o **Time investment**: Most certifications require a significant time investment for preparation. Depending on your prior knowledge and experience, preparation can take anywhere from three to six months. Decide how much time you can realistically dedicate each week to studying.
  - o **Market demand**: Look at current job listings and industry trends. Cloud computing certifications, particularly in AWS, Azure, and Google Cloud, are in high demand. Understanding which certifications are valued in your target market or by your current employer will help you focus your efforts effectively.

Preparing for certifications

Successful preparation for certifications involves a combination of structured study, hands-on practice, and test-taking strategies. Some resources and tips are as follows:

- **Study resources**:
  - o **Online courses**: Platforms like Coursera, Udemy, LinkedIn Learning, and A Cloud Guru offer comprehensive courses specifically designed to prepare you for certification exams. These courses often provide video lectures, quizzes, and hands-on labs to reinforce learning.
  - o **Bootcamps**: Intensive bootcamp programs provide a more structured, immersive approach to preparing for certifications. They often include live instructors, real-world labs, and practice exams to fast-track your preparation.

- o **Practice tests**: Taking practice exams is one of the most effective ways to gauge your knowledge and identify weak areas. Most certification providers, such as AWS and Google Cloud, offer practice exams. You can also find practice tests on platforms like Whizlabs or ExamPro.

- **Tips for effective exam preparation**:
  - o **Follow a study schedule**: Dedicate a fixed number of hours each week to your certification preparation. Break your study into manageable segments, focusing on specific topics or services each week.

  - o **Hands-on labs**: Cloud certifications require practical experience. Set up a free-tier account with AWS, Azure, or Google Cloud to gain hands-on experience with services such as EC2, VMs, or storage solutions. This will deepen your understanding and provide real-world experience.

  - o **Join study groups or forums**: Online communities like Reddit, LinkedIn groups, and certification-specific forums can offer insights, study tips, and moral support. These groups can also help you resolve doubts and clarify complex topics.

Maintaining certifications

Your work is not complete once you have obtained a certification. Continuous professional development is essential to ensure your certifications remain valid and relevant in a constantly changing tech environment. Refer to the following list for more details:

- **Importance of recertification**: Many certifications, particularly cloud certifications, require periodic recertification. Cloud service providers like AWS and Azure require professionals to recertify every two to three years. This ensures that architects stay up to date with new services, features, and best practices.

- **Leveraging professional development units**:
  - o **Tracking PDUs**: Certifications like TOGAF and AWS Solutions architect provide the option to accumulate PDUs by participating in conferences, webinars, or completing relevant courses. These PDUs count toward recertification and demonstrate a commitment to professional development.

  - o **Continuous education programs**: Take advantage of continuous education programs offered by certification bodies or employers. These programs are often structured to help professionals stay ahead of trends, learn new methodologies, or gain deeper insights into emerging technologies.

By continuously updating your certifications and participating in professional development, you reinforce your role as an expert in the field and demonstrate your commitment to lifelong learning.

In solutions architecture, certifications serve as an essential benchmark of proficiency and expertise. They not only validate your skills but also provide opportunities for career growth and industry recognition. Continuous learning, through certifications and professional development, ensures that solutions architects remain competitive and prepared for the challenges of an ever-changing technology landscape. Whether you choose cloud certifications or enterprise architecture frameworks like TOGAF, each certification will serve as a stepping stone to mastering new technologies and delivering innovative, business-aligned solutions.

Certifications offer a structured path for validating expertise, but staying informed about emerging trends is equally important. The following section explores how solutions architects can track and incorporate evolving technologies into their solutions.

Keeping up with industry trends

In the dynamic field of solutions architecture, staying abreast of industry trends is not merely an option. It is a necessity. Emerging technologies and methodologies continuously reshape the landscape, influencing how organizations design and implement their systems. Solutions architects must be proactive in tracking trends, understanding their implications, and incorporating them into their practices. This section explores strategies for staying informed, integrating trends into architectural designs, and developing skills to maintain a competitive edge.

Tracking emerging technologies

To remain relevant, solutions architects must keep a close watch on technological advancements and understand how these innovations impact business and architecture. The industry trends and resources are as follows:

- **Overview of current industry trends**:
    - o **AI/ML**: AI/ML is revolutionizing industries by enabling predictive analytics, intelligent automation, and personalized user experiences. Technologies like OpenAI's models, TensorFlow, and PyTorch are gaining traction across sectors.
    - o **Blockchain**: Beyond cryptocurrency, blockchain is being adopted for secure data sharing, supply chain transparency, and decentralized applications.
    - o **Quantum computing**: Although still in its infancy, quantum computing promises breakthroughs in optimization, cryptography, and complex simulations.
    - o **DevOps and platform engineering**: Practices like GitOps, IaC, and **continuous integration/ continuous deployment (CI/CD)** are becoming standard for modern software delivery.
    - o **Edge computing and serverless architecture**: These trends emphasize reducing latency and enhancing scalability by moving processing closer to the user or adopting event-driven computing.
- **Resources for staying informed:**
    - o **Industry reports**: Publications like Gartner's Magic Quadrant, Forrester Wave, and IDC MarketScape offer in-depth analyses of emerging trends and vendor capabilities.
    - o **Webinars and podcasts**: Platforms like AWS Summit, Google Cloud Next, and industry-specific podcasts provide insights into the latest developments and practical use cases.
    - o **Whitepapers and blogs**: Companies such as AWS, Microsoft Azure, and Google regularly publish whitepapers and blog posts detailing best practices and success stories related to their technologies.

By consistently engaging with these resources, solutions architects can stay ahead of the curve and make informed decisions about adopting new technologies.

Incorporating trends into practice

Understanding trends is only the first step; applying them effectively in real-world scenarios is the hallmark of a successful solutions architect. Some techniques and case studies are as follows:

- **Techniques for integrating new trends**:
    - o **Proof of concept (POC)**: Before full-scale adoption, create POCs to evaluate the feasibility, performance, and ROI of new technologies. For instance, test serverless architecture for handling specific workloads to determine cost-efficiency and scalability.
    - o **Incremental adoption**: Gradually integrate new technologies into existing systems to minimize disruption. For example, adopt edge computing for latency-sensitive applications while retaining centralized systems for less critical workloads.

- o **Collaboration with teams**: Involve cross-functional teams early in the evaluation and implementation process to align technological advancements with business goals.
- **Case studies**:
  - o **Case study 1 (Adopting serverless computing):**
    - ▪ **Scenario**: A retail company struggling with seasonal traffic surges adopted AWS Lambda for serverless computing.
    - ▪ **Approach**: The architecture was redesigned to offload non-critical tasks to Lambda, enabling autoscaling without manual intervention.
    - ▪ **Outcome**: The solution reduced operational costs by 30% and improved system resilience during peak traffic.
  - o **Case study 2 (Implementing edge AI for real-time analytics):**
    - ▪ **Scenario**: A logistics company needed to analyze real-time data from IoT sensors in remote locations.
    - ▪ **Approach**: Edge AI was deployed using NVIDIA Jetson devices to process data locally and transmit actionable insights to the central system.
    - ▪ **Outcome**: The solution reduced latency by 50% and minimized data transfer costs.

These examples illustrate the tangible benefits of adapting architectural practices to leverage emerging trends effectively.

Skill development

To effectively navigate and implement industry trends, solutions architects must continuously refine both their technical and soft skills.

Refer to the following list for more details:

- **Focus on technical skills**:
  - o **Enterprise architectural and design patterns**: Enterprise architectural and design patterns provide structured methodologies for building scalable, maintainable, and resilient systems. Understanding patterns such as microservices, event-driven architecture, and **Domain-Driven Design** (**DDD**) enables solutions architects to create cloud-native, AI-driven, data-centric, and secure solutions that align with business and technical requirements.
  - o **Cloud-native design**: Develop expertise in cloud architectures, microservices, and container orchestration tools like Kubernetes and Docker.
  - o **AI/ML fundamentals**: Gain proficiency in using machine learning libraries and frameworks to integrate AI into architectural designs.
  - o **Data-driven decision-making**: Learn to analyze data effectively using platforms like Tableau or Power BI to support architectural decisions.
  - o **Security best practices**: Stay updated on security frameworks, such as Zero Trust Architecture, to protect systems from evolving threats.
- **Focus on soft skills**:
  - o **Stakeholder communication**: Strengthen the ability to explain technical concepts to non-technical audiences and align project goals with business needs.

- ○ **Conflict resolution**: Enhance negotiation and conflict resolution skills to manage competing priorities and drive consensus among teams.

  ○ **Leadership**: Cultivate the ability to mentor team members and foster a culture of continuous learning and innovation.

- **Recommendations for learning platforms**: To stay updated with evolving technologies and best practices, leveraging diverse learning platforms is essential. The following categories provide structured learning opportunities for solutions architects:

  ○ **Online learning platforms**: Offer structured courses on cloud computing, DevOps, AI/ML, and architectural principles.

  ○ **Professional development courses**: Provide certifications and specialized training on emerging technologies such as cloud security, blockchain, and data analytics.

  ○ **Self-paced and interactive learning**: Platforms with hands-on labs, coding exercises, and real-world case studies enhance practical understanding.

  ○ **Workshops and conferences**: Industry events and in-person workshops offer hands-on experience, exposure to new technologies, and opportunities to engage with experts.

By focusing on continuous skill development and leveraging these platforms, solutions architects can build a versatile skill set that enables them to adapt to emerging trends and deliver innovative solutions.

Keeping up with industry trends is integral to the role of a solutions architect. By tracking emerging technologies, incorporating them into architectural practices, and continuously developing technical and soft skills, architects can ensure they remain at the forefront of innovation. Staying informed and proactive not only enhances individual performance but also drives the delivery of scalable, efficient, and future-ready solutions for organizations.

Tracking industry trends is essential, but connecting with other professionals provides additional insights and valuable opportunities to exchange ideas. The next section explores strategies for networking and sharing knowledge effectively.

Networking and knowledge sharing

In the field of solutions architecture, networking and knowledge sharing are invaluable for professional growth. Building relationships within the industry not only provides access to diverse perspectives and opportunities but also fosters continuous learning through collaboration. Sharing knowledge with the community enhances personal credibility while contributing to collective progress in the field. This section gets into strategies for building a professional network, engaging in knowledge sharing, and exploring collaborative learning opportunities.

Building a professional network

A robust professional network is essential for career advancement and staying informed about industry developments. It creates avenues for mentorship, collaboration, and learning from the experiences of others.

Refer to the following list for more details:

- **Importance of mentorship and peer relationships**:

  ○ **Mentorship**: Mentors provide guidance, share industry insights, and offer support during career transitions or challenges. For instance, an experienced solutions architect might guide a junior professional on certifications, technical challenges, or navigating organizational dynamics.

  ○ **Peer relationships**: Collaboration with peers fosters the exchange of ideas and best practices, enabling professionals to refine their approaches and gain new perspectives.

- o **Community engagement**: Active participation in professional communities allows individuals to stay updated on emerging trends and expand their horizons.

- **Strategies for effective networking**:

  - o **Attending conferences and industry events**:

    - Conferences like AWS re:Invent, Google Cloud Next, or TOGAF Summits provide opportunities to connect with industry leaders and peers.

    - Participating in panel discussions or breakout sessions can facilitate meaningful conversations and knowledge sharing.

  - o **Joining meetups and local groups**:

    - Meetup platforms host tech-centric gatherings where solutions architects can discuss challenges, share solutions, and explore innovations.

    - Local meetups offer a less formal environment for building relationships.

  - o **Engaging on LinkedIn**:

    - LinkedIn is a powerful tool for connecting with professionals, joining industry groups, and sharing personal achievements or insights.

    - Regularly commenting on and sharing relevant posts helps establish a visible and respected online presence.

- **Proactive networking approach**:

  - o Prepare an elevator pitch that highlights your role and interests to initiate meaningful conversations.

  - o Follow up with contacts after networking events to nurture relationships and explore collaboration opportunities.

Knowledge sharing practices

Knowledge sharing not only enhances personal credibility but also strengthens the professional community. It creates a cycle of learning and contribution that benefits all participants.

Refer to the following list for more details:

- **Benefits of knowledge sharing**:

  - o **Reinforcement of expertise**: Articulating concepts for an audience deepens understanding and reinforces knowledge.

  - o **Building credibility**: Consistent contributions to the professional community establish a reputation as a thought leader.

  - o **Driving innovation**: Sharing ideas sparks discussions that lead to creative solutions and new insights.

- **Methods for sharing insights**:

  - o **Blogs and articles**:

    - Platforms like Medium or LinkedIn allow professionals to write about their experiences, challenges, and solutions in solutions architecture.

      For example, a solutions architect could write a blog on *Migrating Legacy Systems to Cloud-Native Architectures* to share practical insights and lessons learned.

- o **Webinars and public speaking**:
  - ▪ Hosting webinars or speaking at events builds visibility and demonstrates expertise.

    For example, conducting a webinar on *Implementing DevSecOps in Hybrid Cloud Environments* to educate peers on best practices.

- o **Community contributions**:
  - ▪ Answering questions or contributing to discussions on forums like Reddit or Stack Overflow helps build a reputation as a helpful and knowledgeable professional.

    For example, sharing optimized design patterns for API gateways in a Reddit architecture group.

- **Platforms for sharing knowledge**:
  - o **GitHub**: Ideal for sharing open-source projects, scripts, or templates.
  - o **Medium and LinkedIn**: Effective for publishing detailed articles and professional updates.
  - o **Reddit and industry forums**: Provide platforms for engaging in discussions, answering queries, and sharing quick tips or advice.

While sharing insights strengthens your credibility, engaging in collaborative learning opportunities takes knowledge-building to the next level. The following section covers effective collaboration strategies that drive innovation and teamwork.

Collaborative learning opportunities

Collaboration is a powerful way to enhance skills, solve problems, and gain diverse perspectives. Engaging in collaborative events and projects fosters a shared learning experience.

Refer to the following list for more details:

- **Participating in collaborative events**:
  - o **Hackathons**: Competitive yet collaborative, hackathons challenge participants to solve problems or build solutions within a time limit. They offer hands-on experience with emerging technologies and foster teamwork.

    For example, participating in an AWS-hosted hackathon to design serverless solutions for real-world challenges.

  - o **Study groups**: Learning with peers enhances understanding through discussion and diverse viewpoints. Study groups for certifications or technical topics provide motivation and structure.

  - o **Bootcamps and workshops**: Intensive sessions focus on building specific skills or solving problems, providing actionable knowledge in a short time.

- **Learning through community projects**:
  - o **Open-source contributions**:
    - ▪ Contributing to open-source projects on platforms like GitHub enables collaboration with a global community while gaining hands-on experience.
    - ▪ For example, collaborating on a cloud-native monitoring tool or API development project.

  - o **Industry challenges**:
    - ▪ Participating in initiatives like Google's AI Challenge or Microsoft's Imagine Cup provides opportunities to work on cutting-edge projects while gaining exposure to industry expectations.

- **Benefits of collaborative learning**:
    - ○ Develops practical skills in a team-based environment.
    - ○ Offers exposure to different tools, methodologies, and perspectives.
    - ○ Builds relationships with like-minded professionals and potential mentors.

Networking and knowledge sharing are essential pillars of continuous professional growth for solutions architects. By building a strong professional network, sharing insights with the community, and participating in collaborative learning opportunities, architects can enhance their expertise and remain at the forefront of the field. These practices not only foster personal development but also contribute to the broader community of professionals striving to deliver innovative, impactful solutions.

Conclusion

Continuous learning and improvement are not just professional obligations for solutions architects, but they are essential drivers of long-term success in a rapidly changing industry. This chapter has outlined the critical components of lifelong learning, from obtaining relevant certifications to staying informed about industry trends and actively participating in professional networks. By embracing these practices, solutions architects can adapt to new challenges, leverage emerging technologies, and maintain their competitiveness in a demanding market.

Ultimately, the journey of learning and growth is ongoing. By committing to continuous improvement, solutions architects can build resilience, inspire innovation, and consistently deliver value to their organizations and clients. Let this chapter serve as a guide and motivation to invest in your development, ensuring that your skills and expertise remain at the forefront of the solutions architecture profession.

As you continue this journey, the next critical step is to effectively communicate your expertise during the solutions architect interview process. In the following chapter, you will discover proven strategies to excel in various interview formats, tackle challenging technical problems, and present your portfolio with confidence. Mastering these techniques will enable you to showcase your skills and make a lasting impression in interviews, bringing you closer to your next big opportunity.

Key takeaways

The takeaways are as follows:

- **Embrace lifelong learning**: Continuous learning is essential for staying relevant in a dynamic field like solutions architecture.

- **Pursue certifications**: Industry-recognized certifications validate expertise and provide a structured path for skill enhancement.

- **Track industry trends**: Stay informed about emerging technologies and methodologies to ensure your architectural practices remain innovative.

- **Develop soft skills**: Balance technical expertise with communication, leadership, and collaboration skills for a well-rounded professional profile.

- **Build professional networks**: Engage with peers, mentors, and industry leaders through events, forums, and online communities to exchange ideas and opportunities.

- **Engage in knowledge sharing**: Contribute to the professional community by sharing insights through blogs, webinars, and collaborative projects.

- **Leverage collaborative learning**: Participate in study groups, hackathons, or community initiatives to learn from diverse perspectives and enhance problem-solving skills.

- **Adapt to change**: Continuously integrate new knowledge and trends into your architectural designs to remain Agile and future-ready.

CHAPTER 18

Preparation for Solutions Architect Interview

Introduction

It is time to sharpen your interview skills. Having spent a lot of hours studying, developing competency, and perfecting the resume, the time has arrived for the interview. This is the moment to demonstrate your knowledge, show your problem-solving abilities and how you can drive business success.

The role of a solutions architect demands a combination of technical excellence, leadership, strategic thinking, and excellent communication skills. Preparing for an interview typically becomes more about displaying the ability to think beyond mere technical problem solving, but to be able to solve complex, heterogeneous problems and to align technical solutions with business goals.

This chapter will comprehensively walk you through the different stages of a solutions architect interview. From understanding what types of interviews, you may encounter to how to present your portfolio, this chapter is designed to give you the strategies and insights required to perform at your best.

You will learn effective strategies for solving difficult technical problems, how to present your response for maximum impact, and how to demonstrate your experience and skills in a manner appealing to interviewers. Whether it is a behavioral interview, a technical deep dive, or a design challenge, you are sure to be best prepared systematically and with confidence for that challenging interview.

Structure

This chapter covers the following topics:

- Types of interviews
- Handling technical challenges during interviews
- Presentation of your portfolio

Objectives

By the end of this chapter, readers will be able to understand each of the crucial areas of the solutions architect interview and the strategies required to ace every stage. You will learn about various interview types that range from behavioral, technical, and design challenges, and get armed with adequate preparation tips for each. This chapter will guide you on how to answer a complex technical question with practical answers, structure responses using frameworks such as the **situation, task, action, result (STAR)** technique, and show a portfolio to exhibit relevant skills and accomplishments. You will learn how to align your technical skills with business objectives. Finally, this chapter equips and empowers you with the skills and the confidence to sail through the interview process.

Keeping these objectives in mind, let us understand the first critical aspect of interview preparation, that is, to know the different types of interviews you might face.

Types of interviews

In your solutions architecture journey, you will face the following types of interviews, each targeting specific competencies. Each type of interview has a different focus and expectations, so knowing where to focus for that specific type of interview is important. This section covers the three main types of interviews, that are, behavioral, technical, and design challenges, outlining their purpose and areas of focus as noted in *Figure 18.1*:

Solutions Architect Interviews

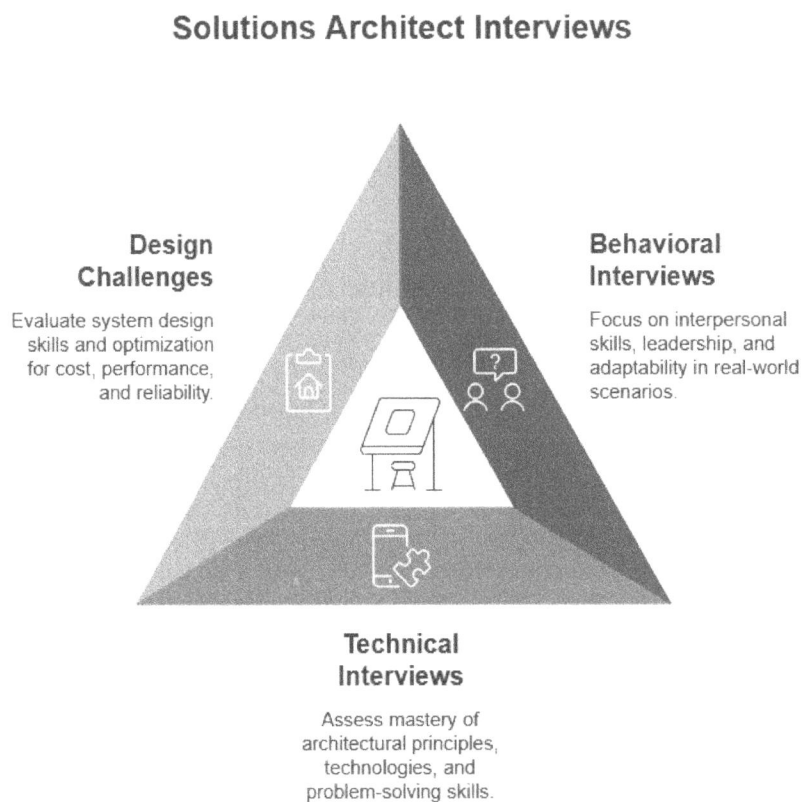

Design Challenges

Evaluate system design skills and optimization for cost, performance, and reliability.

Behavioral Interviews

Focus on interpersonal skills, leadership, and adaptability in real-world scenarios.

Technical Interviews

Assess mastery of architectural principles, technologies, and problem-solving skills.

Figure 18.1: Types of interviews

Behavioral interviews

The behavioral interview is part of the standard recruitment process in which you are inquired about how you have handled real-world situations. These interviews are meant to assess your interpersonal skills and leadership abilities in relation to how you handle problems, work within a team, or coordinate your actions to achieve organization-wide goals.

The details are as follows:

- **Purpose**: Behavioral interviews examine your soft skills and your leadership, teaming, and change adaptability skills. Hiring managers want to know how you manage stakeholders, resolve conflicts, and make decisions in the presence of stressors.

- **Key focus areas**:

    o **Stakeholder management**: Interviewers will ask you questions about how you engage with different stakeholders in terms of technical teams, business leaders, and clients. They would like to see how you balance related competing priorities and build consensus.

    o **Conflict resolution**: You might be asked about situations where you resolved disputes within a team or between different stakeholders. Being proactive with empathy is what counts.

    o **Adaptability and decision-making under pressure**: Solutions architects rarely know in advance what their challenges will be. Hiring managers are interested in hearing how you can maintain your cool and make good choices in intense environments.

    Example question: *Tell me about a time you had to balance conflicting expectations from multiple stakeholders. How did you resolve it?*

- **Preparation tips**:

    o When answering, use the STAR method.

    o Think of instances in which you have had to lead people and adapt.

    o Practice articulating your thought process clearly and concisely.

Technical interviews

Technical interviews are there to test how much you know about core architectural principles, technologies, and patterns. In most cases, this involves solving complex technical problems, analyzing trade-offs, or demonstrating a role in designing scalable and secure systems.

The details are as follows:

- **Purpose**: The purpose is to evaluate the depth of your knowledge about the technical issues you solve and problem-solving skills. The interviewers want to ascertain if you can apply theoretical knowledge to practical scenarios.

- **Key focus areas**:

    o **System design and architecture**: You will be asked to design systems that meet specific functional and non-functional requirements. This could include designing a web application, a data pipeline, or microservices-based architecture.

    o **Cloud-native technologies**: Expect questions on cloud platforms like AWS, Azure, or Google Cloud. Be prepared to discuss services such as Kubernetes, serverless computing, and **infrastructure as code (IaC)**.

    o **Security, scalability, and performance tuning**: You will often be asked how you guarantee a system is secure, scalable, and performant. For example, you might be questioned as to how to protect an API or fine-tune a database for high traffic.

    Example question: *How would you design a system to handle millions of concurrent users while ensuring high availability?*

- **Preparation tips**:

    o Practice whiteboarding or online diagram tools to visually explain your system designs.

     o   Refresh of fundamental architectural patterns and cloud services.

     o   Be prepared to discuss the trade-off for their design choices.

Design challenges

Design challenges are similar to real-life situations that will challenge your thinking ability as an architect. They generally involve translating vague business requirements into concrete, scalable, and cost-efficient solutions.

The details are as follows:

- **Purpose**: Evaluate the design skills of a system, the ability to consider the views of several different people, and the knack for optimizing systems for cost, performance, and reliability.

- **Key focus areas**:

     o   **Design for high availability and disaster recovery**: You might be required to design a system which would have a minimum amount of downtime and fast recovery from failure.

     o   **Selecting the correct technologies with trade-off analysis**: Demonstrate that you can pick the most appropriate technology for the job, with trade-offs being something such as cost, performance, and complexity.

     o   **Cost and performance**: Interviewers will check how you balance performance with cost-effectiveness to ensure that designs are both robust and financially viable.

             Example question: *Design an e-commerce platform that can handle flash sales and high traffic spikes while keeping operational costs low.*

- **Preparation tips**:

     o   Familiarize yourself with common architectural trade-offs as well as the best practices for high availability as well as disaster recovery.

     o   Practice responding to design challenges by using tools like Miro or Lucidchart to create detailed architecture diagrams.

     o   Emphasize the specific reasoning for all your design decisions so that it really shows your knowledge of the technical and business considerations.

Each type of interview will play a significant role in evaluating your readiness for the solutions architect role. Behavioural interviews check your leadership and interpersonal skills, technical interviews measure your problem-solving and technical acumen, and design challenges test whether you have what it takes to architect efficient and cost-effective solutions. With an understanding of each type of interview and its purposes as well as focus areas, you will prepare yourself accordingly to excel in every aspect of the hiring process.

Understanding the types of interviews is a good starting point, but acing these often comes down to how well you can solve tricky technical problems. Now let us walk through some practical strategies for solving such problems and how you should approach solving these issues so that you can present your problem-solving skills at a technical or design challenge interview with confidence.

Handling technical challenges during interview

The solutions architect interview may include answering some of the most complex technical problems ever, that, besides testing your technical knowledge, even test critical thinking, effective communication, and the ability to adapt to fast-changing situations. This section provides practical guidelines on how to answer such questions.

Problem-solving approach

A structured approach is of the essence; it should not deter from coming up with creativity when the problem needs solutions which are novel. Interviewers are interested in how you think and analyze, and how you articulate the process, rather than whether you finally arrive at the correct solution. *Figure 18.2* will help you understand the approach better:

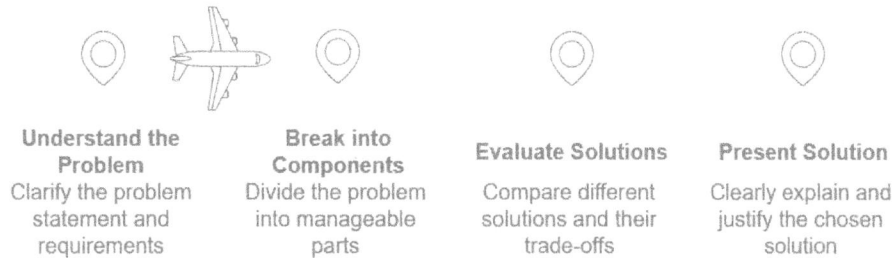

Understand the Problem	Break into Components	Evaluate Solutions	Present Solution
Clarify the problem statement and requirements	Divide the problem into manageable parts	Compare different solutions and their trade-offs	Clearly explain and justify the chosen solution

Figure 18.2: Problem-solving approach

Refer to the following steps:

1. **Understand the problem**: Listen to the problem statement. Be sure that you understand the scope and requirements. Misunderstand the problem, and you are sure to get the wrong answer so take time to clearly define the problem.

   The key actions are as follows:

   - Ask about the expected outcome, constraints, and priorities (e.g., performance versus cost).
   - Confirm your understanding by paraphrasing the problem to the interviewer.
   - **Example**:

     Interviewer: *Can you develop a real-time data processing system?*

     Candidate: *Confirm the understanding, like, are we dealing with streams of data coming from sensors, and should our system be low-latency or cost-effective?*

2. **Break the problem into parts**: Big problems appear daunting when taken as one big problem. Divide the large problem into smaller, more understandable pieces. Working on each piece contributes to a whole solution.

   The key actions are as follows:

   - Identify the core components of the system, such as data ingestion, storage, processing, and output.
   - Solve the problem for individual components separately before interlinking them into a more comprehensive system.
   - **Example**: For a real-time analytics platform, you may break down the problem into:
     - Data ingestion from multiple sources.
     - Stream processing for real-time analytics.
     - Data storage for historical analysis.

3. **Evaluating multiple solutions and their trade-offs**: Rarely is there a single correct solution in architecture. Interviewers expect you to discuss multiple approaches, weigh their trade-offs, and select one that best meets the needs in the context of the problem at hand.

The key actions are as follows:

- Present two or more possible solutions with some pros and cons.
- Highlight trade-offs concerning performance, cost, scalability, and complexity.
- **Example**:
  - o **Option 1**: Use Apache Kafka for stream processing as it can be very high throughput but requires expertise to manage.
  - o **Option 2**: Use AWS Kinesis as it is easier to manage but could possibly be costlier at scale.

4. **Present your solution clearly and justify your choices**: After choosing your solution, present it in a logical and well-coherent structure. Explain at length how the chosen solution solves the problem and explain the reasons behind your choices given the requirements and constraints.

The key actions are as follows:

- Use a logical flow to tell your solution, which covers each component and its role.
- Justify your decisions with data or experience, such as why you chose one technology over another.
- **Example**: *Our system uses Apache Kafka for its scalability and low-latency capabilities. While it introduces some operational overhead, its benefits in handling high throughput align with the system's real-time processing requirement.*

Real-time scenarios

Adaptability is a core skill for solutions architects, especially in dynamic environments where requirements frequently shift. This tests your ability to adapt and prioritize under pressure.

The details are as follows:

- **Strategy**: Stay adaptable and focus on delivering incremental improvements to your solution. Be prepared to iterate based on new information or feedback from the interviewer.
- **Handling changing requirements**:
  - o **Prioritize key requirements**: Identify which aspects of the problem are critical and must be addressed first.
  - o **Refine your solution**: In case of new constraints or requirements coming in during the discussion, redesign your solution.
  - o **Convey your thought process**: Explain how you are refining your solution and why changes are being made.
  - o **Example**:

    Interviewer: *Suppose the system needs to suddenly process a shock load of data.*

    Candidate: *Under this new constraint, I would add auto-scaling and adjust the data partitioning approach to maintain the required performance.*

Whiteboard techniques

Whiteboarding is pivotal in technical interviews, especially with design challenges. Always engage your interviewer by encouraging questions or even feedback as you present; thus, making the session interactive and collaborative.

The details are as follows:

- **Importance of visuals**: Diagrams help interviewers understand your choice of design at a glance. They also provide you with an opportunity to highlight the main components, data flows, and interactions within your system.

- **Effective use of whiteboard**:

  o **Start with a high-level overview**: Begin by sketching the overall architecture, showing the major components and how they interact.

  o **Label components clearly**: Clearly label each part of your system (e.g., databases, APIs, load balancers) to avoid confusion.

  o **Highlight data flows**: Use arrows to indicate the flow of data between components. This helps interviewers visualize how your system processes information.

  o **Iterate as needed**: As the conversation unfolds, update your diagram to reflect changes or new ideas.

  o **Example**:

  For a cloud-based e-commerce platform, your diagram may contain:

  ▪ Frontend systems (user interface).

  ▪ Backend services (product catalog, order processing).

  ▪ Databases (user data, inventory).

  ▪ External integrations (payment gateway, delivery services).

  ▪ Lines connecting these components illustrate how data progresses from user input to order fulfillment.

- **Best practices of whiteboarding**:

  o Use color-coding or use different shapes to distinguish compute, storage, and networking parts.

  o Keep it clean and organized; do not overcrowd the board with too much information that is not crucial.

  o You can also tell the story of your diagram as you draw it and describe the different components' purpose and role.

Any interview that involves complex technical issues requires structured thinking, the flexibility of mind, and a good ability to communicate. Provided that one can comprehend the problem, divide it into reasonable portions, evaluate relevant trade-offs, and express it persuasively, then they will be able to show experience and problem-solving skills. The addition of real-time adjustments plus the use of visual aids such as whiteboarding only increases the candidate's ability to speak about ideas and to be effective in the interview process.

While problem-solving showcases your technical capabilities, your portfolio needs to portray your experience and impact just as well. So, let us discuss how to write and tailor a great portfolio for your interviews.

Presentation of your portfolio

Use your portfolio to tell a compelling story of your technical journey, including challenges you faced, solutions you implemented, and the business value that you delivered. Your presentation of a portfolio allows you to stand out as a candidate who will translate complex technical concepts into actionable business solutions.

Building a strong portfolio

A good portfolio demonstrates your skills in designing and implementing solutions. It should display technical feats, but with the business objective in mind. Let us learn to make a portfolio that leaves an indelible mark. A good portfolio contains:

- **Summary of projects along with architecture diagrams**:
    - o Briefly explain each project's objective, along with a high-level architecture diagram. This will help interviewers get the scope and complexity of the work at hand from the word go.
    - o For instance, when you worked on multi-region deployment, include diagrams about how different regions interact, emphasizing redundancy and load balancing.

- **Quantifiable outcomes**:
    - o Include, wherever possible, metrics that highlight the results of solutions. This includes instances like scaling the system by 30% or reducing page load times by 50%. Quantifiable outcomes show your ability to produce tangible value.
    - o Use before-and-after comparisons to highlight the best performance improvements as well as cost savings achieved because of your solutions.

- **Technical challenges and solutions**:
    - o Every project runs into obstacles. Describing these problems and how you tackled them showcases your problem-solving abilities and grit.
    - o For example, when you encountered a bottleneck in processing data, discuss how you identified the problem, proposed a solution, for example, asynchronous processing, to validate its effectiveness.

- **Business value and alignment**:
    - o Discuss how your technical solutions were aligned with and supported business objectives.
    - o For example, discuss how optimizing system performance contributed to increased user engagement or how automating deployment pipelines reduced time-to-market for new features.

Tailoring the portfolio for interviews

A generic portfolio will not resonate with every interviewer. To make a lasting impression, customize your portfolio for each interview, aligning it with the company's goals, industry, and the specific role you are applying for.

Steps to tailor your portfolio are as follows:

- **Research the company and role**:
    - o Understand the company's mission, industry, and tech stack. Study the job description to identify what key competencies they are looking for.
    - o For cloud-heavy roles, focus on projects involving cloud-native architectures, serverless computing, or containerization.

- **Highlight relevant projects**:
    - o Pick projects that demonstrate your expertise in areas that are critical to the company.
    - o For instance, if scalability is a priority for the company, point out a project where you employed auto-scaling or optimized it for high traffic.

- **Speak their language**:
  - o Use terms and concepts from the company's space. So, for example, if interviewing at a fintech company, highlight your experience in handling securely and compliance frameworks such as PCI DSS.

- **Highlight soft skills**:
  - o If the job requires leadership or a stakeholder-facing role, include instances of how you enabled cross-functional collaboration or how you presented solutions to non-technical stakeholders.

Tools and best practices

Using professional tools and best practices can improve the quality of your portfolio, making it more impactful and accessible.

Recommended tools for creating visuals are as follows:

- **Lucidchart**: Ideal for creating detailed architecture diagrams. It is a cloud-based platform with real-time collaboration and an easy share feature.

- **Miro**: Excellent for brainstorming and presenting user flows or system interactions using the intuitive whiteboard interface.

- **Microsoft Visio**: Designed for professional grade diagrams; useful for organizations with a deep interest in the Microsoft stack.

Showcasing your work using version control:

- Use repositories such as GitHub or GitLab to store and publicly display your code and project documentation.

- Have a specific repository for every project, including:
  - o Architecture diagrams
  - o Code snippets that illustrate the most important functionalities
  - o README files explaining the project goals, tools used, and results

Best practices for a portfolio display are as follows:

- **Organization**: Organize your portfolio well, with an easy-to-follow structure from which interviewers can glance through at ease. Use sections for projects and include an index or table of contents.

- **Interactivity and engagement**: Make your portfolio interactive if possible. For example, link to live demos or hosted applications to demonstrate your solutions in action.

- **Consistency and branding**: Keep your portfolio looking consistent and uniform within a design and format. This will mean keeping a few colour schemes, fonts, and layouts. A professional look attests to your focus on details.

- **Accessibility**: Make sure to make your portfolio available in both digital and hard copy formats if appropriate. The digital versions should be in widely accessible formats (for example, PDF) and easy to share during virtual interviews.

A great portfolio does more than just show your technical skills; it tells a compelling story of your journey as a solutions architect. It is in well-curated portfolios, tailored to every interview, and supported by professional tools that you will be able to present your skills and achievements comprehensively and effectively. Besides the enhanced performance during the interview, this makes you stand out as a candidate with both technical expertise and strategic business value.

You will stand out in your proposal based on strong problem-solving skills, and a well-prepared portfolio in front of the interview panel. Let us summarize the takeaways from this chapter to reinforce your preparation strategy as we reach the end.

Conclusion

Excelling at interviews is not a one-off but a continuous journey of learning and growth. You are seen to be able to approach problems holistically, set business goals for technical solutions, and communicate effectively with diverse stakeholders. This chapter has given you the tools to knock an interview out of the park at behavioral, technical, and design challenges by emphasizing some of the key skills, such as problem-solving, adaptability, and strategic thinking.

Interview success hinges on both the ability to solve complex technical problems and on how well to present experiences and thought processes. Whether it is through structured responses, dynamic whiteboard presentations, or a well-crafted portfolio, it is essential to present unique value to the candidate.

Remember that this is a mutual process in an interview. While it assesses your fit for the role, it also gives you an opportunity to assess whether the organization aligns well with your career aspirations. Every interview, successful or not, provides learning moments that can help fine-tune skills and build on performance.

To maximize your chances of success, strategic preparation is crucial. The next chapter introduces a structured 30-day interview preparation plan, designed to help you build technical depth, strengthen your problem-solving approach, and sharpen your communication skills. By following this guided plan, you will gain the confidence and readiness to excel in even the most demanding solutions architect interviews.

Key takeaways

The takeaways are as follows:

- **Understand the types of interviews**: Master the behavioral, technical and design challenge interviews, their purpose and focus areas. Highlight relevant skills to fit each of the types.

- **Problem solving skills**: Be equipped with structured methodologies to crack technical problems, breaking a complex problem into manageable component parts and evaluating multiple solutions. Ready yourself to adapt to real time changes in an interview.

- **Portfolio presentation**: Construct a comprehensive portfolio along with detailed summaries of projects and quantifiable outcomes. Tailor it for every interview by aligning it with the specific needs and focus areas of the company.

- **Use visual communication**: Whiteboard visually to present system designs and solutions clearly. The whiteboard is effectively helpful for the interviewer to get a quick understanding of the most complex ideas. The presentation also is more interesting and captivating.

- **Showcase business acumen and soft skills**: Discuss how your technical solution has propelled a business to success. Share experiences related to leadership, team management, and stakeholder interactions.

- **Continuous improvement**: Treat each interview as an opportunity to learn. Reflect on your performance, solicit feedback, and iterate in your preparation strategy to help improve your skills and confidence.

Model interview questions and answers

These sample questions and answers show how to prepare for behavioural, technical, and design challenge interviews. By tuning the answers using the STAR framework and presenting clear, structured answers, you will be in good standing when trying to address even the most challenging interview situations.

Behavioral questions

1. **Tell me about a time when you had to guide a team in a process of massive change.**

   Model answer:

   - **Situation**: Migrate from a monolithic architecture to microservices.
   - **Task**: Adapt the new architecture in such a way that the system will be stable.
   - **Action**: Held workshops, hands-on training, and meetings with regular check-ins.
   - **Result**: The migration was completed two weeks ahead of schedule and with a 20% improvement in system performance.

2. **Can you give me an example when you had to make a difficult decision with not enough information to support it?**

   Model answer:

   - **Situation**: Your database went into failure at the high traffic event.
   - **Task**: Given the time constraint, it was either to scale up or to optimize queries.
   - **Action**: Scaled up temporarily and analyzed later.
   - **Result**: Downtime was avoided, and later the queries were optimized to deal with similar loads.

3. **Tell me about a time when you improved a process in your team.**

   Model answer:

   - **Situation**: In your Agile cycles, the time for deployment caused a delay.
   - **Action**: Implemented CI/CD pipelines using Jenkins and automated testing.
   - **Task**: Reduce deployment time to meet sprint goals.
   - **Result**: Reduced deployment time by 40% thus improving delivery speed.

4. **Tell me about a project where you had to juggle priorities.**

   Model answer:

   - **Situation**: Marketing wanted features urgently while QA needed thorough testing.
   - **Task**: Balance between speed and quality
   - **Action**: Implemented feature flagging for gradual rollouts and parallel testing.
   - **Result**: Some critical features were implemented without losing quality. Satisfied both teams.

5. **Tell me about a time you had to navigate stakeholder resistance.**

   Model answer:

   - **Situation**: Stakeholders resist shifting from an on-premise solution to the cloud.
   - **Task**: Bring them on board while addressing all their apprehensions.
   - **Action**: Developed a detailed cost-benefit analysis and did a Pilot.
   - **Outcome**: Achieved acceptance of the stakeholders as it reduced the operational cost by 25%.

Technical questions

6. **How would you design a system to handle real-time stock trading?**

   Model answer:
   - **Architecture**: Implement event-driven architecture with Apache Kafka for message streaming.
   - **Scalability**: Use Kubernetes for container orchestration and horizontal scaling.
   - **Reliability**: Include multi-region deployments for fault tolerance.

7. **How would you secure an API used by a mobile banking app?**

   Model answer:
   - **Security measures**: Implement OAuth 2.0 authentication, enforce HTTPS, and include rate limiting.
   - **Data encryption**: Encrypt sensitive data with the help of TLS and AES-256.
   - **Monitoring**: Configure logging and monitoring to detect threats in real-time and respond to them.

8. **How would you optimize a database for a high-read, low-write workload?**

   Model answer:
   - **Optimization**: Use indexing and caching layers like Redis.
   - **Partitioning**: Do horizontal partitioning for large tables.
   - **Read performance**: Use read replicas to distribute the load.

9. **Describe how you would implement a disaster recovery plan for a SaaS application.**

   Model answer:
   - **Backups**: Schedule automated backups and store them in multiple regions.
   - **Failover**: Use active-passive failover with load balancers.
   - **Testing**: Conduct regular disaster recovery drills to ensure readiness.

10. **How would you ensure data consistency in a distributed system?**

    Model answer:
    - **Approach**: Use consensus algorithms like Paxos or Raft.
    - **Techniques**: Implement eventual consistency using tools like Apache Cassandra.
    - **Monitoring**: Set up alerts for data synchronization issues.

Design challenge questions

11. **Design a recommendation system for an e-commerce platform.**

    Model answer:

    Key considerations:
    - **Personalization**: Use collaborative filtering or content-based filtering.
    - **Data processing**: Use Apache Spark for batch processing and real-time recommendations.
    - **Scalability**: Cloud-native services like AWS SageMaker can be used for ML model deployment.

12. **How would you design a multi-tenant SaaS application?**

    Model answer:

    Key considerations:

    - **Isolation**: Make use of a separate database schema per tenant.
    - **Customizability**: Provide tenants the scope of deciding features by using a centralized settings service.
    - **Security**: Implement tenant-specific encryption along with **role-based access control (RBAC)**.

13. **Build a system for server failure monitoring and prediction.**

    Model answer:

    Key considerations:

    - **Monitoring**: Use Prometheus and Grafana for real-time monitoring.
    - **Prediction**: Integrate machine learning models for failure prediction using historical data.
    - **Redundancy**: Implement auto-healing with AWS Auto Scaling.

14. **Design a scalable video streaming platform.**

    Model answer:

    Key considerations:

    - **Streaming**: Use a **content delivery network (CDN)** to reduce latency.
    - **Storage**: Use object storage like AWS S3 for video storage.
    - **Scalability**: Implement auto-scaling based on traffic patterns.

15. **How would you design an IoT system for smart home devices?**

    Model answer:

    Key considerations:

    - **Data collection**: Use MQTT for lightweight messaging.
    - **Edge processing**: The utilization of edge computing to keep response times close to zero.
    - **Cloud integration**: Leverage the cloud platforms, like Azure IoT Hub, to manage all devices centrally.

Join our Discord space

Join our Discord workspace for latest updates, offers, tech happenings around the world, new releases, and sessions with the authors:

https://discord.bpbonline.com

CHAPTER 19

The 30-day Interview Preparation Plan

Introduction

In the competitive landscape of technology, preparing for a solutions architect interview is not just about technical acumen; it is about demonstrating a comprehensive understanding of how to design, implement, and oversee scalable, efficient, and business-aligned systems. The role of a solutions architect demands a balance between high-level strategic thinking and practical execution, with a strong focus on aligning technology solutions to business objectives.

This chapter is designed to guide you through a structured 30-day interview preparation journey. Unlike traditional study plans, this approach emphasizes both depth and breadth, covering critical technical domains, real-world problem-solving, and the soft skills necessary to navigate complex stakeholder environments.

This plan combines checklists, practical exercises, and mock scenarios to ensure your preparation is both structured and aligned with industry best practices. From mastering architectural principles and cloud-native patterns to refining your ability to communicate complex ideas clearly, this chapter equips you to excel in every aspect of the solutions architect interview process.

Whether you are starting fresh or refining your expertise, this plan offers a roadmap to becoming a well-rounded solutions architect prepared for high-stakes challenges.

Structure

This chapter covers the following topics:

- 30-day solutions architect interview prep plan
- Maximizing the 30-day plan

Objectives

By the end of this chapter, readers will have a comprehensive understanding of the systematic approach required to prepare for a solutions architect interview. They will be equipped with the tools and techniques to align technical solutions with business objectives, ensuring value delivery and stakeholder consensus.

Readers will gain practical knowledge of core architectural principles, including scalability, performance, and security. They will master cloud-native design patterns and learn how to evaluate and implement technology stacks effectively. The chapter will also provide insights into building and optimizing CI/CD pipelines, utilizing **infrastructure as code (IaC)** for automated deployments, and designing systems for high availability and disaster recovery.

Moreover, readers will explore critical soft skills such as effective communication and stakeholder management, learning how to present complex technical solutions in a clear and compelling manner. Advanced topics, including FinOps for cost management and DevSecOps for integrating security across the development lifecycle, will be covered.

By the end, readers will be well-prepared to tackle real-world architectural challenges, excel in technical and behavioural interview scenarios, and confidently assume the role of a solutions architect in any organization.

30-day solutions architect interview prep plan

This comprehensive plan integrates technical knowledge, strategic thinking, and communication skills, ensuring well-rounded preparation. Each week builds on foundational concepts, progressing toward advanced topics, real-world applications, and mock interviews.

Figure 19.1 provides a visual roadmap of the 30-day solutions architect interview preparation plan, outlining key focus areas for each week to ensure comprehensive readiness:

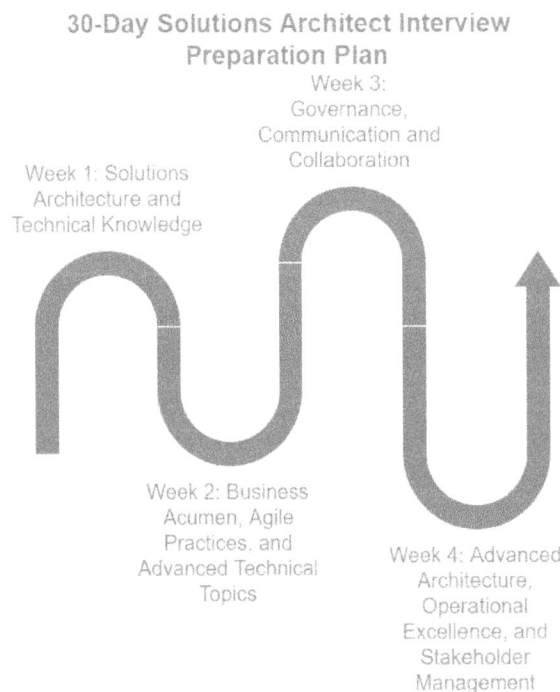

Figure 19.1: 30 days solutions architect interview preparation plan

Week 1: Solutions architecture and technical knowledge

The focus of *Week 1* is to understand the fundamental role of a solutions architect, emphasizing business alignment, stakeholder management, and requirement analysis. The following table highlights the details about the same:

Day	Topics to learn	Chapter reference
One	• **30-day interview preparation plan**: Create a tracker for the next four-five weeks with sections like goals for the day, resources to use, progress status, roadblocks and questions • Solution architecture and its key principles • Need for a solution architecture • Relationship between business architecture, goals and solution architecture • Assessment of a solution architecture (build worthiness) • Attributes of solution architectures	19 1
Two	• Understanding checklists and their advantages • Using a checklist for business stakeholder management and communication • Make notes on how stakeholder communication is managed within your project in conjunction with the checklist • Using a checklist for requirements management • Relate the requirements management checklist to your current project • Using the project development checklist • Mapping different roles and activities within the project to the checkpoints in the checklist	2
Three	• Make notes on different nonfunctional requirements in your project • Understand the DevOps checklist • Learn how to use the performance and security checklist • Use the availability, reliability and usability checklist • Make notes on how performance, security and availability are ensured within your application • Make notes on how certain problems in your project could be solved with automation	2
Four	• Architectural styles versus architectural patterns • DDD • Take a sample e-commerce domain and apply DDD to it • Understand API first design and AI first design • **Gang of Four** (**GoF**) design patterns that are creational, structural and behavioral • Relate GoF patterns to problems in your project • Enterprise application design patterns • Analyze how many enterprise application patterns are used in your project • Design principles; SOLID and 12 factor app	3
Five	• Cloud computing essential knowledge • Database management essential knowledge • Networking essential knowledge • Generative AI, blockchain and quantum computing basics • Make a chart on the different popular GenAI models available • Identify uses cases in your project where GenAI can be applied	3

Day	Topics to learn	Chapter reference

Six	• Drivers of a solution architecture
	• Solution architecture patterns
	   o Pipes and filters
	   o Hexagonal architecture
	   o Monolith
	   o Layered architecture
	   o Service oriented architecture
		4

Seven	• Solution architecture patterns
	   o Event-driven architecture
	   o Microservices architecture
	   o Serverless architecture
	• API design
	   o REST
	   o SOAP
	   o gRPC
	   o GraphQL
		4

Table 19.1: Week 1 overview

Key highlights for week 1

The key highlights are as follows:

- **Fundamental concepts**: Gain a solid understanding of the role and principles of solutions architecture, including stakeholder management, requirement analysis, and architectural assessment.

- **Hands-on exercises**: Analyse real-world projects to identify non-functional requirements, apply DDD, and explore design patterns to solve complex architectural challenges.

- **Practical tools**: Leverage checklists for stakeholder communication, requirements management, and project development. Utilize tools like Lucidchart for diagramming and documentation aids to visualize architectural concepts effectively.

This structured plan sets a strong foundation in essential skills for solutions architects, providing the technical and analytical base necessary for advanced topics and interview preparation.

Week 2: Business, Agile, and technical topics

This week focuses on aligning technical solutions with business goals, mastering Agile methodologies, and delving into advanced concepts like legacy modernization, DevOps practices, performance optimization, and data management. These topics are essential for developing a holistic approach to solutions architecture and excelling in interviews. The following table gives more details:

Day	Topics to learn	Chapter reference

Eight	• Translating business requirements into technical solutions
	• Techniques for requirements gathering (workshops, interviews, business process modelling)
	• Cost management and project budgeting
	   o Cost vs. benefit analysis
	   o Cloud cost optimization
	   o Tracking and managing budgets
	   o Forecasting future costs
	• Project management essentials
	   o Agile vs. Waterfall
	   o Managing risks and technical dependencies
	• Integration solutions during mergers and acquisitions
	   o Assessing technical landscape
	   o Identify redundancies, gaps
	   o Prioritizing integration efforts
	   o Data and system integration strategies
	   o Best practices of M&A
	• Relate these practices to your current or previous projects and identify improvement areas
		5

Nine	• Overview of Agile methodologies
	• Core Agile principles
	• Key Agile frameworks
	   o Scrum: Know all ceremonies, roles, deliverables
	   o Kanban
	   o XP
	   o SAFe
	• Role of solutions architects in Agile teams
	• Architectural spikes
	• Aligning architecture with Agile development cycles
	   o Modular and incremental design
	   o Continuous refactoring and technical debt management
	• Automation in Agile
	• Tools for Agile management
	   o Jira
	   o Confluence
	• Best practices
		6

Day	Topics to learn	Chapter reference
Ten	**Legacy modernization, part 1** • Role of solutions architect in legacy modernization • Challenges in modernization • Drivers for modernization • Legacy modernization strategies o Rehost o Replatform o Rearchitect o Refactor o Rebuild o Replace • Best practices for modernization	7
Eleven	**Legacy modernization, part 2** • Legacy modernization on cloud • Mainframe modernization • AI in legacy modernization • Roadmap to legacy modernization • Checklist for legacy modernization	7
Twelve	• DevOps essentials o Culture and practices • Platform engineering • IaC with DevOps o Tools comparison o IaC in CI/CD • Continuous integration and continuous deployment o End-to-end CI/CD stages o Tools used in CI/CD o GitOps • **Hands-on exercise**: Build an end-to-end CI/CD pipeline using any of the tools like Jenkins and Azure DevOps for any technology stack like Java and .NET • Monitoring and logging strategies • Explore different tools available in the industry and various metrics to be monitored, especially for cloud-native and container-based applications. • Understand AIOps and its necessity • Understand FinOps and its necessity • DevSecOps, security in DevOps • Explore different DevSecOps tools (SAST/DAST) • QA in DevOps	8

Day	Topics to learn	Chapter reference
Thirteen	**Performance and scalability, part 1** • Performance strategies for solutions architect • Types of application performance testing • Application performance monitoring • Key performance metrics	9
Fourteen	**Performance and scalability, part 2** • Types of scaling • Application scalability strategies for solutions architect • Performance and scalability on the cloud • AI in performance and scalability	9
	Synthesis of advanced topics • Revisit the DevOps tools, legacy modernization techniques, Agile frameworks	6, 7, 8

Table 19.2: Week 2 overview

Key highlights for week 2

The key highlights are as follows:

- **Advanced concepts**: Focus on implementing business acumen, Agile and DevOps methodologies, and advanced technical practices in architecture for performance, scalability.

- **Practical tools**: Explore tools like Jira for Agile workflows, Terraform for IaC, and other DevOps tools for CI/CD, monitoring.

This structured plan ensures you build a strong foundation in essential skills for solutions architects, while progressively preparing for interview questions and real-world challenges.

Week 3: Governance, communication, collaboration

In week 3, the focus shifts to data management, user experience and essential soft skills, governance and compliance, and business continuity considerations. Solutions architects must excel in stakeholder communication, team leadership, and ensuring that their designs cater to user needs. This week builds on technical knowledge by integrating human-centric and operational perspectives. The following table explains the same in more detail:

Day	Topics to learn	Chapter reference

Fifteen	**Data management and analytics, part 1**
	• Data architecture design
	• Types of data architectures: comparison study
	• Data architecture principles
	• Data storage and modeling techniques
	   o Relational vs. non-relational storage
	   o Structural vs. semi-structured vs unstructured
	   o Design data models
	   o Data modeling for performance optimization
	Data security and compliance
		10

Day	Topics to learn	Chapter reference

	Data management and analytics, part 2
	• Data storage and architecture patterns
	• Tools for data architecture design
	• Data integration and management
	    ○ Tools
	    ○ Best practices
	• BigData solutions
	• Analytics for business insights
	• **Hands-on exercise**: Explore different data solution tools especially serverless data storage like BigQuery of GCP or other equivalent services in other hyperscaler and analytics dashboard like Looker or Tableau.
		10

Sixteen	• Understanding the role of UX in solutions architecture • Human centric design in architecture • Design thinking in solutions architecture • Designing for accessibility and usability • Best practices in solutions architecture for UX • Future trends in UX	11
Seventeen	• Importance of BCP and DR in solutions architecture • Important concepts: RTO, RPO, DRP, BCP • Difference between BCP and DR • DR planning for solutions architect • IaC for DR • Implementing effective backup solutions • Types of backup strategies • DR architecture and failover strategies • BCP for high availability	12
Eighteen	• Governance and compliance in solutions architecture • Understanding governance frameworks • Centralized vs decentralized governance • Continuous monitoring and auditing tools for governance • Different compliance standards to be aware of • How to design for compliance • Risk management in governance and compliance • Governance and compliance in cloud	13
Nineteen	• Types of stakeholders and how to communicate effectively with tailored approach • Conflict management and active listening techniques • Explore different tools for communication and collaboration • Difference types of documentation which is essential for solutions architect: HLD, LLD, Decision logs, requirements • Know the key elements in each of the documents especially in HLD • Presentation and storytelling techniques	14

Day	Topics to learn	Chapter reference
Twenty	• Analytical thinking in architecture • Real-world problem-solving scenarios • Innovation in solutions architecture • Risk management strategies	15
Twenty-one	• Revisit the key items like HLD elements for documentation, DR and BCP strategies, governance and compliance standards and frameworks, data management architectures, UX; design thinking and trends.	10, 11, 12, 13, 14, 15

Table 19.3: Week 3 overview

Key highlights for week 3

The key highlights are as follows:

- **Soft skills mastery**: Develop advanced communication and team leadership capabilities to engage diverse stakeholders and foster collaboration. Learn to create effective, visually enriched documentation that bridges technical and non-technical audiences.

- **Data management**: Develop the skill in data management and advanced analytics skills for data modelling for different storage.

- **UX and business continuity**: Emphasize user-centric design principles and resilience planning to ensure systems are accessible, usable, and robust against disruptions.

This structured plan ensures you build a balance of technical, human-centric, and operational skills crucial for a well-rounded solutions architect profile.

Week 4: Advanced architecture and management

Week 4 integrates advanced architectural practices, operational excellence principles, and stakeholder and vendor management strategies. This week sharpens your ability to deliver enterprise-grade solutions that balance technical sophistication with effective collaboration and management. The following table gives more details:

Day	Topics to learn	Chapter reference
Twenty-two	• Operational excellence: Principles, best practices, metrics • Designing for scalability and resilience • Designing for maintainability and efficiency • Modular architecture and clean coding practices • Role of SRE • Operational excellence in modern architecture	21
Twenty-three	**Cloud-native architecture, part 1** • Considerations for cloud-native architecture • Containerization and orchestration • Principles of cloud-native architecture • Cloud-native reference architecture	22

Day	Topics to learn	Chapter reference
Twenty-four	**Cloud-native architecture, part 2** • Migrating from non-cloud to cloud-native architecture • Design patterns • Security in cloud-native architecture	22
Twenty-five	**Stakeholder and vendor management** • Managing vendor relationships • Selecting and managing third-party vendors • Vendor negotiation and integration • Stakeholder management techniques	16
Twenty-six	**Production support processes, part 1** • Role of solutions architect in production support • Production support scope, that is, platform, application, operational • Production support lifecycle • Types of production support • Levels in production support: L0, L1, L2, L3	23
Twenty-seven	**Production support processes, part 2** • Production support framework • Production support metrics • Production support in Agile environment • AI and ML in production support • KPI in production support • Production support checklist	23
Twenty-Eight	**Synthesis of advanced topics** Reference architecture of cloud-native application in cloud, metrics and KPIs of production support, design patterns	21, 22, 23, 16

Table 19.4: Week 4 overview

Key highlights for week 4

The key highlights are as follows:

- **Operational excellence**: Gain expertise in building and maintaining scalable, resilient, and efficient systems.

- **Cloud-native design**: Master advanced patterns like microservices, serverless, and service mesh, along with their real-world implementations.

- **Vendor and stakeholder management**: Learn strategies to align stakeholder objectives, negotiate effectively with vendors, and ensure successful collaborations.

- **Production readiness**: Develop skills to monitor, troubleshoot, and stabilize live systems proactively.

This week prepares you to manage complex enterprise architectures while fostering stakeholder and vendor alignment, ensuring project success and long-term system reliability.

Week 5: Final touches and long-term success

The final week focuses on refining your interview readiness while preparing for long-term success in your solutions architect journey. This includes honing interview strategies, understanding industry expectations, and planning for continuous learning and improvement. Chapters on expert insights, common pitfalls, and professional growth are covered alongside a wrap-up of key takeaways and resources for ongoing development. The following table gives more details:

Focus areas	Key items to learn	Chapter reference
Twenty-nine	**Continuous learning and professional development** • Importance of continuous learning for solutions architects • Explore the available Certifications in cloud and architecture like AWS, Azure, GCP, TOGAF, and DevOps • Staying updated with industry trends in AI, cloud, and microservices • Importance of building a professional network and knowledge-sharing practices **Preparing for solutions architect interviews** • Types of interviews: Behavioral, technical, and design challenges • Structuring answers using frameworks like STAR for behavioral questions • Mock exercises for design scenarios and technical problem-solving	17, 18
Thirty	**Expert insights and common pitfalls** • Key traits and qualities industry leaders look for in top candidates • Common mistakes during interviews and practical strategies to avoid them **Resources and tools for future reference** • Glossaries, templates, and checklists for quick reference	20, 25, 24

Table 19.5: Week 5 overview

Key highlights for week 5

The key highlights are as follows:

- **Interview mastery**: Strengthen strategies for behavioural, technical, and scenario-based interviews.

- **Insights and avoiding pitfalls**: Gain practical advice from industry leaders and understand common mistakes to avoid.

- **Career planning**: Learn how to sustain professional growth, build networks, and stay ahead in the evolving field of solutions architecture.

- **Final wrap-up**: Consolidate key takeaways and resources from the book for future reference.

This structured plan for week 5 ensures you are thoroughly prepared for interviews while laying the foundation for ongoing success in your career. By focusing on the essentials, this week consolidates your preparation and equips you with the tools to excel both in interviews and in practice.

Maximizing the 30-day plan

To ensure you get the most out of this 30-day preparation journey, follow these strategies to tailor the plan, integrate feedback, and refine your approach:

- **Tailor the plan to your needs**: This plan provides a comprehensive framework, but individualize it to focus on areas where you need improvement.
  - **Identify weak areas**: Prioritize topics where your confidence is low, such as security, Domain-Driven Design, or DevSecOps.
    - **Action**: Spend extra days on these topics or split the sessions for a deeper dive.
  - **Adjust the schedule**: If the target role emphasizes specific areas like cloud-native architecture or cost optimization, allocate more time to those.
- **Leverage feedback**: Feedback is crucial for identifying gaps in your understanding and approach.
  - **Mock interviews**: Conduct mock interviews with peers, mentors, or use platforms like Pramp, Interviewing.io.
    - **Action**: Simulate both technical and behavioural interview scenarios.
  - **Join online communities**: Engage with groups on LinkedIn, Reddit, or Slack for insights and constructive feedback.
- **Integrate real-world experience**: Bring your past project experiences into the preparation.
  - **Reflect on past projects**: Analyse your previous work to identify how you have applied architectural principles.
    - **Action**: Use these reflections to build narratives for behavioural interview questions.
  - **Case studies**: Include industry-specific case studies in your preparation to demonstrate domain expertise.
- **Stay updated with industry trends**: An effective SA stays ahead by keeping up with the latest in technology.
  - **Follow blogs and webinars**: Stay informed about updates in AWS, Azure, Google Cloud, DevOps tools, and emerging technologies like AIOps and GenAI.
    - **Action**: Dedicate 10-15 minutes daily for industry updates.
- **Practice communication and presentation**: A solutions architect must excel in articulating complex ideas to varied audiences.
  - **Visual aids**: Use tools like PowerPoint, Miro, or Lucidchart to create architecture diagrams.
    - **Action**: Practice explaining these diagrams to non-technical stakeholders.
  - **Storytelling techniques**: Master storytelling to make your solutions relatable and engaging.
- **Build a personal knowledge repository**: Creating a structured repository ensures quick access to vital information during interviews.
  - **Notes and templates**: Document key learnings, checklists, and templates.
    - **Action**: Maintain a repository in tools like Notion, OneNote, or simple folders.
  - **Cheat sheets**: Prepare cheat sheets for quick revision of key concepts and frameworks.

Recommendations

To further maximize your preparation, consider these additional recommendations:

- **Domain-specific case studies**: Study case studies relevant to your industry, such as healthcare, retail, or finance, to demonstrate practical knowledge.

- **Behavioural interview techniques**: Use the STAR method to answer behavioural questions effectively.

- **Live system design exercises**: Spend time on live whiteboarding exercises using tools like Miro (**https://miro.com/**) to simulate real interview conditions.

Key items to maximize learning

To ensure effective preparation for your solutions architect interview, adopting structured learning strategies can significantly enhance your retention, understanding, and application of knowledge. The following *Table 19.6* outlines key actions that align with effective learning methods, helping you identify gaps, reinforce concepts, and improve performance through continuous practice and feedback. By integrating these strategies into your study plan, you can maximize your preparation efforts and build confidence for your interview journey. The following table explains in more detail:

Action	Purpose	Tools and methods
Daily recaps	Reinforce learning and identify gaps.	Journaling, mind maps.
Mock interviews	Simulate real scenarios and get feedback.	Pramp, Interviewing.io, peer reviews.
Collaborative learning	Gain diverse perspectives and insights.	Study groups, Slack channels.
Hands-on practice	Apply theoretical knowledge to real problems.	AWS, Azure, GCP free tiers, local environments.
Scenario-based exercises	Develop problem-solving and critical thinking.	Case studies, architecture challenges.
Feedback loop	Continuous improvement through input.	Mentor reviews, community forums.

Table 19.6: Key items to maximise learning

Conclusion

This 30-day study plan offers a comprehensive roadmap to prepare for solutions architect interviews. By following this plan and maximizing it through feedback, real-world application, and continuous learning, you can build the confidence and skills required to excel. With consistent effort and a strategic approach, you will be well-equipped to tackle complex interview scenarios and secure your role as a solutions architect. This 30-day plan ensures you are equipped with the technical skills, strategic thinking, and communication techniques required to excel in your solutions architect interview.

As you continue to refine your preparation, the next chapter explores invaluable insights from industry experts, revealing what top architects look for in candidates and the pitfalls to avoid during interviews.

Join our Discord space

Join our Discord workspace for latest updates, offers, tech happenings around the world, new releases, and sessions with the authors:

https://discord.bpbonline.com

CHAPTER 20

Expert Insights and Common Pitfalls

Introduction

These are transformative times for technology, where the solutions architect's role has become pivotal in driving innovation and aligning technology with business objectives. An architect is expected not only to have solid technical expertise but to align technology strategies with business goals as well, navigate complex systems, and lead teams in crafting scalable, reliable, and secure solutions. Such a balance requires not only profound technical knowledge but also an acute understanding of business needs and the dynamics of stakeholders.

This chapter prepares you for the multifaceted challenges of a solutions architect interview, based on expert answers and common pitfalls that occur. Successful candidates not only score well in technical evaluations but also show the ability to lead, communicate effectively, and make sound decisions under pressure.

You will learn valuable insights, such as what major architects look for in candidates and how to avoid making the most common mistakes during interviews. This chapter draws on real-world advice and strategies to avoid pitfalls that will prepare you with confidence in navigating the interview process. Show your ability to not only demonstrate your technical expertise but also your leadership potential.

Structure

This chapter covers the following topics:

- Insights from industry experts
- Qualities top architects seek in candidates
- Common pitfalls in interviews
- Strategies to avoid common mistakes

Objectives

By the end of this chapter, readers will have a clear understanding of the key lessons and expectations required to excel in solutions architect interviews. They will acquire valuable insights into what industry leaders value most in their candidates, including technical acumen, good strategic fit to the business objectives, and savvy stakeholder management.

Readers will learn how to recognize and avoid common pitfalls in interviews, thus avoiding embarrassment and confusion when representing their skills and experience. Real-life tips by the authors, who are seasoned architects, on the best way to answer tricky technical and behavioural questions will be discussed in the chapter.

The chapter also discusses the importance of demonstrating leadership, communication, and decision-making in an interview. It will prepare readers for techniques in handling high-pressure situations, alignment of technical solutions with business goals, and articulation of thought processes. Readers will be well-equipped by the end of this chapter to navigate through the interview process, avoid the common mistakes that other people make, and shine as top-tier candidates for solutions architect roles.

Insights from industry experts

Learning directly from experienced architects equips candidates with the perspective to anticipate challenges and proactively address them. Expert insights highlight the importance of aligning technical solutions strategically with evolving business goals, ensuring long-term success.

Importance of expert insights

In the rapidly evolving world of technology, to remain relevant as a solutions architect calls for more than technical knowledge; it demands experiential wisdom. Here, insight from an expert becomes invaluable. This could include industry veterans who have encountered a wide range of architectural challenges across different domains that include finance, insurance, health care, and retail.

These challenges require a unique approach, blending strategic foresight with hands-on problem-solving. Besides running evaluations based on current requirements, expert architects predict future requirements to ensure that the systems are scalable, reliable, and adaptable.

Critical highlights for expert mindset

This requires a mindset that goes well beyond solving immediate technical problems. Industry leaders bring to the table a strategic view of their solutions, ensuring current requirements are met but also that expected future challenges are addressed. Top architects are distinguished from others by their proactive and holistic approach.

Here are the essential elements of the expert mindset that aspiring architects need to develop:

- **Risk mitigation**: Good architects proactively identify system failures, security vulnerabilities, and performance bottlenecks in their design. They put into place strategies such as redundancy, failover mechanisms, and security controls so that systems may better withstand and recover from potential disruptions.

- **Future-proofing**: As the technology landscape continues to accelerate, architects have the challenge of designing systems that are inherently future-proof. This includes designing modular and scalable architectures that accommodate growth and seamlessly integrate new tools or services as they emerge.

- **Stakeholder alignment**: A top architect knows that technical decisions should return business value. Aligning technical solutions with the organizational goals of its work ensures that they support broader business objectives, like enhancing customer satisfaction, achieving higher operational efficiency, or generating revenue growth.

These points underscore strategic foresight, flexibility, and business acumen in the solutions architect role.

Key takeaways from top architects

Drawing on five decades of combined experience, we distill the core lessons that set successful solutions architects apart:

- **Building scalable and reliable systems**: Scalable and reliable architecture is placed at the top of the list from day one. While designing a system for a startup or for a global enterprise, the ability to handle increased load without compromising performance is not negotiable.

  Key takeaway: Use modular designs and leverage cloud-native services such as auto-scaling, load balancing, and multi-region deployments to achieve scalability and high availability.

- **Adapting to emerging trends**: Technology evolves rapidly. Top architects stay ahead by adopting trends like DevSecOps, cloud-native architecture, and AIOps. These approaches streamline operations, enhance security, and improve system observability.

  Key takeaway: Commit to continuous learning. Regularly assess how emerging trends can solve current bottlenecks or make the system better.

- **Balance technical depth with business alignment**: A good architect is an interface between technical teams and business leaders. They explain technical concepts in business terms so that stakeholders understand the value that proposed solutions would drive.

  Key takeaway: Understand the business domain deeply so that every technical decision drives business outcome.

Successful architectures examples

Let us look at a few examples.

Retail industry

Let us consider a scalable e-commerce platform. A retail chain was suffering huge losses during sales events due to the heavy traffic on its platform. It used microservices architecture, orchestrating container systems with Kubernetes.

The salient features and success factors are as follows:

- **Salient features**:
  - Auto-scaling ensured that the platform could recover from traffic surges.
  - The ordering process is made much more responsive due to event-driven systems.
  - AI-based recommendation systems seamlessly integrated with the platform, which enhanced the average order value.

- **Success factors**: Scalability, fault tolerance, and non-obstructive user experience promoting business growth.

Healthcare vertical

Let us consider a secure HIPAA Compliance Patient Record Management System. A health services company needed a solution to handle sensitive patient information in compliance with HIPAA regulations. The architectural design was laid on a hybrid cloud model where secure data transfer was ensured, and encryption was integrated for sensitive information.

The salient features and success factors are as follows:

- **Salient features**:
  - Role-based access control ensured data privacy.
  - Disaster recovery mechanisms minimized the downtime during the critical operations.
  - Integration with wearables provided real-time health monitoring.

- **Success factors**: Emphasis on security, compliance, and integration capabilities ensured the protection of patient data while enhancing care delivery.

Financial services

Let us consider a real-time fraud detection system. A financial service organization had the requirement of being able to detect fraudulent transactions in real time. The architecture used a combination of machine learning models along with a low-latency event processing system.

The salient features and success factors are as follows:

- **Salient features**:
  - Stream processing with Apache Kafka enables real-time data ingestion.
  - ML models deployed in production flagged anomalies within milliseconds.
  - Continuous monitoring provided system health insights and minimized false positives.

- **Success factors**: Its ability to detect and prevent fraud in real time protected the institution's reputation and saved millions in potential losses.

These examples highlight the value of technical excellence blended with an in-depth understanding of the business context. Learning from these successes can serve aspiring solutions architects as a blueprint for designing impactful systems.

With these expert insights in mind, let us now examine the specific qualities top architects seek in candidates.

Qualities top architects seek in candidates

Solutions architects are arguably the people who connect business requirements with technical deliverables. The definition of this role is not entirely about technical skills but about strategic thinking, leadership, and problem-solving abilities. This section outlines the core competencies that top architects and hiring managers look for in a candidate during the interview process.

The essential competencies assessed by top architects are technical expertise, strategic thinking, communication skills, leadership, adaptability, and evaluating trade-offs. They are illustrated clearly in *Figure 20.1*:

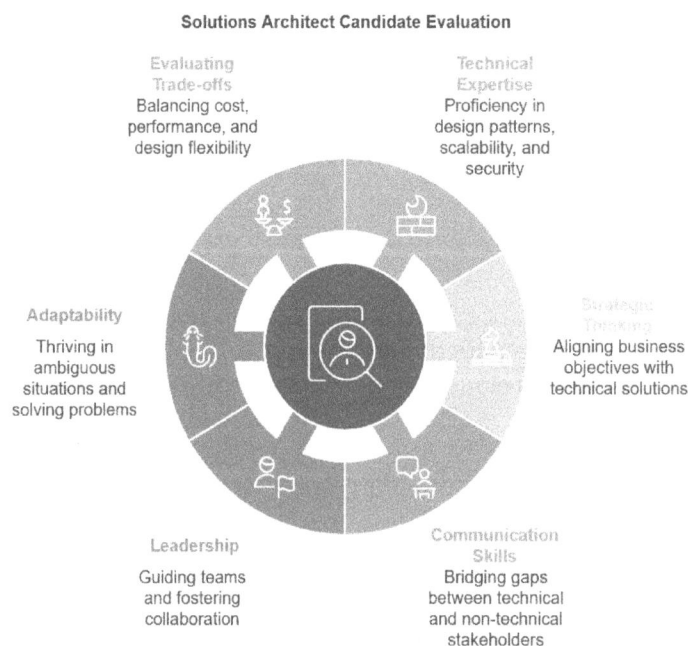

Solutions Architect Candidate Evaluation

- Evaluating Trade-offs: Balancing cost, performance, and design flexibility
- Technical Expertise: Proficiency in design patterns, scalability, and security
- Adaptability: Thriving in ambiguous situations and solving problems
- Strategic Thinking: Aligning business objectives with technical solutions
- Leadership: Guiding teams and fostering collaboration
- Communication Skills: Bridging gaps between technical and non-technical stakeholders

Figure 20.1: Solutions architect candidate evaluation parameters

Core competencies

Successful solutions architects possess a balanced mix of technical expertise, strategic thinking, and strong communication skills. Excelling in these core areas enables candidates to design scalable solutions, align technical decisions with business goals, and effectively manage stakeholder expectations.

Technical expertise

One of the most critical aspects of a solutions architect is their technical proficiency across multiple domains. They are as follows:

- **Design patterns**: Demonstrating familiarity with industry-standard design patterns (e.g., Factory, Singleton, Event Sourcing) and their appropriate application. Skilled architects leverage advanced design paradigms to build robust, scalable solutions that meet both current needs and future demands. New trends, like **Domain-Driven Design (DDD)**, model complex domains closely aligned with business processes. This would help to create clear reusable interfaces as the base for scalable systems, while AI-led design introduces machine learning and AI as core components to architectural strategies. It is about automating decision-making with good predictive capabilities. The technical depth and forward thinking would be very well evidenced through understanding these approaches and their application in the right contexts.

- **Example use cases**:

  o DDD in a retail application can thus ensure that product catalog and inventory modules are aligned with business rules, thereby producing fewer inconsistencies.

  o API-first design guarantees seamless integration with third-party services, such as payment gateways or shipping providers, because the contracts are defined upfront.

  o AI-led design enables the optimization of fraud detection systems in financial services through direct integration of machine learning models in architecture to make real-time predictions.

- **Scalability**: The ability to design a system that scales with business growth and user demand.

- **Security**: Use of best security practices, including authentication, authorization, and data protection.

For instance, a strong candidate should explain not only what a microservices architecture is but also when and why it is preferable to a monolithic architecture, considering scalability and maintainability.

Strategic thinking and decision-making skills

What hiring managers value most about candidates is the ability to think beyond the current technical problem.

A lead solutions architect is also a generalist who can connect the dots between multiple domains, technologies, and methodologies. While depth in specific areas is valuable, the ability to evaluate and compare different technologies, adapt to new trends, and merge diverse systems with each other is equally important. To give examples, understanding the trade-offs between relational databases and NoSQL, or deciding between containerization and serverless computing, can significantly impact the success of a solution.

Top architects consistently look for candidates who demonstrate strategic foresight and the ability to align technical solutions effectively with business goals. Specifically, they seek candidates who exhibit:

- **Business alignment**: Understand business goals and set technical solutions to line up with those goals.

- **Decision-making frameworks**: Leverage structured approaches to architectural decisions, for instance, trade-off analysis or impact assessment.

For example, in a discussion about cloud migration strategy, the candidate should then consider cost, performance, or compliance implication in order to recommend the most appropriate approach.

Effective communication and stakeholder management

As such, a solutions architect must bridge the gap between technical teams and business stakeholders, as is explained in the following list:

- **Clear articulation of technical concepts**: Explaining complex technical solutions in a manner that non-technical stakeholders can understand.

- **Active listening**: Understanding stakeholder concerns and incorporating their feedback into solutions.

For example, a top candidate can present an architectural proposal to a mixed audience, addressing technical details for engineers while highlighting business value for executives.

Soft skills

Beyond technical expertise, solutions architects must excel in soft skills such as leadership, team collaboration, adaptability, and problem-solving under pressure to effectively manage diverse teams, respond swiftly to challenges, and ensure successful outcomes.

Leadership and team collaboration

Strong leadership skills are essential for guiding teams and influencing stakeholders, such as:

- **Mentorship**: Assisting junior team members in sharing knowledge and best practices.

- **Facilitating collaboration**: It enables cross-functional collaboration with development, operations, and business teams.

For example, a high-performance solutions architect resolves conflicts between teams, ensures the teams are aligned on common goals, and creates a healthy team environment.

Adaptability and problem solving under pressure

Adaptability is a key competency in the fast-paced tech setting. The details are as follows:

- **Uncertainty management**: The capability to remain composed and resourceful while working with incomplete information or changing priorities.

- **Rapid problem solving**: The ability to think on the spur of the moment and respond to unexpected problems on time.

For example, a critical system component fails during peak hours. The candidate should be able to rapidly identify the problem, suggest a possible solution, and communicate a recovery plan.

Real-world problem solving

The details are as follows:

- **Ambiguity tolerance**: Leading architects look for individuals who can thrive in ambiguity, where instructions are not clearly defined or complete information is lacking.

- **Navigating complex problem spaces**: Breaking down ambiguous or ever-changing requirements into workable solutions.

  For example, when faced with a fuzzy requirement such as optimizing system performance, a good candidate should point out specific bottlenecks in performance, ascertain metrics for improvement, and implement targeted optimizations.

- **Evaluating trade-offs in design decisions**: All architectural decisions entail trade-offs, and great candidates can analyse and explain such trade-offs well.

    o   **Cost versus performance**: The desire to minimize operational costs in bounding performance.

    o   **Simple yet flexible**: Design of noncomplex flexible systems.

For example, a candidate discussing the database solution may weigh the pros and cons of a NoSQL database versus a relational database in consideration of factors such as query flexibility, required scalability, and required consistency.

Candidates have honed their skills in these fields, so they can fulfil the multi-dimensional role of solutions architect. They make sure that the designs they come up with are technically sound as well as consistent with business objectives and practical constraints.

Understanding these desired competencies helps avoid common pitfalls candidates often encounter during interviews, which we will discuss next.

Common pitfalls in interviews

Solutions architect interview process is highly demanding, involving not only technical ability but also strategic thinking and good communication skills, as well as the alignment of solutions with business objectives. Many candidates struggle to balance these factors. The next section discusses some common mistakes interviewees make and ways to avoid them.

Typical pitfalls candidates encounter in solutions architect interviews, such as overemphasis on technology, unclear communication, weak stakeholder management, ignoring non-functional requirements, and inadequate system design, are summarized in *Figure 20.2*:

Figure 20.2: Common mistakes occur in solutions architects interviews

Overemphasizing technology

The most common mistake that the candidates make is becoming over focused on technical specifics of a particular tool or framework, forgetting the big picture, that is, the larger business objectives. Refer to the following list for more details:

- **Pitfall**: Describing the architecture in terms of the technologies that it includes, such as describing an architecture in terms of Kubernetes or Terraform without considering how those technologies help get to business objectives, like time-to-market, system reliability, and other relevant outcomes.

- **Avoidance strategy**: Always relate your technical decisions to relevant business outcomes. For example, if you are proposing the architecture of microservices, let them know how it will support scalability and rapid feature development, all of which are ways to accelerate business growth.

Communicating ineffectively

This section discusses the pitfalls of using excessive technical jargon.

Effective communication is the backbone of a solutions architect's role. Many candidates often fail to engage the audience if they fill a response too dense with technical terms or do not change their communication mode to suit the interview panel. Refer to the following list for more details:

- **Pitfall**: Elaborating on a solution in highly technical language without confirmation that the panel, which can consist of people lacking the technical background, understands its merit.

- **Avoidance strategy**: Plan your language according to the audience. When talking through the technical aspects, talk down the technical so that other ideas can be conceptualized. Practice summarizing your solutions in plain talk so that others may understand.

Ignoring conflicting stakeholder requirements situations, typically in the form of an interview, test candidates on their conflict management skills among stakeholders. A candidate talking more about the technical means than the dynamics of stakeholders may be perceived as too detached from the human touch of solution design.

Effectively managing stakeholder conflicts is vital for architects. Candidates must demonstrate their ability to balance competing stakeholder priorities thoughtfully and strategically:

- **Pitfall**: Not demonstrating how you would deal, for example, with a business stakeholder that is demanding fast deployment against the operations team that insists on stability of the system.

- **Avoidance strategy**: Emphasize your ability to mediate between stakeholders. Discuss how you would facilitate workshops to align priorities, propose trade-offs, or build consensus around phased implementations.

Overlooking non-functional requirements

This section addresses the common mistake of overlooking performance, scalability, or security.

A **non-functional requirement** (**NFR**) rich architecture must support both functional and non-functional requirements.

Candidates pay much attention to the functional features while missing out on important NFRs, such as system performance, security, and reliability. Refer to the following list for more details:

- **Pitfall**: Proposing a solution that satisfies functional requirements but neglects scalability, which tends to lead to the applications performing poorly under heavy loads.

- **Avoidance strategy**: In the system design question above, explicitly mention your NFRs.

Explain how your architecture addresses performance (for instance, via caching), security (for example, through role-based access controls), and scalability (for example, auto-scaling based on traffic).

Providing inadequate system design

Candidates often undermine their credibility by not clearly justifying their design decisions. Demonstrating clear reasoning behind architectural choices highlights your analytical thinking and ensures your solutions are credible, robust, and well-aligned with business needs.

Not justifying architectural choices with proper reasoning

Architectural design questions are meant to evaluate your ability to make sound, rational decisions. Often, candidates fail to say why they chose a particular design or technology, which really diminishes the credibility of the solution itself. Refer to the following list for more details:

- **Pitfall**: Provide a high-level design without justification of why a particular architectural style, such as microservices, or a tool, like Redis for caching, was chosen.

- **Avoidance strategy**: Always justify design decisions. Discuss alternative options clearly with explanations on the advantages and limitations of such options for every alternative. For example, when proposing serverless architecture, say how it lessens operational overhead but may cause latencies in initiating cold starts.

The common pitfalls described here can significantly improve performance in solutions architect interviews. Balancing knowledge of technical areas with clear communication, strategic thinking, and a focus on business outcomes will ensure the entire skill set required for the position. What might prove to be useful in avoiding these pitfalls will not only help during the interview process but also set a well-crafted foundation for real-world success as solutions architects.

Having identified these frequent mistakes, let us now explore practical strategies to effectively avoid them and succeed in your interviews.

Strategies to avoid common mistakes

Success in a solutions architect interview is not just a function of technical know-how but also the quality of the solutions presentation and whether the solutions are aligned with the goals of the company. Several candidates make unnecessary mistakes that would hold them back. This section gives practical approaches that would structure your preparation, present your answers well, and consistently show that you are a candidate for success.

Figure 20.3 outlines key strategies for interview success, including tailoring responses, leveraging experience, building a strong narrative, and staying calm under pressure:

How to excel in Solutions Architect interviews?

Tailor Responses
Understand the company's domain, speak their language, and ask clarifying questions.

Leverage Experience
Quantify impact, highlight relevant experiences, and use the STAR approach.

Build Narrative
Frame solutions around business impact, showcase problem-solving skills, and weave a compelling story.

Stay Calm
Pause and think, break down problems, practice mindfulness, and acknowledge uncertainty.

Figure 20.3: Best practices to ace solutions architect interviews

Preparation advice

Effective preparation forms the foundation for a successful interview. After all, inadequate or unsuitable preparation is just a missed opportunity to present one's competency.

Key tips

The key tips are as follows:

- **Preparation aligned to job and organizational ends**

    Starting with a good understanding of the position description and the business requirements of the company. Align your preparation to tackle skills, technologies, and pain areas of relevance to the job.

- o Look up the company's industry, products, and services.

- o Identify some key business challenges like scaling systems, compliance, or cost reduction.

- o Read up on the organization's tech stack and any publicly available information about their architecture.

- **Leverage checklists and frameworks for systematic preparation**

  Make use of the checklists given in *Chapter 2, Solutions Architect Checklist* to ensure that you address all critical areas of solutions architecture.

  - o Use the requirements gathering checklist, checklists on design principles, performance tuning, and security best practices.

  - o Review your preparation regularly, pointing out any gaps.

For example, suppose it is a cloud-native focus for a company. Then, your preparation should include containerization, serverless architectures, and IaC.

Practice and feedback

Theoretical knowledge alone will not suffice if you cannot articulate it under pressure. Mock interviews and constructive feedback are important to hone the delivery.

Key tips

The key tips are as follows:

- **Mock interviews**: Mock interviews simulate real interview scenarios and help you in:
  - o Determining areas to improve, such as aspects of communication or incomplete technical descriptions of solutions.

  - o Developing the ability to clearly express complex solutions.

- **Iterative improvement**: Apply the lessons learned from mock interviews to your preparation. Focus on improving specific aspects, such as answering behavioural questions or diagramming system designs.
  - o Talk to other peers, mentors, or try services like Pramp or Interviewing.io, which can provide professional feedback.

  - o Return and adjust the learning plan based on areas of improvement highlighted in the feedback.

For example, if feedback indicates your answers are too technical, practice tying them to business outcomes, such as cost savings or improved user experience.

Crafting responses

A well-structured answer will make a big difference in how your solutions are perceived. Interviewers prefer the candidate who shows clear thinking and problem-solving abilities.

Key tips

The key tips are as follows:

- **Make use of the STAR framework for behavioral questions**:

  You will be guided to give structured, impactful answers when answering those behavioural interview questions, using the STAR framework.

  - o **Situation**: Set the context.

- o **Task**: Explain your responsibility or challenge.

- o **Action**: Describe the steps you take to accomplish the challenge.

- o **Result**: Outcomes, with metrics as possible.

For example, *Our application was performing poorly during peak hours in a past role (Situation). I was asked to identify and remove bottlenecks (Task). I implemented a Redis caching strategy and optimized database queries (Action), reducing page load times by 50% (Result).*

- **Structure technical answers to demonstrate your reasoning and trade-off analysis**: For technical interview questions, break down your problem-solving approach:

  - o Start with problem analysis and discuss key considerations (e.g., scalability, security, cost).

  - o Outline possible solutions and their trade-offs.

  - o End with your recommended solution with justification.

  For example, when tasked with designing a system that has the availability:

  - o Start with a description of the business need, which will be the minimum downtime.

  - o Discuss Redundancy, multi-region deployment, and load balancing.

  - o Recommend Solution (for example, AWS multi-region architecture) with a focus on continuous business operations and user experience.

Applying these strategies sets the stage for showcasing real-world relevance, essential advice for excelling as a solutions architect candidate.

Real-world tips for interview success

Excelling in a solutions architect interview requires more than technical knowledge; it demands applying your skills in a way that aligns with the company's unique business and technical context. Demonstrating this adaptability and relevance can set you apart from other candidates.

Demonstrating context awareness

One of the most important ways in which you would pass a solutions architect interview is by relating your answers to the unique business and technical context of the job itself. Every organization has distinct requirements and challenges, and demonstrating flexibility and adaptability sets you apart.

Key tips

The key tips are as follows:

- **Know the domain of the company**: Investigate the company's industry, their products, and services before the interview. Pinpoint the technical and business problems they are likely to face.

- **Tailor your language to the domain**: Use industry-specific terminology and align your solutions with their business goals. For instance, a healthcare organization may be sensitive to compliance and data security issues, while an e-commerce firm is bound to be interested in scalability and user experience.

- **Request clarification of the question**: When the interviewer mentions something vaguely, ask a few questions to seek further clarification. This clearly establishes an analytical thinking approach, and this answer, in turn, shows it is relevant.

For example, when asked to design a system for high availability, relate your answer to the company's specific needs. For a retail company, emphasize minimizing downtime during peak shopping hours. For a healthcare provider, focus on ensuring data accessibility for emergency responders.

Leveraging personal experience

Your past work and accomplishments provide concrete proof of your expertise. Talk about your experiences in an interview that coincide with the job requirements.

Key tips

The key tips are as follows:

- **Quantify impact**: Use metrics to showcase the success of your projects. For example, *I implemented a microservices architecture that improved system scalability by 40% and reduced deployment time from 2 hours to 15 minutes.*

- **Emphasize pertinent experience**: Tell stories that apply to the position. If the position focuses on cloud-native architectures, then you talk about your experience with Amazon Web Services, GCP, or Azure.

- **Be specific**: Explain the problem you had, your responsibility, what you did, and the result. The STAR method is very effective.

  For example, *In a previous role, we led the migration of a legacy monolithic application to a microservices-based architecture on AWS. This reduced downtime during updates by 80% and improved overall system performance by 30%.*

- **Storytelling with business impact**: Engage your technical competence with business results. Companies want to see how your technical decisions drive business value.

Key tips

The key tips are as follows:

- **Frame your solutions around business impact**: When discussing a technical solution, always tie it back to the business benefit.

- **Showcase problem-solving skills**: Highlight how you have tackled real-world challenges, such as improving system performance, reducing costs, or enhancing user experience.

- **Weave a compelling story**: Use storytelling to make your achievements memorable. Provide context, detail your approach, and emphasize the positive results.

For example, *When our company faced increasing user complaints about slow application performance, I led an initiative to implement a caching strategy using Redis. This reduced page load times by 50%, improving customer satisfaction and contributing to a 15% increase in sales during the following quarter.*

Keeping cool under pressure

Technical interviews can be intense, especially when faced with complex scenarios or unexpected questions. Your ability to remain composed is as important as your technical knowledge.

Key tips

The key tips are as follows:

- **Pause and think**: Do not rush to answer. Take a moment to gather your thoughts and structure your response. This not only improves your answer but also shows confidence.

- **Break down the problem**: This is especially when you break down complex problems into smaller units. As you break it down, explain your thought process behind working on each part.

- **Practice mindfulness techniques**: Deep breathing or visualization can help manage stress during high-pressure situations.

- **Acknowledge uncertainty**: Show that you do not know the answer honestly and explain how you would solve it. This is a great way of showing off your problem-solving skills as well as your willingness to learn.

For example, having to design a fault-tolerant system on the spot, start with identifying basic components where redundancy will be applied. Discuss possible solutions, their trade-offs, and how you would evaluate them in a real-world scenario. If unsure of any of the details, mention the tools or frameworks you would research to fill the gaps.

These strategies can help you present yourself as a confident, adaptable, and impact-driven solutions architect. Interviews are more about how to think and communicate than the technical skills you have.

Conclusion

Excelling in a solutions architect interview requires more than technical expertise; it demands strategic thinking, effective communication, and the ability to align technical solutions with business goals. Certainly, technical expertise provides a solid platform, but it is the ability to present deep ideas in relatively accessible ways, handle conflicting requirements from various stakeholders, and create systems which balance functionality with non-functional needs that makes top candidates stand out.

By being mindful of common pitfalls such as overemphasizing technology, neglecting stakeholder management, or overlooking non-functional requirements, you can portray yourself as a well-rounded candidate. A solutions architect is not a simple problem solver; they are the bridge between the need in business and the technical means of it to deliver value to the organization.

This holistic approach will not only help you stand out during interviews but also prepare you for the multifaceted responsibilities of the role in real-world scenarios.

In the next chapter, we will explore operational excellence considerations, delving into essential strategies for designing systems that are scalable, resilient, maintainable, and efficient. Understanding operational excellence will further enable solutions architects to consistently deliver high-performing solutions, align technical designs effectively with evolving business goals, and position themselves as leaders capable of guiding organizations toward sustainable technical success.

Key takeaways

The takeaways are as follows:

- **Bridge technical decisions with business value**: Always connect technical decisions with their impact on business outcomes. Clearly articulate how your solutions address real-world problems and deliver measurable value to the organization.

- **Communicate effectively**: Use language according to the audience. Technical and non-technical audiences must understand your vision; Avoid jargons overload.

- **Stakeholder management**: Show your ability to mediate conflicting requirements align stakeholders toward a shared goal.

- **Emphasize NFRs**: Present your designs with performance, scalability, security, and reliability to demonstrate a holistic understanding of architecture.

- **Design justification**: Clearly explain your decisions using trade-offs to demonstrate your analytical thinking.

- **Practice real-life scenario solving**: Practice yourself in simulating interview situations to hone your problem-solving and communications skills under pressure.

Model interview questions and answers

1. **Describe a time when you had to mediate between conflicting stakeholder requirements. How did you resolve the conflict?**

   Model answer:

   - **Situation**: In your last assignment, you were asked to design a new system, maintaining cost-effectiveness in contrast with scalability. One stakeholder was keen on scalability, which would provide head room for future growth, however, the other was concerned about upfront costs.

   - **Task**: Your task was to come up with a solution that satisfies both requirements without compromising the fundamental functionality of the system.

   - **Action**: You held a stakeholder workshop to clarify the priorities. You proposed a phased approach starting with cost-efficient cloud solution with auto-scaling capabilities. This would enable you to save money on the upfront cost while still benefiting from scalability.

   - **Result**: Both stakeholders were satisfied since this would be a solution that has immediate savings while also being prepared for future system growth. It also helps optimize the deployment time.

2. **Describe a project where scalability and performance had to be balanced.**

   Model answer:

   - **Situation**: You were leading the redesign of a customer portal for a retail client experiencing performance issues during peak sales events.

   - **Task**: The goal was to redesign the system to handle traffic surges without degrading performance.

   - **Action**: You adopted a microservices architecture deployed on auto-scaling Kubernetes clusters. You implemented Redis caching for frequently accessed data and optimized database queries to reduce latency.

   - **Result**: The system's performance improved by 40% during peak traffic, with zero downtime reported during the Black Friday sales period.

3. **How to design a high availability system for a crucial health application?**

   Model answer:

   - First thing is to identify key business and technical requirements, namely HA and fault tolerance.

   - **Redundancy**: As redundancy, along with multiple availability zones or regions, there will be continuous operation during a failure.

   - **Load balancing**: Using a load balancer like AWS Elastic Load Balancer or Azure Application Gateway for distributing traffic equally.

   - **Database**: Multi-master database with automatic failover.

   - **Disaster recovery**: Automated backups with regular recovery processes testing.

   - **Result**: Such architecture generates a 99.99% uptime SLA without putting the organisation at risk of potential service disruption.

4. **You are asked to transform a monolith application into a microservices architecture. How would you handle it?**

   Model answer:

   - **Monolith review**: Identify the modules which are very critical and find their dependencies.

   - **Prioritize microservices**: Start with the modules with clear boundaries as well as having the maximum possible impact.

   - **API develop**: Utilize REST or gRPC for the API communication of the microservices.

   - **Containerization**: Develop microservices in containers using Docker and deploy them via Kubernetes to scale.

   - **Data strategy**: Shared or separate database for each and every microservice based on consistency and performance criteria.

   - **CI/CD**: Build CI/CD pipelines such that the entire process can be made non-breakable.

   - **Monitor and iterate**: Apply tools like Prometheus and Grafana in observability and refine further based on the performance metrics.

5. **How would you harden a cloud-native application?**

   Model answer:

   - **Authentication and authorization**: OAuth 2.0 for API access control or RBAC.

   - **Encryption of data**: AWS KMS or Azure Key Vault for data in rest and using TLS for data in transit.

   - **Infrastructure security**: Security groups, NACLs and private subnet.

   - **DevSecOps**: Integrate security into your CI/CD pipeline; you can use, for example, a tool like SonarQube to auto scan for vulnerabilities and analysis of static code.

   - **Audit and compliance**: Audit logging and access monitoring, followed by anomaly detection using AWS CloudTrail or Azure Security Center.

6. **You would prefer relational for an e-commerce site, and NoSQL or vice versa. Explain why you made such a choice.**

   Model answer:

   It depends on your application requirements:

   - **Relational database management system (RDBMS)**: If the application necessitates complex queries, for example transactional consistency across the payments or requires structured data, you will be very likely to use an RDBMS like PostgreSQL.

   - **NoSQL database**: If your primary requirement is scalability and processing of unstructured or semi-structured data, like user behavior logs, then a NoSQL solution like MongoDB or DynamoDB would be ideal.

   - **Recommendation**: In many cases, the hybrid way works better. For example, critical transactions using RDBMS and user sessions and product catalogues by NoSQL.

7. **What is your approach to a trade-off between performance vs cost as part of the cloud deployment?**

   Model answer:

   Approach:

   - **Analyze requirements**: Understand the performance metrics like response time and the budget constraints.

- **Review the cloud service options**: Consider using spot instances or reserved instances to reduce costs by keeping performance consistent.

- **Leverage auto-scaling**: Build auto-scaling policies to optimize resource usage during high and low traffic.

- **Caching**: Utilize caching solutions like Redis to improve performance without incurring too much cost.

- **Final recommendation**: Balance by optimizing workloads to run efficiently during peak and off-peak hours. Cost monitoring using FinOps practices.

8. **How do you align between the technical solution and the business objectives?**

Model answer:

- At first, you get familiarized with the business issues and priorities by discussing these matters with the relevant stakeholders.

- As the work progresses, all your technical decisions match those strategic goals at a later stage.

- For example, if faster time-to-market is the objective, then you would suggest implementing the DevOps practices like CI/CD pipelines, IaC to automate the deployment process.

- Also, implement periodic feedback loops with users to ensure that the solution stays relevant in changing business needs ecosystem.

9. **How do you manage requirements ambiguity?**

Model answer:

Ambiguity is prevalent, and my strategy involves the following:

- **Clarify assumptions**: Get stakeholders to close the gaps and agree on the assumptions.

- **Iterative development**: Starting with a minimal viable solution and then building based on feedback.

- **Using domain knowledge**: Leverage past experiences to enable you to make appropriate decisions when clarity is scarce. For example, *in a recent project, we did not have much clear sight of future traffic patterns. We designed the system modular in nature and scalable so that we can adapt it with the requirements evolving.*

Join our Discord space

Join our Discord workspace for latest updates, offers, tech happenings around the world, new releases, and sessions with the authors:

https://discord.bpbonline.com

CHAPTER 21

Operational Excellence Considerations

Introduction

Operational excellence is the backbone for developing Agile, robust, and efficient software systems that can survive and perform well under changing conditions. It calls for the balancing of performance, reliability, and business needs so that technology creates value and drives innovation. It calls for solutions architects to come up with scalable, robust, maintainable, and efficient systems aligned with the short to medium term goals of the business enterprise in general while at the same time ensuring long-term success.

This chapter discusses the foundational principles and practices of operational excellence, which are scalability, resilience, maintainability, and efficiency-related strategies. It discusses certain topics in detail, such as automation, feedback-driven improvement, incident management, and modern architectural approaches. Taking up these topics will thus arm solutions architects with usable insights and practical tools to properly align technology with changing demands from business and deliver technologically robust and impactful solutions for stakeholders.

This chapter will break down the principles and practices of operational excellence into actionable ones, guiding solutions architects in its deployment across system design, modern architectures, and continuous improvement strategies.

Structure

This chapter covers the following topics:

- Principles of operational excellence
- Designing for scalability and resilience
- Ensuring maintainability and efficiency
- Best practices for continuous improvement
- Role of SRE in operational excellence
- Operational excellence in modern architectures

Objectives

This chapter aims to equip solutions architects with the knowledge and actionable strategies required to design and implement systems that exemplify operational excellence. The chapter will focus on foundational principles, best practices, and real-world implementation techniques to ensure that solutions architects can create scalable, resilient, maintainable, and efficient systems. Furthermore, this chapter also encourages the readers to be well-prepared for interviews, as this would reveal how these concepts can be articulated and thus demonstrate practical application. In conclusion, by the end of this chapter, one will be equipped enough to design and maintain systems that work well and operate successfully while being aligned to business goals and technical requirements.

Principles of operational excellence

Operational excellence is a multifaceted approach incorporating best practices, structured methodologies, and actionable strategies to make sure systems are resilient, adaptable, and efficient. Solutions architects should understand these principles to design systems that not only meet today's needs but also can cope with tomorrow's challenges. Solutions architects must first internalize its core principles to attain operational excellence, the foundation on which systems are designed to thrive in changing conditions.

Core principles

Automation is at the core of operational excellence, as it provides a basis for consistent, efficient, and error-free operations. Organizations reduce manual effort by automating routine tasks like deployments, monitoring, and incident responses, allowing teams to focus on strategic goals. Tools such as **continuous integration and continuous deployment (CI/CD)** pipelines, IaC frameworks, and automated testing suites help streamline workflows and improve overall system reliability. Proactive problem management ensures that potential issues are identified and addressed before they escalate into critical failures. This approach requires robust monitoring systems, predictive analytics, and well-defined escalation protocols. Leveraging tools for metrics collection and log analysis can help detect anomalies early, minimizing downtime and enhancing user experience.

Continuous feedback loops are crucial for driving iterative improvements. With the integration of feedback from end-users, monitoring systems, and stakeholders, organizations can make data-driven decisions that enhance system functionality and performance. Feedback loops foster a culture of learning and adaptation, enabling teams to refine their strategies in alignment with evolving requirements. Another essential principle is adaptability, making sure that the systems are in a position to change according to business needs, regulatory requirements, or technological change. Solutions architects should always use modular design, scalable frameworks, and decoupled architectures for creating flexible and future-proof systems. This adaptation saves time and cost for overhauls and ensures long-term relevance.

Balance innovation and reliability

It involves the balance of innovation and reliability in achieving operational excellence. A practical way of managing this trade-off is to introduce error budgets. Error budgets define an acceptable threshold for system downtime or errors, allowing teams to experiment and innovate without jeopardizing core functionality. This approach empowers teams to explore new solutions while maintaining user trust.

Service level agreements (SLAs), **service level objectives (SLOs)**, and **service level indicators (SLIs)** are crucial elements of this balance. The details are as follows:

- SLAs define commitments to end-users.
- SLOs define measurable performance targets.
- SLIs provide the data required for measuring system performance against these goals.

All these together help organizations monitor reliability, close gaps, and align performance with business objectives.

Best practices for operational excellence

Clear operation goals should be documented. Such a thing is the backbone of operational excellence. Well-defined goals provide a shared understanding of success criteria, guiding decision-making and resource allocation. For instance, goals might include achieving 99.99% system uptime or reducing incident response times to under five minutes.

The establishment of KPIs is equally important. KPIs are measurable benchmarks that help track progress and identify areas for improvement. Metrics such as **mean time to recovery (MTTR)**, **mean time between failures (MTBF)**, and system latency provide actionable insights into operational performance. Regular review and refinement of these KPIs ensure continuous improvement and sustained excellence.

By embedding these principles and best practices into their operational strategies, solutions architects can develop systems that are robust, scalable, and aligned with organizational goals. Such systems not only meet user expectations but also place organizations in the right position to enjoy long-term success in the changing technological landscape.

With these principles in place, solutions architects can now explore how to apply them in designing scalable and resilient systems that meet the demands of dynamic workloads.

Designing for scalability and resilience

To ensure systems remain effective in dynamic environments, solutions architects must design for both scalability and resilience. Scalability addresses the system's ability to handle growth, while resilience focuses on ensuring stability during failures. By combining both strategies, architects can build systems that scale seamlessly to meet rising demands while maintaining high availability and performance.

The following sections explore key strategies for achieving scalability and resilience in modern system design.

Designing for scalability

Scalability is a key aspect of operational excellence as it allows systems to scale with increasing workloads without degrading performance. The solutions architect will need to design scalable systems to consider both horizontal and vertical scaling options. Horizontal scaling adds more instances or nodes to distribute the workload, giving flexibility and redundancy. Vertical scaling increases the capacity of existing resources by upgrading hardware or allocating more memory and CPU. For further information on application scaling strategies, refer to *Chapter 9, Performance and Scalability*.

Scalability patterns include sharding, load balancing, and microservices. Sharding distributes data across multiple databases or partitions, ensuring that data access and storage are very efficient. Load balancing distributes incoming requests evenly across servers, avoiding bottlenecks and ensuring consistent performance. Microservices architecture allows independent scaling of specific components, so resource allocation aligns with workload demands.

In cloud-native environments, auto-scaling mechanisms automatically adjust resource allocation based on real-time demand. Tools such as AWS Auto Scaling and Azure Scale Sets automate the process, thus keeping systems cost-efficient and responsive to traffic spikes. Auto-scaling minimizes manual intervention, allowing teams to focus on strategic initiatives.

Ensuring resilience

Resilience ensures that systems can withstand and recover from failures. Solutions architects must design for fault tolerance by incorporating redundancy and failover mechanisms. Redundant components ensure continuous availability, while failover mechanisms automatically switch to backup systems during outages.

There is always a requirement to maintain stability within the system; hence, error-handling strategies are circuit breakers, retries, and timeouts. Circuit breakers prevent failures from cascading while ensuring that service-to-service communications are robust because of retries and timeouts. In conclusion, such error-handling strategies can mitigate transient errors and further increase reliability overall.

Leveraging cloud-native resilience features enhances system robustness. Services like AWS Auto Scaling, Azure Availability Zones, and Google Cloud Load Balancer offer built-in mechanisms to distribute workloads and recover from failures seamlessly. These features reduce the risk of downtime and improve user experience.

Practical tips

Implementing scalability and resilience effectively requires thoughtful planning and proactive strategies. The following practical tips provide actionable guidance for solutions architects to design systems that can efficiently manage dynamic workloads while ensuring stability and performance:

- **Start with predictable workloads**: Begin by analyzing usage patterns and scaling incrementally to avoid overprovisioning resources.

- **Use load testing tools**: Use tools like Apache JMeter or Locust to identify bottlenecks and optimize system performance.

- **Monitor system health**: Continuously monitor resource utilization, latency, and error rates to catch issues early.

- **Hybrid scaling**: Implement a combination of horizontal and vertical scaling to deal with the fluctuations in workload.

- **Peak loads preparation**: Use predictive analytics to predict traffic spikes and make sure that the required resources are in place.

Using such strategies can help solutions architects design systems that are not only scalable and resilient but also in accord with business and user expectations.

Scaling and resiliency thus obtained; these systems must be maintained for their lifetime by keeping them in a good operating state.

Ensuring maintainability and efficiency

Operational excellence is incomplete without a strong focus on maintainability and efficiency. These two attributes ensure that systems remain robust, adaptable, and cost-effective throughout their lifecycle. Solutions architects must prioritize clean designs, effective resource utilization, and proactive monitoring to deliver systems that stand the test of time.

Designing for maintainability

Maintainability refers to the ease with which a system can be modified, updated, or repaired. A maintainable system reduces operational overhead, enhances developer productivity, and ensures long-term adaptability. Let us look at the essential strategies.

Modular architecture and clean code practices

A modular architecture breaks down complex systems into smaller, self-contained components. These modules can be developed, tested, and deployed independently, reducing interdependencies and improving fault isolation.

Some more details are as follows:

- **Benefits**: Implementing a modular architecture and adhering to clean code principles offer several advantages that improve system stability, scalability, and maintainability. Key benefits include:

  o   Easier debugging and troubleshooting.

  o   Enhanced scalability through independent updates.

  o   Simplified onboarding for new team members.

  Clean code practices further reinforce maintainability. Developers should adhere to principles like **don't repeat yourself (DRY)** and **keep it simple, stupid (KISS)**, ensuring code is readable, concise, and consistent.

- **Example of best practices**: Adopting clean code principles ensures that the codebase remains organized, readable, and easy to maintain. The following best practices help developers write efficient and scalable code:

  o   Use meaningful variable and function names.

  o   Limit function sizes to focus on single responsibilities.

  o   Implement consistent formatting and documentation.

Comprehensive documentation and knowledge sharing

Documentation acts as the backbone of maintainability, bridging the gap between different teams and stakeholders. Comprehensive documentation should cover:

- **System overview**: High-level architecture diagrams and descriptions.
- **Codebase details**: Comments, API documentation, and configuration guides.
- **Operational playbooks**: Incident response protocols, SLAs, and troubleshooting steps.

Collaboration tools like Confluence or Git-based wikis can centralize knowledge, enabling teams to access and update documentation seamlessly.

Optimizing efficiency

Efficiency in system design ensures optimal use of resources, reducing costs while maintaining performance. It requires careful planning, monitoring, and continuous improvement.

Resource utilization

Efficient systems maximize resource use without overprovisioning or underutilization. Right-sizing instances and minimizing idle capacity are key.

Key strategies include:

- **Right-sizing instances**: Select instance types and sizes that align with workload requirements. Tools like AWS Cost Explorer or Azure Advisor can provide insights into optimal configurations.
- **Minimizing idle capacity**: Implement auto-scaling to match resource allocation with demand, avoiding wastage during low-traffic periods.

Performance monitoring and optimization

Performance monitoring identifies bottlenecks, while optimization ensures sustained efficiency. The details are as follows:

- **Tools for monitoring**:
    - ○ **Prometheus**: For collecting real-time metrics.
    - ○ **Grafana**: For creating dashboards and visualizing performance data.
    - ○ **New relic**: For end-to-end performance tracking.
- **Optimization techniques**:
    - ○ Use caching layers like Redis or Memcached to reduce database load.
    - ○ Optimize query performance with indexing and query profiling.
    - ○ Leverage **content delivery networks (CDNs)** to reduce latency for global users.

Operational excellence metrics

Measuring system performance is crucial to maintainability and efficiency. Metrics provide actionable insights and guide improvement efforts.

Key metrics

To effectively assess system performance and ensure operational excellence, solutions architects should focus on the following key metrics:

- **Mean time to recovery**: Measures the average time to restore services after a failure. Lower MTTR indicates effective incident response.
- **Mean time between failures**: Tracks the average time between system failures, reflecting system reliability.
- **Resource utilization metrics**: CPU, memory, and disk usage trends highlight potential overprovisioning or underutilization.

Real-time monitoring

Real-time monitoring tools ensure proactive identification of issues:

- **Synthetic monitoring**: Simulates user interactions to detect issues before they affect real users.
- **Distributed tracing**: Tracks requests across services to identify bottlenecks in microservices architectures.

Practical tips

To ensure maintainability and efficiency, solutions architects should:

- **Conduct regular code reviews**: Identify inefficiencies, enforce coding standards, and share feedback across teams.
- **Implement CI/CD**: Automate testing and deployments to ensure faster, error-free updates.
- **Use synthetic monitoring**: Simulate user interactions to identify potential performance issues proactively.
- **Encourage team collaboration**: Host regular knowledge-sharing sessions and retrospectives to identify improvement areas.

By prioritizing maintainability and efficiency, solutions architects can ensure their systems remain Agile, cost-effective, and aligned with business goals. These practices not only reduce operational overhead but also enhance user satisfaction by delivering consistent, high-quality services.

Maintaining systems is not a one-time effort; it requires continuous improvement driven by feedback, observability, and proactive incident management.

Best practices for continuous improvement

Continuous improvement is a cornerstone of achieving operational excellence, ensuring that systems and processes evolve to meet changing business demands, user expectations, and technological advancements. Solutions architects play a pivotal role in fostering a culture of continuous learning and adaptation, enabling their organizations to remain competitive and resilient. This section gets into the best practices for embedding continuous improvement into systems, focusing on building a feedback-driven culture, leveraging observability, and managing incidents proactively.

Building a feedback-driven culture

To effectively understand user needs and drive continuous improvement, it is essential to establish robust mechanisms for gathering and acting upon feedback. This includes:

- **User feedback**: Regularly gather insights from end-users through surveys, usability tests, and behaviour analytics. This feedback helps prioritize features, refine workflows, and enhance user experience.

- **Stakeholder feedback**: Engage business stakeholders in reviews and planning sessions to ensure system designs align with strategic objectives.

- **Team feedback**: Encourage cross-functional teams to share insights during retrospectives or brainstorming sessions. Development, operations, and quality assurance teams can uncover hidden inefficiencies or risks.

Feedback loops promote transparency, accountability, and a shared commitment to continuous improvement. They ensure that all voices are heard and that enhancements are guided by data and diverse perspectives.

Role of observability

Observability is a critical enabler of continuous improvement, providing the visibility needed to understand system behaviour and diagnose issues. While often confused with monitoring, observability offers a broader perspective, emphasizing the collection and interpretation of data to answer questions about a system's state. Refer to the list for more details:

- **Observability versus monitoring**: Monitoring focuses on predefined metrics and alerts, while observability seeks to provide a comprehensive understanding of system behaviour. Observability enables teams to troubleshoot novel issues, while monitoring handles known failure scenarios.

- **Key observability practices**: To gain comprehensive insights into system behavior and performance, it is essential to implement key observability practices. These practices include:

  o **Distributed tracing**: Track requests as they flow through a system, pinpointing bottlenecks and latency issues.

  o **Log aggregation**: Centralize and analyse logs to identify patterns and anomalies.

  o **Metrics collection**: Measure critical performance indicators such as CPU usage, memory consumption, and response times.

Adopting observability platforms like Honeycomb or OpenTelemetry early in the development cycle ensures seamless integration and robust visibility into system operations.

Proactive incident management

Proactive incident management is vital for minimizing downtime, maintaining user trust, and fostering a culture of resilience. It emphasizes preparedness, automation, and learning from failures. To ensure effective and timely responses to disruptions, it is crucial to establish robust incident response plans. These plans should encompass:

- **Incident response plans**: Develop and document clear response protocols for various incident scenarios. Include escalation paths, communication plans, and recovery steps.

- **Automating recovery actions**: Implement self-healing mechanisms that detect and resolve common issues without human intervention. For instance, auto-scaling policies can mitigate performance degradation during traffic surges.

- **Postmortems and root cause analysis**: Conduct thorough postmortems after incidents to identify root causes and implement corrective actions. Postmortems should focus on learning, not blaming, and aim to prevent recurrence.

Practical tips for continuous improvement

This section focuses on practical strategies to embed continuous improvement into organizational workflows, emphasizing observability, iterative changes, and team retrospectives. These practices build a foundation for adopting advanced methodologies like **site reliability engineering** (**SRE**).

To foster a culture of ongoing enhancement and adaptation, consider these practical tips for continuous improvement:

- **Introduce observability platforms early**: Ensure that observability tools are incorporated into the system design phase to capture relevant data from the outset.

- **Schedule regular retrospectives**: Facilitate periodic reviews with cross-functional teams to discuss challenges, successes, and opportunities for refinement.

- **Iterate incrementally**: Make small, manageable changes that can be monitored and evaluated before scaling improvements across the system.

- **Celebrate successes**: Recognize and reward teams for contributions to continuous improvement initiatives, reinforcing a positive feedback loop.

By embedding these best practices into organizational workflows, solutions architects enable teams to evolve their systems proactively, ensuring they remain efficient, reliable, and aligned with user needs. Continuous improvement is not a one-time activity but a mindset that drives sustained operational success.

These best practices lay the groundwork for incorporating advanced operational strategies, such as those advocated by SRE, to further enhance system performance and reliability.

As continuous improvement becomes embedded in system operations, integrating SRE principles provides a structured approach to balance reliability and innovation.

Role of SRE in operational excellence

SRE has emerged as a transformative discipline that bridges the gap between software engineering and operations, ensuring systems remain reliable, scalable, and efficient. By incorporating SRE practices into their design, solutions architects can enhance system performance, reduce downtime, and enable seamless scalability. This section explores the foundational principles of SRE, its alignment with operational excellence, and practical strategies for collaboration between SRE teams and solutions architects.

Introduction to site reliability engineering

SRE was pioneered by *Google* as an engineering-driven approach to maintaining system reliability. Unlike traditional operations, which often focus solely on system stability, SRE emphasizes balancing reliability with innovation. This is achieved by embedding software engineering practices into operational workflows, allowing teams to automate repetitive tasks, monitor systems effectively, and respond proactively to incidents.

SRE's focus aligns seamlessly with the goals of operational excellence by addressing scalability, resilience, and efficiency. Solutions architects who understand and apply SRE principles can design systems that meet reliability objectives without sacrificing agility or innovation.

Key SRE practices aligned with operational excellence

SRE offers a structured approach to achieving operational excellence by focusing on reliability, automation, and data-driven decision-making. Here are key SRE practices aligned with operational excellence:

- **Establishing service level objectives and managing error budgets**:

    o **Service level objectives**: SLOs define measurable targets for system performance and availability. For instance, an SLO might specify that a service should achieve 99.95% uptime over a given period. These objectives ensure teams focus on what matters most to users.

    o **Error budgets**: An error budget represents the permissible threshold of unreliability within an SLO. For example, if the SLO allows 0.05% downtime, that equates to a specific duration of allowable downtime (e.g., 21.6 minutes per month). Error budgets encourage teams to balance innovation and reliability by permitting controlled experimentation while staying within acceptable limits.

- **Automating repetitive tasks to reduce human error**:

    Automation is central to SRE, as manual interventions often lead to inconsistencies and errors. Common automation practices include:

    o **Infrastructure as code (IaC)**: Automating infrastructure provisioning using tools like Terraform or CloudFormation.

    o **Automated incident response**: Configuring systems to detect anomalies and trigger predefined recovery actions without human intervention.

    o **CI/CD**: Streamlining code integration and deployment to minimize disruptions.

    o By reducing manual workloads, teams can focus on higher-value tasks such as system optimization and feature development.

Solution architects and SRE teams collaboration

Solutions architects and SRE teams share a common goal of delivering reliable, scalable, and efficient systems. Effective collaboration will ensure that the operational considerations are integrated during the design phase and reduce the likelihood of issues during deployment or production. Some areas of collaboration include:

- **System design validation**: Solutions architects can utilize SRE expertise to validate design against operational requirements. For example, SREs might review failover mechanisms, scaling strategies, or monitoring frameworks to ensure they align with reliability goals.

- **Capacity planning**: SRE teams bring insights into workload trends and system bottlenecks, helping Solutions architects design architectures that accommodate current demands while planning for future growth.

- **Incident response frameworks**: SREs can assist solutions architects to design systems with strong incident response protocols, including automated alerts and escalation paths.

Practical tips for leveraging SRE principles

This section outlines practical steps for implementing SRE principles, emphasizing the importance of clear SLOs, error budgets, and automation. It highlights the collaborative role of solutions architects and SRE teams in achieving operational excellence in modern, complex architectures.

To effectively integrate SRE principles into your operational strategy, consider these practical tips:

- **Start with clear objectives**: Define SLOs early in the design process to align system reliability with business priorities.

- **Implement error budgets**: Use error budgets to foster innovation while maintaining user trust. Monitor these budgets actively and adjust operational strategies as needed.

- **Automate from the outset**: Incorporate automation into deployment pipelines, monitoring systems, and incident responses to minimize human error and streamline operations.

- **Foster collaborative reviews**: Schedule regular design and operational reviews involving both SREs and solutions architects to ensure alignment on goals and expectations.

- **Prioritize high-impact improvements**: Focus on changes that deliver the greatest reliability or scalability benefits, guided by SRE principles and data-driven insights.

By adopting SRE practices and fostering close collaboration between solutions architects and SRE teams, organizations can achieve a robust balance between innovation and reliability. This alignment not only enhances system performance but also ensures long-term scalability and user satisfaction, fulfilling the principles of operational excellence.

The integration of SRE practices is particularly valuable in modern architectures, where cloud-native, multi-cloud, and hybrid environments demand robust and adaptable designs.

Modern architectures require not only operational robustness but also seamless integration of advanced tools and practices, as explored in the context of SRE.

Operational excellence in modern architectures

Modern architectures demand systems that are not only efficient but also adaptable to the rapidly evolving technological landscape. Operational excellence in such environments is achieved by embracing cloud-native practices, addressing multi-cloud and hybrid challenges, and aligning DevOps principles with operational goals. This section explores the strategies for achieving operational excellence in modern architectures, emphasizing the role of cutting-edge tools, best practices, and practical approaches.

Designing for cloud-native environments

Cloud-native environments are the cornerstone of modern architectures, enabling scalability, resilience, and efficiency. By leveraging technologies like Kubernetes, serverless computing, and container orchestration, organizations can build systems optimized for dynamic workloads and rapid innovation.

The following approaches play a crucial role in building robust cloud-native systems:

- **Kubernetes for orchestration**: Kubernetes serves as a powerful container orchestration platform, enabling automated deployment, scaling, and management of containerized applications. With its support for declarative configurations, Kubernetes ensures consistency and flexibility in managing workloads. Key features include:

  o **Self-healing capabilities**: Automatically restarts failed containers and replaces unhealthy nodes.

- o **Horizontal scaling**: Dynamically adjusts the number of pods based on workload demands.

- o **Namespace isolation**: Segregates workloads for security and efficient resource management.

- **Serverless computing for flexibility**: Serverless platforms like AWS Lambda, Azure Functions, and Google Cloud Functions allow developers to focus on code rather than infrastructure. Serverless computing offers:

  - o **Event-driven execution**: Triggers code in response to events, reducing resource usage during idle periods.

  - o **Cost efficiency**: Charges are based on actual usage, eliminating the overhead of idle resources.

  - o **Scalability**: Automatically scales with demand, ensuring consistent performance under varying loads.

- **Efficiency through containerization**: Containers encapsulate applications with their dependencies, ensuring consistent performance across environments. Docker and container orchestration tools like Kubernetes provide lightweight, portable solutions that enable rapid development and deployment cycles.

By combining these technologies, organizations can achieve operational efficiency while reducing time-to-market for new features and applications.

Operational challenges in multi-cloud and hybrid architectures

Organizations increasingly adopt multi-cloud and hybrid architectures to balance cost, flexibility, and resilience. However, these architectures introduce operational challenges that require careful planning and robust strategies. They are as follows:

- **Ensuring interoperability**: Multi-cloud environments often involve diverse platforms with different APIs, configurations, and capabilities. Solutions architects must design systems that are interoperable by adopting standards such as:

  - o **Open APIs**: Use standardized APIs to ensure compatibility across platforms.

  - o **Containerization**: Leverage portable containers to run applications consistently on any cloud provider.

- **Resilience across platforms**: Ensuring system reliability in multi-cloud setups requires redundancy and failover mechanisms across clouds. Techniques include:

  - o **Active-active architectures**: Distribute workloads across multiple clouds to prevent single points of failure.

  - o **Data replication**: Use tools like AWS Global Accelerator or Azure Traffic Manager to synchronize data and direct traffic during outages.

- **Hybrid integration challenges**: Hybrid architectures that combine on-premises and cloud systems face latency, security, and compatibility issues. Address these challenges by:

  - o **Using hybrid cloud platforms**: Tools like Azure Arc or AWS Outposts unify management across environments.

  - o **Implementing secure gateways**: Use VPNs or dedicated connections like AWS Direct Connect for secure data transfer.

Aligning DevOps and operational excellence principles

To successfully align DevOps practices with operational excellence, solutions architects should adopt key strategies that enhance automation, collaboration, and system reliability. The following practices are essential for achieving these goals:

- **CI/CD pipelines for continuous delivery**: CI/CD pipelines make integration, testing, and deployment processes more streamlined for code. Benefits include:

  o **Decreased deployment times**: Automating builds and deployments will speed up iterations.

  o **Improved reliability**: Automated tests catch the errors early on in the development cycle.

  o **Increased collaboration**: Shared pipelines increase visibility and accountability between teams.

- **Automated monitoring and observability**: DevOps focuses on real-time monitoring and observability to detect and resolve issues proactively. Tools like Prometheus, AWS CloudWatch, and Azure Monitor offer:

  o **Comprehensive dashboards**: Visualize system performance and identify bottlenecks.

  o **Alerting mechanisms**: Notify teams of anomalies before they impact users.

- **Infrastructure as code**: IaC allows for the automation of infrastructure provisioning using tools like Terraform or Ansible. This approach ensures consistent environments across development, testing, and production.

Practical recommendations

Achieving operational excellence in modern architectures requires not just theoretical knowledge but actionable strategies that can be applied during system design, implementation, and operation.

The following is a set of practical recommendations placed in context, giving direction for solutions architects toward robust, scalable, and efficient systems:

- **Adopt cloud-native tools**: Cloud-native tools can be very powerful in monitoring, observing, and optimizing system health. Observability platforms such as AWS CloudWatch, Azure Monitor, and Google Cloud Operations Suite allow for the real-time tracking of system performance, resource utilization, and error rates. These tools empower teams to detect anomalies early, address issues proactively, and maintain high availability. For example, you can set up alarms and dashboards for tracking metrics with AWS CloudWatch so that you can react in time to potential bottlenecks.

- **Standardize across platforms**: Standardization is easier in multi-cloud and hybrid environments. The use of Kubernetes and containerization makes deployments platform-agnostic, making it easy to move and scale workloads between various cloud providers. This way, vendor lock-in is minimized, and the process of system upgrades is streamlined. For instance, using Docker containers managed by Kubernetes allows teams to run workloads consistently on AWS, Azure, and on-premises data centers.

- **Automate early**: Automation enhances operational efficiency and reduces human error. CI/CD pipelines and IaC during the designing phase streamline deployments and ensure consistent environments. Tools like Jenkins, GitHub Actions, Terraform, and Ansible automate code integration to infrastructure provisioning that accelerates development cycles and improves systems' reliability.

- **Test for resilience**: Resilience testing ensures systems can handle unexpected failures without significant disruption. Chaos engineering exercises, using tools like Gremlin or Chaos Monkey, simulate real-world failure scenarios to evaluate system robustness. These tests identify vulnerabilities in failover mechanisms, redundancy setups, and error-handling strategies, allowing teams to address weaknesses before they impact users. For example, injecting latency into database connections during a test can reveal how well your application handles degraded performance.

With these strategies, solutions architects will be able to design systems aligned with technical and business goals while preparing for the real world.

Organizations will achieve operational excellence in modern architectures by integrating cloud-native technologies, addressing multi-cloud and hybrid challenges, and aligning DevOps principles with operational goals. These strategies will ensure that the systems are resilient, scalable, and able to withstand the demands of today's dynamic technological landscape.

Conclusion

Operational excellence is not a one-time achievement but an ongoing commitment to improvement. Solutions architects play a pivotal role in embedding operational efficiency, scalability, resilience, and maintainability into system designs. By strategically leveraging cloud-native technologies, fostering a feedback-driven culture, and embracing modern DevOps practices, solutions architects can create systems that remain Agile, responsive, and aligned with evolving business needs.

Incorporating SRE principles further strengthens reliability by simplifying operational complexity and reducing downtime. Together, these strategies enable organizations to build high-performing, user-centric systems that thrive in fast-paced, ever-evolving technological landscapes.

Looking ahead, the next chapter gets into cloud-native architecture and design, which is a critical approach for developing applications that fully harness the power of cloud platforms. This upcoming chapter will guide you through designing cloud-native systems, implementing containerization and orchestration strategies, and adopting reference architectures that enhance scalability, flexibility, and performance in modern cloud environments.

Key takeaways

The takeaways are as follows:

- **Principles of operational excellence**: Automation, feedback loops, and adaptability are key to efficiency and resilience.

- **Cloud-native and modern architectures**: Adopt Kubernetes, serverless technologies, and CI/CD pipelines for scalable, efficient systems.

- **Resilience practices**: Employ fault tolerance mechanisms like redundancy, failover systems, and circuit breakers to gracefully handle failures.

- **Culture of continuous improvement**: Build a feedback-driven culture with robust incident management and regular retrospectives to ensure continuous improvement.

- **Collaboration**: Use SRE practices to collaborate between engineering and operational teams to bridge the gaps and drive innovation in the solutions.

Model interview questions and answers

1. **How would you design a scalable and resilient system for an application with unpredictable traffic spikes?**

   Model answer:

   To design a scalable and resilient system:

   - **Scalability**: Use auto-scaling groups in cloud platforms like AWS or Azure to handle traffic spikes. Horizontal scaling is preferred for stateless applications. Implement load balancing to distribute traffic across servers.

- **Resilience**: Design fault-tolerant systems using redundant components and failover mechanisms. Use database replication and caching to ensure data availability.

- **Example**: For a streaming service, use a **content delivery network (CDN)** for edge caching and auto-scaling for backend services.

2. **How do you ensure the maintainability of a complex enterprise application?**

    Model answer:

    - **Modular architecture**: Adopt microservices or Domain-Driven Design to break the system into manageable components.

    - **Clean code practices**: Enforce coding standards and conduct regular code reviews.

    - **Comprehensive documentation**: Maintain updated architecture diagrams, API specifications, and operational runbooks.

    - **Example**: For an e-commerce application, separate payment, inventory, and order management services for independent updates and scalability.

3. **What tools would you use to monitor a distributed system and why?**

    Model answer:

    - **Monitoring tools**: Use Prometheus for metrics collection, Grafana for visualization, and **Elasticsearch, Logstash, and Kibana (ELK)** stack for log analysis.

    - **Observability tools**: Implement OpenTelemetry for distributed tracing to identify bottlenecks.

    - **Example**: For a microservices architecture, use Prometheus to monitor individual service performance and Grafana for centralized dashboards.

4. **How do you balance innovation with reliability in a production system?**

    Model answer:

    - Introduce error budgets to quantify acceptable risks, allowing innovation while maintaining reliability.

    - Use blue-green deployments or canary releases to minimize the impact of new features.

    - Conduct extensive testing in staging environments before production rollout.

    - **Example**: For a banking application, test new features in a sandbox environment and release them incrementally with real-time monitoring.

5. **How would you handle a system outage caused by a critical component failure?**

    Model answer:

    - **Immediate action**: Trigger incident response protocols and notify the on-call team. Use monitoring tools to isolate the issue.

    - **Temporary mitigation**: Redirect traffic using a failover mechanism or revert to a previous stable version.

    - **Postmortem analysis**: Conduct root cause analysis and implement preventive measures like better monitoring or more redundancy.

    - **Example**: For an API outage, switch to a backup instance and analyse logs to pinpoint the failure cause.

CHAPTER 22

Cloud-native Architecture and Design

Introduction

Cloud-native architecture is about architecting and designing applications for the cloud. With the cloud becoming an inevitable option over the last decade, all enterprises, large or small, have roadmaps to move their workloads to the cloud. The cloud importantly provides a scalable environment that modern-day enterprises need to grow their businesses at a global scale. The cloud provides predictability of infrastructure and platforms on which enterprises deploy their applications. The cloud-native applications are specifically designed to leverage the dynamic nature of the cloud and take full advantage of the services provided by the cloud. Applications tend to gain a lot when they are architected and designed, using industry accepted principles and reference application architectures that have been created and refined over a period and have been adopted by numerous enterprises.

Structure

This chapter covers the following topics:

- Cloud-native architecture preview
- Considerations for cloud-native architecture
- Containerization and orchestration
- Deep dive into cloud-native architecture
- Taking advantage of cloud-native architecture
- Cloud-native reference architecture
- Migrating non-cloud workloads to a cloud-native architecture
- Cloud-native application design patterns
- Security in a cloud-native architecture

Objectives

In this chapter, readers will get an overview of the cloud-native architecture and the broad types of services offered on the cloud. The chapter will cover the factors a solutions architect should consider while architecting applications for the cloud, including prerequisites such as containerization and orchestration technologies. The chapter will discuss containerization and orchestration in detail, which are the underpinning technologies behind cloud-native applications. We will also cover the design principles guiding cloud-native architecture and the characteristics of cloud-native applications. We will further move on to discuss application reference architecture for the cloud with a specific example of it on a major cloud provider, Azure. Along with the cloud-native architecture, we will also look at best practices for migrating a non-cloud workload to a cloud-native format. We will also look at the design patterns that cloud-native applications can use to make the architecture robust, modular, and maintainable. We will also cover cloud application security using the OAuth 2.0 framework, which is commonly used to secure cloud-native applications.

Cloud-native architecture preview

The cloud has transformed the way applications are conceptualized, designed, built and deployed. A cloud-native architecture is one in which the architect takes full advantage of the features offered by the cloud provider to blueprint the solution as a set of loosely coupled services. In *Chapter 3, Technical Proficiency Essential Knowledge,* we discussed the following four types of computing models offered by popular cloud providers. They are:

- IaaS
- PaaS
- SaaS
- Serverless computing

Solutions architects leverage one or more of these capabilities offered in the cloud to blueprint and develop cloud-native applications. Cloud-native applications differ from other applications in that they are developed by keeping the cloud offered services as the first option in a given list of choices.

Cloud-native applications are developed as independent software components and, to a large extent, make use of the compute, integration, and data services available on the cloud to build their capabilities rather than getting an external software platform or service to be deployed on the cloud to fulfil the required capability. Cloud-native applications are born on the cloud and are deployed on public or private clouds offered by providers like **Amazon Web Services** (**AWS**), Microsoft Azure, and **Google Cloud Platform** (**GCP**).

Having got an overview of cloud-native architecture, we will look at the factors to be considered for cloud movement and architecting applications for the cloud.

Considerations for cloud-native architecture

The cloud is a very dynamic environment, providing a host of services for different capabilities that are required to build and host applications. Before embarking on a journey into the cloud, it is important to understand the factors that influence the development and deployment of applications on the cloud.

It is important for a solutions architect to know these factors to decide the suitability of hosting applications on the cloud. We can categorize the factors as operational and technical. The operational factors relate to regulatory compliance, choice of the cloud provider, organization readiness for the cloud, and the costs associated with the cloud. The technical factors include application complexity, automation readiness, DevOps adoption, and the ability to monitor and maintain applications on the cloud for the long term.

The operational factors that will influence the movement to cloud and the cloud architecture to be adopted are as follows:

- **Regulatory compliance**: This relates to adhering to the laws of the region. In cloud-native architecture, all the application components reside on the cloud, including the data generated and used by the application. If the application deals with sensitive and private data pertaining to customers, there could be regulations that prevent storage of such data on the cloud infrastructure. The solutions architect should be aware of such regulatory implications before coming up with an application architecture that works on the cloud.

- **Stakeholder buy-in**: The enterprise should initially prepare for cloud migration. This requires an assessment of their application inventory and prioritizing them based on their mission critical nature. It is not just an architectural decision to move workloads to the cloud. There are business stakeholders who should be kept informed of their applications moving to the cloud, and their buy-in to move to the cloud becomes very critical. There could be multiple levels of approval required from both the business and technology side before a decision to move to the cloud is taken. For enterprises embarking on their cloud journey, it makes more sense to move some of their non-critical workloads to the cloud to test the waters before they move their mission critical applications to the cloud.

- **Choice of cloud providers**: All the major cloud providers offer a similar set of services on their cloud. Once an application is deployed on the cloud, it takes effort and time to move applications to another cloud provider. Therefore, the decision to choose a cloud provider becomes very tricky and important. The cost of ownership and vendor support could be one of the driving factors in choosing a cloud provider. Some of the enterprises might already have an ongoing contract with an existing vendor, based on which the vendor may offer competitive pricing for the enterprise. Another factor that could affect the choice is the pace and ability of the cloud provider to roll out new services on the cloud.

- **Cost and budget**: The cloud gives you pay as you go model. The enterprise must understand the overall cost of ownership to run and maintain its workloads on the cloud. Some of the cloud providers offer discounted pricing models if the enterprise could commit to a set of infrastructure (reserved instances) usage annually. There are also options in which the customer can avail themselves of discounts if a certain amount is paid upfront. The solutions architect, hence, should have an overview of the different pricing models available for the enterprise moving to the cloud. The solution architect should also look at some of the exclusive and expensive services that the application might need on the cloud and suggest an appropriate solution or an alternative to it. Some of the cloud providers also provide spot instances, which can be used for jobs that can be terminated and continued based on infrastructure availability. Such infrastructure is offered at very low prices to the customer. An architect should carefully craft their solution to make use of the different options available on the cloud, which will reduce the overall cost of application development, deployment, and maintenance on the cloud.

After addressing operational factors, solutions architects must also assess the technical feasibility to ensure optimal cloud deployment and long-term maintenance.

The following are the technical considerations for an architect while architecting solutions on the cloud:

- **Application architecture considerations**: Cloud-native architecture warrants that the applications be built as smaller components or microservices. Most of the applications born on the cloud make heavy use of containerization to scale up or scale down the infrastructure depending on the load to the application. A solutions architect should keep this in mind and assess the suitability of the application being architected on the cloud. They should carefully weigh the requirements for cloud suitability and recommend whether the application can be architected for the cloud. There are other options available on the cloud where applications can be directly deployed using managed services like an Azure App Service or an AWS Elastic Beanstalk. The solutions architect, hence, plays a key role in deciding the appropriate solution for building and deploying applications on the cloud.

- **Automate everything**: The cloud is a very dynamic environment. Infrastructure can virtually be scaled infinitely. When it comes to cloud-native architecture, the applications are built and deployed as independent components. The cloud gives an immense advantage for hosting these kinds of components. However, for provisioning infrastructure and ensuring their scalability, automation plays a key role. Architects need to consider tools like Terraform, Azure resource manager, to help create the required infrastructure for applications. When applications are built, there must be proper DevOps pipelines built alongside to support automated building, testing, and deployment of the cloud-native applications. The architect also needs to configure the infrastructure to scale as appropriate automatically using rules provided by the cloud provider. For instance, you can configure a rule to increase the memory of the computing instance from 8GB to 16GB based on usage.

These cloud-native application components, being granular, lend themselves very well to the cloud environment and can scale extremely fast without having to depend on any external libraries or platforms.

- **Application security considerations**: Cloud offers a shared security model. The cloud provider is responsible for the security of the infrastructure provided. The customer is responsible for the security of the applications deployed on the cloud. The architect needs to have a clear understanding of the security measures that need to be put in place for the applications being deployed on the cloud. The architect also needs to understand industry accepted standards that are required for the specific data that is being handled and stored, and ensure that the cloud infrastructure and the platform comply with those standards. For instance, PCI DSS is the widely accepted standard for handling credit card data. The architect needs to ensure that the cloud provider is PCI DSS compliant before choosing to deploy and run their applications on that cloud. The architect also needs to think of solutions for allowing third party partners and applications to access the enterprise's cloud-native applications being deployed on the cloud.

- **Observability considerations**: Given the dynamic nature of the cloud infrastructure, the architect must devise approaches for monitoring the moving parts of the cloud infrastructure, performance of the applications deployed, and the continued security posture of applications. Popular cloud providers offer the required tools for monitoring the infrastructure and application performance on the cloud. There are services to check if the infrastructure and other services used comply with a specific configuration as per the enterprise requirements. Any deviations from the required configuration can result in support or the development team being notified for corrective action to be taken. As for the cloud-native applications, the architect should leverage the right services for a distributed tracing of the request flow across components.

Having discussed the factors that an architect should consider for deploying applications on the cloud, we will move to the next section to understand how cloud-native applications are architected and developed on the cloud. Containerization is an important concept that allows these components to be packaged and deployed on the cloud. In the following section, we will discuss containerization in detail and its counterpart, the virtual machine. We will also discuss the topic of orchestration, which helps to manage the instances of an application service deployed on the cloud in the most optimal way as required by an enterprise.

Containerization and orchestration

The way software is developed, packaged, and deployed has changed drastically in the last decade. Containerization and container orchestration have transformed the development, deployment, and management of software components. From large compilation units like a **web archive (WAR)** or an **enterprise archive (EAR)** file containing all the code and configuration artefacts, the software packaging mechanism has come a long way to bundle them as images and run as containers.

Orchestration is the way the containers are managed within the container runtime. Orchestration tools help to manage the deployed software units, ensuring optimum infrastructure usage and continuous uptime of applications.

Containerization and orchestration have become an integral part of cloud-native architecture. They make use of cloud capabilities like hardware clustering and autoscaling to provide the required quality of services that modern day enterprises need for their software applications.

Virtual machines

It is important for a solutions architect to understand the difference between virtual machines and containers, as there is still an ambiguity between the two and they are used interchangeably.

Virtual machines fundamentally virtualize the hardware component of a server or a host. This helps us to install multiple guest operating systems on the host machine. For instance, you can install a flavor of the Unix operating system on a host running Windows with the help of the virtualization software. There are multiple choices of virtualization software available, such as Oracle VirtualBox and Microsoft Hyper-V.

The following figure depicts the organization of components in a virtual machine:

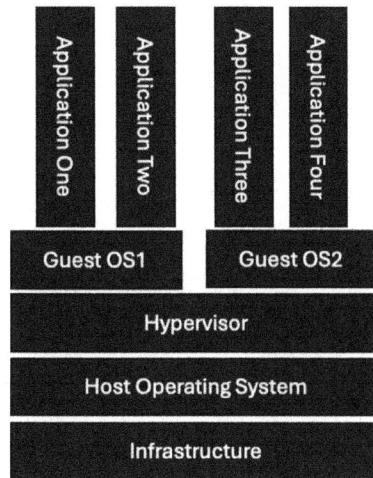

Figure 22.1: Virtual machine

The guest operating systems within a single server take up their own resources on the host in terms of memory and computing power. When a virtualization software is installed on a machine, it installs a component called the hypervisor, which acts as an interface layer between the guest operating systems and the host operating system. The hypervisor interprets the commands of the guest operating system and passes on the commands to the host operating system. It also provides other services to the guest operating system, like networking and resource allocation. Though the virtual machines help to run multiple guest operating systems on the host, the guest operating systems take a good chunk of resources on the host machine, making them heavier and inefficient from a resource usage perspective. Despite the consumption of resources by individual guest operating systems, virtual machines was a disruptive thought in the direction of hardware utilization. Virtual machines helped to run multiple operating systems on powerful machines, providing efficient utilization of hardware and optimization of cost. They importantly laid the foundation for cloud computing by introducing the concept of sharing computing power by multiple users. They also showcased that these individual partitions can be run in an isolated manner, so that the security concerns of one virtual machine do not affect the other virtual machine. The virtual machines also provided fault tolerance, in which the failure of one of the virtual machines did not affect the other virtual machines running on the host.

The hardware virtualization was taken a step further to give way for the concept of containerization, in which the host system operating system is virtualized rather than the hardware of the host system. We will discuss containerization in detail in the next section.

Containerization

Containerization is packaging of software components in a way that they are independent and self-contained. The packaged software that can be executed or run using specific commands is called an image. The software component is packaged(image) along with all its dependencies so that it can be deployed and run independently. The salient feature of containerization is its ability to create images that are portable and can be run in any hardware and software configuration that has a standardized container run time. When the images are run, the images are called containers. The images are run in a specific environment called the container runtime, which offers a specialized layer over the operating system to host and execute these software containers. Docker is one of the popular containers run time that is being used by many of the enterprises. These containers run times are available for most of the popular operating systems like Linux and Windows and the containers deployed and tested in a developer's laptop can be seamlessly deployed on any other machine running the container run time without any changes.

The following figure depicts the containerization of software components:

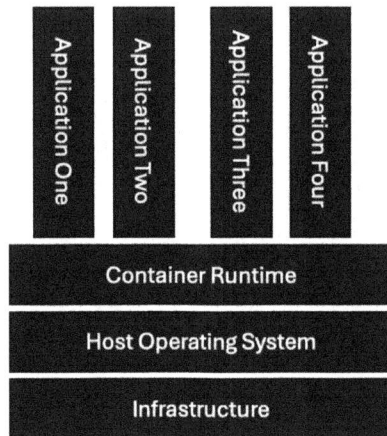

Figure 22.2: Container organization

Orchestration

Orchestration is an approach using which the containers (microservices) on the cloud are managed in a cloud-native architecture. Once the application is deployed as a set of containers on the cloud infrastructure, there will be multiple instances of the container running on the cloud, based on a scalability factor. This is to avoid a single point of failure and to spread the load across multiple redundant instances of the microservice. The container instance in some cases runs on a separate physical machine (though it can be shared) to have a standardized configuration for the instance of the container. Using a container orchestration tool is one of the best ways to manage clusters (group of servers or nodes) and containers on the cloud. The orchestration tool ensures that there is optimum utilization of hardware resources in terms of how the containers are deployed and managed within the nodes on the cloud. It also provides a completely automated way to keep the desired number of container instances of a microservice running on the cloud. If one of the containers gets terminated due to a technical glitch, the orchestration tool immediately spins up a new container of the microservice thereby keeping the number of container instances at a level required to service customer requests within accepted levels of performance. It also helps to route requests from one microservice container to another in the most optimum way so that the load on the system is kept in balance. The orchestration tool also exposes a feature in the form of APIs to take inputs from the user to increase or decrease the desired number of container instances for a specific microservice in a cluster.

Figure 22.3 depicts the major components of an orchestration engine. This is based on Kubernetes, a popular container orchestration tool available to manage clusters and containers both on the cloud and on premise as well.

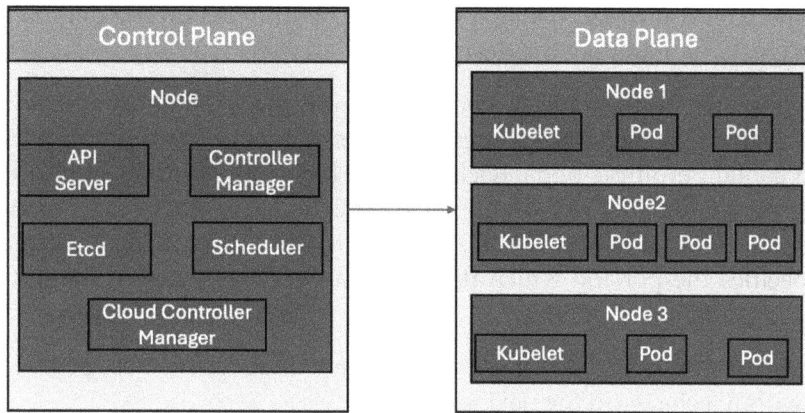

Figure 22.3: Kubernetes orchestration components

The architecture of the orchestration tool is divided into a control plane and a data plane. The control plane has the components necessary to manage the entire cluster and to keep it in a state of equilibrium based on the needs of the application. The data plane has nodes into which the microservices containers are deployed and run. The control plane has total control of the data plane and keeps track of all activities that happen within the data plane.

The components of a control plane are as follows:

- **API server**: This component of the control plane exposes a feature to take inputs through APIs or command line (a tool like kubectl) from the user to create new containers on the cloud and to increase or decrease the number of already running container instances of a microservice at the required level. The API server is internally wired with other components of the control plane to achieve this.

- **Controller manager**: The controller manager monitors the state of the cluster and keeps the nodes and the containers in each node to the desired state as required by the application. This also enables internode communication by enabling the routes required. In the cloud environment, it manages the load balancers required for each service pertaining to the deployment containing a group of pods. Each pod is a computational unit in a host within which one or more containers reside. A group of pods is clubbed as a deployment. A service is an artefact created to interact with deployment in the cluster.

- **Scheduler**: The scheduler schedules new pods into the nodes based on the resource availability within the cluster. This component continuously assesses the requirements of the application within the cluster and assigns the pod to a node that has the least load at that point in time. It ensures optimal usage of the cluster.

- **Etcd**: This is a distributed key value storage which stores the current state of the cluster. It is a central point of information for the scheduler and controller manager to understand how many nodes and pods are operational in the cluster. Any input from the user through the API server updates the etcd database so that the controller manager and the scheduler can pick it up and act on it to adjust the state of the cluster based on the application needs.

- **Cloud controller manager**: This is a component of the control plane that has cloud specific logic. It links the cluster with the cloud providers APIs. It separates the components in the cluster that interact with the cloud versus others that do not need to interact with the cloud provider. The cloud controller manager component is specifically for the cloud and is not installed when the cluster is installed on premises.

The components of a data plane are as follows:

- **Kubelet**: This is an agent that is present in each of the nodes in the cluster. This transmits any changes to the nodes and the pods in those nodes to the control plane. Any node or pod failure is informed to the control plane. The controller manager and the scheduler act on the data to accordingly to adjust the state of the cluster to maintain the desired state.

- **Pods**: The data plane of the cluster comprises multiple worker nodes. A pod is the minimal computational unit within the node, inside which a container of the application runs. Each node in the data plane can contain multiple pods. Each pod can have one or more containers. As stated earlier, a set of pods is grouped together as a deployment, which enables them to be managed as a single unit. The deployment is exposed to applications external to the cluster using an artefact called the service. The service specifies the port on which the pods can be reached from the outside world in a load balanced way.

Having seen the components of an orchestration engine, we will cover the best practices for deploying and managing containers within a cluster in the next section.

Best practices for application deployment

Once the microservices are developed as containers, the following are some of the best practices a solutions architect can recommend to ease deployment, enable health checks, ensure security, and group resources. It is applicable to Kubernetes, a popular container management tool that is being used widely by enterprises. The details are as follows:

- **Grouping pods as namespaces**: Once the application has been containerized as microservices, as a best practice, we can logically group pods in a cluster using a concept called a namespace. The namespace is a virtual cluster within the overall larger cluster that allows you to create separate environments for the ease of managing the resources. We can have namespaces for different environments like development and testing within the cluster. Namespaces can also be used to segregate type of components like pods containing business logic versus pods that hold database logic. Namespaces also provide role-based access that help to assign permissions at each namespace level. We can also use namespaces to assign resource limits such as memory and computation power.

- **Use secrets for secure data**: Each application uses confidential information like user IDs and passwords to connect to the database and API keys for connecting to external APIs. Instead of hardcoding this information within application code., Kubernetes secrets can be used to store them. This is done by creation of an encryption configuration file and enabling encryption in the API server of the control plane.

- **Using configmaps for application configuration data**: In Kubernetes, application configuration data can be stored in configmaps. It can be used to store environment specific data, which can help write cleaner code within the application. However, it needs to be noted that the data stored in a configmap is not encrypted. The configmaps should not be used to store sensitive information. Any update to the configuration information inside the configmap does not automatically reflect in the microservices code deployed as a pod. Hence, the pods need to be restarted in case of configuration updates.

- **Implement health checks for microservice container pods**: Readiness and liveness probes can be included as part of the pod specification. Readiness tells Kubernetes that a pod is ready and operational to service requests from the client. Liveness probes inform Kubernetes about the problems encountered by a pod in operation. Kubernetes decides either to restart the pod or to destroy it and create a new pod for the microservice.

- **Use Helm for application management**: Helm is a package manager for Kubernetes. It aids in packaging different artefacts of Kubernetes like deployments, services and configmaps into a single package called the helm chart. Usage of Helm charts can help to seamlessly package and deploy applications on the cluster. They also help in maintaining multiple versions of a microservice.

- **Use horizontal pod autoscalers (HPA)**: Kubernetes can be instructed to scale up the number of pods based on resource usage. HPAs compute the replica count (desired number of pods) based on a threshold resource utilization. If the resource utilization exceeds the threshold, Kubernetes increases the number of pods. Similarly, if the current utilization of resources falls below the threshold limit, it reduces the number of pods, thereby making optimal use of resources. HPAs can be set up through command line tools (kubectl) or through YAML configuration.

Now that we have seen containerization and orchestration, the central concepts to cloud-native architecture, and the best practices for their usage, we will go deeper into the principles of cloud-native architecture and how cloud-native applications are developed.

Deep dive into cloud-native architecture

Cloud-native architecture is an approach in which the application is built as microservices and deployed as containers, making use of the compute, data storage, networking, and integration services of the cloud provider. Microservices and containerization together provide the backbone of a cloud-native application architecture overseen by an orchestration engine for optimal performance on the cloud. We have seen the microservices architecture, its advantages, and applicability in *Chapter 4, Technical Solutions Architecture and Design*. The microservices architecture takes advantage of the dynamic nature of the cloud infrastructure, along with other engineering principles like DevOps, to provide the required functionality and quality of services to the end customer.

Cloud-native architecture lets the solutions architects and developers make use of several features offered by the cloud like infrastructure redundancy, virtually infinite scalability, a shared security model and reliability of hardware and software platforms. Cloud-native architecture also stands out in the way they respond to failure situations.

The following are the key principles of cloud-native architecture according to the **Cloud Native Council Foundation (CNCF)**, an organization that promotes the adoption of cloud-native applications and supported by cloud providers like Microsoft, Google and Amazon Web services. These principles are fundamental to the adoption of cloud and building cloud-native applications. Each cloud provider offers a rich set of run time options and tools to build, deploy and monitor cloud-native applications in a standard way. For instance, Azure provides **Azure Kubernetes Service (AKS)** and AWS provides a similar service called **Elastic Kubernetes Service (EKS)** to deploy and run cloud-native applications on the cloud. Moreover, they provide the required auxiliary services for a continuous monitoring of these deployed applications thereby providing a control of how applications should be run and managed on the cloud.

Figure 22.4 depicts the principles of cloud-native architecture for a quick reference:

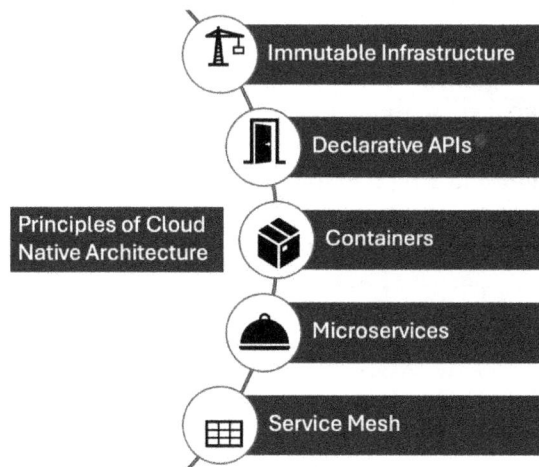

Figure 22.4: Principles of cloud-native architecture

The principles of a cloud-native architecture explained as follows helps in blueprinting applications that can lend themselves to be deployed on any of the cloud providers without major customization:

- **Immutable infrastructure**: An immutable infrastructure is one which does not undergo any changes after it has been created. If the infrastructure after deployment of the application needs a change, the existing infrastructure is torn down, and new infrastructure is provisioned, and the application gets deployed on the new provisioned infrastructure. For instance, if a microservice needs a higher compute capacity due to a demand in throughput, the existing server is destroyed and the microservice gets deployed in a server with multiple cores. This promotes automation which is very important for a dynamic environment like the cloud where manual management of the cloud resources could be laborious and error prone. Immutable infrastructure also provides scalability, fault isolation, ease of deployment, and rollback, along with reduced operational tasks.

- **Declarative APIs**: Declarative APIs are APIs that take inputs from the users and help them to realize the end state on the cloud infrastructure, without having the users know how the API works internally. Declarative APIs are more about what users want rather than how it is achieved. Declarative APIs are very relevant to cloud-native architecture as they help in scaling infrastructure through instructions (infrastructure as code) provided. They promulgate the acceleration of automation within the cloud infrastructure that can be made use by microservices in provisioning the required infrastructure for their operations. These APIs also help achieve consistency of configuration of the provisioned infrastructure across different environments like development, testing, staging, and production, thereby bringing predictability to the cloud environment. Examples of declarative APIs include the APIs exposed by the Kubernetes control plane, which help to provision the required resources like pods or services within the Kubernetes data plane.

- **Containers**: We have already discussed the working of containers in the section *Containerization and orchestration*. Containerization platforms provide the required runtime for cloud-native architecture in which applications are developed as microservices. In addition to optimizing resources, containerization also standardizes the platform on which the microservices reside. This means that a microservice image behaves the same way on a container run time, irrespective of the hardware. This results in a huge benefit in terms of testing the software early in the lifecycle. A microservice developed as an image, run as a container, and tested in a developer's laptop with a container runtime behaves the same way across different cloud provider environments.

- **Microservices**: Microservices architecture lend themselves very well to cloud-native architecture because of their ability to be deployed independently and be scaled without the need to be dependent on external factors like the hardware configuration or the operating system.

- **Service mesh**: A service mesh is a software layer that manages many of the cross-cutting concerns like networking, inter service communication, security and observability. A service mesh makes more sense in the case of a cloud-native application because of the way the application is divided into multiple smaller components(microservices) and the dynamic way in which multiple instances of those components are managed within the cloud infrastructure. An extra layer of the service mesh software becomes necessary to manage the capabilities of networking, security of communication between components and monitoring the usage of services and the nodes in an optimal way. Hence, a service mesh is one of the prescribed layers of software in cloud-native architecture. Istio and Linkerd are the popular service meshes used by enterprises while deploying cloud-native applications on the cloud.

Having looked at the principles behind cloud-native architecture, the following are the key characteristics of cloud-native applications:

- **Distributable**: To reemphasize, cloud-native applications are built as loosely coupled components or microservices. This is to take advantage of the virtually infinite scaling of infrastructure provided by the cloud. Smaller components are easier to scale with minimum startup times.

- **Observable**: A request to a cloud-native application span across multiple microservices and the requests flowing through them are tracked using special software or a cloud provider service. For example, AWS X-Ray is a service which provides distributed tracing of cloud-native applications. This helps the developer and production support teams to very easily debug technical problems and fix them quickly.

- **Portable**: The cloud-native application does not have a lock in with a particular cloud provider and they are built to be vendor neutral and can be ported to any cloud provider with minimum effort.

- **Interoperable**: All the microservices in the cloud-native application expose their functionality using well designed APIs, which can be consumed by other services using standard application protocols.

- **Available**: The cloud-native applications have high availability because of features like auto scaling which kick in if an instance of the service is down. Another identical instance of the service is automatically created.

Having discussed what cloud-native architecture is and the key principles behind it, let us move on to see how a cloud-native architecture benefits from the unique features of the cloud.

Taking advantage of cloud-native architecture

Applications on the cloud can benefit from unique models and services that are inherent to the cloud. These are offered by popular cloud providers under various names. We make use of them in our applications depending on the nature, complexity and the requirements of the application.

Multi-cloud deployment

Cloud-native architecture lends itself easily to a multi-cloud deployment arrangement. In a multi-cloud architecture, applications can be deployed across two or more cloud providers to avoid vendor lock-in. They also help to adhere to regulatory compliance for workloads in which a single provider may not be able to fulfill all requirements. A multi-cloud architecture provides cost advantages for workloads in which expensive services could be moved to a cloud provider that provides them at a lower cost. Cloud-native architectures built as containers and orchestrated using market popular orchestration tools (Kubernetes) provide the enterprise with the flexibility to deploy their workloads across multiple clouds. They also provide the advantage of moving the application from one cloud provider to another with minimum effort.

Serverless computing

As stated earlier, cloud-native architectures can take advantage of the serverless computing model on the cloud. In a serverless computing model, the developers only need to write code and deploy it in the software platform of their choice. The hardware and software platforms are maintained by the cloud provider. Microservices and event-driven architecture hugely benefit from the serverless computing model. AWS Lambda and Azure functions are some of the examples of the serverless computing model.

Edge computing

Edge computing is a model in which the resources, like computing power and storage space, are brought closer to the applications that need them rather than deploying the application to a specific region on cloud. Given the complexity of data formats and limitations in the network band width, the edge computing model provides greater performance by getting near the application and source of data. The edge computing model is very prevalent in health care and manufacturing applications where the sensitivity and volume of data are high. The edge computing model provides high performance at locations where the network bandwidth is a challenge. It also helps to adhere to data protection laws, which prohibit the movement of data to locations other than where it was produced. Edge computing is also useful in applications where large amounts of data are produced, analyzed, and acted upon quickly.

Content delivery network

The cloud offers a feature called the **content delivery network** (**CDN**) to cache the content across multiple points of presence of the cloud provider across the globe. When a user requests content, the request is routed to the cache location that is nearest to the user, and the content is served from that location. When an application is deployed on the cloud, the back-end services can be configured to use the CDN to serve the data to the user. If there is a cache miss, the request is routed to the backend service, and in the round trip, the data is cached in the CDN for future requests. CDN offers the capability to cache content based on a set of keys that can be used to fetch the response. It is used by applications in which the user needs to download large files, such as videos and images. This feature is particularly useful for applications offering educational content to users. The content delivery network also provides a capability to demarcate content that is downloadable free of cost versus a download that is allowed only for subscribed users. The CDN can also be configured to make use of secure protocols like **transport layer security** (**TLS**) that we discussed in *Chapter 3, Technical Proficiency Essential Knowledge*.

Financial operations

Financial operations (**FinOps**) for short, is a framework that lets different divisions in the enterprise work together to continuously innovate ways of optimizing resources to reduce the total cost of the cloud. Cloud is a very dynamic environment, and in large enterprises where multiple units move their workloads to the cloud, the enterprise can lose sight of the cloud services usage, and the costs can shoot up very quickly. It is therefore mandatory for the enterprise to lay down principles of usage for resources on the cloud. Teams from information technology, business, and finance work closely to gain real time visibility into the usage of the cloud and help the enterprise to make informed decisions to increase or limit the spending on the cloud. FinOps encourages a shared responsibility model in which the budget is allocated by the finance team. The business teams prioritize their application features based on the budget allocated. The technology team makes judicious use of the allocated budget in provisioning infrastructure and other services on the cloud to build applications offering maximum business value to the enterprise and its customers.

Infrastructure as code

One of the advantages of the cloud is its elasticity. Infrastructure can be created or terminated at will, based on user requirements. Cloud providers offer the capability to express the infrastructure requirement as code. Each cloud provider has its own syntax to represent their services along with attributes to describe their initial setup and configuration. This is a huge shift in terms of how enterprises deal with their infrastructure requirements on the cloud. When the enterprise wants to make a change to the existing infrastructure, the cloud provider allows the enterprise to visually compare the existing and new setups, which helps in making sure that there are no gaps that could cause a potential infrastructure or application outage. AWS CloudFormation and Azure resource manager templates are examples of services that help in defining infrastructure as code.

Cloud-native reference architecture

A reference architecture is a sample blueprint that has all the best practices and industry standard guidelines built into it. Reference architecture for specific technologies or platforms is published by leading engineering companies or organizations formed as a conglomerate of multiple top engineering firms in the world. The reference architecture is vendor neutral and offers guidance to build an architecture. Enterprises can use reference architecture to build applications with the most appropriate technology stack for each of the layers or components in it. Take a look at the following figure for a better understanding:

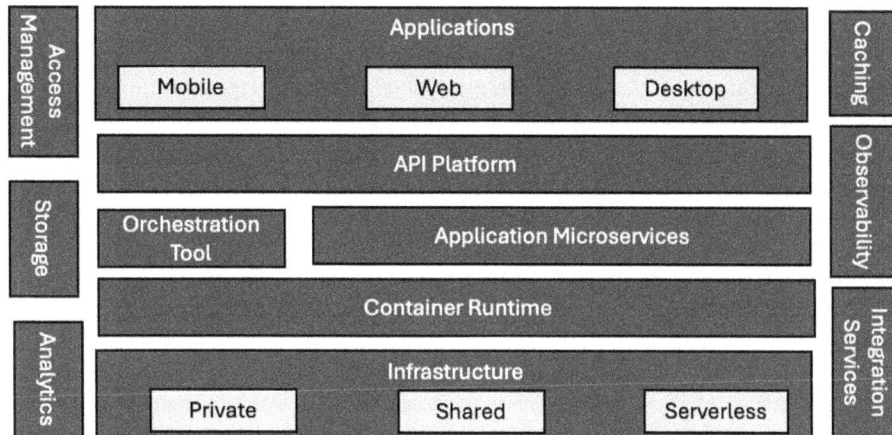

Figure 22.5: Cloud-native architecture

The key components of the reference architecture are as follows:

- **Infrastructure layer**: This provides the required hardware for running the cloud-native applications. The infrastructure can be provisioned to be dedicated (private) for a single customer, or it can be shared (public) with multiple customers (called multitenancy). The cloud also provides a serverless computing model in which the hardware and software platforms are completely managed by the cloud provider, and the developer just needs to write and run the code.

- **Container runtime**: The container run time provides the required platform to deploy and manage the microservices of the application. Each microservice is created as an image using popular container platform tools like Docker. These images are deployed and run within the container run time whose instances can be controlled using configuration files. The image is packaged to have all the dependencies (libraries) required for the microservice to operate and scale independently.

- **Microservices**: These are the application microservices within the cloud-native application. These microservices comprise business capabilities that are exposed using well defined interfaces. Microservices lend themselves very well to the cloud environment. Microservice instances can be scaled up or down based on business needs.

- **Orchestration tool**: As seen earlier, this manages the number of instances (containers) of the microservices on the cloud. It is responsible for creating the required number of containers within the cloud based on the desired state. The orchestration tool makes sure that the number of instances of a microservice does not go below the desired count. The user can increase or decrease the number of instances in the desired state through command line tools or through APIs. The orchestration tool will automatically scale up or scale down the number of container instances based on that user input. As discussed before, the orchestration tool is also supplemented with a service mesh that provides additional capabilities such as security for interservice communication and enhanced monitoring.

- **API gateway**: This is the component that exposes the application to internal and external parties. The APIs are created and deployed to aggregate the calls to the microservices based on business requirements. The API platform also provides security by authenticating the requests made to the application by interfacing with the identity provider. The API platform has the capability to throttle requests to the microservices, thereby avoiding flooding of requests to the application components. API platform supports policies that regulate the number of requests to the application in each period (per minute or per hour).

- **Integration services**: The integration services bring different components in the application together to realize a particular business function. Each microservice communicates with other microservices through this integration layer by exchanging messages. Azure service bus, AWS simple queue service, and AWS simple notification service are some examples of integration services.

- **Observability layer**: This layer provides the required capability to monitor microservices. This layer constantly observes the resource utilization for a particular component. If the resource usage exceeds the threshold, then this data is used to trigger the auto scaling mechanism to spin up additional containers of the service to bring the resource consumption to normal levels. This layer also helps to keep track of requests routed across multiple microservices based on functional requirements.

- **Caching**: This layer caches the data returned as part of the API response. All APIs are built to be stateless in a cloud-native architecture. This is an essential design principle of the cloud wherein the infrastructure can be created or destroyed dynamically. This quality of the cloud necessitates that the applications (microservices) on the cloud are created as stateless services to take full advantage of the dynamic nature of the cloud for scalability.

- **Access management**: Identity providers are platforms that provide authentication and authorization services for applications on the cloud. Different types of users might have different entitlements within the system. This is managed by the identity provider, which in most cases integrates with the API layer to provide the required permissions to the users of the application. Many a time, the permissions are managed as **JSON Web Tokens** (**JWT**), which encode all the permissions that a user has within the application. When the user logs in, a JWT is created by the application through the identity provider and sent to the user. The user sends this JWT as part of every request (as a bearer token) to be allowed access till the active session with the application is terminated for the user.

- **Storage**: In cloud-native architecture, all microservices have their own database schema and instance. This enables the solutions architect to choose the type of database for the microservice based on the data it handles. For instance, a microservice handling a financial transaction might store the data in a relational database, whereas a microservice handling a document would store it in a document database like an AWS DocumentDB instance. The storage layer also includes capabilities like Azure Blob Storage or an AWS S3 to store file and image objects.

- **Analytics layer**: This layer of architecture provides insights about all the services included as part of the cloud-native application. A cloud-native application makes use of the native services offered by the cloud provider. For each period, this layer generates reports that can be used to assess the cost of deploying the application on the cloud. This helps with a continued improvement of the solution to reduce the deployment and maintenance costs. This layer also helps to procure or allocate a budget for running the application on the cloud for a future period. The solutions architect also gets insights into the most expensive services being used and can look at alternatives or redesign the solution to reduce the overall cost.

In this section, we covered the reference architecture for the cloud. In the next section, we will take this reference architecture and see how we can deploy the same in Azure, which is one of the popular cloud providers that is being adopted by many of the large enterprises.

Cloud-native reference architecture on Azure

The following is a depiction of the reference cloud-native architecture using Microsoft Azure Kubernetes Service. It depicts a mapping of the components between the reference architecture and Azure. We have taken a few microservices (order, shipping, and invoice processing) from the e-commerce domain as examples for depiction. The reader needs to note that the other popular cloud providers, like AWS and Google, also provide similar components that can be mapped to the reference architecture.

Additionally, note that in this section, we have used **Azure Kubernetes Service** (**AKS**) to realize the reference architecture. It is to be noted that there are other options available with Azure and other cloud providers like AWS and Google. For instance, **Azure Container Instances** (**ACI**) is a serverless model to deploy microservice containers on the cloud. In this case, the infrastructure and the software platforms are managed by the cloud provider. Similarly, AWS provides a choice of **Elastic Container Service** (**ECS**) and Fargate to deploy containerized applications. ECS provides a managed service option to run containers without the need for Kubernetes, and Fargate is a serverless option to run containers without the customer having to provision any infrastructure. Likewise, Google Cloud provides Google Cloud Run service that can be used to deploy containerized applications. It is a serverless model in which the number of instances is scaled down when the application is not in use. The choice of the cloud service used to deploy containerized apps on the cloud depends on factors like cost, complexity of the application and the available expertise to manage these applications independently on the cloud. Take a look at the following figure:

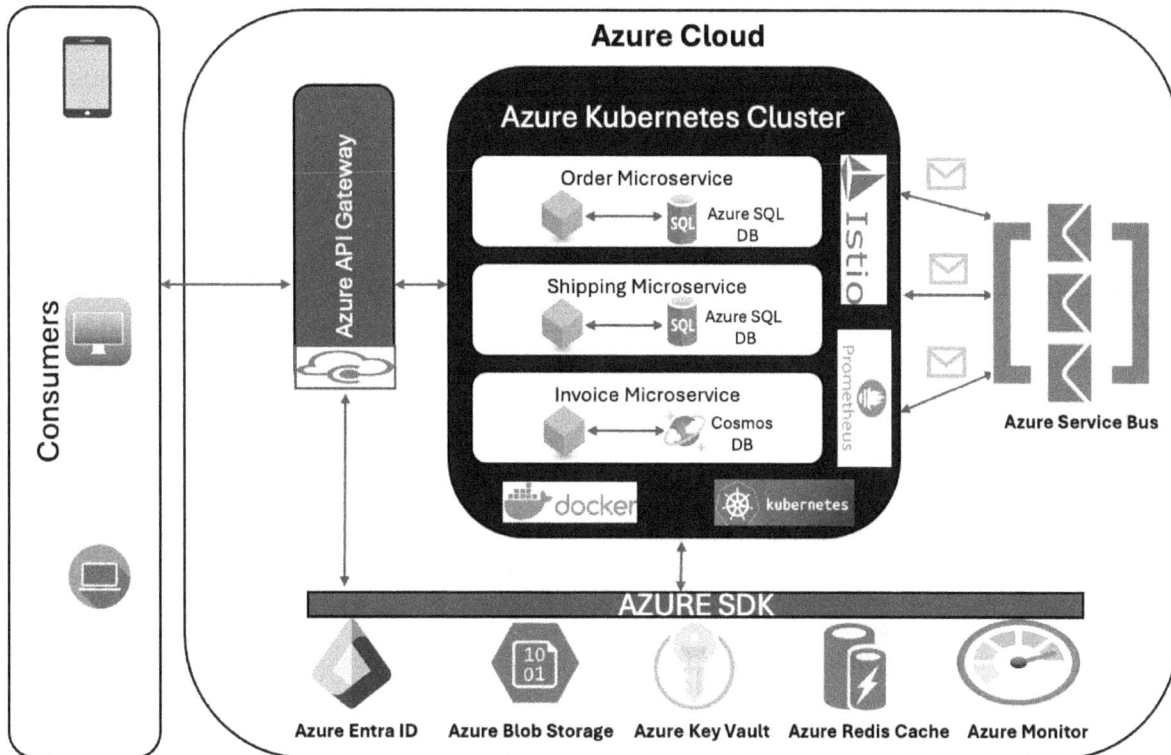

Figure 22.6: Cloud-native architecture on Azure

The salient features of the reference architecture for an e-commerce application deployed on the Microsoft Azure platform are as follows:

- The Azure Kubernetes Service is the Azure managed service that provides the required container runtime and the orchestration capabilities for architecture.

- Istio is installed for secure inter services communication and enhanced monitoring of the application services. Istio injects its envoy pods alongside the application pods (sidecars) and enables generation of telemetry data. We can optionally install Prometheus as part of the Istio installation to collect telemetry data from the Kubernetes cluster. Prometheus collects telemetry data from these injected side cars about the traffic moving in and out of the microservice pods, thereby enhancing the overall observability of the cluster.

- Azure manages the control plane of the architecture, and all the application microservices are deployed on the data plane of the cluster.

- Each microservice has its own data store depending on the nature of the data it handles. For instance, the order and shipping microservices use a relational SQL server database, and the invoice microservice uses an Azure Cosmos NoSQL database.

- The microservices communicate with each other using a services bus. This capability can be leveraged using the Azure Service bus. The Azure service bus provides both the capability of a point-to-point communication (queue based) between two microservices and a broadcast style communication(topic based) between microservices.

- The business capabilities of the application are exposed by the microservices as well-defined interfaces. These interfaces are exposed to the outside world using the API gateway.

- The Azure API gateway provides the required API capabilities to the system. It helps to throttle the number of requests per client. The API gateway provides policy configuration that can be used to define usage patterns (consumption per minute, per hour, etc.) for different types of consumers.

- The Azure API gateway also connects to the Azure Entra ID service for providing the required authentication and authorization features to the application. The API gateway also provides support for **http** responses generated by the APIs, to be served again to the users who make a request with the same payload.

- The Azure Redis cache provides the required support to cache information that is quickly required for any transaction based on business requirements. The REDIS caches provide the ability for the application to respond to users in a performant manner.

- The Blob Storage used in the architecture can be used to store object-based artefacts like documents, images, and video files. This acts as persistent storage to hold supporting data in addition to the transactional data stored in the relational database.

- The Azure Entra ID also helps to define role-based access control for the system. When a user logs in it authenticates the user and issues a JWT access token based on user's permissions. This token can be used to access the application APIs and resources for a period, till it expires.

- Azure key vault in the architecture is used to store confidential information like database credentials and API keys. They provide a cleaner and a secure way of organizing information within the application.

- Azure monitor collects data pertaining to health, availability and performance of the different services used in the architecture. It collects application data as well as telemetry data about different services used by the application within the azure cloud. It also monitors and collects data pertaining to the usage of the subscription accounts within the enterprise. Azure monitor provides a log analytics feature to query and visualize the data collected by Azure monitor. Azure monitor has a built-in feature called application insights to monitor the performance metrices like response time, error rates and throughput of the deployed services.

Having seen the implementation of a cloud-native architecture with one of the popular cloud providers (Azure), we will now discuss the principles and best practices around Migrating non-cloud workloads to a cloud-native architecture.

Migrating non-cloud workloads to a cloud-native architecture

Moving a non-cloud workload to a cloud-native architecture involves a host of different factors such as organization readiness, willingness to adopt a distributed architecture like microservices, embracing a DevOps culture and structuring teams to align to cloud-native architecture.

The following are the best practices that a solutions architect can apply to transform a non-cloud architecture into cloud-native architecture:

- Perform assessment of the applications that are candidates to adopt a distributed architecture.

- Leverage methodologies like Domain-Driven Design to identify the microservices required for the application. The microservices denote the business capabilities required in the application.

- Use an architectural pattern like event-driven architecture for inter services communication. A service like an Azure event bus can be used for this purpose.

- Use industry standard design patterns such as 12 factor app design and microservice design patterns to address cross cutting concerns like transaction management, secure inter service communication, and response aggregation from multiple services. Choose an appropriate storage mechanism for each of the microservices.

- Use a service mesh to provide the required capabilities to the cluster for enhanced monitoring and secure communication between services.

- Use an API gateway to enable path-based routing to the services within the application. Create policies to limit the number of requests to each service based on customer needs.

- Choose an identity provider that will provide the authentication and authorization capabilities to the application. Azure Entra ID and AWS Cognito are popular choices for an identity provider.

- Enable application security by using industry standard frameworks like OAuth 2.0. Many identity providers, such as Azure Entra ID, provide out of the box support for an OAuth 2.0 implementation within the application. We will discuss OAuth 2.0 in detail in the section cloud application security.

- Provision TLS certificates for end-to-end secure transmission of data across different layers of the application, such as API gateway, load balancers, containers, and data storage services.

- Automate infrastructure provisioning for these microservices by using Infrastructure as code principles. AWS CloudFormation, Google cloud deployment manager and Azure resource manager templates are popular choices to provision infrastructure using code.

- Choose and configure features like a CDN or edge computing to ensure faster delivery of services to the users of the application.

- Build the required CI/CD pipelines for the microservice components to be easily developed and deployed in the cloud environment.

- Package each microservice as a container image with all the dependencies packaged as part of the image.

- Provision appropriate security checks across the layers of the application. For instance, the API gateway can be secured using a **Web Application Firewall** (**WAF**). The inter services communication can be made secure by enabling mutual TLS between the components. This capability is provided out of the box by a software-like service mesh.

- Choose a suitable container and orchestration platform to deploy microservices. Azure Kubernetes Service, AWS elastic Kubernetes services are examples of such platforms.

- Leverage the serverless computing model for the application components. Serverless models lend themselves extremely well to microservices and event-driven architectures.

- Assess the performance requirements of each of these individual microservice components to provision the required infrastructure and the number of instances required.

- Use a canary or blue green deployment strategy to deploy the microservices on the cluster. This strategy will reduce the downtime at the time of application upgrades.

- Enable distributed tracing using tools like AWS X-Ray for easier debugging during problems. Leverage tools like ELK to centrally store, aggregate, and visualize application logs.

- Enable telemetry data collection and monitoring using tools like Istio and Prometheus for optimized resource usage and to ensure performance of the application within accepted levels.

Having seen the principles behind moving a non-cloud application to a cloud-native architecture in this section, we will now discuss the industry standard patterns that can be adopted while designing and developing cloud-native applications.

Cloud-native application design patterns

The cloud-native design patterns in general apply to microservices architecture. The solutions architect needs to be conversant with these patterns, internalize them, and identify scenarios for their application during design and development of cloud-native applications. These patterns, when applied, make the solution robust, increase reliability, and enhance scalability. The most adopted microservices design patterns that apply to cloud-native applications built as loosely coupled microservices are as follows:

- **Decompose by business capability**: This pattern emphasizes that the microservices in an application can be identified based on the business capabilities required. Once we have a subdomain, which identifies a portion of the business within the larger domain. The services within the domain can be identified by capabilities that create value for the business and its customers. For example, an order subdomain could have services like customer quote management and order management. Each of these microservice in turn support several operations.

- **Api gateway pattern**: The API gateway pattern emphasizes the inclusion of an API gateway in the microservices architecture. The API gateway acts as an entry point for the application. It performs data transformation, provides routing and response aggregation logic (of multiple microservices), authenticates and integrates with an identity provider for authentication and authorization. It also provides a request throttling mechanism while exposing the application to third party clients. The API gateway also provides caching capabilities and makes the application performant.

- **Circuit breaker pattern**: This pattern helps with graceful degradation when one or more microservices fail within the application. This pattern isolates the fault and does not route the request to the service that is down. It has a fallback mechanism that provides an alternate service (response) till the time the called microservice (backend system) comes back to operation.

- **Database per service**: This microservice pattern prescribes that each microservice should have its own data store. This enables the microservice to handle and store data that is more aligned with the business capability being built within the microservice. A microservice that deals with bank account information can use a relational database as its data store, whereas a microservice dealing with a social media platform can store its data using a graph database like AWS Neptune.

- **Domain events**: This pattern is used by an application composed of microservices that communicate with each other using a service bus. Each microservice, when it updates its database, emits a domain event, which is consumed by other interested services to act and accordingly update their database to keep the whole system in harmony.

- **Event sourcing**: Instead of storing the current state of the application in a persistent data store, state changes can be stored as a series of events. This helps the application to replay the changes that have happened over a period and helps to move to a particular state as required by the business capability. The events can be stored in an event store like Apache Kafka.

- **Command Query Responsibility Segregation (CQRS)**: This pattern helps to segregate the database for read and write operations separately. This helps to normalize the read database depending on the type of queries. Each microservice has its own read database that it queries for fetching business information relevant to the subdomain that it is part of. This pattern helps to improve the performance of the microservice. The read database is updated using domain events every time the write database is inserted, updated, or deleted.

- **Saga pattern**: The saga pattern defines the principle to manage transactions across microservices. Orchestration and choreography are the two different ways in which transactions can be managed in the microservices architecture. In the choreography pattern, each microservice responds to an event and then drops a message in the event bus to be picked up by the next microservice. This continues till the transaction is completed. In the orchestration pattern, there is an orchestrator component which calls each of the microservice taking part in the transaction and issues a signal to either commit or rollback the transaction.

In this section, we covered the important patterns that can be used in cloud-native architecture. This will help the solutions architect to solve some of the commonly occurring problems in a microservices application that can be deployed on the cloud. In the next section, we discuss OAuth 2.0 that deals with the security of an application built in a cloud-native way.

Security in a cloud-native architecture

Contemporary cloud-native applications use a cloud security model called the Zero Trust model in which no component of the architecture assumes implicit security, and all the parts of the application need to be secured explicitly. In the cloud, the application is made up of moving parts from a hardware and software platform perspective. Hardware gets provisioned and torn down based on application non-functional requirements like performance and scalability. Software platforms get patched regularly as new versions get released. It is inevitable that these are monitored continuously, and security controls are updated on a regular basis to maintain the security posture of both the provisioned cloud services and applications that use them. In the following sections, we will look at ways in which we can maintain the security posture within cloud-native applications.

Role-based access control

RBAC determines the permissions assigned to a group of users to access resources on the cloud. Each cloud provider offers their own implementation of the identity and access management services that provide end to end capabilities to manage users and roles on the cloud. AWS provides the **identity and access management** (**IAM**) service, and Azure provides an equivalent service called **Azure Entra ID**. In practice, a role is created, and a set of policies is assigned to the role. Each assigned policy can have permissions to access one or more resources on the cloud. The role is assigned to a group of users, enabling them access to their entitled resource group. As a best practice, adopt the principle of least privileges, wherein the principal is assigned minimum permissions just enough to perform the required operations within the cloud and application ecosystem.

Container security

All microservices in a cloud-native application live as containers inside the cloud environment. It is important that the containers are kept secure, and they continue to be monitored for any unusual behavior. Kubernetes and Istio help to define network policies that limit the inter service and service to outside world communication to required levels. In the cloud, where immutable infrastructure is the norm, containers should never be modified once created. Containers should be torn down and created afresh if changes are required to the image or the running containers. Kubernetes namespaces can be used to group and isolate related resources in the cluster and that they do not overlap with each other. Use a stringent audit trail process to capture all the behavioral changes happening within the system. Do not expose sensitive information like database passwords and API keys, and store them in services meant for them on the cloud. **AWS Secrets Manager** and **Azure Key Vault** are some of the choices for storing this kind of information. Continuously monitor the security of infrastructure using cloud services providing this capability. **AWS GuardDuty and Microsoft Defender** for cloud helps in monitoring the application resources and the underlying infrastructure and flag unusual behavior, if any.

Data security

Data security pertains to the security of data when it is stored and while it is in transit. We looked at the approaches for both in *Chapter 3, Technical Proficiency Essential Knowledge*. All the cloud providers offer mechanisms to encrypt data when it is stored. AWS, Azure, and GCP provide their own encryption mechanism while the data is being stored in their respective persistence storage services. This applies to both transactional data stored in a relational database and artefacts stored as part of their object storage system. For instance, AWS S3, an object-based storage, offers different types of encryption. The user can opt to use the default encryption S3 provides out of the box. The other option is for the customer to create their own key for encryption within the cloud and use it to encrypt objects before they are stored. There is also a client-side encryption mechanism in which the customer can encrypt objects on the client side before they are stored. As stated in the previous section, sensitive information like database credentials and API keys must be stored in the managed services like secrets manager provided by AWS and Google cloud platforms.

Cloud-native application security

In this section, we will look at OAuth 2.0, a framework that is most used in the authentication and authorization of cloud-native applications made of microservices. It delegates the authentication and authorization to an authorization service (an identity provider) that is integrated with the application. It helps to assign the required permissions to users based on the role assigned to them by the enterprise. The permissions are granted in the form of an access token (JSON Web token), which is sent to the user, and it can be passed along with subsequent requests. The access token is validated (based on the timestamp) for every request, and the user is authorized based on their permissions described within the token payload.

Figure 22.7 depicts the OAuth 2.0 authorization code grant flow, which is used in the context of authentication and authorization of microservices. It becomes imperative for the solutions architect to understand OAuth 2.0 from an application security and a solutions architect interview perspective. Let us walk through the OAuth 2.0 authorization code grant flow as depicted in the following figure:

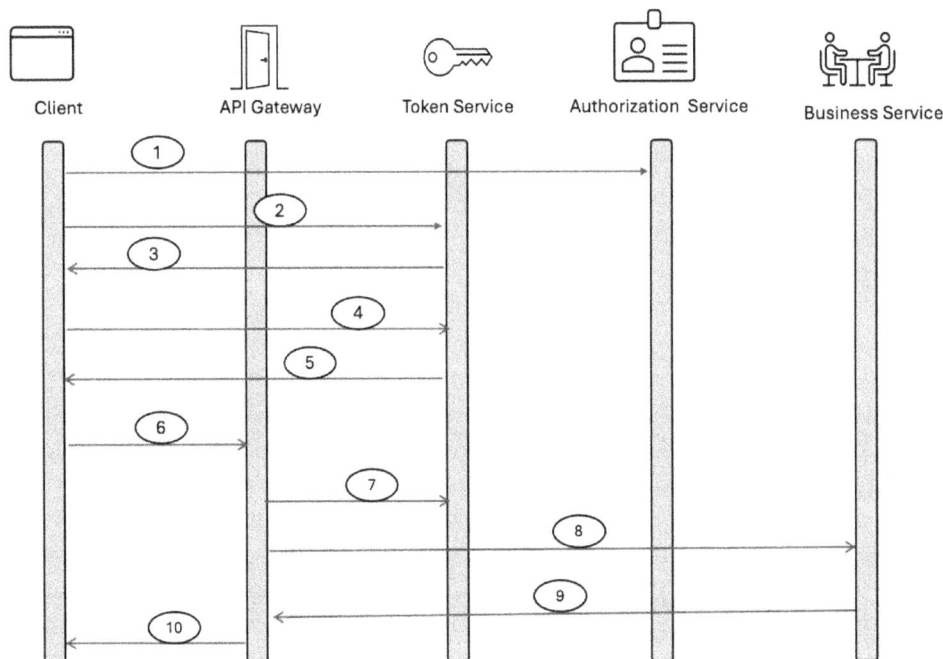

Figure 22.7: *OAuth 2.0 authorization code grant flow*

The steps can be explained as follows:

1. The user (through a client application) wants to access a business service. It calls the authorization endpoint of the application to sign in.

2. The user is redirected by the authorization end point of the application to a token endpoint (An identity provider like Azure Entra ID or AWS Cognito). The user is requested by the token endpoint (through a login page) to enter their credentials.

3. The user enters their credentials, and it is validated by the token service. Once the user login is successful. The token service sends an authorization code to the client application.

4. The client application sends the authorization code back to token service (identity provider) to exchange the authorization code for an access token.

5. The token service sends an access token to the client application. This access token becomes the bearer token for the user. This access token can be in the form of a JWT.

6. The client application makes the next request to access a business service. It sends the access token in the authorization header. The request is routed through the API gateway.

7. The API gateway validates the access token for validity by interacting with the token service (identity provider).

8. Once the token is validated for success, the request is forwarded to the business service for necessary business action, such as an order retrieval or a payment.

9. The result of the business action (success or failure) is returned to the API gateway.

10. The API gateway forwards the result of the business service call to the client application.

The advantage of the authorization code grant is that it is more secure as it involves a two-step process of generating an authorization code and then exchanging it for an access token.

In the case of mobile and single page applications, the security is achieved using a technique called **Proof Key for Code Exchange** (**PKCE**). It prevents an authorization code interception attack on the mobile device. PKCE is the same as the authorization code grant flow with some minor variations.

The following are the salient features of the PKCE flow:

*   When the client submits the credentials to the token service (identity provider), it also creates a random string, hashes it, and sends it as part of the request.

*   The token service then returns the authorization code to the mobile application.

*   The mobile application then sends the authorization code along with the original plain random string value to the token service and requests for the access token.

*   The token service compares the plain text random string with the hashed value that was initially sent by the client. If they match, the access token is issued to the client.

The other flow that is used for mobile and single-page applications is the implicit grant in which the client is given the access token after signing in with credentials. There is no authorization code involved in this type of OAuth flow. However, this method is less secure than the authorization code grant.

Implementing an OAuth 2.0 authorization code flow

In this section, we will look at the steps to implement the OAuth 2.0 authorization code grant flow with the Azure identity provider, namely the Azure Entra ID. Azure Entra ID has been taken as a reference Identity provider here on the Azure cloud. OAuth 2.0 is a specification, and these steps to implement OAuth 2.0 are pretty much the same using any of the popular Identity providers. It requires registration of the app with Azure Entra ID service and providing a redirect URL within the application to which the authorization code will be sent. The application exchanges the authorization code for the access token.

The steps are as follows:

1. Register the application with the Azure Entra ID service. Let us call our application **My Sample App 1**.

2. As part of the registration process, the developer enters a redirect URL. This is the URL within the application to which Azure Entra ID will redirect the user, along with the authorization code as a request parameter, after successful authentication. Let us call this redirect URL **https://mysampleapp1. com/callback**. The registration page within Azure is shown in the following figure:

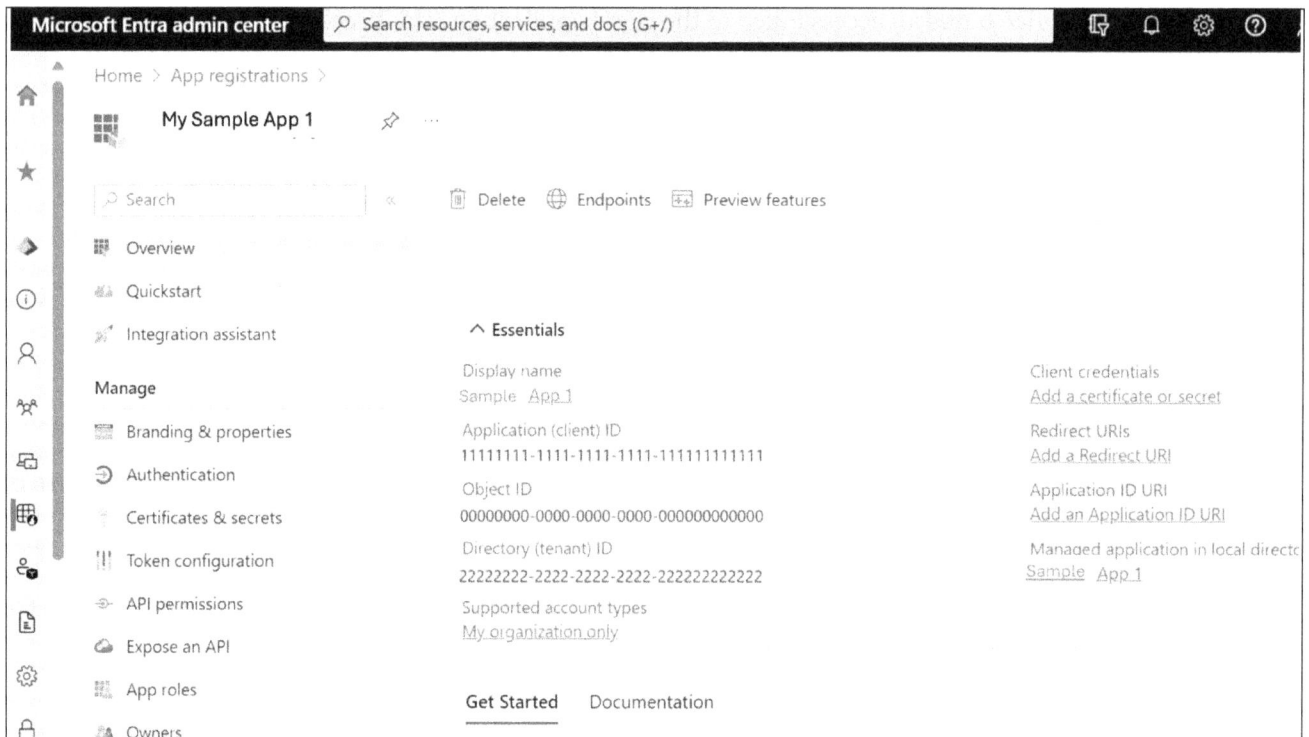

Figure 22.8: Implementing OAuth 2.0 with Azure Entra ID

3. After configuring the redirect URL, generate a client secret for the application under **Certificates & Secrets**. The secret is used by the client to authenticate itself with Azure Entra ID and exchange the authorization code for the access token.

4. Click on **API permissions** and include the APIs and resources which needs to be accessed with the access token issued by the Azure Entra ID. These are the APIs and resources the application can access on behalf of the user using the access token issued by Azure Entra ID.

5. Create a client login page in the application. When the user tries to login, redirect the user to the Azure Entra ID authorization endpoint as follows: **https://login.microsoftonline.com/{tenant}/oauth2/v2.0/authorize**.

   Note: **Tenant is the unique ID of Azure Entra ID that the organization received when it signed up with Microsoft for the cloud service.**

6. Include the following parameters as part of the redirection mentioned previously:

   a. **client_id**: The client ID is the application ID generated as part of the application registration process.

   b. **response_type; code**: This indicates that we want an Authorization code from the authorization endpoint.

   c. **redirect_uri**: The redirect URI that we entered as part of the app registration.

   d. **scope**: The data permissions required (e.g. profile, email).

   e. **state**: Any string value that we want to preserve between authentication and redirection.

7. The Entra ID service will ask for the users to authenticate themselves. Once the users enter their user ID and password, Azure Entra ID will validate them, and if authentication is successful, it redirects to the URL given as part of the application registration process.

   https://mysampleapp1.com/callback is the redirection URL as configured during the application registration.

8. The redirect URL will contain the authorization code as a request parameter. The redirection endpoint will exchange the authorization code for an access token by making a POST request to the Microsoft token endpoint as follows:

   https://login.microsoftonline.com/{tenant}/oauth2/v2.0/token

9. Include the following parameters in the request body while calling the token end point to exchange the authorization for the access token:

   a. **client_id**: Client ID is the application ID generated as part of the application registration process.

   b. **client_secret**: Client secret generated as part of the registration process.

   c. **code**: Authorization code received from Azure Entra ID.

   d. **redirect_uri**: The redirect URL that was used in the authorization request.

   e. **grant_type**: Should be `authorization_code`.

10. Use the access token received to access the APIs and other resources to which permissions were given within the application.

Now that we have covered the required knowledge areas for cloud-native architecture, we will look at the possible questions that can be asked in a solutions architect interview.

Conclusion

The cloud has become an inevitable proposition in the technology roadmap of large enterprises. It is important for solutions architects to understand the nuances of cloud native architectures, including factors that influence the migration of on-premise workloads to the cloud.

In this chapter, we discussed the different computing models like IaaS, PaaS, and SaaS offered by cloud providers. We looked at the factors to be considered by a solutions architect before moving workloads to the cloud or blueprinting a new application for the cloud.

We explained the concepts of containerization and orchestration, understanding of which is important for cloud-native architectures. We also looked at the difference between virtual machines and containerization, along with the advantages that containers offer over virtual machines. We also looked at the principles governing cloud-native architectures like immutable infrastructure, declarative APIs, and Microservices. We went on to discuss computing models and services offered by the cloud to make applications robust enough to address the required quality of services. We went on to discuss a reference architecture based on Azure to explain the different components that make up cloud native architecture. We also covered important design patterns required to come up with a robust cloud-native architectural blueprint.

Security considerations are paramount while blueprinting cloud-native architectures. We covered aspects for implementing a security framework on the cloud using the OAuth 2.0 specification.

In the next chapter, we will cover the process related to effectively managing applications once they have moved into production.

Key takeaways

The takeaways are as follows:

- **Considerations for cloud-native architecture**: understand important factors to be considered such as regulatory compliance, cost, cloud provider choices and application security before architecting applications for the cloud.

- **Containerization and orchestration**: Containerization and orchestration are important capabilities required for cloud-native applications. Containerization lends itself to scalability, which is a fundamental characteristic of the cloud. Orchestration helps in managing scalability on cloud.

- **Cloud-native architecture**: Break down the application into loosely coupled microservices. Use Domain-Driven Design to come up with sub domains and microservices. Understand the reference architecture for the cloud and the equivalent technology components provided by cloud providers to realize the reference architecture. Understand and adopt best practices to move non-cloud workload to a cloud-native architecture. Leverage unique capabilities of the cloud to build cloud-native applications.

- **Microservice design patterns**: Understand the design patterns that make business microservices scalable, resilient and available. Understand how to manage transactions in a distributed architecture like microservices on the cloud.

- **Cloud-native security**: Understand the implementation of security for the infrastructure, data, and applications. Understand OAuth 2.0 framework to implement authentication and authorization for cloud-native applications. Understand the different flavors of the OAuth 2.0 implementation and their applicability to different types of applications.

Model interview questions and answers

1. **What is the difference between virtual machines and containerization?**

   Model answer:

   - Virtual machines are fundamentally a technique for hardware virtualization, whereas containerization virtualizes the operating system of a node or server.

   - In a virtual machine, you can install multiple operating systems on a host called guest operating systems. A hypervisor sits between the host operating system and the guest operating systems, interpreting the commands and providing networking services through the host operating system.

   - In containerization, a container run time sits on top of the host operating system and provides an environment for the software containers to run. This results in optimization of resources as no guest operating systems are required.

   - Docker is a very popular containerization platform, whereas Hyper-V by Microsoft and VirtualBox by Oracle are popular virtual machine software.

2. **What are the design principles behind cloud-native architecture?**

   Model answer:

   - The infrastructure of cloud-native architecture is immutable. It means that the infrastructure is never modified once created. If any changes are required, the infrastructure is destroyed and recreated.

   - It makes use of declarative APIs that take input from the users and help them to realize the end state on the cloud infrastructure, without having the users know how the API works internally.

   - The cloud-native architecture is made up of loosely coupled components (microservices).

   - The cloud-native architecture has a service mesh which helps in secure inter microservice communication and enhances the observability of the solution.

3. **What are the salient features of a cloud-native application?**

   Model answer:

   - In cloud-native architecture, the application is made up of individual microservices.

   - The microservices are deployed as containers in the cloud environment.

   - Each container is packaged to contain all the dependencies (libraries) of the microservice.

- The containers are managed using an orchestration tool like Kubernetes.

- Azure Kubernetes Service and Amazon Elastic Kubernetes Services are some of the managed services that can be used to deploy cloud-native applications.

4. **What is the requirement for an orchestration tool in a cloud-native architecture?**

Model answer:

- An orchestration tool provides the required capability for scheduling and controlling the microservice containers inside a cluster.

- The orchestration tool has two main components, a control plane and a data plane.

- The control plane has the administrative components of the orchestration tool, like a controller manager, scheduler, API server, and data storage component.

- The scheduler schedules new containers in the cluster, and the controller manager maintains the required number of instances of the application containers.

- The API server is used to take user inputs to manage the cluster according to the customer application requirements (scale up or scale down the number of container instances of a microservice). The data storage component stores the current state of the cluster.

- The data plane is the area (nodes or servers) in which the business application microservices reside as containers. The data plane is controlled by the control plane.

- The orchestration tool has an indispensable place in the cloud environment where the infrastructure creation and termination are very dynamic, and we need an automated way to scale up and scale down container instances based on application load.

- Kubernetes is one of the popular container management and orchestration tools being used by enterprises.

5. **How will you manage transactions in a cloud-native microservices architecture?**

Model answer:

- A cloud-native microservices architecture follows a model called an eventual consistency.

- The saga pattern can be used to manage distributed transactions in a microservices architecture. The saga pattern has two different flavors, choreography and orchestration.

- In the choreographed mode, each microservice emits an event that is consumed and processed by the other microservice in the sequence. If the processing is successful, it emits a success message; otherwise, it emits a failure message that is picked up by the first microservice, and it rolls back its changes.

- In the orchestrated mode, an orchestrator calls each microservice in the sequence and manages the success and failure modes of each microservice involved in the transaction.

6. **How can you achieve graceful degradation of the application in cloud-native microservices architecture?**

Model answer:

- In a microservices architecture, you can use a circuit breaker pattern to prevent routing calls to a microservice that is failing.

- The circuit breaker pattern helps to define a fallback function that is called in lieu of the failed microservice for fault isolation and graceful degradation.

- The fallback function helps to handle the failure scenario with an alternate functionality or response till the time the failed microservice is up and running.

- The circuit breaker uses rate limiting to throttle the requests to microservices, reducing load on a microservice that is already under heavy load, due to which it can fail. This improves the resilience of the system.

- Libraries like Reslience4J (Java based) can be used to implement the circuit breaker pattern in Java.

7. **How will you come up with the required microservices in the sub domain of the application?**

Model answer:

- Sub domains are business areas constituting the main domain. The overall business domain is divided into core and supporting sub domains.

- For each sub domain, a domain model is created containing entities and aggregates. It also uses ubiquitous language for uniformity of vocabulary within the sub domain.

- Each sub domain comprises of business capabilities. For instance, in an e-commerce application(domain), order management, inventory control, payment management order shipping can be the sub domains. Within order management sub domain, track order, cancel order could be the business capabilities.

- Each of the business capabilities can in turn be represented as a microservice exposing the required operations for exposure to the channel systems for consumption.

8. **What is the need for an API gateway in cloud-native architecture?**

Model answer:

- The API gateway provides path-based routing of request to the required business microservices of the cloud-native application.

- The API gateway also provides service aggregation in which a request needs to communicate with multiple microservices to process a user request.

- The API gateway also interacts with the identity provider to validate whether the access token sent by the client application is valid and has not been tampered with.

- The API gateway provides throttling capability to limit the requests to microservices, thereby limiting the load on the system. The limits could be set based on user and time (requests per minute, etc.).

- The API gateway also provides a caching mechanism to cache responses, which reduces the overall load on the application.

9. **Can you explain the authorization code grant flow of OAuth 2.0 to implement authentication and authorization for a cloud-native application?**

Model answer:

- OAuth 2.0 is an authorization framework that helps in a secure delegated authorization mechanism for cloud-native microservice applications.

- The authorization code grant starts with redirecting the user to an authorization server to authenticate themselves.

- Once the user authenticates, an authorization code is sent to the client, which they exchange for an access token (JWT) and use it as part of subsequent requests to access the application.

- The access token is the bearer token that the client sends as part of the request authorization header to identify itself as an authentic user.

- The API gateway picks up the access token from the request header and validates it against the authorization server. The user is allowed access if the access token is valid.

CHAPTER 23
Production Support

Introduction

Production support includes the set of activities to maintain applications after they have been developed, tested, and deployed into production. Long term support of applications is an area where most enterprises spend millions of dollars every year. The production support team is the face of the enterprise to the outside world. The quality and timeliness of the response to queries of customers regarding system usage and resolution to incidents raised becomes one of the important factors for the continuance by customers with the product or services offered by an enterprise. Effective production support involves the right mix of people, process, and technology to come together. Production support is an area that is evolving fast, like any other within the software world. Innovative processes supplemented by state-of-the-art tools are continuously disrupting the way production support is being carried out in large enterprises.

Structure

This chapter covers the following topics:

- Production support overview
- Solutions architect's role in production support
- Types of maintenance
- Levels of production support
- Production support lifecycle
- Artificial intelligence in production support
- Key performance indicators in production support
- A production support checklist

Objectives

In this chapter, we will discuss what production support is and the terminology used in the production support arena of software applications. We will understand the role of solutions architects in the production support function and how they can help improve process efficiency.

We will discuss the types of maintenance carried out by enterprises to address current problems reported and to future proof the system from failures. Following this, different types of support provided by enterprises to customers regarding product and service usage will be covered.

We will also cover the lifecycle of a product in production support and responsibilities for each of the phases in the lifecycle. A section highlighting how machine learning and artificial intelligence have made production support processes more innovative and productive has been discussed.

Moreover, we will cover key performance indicators and factors for the efficient functioning of the production support team, followed by a checklist for the production support team. Finally, we will discuss questions and pointers to answers to prepare solutions architects for interviews in which they may be expected to know the breadth of **software development life cycle** (**SDLC**) from software architecture to development and maintenance.

Production support overview

Production support comprises all activities required to keep a software system in the desired state of operation after it has been moved to production. The activities vary from setting up a help desk for customer support to answer queries regarding the usage of the products and services of an enterprise to analyzing major application gaps reported by users and giving them workarounds till the issues are fixed by the development team. Production support also includes monitoring the application configuration and fixing any deviations from the ideal set as given by the development team. The production support team also supports new releases by monitoring the deployed application and reporting any anomaly that could have an impact on the quality of services, like performance and availability.

Apart from monitoring and maintaining applications in a desired state, the production support team also takes care of the operational side of things. They maintain the infrastructure in an ideal state as required by the application. They quickly respond to triggers emitted by the hardware and software platforms and take immediate action to prevent failures. The production support also regularly patches the platforms on which the application is deployed to keep the platform current and prevent any performance and security related incidents. They also provide the required professional support to understand user expectations and see if there are any gaps in the application. These gaps are analyzed and reported to the development team on a regular basis, who, in turn, close those gaps by introducing code fixes or additional features in the application. Thus, the production support teams act as a bridge between the users of the application and the development team. They also provide regular reports to the management stakeholders about the type of incidents being reported and solved to give a clear picture of the quality of service and ensure that the business goals of the enterprise are met.

Solutions architect's role in production support

A solutions architect plays a key role in realizing the vision of a software project. They blueprint and design software applications. They have a combined knowledge of the business domain and the technology landscape. They are positioned very well to assist different teams during all phases of the software development lifecycle, including production support. In turn, software architects having a deep understanding of the production support function help them to design features that lend themselves to easier long-term support.

Essential knowledge for solutions architects

Solutions architects in modern day enterprises are expected to possess knowledge of areas that help application stability, efficiency, and availability in production, and artefacts that help the production support personnel to efficiently troubleshoot reported issues.

These areas are as follows:

- **Log management in production**: Log and audit trails are the guiding light for the development and support teams to troubleshoot issues reported in production. Knowledge of different types of log files and the production support team's expectations in their structure and granularity needs to be understood by the architect to incorporate them as a nonfunctional requirement within the system. The architect also needs to understand how the log files are being indexed and searched within the production support environment to incorporate the right log structure and content.

- **Deployment architecture**: The solutions architect needs to be conversant with different types of deployment architecture that can help the company to quickly overcome failures and ensure business continuity. They need to understand the criticality of the system in conjunction with the deployment architecture patterns to come up with an optimum deployment option. For instance, the solutions architecture can suggest a cold or a warm standby depending on the criticality of the different components within the application. The solutions architects will also be in the best position to recommend the number of instances of microservices in production in collaboration with the performance architect, since they have knowledge of the service level agreement for different qualities of services of the software system.

- **Business continuity**: The solutions architect needs to be aware of the vocabulary used in the production support domain to contribute actively to the preparation of disaster recovery and business continuity plans. Solutions architects need to understand the **recovery time objective** (**RTO**) and **recovery point objective** (**RPO**), and this helps them to make necessary changes to the architectural blueprint to support them. Based on the architecture, the architect needs to be aware of the different disaster recovery and business continuity strategies to suggest the right deployment architecture and backup plans to quickly recover from failures and disasters.

- **Service level agreements (SLAs)**: The solutions architect needs to be conversant with different metrics using which the hardware and software components are provisioned in the production environment. Based on the agreed levels for these metrics, the solutions architect can help to size the hardware in production. For example, the solutions architect needs to be aware of metrics like response time, throughput, read-write per minute, etc., to help the support team provision the right amount of hardware for optimal performance.

Solutions architects role in production support

Solutions architects can play an important role in preparing the enterprises to efficiently manage applications in production. The following are the ways in which a solutions architect can provide required assistance to support teams to ensure a smooth maintenance phase for software projects:

- **Help identify vulnerable points within the application**: Having a context of the domain and technology is key for the production support personnel to perform their duties effectively. The solutions architect can impart knowledge of the overall system parts and their integration touchpoints, both within the application and with external applications. This helps the production support teams to place the right probes at points within the application that are vulnerable to failure.

- **Aid with required skillset**: The solutions architect can assist the enterprise management in recommending the type of skills required for the production support team based on the technical nature of the application. For example, if the architecture is heavily event driven and the application makes use of multiple message queues, the architect can accordingly suggest the team composition to have the required skills or train existing personnel to acquire the required knowledge about message driven applications and message queues.

- **Guidance with monitoring**: The architect can also educate them on different logging mechanisms available within the application. They can also guide them on the type of log files generated within the system so that the production support team can use the right log files to debug based on the issue reported. The architect can guide them on the structure and content of the log files and the conditions in which the entries are made within the log files.

- **Preparation of operations manual and cookbooks**: The operations manual helps the production team to know the working of different parts of the application, including infrastructure setup. Though the manuals may be written by technical writers with inputs from the development team, solutions architects can play a role in creating the structure and help in including the important workings of the system, which will help in a better understanding of the system by the production support personnel. They can help in documenting production support, cookbooks, procedures, and practices for troubleshooting issues that may arise in the system.

- **Business continuity and disaster recovery plans**: We got into the details of business continuity and disaster recovery in *Chapter 12, Disaster Recovery and Business Continuity*. Solutions architects blueprint and design the software system. They understand the failure points within the application more than others. They can work with infrastructure architects and come up with an application deployment architecture that helps with business continuity in case of a catastrophic failure of the hardware or the software platforms. They can also recommend approaches to quickly recover from failures by suggesting appropriate technical risk mitigation strategies and backup plans.

Types of maintenance

The maintenance of a software system once it has moved to production is one of the very important phases of a software lifecycle. Though it is important to architect, design, and develop a system as per industry standards, it is also important to make sure the software is maintained in a state that continues to serve the customers of the enterprise, thereby adding value to the business that spent money in creating the software.

The maintenance of a software system needs to be looked at from three different dimensions, which are as follows:

- Changes to the software system because of possible errors or issues.
- Changes to the environment hosting the software, including the hardware and software platforms.
- Changes in the expectations from the software system.

From the mentioned types of changes, it becomes clear that it is not enough to make changes to the software system only from a defect-fix perspective. We also need to look at maintenance from a platform and change management perspective.

The following figure captures the different types of maintenance undertaken by the production support team:

Corrective Maintenance	Changes done to resolve issues reported within the application from time to time
Preventive Maintenance	Changes to the hardware, software platforms and applications to prevent failures
Adaptive Maintenance	Changes to the application to ensure they work in harmony with environment changes
Perfective Maintenance	Adding new features to the application to changing market and customer needs

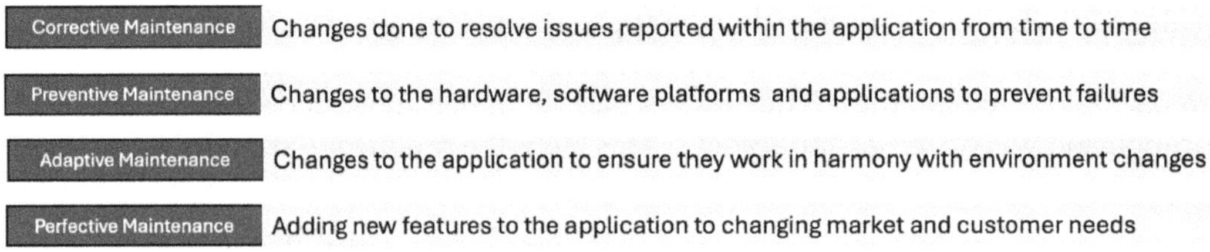

Figure 23.1: Types of software maintenance

In modern day enterprises, the line between development and operations has blurred, which has created a situation in which architects and developers must work closely with the production support team. For a solutions architect, it is important to understand the nature of the application, its run time dependencies, and the changing business expectations to work with the production support teams to recommend a maintenance strategy for long term support, including the process to be followed and the monitoring tools to be used.

A software system might require one or more of the following types of maintenance. This depends on the phase of maintenance the software is in and the software platform on which the application is deployed.

Corrective maintenance

Software systems, irrespective of the testing rigor followed during development, are bound to have issues. These issues could arise due to misunderstood requirements by developers and testers that manifest themselves in the form of incorrect code logic and design gaps that result in a technical glitch within the system. A software system, hence, undergoes corrective maintenance right from the time it is deployed into production till the time it is sunset. It is important to have standard procedures in place to provide a resolution to customer issues within a reasonable amount of time.

Preventive maintenance

Preventive maintenance is also done to prevent failures from happening. For example, the production support team may act on a sudden spike in user load on the application by increasing the number of nodes so that the application does not become extremely slow or go down unexpectedly. This type of maintenance also includes scheduling windows for patching operating systems and the software platforms on which applications run. These are required to ward off any known security vulnerabilities and to make use of the enhancements made to the operating systems and run time platforms. This type also includes making changes to application configuration depending on the usage levels to ensure optimum service levels.

Adaptive maintenance

Adaptive maintenance includes changes made to the application so that it continues to work in harmony with the changing hardware and software environments. This also includes upgrades to hardware and software platforms in production. For example, the upgradation of Java 11 to Java 16 is a type of adaptive maintenance done. This type of maintenance ensures continued usability of the application, and it also provides the required quality of services like scalability and availability. This type of maintenance is also done to keep the system in alignment with changing laws of the land and to synchronize its interaction with external systems depending on the changes in those systems.

Perfective maintenance

Perfective maintenance includes changes to the applications, software, and hardware platforms in tune with the anticipated changes in business operations and customer application usage in the future. Perfective maintenance can be predictive or prescriptive. Predictive maintenance is about predicting failures using advanced analytics techniques based on the usage data of the system. For instance, machine learning models can predict a spike in the memory or CPU usage of a system. Prescriptive maintenance takes predictive maintenance a step further by not just predicting failures but also giving a prescription to avoid failures that are bound to happen in the near term. Prescriptive maintenance requires developing models on a huge amount of data produced by the hardware and software platforms on which the application runs.

Levels of production support

Production support is divided into different levels from L0 to L3. This division makes it easier to categorize the types of problems that each level can solve. It also helps the enterprise to stack up each level with the required skills and train the personnel in the right tools that keep evolving, to address issues that are routed to the appropriate level within the production support team. The division also enables the organization to put in place a communication structure between different teams. There are also timelines associated with each level so that the users of the service can benefit by getting a resolution within the shortest possible time. This enables the enterprise to provide a positive customer experience and improve customer retention rates. This structure also helps to consolidate product improvement suggestions gathered from the users and to continuously upgrade the application, that helps to grow the business strategically.

The following figure represents the different levels of support provided by enterprises to address customer reported issues:

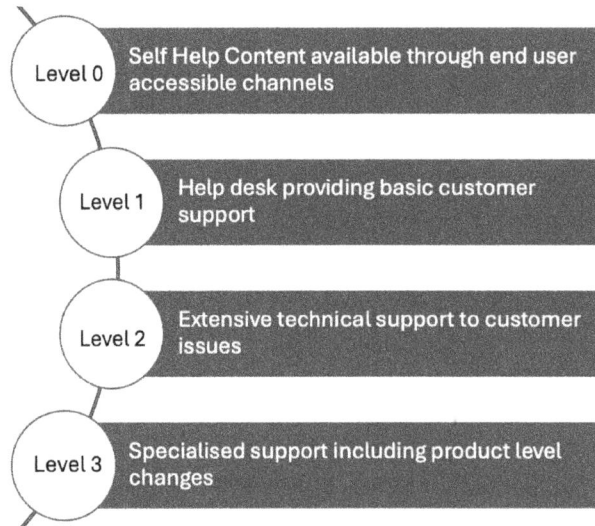

Figure 23.2: Levels in production support

Level 0 support

Level 0 support aims to resolve customer application issues by providing a self-help mechanism without a need for any external assistance from the production support team. This is the first level of support when customers face an issue while using a service or a product rolled out to them. Level 0 support includes self-help troubleshooting guides, videos to explain product and service usage. This level also creates moderated forums in which customers discuss their issues and search for possible solutions to their problems. This level of support also includes AI-powered chatbots which query a vast body of information about the services and provide relevant answers to customer questions. Users are also encouraged to refer to blog posts and frequently asked questions in user portals maintained by the enterprise which are updated from time to time.

Level 1 support

This level of support requires the set-up of a service desk that provides answers to basic queries and helps customers to solve minor usage-related issues of the application. They provide the first level of interface between the customers and the enterprise when it comes to resolving any application usage problems. For example, you call the service desk of a bank to understand what to do if your user account has been locked after the maximum number of password retries. The personnel at this level do not possess any technical knowledge, as they provide basic support for usage. The personnel in this tier are trained in the usage of the application, along with the common challenges the customers might face while using the application. The personnel also have access to the operations manual to keep their knowledge up to date about new features introduced. They also have AI-powered chatbots at their service to retrieve information and answer customer queries regarding the usage of products and services. This level also supports answering queries to customer emails, classifying and route issues to higher levels, if it is not within their scope of resolution.

Level 2 support

Level 2 is an escalated level of support for issues that have not been able to be solved by level 1 personnel. It involves deep analysis and troubleshooting of the issue reported by the customer. Level 2 support personnel have access to all the hardware and software components within the application to troubleshoot the issue and take the required action to sort it out. The personnel at this level possess deep technical knowledge with regard to the application, software, and hardware platforms. They collaborate with the developers and architects, discuss the root cause analysis, and get approvals for making changes required to correct the reported problem. The solutions to problems could include minor changes to application configuration, provisioning additional nodes in consultation with the development team to solve load related issues.

Apart from resolving customer technical issues, they monitor the application continuously using application monitoring tools, identify anomalies, and take corrective action based on standard operating procedures given to them. They also plan maintenance windows for patching operating systems, software platforms, and hardware upgrades in consultation with the development team and business stakeholders. They also work with different stakeholders within the enterprise and are running points to get the required approvals for making changes to the application environment.

Level 3 support

Level 3 support offers the highest level of support for any issue escalated by the level 2 personnel. Level 3 support is made up of highly skilled production support personnel who work with developers of the application and solutions architects. Complicated issues and gaps in the application logic warrant the support of the level 3 team. This level of support requires in-depth technical and domain skills and mostly requires a change in the design or the code within the application. They are also in charge of deploying advanced tools and techniques for continued and effective monitoring of the production environment. They also make decisions regarding hardware and software platform upgrades, thereby performing preventive and perfective maintenance. They also adopt techniques like AIOps to forecast application issues and quality metric changes like response time and throughput, and accordingly carry out changes in the application environment. The L3 support team also participates in daily standups along with the development teams to prepare production deployment environments for the upcoming releases of the software. They also work with solutions architects, development teams, and business stakeholders for the joint preparation of disaster recovery and business continuity plans.

Having seen the different levels of support provided, we will now look at the different stages of the production support lifecycle.

Production support lifecycle

Applications after being deployed in production continue to service customers within the accepted service levels. However, issues do arise from time to time in application functionality, software platforms used by the application and the underlying hardware. **Information Technology Infrastructure Library (ITIL)**, a universally accepted framework for software delivery and servicing provides guidelines for the effective maintenance of a software application and its environment. *Figure 23.3* depicts the different stages of the production support lifecycle:

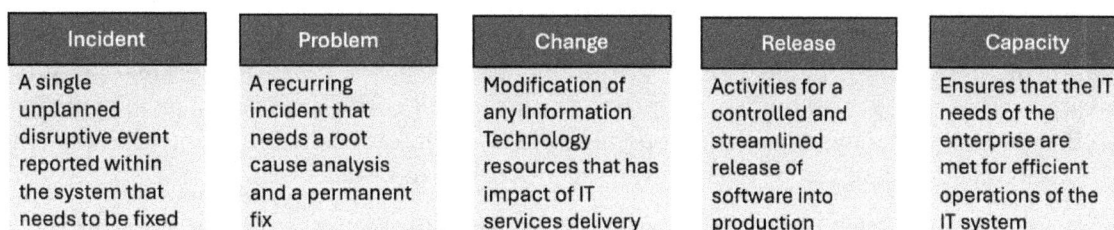

Incident	Problem	Change	Release	Capacity
A single unplanned disruptive event reported within the system that needs to be fixed	A recurring incident that needs a root cause analysis and a permanent fix	Modification of any Information Technology resources that has impact of IT services delivery	Activities for a controlled and streamlined release of software into production	Ensures that the IT needs of the enterprise are met for efficient operations of the IT system

Figure 23.3: Production support lifecycle

Let us look at the different stages of how an issue reported by the customer is managed within the production support function.

Incident management

ITIL defines incident as a single unplanned event causing a service disruption to the customer. It is a situation which requires immediate action to get the services back. Any incident reported has a direct correlation with the business reputation and monetary loss and needs to be resolved at the earliest possible time. Incident management is the process that is used to respond to the event to bring back the service into operation. This process involves the steps of identifying, analysing and resolving the reported incident. Incident management includes a fix that immediately resolves the issue.

The steps of incident management are as follows:

- **Incident identification**: This is the step where the incident is identified. This step can either be automated or manual. An incident could be reported by a user over email or could be triggered by a system that uses automation to notify the production support team. The identified incident is formally recorded into an incident recording system with the description of the incident along with the date and time received and with possible resolution information.

- **Incident prioritization**: When incidents arrive at the queue, the team should look at the severity of the issue in terms of its impact on the business and prioritize the incident for resolution. An incident involving login failure for a certain set of users takes priority over an issue wherein some of the users did not get mobile notification for their banking transactions.

- **Incident analysis**: The team quickly analyses the issues and comes up with the fixes required. The incident management team also makes sure that the incident does not spread and acts so that it does not affect application availability or uptime. The team will also use their existing error knowledgebase to see if there are prior instances and draw possible reasons for the incident.

- **Incident resolution**: The incident resolution depends on the analysis of the incident. The incident will be resolved by provisioning additional hardware or making any configuration changes to the application. For example, if the CPU consumption is very high for a particular transaction, the component is moved to a node with multiple cores. Teams use automation tools and AIOps to quickly resolve issues.

- **Incident documentation**: The details of the resolution for the incident are documented in detail. This helps to make sure that any instances of such incidents in the future can be resolved quickly without having to spend time on analysis and troubleshooting. The details of the resolution will also go into error knowledge bases, which will be used to train chatbots to provide answers to customer queries for similar problems.

With regard to the type of incidents, they are divided into major and minor incidents:

- **Major incident management**: These are incidents that result in a disruption of business operations and need to be addressed immediately. A security breach in a banking application is a major incident. These are issues that are highly critical and warrants immediate analysis and action sometimes in the form of quick fixes to overcome the issue. The objective of major incident management is to get the business operations back within the recovery time objective and recovery point objective.

- **Minor incident management**: These are incidents that does not affect the normal operations of the business. These are solved by the production support team within the service level agreement based on the severity of the incident. A non-operational branch locator functionality within the application is a minor incident that can be fixed within the SLA when reported.

Organizations use mature DevOps processes to identify incidents and fix incidents early in the software development lifecycle. DevOps encourages continuous monitoring and improvement of applications.

Development and production teams are alerted for any deviations from set thresholds noticed in the application. The development and the production support teams work together to quickly identify resolution and fix issues.

Problem management

There could be incidents that are recurring in nature. Recurring incidents becomes a problem. Though they are addressed at the point in time they occur, the team needs to perform a **root cause analysis (RCA)** of the recurring incident and ensure that a permanent solution has been found to stop the incident from occurring again. Teams perform RCA using tools like fish bone diagrams and **Failure Mode And Effects Analysis (FMEA)**. Problem management can be both reactive and proactive. In reactive problem management, the teams work to find the resolution and the root cause of the problem and fix it. In a proactive mode, the observability of the system is enhanced to ensure that incidents are identified early and an analysis ensues if they would become a problem. Incidents that could potentially become problems are categorized and addressed accordingly.

Like incident management problem management is also divided into different steps like problem identification, analysis, resolution and documentation that is contextual to the problem being solved.

Change management

According to ITIL, change management is the addition, modification, and removal of anything that could have an impact on IT services delivery. IT change management provides the process to modify the IT infrastructure and software platforms in a standardized and systematic manner to minimize disruptions in system operation. It is a well-planned process comprised of various stages and statuses that IT changes can go through. Change management aims to reduce the number of incidents in production. Change management is also carried out to plan and implement certain changes required in the system to adhere to regulatory compliance and industry standards. The change management process considers all the possible risks associated with the change and there are plans in place to mitigate them in order to make sure that there is no disruption to the business operations.

Release management

In modern day enterprises, new features are introduced every other week. Apart from new features, patches related to the application defect fixes also need to be released into production for a stable and efficient functioning of the application. Release management comprises of all activities for a controlled and streamlined release of software into production environment. It requires careful planning, testing and an informed deployment of software. The release is planned in such a way that there is no or very minimal downtime of the application. Deployment strategies like blue green deployment and canary deployment ensure minimum downtime when new software versions are released into production.

Blue green deployment creates an environment (green) with the newer version of the software which takes part of the load, and the old environment (blue) continues to serve other users. Once the green environment is proven to be faultless and stable, all users are redirected to the green environment and the blue environment is shut down.

Automation plays a very key role in deploying newer releases to the production environment. The whole deployment process is automated and provisioning and balancing between the blue and green environments is done in an automated manner. Release management is not only about software releases. but it also includes activities to create operational manuals for use by production support personnel and training the production support team.

Capacity management

Capacity management is the process that ensures that the infrastructure needs of the enterprise are met for efficient operations of the IT systems to realize the current and future business goals. It deals with managing both hardware and software demands of the organization so that the applications in production perform with the acceptable levels of service.

Capacity management broadly is made up of the following areas:

- **Business capacity management**: This ensures that the IT infrastructure can support the future growth of business. It involves capacity planning in line with the business goals of the enterprise.

- **Services capacity management**: This aims to ensure that there is enough Infrastructure capacity to deliver IT services of the enterprise by monitoring and analysing the collected data. Software applications are expected to function within their accepted service level agreements when it comes to measuring their quality of services. Services capacity management ensure if there is enough capacity to meet the accepted service level agreements.

- **Component capacity management**: Component capacity management deals with different types of components, like databases and networks. This process aims to optimally use the resources available to provide customer services within the required levels.

In this section, we looked at the different stages of the production support life cycle. we will now discuss how AI and ML are transforming the production support function in the next section.

Artificial intelligence in production support

AI and ML have disrupted different areas within the software industry, including production support. In the development phase, AI models generate code in modern day programming languages for different business functions. They also generate DevOps pipelines, create test scripts, and execute them. Models are often deployed to read user stories and generate design artefacts for the software applications. A lot of enterprises use tools like GitHub Copilot for generating code for their software applications.

Production support has long been an area comprising tasks that are manual and laborious in nature. There are applications that need to be physically monitored for long periods of time through monitoring tools that emit data based on the state of the application at a given instant of time. However, AI and ML have transformed many of these manual tasks to become automated, thereby reducing manual effort. Machine learning algorithms analyse data produced by monitoring tools and log files to identify outliers and forecast any issues that could happen in production systems in the near term.

AIOps is the use of AI for automated monitoring and management of IT operations in an enterprise. This is an area that is becoming prevalent within enterprises to identify, analyse, and resolve issues both in a proactive and a reactive manner.

Ways in which ML and AI have transformed the production support function are as follows:

- **Predictive maintenance**: Machine learning algorithms are trained on a large amount of data to create models that can forecast any untoward events that can occur within the applications in the near term. For instance, a model trained on the last six months of data could understand the patterns and forecast occurrence of a spike in **major garbage collections** (**major GC**) happening within microservices. This could alert the production support team about the possible spike and the team could respond by increasing the memory configuration of the hardware or the memory allocated to the container.

- **Anomaly detection**: Anomaly detection is the identification of patterns that are deviating from the normally seen and accepted patterns within an application, about any quality of service being measured, like performance and security. Many of the application monitoring tools monitor traffic to systems for a period and baseline normal patterns as a machine learning model. They use this baselined model to detect any unusual behaviour within the system. This could be in terms of an unusual spike in the load on the system at specific times of the day, entries in the log files that normally do not happen, requests coming from IP addresses apart from regions where the enterprise runs its business, etc. These models continuously monitor the oncoming data into the system and flags off any data point that are outside of the baseline range.

- **Intelligent bots**: Usage of intelligent chatbots built using the principles of AI has become a regular feature in the resolution of customer issues. Production support personnel also use intelligent chatbots to search through huge corpus of known error knowledge bases to get the right content pertaining to the solution of customer reported issues. Chatbots are also deployed to interpret customer problems and create support tickets based on the type of issue reported. They also create a workflow and trigger appropriate teams to attend to issues if the issue resolution requires manual intervention. Chatbots are useful when integrated with services to support multiple languages or perform language translation to answer queries in the user's language of choice.

- **Self-healing**: Many AI based automated solutions deployed in the production environment can continue monitoring data points from application monitoring tools and can act on deviations seen in the normal functioning of applications. An AI based monitoring solution can switch on the caching feature within the application during the peak hours of application usage to reduce the load on the application's database or operational systems.

- **Cost optimization on cloud**: Intelligent algorithms continuously assess the usage of the infrastructure on cloud platforms and can provide suggestions to scale down or terminate hardware that is not used. Alternatively, it can also provide recommendations to use aggregated or enhanced sizes of compute machines based on their current configuration and their usage by the application.

Key performance indicators in production support

Key performance indicators (**KPIs**) are used to measure the efficiency of production support operations within the enterprise. It helps to understand how well each one of the support levels (L0 to L3) works. The cost increases for the enterprise as the issues reported escalate up the support chain from L0 to L3. It is important to measure the response time and quality of support provided at each level and ensure that the customer is provided with the required support at the earliest possible opportunity and time. The KPIs also help to understand the gaps in training, and the enterprise can choose to introduce new tools or upskill the support personnel at each level to close the gaps.

KPIs that can be used to measure the efficiency of the production support function are as follows:

- **Incident volume**: Number of incidents reported in a period. It helps to categorize the type of incidents and helps in addressing areas where there are regular incidents being reported. This indicates the cost of quality incurred in the build and maintenance of the software.

- **Mean time to resolve**: This is the average time taken to resolve the incidents reported. This measures the efficiency of the resolution process. This metric helps to understand if additional training and resources are required within the team. This also helps to see if all incidents are resolved within their SLA.

- **Mean time for RCA**: Average time taken to perform root cause analysis of incidents. The team aims to reduce the time taken for root cause analysis. RCA helps to make permanent fixes to prevent similar incidents from recurring.

- **Service uptime**: This is the time during which the software application was operational within a given period. It is important for production support teams to keep services up as per the service level agreement and ensure that planned downtime is kept to a minimum.

- **Incidents re-opened**: This metric ensures that the incidents re-opened by the customers are kept to a bare minimum, as it is directly related to the business reputation and money spent on support activities.

- **Incidents responded to within SLA**: This is the end-to-end time between raising an incident and the resolution provided, including possible escalations. This needs to be kept to a bare minimum and translates to customer satisfaction.

- **Known error database (DB) usage rates**: This metric is used to identify the effectiveness of the known error DB usage. It can also be used to assess the number of misses from the known error DB that points to new types of incidents being reported regularly.

- **Customer satisfaction index**: This is the overall customer satisfaction score with regard to the support provided for the services and products offered by the enterprise. This can be collected through formal customer satisfaction surveys.

Having seen the important metrics to measure the efficiency of the production support process, we will now discuss the factors that contribute to the success of a production support function.

Improving production support efficiency

Production support is about continuous improvement of the process to reduce the time it takes to resolve customer issues.

The factors that can considerably improve production support in terms of the efficiency with which a resolution is provided to the users of the application are as follows:

- **Domain knowledge**: Imparting domain knowledge of the application to the production support team becomes a key to understanding issues better. Without the functional knowledge of the application, the production support personnel treat incidents as one-off technical issues, which may reduce the overall efficiency of the process.

- **Trend sensing**: A continuous analysis of the incidents reported, and patterns drawn from those incidents reported in the system helps the production support team to be prepared for seasonal issues. For example, there will be a spike in the load of e-commerce applications during festival times, and performance issues could be reported.

- **Knowledge management**: The team needs to continuously build a known error database which has all the analysis and resolution details for the incidents reported within the system. This helps in the long run to quickly analyze issues without having to start all over again. Many production support teams also build sophisticated chatbots and roll them out to the production support team to query the known error database to quickly resolve issues.

- **Self-help mechanism**: To create efficiency within the production support function, it is imperative to build an effective self-help mechanism, using which the users can solve many of the problems themselves. Enterprises end up spending additional dollars for each of the support calls reaching higher up the support chain. The production support team, in discussion with the development team, should create content that users can help themselves with most of the commonly occurring problems while using the application. These could include videos explaining the usage of services, FAQs to contain answers related to common issues customers face, and a self-help portal where users can discuss possible solutions to their problems and refer to blogs about the usage of newly introduced features.

- **Modern engineering practices**: Enterprises should adopt modern engineering practices like DevOps to help improve the cost of quality. If an issue is found and fixed earlier in the development lifecycle, it lessens the cost of quality. Each team should have the required quality gates to ensure that the product rolled out to production is bug free. The quality gates pertain to not just validation of functional requirements but also other quality of services like performance and security which are important from a customer usability perspective.

Having seen the factors that make the production support function effective, we will now look at a checklist that the production support personnel can use to measure efficiency, reduce gaps, and improve the process continuously.

A production support checklist

The following is a checklist based on modern day production support operations. This can be used by production support teams to make their process effective and productive.

The checklist is as follows:

- The production support team has been trained on the application domain and required technology.

- The support team has access to a quality operations manual pertaining to the working of the application and possible workarounds in case of issues reported.

- The production support has standard operating procedures for different types of issues that could be reported within the application in production.

- The production support team has a well-defined escalation matrix depending on the type of issue reported.

- The production system has a robust framework for release management.

- The production support team has documented the procedure for release management and socialized it with the solutions architects and development teams.

- The production support team runs a self-help portal for the customer to perform the first level of troubleshooting.

- Production support has a schedule to perform regular adaptive maintenance to keep the application environment in sync with changes in hardware and software platforms.

- Production support team performs regular preventive maintenance to avoid failures from occurring.

- The production support team has created a known error database and continually updates it.

- The production support team performs regular root cause analysis of the issues reported and resolved in the system.

- The production support team is being regularly trained with the latest application monitoring tools in the industry.

- The production support team deploys machine learning algorithms to forecast deviations in the quality of services like performance.

- The production support team uses intelligent bots to get answers to customer problems to save cost and time.

- The production support team has automated the creation of tickets, set up workflows, and triggered manual intervention for issues reported by users.

- The production support team uses AI based application monitoring tools to set baselines for normalcy and identify deviations from normal operations.

- The L3 team regularly participates in Agile standups to collaborate with the development team to prepare for the release of new software versions and applications.

In modern day enterprises, the solutions architect plays a key role from architecture definition to application development and deployment of applications to production. Hence, in a solutions architect interview, a solutions architect might be expected to explain their contribution to the movement of applications to production and their recommendations for effective long-term support and continuous improvement. Therefore, it is important for a solutions architect to be conversant with the production support process.

Conclusion

In this chapter, we looked at different aspects of the production support function. This is one of the areas that the solutions architects and developers pay less attention to. However, the knowledge of this area helps the solutions architect to contribute to making the production support function effective, productive and innovative. With that in mind, in this chapter, we covered the important topics like stages, levels and types of support offered by enterprises. We also discussed the lifecycle of the production support process followed by KPIs that help to continuously improve the production support function. Finally, we discussed as to how AI is transforming the production support function by offering innovative ways of monitoring and managing software systems in production.

In this book, we had so far looked at different facets of the skills required for a solutions architect to not only ace their interviews but also succeed in their job. We covered important technical concepts regarding software architecture and design, soft skills required and operational techniques that can help them to navigate easily through the complexities of modern age software enterprises. The learning and expertise that you have acquired through this book will provide a foundation for a successful solutions architect career. The next chapter will reflect on the journey to interview success and will discuss the path ahead from here.

Key takeaways

The takeaways are as follows:

- Understand how solutions architects can help improve efficiency of a production support function.

- Learn the different types of maintenance carried out by enterprises to address current problems reported and futureproof their application from failures.

- Understand different types of support provided by enterprises to customers regarding product and service usage.

- Learn the lifecycle of a product in production support and responsibilities for each of the phases in the lifecycle.

- Understand the role of machine learning and artificial intelligence in production support processes making them innovative and productive.

- Learn the key performance indicators and a checklist for an efficient functioning of the production support function.

Model interview questions and answers

1. **How can a solutions architect help in improving the efficiency of production support teams?**

   Model answer:
   - The solutions architect can educate and train the production support technical team on the architecture of the system and the integration touch points between the layers of the application.

   - The solutions architect can design appropriate log mechanisms within the application that can help to troubleshoot issues. This can include relevant attributes to index and search, content to be logged, and appropriate log levels.

   - The solutions architect can suggest appropriate application monitoring tools like AppDynamics and Splunk for effective monitoring of the application.

   - The solutions architect can recommend production support teams in the areas of preventive and perfective maintenance.

2. **What are the different levels of support provided by production support teams?**

   Model answer:

   - Production support in general consists of four levels of support from level 0 to level 3.

   - Level 0 support aims to equip the application users with self-help content to troubleshoot issues.

   - Level 1 is the basic help desk support to help users with navigational issues, carrying out simple business functions within the application.

   - Level 2 provides technical support with resolving incidents by making simple application configuration and minor fixes.

   - Level 3 team provides expert support on issues escalated by level 2 teams and involves application design changes, addition of new hardware, and software platforms. They also plan for new software releases by working closely with the solutions architects and the development team.

3. **What is the difference between preventive maintenance and perfective maintenance?**

   Model answer:

   - Preventive maintenance is done to prevent failures from happening.

   - Perfective maintenance is done to help the application perform better than its current performance.

   - An example of preventive maintenance is the addition of extra hardware to counter the sudden spike in the load and deterioration of response time.

   - Perfective maintenance could be an addition of a caching layer within the application to improve the response time of the read operations.

4. **What are the different types of maintenance of an application?**

   Model answer:

   - Corrective, adaptive, preventive, and perfective maintenance are the four types of maintenance carried out in the production environment.

   - Corrective maintenance deals with analyzing and fixing issues reported by users within the application.

   - Adaptive maintenance is done to keep the application up to date with changing hardware and software platforms in the industry.

   - Preventive maintenance is carried out to prevent any failures from occurring. This includes the incorporation of health checks and monitoring of critical components within the system.

   - Perfective maintenance is done to make the application perform better in terms of performance, scalability, security, and reliability.

5. **What are the stages in the production support lifecycle?**

   Model answer:

   - Incident management, problem management, change, capacity, and release management are the different stages within the production support lifecycle.

   - Incidents are issues reported by the users of the application, and recurring incidents become a problem for which a root cause analysis needs to be done and a permanent fix needs to be made.

   - According to ITIL, change management is the addition, modification, and removal of anything that could have an impact on IT services (applications) delivery.

- Release management comprises all activities for a controlled and streamlined release of software into the production environment.

- Capacity management is the process that ensures that the infrastructure needs of the enterprise are met for efficient operations of the IT systems so as to realize the existing and future business goals of the enterprise.

6. **How can we proactively avoid issues in production systems?**

   Model answer:

   - Proactive support can be implemented using machine learning models that have learnt from past data and can forecast problems that can happen in the near term. For example, an ML model deployed can forecast the occurrence of a series of major GC within the application and can trigger a warning email to the production support team.

   - Application monitoring tools can be configured for proactive monitoring. Tools listen to the oncoming traffic to the application for a set period and create a baseline. It can then flag data points which are deviating from the set thresholds using the baseline. This could include throughput, response time, number of errors, and exceptions within the system.

7. **Can you list four important key performance indicators used by production support teams?**

   Model answer:

   - **Mean time to resolve**: This is the average time taken to resolve the incidents reported. This measures the efficiency of the resolution process. The team makes every effort to reduce this.

   - **Service uptime**: This is the time during which the software application was operational within a given period. This KPI helps to ensure that the business operations are not impacted.

   - **Incidents reopened**: This metric ensures that the incidents reopened by the customers are being kept to a minimum.

   - **Incidents responded within SLA**: This is the end-to-end time between raising an incident and the resolution provided within the SLA. This helps to retain customer confidence.

8. **What role does artificial intelligence play in long term support of applications?**

   Model answer:

   - Artificial intelligence can create baselines of quality of services of applications, like performance and security, and flag off anomalies from normalcy.

   - AI and ML can help create models that can forecast problems that can happen in the near future. For example, ML models can be deployed to forecast frequent major garbage collection happening in the application.

   - Intelligent chatbots can search through massive amounts of resolution related content and provide answers to customers and production support personnel.

   - AI bots can create tickets based on issue types and can initiate workflows for effective tracking and resolution of issues reported.

CHAPTER 24
Strategic Future for Architects

Introduction

The journey to mastering solutions architecture is one that combines technical excellence, strategic thinking, and the ability to drive business outcomes. As you approach the end of this book, you are not merely closing its pages; you are stepping into a world of new opportunities, equipped with skills, insights, and a growth mindset that will define your career.

This chapter reflects on the journey you have undertaken, emphasizing the essential qualities that will empower you to excel as a solutions architect. From mastering technical skills to building strong relationships and embracing innovation, this conclusion highlights the mindset and actions required to thrive in this dynamic profession.

The final insights provided here will prepare you not only for interview success but for long-term career growth, ensuring you remain adaptable and impactful in an ever-evolving industry.

Structure

This chapter covers the following topics:

- Reflecting on the journey to interview success
- The journey beyond the interview
- Solutions architect's role in shaping the future
- Strategies for continuous improvement
- Final thoughts
- Creating value beyond systems
- Staying curious and embracing challenges
- Inspiring the next generation
- Key takeaways from the book
- A journey of impact and progress

Objectives

By the end of this chapter, you will have a consolidated understanding that prepares you for a thriving career as a solutions architect. You will be able to synthesize and articulate the core principles and key takeaways from the entire book, recognizing their importance in achieving success. You will learn to identify and effectively implement continuous improvement strategies, ensuring ongoing skill development, knowledge expansion, and professional networking. Ultimately, the goal is for you to formulate a personalized roadmap for your continued journey as a solutions architect, embracing lifelong learning and adapting proactively to the evolving demands of the industry.

Reflecting on the journey to interview success

As you turn the final pages of this book, you are not just finishing a book with chapters to prepare for an interview; you are starting on an exciting new chapter in your professional life. The journey has not been about just cracking an interview but rather bringing together the skills, strategies, and mindset one needs to possess in a role as pivotal as that of an indispensable bridge between technology and business.

Being a successful professional solutions architect from an aspirant solutions architect requires not only technical skills and expertise but strategic thinking, effective communication, and adaptability to emerging technologies.

This book accompanied you through navigating the multi-disciplinary world of solutions architectures. Each chapter has been designed to enable readers to gain a deep understanding of what solutions architecture is and go through the principles from which system design will evolve; more advanced topics include aspects like cloud-native architectures, DevOps practices, or data analytics. All in all, you have been armed with expertise in the formation of robust, scalable, business-objective aligned architecture and providing measurable value from it.

The solutions architect role, however, has not limited itself to merely the technical scope. It requires deep insight into the broader business environment and the ability to marry technology with organizational objectives. What you have learned through this book is how to take business requirements and convert them into actionable technical solutions; it has taught you how to control your costs and ensure that the design you produce will deliver real-world value.

In addition to technical skills, the book has highlighted the need for critical soft skills. You will cross paths with many teams and stakeholders as a solutions architect. Communication of complex ideas in an easy-to-understand manner, working with different groups, and leading with confidence will be as important as your technical skills. Such skills will help you create trust, bring teams together to a shared vision, and encourage innovation in your organization.

This journey has focused on a good amount on the adoption of DevOps principles and practices, including CI/CD. These methodologies enable you to build your features in an Agile, efficient manner, aligned with modern development practices. Thus, the integration of DevOps within your approach is going to help streamline processes, reduce the time-to-market, and ensure that the solutions remain adaptable to rapidly changing technological landscapes.

The structured 30-day interview preparation plan provided a roadmap to success and made what otherwise would have been an overwhelming process clear and actionable. It helped break your preparation into manageable tasks and allowed you to build confidence, refine knowledge, and approach the interview with a strategic mindset. This structure not only prepared you for interviews but also helped you embrace discipline, focus, and practice within yourself that would be super useful for you in your career.

Now, as you walk into the interview room and out of it, you take with you a growth mindset that comes in the form of embracing challenge as an opportunity for learning, adjustment, and innovation. You have honed your ability to take on challenging problems and adapt your strategy as necessary. These, along with your technical and strategic skills, make you ready to communicate your knowledge, demonstrate your accomplishments, and present solutions that are compelling both in terms of technology and business.

This is just the start. The learning and expertise that you have acquired through this book will provide a foundation for a solutions architect career. Keep going on your journey with more learning, collaboration, and challenging yourself to reach new heights. Solutions architecture is a dynamic and ever-changing field, and with the tools at your fingertips, you are prepared to put your stamp on it. The way forward is yours to decide, so be confident, curious, and committed to excellence.

Journey beyond the interview

Your success as a solutions architect does not end with just landing a job; it begins there. The interview may have tested your knowledge, problem solving abilities, and communication skills, but the real challenges lie in applying these skills to deliver value in the dynamic, fast paced environments you will encounter in your day-to-day activities. As industries and technologies advance and business needs change, your role as a solutions architect will be continuously evolving in terms of learning, adaptability, and innovation.

Curiosity and continuous learning

The field of solutions architecture operates on the premise of never-ending innovation. Technologies that look revolutionary today will be obsolete tomorrow. To continue being effective and relevant, you must be committed to learning for a lifetime.

Embrace the following strategies to fuel curiosity and expand your expertise:

- **Exploring frontier technologies**: As a solutions architect, you are placed at the bleeding edge of technology. Get into innovative trends such as GenAI, low-code no-code platforms, edge computing, and serverless architectures. Not only is it the future, but also solving problems in ways never possible previously.

- **Attending conferences to hear industry leaders present**: You often learn insights from emerging best practices and new tools from industry thought leadership. Stay ahead of what is coming through these opportunities while you make contact with people who may provide additional perspective. Opportunities for you include conferences like AWS re:Invent, Microsoft Ignite, and Google Cloud Next, where you explore the very latest innovation.

- **Deep diving into topics of interest**: Your career is as much about depth as breadth. Whether your passion lies in security architecture, data analytics, or cloud-native patterns, allocate time to develop specialized expertise. This not only enhances your value but also makes your work more fulfilling.

With continuous learning and curiosity, you position yourself as a visionary architect who not only reacts to change but creates it. Every new skill or concept that you master equips you to shape solutions that can meet future needs and have a greater impact in the long term.

Building and nurturing relationships

Being a successful solutions architect is all about collaboration. Your job often entails aligning disparate teams, such as those of developers, stakeholders, and executives, toward a common goal. Therefore, building and maintaining such strong relationships is essential for your long-term success. Consider these strategies to build and nurture relationships effectively:

- **Join professional communities**: These would be ones like CNCF, Open Group, or specific to clouds like user groups (AWS, Azure, GCP), where the thought leadership and learning from peers through ideation and knowledge can occur in those environments. It connects with other members in the community for general understanding and collaboration.

- **Mentoring and giving back**: Sharing your expertise with aspiring professionals helps them grow, but more importantly, it sharpens your skills. Teaching forces you to articulate your knowledge clearly and to keep up with industry trends. Mentorship creates a ripple effect that strengthens the field and brings in innovation.

- **Develop stakeholder relationship**: Here, the solutions architect becomes a liaison between the technical and business domains. Building trust and rapport with stakeholders will ensure that the solutions designed reflect the goals of the business. Strong relationships lead to smoother collaboration, more effective problem-solving, and better overall outcomes.

It not only makes a project run more smoothly, but it also creates a collaborative ecosystem and gives way to innovation. By building trust through connection, you help create a culture of creativity and progress that defines the future of solutions architecture.

Sparking innovation

At its core, the role of a solutions architect is about solving real-world problems through technology. Innovation is not a one-time act but a mindset you carry into every project, meeting, and conversation. To ignite innovation in your role, consider the following approaches:

- **Challenging the status quo**: As a solutions architect, you are uniquely positioned to question established practices and propose more efficient or effective alternatives. Use your technical expertise to push boundaries and identify areas for improvement in existing processes, systems, or designs.

- **Creating tangible value**: Whether you are optimizing supply chains, enhancing customer experience, or enabling sustainability efforts, focus on delivering solutions that have a measurable impact. Technology should not just work. It should make a difference.

- **Fostering a culture of innovation**: Encourage your team to think creatively and embrace experimentation. Cultivate an environment where failure is seen as a learning opportunity, and success is celebrated as a shared achievement. By fostering innovation, you not only improve outcomes but also inspire those around you to strive for excellence.

Your innovative solutions have the power to redefine how industries operate, opening doors to possibilities that were previously unimaginable. With each project, you not only solve current problems but also set the stage for what is to come, leaving a lasting mark on the technological landscape.

Embracing feedback and adaptability

Growth as a professional requires self-awareness and the ability to adapt. Feedback, both positive and constructive, is one of the most powerful tools for self-improvement.

To foster continuous improvement, consider the following strategies:

- **Reflecting on your work**: After completing a project or initiative, take time to analyze its outcomes. Identify what worked well and areas where improvements are needed. This reflection not only fine-tunes your approach but also prepares you for future challenges.

- **Seeking constructive criticism**: Actively invite feedback from peers, stakeholders, and mentors. A fresh perspective can uncover blind spots and provide valuable insights into areas you might not have considered.

- **Applying lessons learned**: Use the insights gained from feedback to inform your future projects. Adaptability is not just about reacting to change. It is about anticipating it and proactively evolving to meet new demands.

By embracing feedback and cultivating adaptability, you ensure that every experience contributes to your growth as a solutions architect.

The path ahead

Solutions architecture is an entity where you have to shape the technological landscape, influence business outcomes, and drive meaningful change; it is all about curiosity, relationship building, innovation, and adaptability that puts you in a position for long-term success in this dynamic field.

Reminding yourself, a solutions architect's job is about continuous learning, collaboration, and also skills or technical know-how. Your journey ahead will be strewn with challenges, lessons you will learn, and even possibilities in serving, and that is all pretty important. You are equipped today with the tools, your knowledge, your skills, and your mindset.

Solutions architect's role in shaping the future

Working in this role as a solutions architect, you are tasked beyond the immediate needs and obstacles facing people today. Every solution and every problem you solve puts a mark on the path for tomorrow's technological architecture. You are not just building solutions for today's businesses, but also are building that structure for innovation, for efficiency, and for improvement to define the future.

Creating impactful solutions

As a solution architect, the solutions that you design have deep implications. It is not just a tool designed for a particular problem; rather, it is a driver of innovation across industries to bring change. To maximize your impact, focus on the following key areas:

- **Enabling digital transformation**: One of the biggest contributions you make is enabling smooth digital transformation for organizations. This could be in the form of migrating legacy systems to the cloud, optimizing infrastructure for scalability, or integrating cutting-edge technologies like AI and ML. These transformations enable businesses to adapt to market changes, deliver superior customer experiences, and achieve strategic objectives.

- **Improving accessibility**: Technology has the power to bridge gaps, and your work as a solutions architect plays a crucial role in making solutions accessible to underserved communities. Whether it is designing platforms that prioritize inclusivity or creating systems that extend services to remote areas, your work ensures that technology benefits a broader audience.

- **Driving industry innovation**: Your designs shape how businesses function and innovate in healthcare, finance, education, and across the board. Example: A modern data analytics system in healthcare would lead to improved patient care, and a robust supply chain solution in healthcare would help reduce waste and contribute toward higher efficiency and sustainability.

Designing impactful solutions is one of the key differentiators in the competitive field of technology. Whether it is about optimizing processes for efficiency or enabling digital transformation, the solutions you create show your value and make you a leader in innovation.

Leading with confidence

Leadership is integral to your being a solutions architect; it is the art of inspiring trust, moving teams toward achieving results that inspire stakeholders. Leading with confidence involves several key practices:

- **Guiding teams**: For executing the most complex project, clarity and purpose characterize the way you lead the teams. And you will communicate a proper vision in such a fashion that there will be real collaboration for achieving common ends.

- **Engaging stakeholders**: As a bridge between the technical teams and business leaders, you need to articulate solutions in ways that resonate with very different audiences. Whether it is a detailed technical presentation for engineers or a high-level strategic overview for executives, your ability to confidently convey ideas makes you crucial.

- **Leading initiatives**: As a leader, you are often responsible for initiating new ideas, from innovative projects to transformative solutions. It requires confidence in decision-making, flexibility, and the strength to face challenges.

As a leader, you not only deliver solutions; you lead people, gain stakeholders' trust, and create excellence in your organization.

Leaving a legacy

The impact of a solutions architect extends well beyond individual projects. It shapes the future of technology, business, and society. By fostering innovation, guiding future professionals, and driving positive changes, you leave a lasting imprint that continues to influence long after your direct involvement ends.

Key ways to build a meaningful legacy include:

- **Encourage innovation**: Creating a culture of creativity and experimenting within your teams provides you with the foundation for continued innovation. Often, the solutions created today lead to the breakthroughs of tomorrow.

- **Mentoring the next generation**: Teaching aspiring solutions architects your expertise and experience creates a ripple effect by empowering others to carry on the torch of innovation. Mentorship ensures that the field will continue to grow, evolve, and attract diverse talent.

- **Driving meaningful change**: More than technical accomplishments, your work determines how technology improves the quality of life in society. Whether that is through sustainable advancement, user experience improvement, or building systems that increase operational efficiency, your work drives progress that lasts.

A legacy built on innovation, collaboration, and meaningful contribution lasts. Each project you lead and every problem you solve adds to this lasting impact.

Strategies for continuous improvement

Your growth as a solutions architect does not stop at mastering the basics. To remain effective and impactful, you must commit to continuous improvement, and some factors to do that include:

- **Lifelong learning**: Stay curious and proactive in exploring emerging technologies. Pursue certifications, attend workshops, and dedicate time to understanding new methodologies and tools that can enhance your skill set.

- **Hands-on practice**: Theory alone is not enough. Engage in personal projects, contribute to open-source initiatives, and experiment with innovative ideas to solidify your understanding and keep your skills sharp.

- **Reflection and feedback**: Regularly assess your performance. Seek constructive feedback from mentors, peers, and stakeholders to identify areas for improvement. Reflection ensures that every experience becomes an opportunity for growth.

- **Networking and knowledge sharing**: Participate in professional communities, share insights through blogs or talks, and collaborate with others in the field. Networking not only broadens your perspective but also keeps you connected to the pulse of the industry.

By integrating these strategies into your routine, you ensure that your career remains dynamic, fulfilling, and aligned with the evolving needs of the industry.

In today's competitive job market, staying ahead requires a proactive approach to learning and growth. Employers are increasingly seeking professionals who not only understand the latest technologies but can also apply them to create value. These strategies ensure you remain relevant and indispensable in a rapidly evolving industry.

Final thoughts

The journey to becoming a solutions architect is not merely a destination; it is a lifelong process of learning, adapting, and growing. Each milestone you achieve in your career serves as a stepping stone toward greater challenges and opportunities. As you reflect on what you have learned and accomplished, remember that the true essence of this role lies in its dynamic nature, requiring you to evolve continuously with the technologies, industries, and people you serve.

Through this book, you have gained a foundation of knowledge, honed critical technical skills, and developed a mindset that prioritizes innovation, problem-solving, and collaboration. These qualities are not just tools to help you succeed; they are the cornerstone of a career that can drive significant change in the world of technology and beyond.

The future is shaped by those who dare to innovate and embrace change. As a solutions architect, you are uniquely positioned to lead this charge. Step forward with confidence, creativity, and a commitment to excellence, and let your work inspire the next wave of innovation.

Creating value beyond systems

Success as a solutions architect extends far beyond the systems you design. It is about the value you bring to businesses, users, and society as a whole. Consider the following key areas where your role can make a lasting impact:

- **Empowering businesses**: The solutions you design have the power to transform how organizations operate, innovate, and grow. By aligning technology with business objectives, you enable companies to overcome challenges, achieve their goals, and remain competitive in a fast-paced digital landscape.

- **Enhancing user experiences**: At the heart of every great solution is the user. Whether you are designing a customer-facing application or an internal system, the experience of the end-user should always be a priority. By focusing on usability, accessibility, and responsiveness, you can create solutions that make technology intuitive and impactful.

- **Driving societal progress**: As a solutions architect, you can contribute to broader societal goals. Whether it is through advancing sustainability, improving healthcare systems, or enabling educational access through technology, your work can create a ripple effect that benefits communities and shapes the future.

Every solution you design represents a step toward creating a better, more connected world. Keep this perspective at the forefront of your work to ensure your impact reaches beyond the immediate technical challenge.

Staying curious and embracing challenges

To thrive as a solutions architect, cultivating curiosity and embracing challenges is essential. Curiosity fuels innovation, while challenges present valuable opportunities for growth and learning. Consider the following approaches to nurture these qualities:

- **Exploration fuels growth**: Dive into topics that intrigue you, from advanced machine learning models to cutting-edge cloud-native design patterns. Let your curiosity guide you toward areas where you can expand your expertise and uncover innovative ways to solve problems.

- **Challenges are opportunities**: Every challenge you face is an opportunity to grow, adapt, and innovate. Whether it is a complex technical hurdle, a demanding stakeholder, or a high-pressure deadline, approach these situations with a mindset of resilience and creativity. These experiences will refine your skills and prepare you for even greater responsibilities in the future.

Embracing curiosity and challenges with enthusiasm will ensure that you remain Agile and effective in an ever-evolving landscape.

Inspiring the next generation

As you grow in your career, your journey will naturally become a source of inspiration for others. The lessons that you have learned and the skills you have mastered are invaluable not only to your success but also to the development of the next generation of solutions architects.

Here are key ways to inspire and guide others:

- **Mentorship**: Share your knowledge and experiences with aspiring professionals. Guiding others not only strengthens the field as a whole but also reinforces your own understanding and expertise.

- **Thought leadership**: Use your platform, whether through blogs, presentations, or community engagement, to share insights, best practices, and innovative ideas. Your voice can help shape the conversation around the future of solutions architecture.

- **Collaboration**: Lead by example in fostering an environment of collaboration, respect, and innovation within your teams. Demonstrating how to navigate challenges and seize opportunities will leave a lasting impression on those you work with.

By inspiring others, you extend your influence and contribute to a legacy that promotes growth and innovation in the field.

Key takeaways from the book

Reflecting on your journey through this book, here are some of the key takeaways that summarize the characteristics of being a solutions architect:

- **Technical mastery**: Understand core technologies, architecture patterns, and best practices to build scalable, resilient, and efficient systems.

- **Business alignment**: Bridge the gap between technology and business by designing solutions that deliver measurable value and support strategic goals.

- **Soft skills**: Identify the value of communication, teamwork, and leadership in the process of working with diverse teams to influence stakeholders.

- **Continuous improvement**: Learn from experience and adapt to an ever-changing technological environment by accepting feedback.

- **Preparation**: Use structured preparation when approaching a challenge, be it an interview or an enormous project, to ensure you are clear and focused.

These pillars of success will help guide you through your role and career growth.

A journey of impact and progress

This vast and dynamic area of solutions architecture holds incredible opportunities for a difference-maker to make it big. In this case, it matters whether one is designing scalable systems, solving complex problems, or even mentoring future professionals about the correct way of technology in society.

Bring to this new phase of your journey the lessons learned, the mindset developed. Stand upon the principles of curiosity, collaboration, and continuous improvement as a solid foundation for developing solutions to push meaningful progress forward. Go forth with confidence, creativity, and a commitment to excellence.

Your journey as a solutions architect is not only about achieving personal success but also about leaving a legacy of innovation, inspiration, and impact. The world awaits your contribution, step into your role with purpose and pride, and let your work shape a brighter future for technology and society.

As you continue your journey, having the right tools and references will be crucial for overcoming challenges and delivering impactful solutions. The next chapter consolidates essential resources, templates, troubleshooting guides, and practical insights to support your ongoing growth as a solutions architect. Whether you are preparing for technical challenges, refining your design strategies, or seeking curated reading materials, *Chapter 25, Appendix* provides valuable resources to ensure you are well-equipped for success in your role.

Conclusion

With this chapter, you complete the journey through the *Solutions Architect Interview Guide*. You have gained not only the knowledge to succeed in interviews but also the mindset to thrive as an architect who bridges technology and business with impact. Use the roadmap, checklists, and tools provided to continuously sharpen your skills and embrace the challenges ahead.

The role of a solutions architect is one of influence, innovation, and leadership. Step forward with confidence and curiosity. Your work has the power to shape technology, businesses, and society. This is where your journey towards being a solutions architect begins; go and architect the future.

Join our Discord space

Join our Discord workspace for latest updates, offers, tech happenings around the world, new releases, and sessions with the authors:

https://discord.bpbonline.com

CHAPTER 25
Appendix

Introduction

This chapter serves as a comprehensive resource hub for solutions architects, consolidating essential tools, templates, references, and practical guides. It is designed to complement the knowledge shared in the previous chapters, offering hands-on materials that are invaluable for both preparation and execution in professional roles. From troubleshooting cheat sheets and cloud service comparisons to high-level design templates and recommended reading lists, this chapter equips solutions architects with actionable resources to excel in their careers. Whether you are preparing for an interview, tackling real-world challenges, or exploring specialized roles, the appendix provides the critical resources to support your journey.

Structure

This chapter covers the following topics:

- Troubleshooting cheat sheet
- Cheat sheet for cloud service comparisons
- Essential resources for solutions architects
- Recommended reading for solutions architects
- Software system vision document

Objectives

The objective of this chapter is to serve as a practical toolkit for solutions architects by consolidating essential resources, templates, and references that bridge theoretical knowledge with real-world applications. It aims to equip professionals with high-value tools such as **high-level design** (HLD) templates, troubleshooting guides, and cloud service comparisons, enabling efficient problem-solving and design planning. The chapter also emphasizes continuous learning and career growth by highlighting key certifications, recommended reading, and curated learning platforms. By simplifying complex scenarios and offering actionable insights, the appendix supports solutions architects in staying competitive, mastering emerging technologies, and excelling in their professional roles.

Troubleshooting cheat sheet

Troubleshooting is a critical skill for solutions architects, enabling them to quickly identify and resolve technical issues across cloud platforms, networks, applications, databases, and performance bottlenecks.

Table 25.1 provides a practical cheat sheet for common troubleshooting scenarios, including recommended commands or tools, solutions, and why each step is important. This resource serves as a quick reference guide to help solutions architects efficiently address system issues, minimize downtime, and maintain optimal performance in complex environments.

Area	Context or issue	Command or tool	Solution	Why it matters
Networking	Server unreachable	`ping <ip/domain>`	Verify response times. Investigate firewalls or DNS issues if unreachable.	Ensures basic connectivity and identifies network outages.
	Trace the route to identify bottlenecks	`traceroute <ip/ domain>`	Locate where the connection is failing.	Diagnoses intermediate routing issues affecting latency or connectivity.
	Port closed or unreachable	`telnet <ip> <port>`	Check firewall rules or service configurations.	Validates open ports for application communication.
	DNS resolution failure	`nslookup <domain> or dig <domain>`	Verify DNS server responses and configurations.	Ensures proper domain resolution for services or applications.
Application	API returns errors	`curl -I <url>`	Inspect HTTP response codes for insights.	Helps debug issues like incorrect endpoints or server-side errors.
	Debug API with headers	`curl -X GET <url> -H "Authorization: Bearer <token>"`	Test authentication and payload format.	Validates API authentication and data exchange.
	Application logs reveal runtime errors	`tail -f /var/ log/<app>.log`	Identify specific error messages or stack traces.	Enables targeted fixes for application issues.
Database	Unable to connect	`mysql -h <host> -u <user> / psql -h <host>`	Verify credentials, firewall rules, and port configurations.	Ensures database availability and accessibility.
	Queries running slowly	Explain select	Analyze execution plans to optimize performance.	Pinpoints query inefficiencies for tuning indexes or joins.
	Replication lag	Platform-specific commands	Check replication configurations and latency.	Ensures database redundancy and consistency in real-time environments.
Cloud	Instance not running	`AWS: aws ec2 describe- instance-status`	Check and restart instance if necessary.	Restores compute resources for critical applications.
	S3 bucket access denied	`aws s3api get- bucket-acl --bucket <name>`	Verify IAM roles and bucket policies.	Ensures proper access control for data storage.

Area	Context or issue	Command or tool	Solution	Why it matters
	GCP instance misconfigured	`gcloud compute instances describe <name>`	Validate instance configurations and metadata.	Ensures that compute instances are properly set up for workloads.
Containers	Container crashes	`docker ps -a / kubectl get pods`	Inspect container health and recent changes.	Identifies errors in containerized application deployments.
	Logs show application-specific errors	`docker logs <id> / kubectl logs <pod>`	Check logs for runtime issues or missing dependencies.	Debugs containers in isolated environments.
Performance	High CPU or memory utilization	`top / htop`	Locate resource-hogging processes.	Addresses resource allocation for performance optimization.
	Disk space full	`df -h / du -sh / path/*`	Clear temporary files or allocate additional storage.	Prevents downtime due to full disk capacity.

Table 25.1: Common troubleshooting commands

Cheat sheet for cloud service comparisons

With the increasing adoption of multi-cloud strategies, solutions architects often need to evaluate and compare cloud services across platforms.

Table 25.2 provides a detailed comparison of key cloud services, highlighting their features, descriptions, and common use cases. This comparison serves as a valuable reference for architects navigating multi-cloud strategies, ensuring informed decisions that align with business and technical goals.

Feature	AWS	Azure	GCP	Multi-cloud or open-source	Description	Use case
Compute	EC2, Lambda, ECS, Fargate, EKS, Batch	VMs, Functions, App Service, AKS, Azure Batch, Container Instances	Compute Engine, Cloud Functions, App Engine, GKE, Cloud Run	Azure Arc, Anthos	On-demand instances, serverless compute, container orchestration.	Hosting applications, batch jobs, microservices.
Storage	S3, EBS, EFS, Glacier, FSx (Lustre/ NetApp/ Windows), Storage Gateway	Blob Storage, Disk Storage, File Storage, Data Lake Storage	Cloud Storage, Persistent Disks, Filestore, Cloud Storage for Firebase	NetApp ONTAP	Object, block, or file storage for varied workloads.	Backup, archival, data lakes, and databases.
Networking	VPC, Direct Connect, Global Accelerator, Cloud WAN	VNet, ExpressRoute, Azure VPN Gateway, Azure Load Balancer	VPC, Interconnect, Cloud VPN, Global Load Balancer	Aviatrix	Secure and scalable networking options.	Enterprise-grade connectivity and hybrid cloud setups.

Feature	AWS	Azure	GCP	Multi-cloud or open-source	Description	Use case
AI/ML	SageMaker, Bedrock, Rekognition, Transcribe, Comprehend, Polly, CodeWhisperer	Azure ML, Cognitive Services, Document Intelligence, Azure OpenAI, Bot Framework	Vertex AI, Vision API, AutoML, GenAI Studio, Natural Language API	None	Tools for building, training, and deploying ML models.	Predictive analytics, NLP, computer vision, personalization.
Monitoring	CloudWatch, CloudTrail, X-Ray	Azure Monitor, Log Analytics, Application Insights	Cloud Monitoring, Logging, Trace, Error Reporting	Grafana, Prometheus	End-to-end monitoring, logging, and alerting.	Troubleshooting, performance tuning, compliance monitoring.
Serverless	Lambda, Step Functions, EventBridge	Functions, Logic Apps	Cloud Functions, Cloud Run, Eventarc	OpenFaaS, Knative	Fully managed services to run code without provisioning.	Event-driven processing, automation, lightweight APIs.
Big data and analytics	Redshift, Athena, EMR, Glue, QuickSight	Synapse Analytics, Data Factory, Azure Databricks, Azure Analysis Services	BigQuery, Dataflow, Dataproc, Looker	Snowflake, Databricks	Tools for large-scale data processing and analysis.	ETL pipelines, real-time analytics, data warehouses.
IoT	IoT Core, Greengrass, SiteWise	IoT Hub, Azure Sphere, Azure Digital Twins	Edge services, IoT Edge (Cloud IoT Core deprecated, edge-compute alternatives)	None	IoT device management and edge computing.	Smart devices, industrial IoT, real-time telemetry.
Identity and access	IAM, Cognito, AWS SSO	Azure Active Directory, Managed Identities	Cloud Identity, IAM, BeyondCorp Enterprise	Okta, Auth0	Manage user identities and access permissions securely.	Secure access to cloud resources and applications.
Network security	AWS Shield, WAF, Firewall Manager	Azure DDoS Protection, Web Application Firewall	Cloud Armor, Security Command Center	Palo Alto Prisma, Zscaler	Protect applications from DDoS attacks and web vulnerabilities.	Securing applications from threats.
Database services	RDS, DynamoDB, Neptune, Aurora, Redshift	Azure SQL Database, Cosmos DB, Azure Database for MySQL/ PostgreSQL, Azure Cache for Redis	Cloud SQL, Firestore, Spanner, Memorystore	Yugabyt-eDB, Cock-roachDB	Managed database services for SQL and NoSQL.	Storing structured/ unstructured data, high availability.

Feature	AWS	Azure	GCP	Multi-cloud or open-source	Description	Use case
DevOps tools	CodeCommit, CodeBuild, CodePipeline, CodeDeploy	Azure DevOps, GitHub Actions	Cloud Build, Artifact Registry, Cloud Source Repositories	Terraform, Jenkins	Tools for CI/CD and version control.	Automating software delivery pipelines, faster releases.
CDN	CloudFront	Azure CDN	Cloud CDN	Akamai, Fastly	Low-latency, global content delivery.	Delivering static content quickly worldwide.
Edge computing	AWS Outposts, Wavelength, Local Zones	Azure Stack, Azure Edge Zones	Google Distributed Cloud Edge	None	Compute and storage at the edge for low-latency applications.	Smart cities, AR/VR, industrial IoT.
Security and compliance	AWS Config, Macie, GuardDuty, Inspector	Azure Security Center, Microsoft Defender for Cloud	Security Command Center, Assured Workloads	IBM QRadar, Splunk	Security services for compliance and threat detection.	Threat detection, compliance, data protection.
Quantum computing	Braket	Azure Quantum	Quantum AI	None	Cloud-based quantum computing for R&D.	Optimization problems, cryptography, advanced research.

Table 25.2: *Comparison of cloud services*

Essential resources for solutions architects

To excel as a solutions architect, having quick access to essential resources is vital. These resources provide a comprehensive toolkit for staying informed, learning new skills, engaging with the community, and preparing for interviews and certifications. A categorized table of must-bookmark resources for every solutions architect is as follows:

Category	Resource name	Description
Official documentation	AWS Well-Architected Framework	Best practices for designing cloud-native solutions on AWS.
	Azure Architecture Center	Guidelines and patterns for building solutions on Microsoft Azure.
	Google Cloud Architecture Framework	Strategies for optimizing solutions on Google Cloud.
	TOGAF Standard by The Open Group	Enterprise architecture framework for strategic IT solutions.

Category	Resource name	Description
Community forums	Stack Overflow	Q&A platform for technical challenges across technologies.
	Reddit: r/aws, r/azure, r/cloudcomputing	Communities for discussions on AWS, Azure, and general cloud computing topics.
	Solutions architect LinkedIn Groups	Professional groups for networking and discussions related to solutions architecture.
	Dev.to	Community-driven platform for developers and architects to share knowledge and articles.
Learning platforms	A Cloud Guru	Cloud computing and certification preparation courses.
	Pluralsight	Skill-based learning for cloud, DevOps, and architecture roles.
	Coursera	University-backed courses on emerging technologies and architecture best practices.
	edX	Access to certifications and courses on enterprise architecture and cloud.
	LinkedIn Learning	Professional courses on architecture, communication, and leadership.
Mock interview platforms	Pramp	Practice mock interviews for technical and architecture roles.
	Exponent	Mock interview practice tailored for technical and leadership roles.
	TechMockInterview	Platform for preparing for architecture interviews through realistic scenarios.
Design tools	Lucidchart	Cloud-based diagramming tool for architecture workflows.
	Miro	Visual collaboration platform for brainstorming and system mapping.
	Draw.io	Free tool for creating architecture diagrams and workflows.
Industry reports	Gartner Magic Quadrant	Comprehensive market analysis and vendor comparisons across technologies.
	Forrester Wave	Research and insights on cloud platforms, tools, and services.
	IDC MarketScape	Industry-specific reports for evaluating emerging trends and technologies.
Hands-on labs	AWS Hands-On Labs	Practical exercises to build and test AWS solutions.
	Azure Lab Services	Labs for exploring Microsoft Azure solutions.
	Google Cloud Skills Boost	Hands-on labs and quests for learning Google Cloud tools.
	Katacoda	Interactive labs for Kubernetes, Docker, and more.
Certifications	AWS Certification Pathways	Official guide for AWS certification options and paths.
	Azure Certification Guide	Detailed guide for Microsoft Azure certifications.
	Google Cloud Certifications	Certification roadmap for Google Cloud roles.
	TOGAF Certification	Information on TOGAF enterprise architecture certification.

Table 25.3: Essential resources for solutions architects

Table 25.3 ensures solutions architects have access to curated resources for learning, networking, and career advancement. It is a one-stop reference for individuals aiming to stay updated, enhance skills, and prepare for real-world challenges.

Recommended reading for solutions architects

A well-rounded solutions architect stays informed through continuous learning, leveraging foundational and contemporary texts to build expertise. This curated list of books covers key areas of solutions architecture, including scalability, cloud computing, data systems, and operational practices. These resources serve as essential reading for professionals aiming to deepen their understanding and excel in the field.

The following table provides a curated selection of books that cover key focus areas such as architecture design, scalability, cloud computing, DevOps, and automation:

Title	Author(s)	Overview	Focus area
Software Architecture in Practice	*Len Bass, Paul Clements, Rick Kazman*	Foundational text covering architectural concepts and practices to establish a strong framework for software architecture.	General architecture
Clean Architecture: A Craftsman's Guide to Software Structure and Design	*Robert C. Martin (Uncle Bob)*	Explores clean code and software structure principles to build maintainable and extensible systems.	Software design principles
The Art of Scalability: Scalable Web Architecture, Processes, and Organizations for the Modern Enterprise	*Martin L. Abbott, Michael T. Fisher*	Insights into building scalable systems and processes, essential for architects designing solutions to handle growth.	Scalability
Designing Data-Intensive Applications	*Martin Kleppmann*	Comprehensive guide on data systems, including modeling, storage, and processing.	Data architecture
Domain-Driven Design: Tackling Complexity in the Heart of Software	*Eric Evans*	Introduces Domain-Driven Design principles to create systems aligned with complex business needs.	Domain-Driven Design
Building Microservices: Designing Fine-Grained Systems	*Sam Newman*	Practical advice on designing and implementing scalable microservices architecture.	Microservices
Event-driven architecture: How SOA Enables the Real-Time Enterprise	*Hugh Taylor, Angela Yochem, Les Phillips*	Detailed exploration of event-driven architecture, focusing on how SOA supports real-time enterprise operations.	Event-driven systems
Architecting the Cloud: Design Decisions for Cloud Computing Service Models (SaaS, PaaS, and IaaS)	*Michael J. Kavis*	Offers insights into cloud architecture decision-making processes across various service models.	Cloud computing
The Practice of Cloud System Administration	*Thomas A. Limoncelli, Strata R. Chalup, Christina J. Hogan*	Practical guide to managing and operating cloud-based systems, covering infrastructure, scalability, and automation.	Cloud administration
The Phoenix Project: A Novel About IT, DevOps, and Helping Your Business Win	*Gene Kim, Kevin Behr, George Spafford*	Fictional narrative illustrating DevOps principles and IT management practices, providing real-world lessons.	DevOps and IT management

Title	Author(s)	Overview	Focus area
Accelerate: The Science of Lean Software and DevOps	*Nicole Forsgren, Jez Humble, Gene Kim*	Data-driven insights into high-performing DevOps teams, focusing on speed, stability, and business outcomes.	DevOps and performance
Continuous Delivery: Reliable Software Releases through Build, Test, and Deployment Automation	*Jez Humble, David Farley*	Practices for automating software delivery processes to improve deployment efficiency.	CI/CD and automation
Site Reliability Engineering: How Google Runs Production Systems	*Niall Richard Murphy, Jennifer Petoff, Chris Jones*	Essays from Google engineers on site reliability engineering, emphasizing operational excellence and scalable architecture.	Reliability and operations
Infrastructure as Code: Managing Servers in the Cloud	*Kief Morris*	Explains how to implement Infrastructure as Code (IaC) practices for automation and repeatability in managing cloud infrastructure.	Automation and IaC

Table 25.4: Recommended books for solutions architects

These books are invaluable for solutions architects looking to build a strong foundation, stay current with emerging trends, and excel in their roles. Covering a range of topics from scalability and cloud computing to DevOps and design principles, this list serves as a roadmap for continuous professional growth. Bookmark and explore these titles to expand your expertise and deliver impactful solutions.

Specialized solutions architect roles and profiles. The role of a solutions architect varies significantly depending on the domain of specialization, such as security, cloud, DevOps, networking, or integration. While a general solutions architect focuses on creating scalable and efficient architectures, specialized architects concentrate on domain-specific challenges and innovations. This section highlights the differences in responsibilities, technical skills, certifications, and focus areas across these roles, providing a clear understanding for individuals looking to tailor their career paths or prepare for interviews. Let us take a closer look:

- **General solutions architect's role**:
  - **Focus**: Design scalable, secure, and business-aligned solutions.
  - **Key skills**: Cloud platforms (AWS, Azure, GCP), TOGAF, microservices, APIs.
  - **Certifications**: AWS solutions architect Associate, TOGAF Certified, Azure Architect Expert.
  - **Tools**: Lucidchart, Jira, Confluence.
  - **Responsibilities**:
    - Collaborate with stakeholders to define technical requirements.
    - Develop high-level architecture diagrams and roadmaps.
    - Evaluate technology solutions and lead POCs.
- **Cloud architect's role**:
  - **Focus**: Optimize cloud environments for performance and cost-efficiency.
  - **Key skills**: Cloud-native designs, serverless architecture, hybrid cloud strategies.
  - **Certifications**: AWS solutions architect Professional, Azure Architect Expert, Google Cloud Architect.
  - **Tools**: Terraform, CloudFormation, Azure ARM.
  - **Responsibilities**:

- Migrate on-premises workloads to cloud platforms.
- Develop multi-cloud or hybrid cloud strategies.
- Optimize performance and cost for cloud services.

- **DevOps architect's role**:
  - **Focus**: Streamline CI/CD pipelines and automate infrastructure.
  - **Key skills**: CI/CD tools, IaC, monitoring systems.
  - **Certifications**: AWS DevOps Engineer Professional, Kubernetes Administrator.
  - **Tools**: Jenkins, Terraform, Ansible, Prometheus.
  - **Responsibilities**:
    - Automate software delivery processes.
    - Implement observability and monitoring systems.
    - Define scalable infrastructure templates using IaC.

- **Security architect's role**:
  - **Focus**: Implement security frameworks and mitigate risks.
  - **Key skills**: Identity management, encryption, threat modeling, SIEM tools.
  - **Certifications**: CISSP, AWS Security Specialty, CISM.
  - **Tools**: Splunk, Nessus, Palo Alto firewalls.
  - **Responsibilities**:
    - Conduct threat modeling and risk assessments.
    - Define security policies and incident response strategies.
    - Monitor vulnerabilities and ensure compliance (e.g., GDPR, HIPAA).

- **Networking architect's role**:
  - **Focus**: Design and maintain enterprise-level network infrastructures.
  - **Key skills**: LAN/WAN, SD-WAN, firewalls, load balancers, VPNs.
  - **Certifications**: Cisco CCNP, AWS Advanced Networking, Juniper Networks.
  - **Tools**: Cisco IOS, Fortinet, Juniper switches.
  - **Responsibilities**:
    - Plan and optimize enterprise LAN/WAN architectures.
    - Ensure network security and redundancy.
    - Manage capacity planning and scalability for networks.

- **Integration architect's role**:
  - **Focus**: Enable seamless system interoperability and data synchronization.
  - **Key skills**: API gateways, messaging systems, middleware platforms.
  - **Certifications**: MuleSoft Certified Integration Architect, IBM Solution Designer.
  - **Tools**: MuleSoft Anypoint, Apache Camel, RabbitMQ, Kafka.
  - **Responsibilities**:
    - Design and implement APIs and middleware solutions.

- Ensure real-time data synchronization across systems.
- Oversee the integration of legacy systems with modern platforms.

- **AI architect's role (with GenAI Skills)**:
  - **Focus**: Design and implement advanced AI systems, with specialization in GenAI models for scalable and innovative solutions.
  - **Key skills**: GenAI (LLMs, transformers), prompt engineering, AI/ML frameworks (TensorFlow, PyTorch), cloud-based AI platforms.
  - **Certifications**: AWS Certified Machine Learning – Specialty, Google Cloud Professional ML Engineer, Hugging Face Transformers, OpenAI integration courses.
  - **Tools**: Hugging Face, LangChain, MLflow, Kubeflow, Vertex AI, Docker, Kubernetes, Apache Spark.
  - **Responsibilities**:
    - Architect AI-driven systems leveraging GenAI for tasks like content generation, conversational agents, and personalization.
    - Integrate AI models into enterprise systems ensuring seamless interaction with legacy and modern platforms.
    - Optimize training pipelines for LLMs and ensure scalable model deployments.
    - Address ethical AI practices, including bias detection, transparency, and compliance.
    - Collaborate with stakeholders to align AI solutions with strategic goals and measurable ROI.

This section presents each specialized solutions architect role. This way, readers can focus on specific domains without getting overwhelmed, making it easier to identify the unique skill sets and responsibilities associated with each role.

Having mastered all that is required for an end-to-end fulfilment of a software project, let us now create a software system vision document that acts as a reference for all aspects of the project software architecture and design for all stakeholders to ensure success.

Software system vision document

A software system vision document (can be used as HLD template as well) serves as a critical blueprint for a system's architecture, bridging the gap between business requirements and technical implementation. For a solutions architect, it is an indispensable tool to convey the system's overarching structure, enabling stakeholders to align on the vision and providing a clear roadmap for development and deployment. Let us take a closer look:

- **Project title**:
  - **Name of the project**: [Insert project title here]
- **Executive summary**:
  - **Description**: A brief overview of the project, its purpose, and its significance.
  - **Key objectives**: High-level goals the project aims to achieve, such as scalability, performance optimization, or enhanced user experience.
  - **Key outcomes**: Expected benefits and value addition for the organization.
- **Project overview**:
  - **Scope**: Define the boundaries of the project, including what is in and out of scope.

- o **Stakeholders**: Identify key stakeholders, their roles, and involvement.
- o **Dependencies**: Highlight any dependencies on third-party systems, internal teams, or external factors.

- **Architecture overview**:
  - o **High-level architecture diagram**: Include a clear visual representation of the system's architecture, depicting components and their interactions.
  - o **Components and modules**:
    - ▪ Describe each major component (e.g., frontend, backend, database).
    - ▪ Detail their functionality and how they integrate with one another.

- **Technology stack**:
  - o **Programming languages**: List languages being used (e.g., Python, JavaScript).
  - o **Frameworks**: Specify frameworks (e.g., React, Spring Boot).
  - o **Databases**: Mention database types and tools (e.g., PostgreSQL, MongoDB).
  - o **Tools and services**: Include CI/CD tools, cloud providers, and monitoring solutions.

- **Data architecture**:
  - o **Data flow diagram (DFD)**: Visualize how data flows through the system, from input to storage and output.
  - o **Data storage strategy**:
    - ▪ Describe storage solutions (e.g., relational, NoSQL, or data lakes).
    - ▪ Include backup and archival strategies.
  - o **Database schema**: Summarize the structure of the database with key tables and relationships.

- **Security architecture**:
  - o **Security protocols**:
    - ▪ Define encryption standards (e.g., AES-256).
    - ▪ Discuss compliance with standards like GDPR or HIPAA.
  - o **Authentication and authorization**: Detail methods used, such as OAuth 2.0, SSO, or MFA.
  - o **Threat mitigation**: Highlight strategies like WAF, secure API gateways, or intrusion detection systems.

- **Business architecture**:
  - o **Business processes**:
    - ▪ Outline workflows the solution will support.
    - ▪ Include process diagrams if necessary.
  - o **Business rules**: Define key rules that guide operations.
  - o **Alignment with business goals**: Explain how the solution supports organizational objectives.

- **Application architecture**:
  - o **Application design**:
    - ▪ Detail application layers (e.g., presentation, business logic, data access).

- Describe reusable components or microservices.
  - **Integration points**:
    - Specify interactions with external systems or APIs.
    - Include protocols like REST, GraphQL, or SOAP.
  - **Error handling**: Outline strategies for handling errors and ensuring reliability.
- **Infrastructure architecture**:
  - **Infrastructure design**:
    - Describe deployment architecture (e.g., on-premises, cloud, hybrid).
    - Include diagrams for network topology and server layout.
  - **High availability and scalability**: Detail failover mechanisms, auto-scaling configurations, and disaster recovery regions.
  - **Monitoring and logging**:
    - Specify tools for monitoring system health (e.g., Datadog, Prometheus).
    - Include logging mechanisms for debugging and audit trails.
- **Business continuity plan (BCP)**:
  - **Critical services**: Identify components essential for operation during outages.
  - **BCP strategy**: Define strategies to maintain uptime (e.g., active-active failover).
  - **Testing schedule**: Include plans for regular continuity tests.
- **Disaster recovery strategy**:
  - **RTO/RPO goals**:
    - Define acceptable **recovery time objectives (RTO)** and **recovery point objectives (RPO)**.
  - **Backup and restore**: Describe backup processes and frequency.
  - **Failover plan**: Outline steps for activating secondary systems in the event of a failure.
- **Architecture decisions**:
  - **Decision log**: Record key decisions with justification.

    Example:
    - **Decision:** Use AWS RDS for database hosting.
    - **Rationale:** Offers automated scaling, backup, and compliance.
  - **Alternatives considered**: List other options evaluated and reasons for rejection.
  - **Trade-off analysis**: Highlight trade-offs made for critical decisions.
- **Risks and mitigations**:
  - **Identified risks**: List potential risks (e.g., vendor lock-in, scalability bottlenecks).
  - **Mitigation strategies**: Provide actions to address each risk (e.g., multi-cloud strategy to avoid lock-in).
- **Testing strategy**:
  - **Testing types**: Unit testing, integration testing, performance testing.

- o **Tools**: List tools like Selenium, JMeter, or Postman for automated testing.
- o **Acceptance criteria**: Define the metrics for successful implementation.
- **Deployment plan**:
  - o **Deployment process**: Explain CI/CD pipelines and tools (e.g., Jenkins, GitHub Actions).
  - o **Environment details**: Define environments (e.g., Dev, Test, Staging, Production).
  - o **Rollout strategy**: Discuss phased rollouts, blue-green deployments, or canary releases.
- **Appendix**:
  - o **Supporting documents**: Include detailed diagrams, additional resources, or technical specifications.
  - o **Glossary**: Define project-specific terms or acronyms.
  - o **Reference material**: Link to related documents, standards, or APIs.

The factors due to which the template works are as follows:

- **Comprehensive coverage**: Includes all major aspects of design, from architecture to deployment.
- **Clarity**: Clear structure ensures easy understanding by technical and non-technical stakeholders.
- **Customization**: Flexible sections that can be tailored to specific project needs.
- **Focus on continuity and recovery**: Emphasizes robustness with BCP and DR plans.

This standardized HLD template provides a thorough foundation for documenting design decisions, making it suitable for a wide range of projects while meeting stakeholder expectations.

Conclusion

This chapter is a one-stop repository of essential tools, knowledge, and references for solutions architects. It bridges theoretical knowledge and practical application, providing templates, troubleshooting strategies, and curated resources to address challenges across diverse domains. By leveraging the materials in this chapter, solutions architects can enhance their technical acumen, improve problem-solving efficiency, and accelerate their career growth. Whether you are an experienced professional or just starting out, the appendix equips you with the resources needed to thrive in the dynamic world of solutions architecture.

Join our Discord space

Join our Discord workspace for latest updates, offers, tech happenings around the world, new releases, and sessions with the authors:

https://discord.bpbonline.com

Index